MU SHI SHI

5

Yuki Urushibara

Translated and adapted by
William Flanagan

Lettered by
North Market Street Graphics

Ballantine Books ∗ New York

A Del Rey Manga/Kodansha Trade Paperback Original

Mushishi volume 5 copyright © 2004 by Yuki Urushibara
English translation copyright © 2008 by Yuki Urushibara

Published in the United States by Del Rey Books, an imprint of The Random House Publishing Group, a division of Random House, Inc., New York.

DEL REY is a registered trademark and the Del Rey colophon is a trademark of Random House, Inc.

Publication rights arranged through Kodansha Ltd.

First published in Japan in 2004 by Kodansha Ltd., Tokyo.

ISBN 978-0-345-50138-7

Printed in the United States of America

www.delreymanga.com

9 8 7 6 5 4 3 2 1

Translator/adapter: William Flanagan
Lettering: North Market Street Graphics

Contents

Honorifics Explained

Throughout the Del Rey Manga books, you will find Japanese honorifics left intact in the translations. For those not familiar with how the Japanese use honorifics and, more important, how they differ from American honorifics, we present this brief overview.

Politeness has always been a critical facet of Japanese culture. Ever since the feudal era, when Japan was a highly stratified society, use of honorifics— which can be defined as polite speech that indicates relationship or status—has played an essential role in the Japanese language. When addressing someone in Japanese, an honorific usually takes the form of a suffix attached to one's name (example: "Asuna-san"), is used as a title at the end of one's name, or appears in place of the name itself (example: "Negi-sensei," or simply "Sensei!").

Honorifics can be expressions of respect or endearment. In the context of manga and anime, honorifics give insight into the nature of the relationship between characters. Many English translations leave out these important honorifics and therefore distort the feel of the original Japanese. Because Japanese honorifics contain nuances that English honorifics lack, it is our policy at Del Rey not to translate them. Here, instead, is a guide to some of the honorifics you may encounter in Del Rey Manga.

-san: This is the most common honorific and is equivalent to Mr., Miss, Ms., or Mrs. It is the all-purpose honorific and can be used in any situation where politeness is required.

-sama: This is one level higher than "-san" and is used to confer great respect.

-dono: This comes from the word "tono," which means "lord." It is an even higher level than "-sama" and confers utmost respect.

-kun: This suffix is used at the end of boys' names to express familiarity or endearment. It is also sometimes used by men among friends, or when addressing someone younger or of a lower station.

-chan: Thisis used to express endearment, mostly toward girls. It is also used for little boys, pets, and even among lovers. It gives a sense of childish cuteness.

Bozu: This is an informal way to refer to a boy, similar to the English terms "kid" and "squirt."

Sempai/ Senpai: This title suggests that the addressee is one's senior in a group or organization. It is most often used in a school setting, where underclassmen refer to their upperclassmen as "sempai." It can also be used in the workplace, such as when a newer employee addresses an employee who has seniority in the company.

Kohai: This is the opposite of "sempai" and is used toward underclassmen in school or newcomers in the workplace. It connotes that the addressee is of a lower station.

Sensei: Literally meaning "one who has come before," this title is used for teachers, doctors, or masters of any profession or art.

Onee-san/ Onii-san: Normally older siblings are not called by name but rather by the title of older sister (*Onee-san*) or older brother (*Onii-san*). Depending on the relationship, *-chan* or *-sama* can also be used instead of -san. However, this honorific can also be used with someone unrelated when the relationship resembles that of siblings.

Obaa-san/ Ojii-san: Japanese grandparents are called by their titles rather than by name. Grandmothers are called Obaa-san (or Obaa-sama to imply added respect and distance, or Obaa-chan for more intimacy). Likewise grandfathers are called Ojii-san, Ojii-sama, or Ojii-chan.

-[blank]: This is usually forgotten in these lists, but it is perhaps the most significant difference between Japanese and English. The lack of honorific means that the speaker has permission to address the person in a very intimate way. Usually, only family, spouses, or very close friends have this kind of permission. Known as *yobisute*, it can be gratifying when someone who has earned the intimacy starts to call one by one's name without an honorific. But when that intimacy hasn't been earned, it can be very insulting.

蟲

むしし

師
Mushishi
5

Yuki Urushibara

Contents

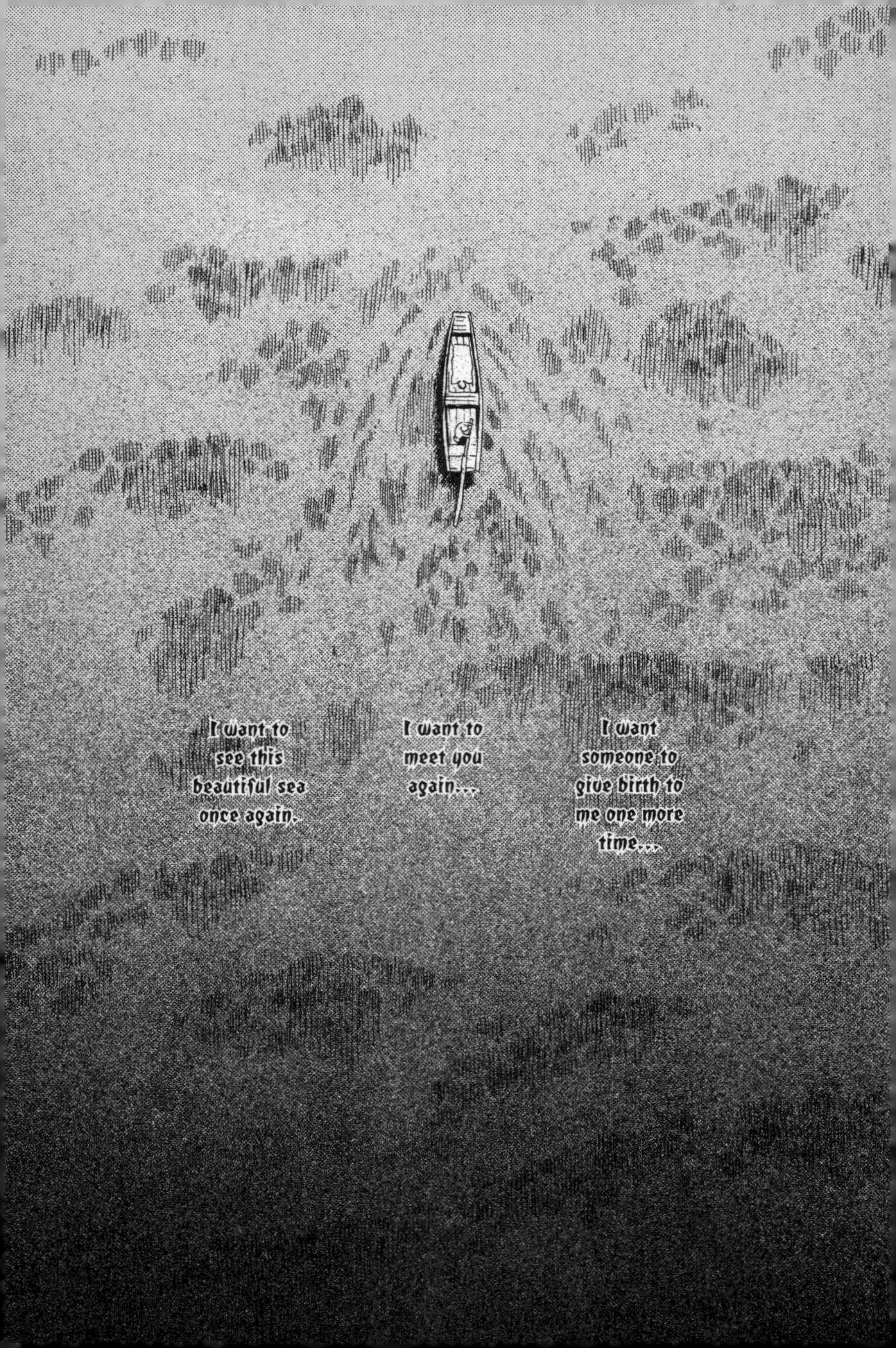
I want someone to give birth to me one more time...
I want to meet you again...
I want to see this beautiful sea once again.

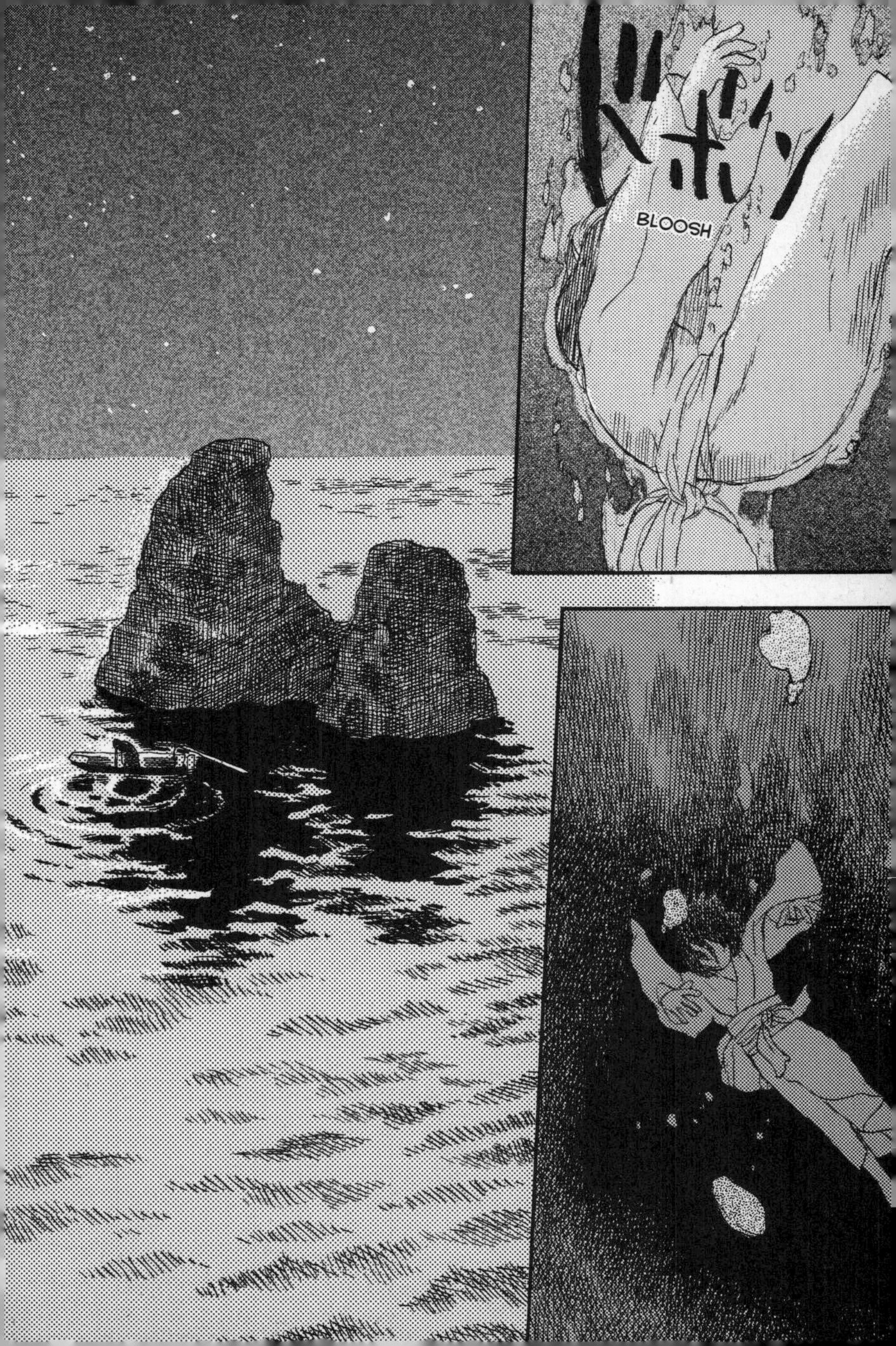
BLOOSH

SUPASH

The Sea Palace

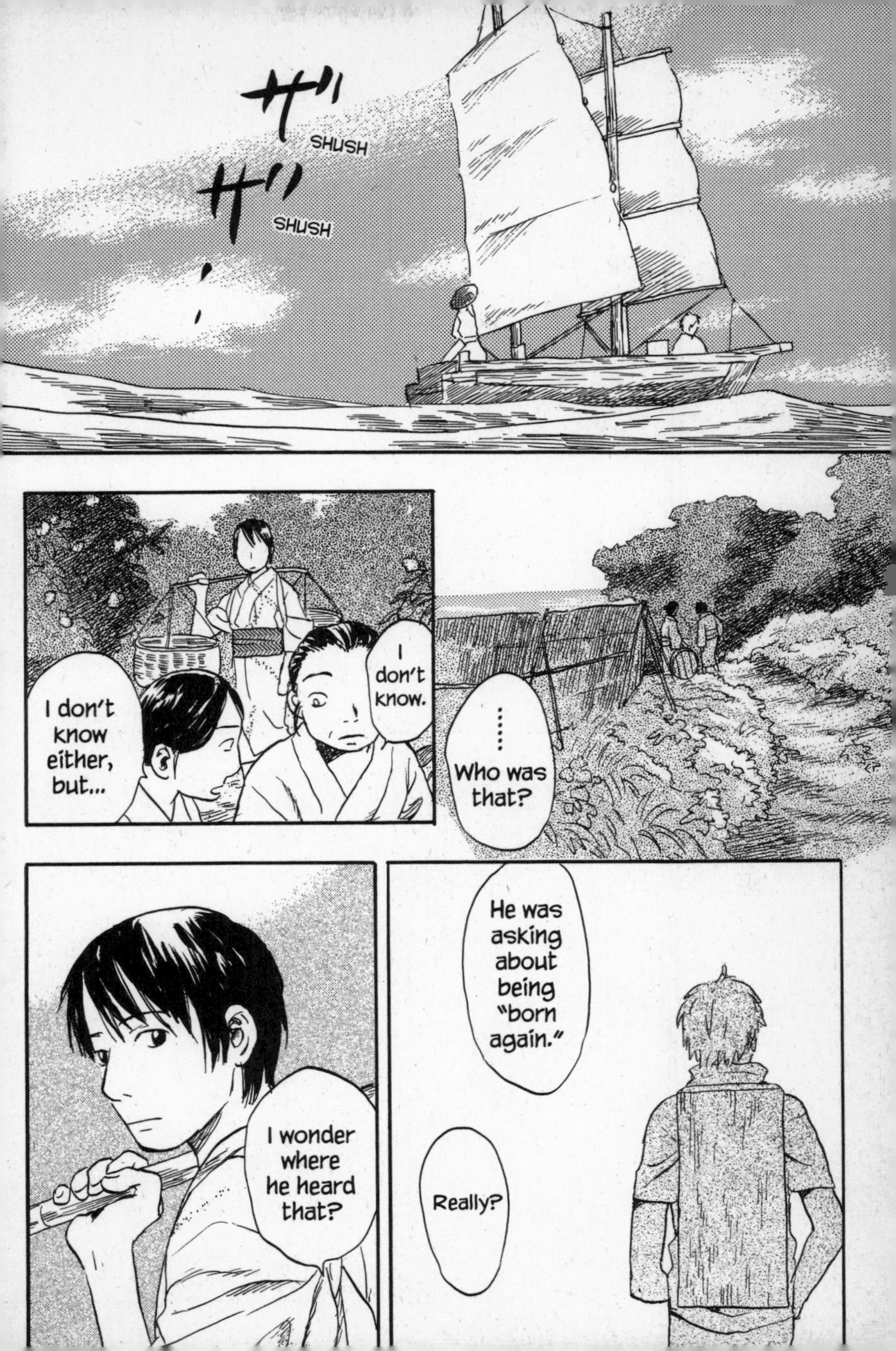
SHUSH
SHUSH
...... Who was that?
I don't know.
I don't know either, but...
He was asking about being "born again."
Really?
I wonder where he heard that?

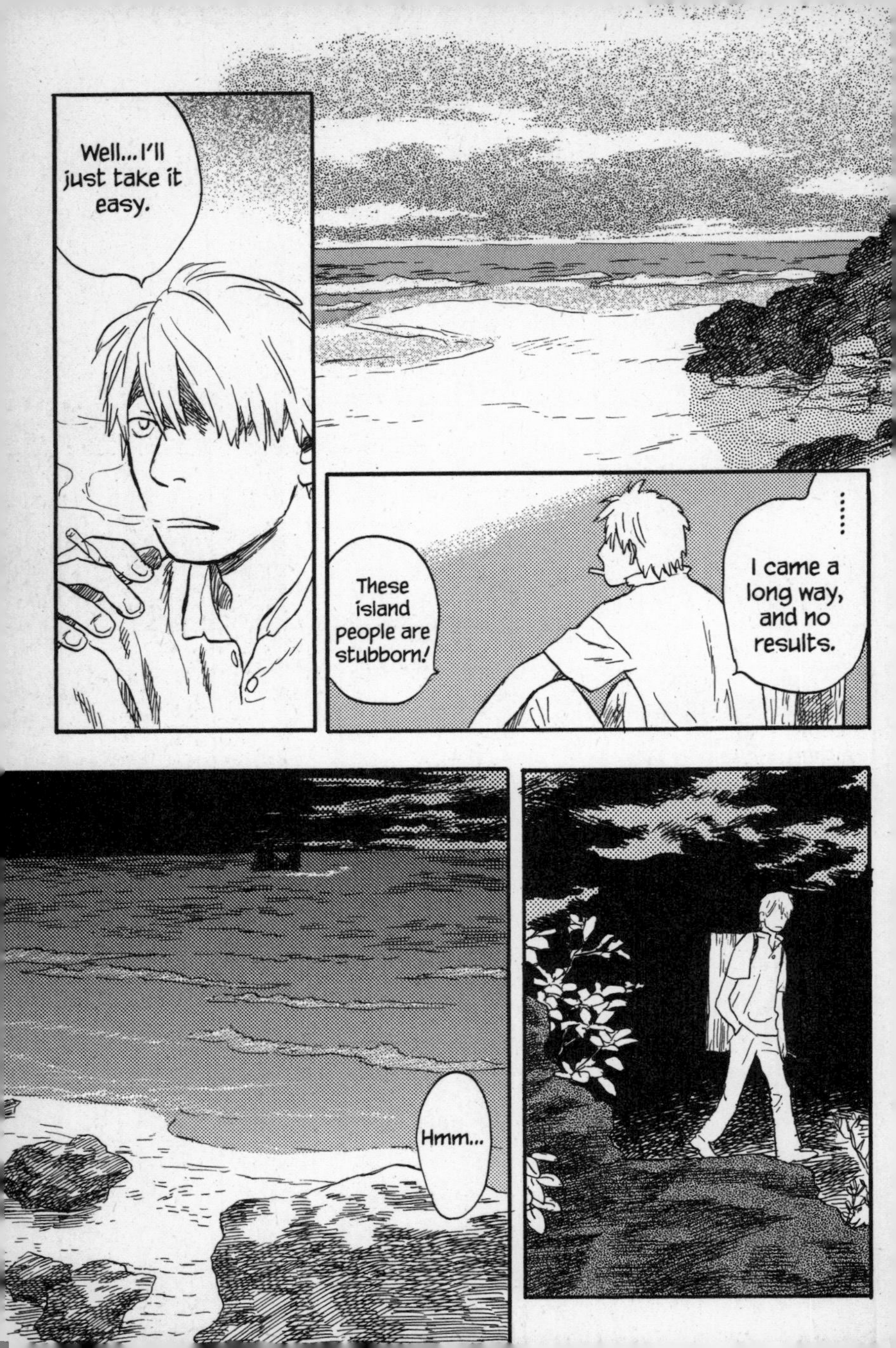
......
I came a long way, and no results.
These island people are stubborn!
Well...I'll just take it easy.
Hmm...

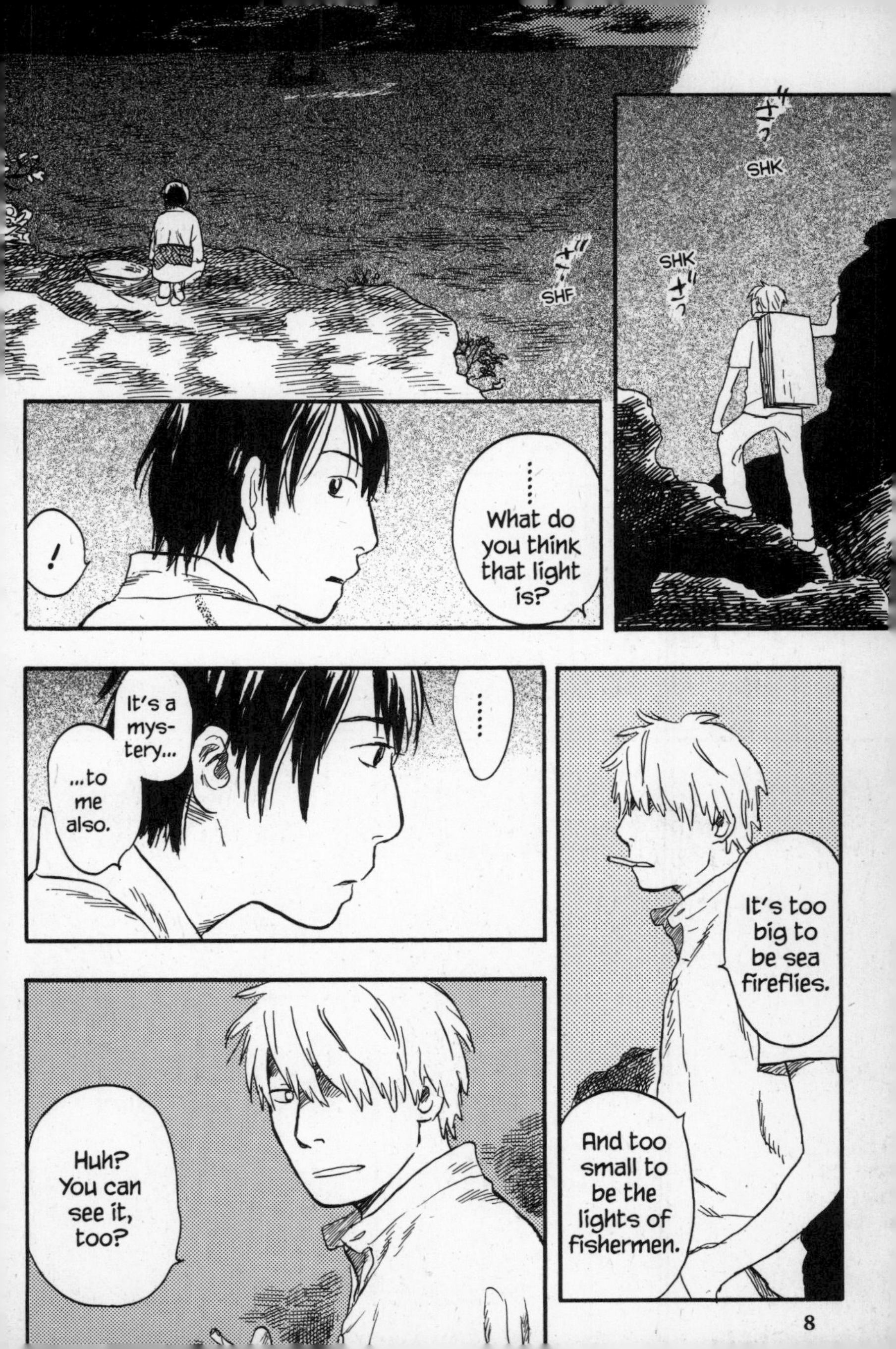
SHK
SHK
SHF
...... What do you think that light is?
!
It's too big to be sea fireflies.
And too small to be the lights of fishermen.
......
It's a mystery...
...to me also.
Huh? You can see it, too?

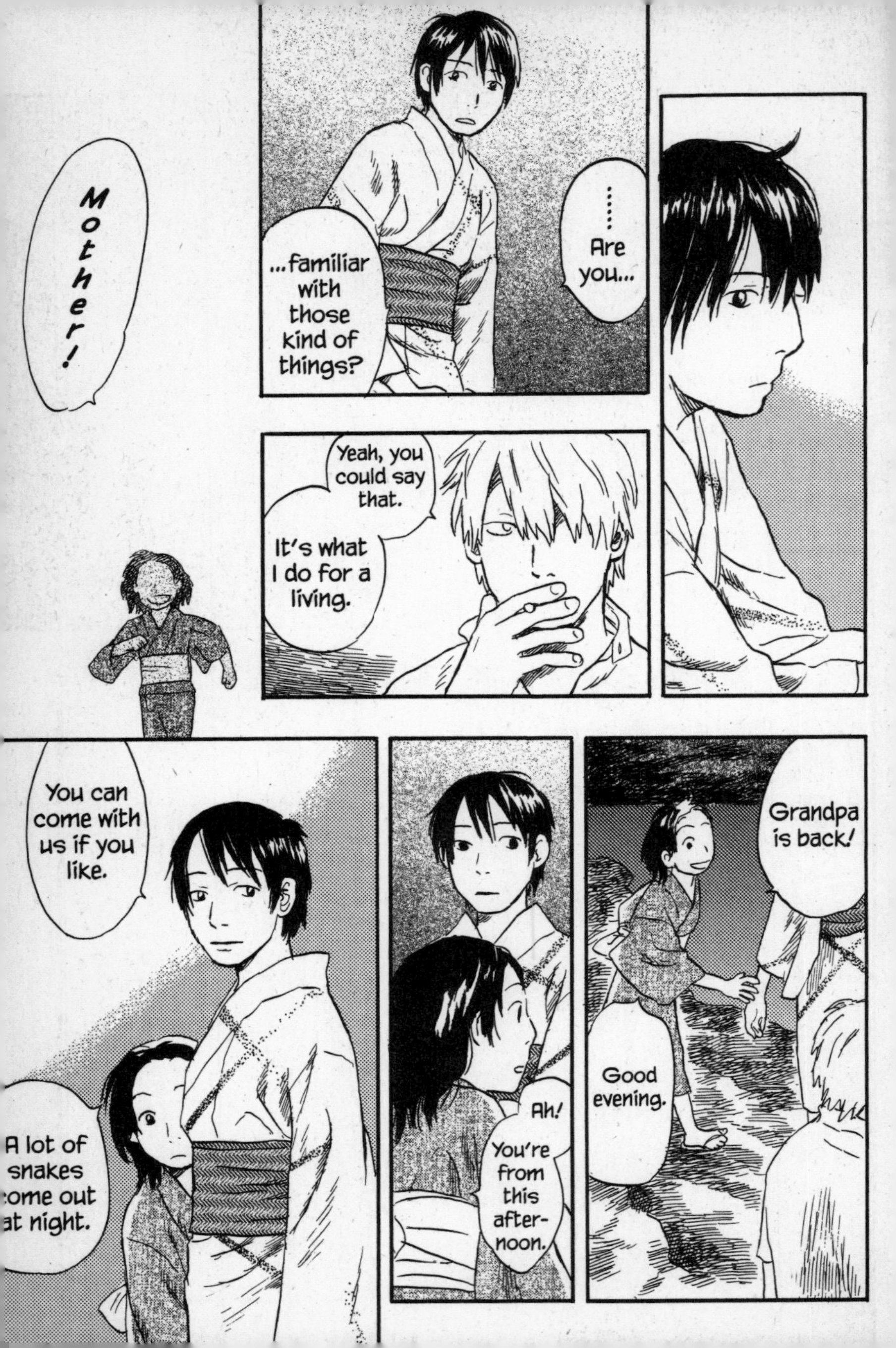

...... Are you...
...familiar with those kind of things?
Yeah, you could say that.
It's what I do for a living.
Mother!
Grandpa is back!
Good evening.
Ah! You're from this afternoon.
You can come with us if you like.
A lot of snakes ome out at night.

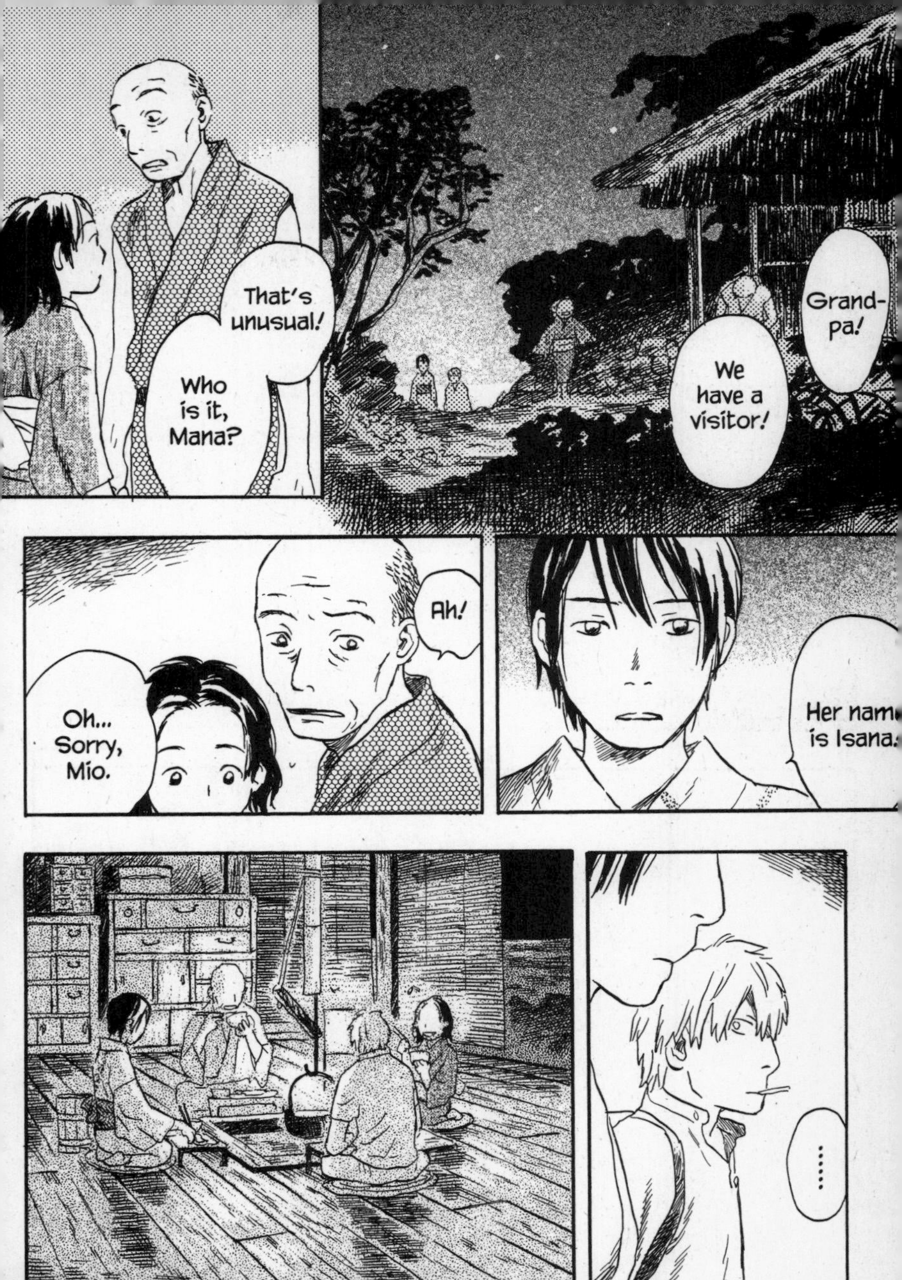
Grand-pa!
We have a visitor!
That's unusual!
Who is it, Mana?
Her nam is Isana.
Ah!
Oh... Sorry, Mio.
......

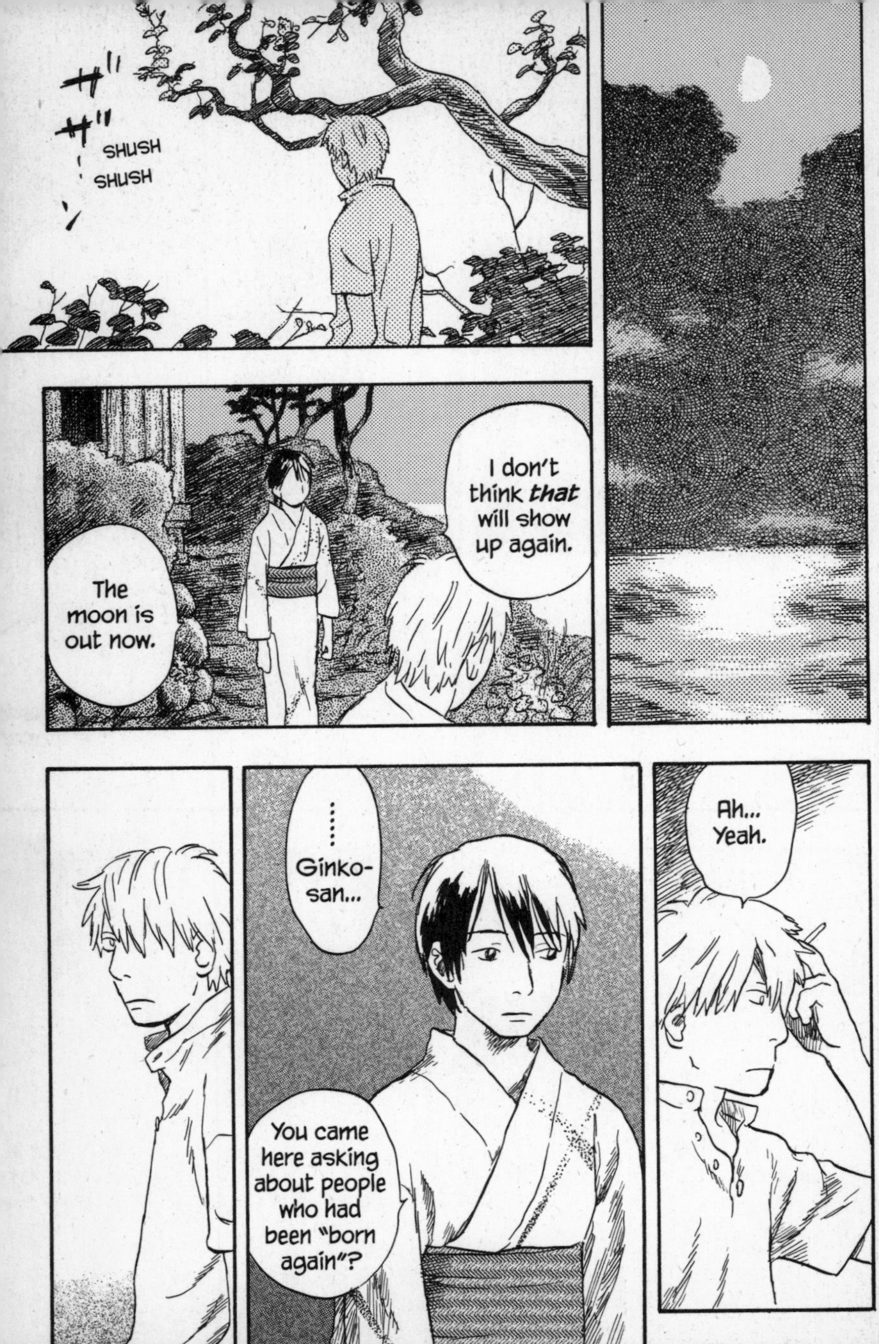
SHUSH
SHUSH
I don't think *that* will show up again.
The moon is out now.
Ah... Yeah.
...... Ginko-san...
You came here asking about people who had been "born again"?

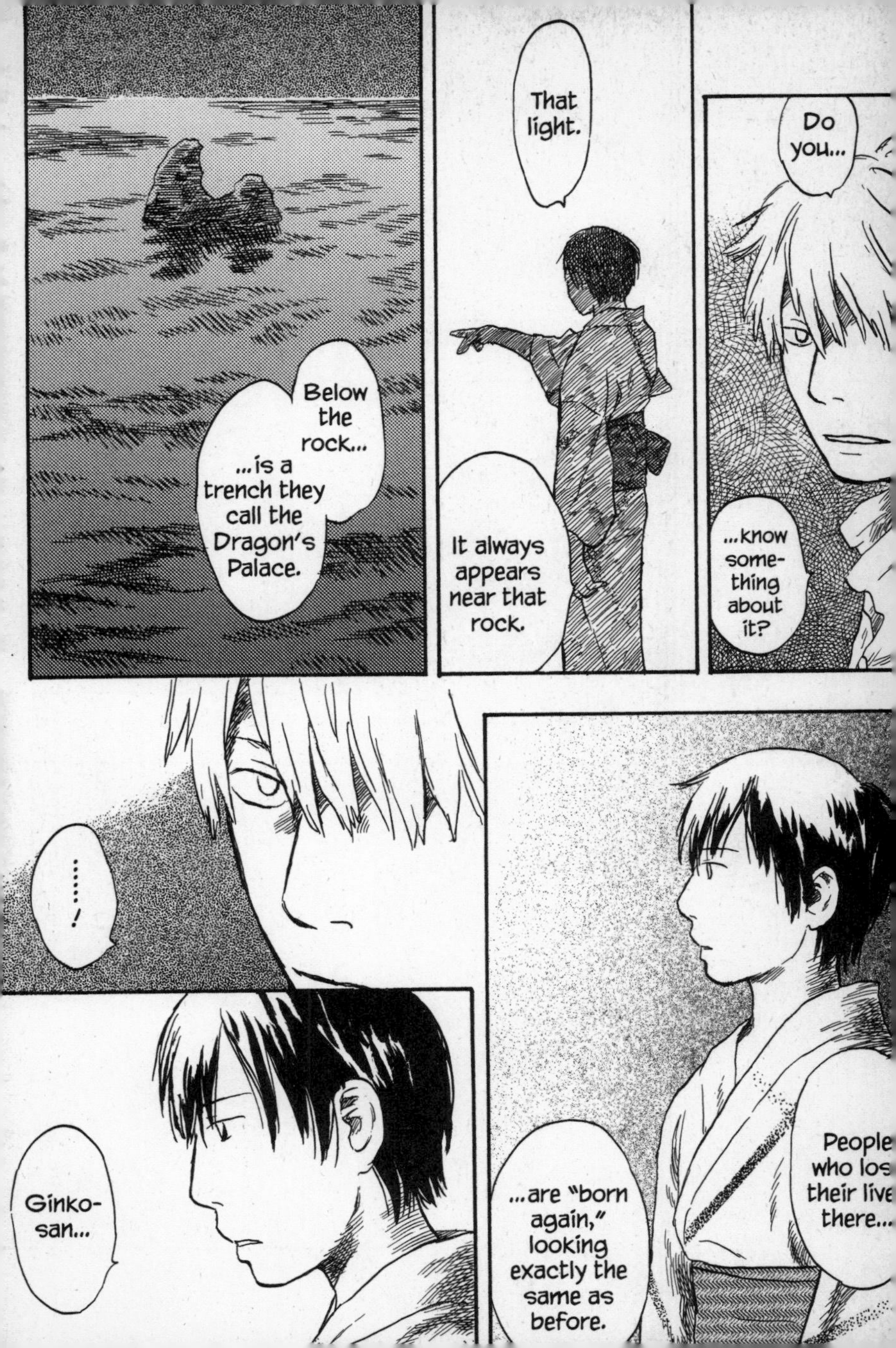

Do you...
...know some-thing about it?
That light.
It always appears near that rock.
Below the rock...
...is a trench they call the Dragon's Palace.
People who los their live there...
...are "born again," looking exactly the same as before.
......!
Ginko-san...

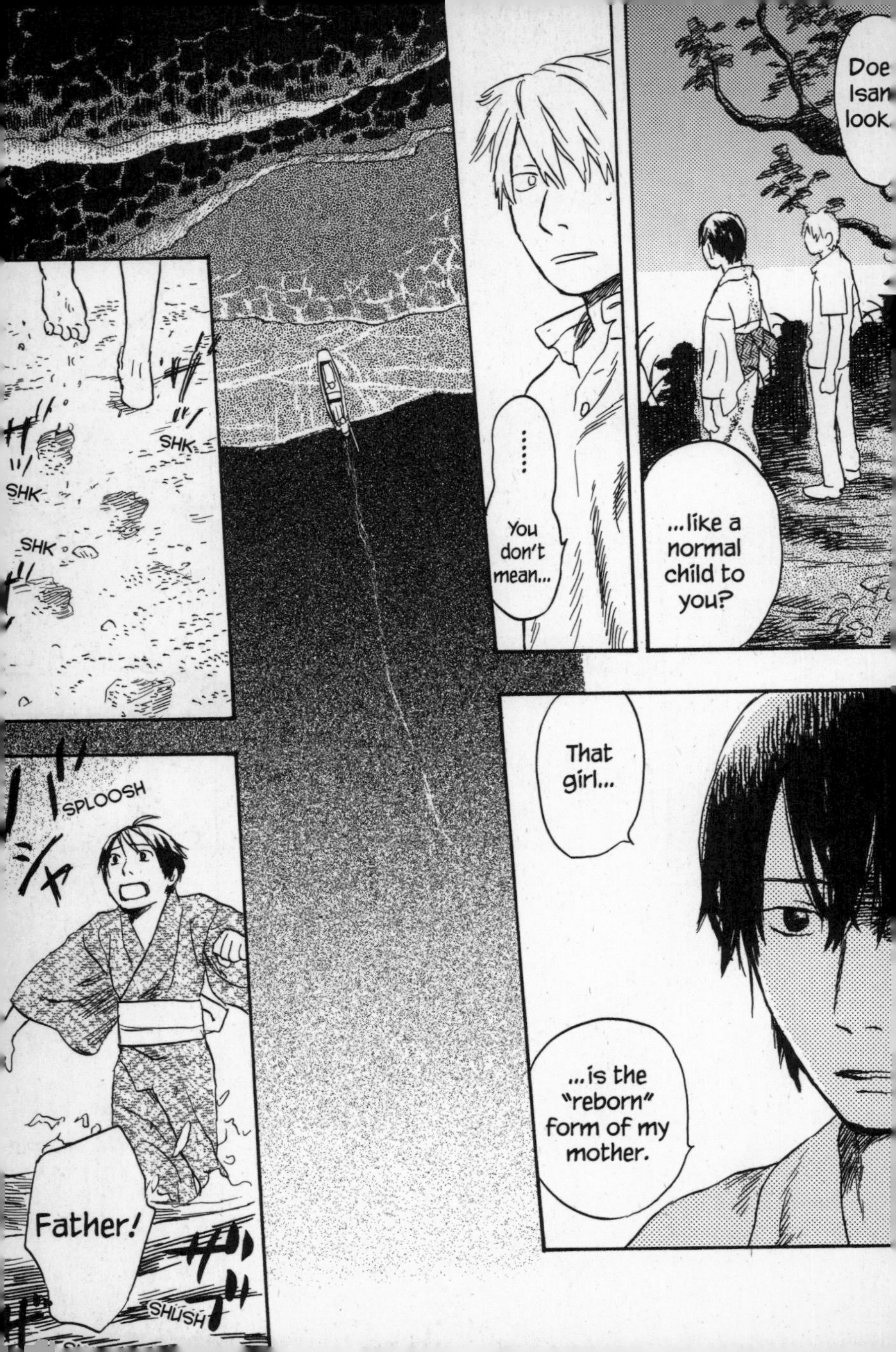
Doe
Isan
look
...like a normal child to you?
......
You don't mean...
That girl...
...is the "reborn" form of my mother.
SHK
SHK
SHK
SPLOOSH
Father!
SHUSH

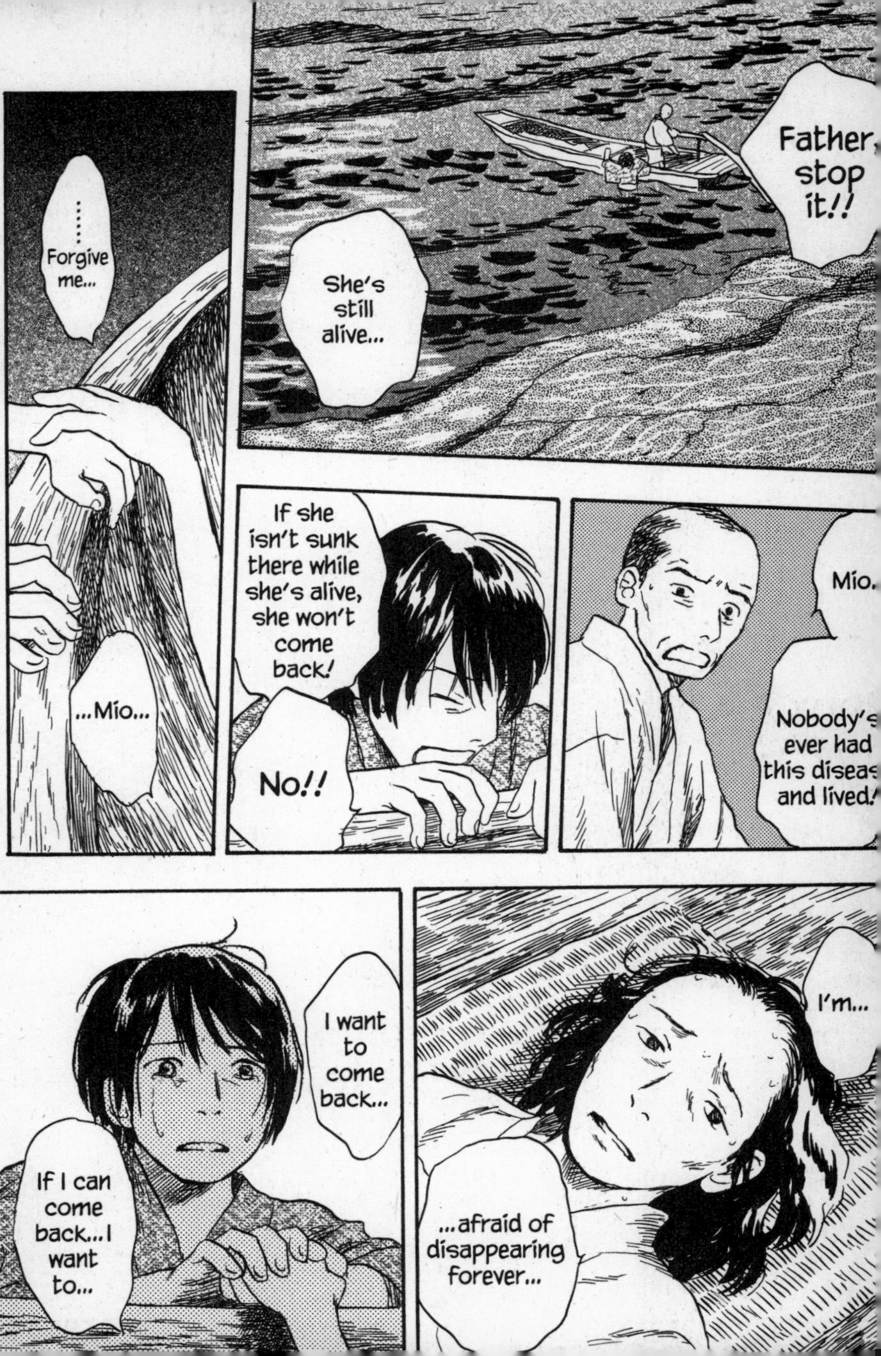
Father, stop it!!
She's still alive...
Mio.
Nobody's ever had this diseas and lived!
If she isn't sunk there while she's alive, she won't come back!
No!!
...... Forgive me...
...Mio...
I'm...
...afraid of disappearing forever...
I want to come back...
If I can come back...I want to...

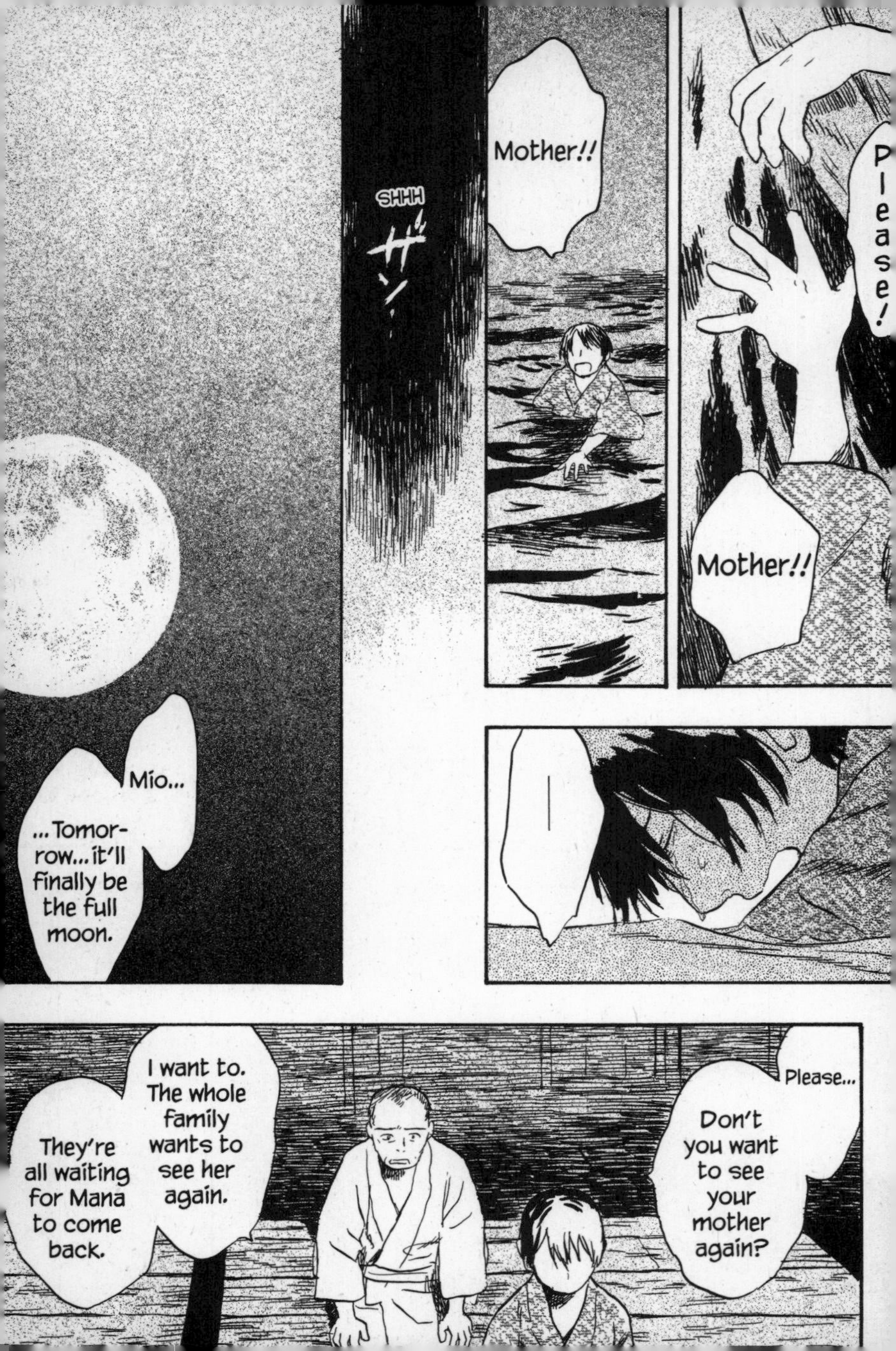
Please!
Mother!!
Mother!!
SHHH
ザン
Mio...
...Tomorrow...it'll finally be the full moon.
Please...
Don't you want to see your mother again?
I want to. The whole family wants to see her again.
They're all waiting for Mana to come back.

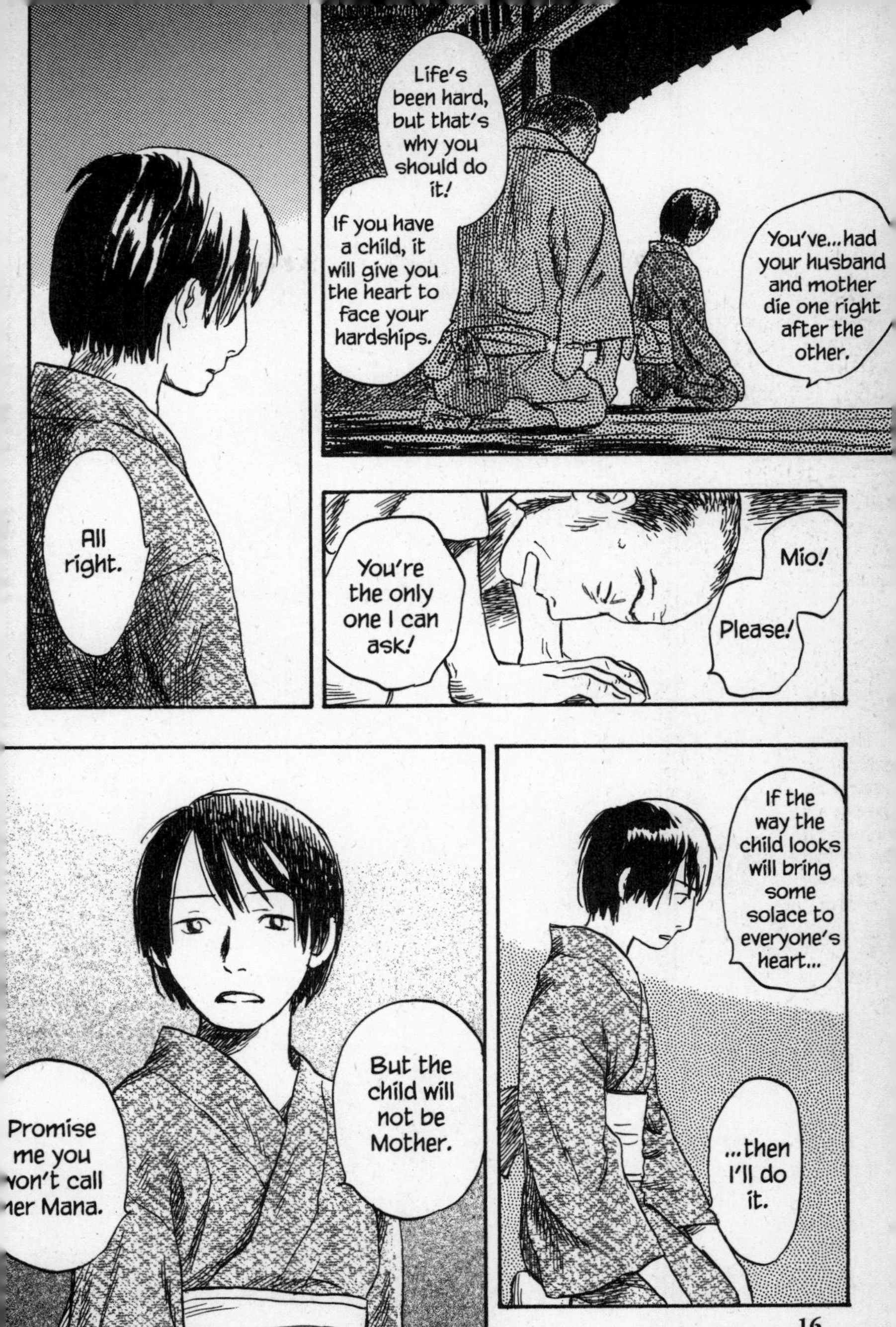
You've...had your husband and mother die one right after the other.
Life's been hard, but that's why you should do it!
If you have a child, it will give you the heart to face your hardships.
Mio!
Please!
You're the only one I can ask!
All right.
If the way the child looks will bring some solace to everyone's heart...
...then I'll do it.
But the child will not be Mother.
Promise me you von't call ner Mana.

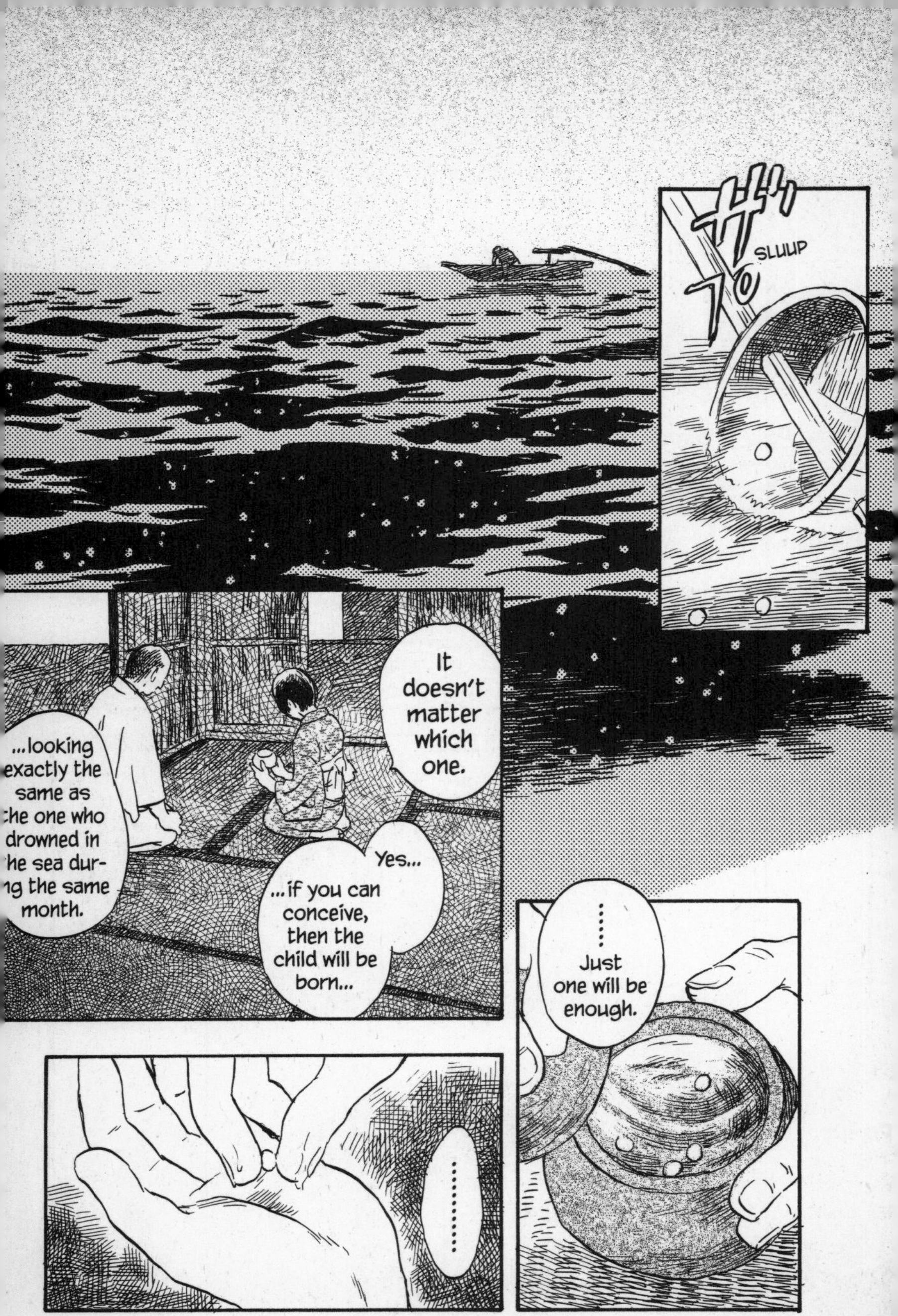
SLUUP
It doesn't matter which one.
Yes...
...if you can conceive, then the child will be born...
...looking exactly the same as he one who drowned in he sea dur- ng the same month.
...... Just one will be enough.
......

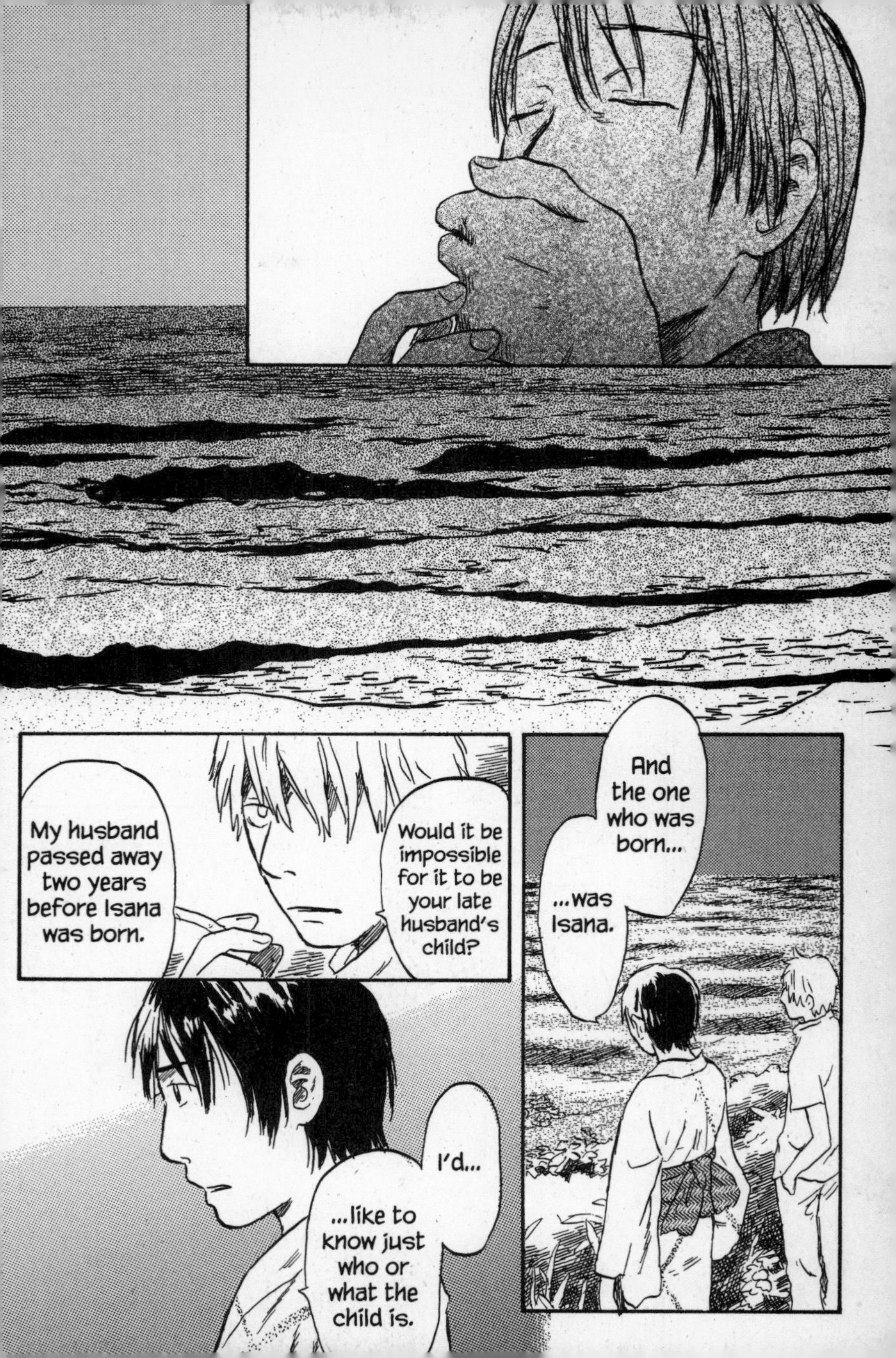

And the one who was born...
...was Isana.
Would it be impossible for it to be your late husband's child?
My husband passed away two years before Isana was born.
I'd...
...like to know just who or what the child is.

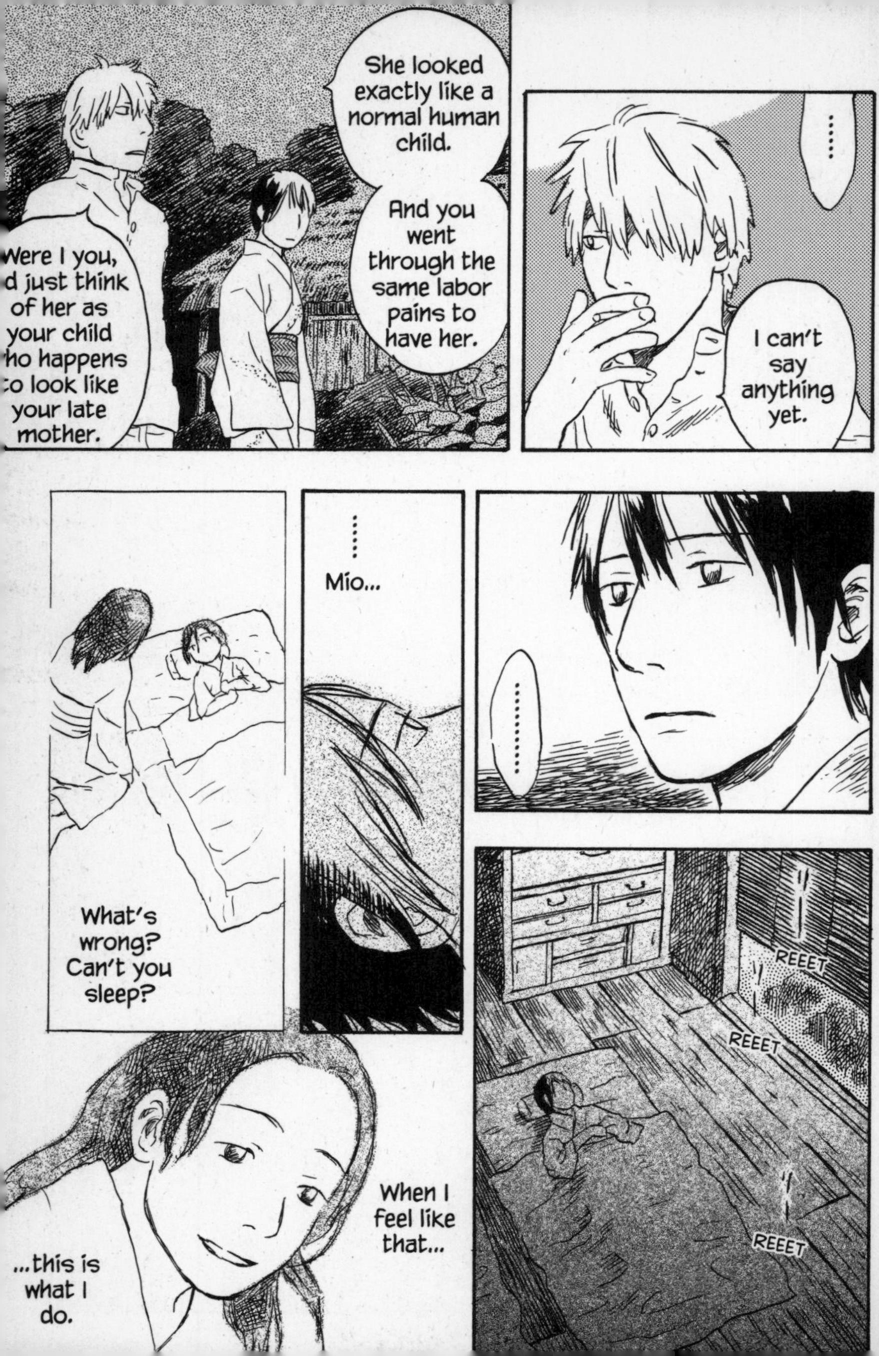
……
I can't say anything yet.
She looked exactly like a normal human child.
And you went through the same labor pains to have her.
Were I you, d just think of her as your child ho happens o look like your late mother.
……
……
Mio...
What's wrong? Can't you sleep?
REEET
REEET
REEET
When I feel like that...
...this is what I do.

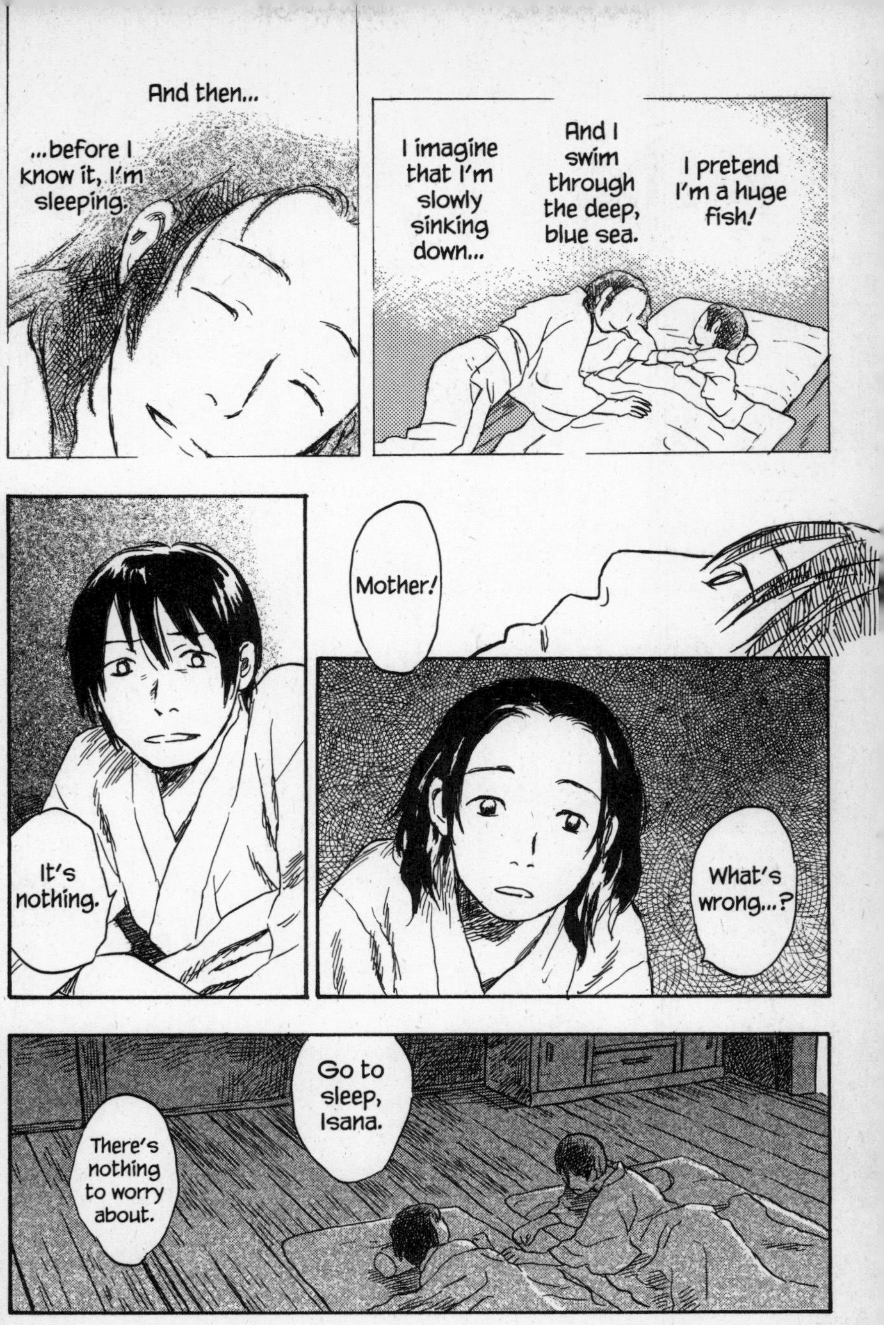
I pretend I'm a huge fish!
And I swim through the deep, blue sea.
I imagine that I'm slowly sinking down...
And then...
...before I know it, I'm sleeping.
Mother!
What's wrong...?
It's nothing.
Go to sleep, Isana.
There's nothing to worry about.

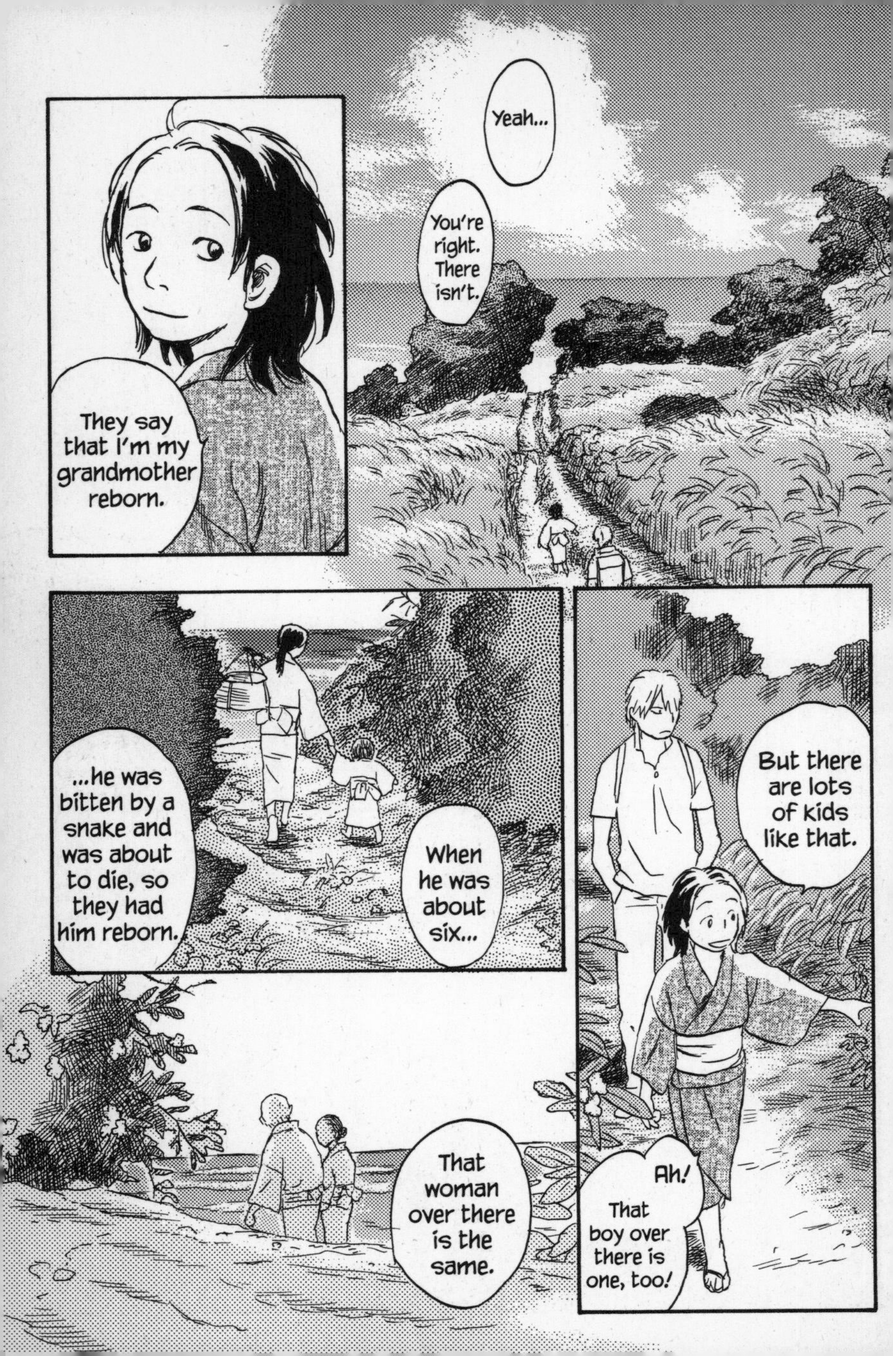
Yeah...
You're right. There isn't.
They say that I'm my grandmother reborn.
But there are lots of kids like that.
Ah!
That boy over there is one, too!
When he was about six...
...he was bitten by a snake and was about to die, so they had him reborn.
That woman over there is the same.

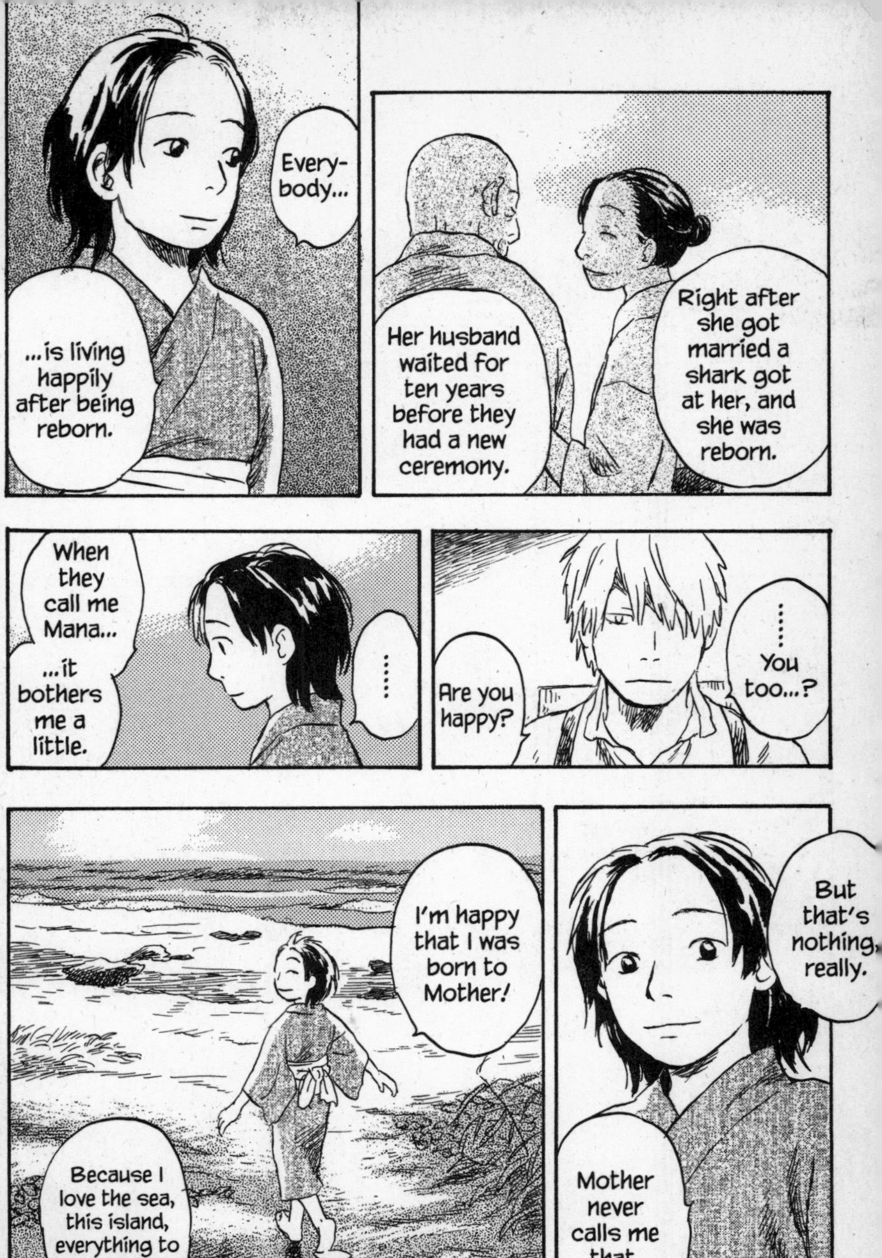
Right after she got married a shark got at her, and she was reborn.
Her husband waited for ten years before they had a new ceremony.
Every-body...
...is living happily after being reborn.
...... You too...?
Are you happy?
......
When they call me Mana...
...it bothers me a little.
But that's nothing, really.
Mother never calls me that, so...
I'm happy that I was born to Mother!
Because I love the sea, this island, everything to do with this place!

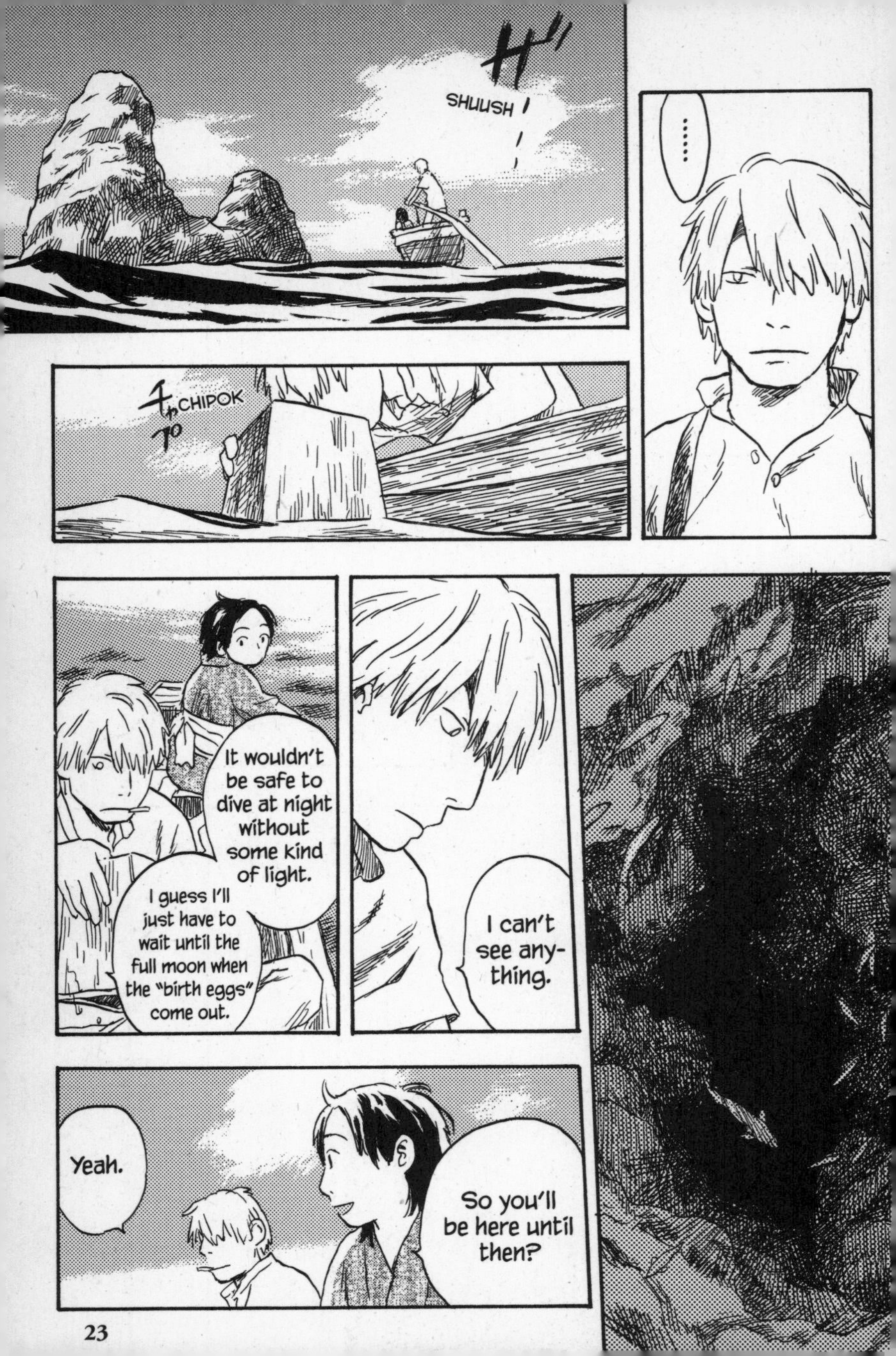
......
SHUUSH
CHIPOK
I can't see anything.
It wouldn't be safe to dive at night without some kind of light.
I guess I'll just have to wait until the full moon when the "birth eggs" come out.
So you'll be here until then?
Yeah.

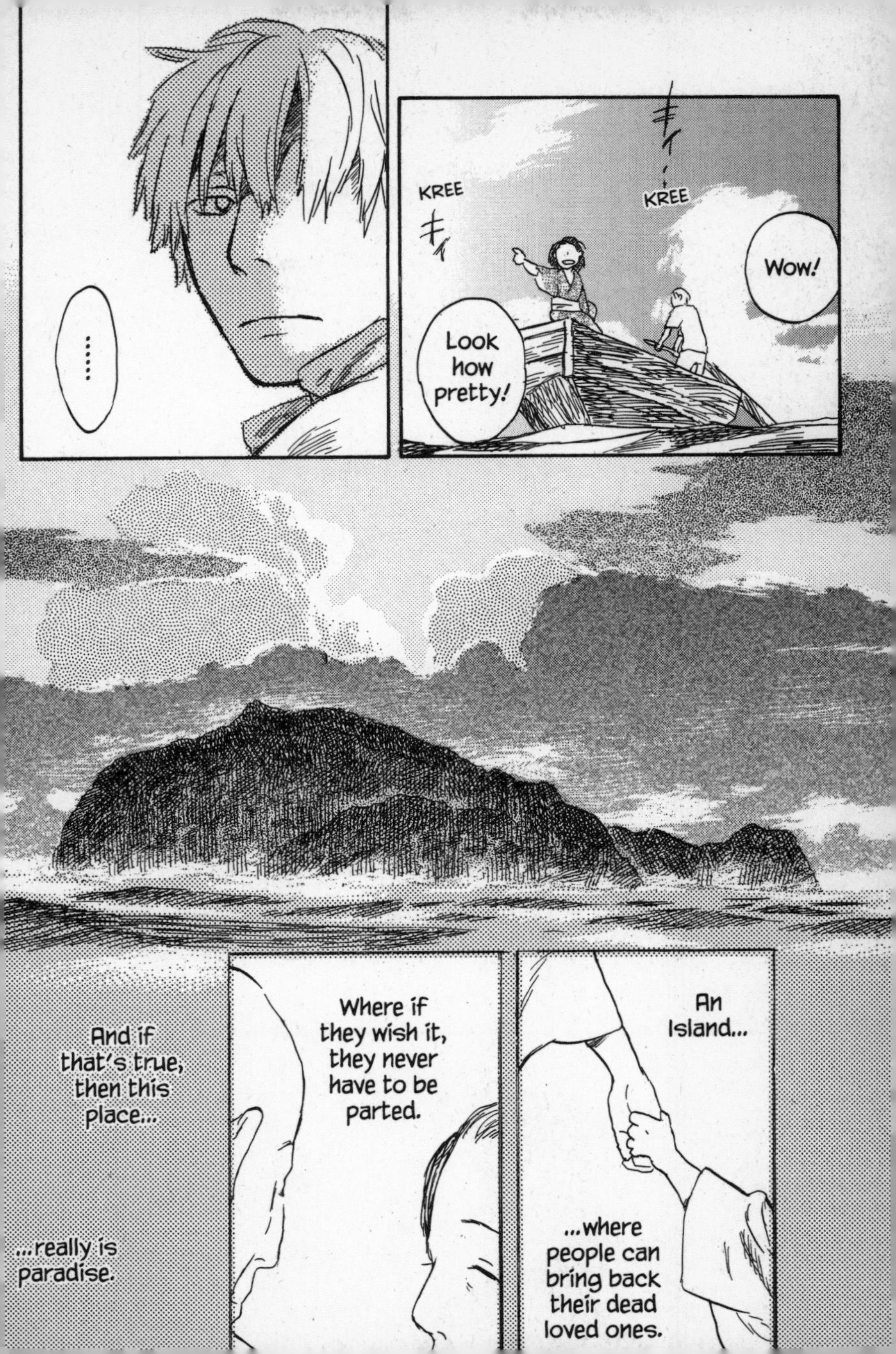
KREE
Wow!
KREE
Look how pretty!
......
An Island...
...where people can bring back their dead loved ones.
Where if they wish it, they never have to be parted.
And if that's true, then this place...
...really is paradise.

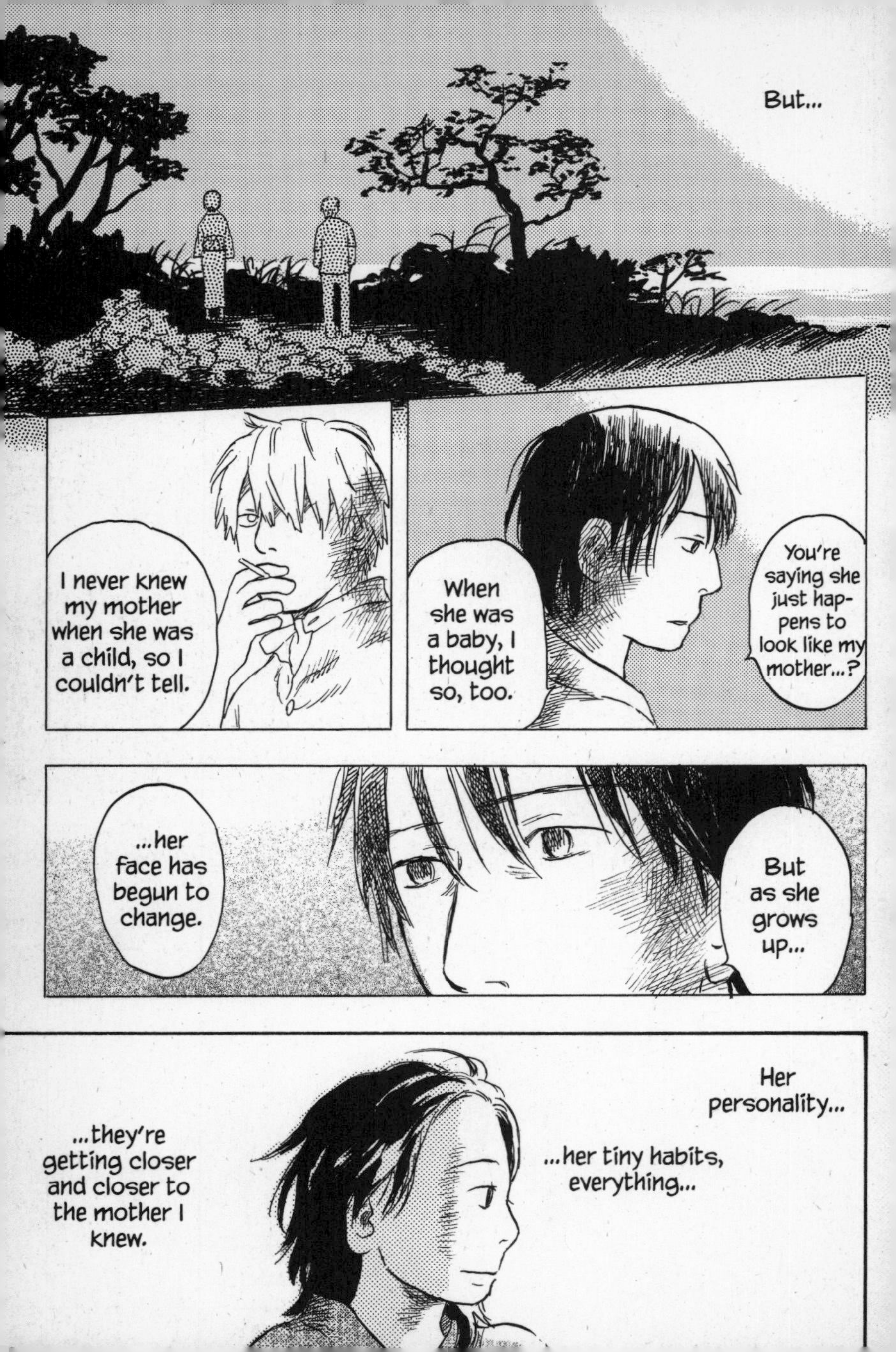
But...
You're saying she just happens to look like my mother...?
When she was a baby, I thought so, too.
I never knew my mother when she was a child, so I couldn't tell.
But as she grows up...
...her face has begun to change.
Her personality...
...her tiny habits, everything...
...they're getting closer and closer to the mother I knew.

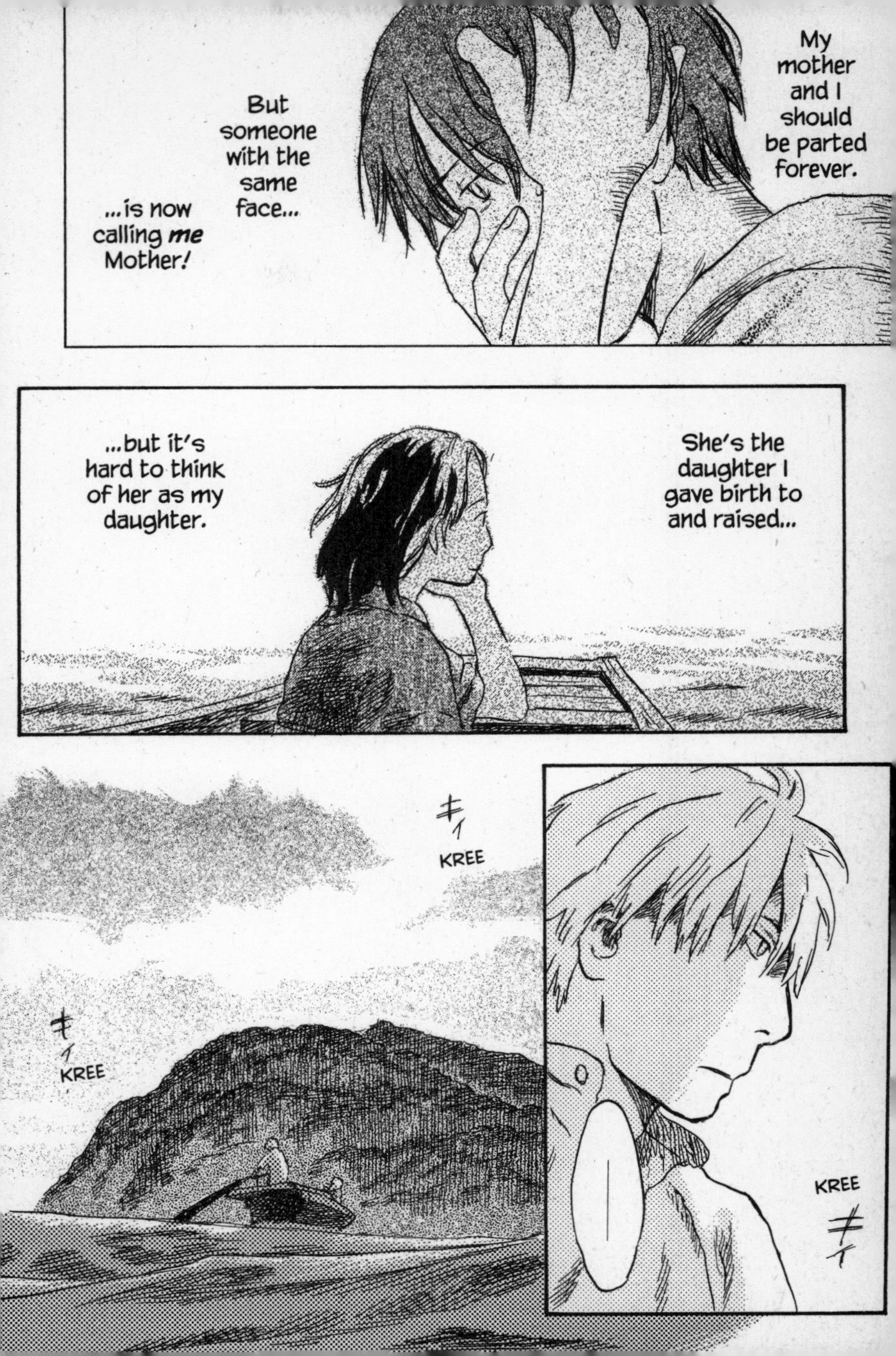
My mother and I should be parted forever.
But someone with the same face...
...is now calling *me* Mother!
She's the daughter I gave birth to and raised...
...but it's hard to think of her as my daughter.
KREE
キイ
キイ
KREE
キイ
KREE

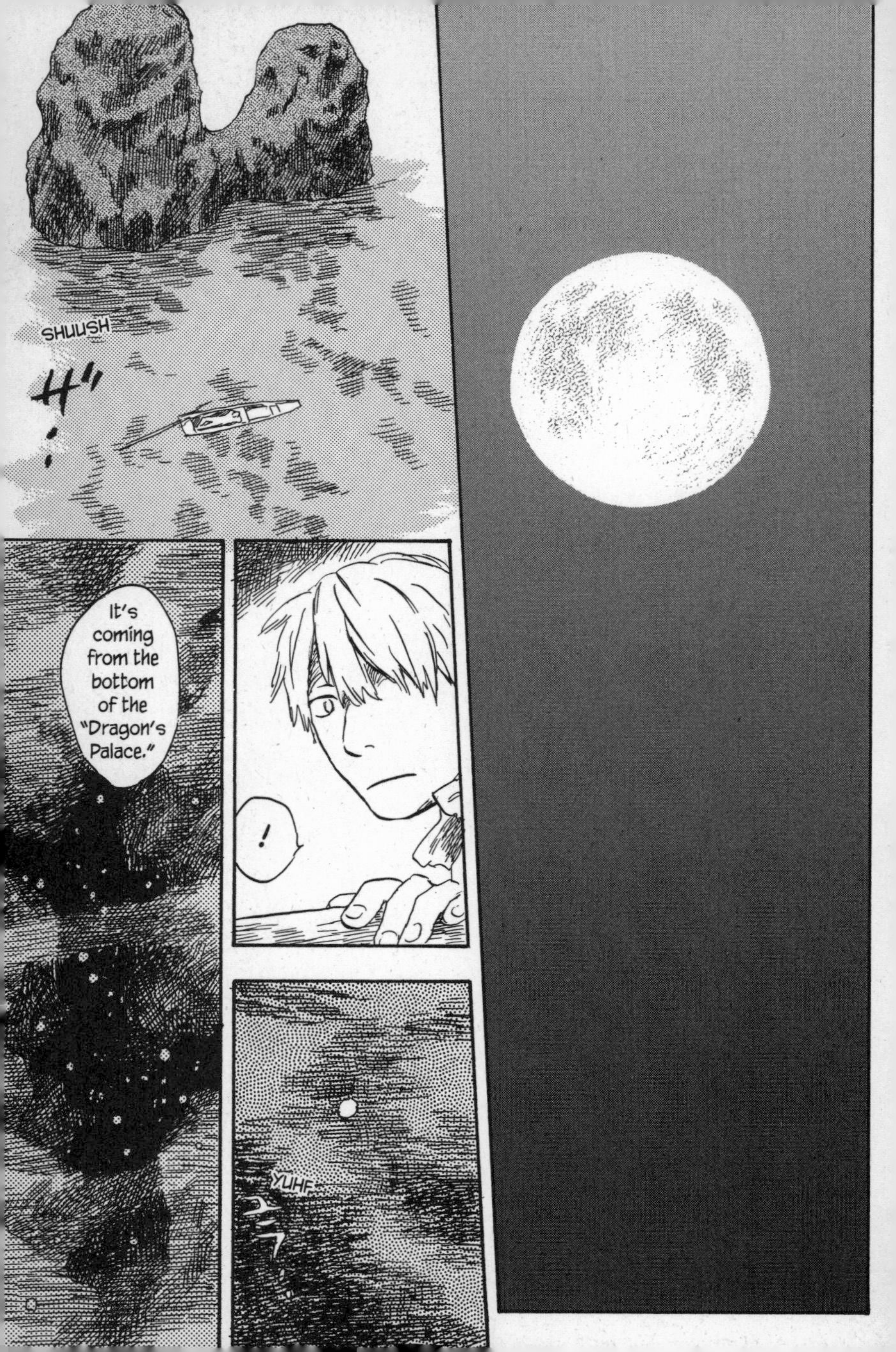
SHUUSH
!
It's coming from the bottom of the "Dragon's Palace."
YUHF

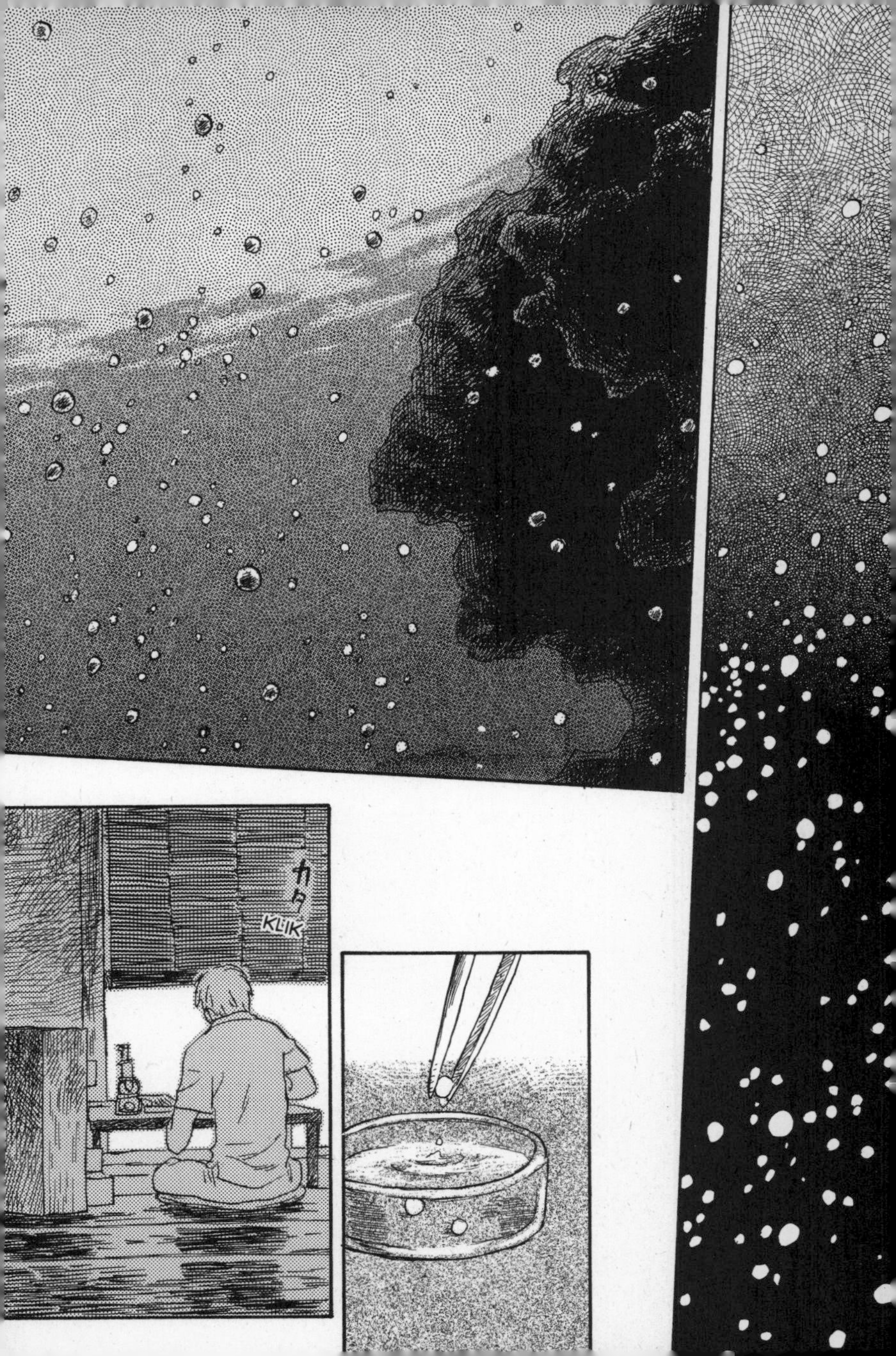
カタ
KLIK

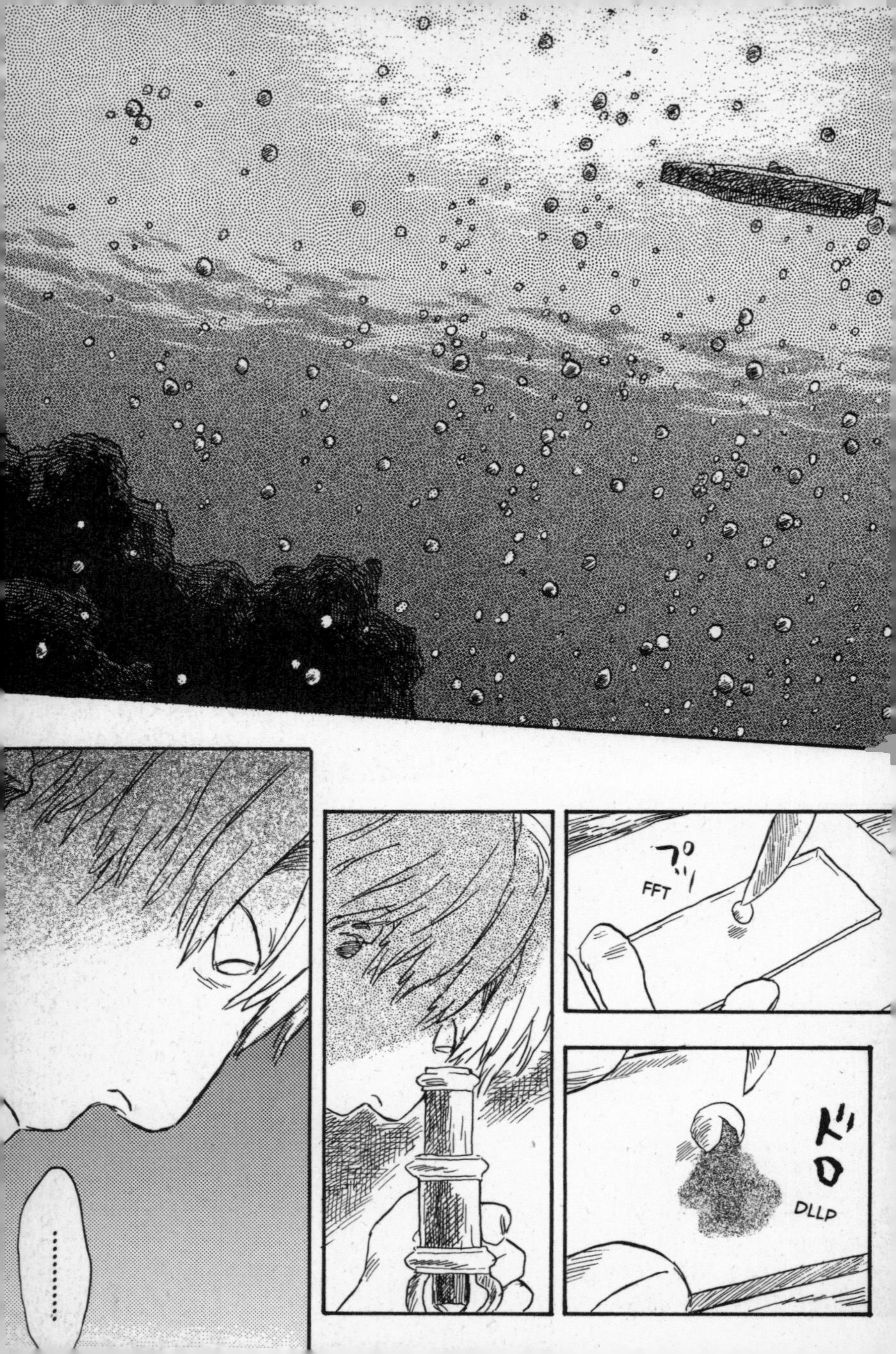
プッ
FFT
ドロ
DLLP
……

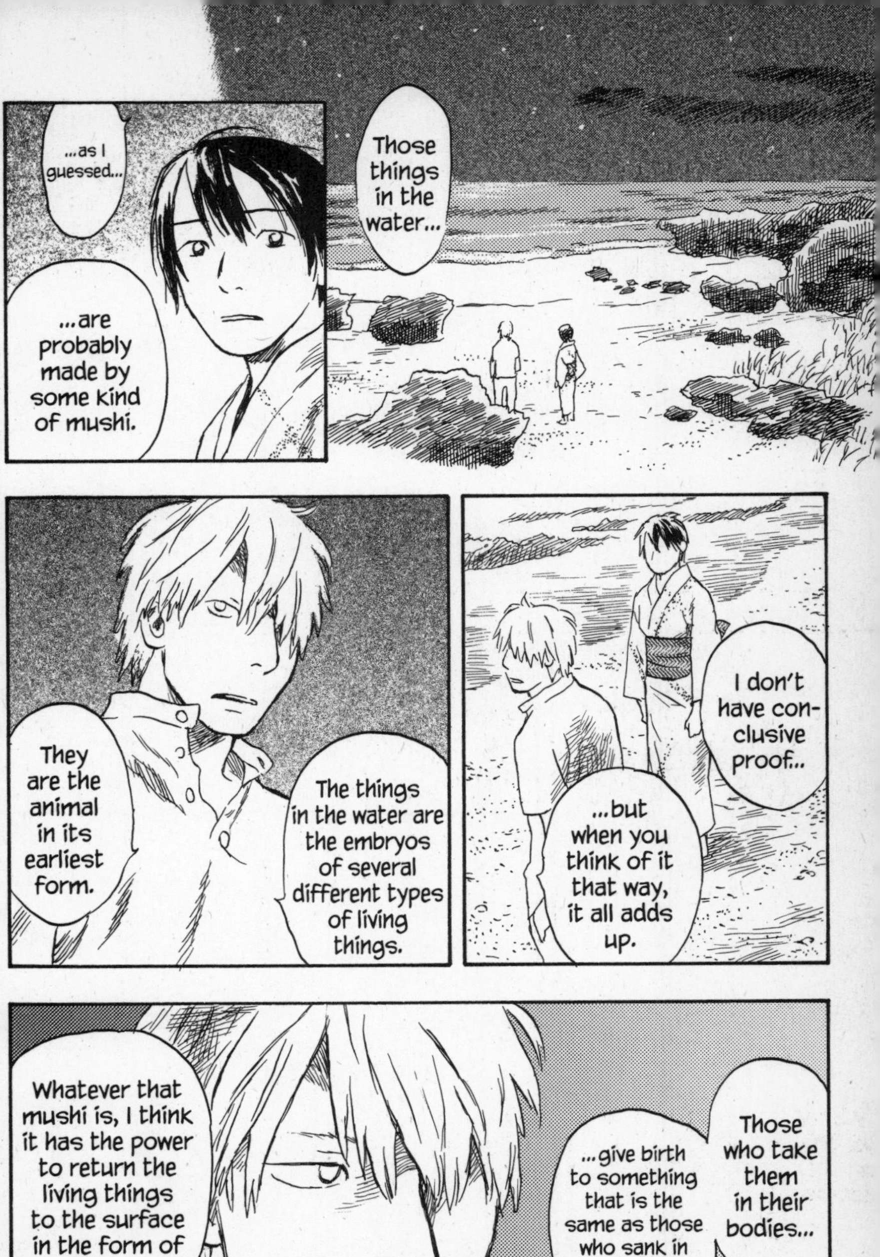
Those things in the water...
...as I guessed...
...are probably made by some kind of mushi.
I don't have conclusive proof...
...but when you think of it that way, it all adds up.
The things in the water are the embryos of several different types of living things.
They are the animal in its earliest form.
Those who take them in their bodies...
...give birth to something that is the same as those who sank in that part of the sea.
Whatever that mushi is, I think it has the power to return the living things to the surface in the form of embryos.

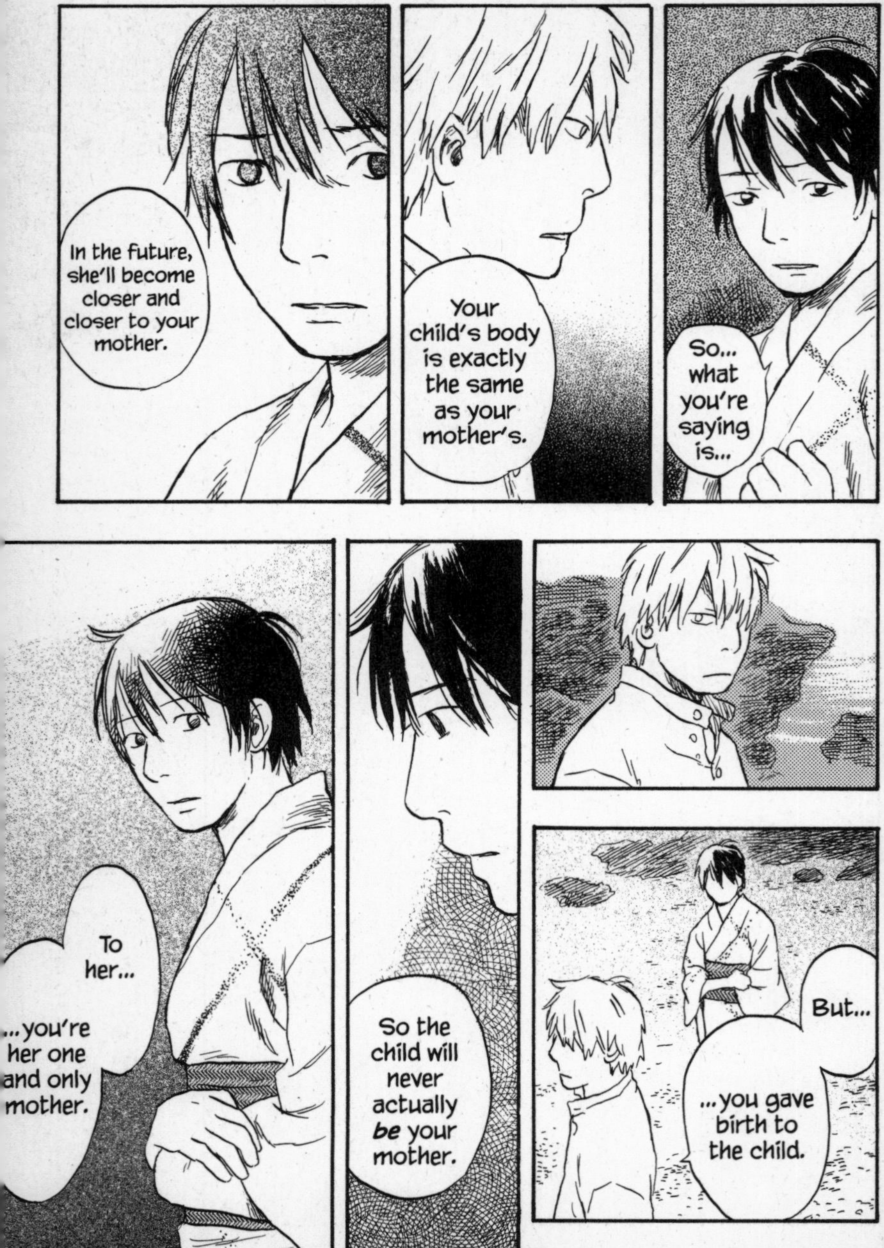
So... what you're saying is...
Your child's body is exactly the same as your mother's.
In the future, she'll become closer and closer to your mother.
But...
...you gave birth to the child.
So the child will never actually *be* your mother.
To her...
...you're her one and only mother.

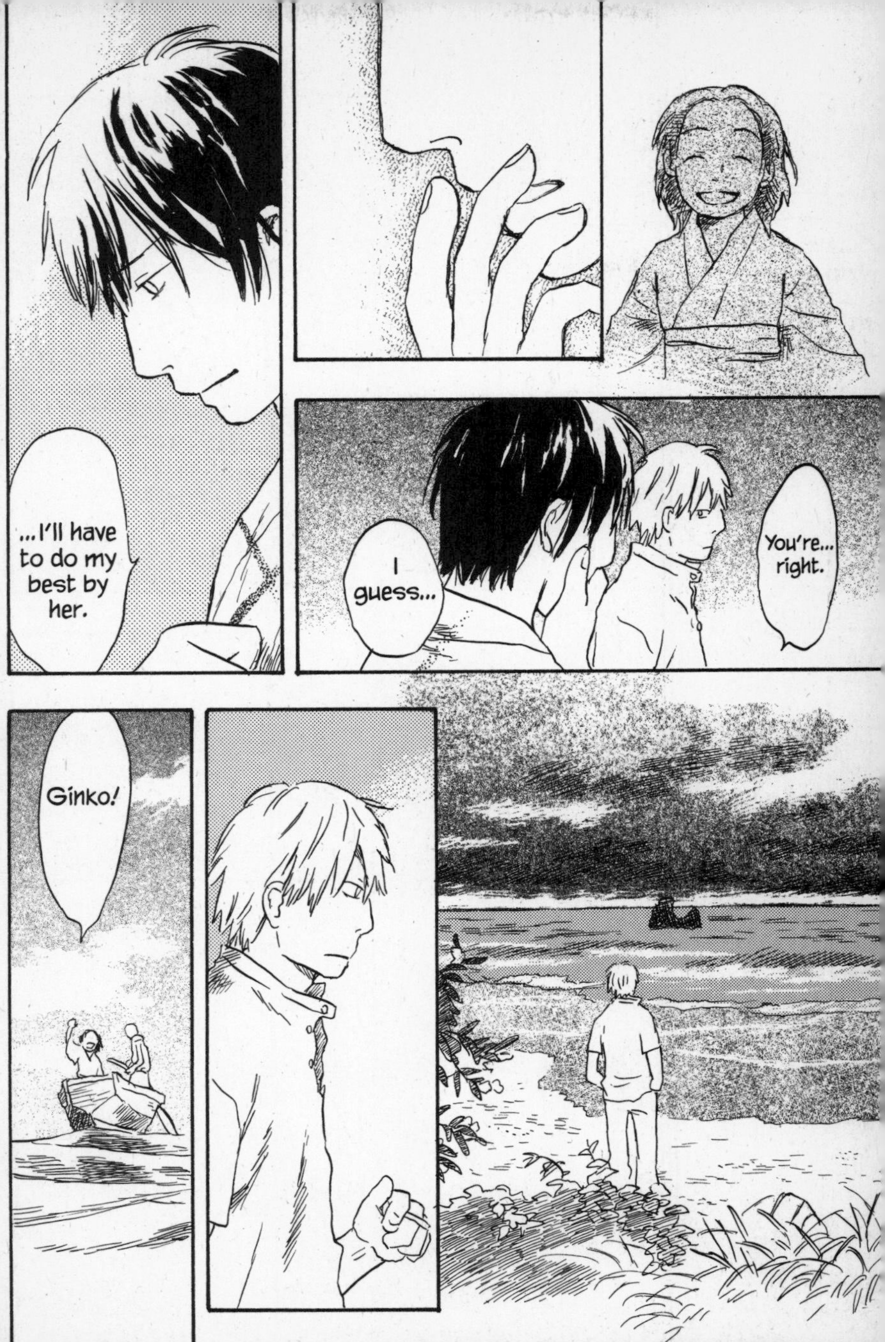
You're... right.
I guess...
...I'll have to do my best by her.
Ginko!

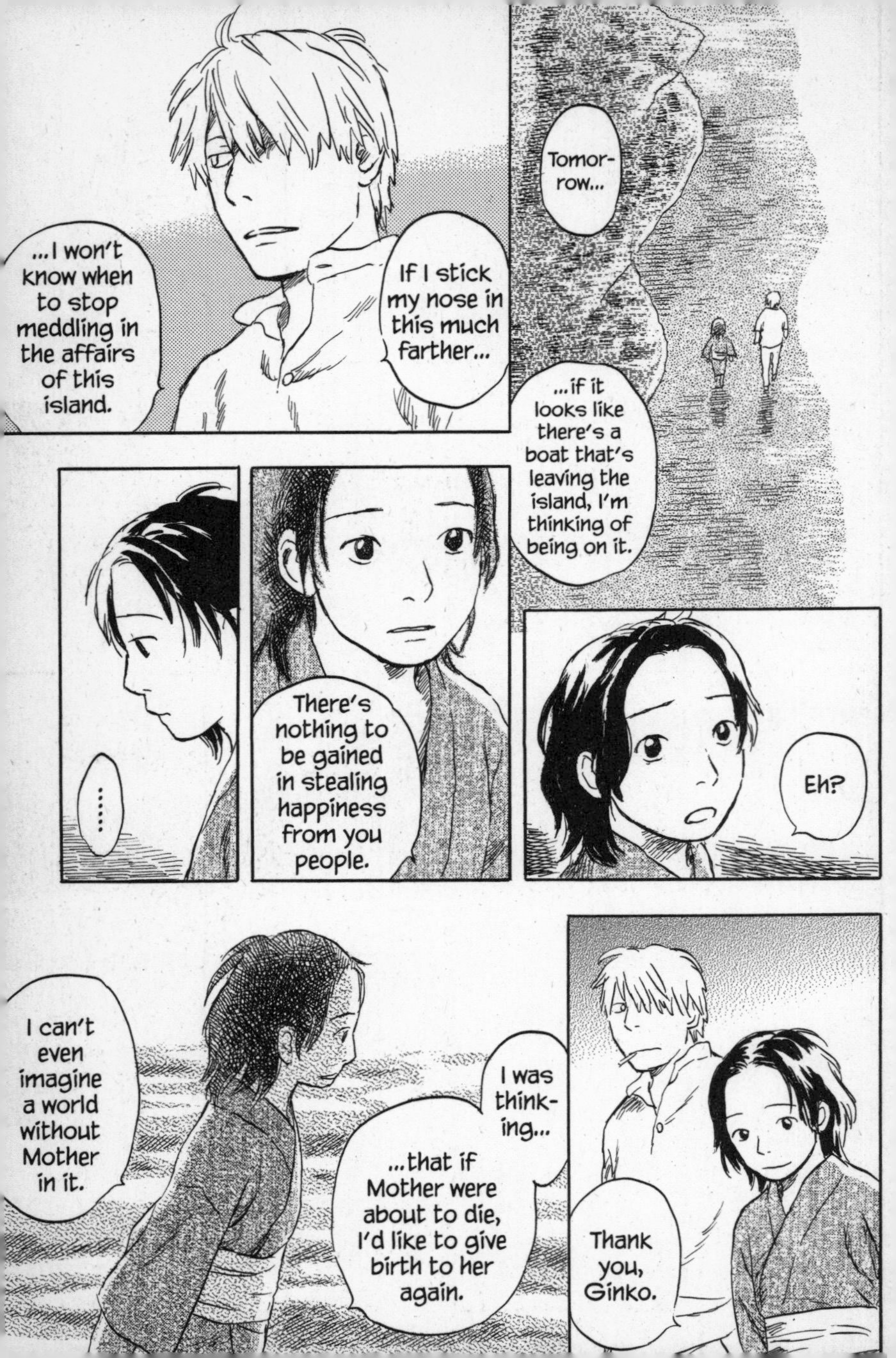

Tomorrow-row...
...if it looks like there's a boat that's leaving the island, I'm thinking of being on it.
If I stick my nose in this much farther...
...I won't know when to stop meddling in the affairs of this island.
Eh?
There's nothing to be gained in stealing happiness from you people.
......
Thank you, Ginko.
I was thinking...
...that if Mother were about to die, I'd like to give birth to her again.
I can't even imagine a world without Mother in it.

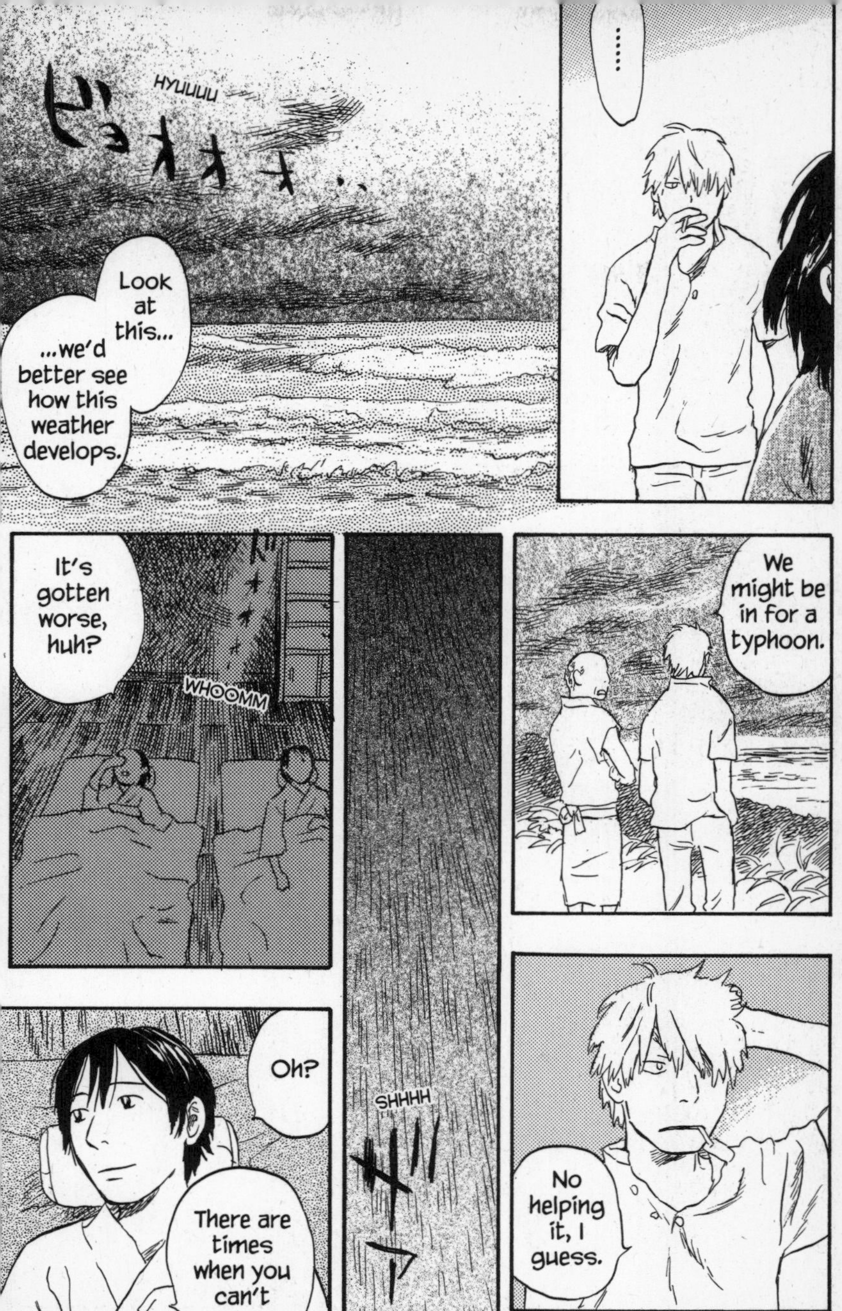
……
HYUUUU
ビョォォォ…
Look at this...
...we'd better see how this weather develops.
We might be in for a typhoon.
No helping it, I guess.
SHHHH
ザァァ
It's gotten worse, huh?
WHOOMM
Oh?
There are times when you can't sleep?

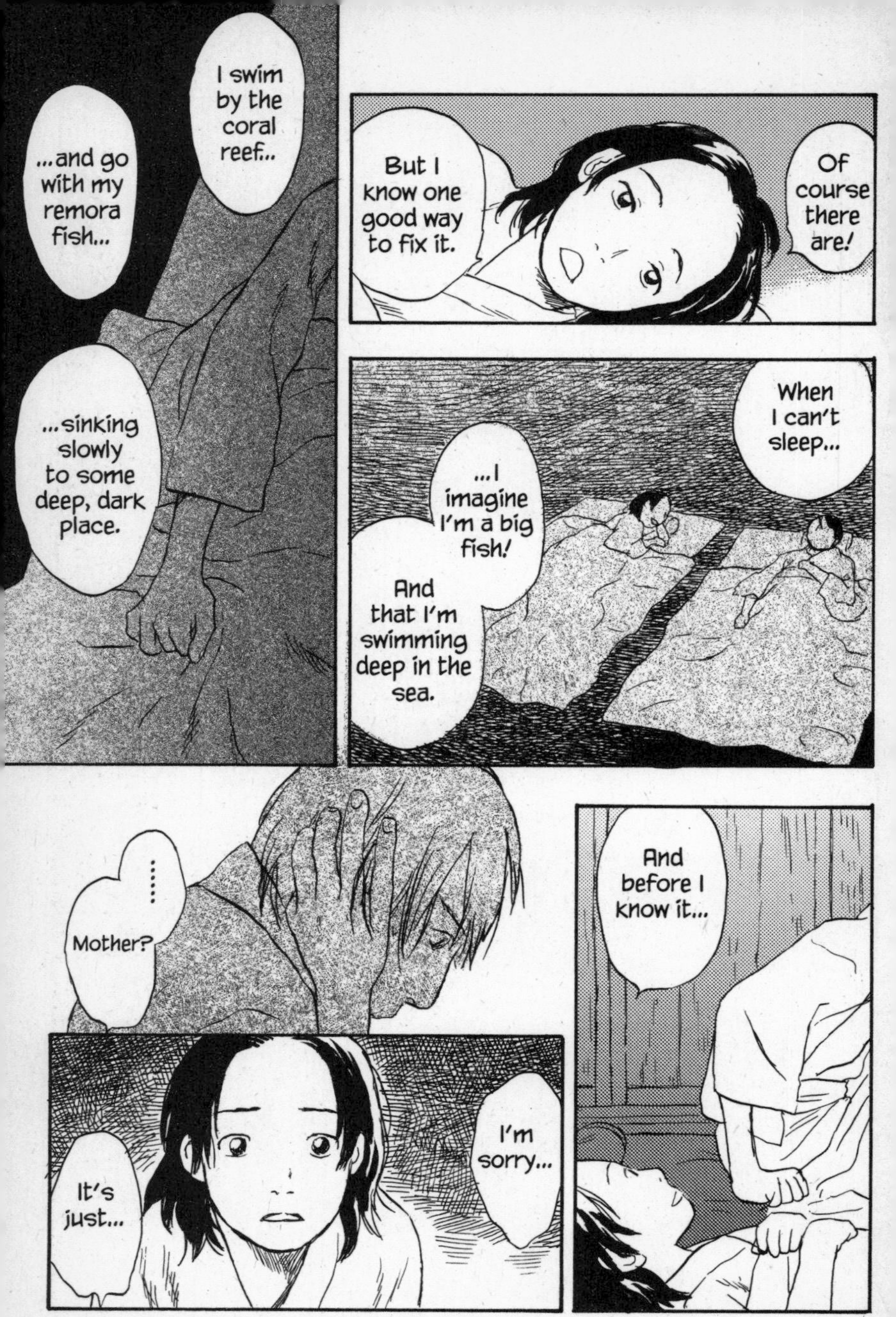
Of course there are!
But I know one good way to fix it.
When I can't sleep...
...I imagine I'm a big fish!
And that I'm swimming deep in the sea.
I swim by the coral reef...
...and go with my remora fish...
...sinking slowly to some deep, dark place.
And before I know it...
......
Mother?
I'm sorry...
It's just...

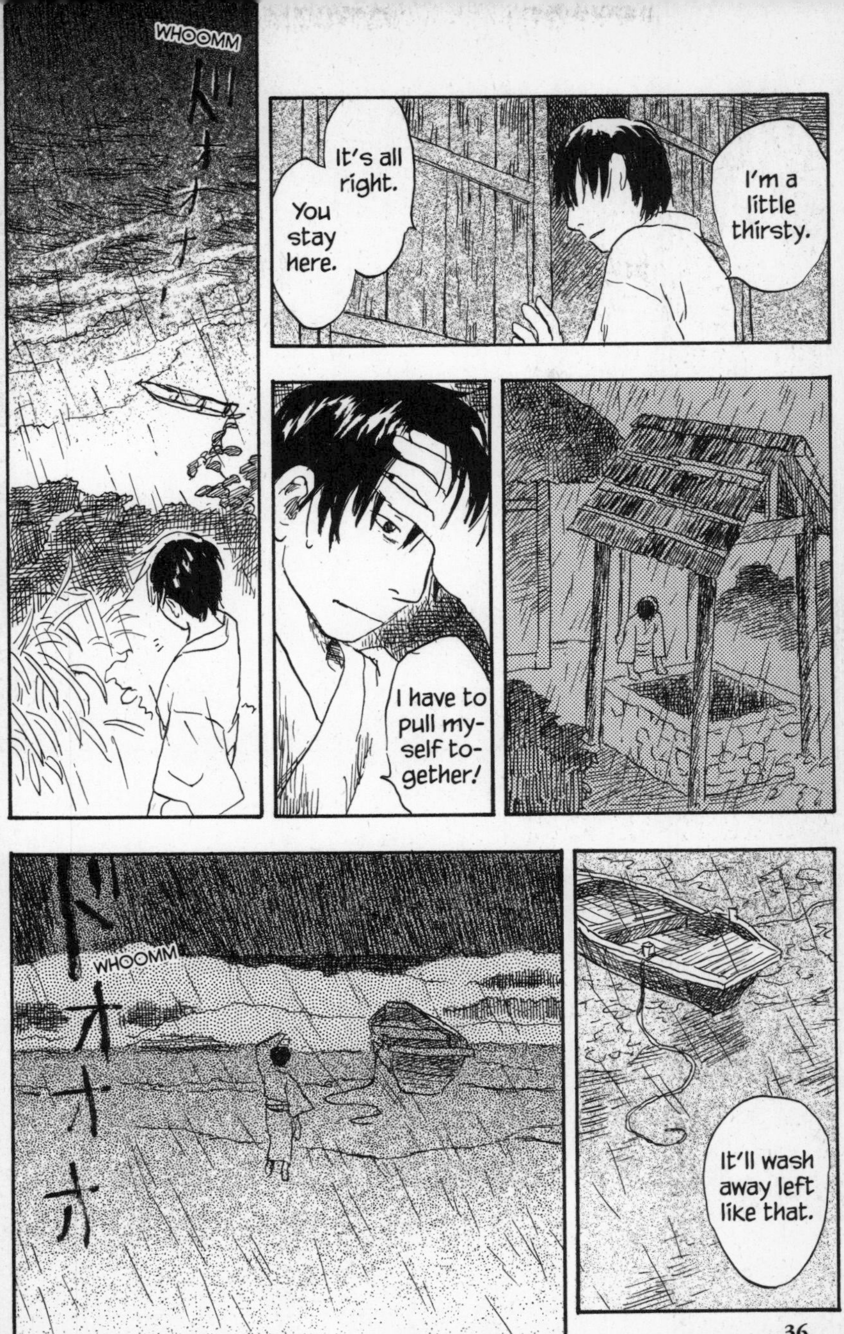
I'm a little thirsty.
It's all right.
You stay here.
I have to pull my-self to-gether!
WHOOMM
ドオオオ！
It'll wash away left like that.
WHOOMM
ドオオオ

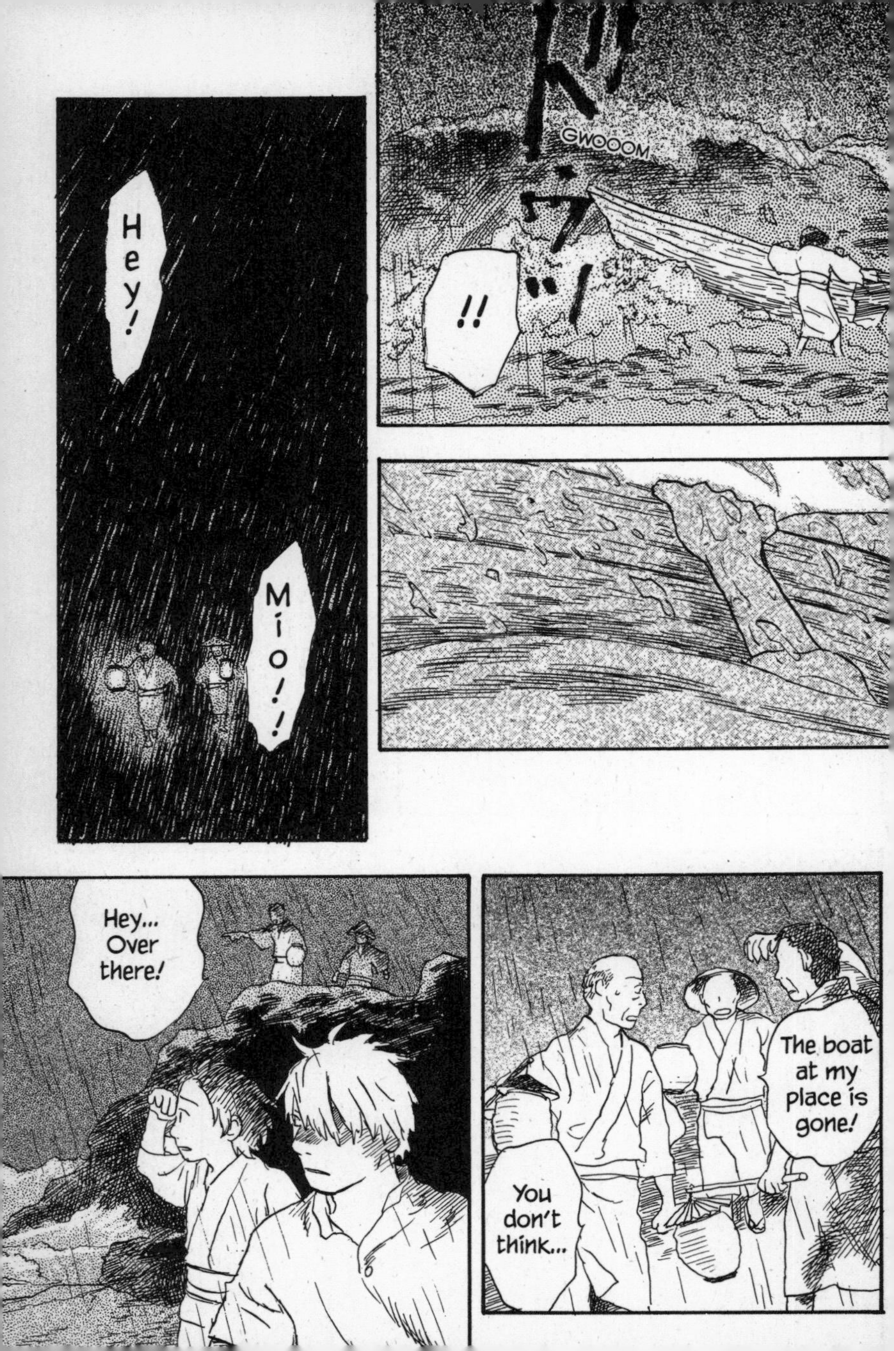
GWOOOM
!!
Hey!
Mio!!
The boat at my place is gone!
You don't think...
Hey... Over there!

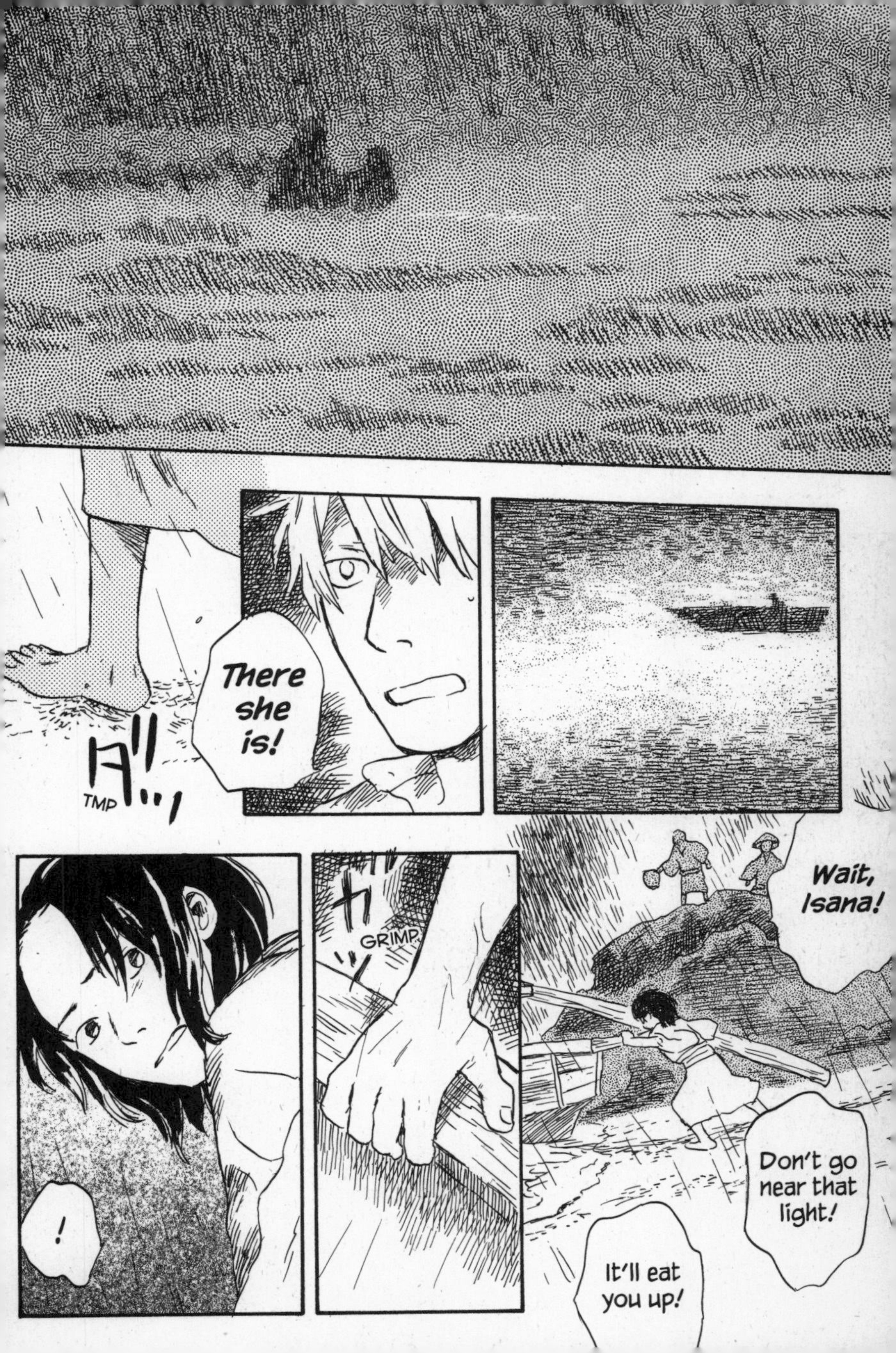

There she is!
TMP
Wait, Isana!
Don't go near that light!
It'll eat you up!
GRIMP
!

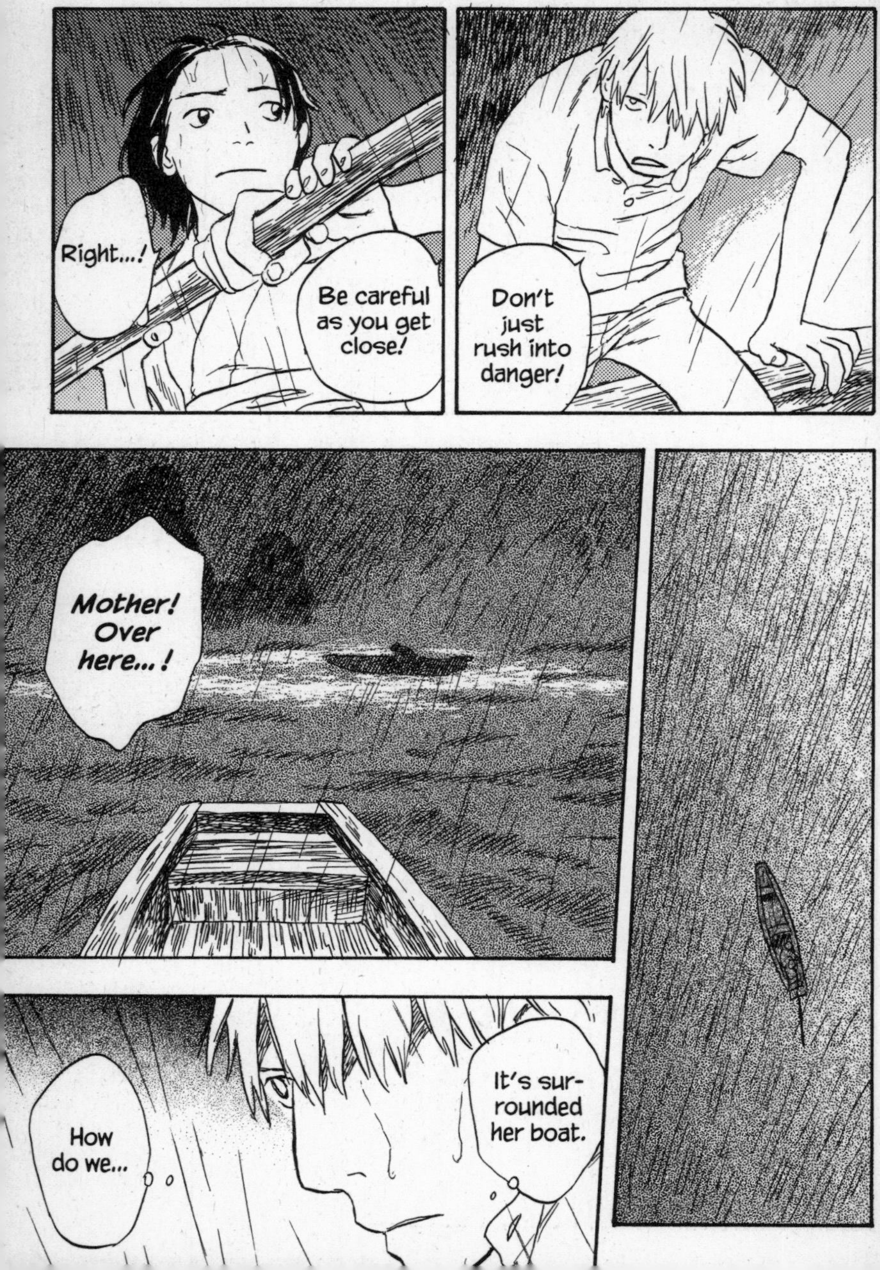
Don't just rush into danger!
Be careful as you get close!
Right...!
Mother! Over here...!
It's surrounded her boat.
How do we...

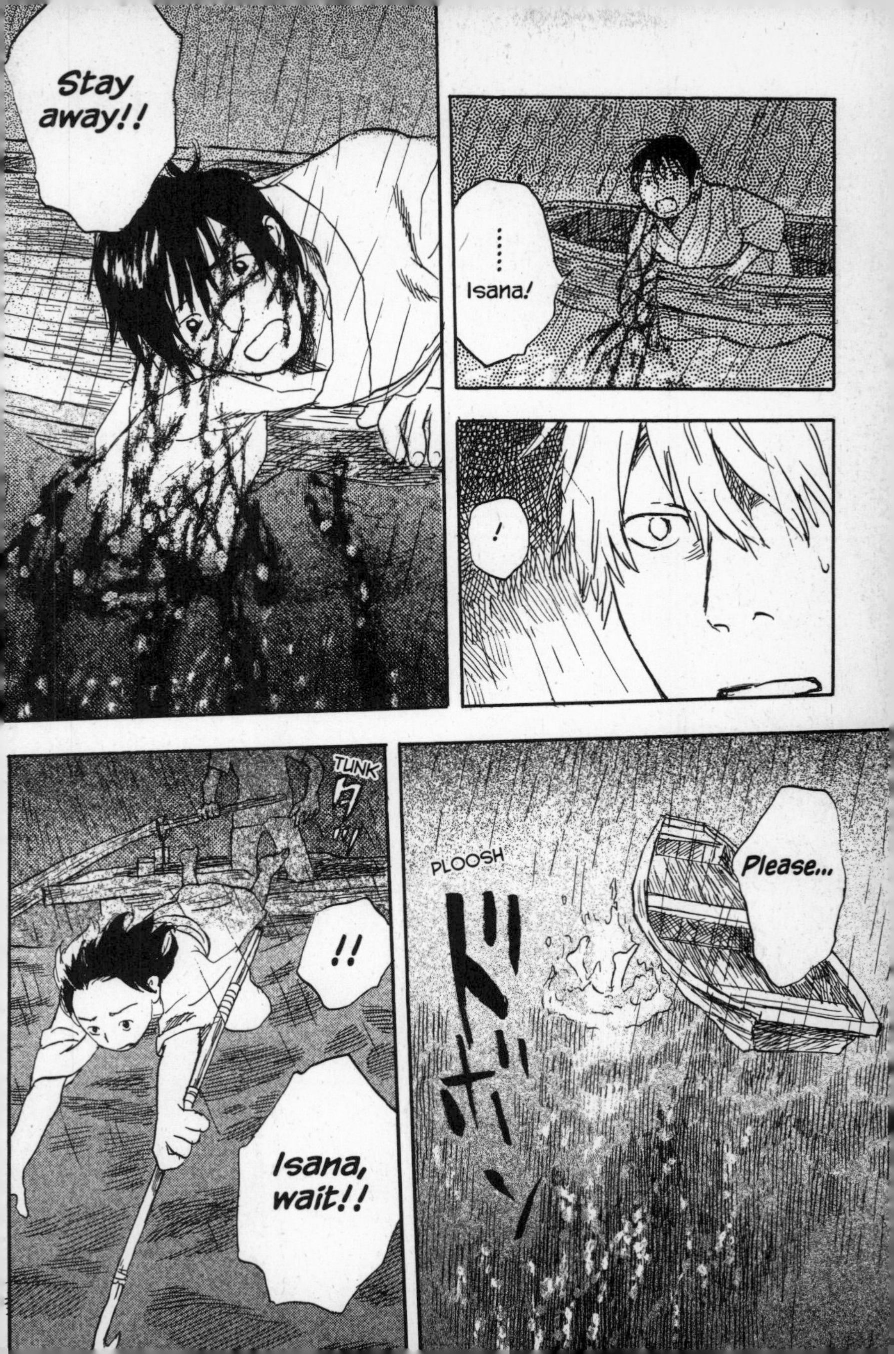
......
Isana!
!
Stay away!!
PLOOSH
Please...
TUNK
!!
Isana, wait!!

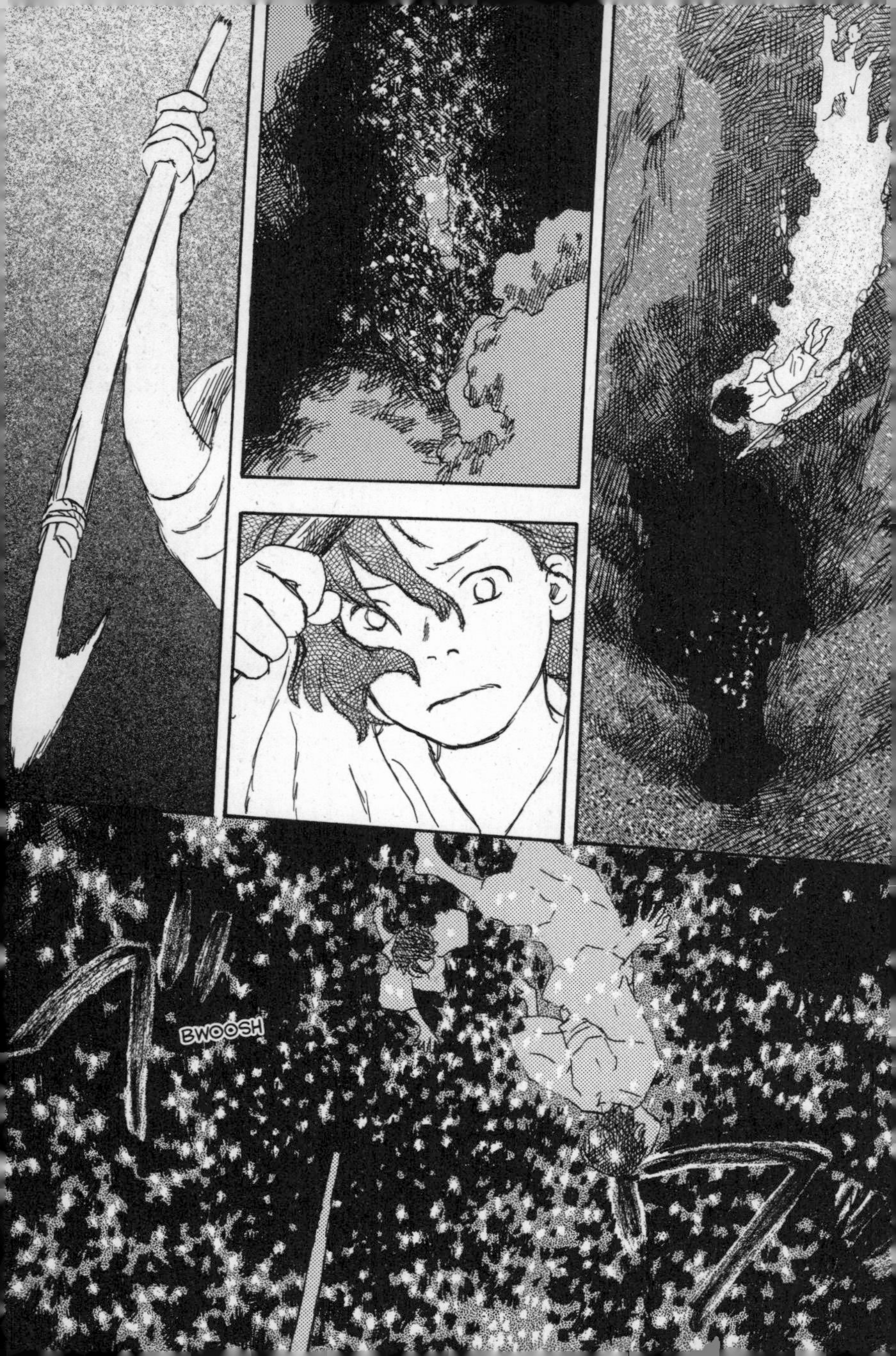
BWOOSH

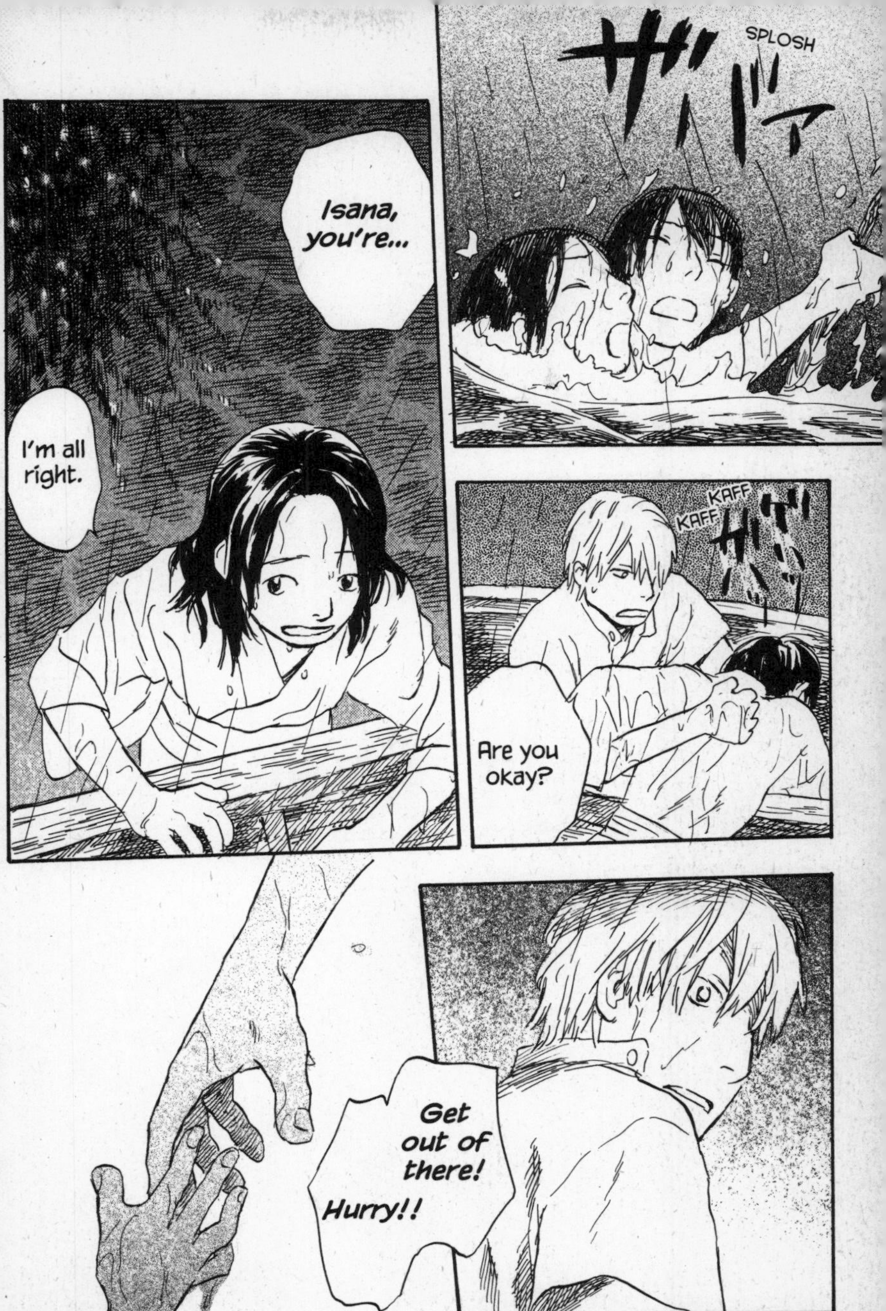
SPLOSH
KAFF KAFF
Are you okay?
Isana, you're...
I'm all right.
Get out of there!
Hurry!!

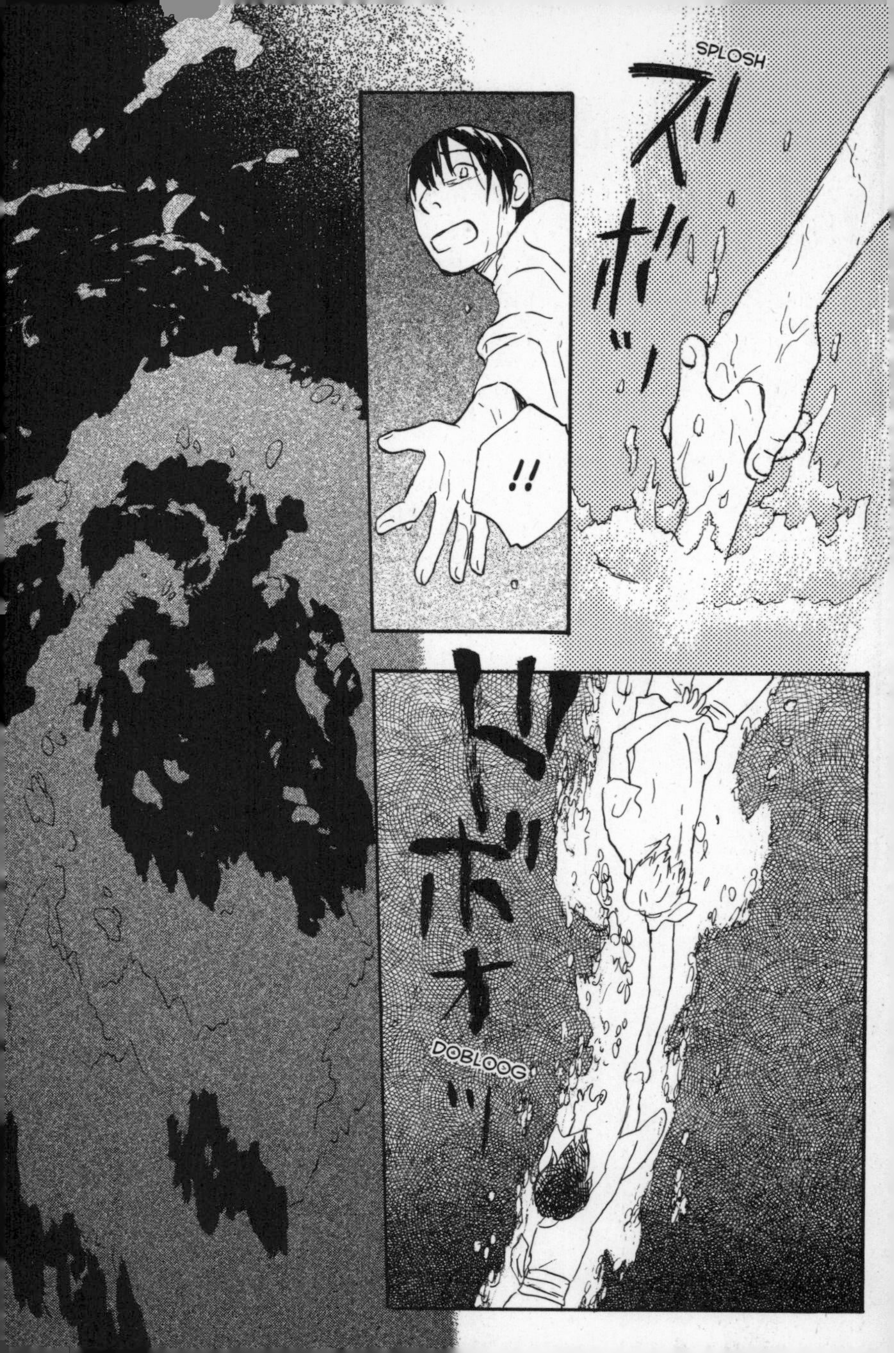
SPLOSH
!!
DOBLOOG

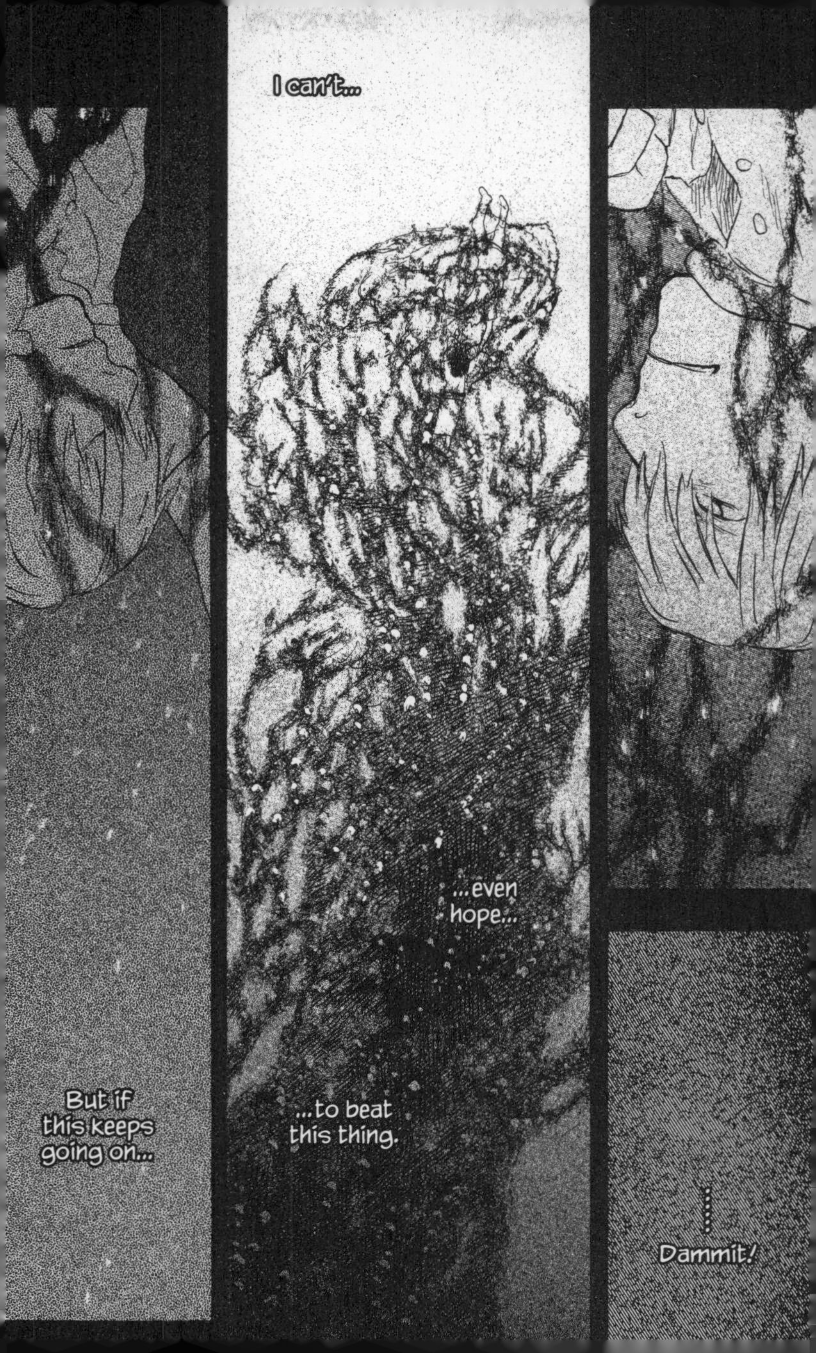
......
Dammit!
I can't...
...even hope...
...to beat this thing.
But if this keeps going on...

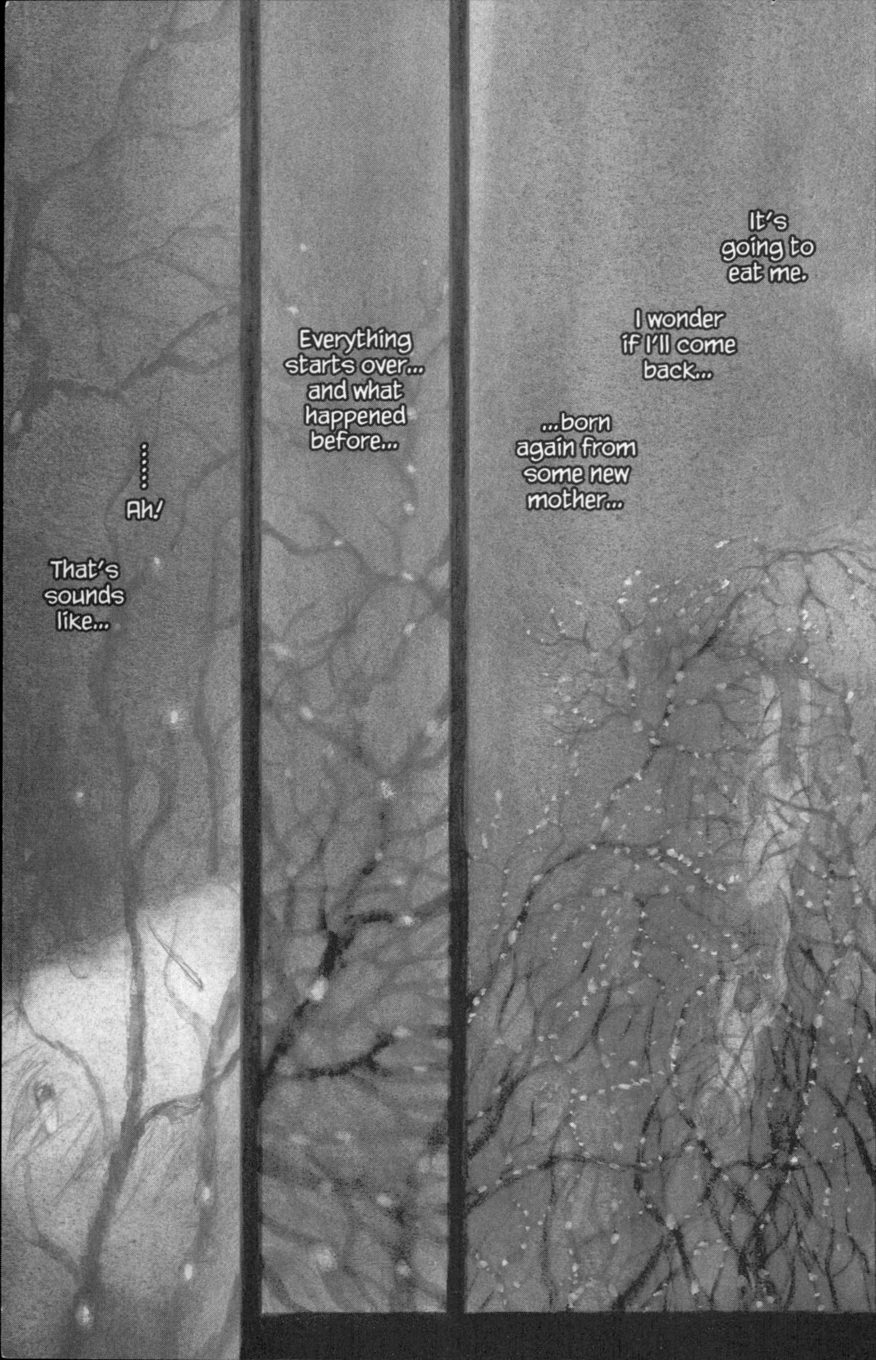
It's going to eat me.
I wonder if I'll come back...
...born again from some new mother...
Everything starts over... and what happened before...
......
Ah!
That's sounds like...

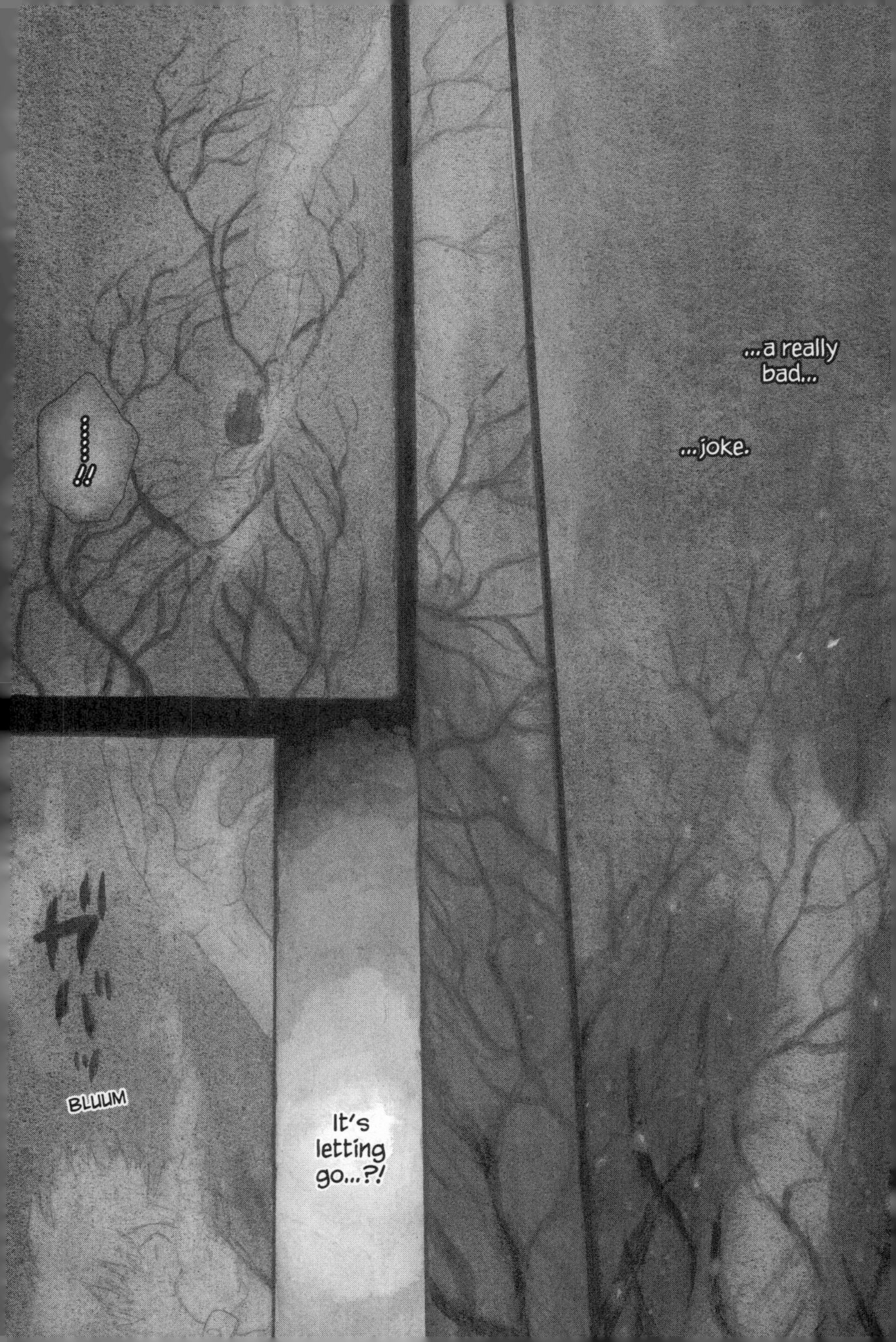
...a really bad...
...joke.
......!!
It's letting go...?!
BLUUM

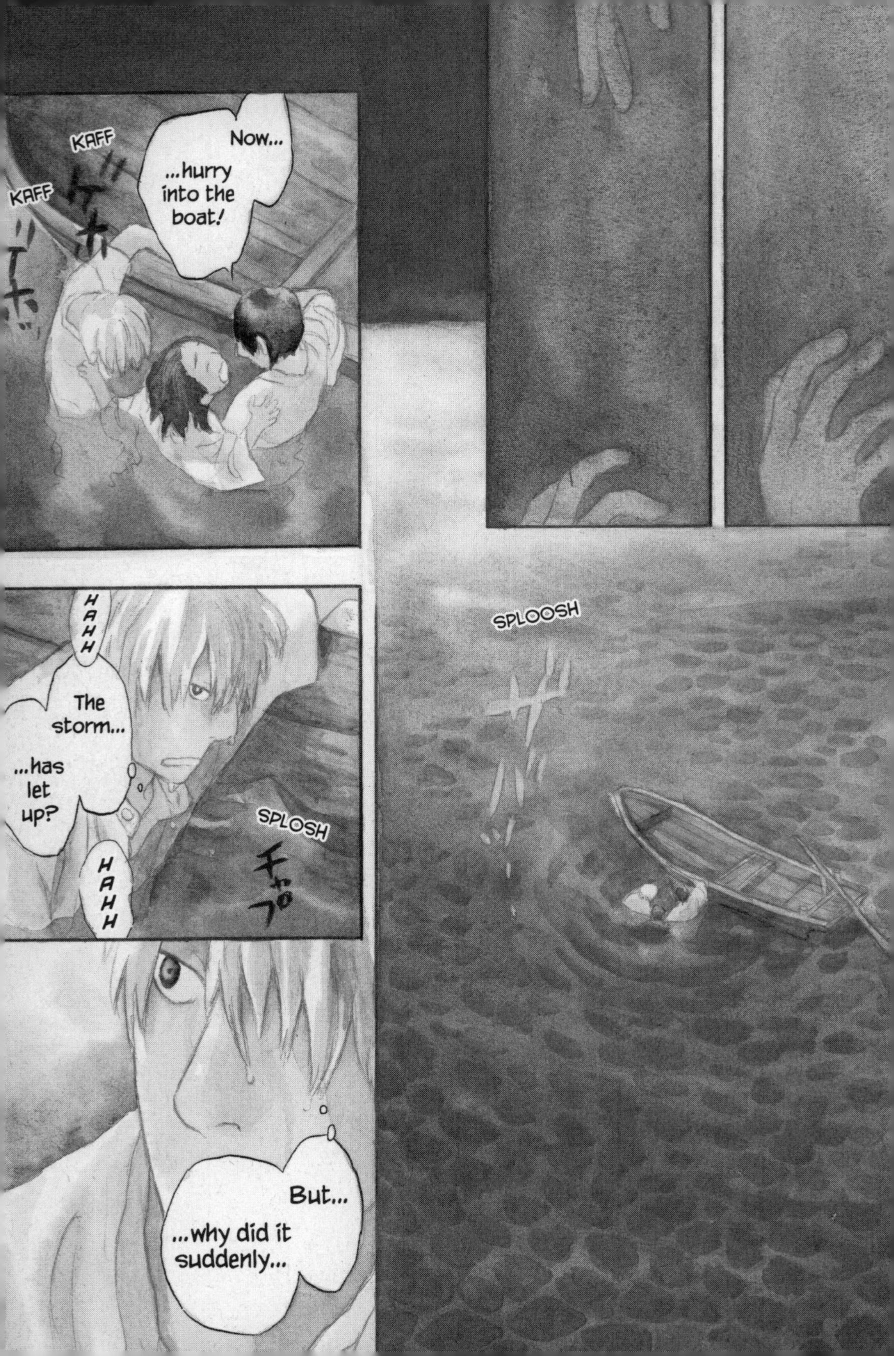
KAFF
KAFF
Now... ...hurry into the boat!
SPLOOSH
HAHH
The storm...
...has let up?
SPLOSH
HAHH
But... ...why did it suddenly...

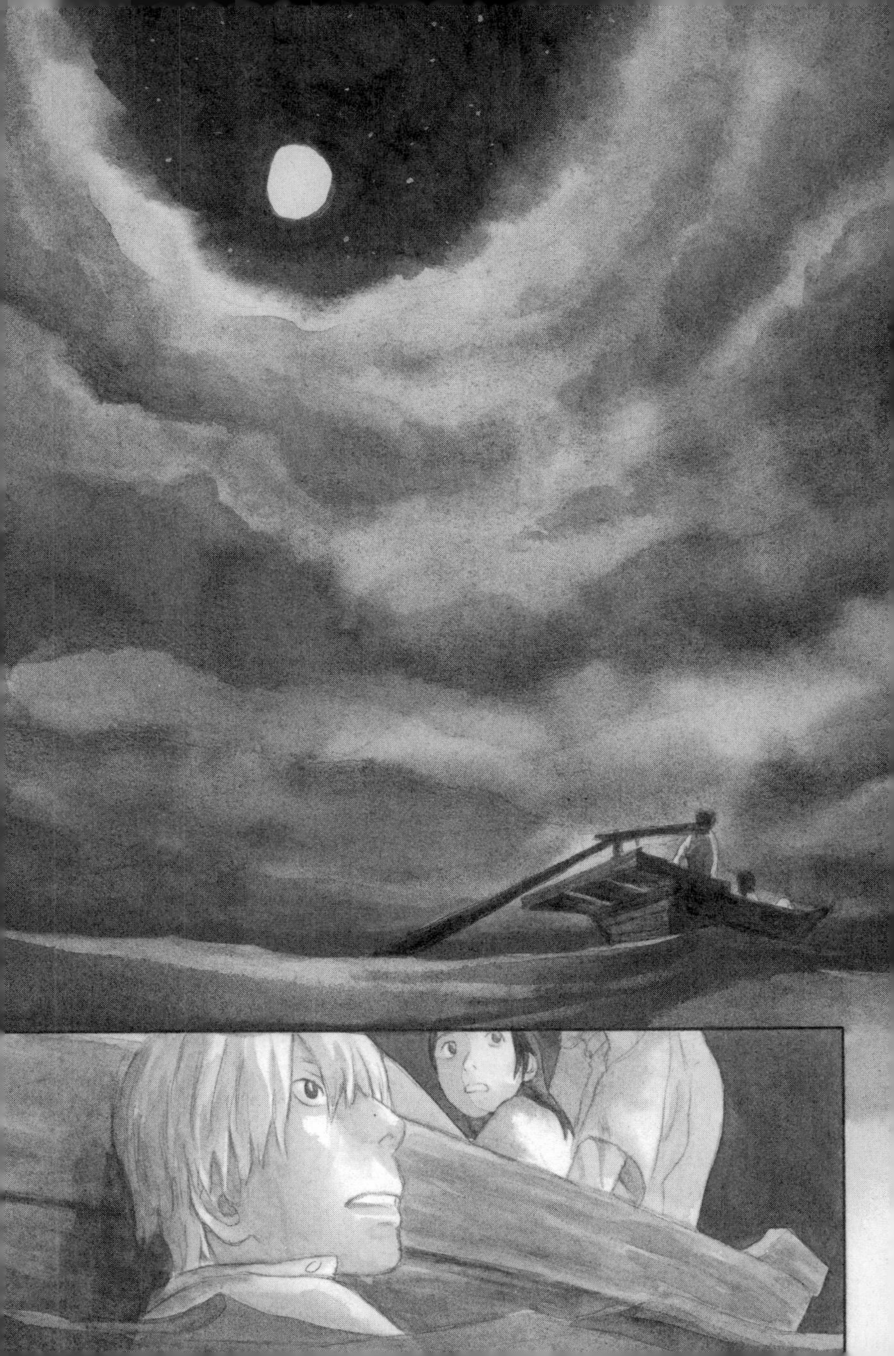

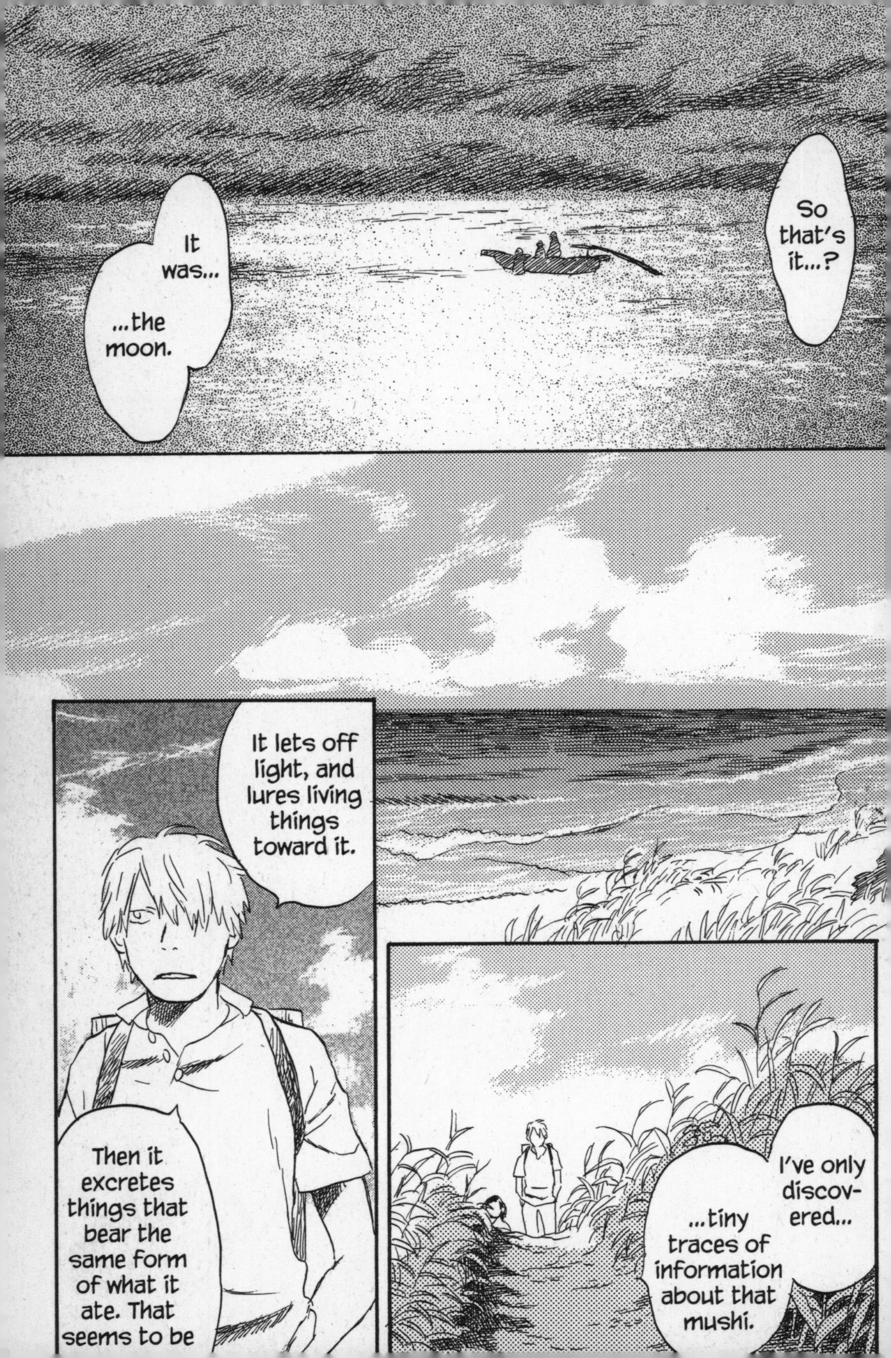
So that's it...?
It was...
...the moon.
I've only discovered...
...tiny traces of information about that mushi.
It lets off light, and lures living things toward it.
Then it excretes things that bear the same form of what it ate. That seems to be

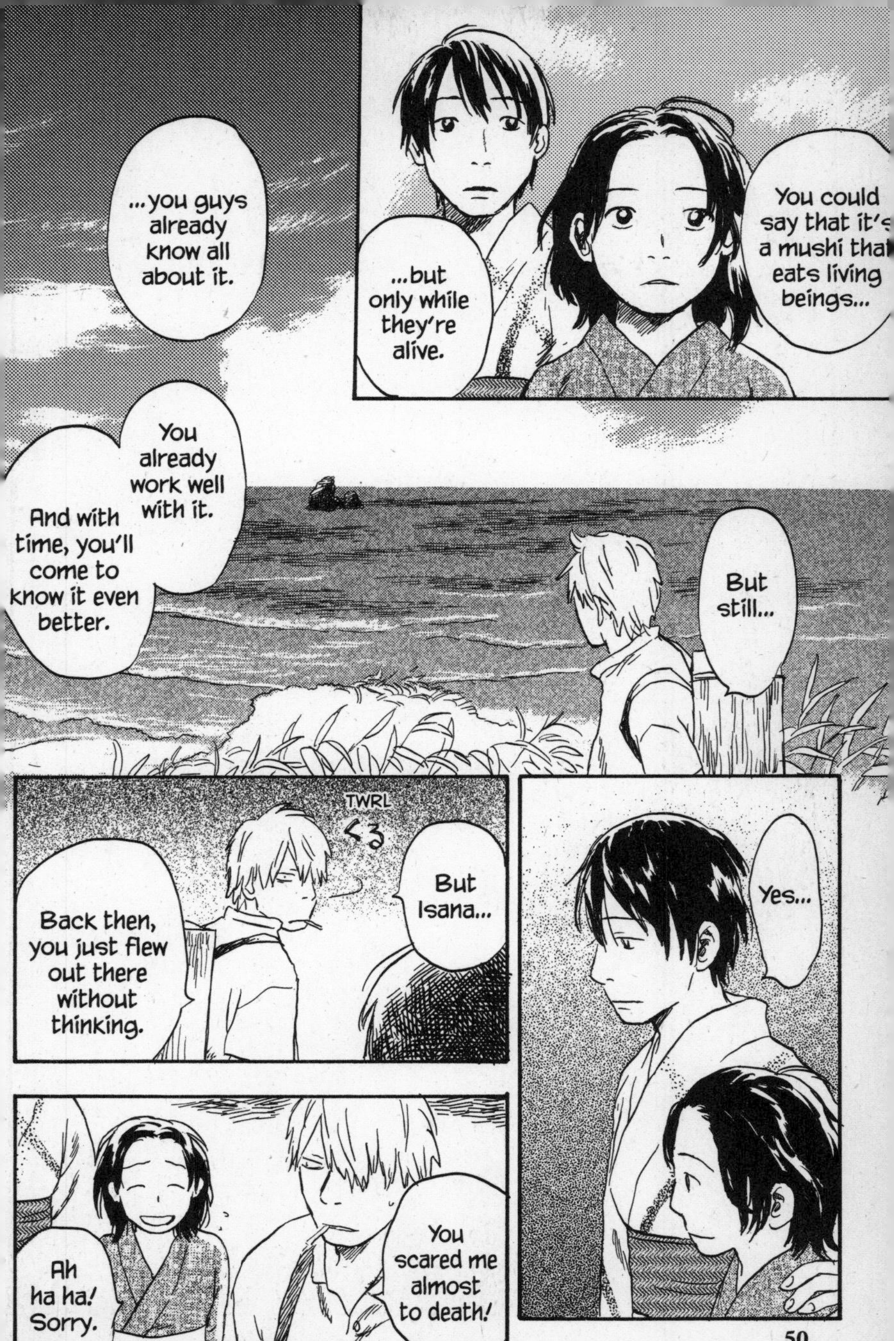
You could say that it's a mushi that eats living beings...
...but only while they're alive.
...you guys already know all about it.
You already work well with it.
And with time, you'll come to know it even better.
But still...
Yes...
TWRL
くる
But Isana...
Back then, you just flew out there without thinking.
You scared me almost to death!
Ah ha ha! Sorry.

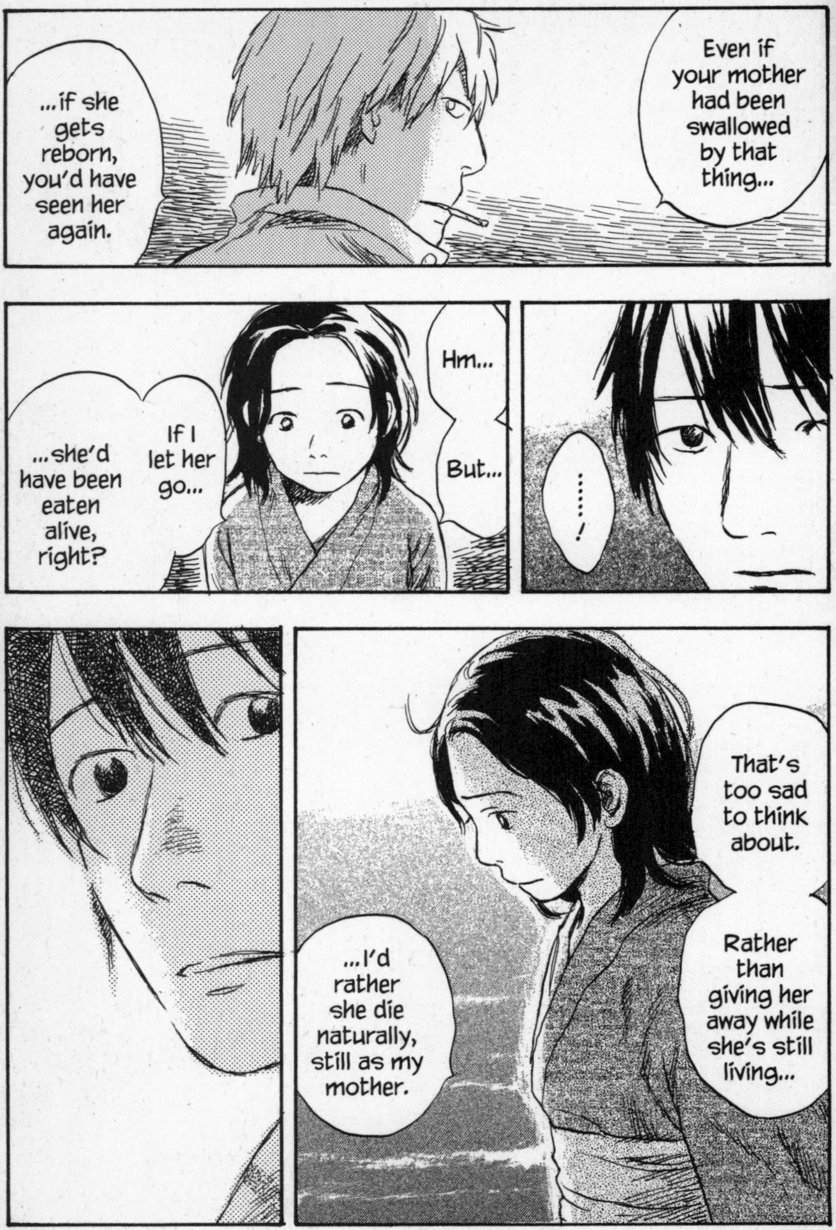
Even if your mother had been swallowed by that thing...
...if she gets reborn, you'd have seen her again.
......!
Hm...
But...
If I let her go...
...she'd have been eaten alive, right?
That's too sad to think about.
Rather than giving her away while she's still living...
...I'd rather she die naturally, still as my mother.

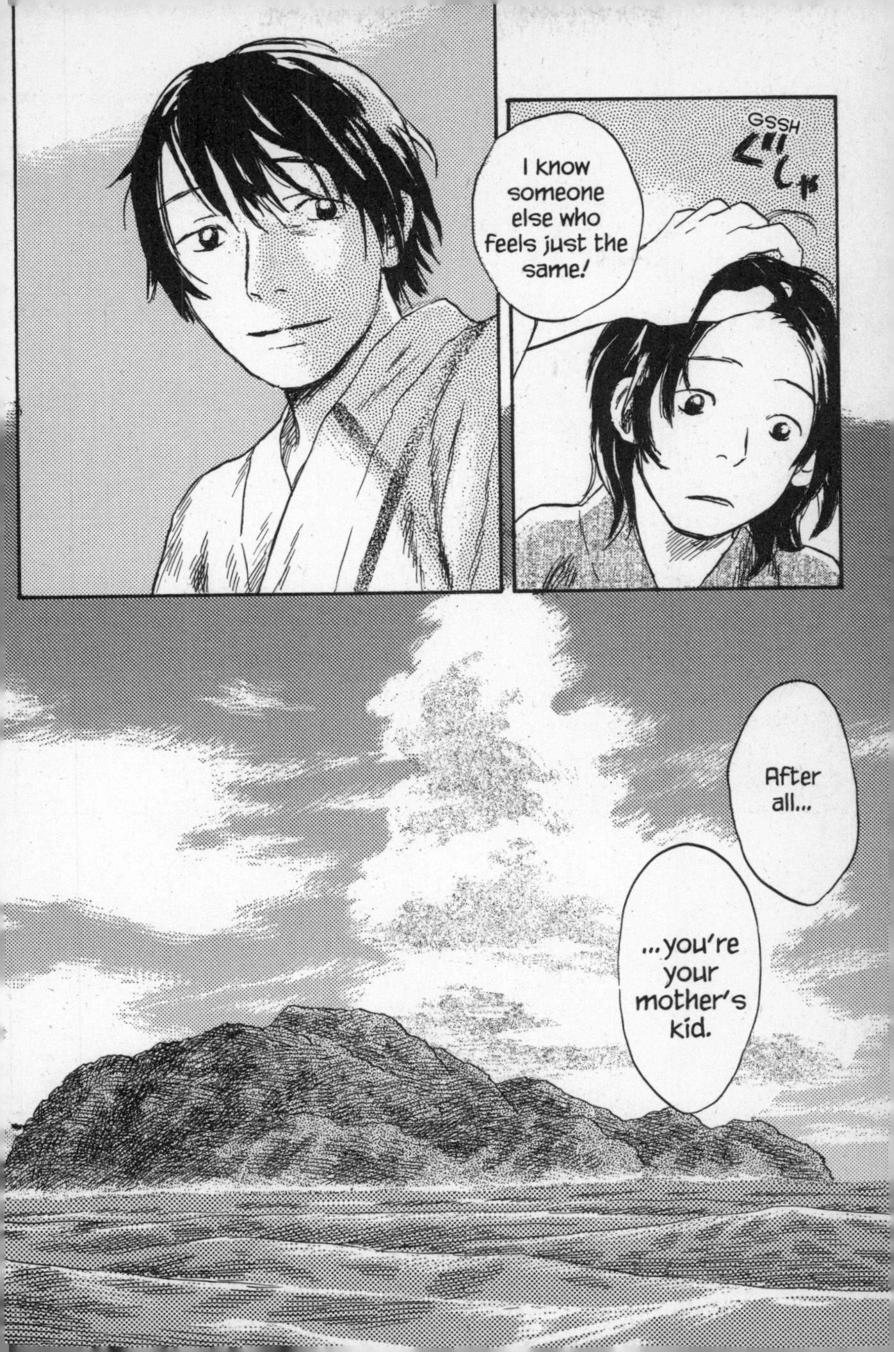
GSSH
I know someone else who feels just the same!
After all...
...you're your mother's kid.

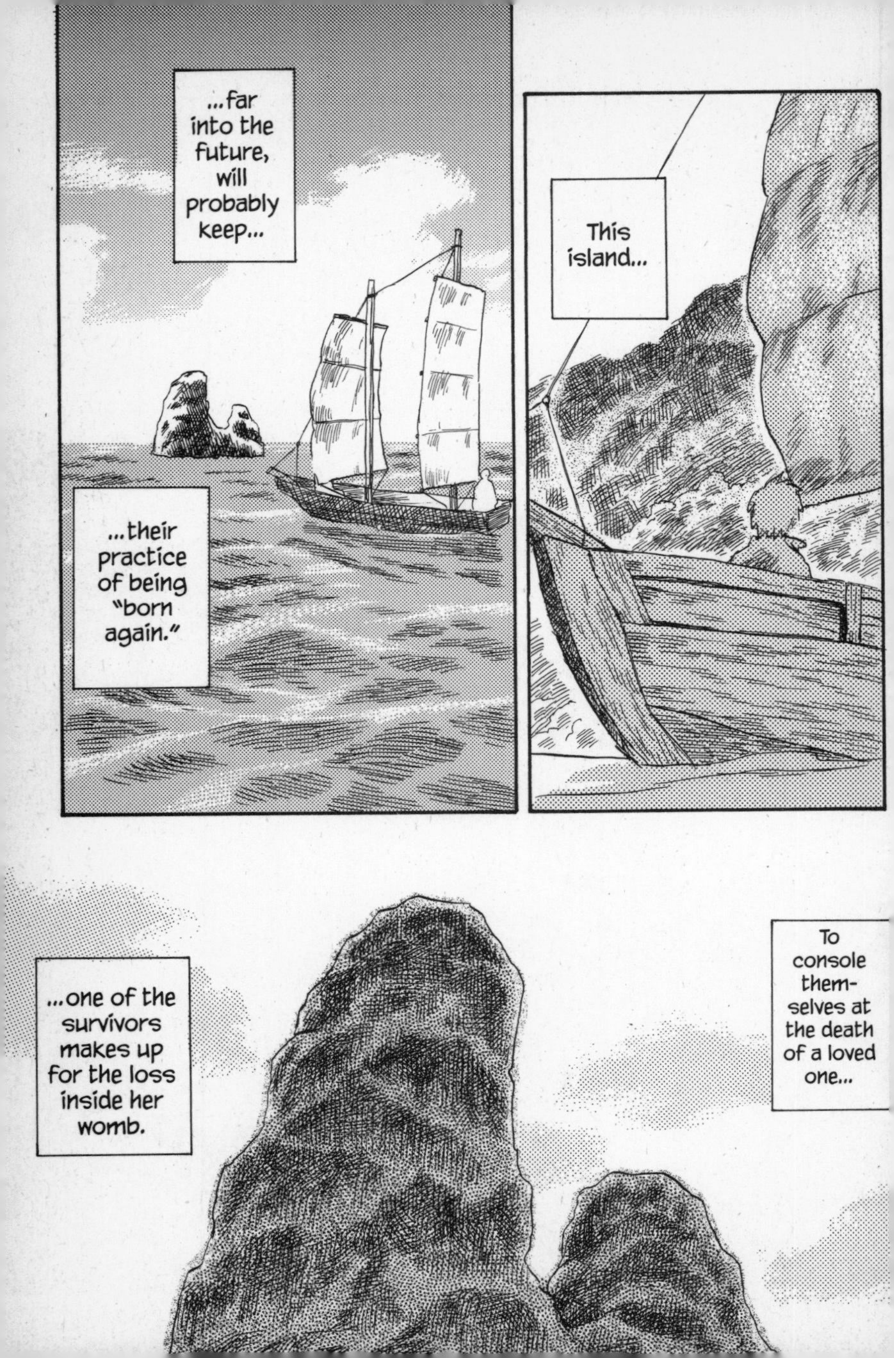
This island...
...far into the future, will probably keep...
...their practice of being "born again."
To console them-selves at the death of a loved one...
...one of the survivors makes up for the loss inside her womb.

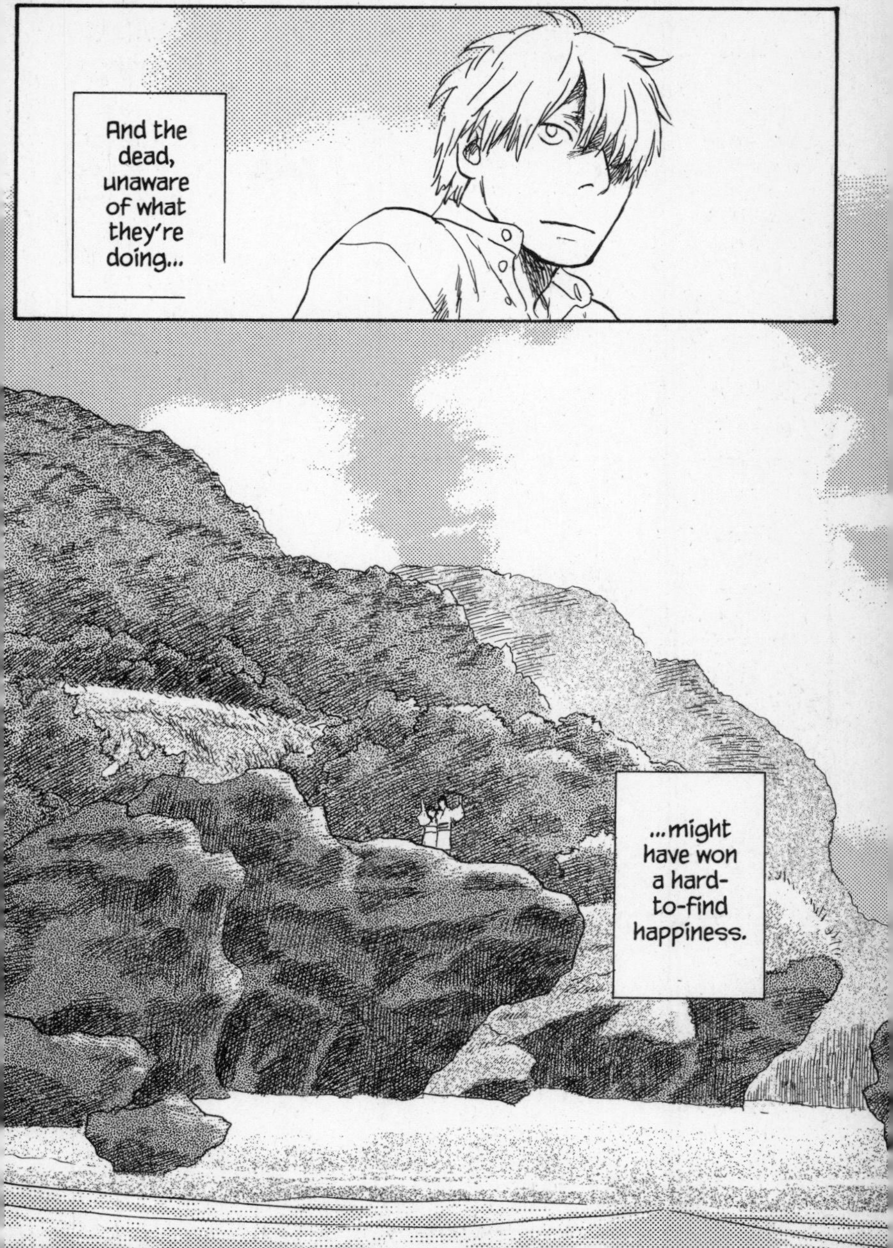
And the dead, unaware of what they're doing...
...might have won a hard-to-find happiness.

Bonus Manga

A Tale of Quite a Long Time Ago

Sounds in the Mountain Chapter

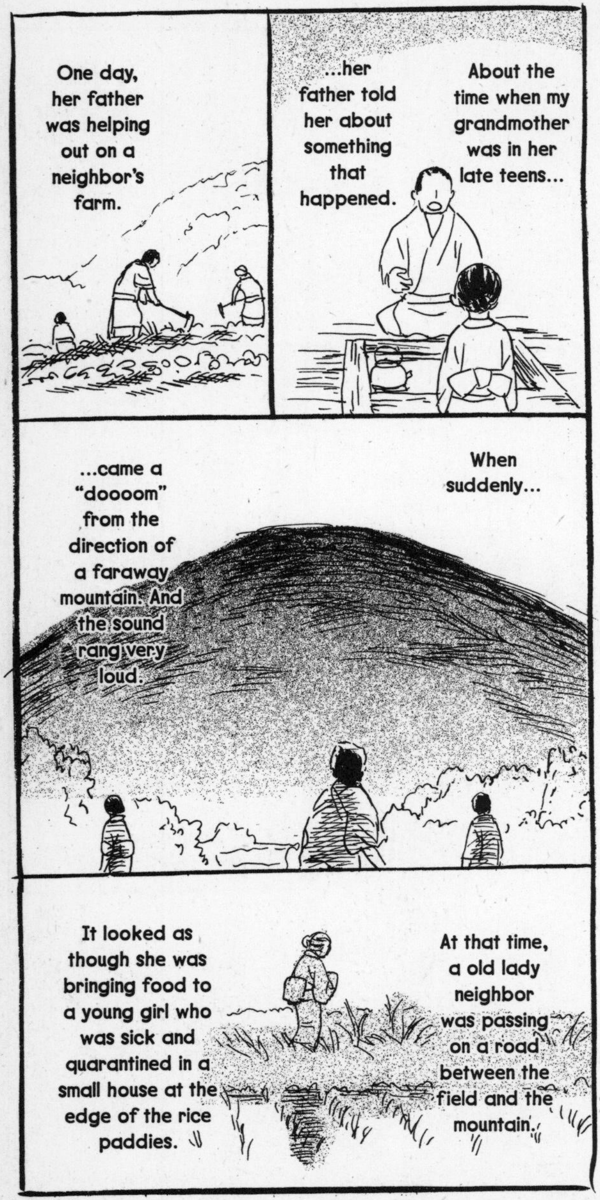

About the time when my grandmother was in her late teens...
...her father told her about something that happened.
One day, her father was helping out on a neighbor's farm.
When suddenly...
...came a "doooom" from the direction of a faraway mountain. And the sound rang very loud.
At that time, a old lady neighbor was passing on a road between the field and the mountain.
It looked as though she was bringing food to a young girl who was sick and quarantined in a small house at the edge of the rice paddies.

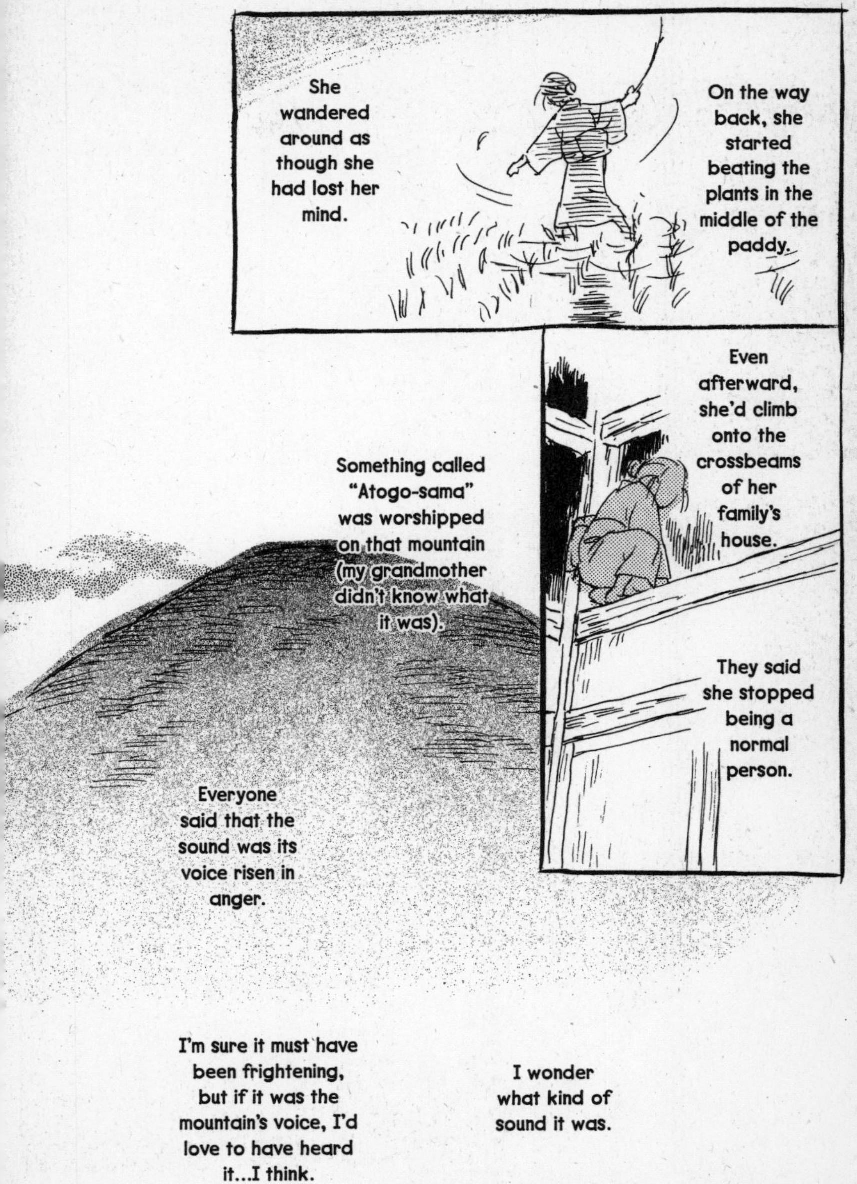
On the way back, she started beating the plants in the middle of the paddy.
She wandered around as though she had lost her mind.
Even afterward, she'd climb onto the crossbeams of her family's house.
They said she stopped being a normal person.
Something called "Atogo-sama" was worshipped on that mountain (my grandmother didn't know what it was).
Everyone said that the sound was its voice risen in anger.
I wonder what kind of sound it was.
I'm sure it must have been frightening, but if it was the mountain's voice, I'd love to have heard it...I think.

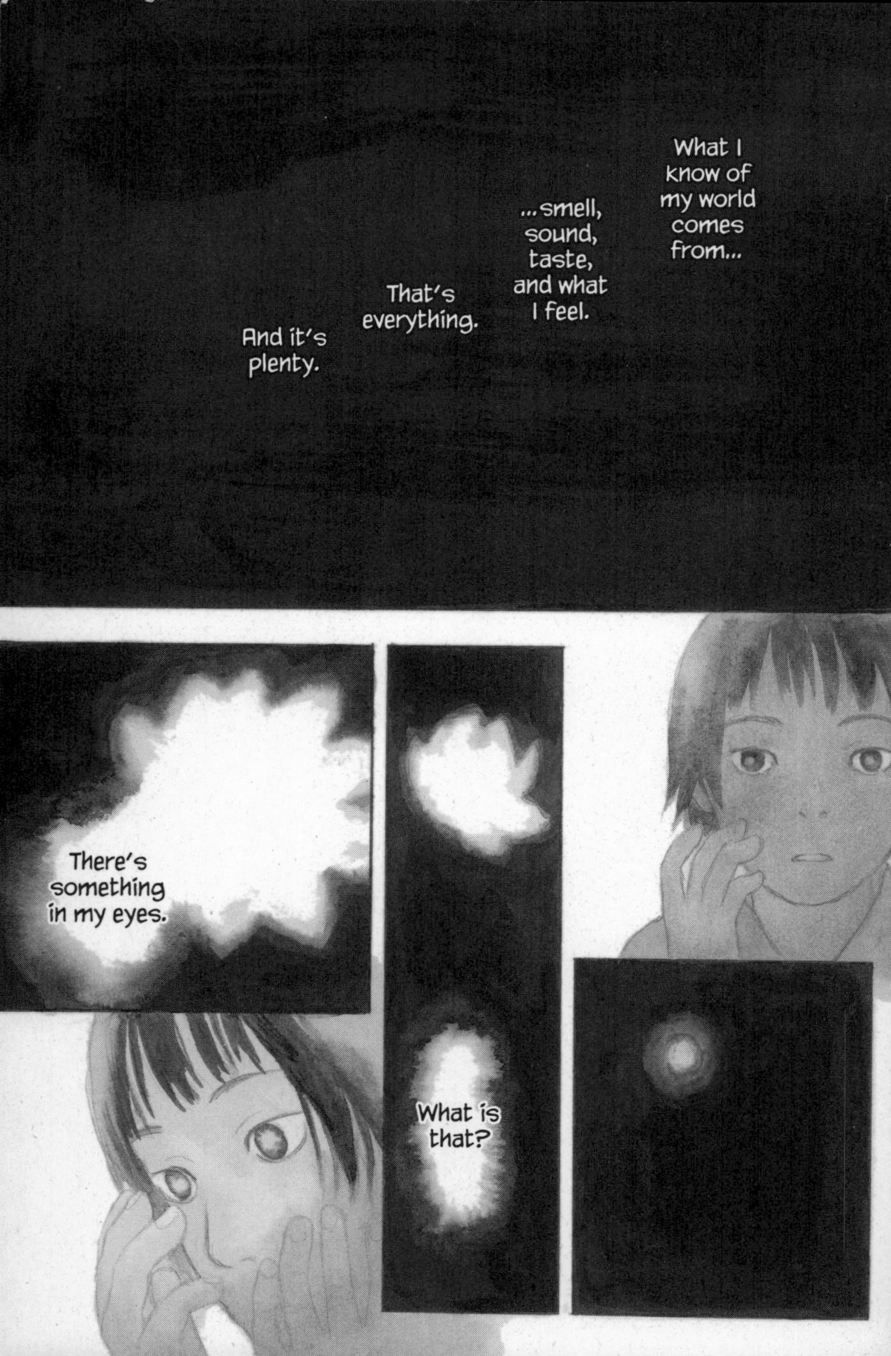
What I know of my world comes from...
...smell, sound, taste, and what I feel.
That's everything.
And it's plenty.
What is that?
There's something in my eyes.

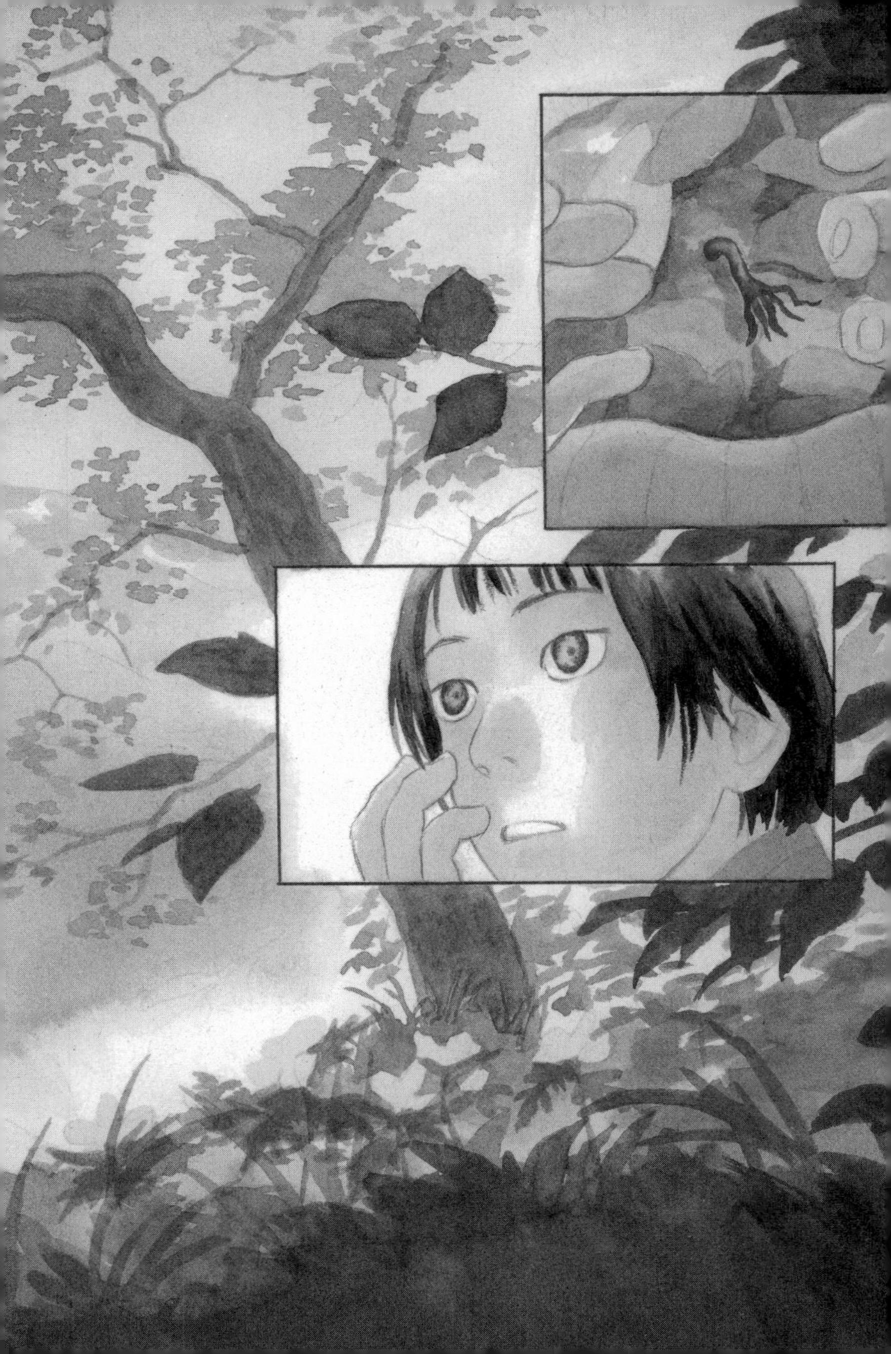

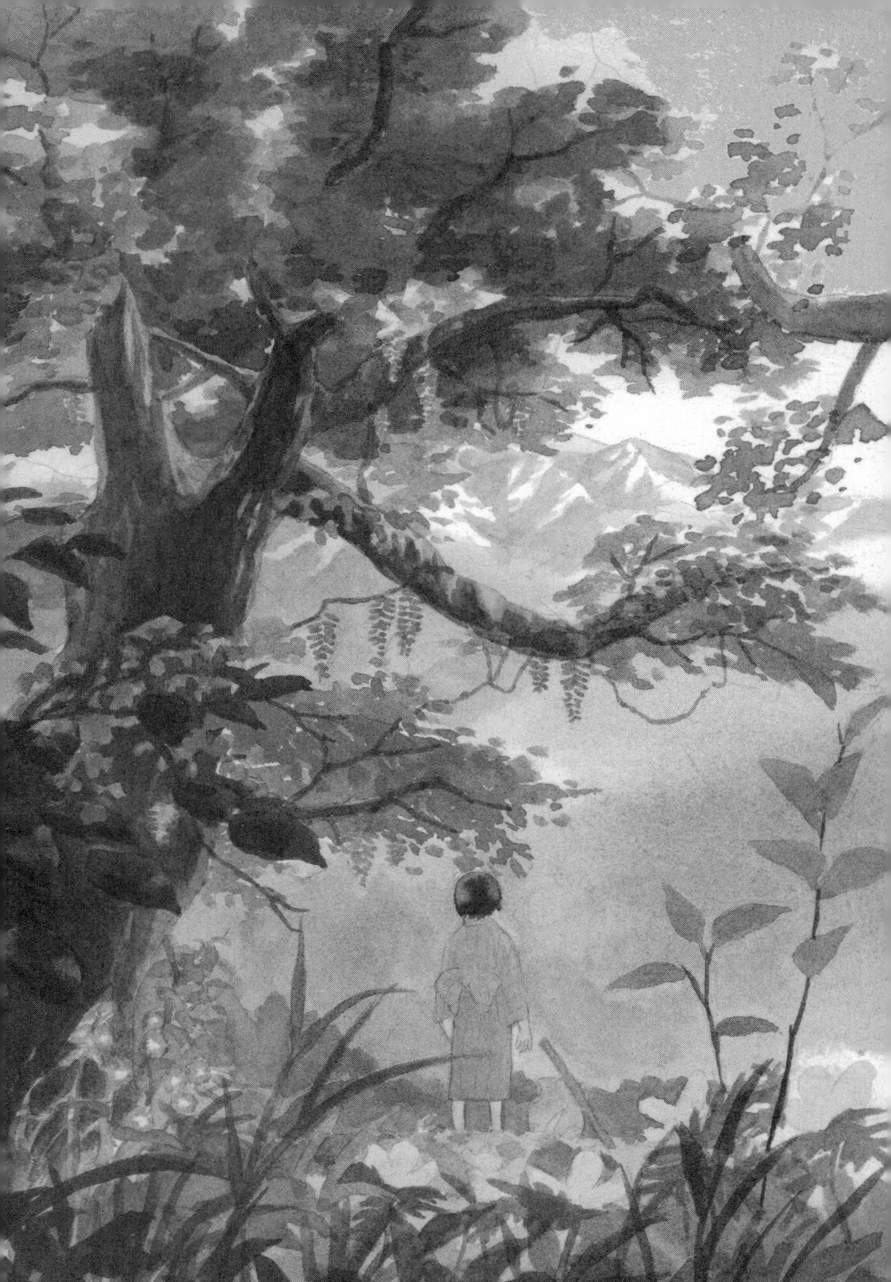

Eve's Fortune, Eve's Misfortune

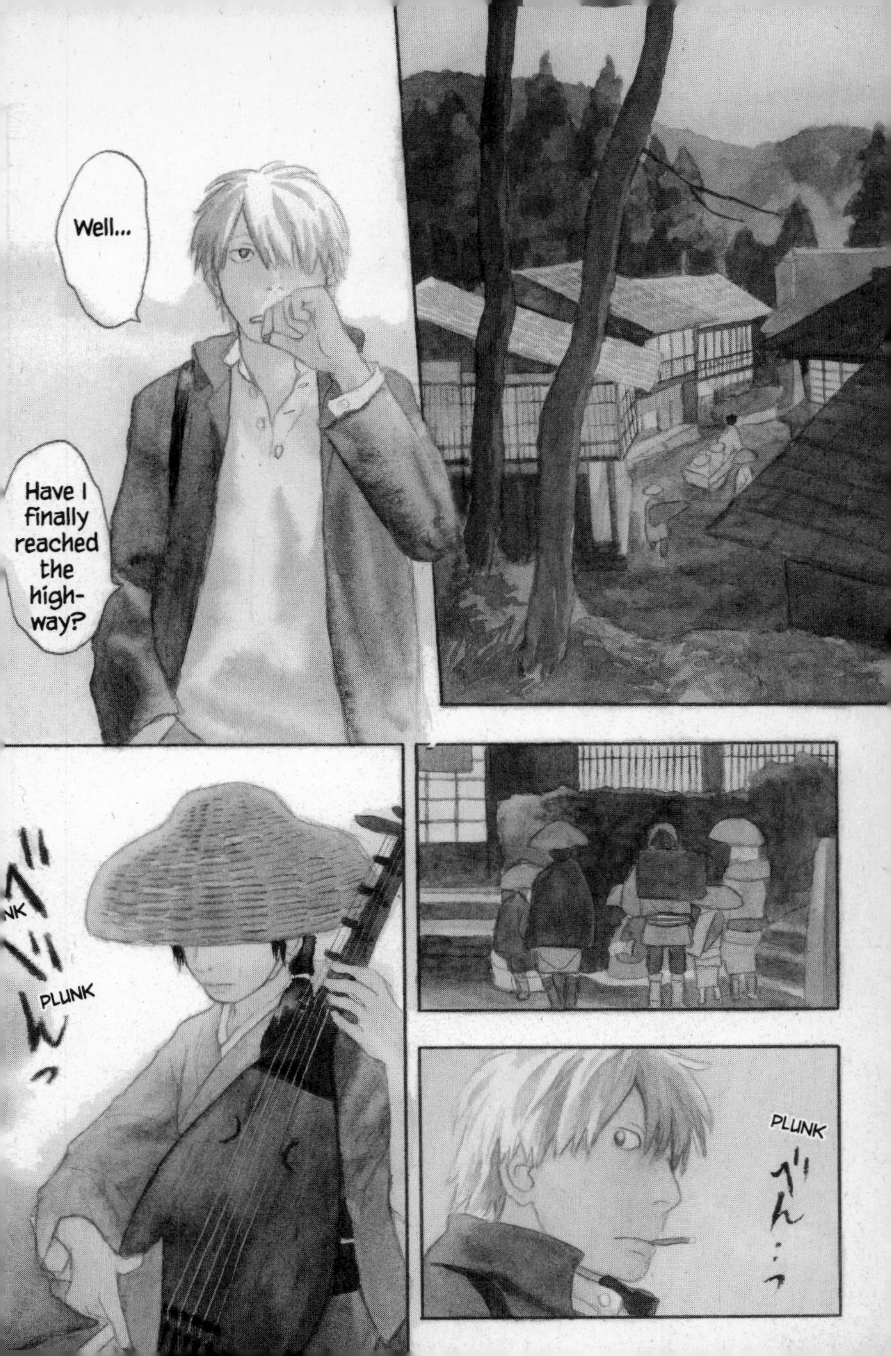
Well...
Have I finally reached the highway?
PLUNK
NK
PLUNK

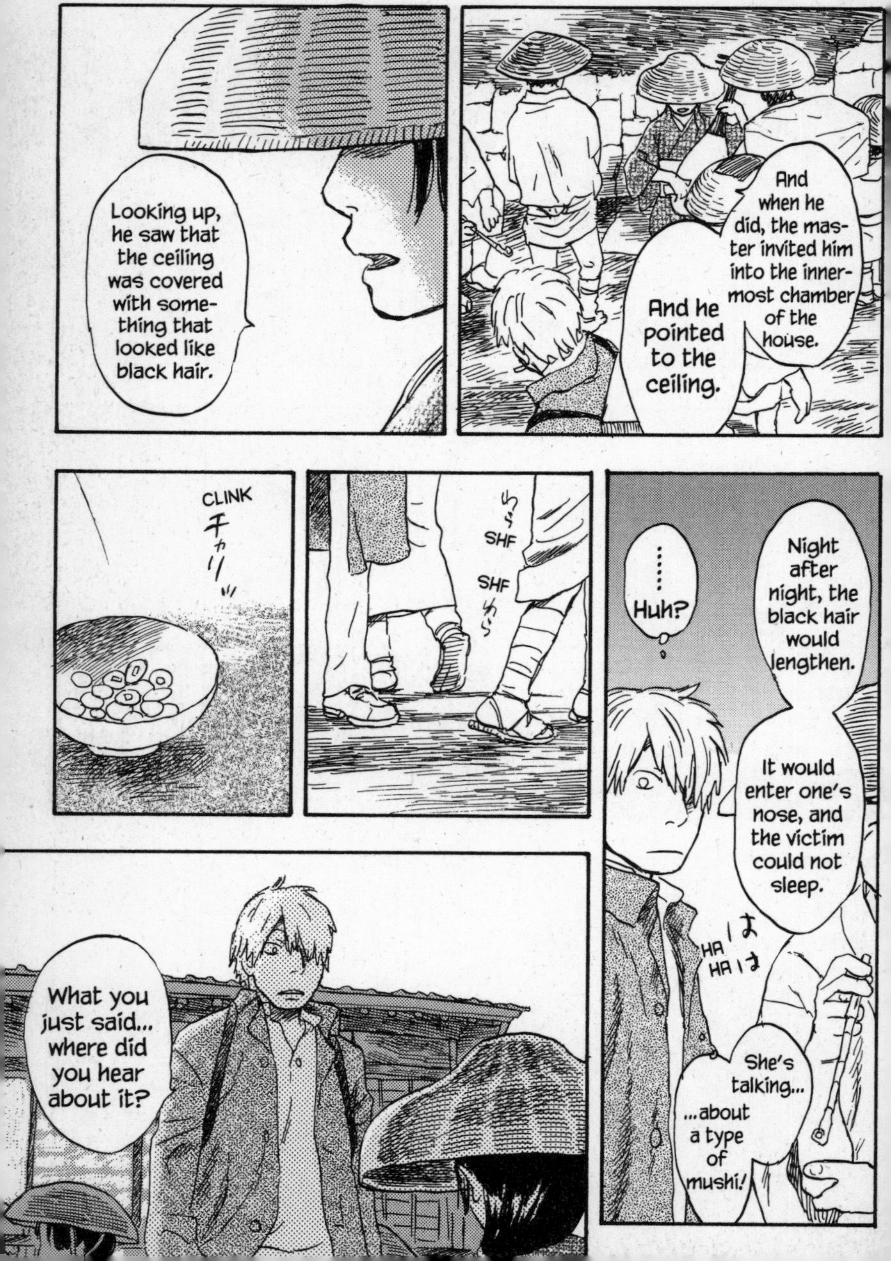
And when he did, the master invited him into the innermost chamber of the house.
And he pointed to the ceiling.
Looking up, he saw that the ceiling was covered with something that looked like black hair.
Night after night, the black hair would lengthen.
...... Huh?
It would enter one's nose, and the victim could not sleep.
HA HA
She's talking... ...about a type of mushi!
SHF SHF
CLINK
What you just said... where did you hear about it?

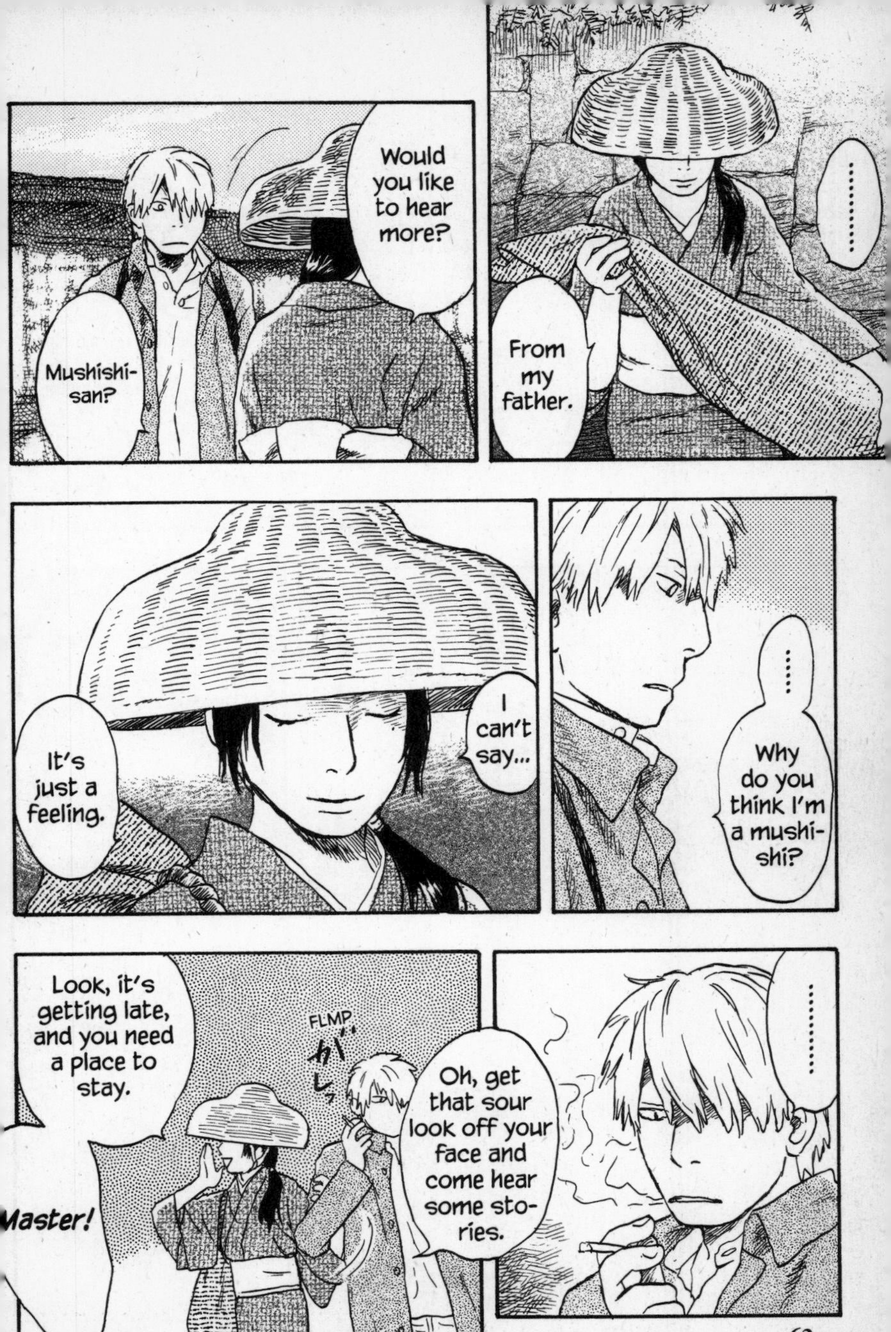
……
From my father.
Would you like to hear more?
Mushishi-san?
……
Why do you think I'm a mushi-shi?
I can't say...
It's just a feeling.
……
FLMP
Oh, get that sour look off your face and come hear some sto-ries.
Look, it's getting late, and you need a place to stay.
Master!

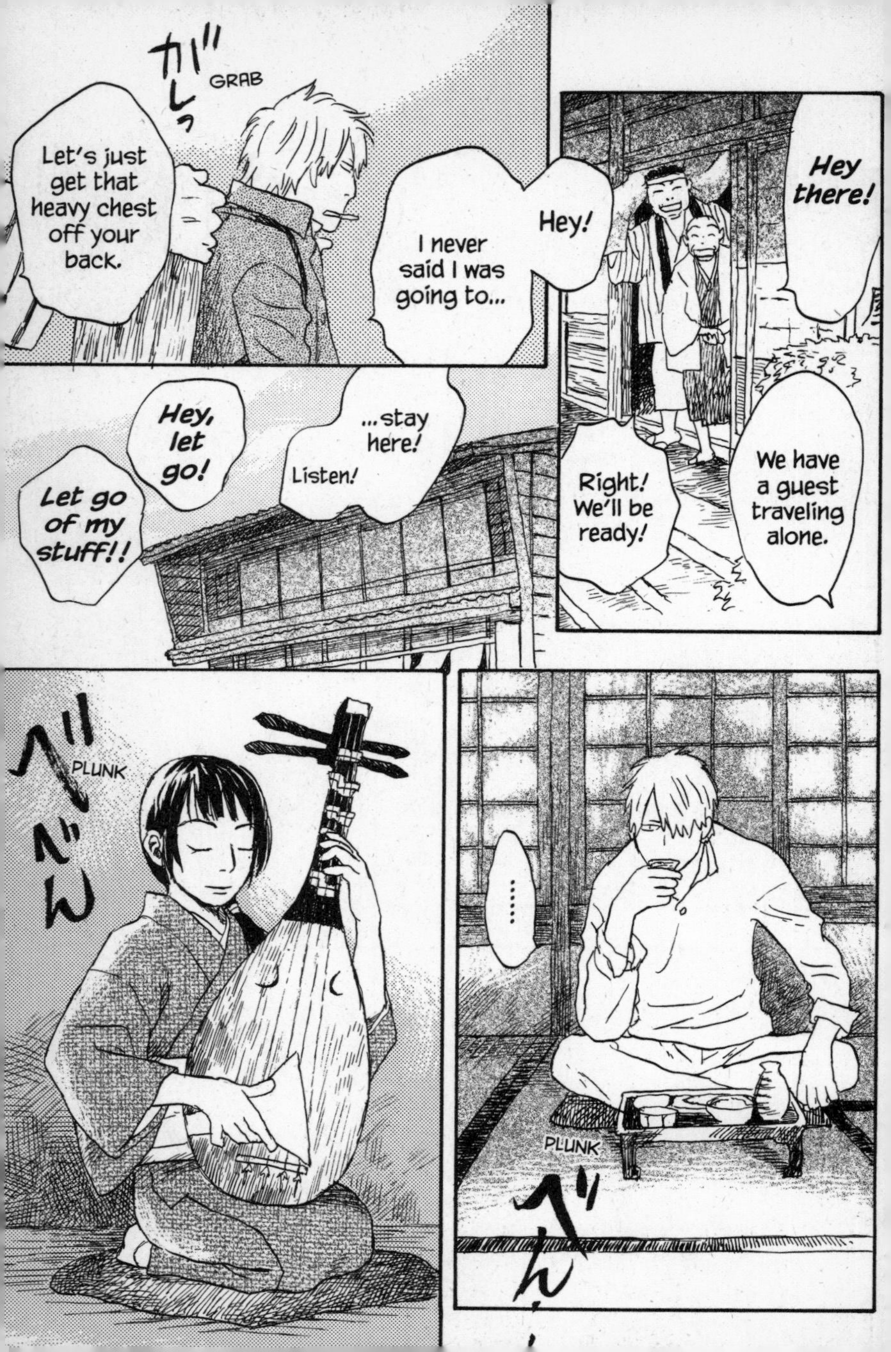

Hey there!
Hey!
We have a guest traveling alone.
Right! We'll be ready!
GRAB
I never said I was going to...
Let's just get that heavy chest off your back.
...stay here!
Listen!
Hey, let go!
Let go of my stuff!!
......
PLUNK
PLUNK

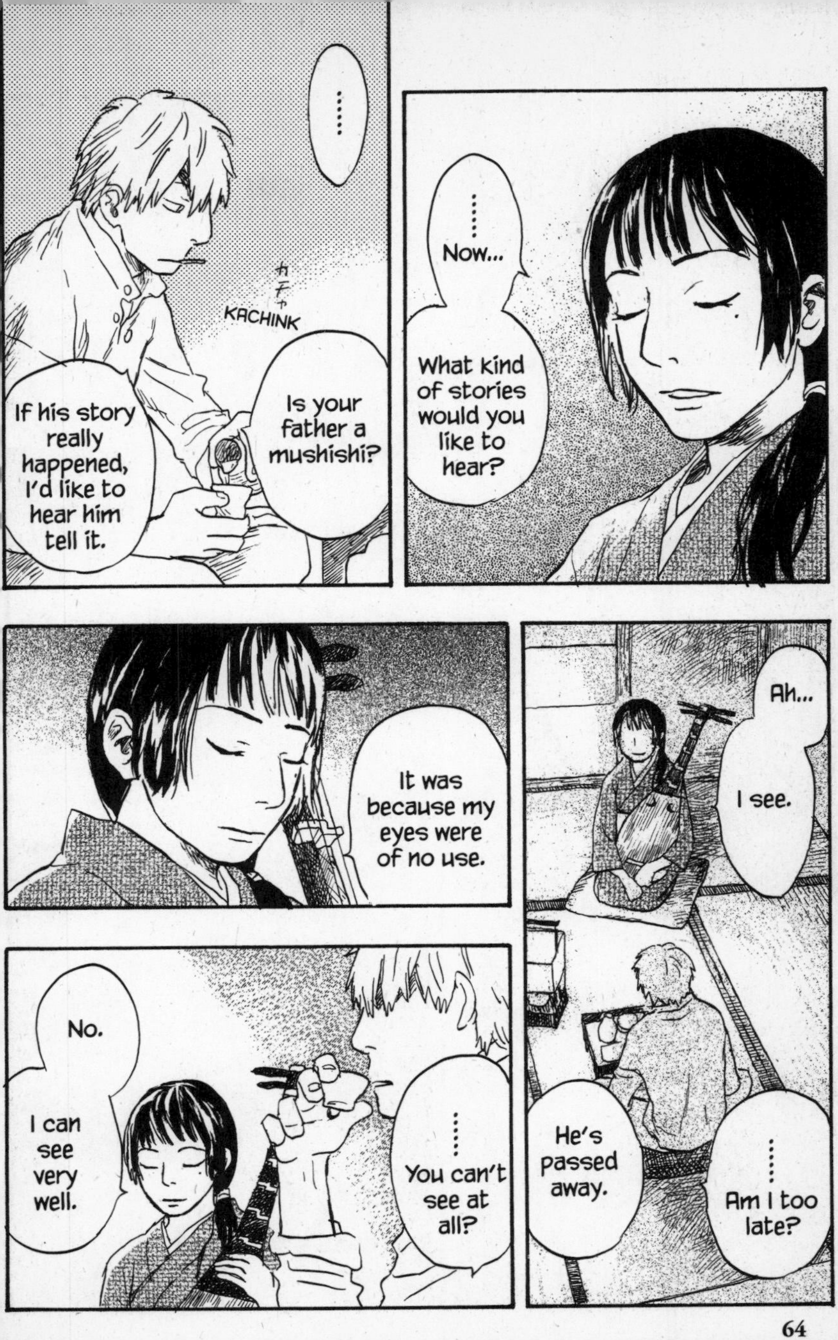

......
Now...
What kind of stories would you like to hear?
......
KACHINK
Is your father a mushishi?
If his story really happened, I'd like to hear him tell it.
Ah...
I see.
......
Am I too late?
He's passed away.
It was because my eyes were of no use.
......
You can't see at all?
No.
I can see very well.

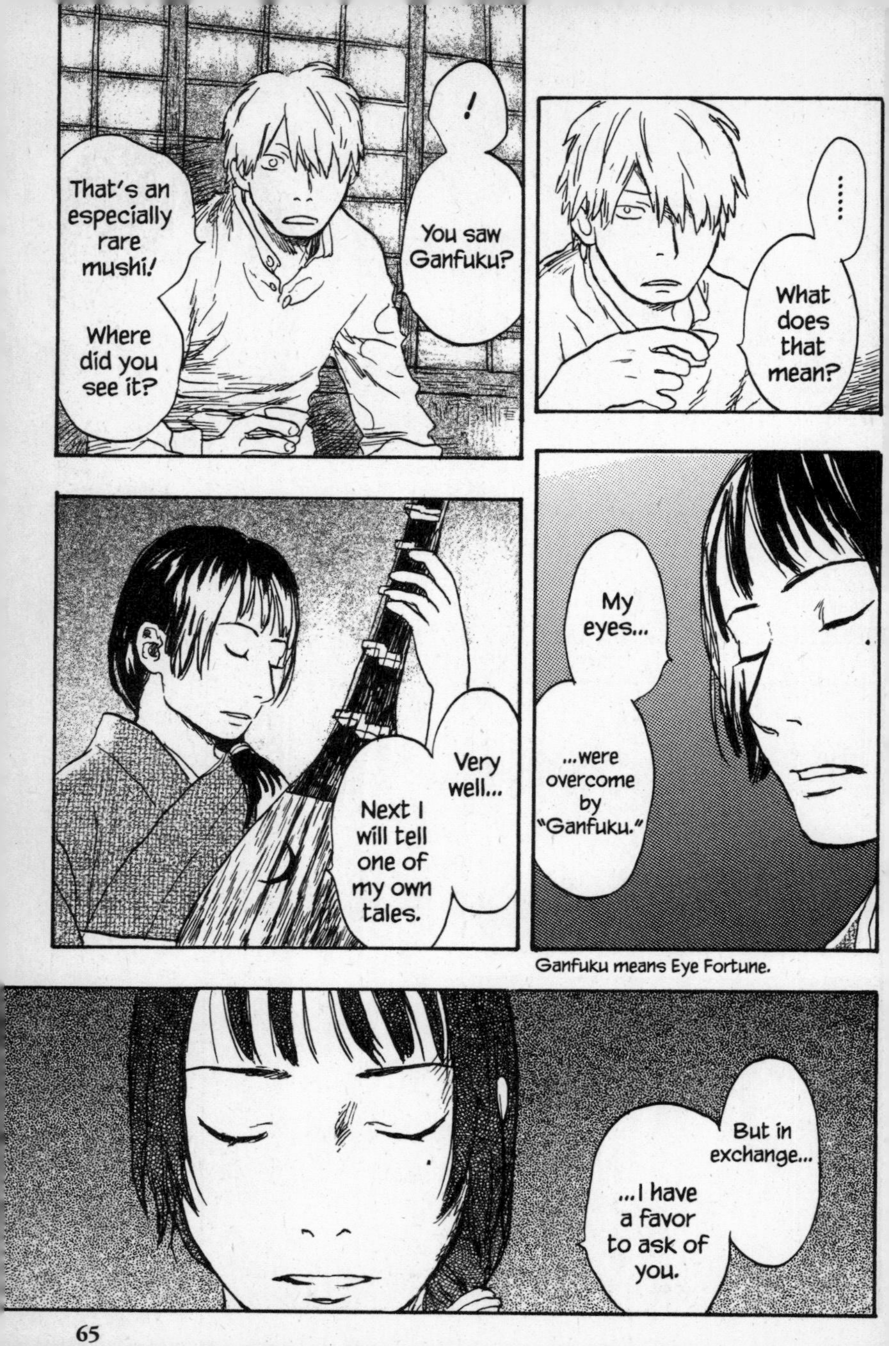
......
What does that mean?
!
You saw Ganfuku?
That's an especially rare mushi!
Where did you see it?
My eyes...
...were overcome by "Ganfuku."
Very well...
Next I will tell one of my own tales.
But in exchange...
...I have a favor to ask of you.
Ganfuku means Eye Fortune.

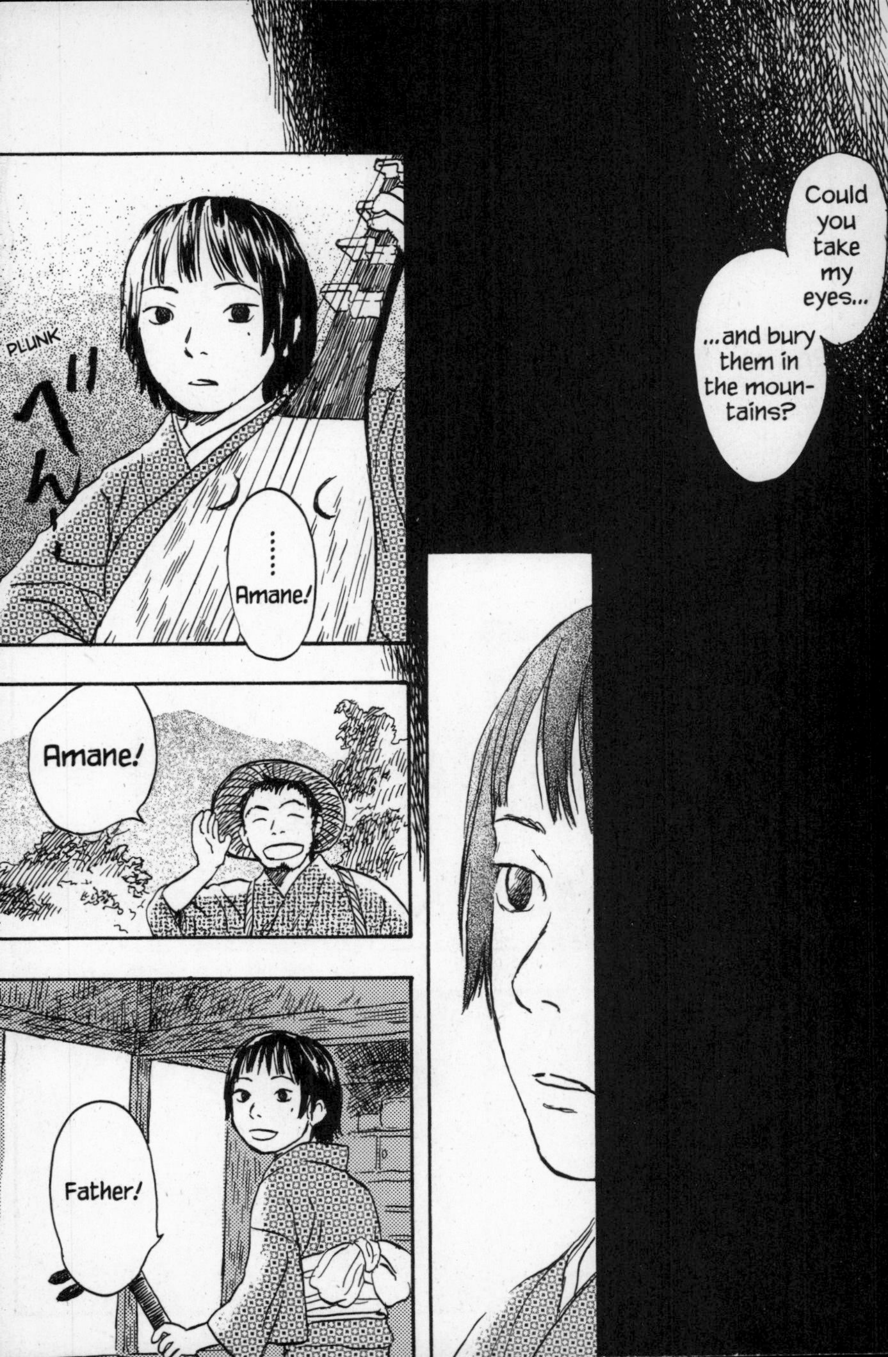
Could you take my eyes...
...and bury them in the moun-tains?
PLUNK
......Amane!
Amane!
Father!

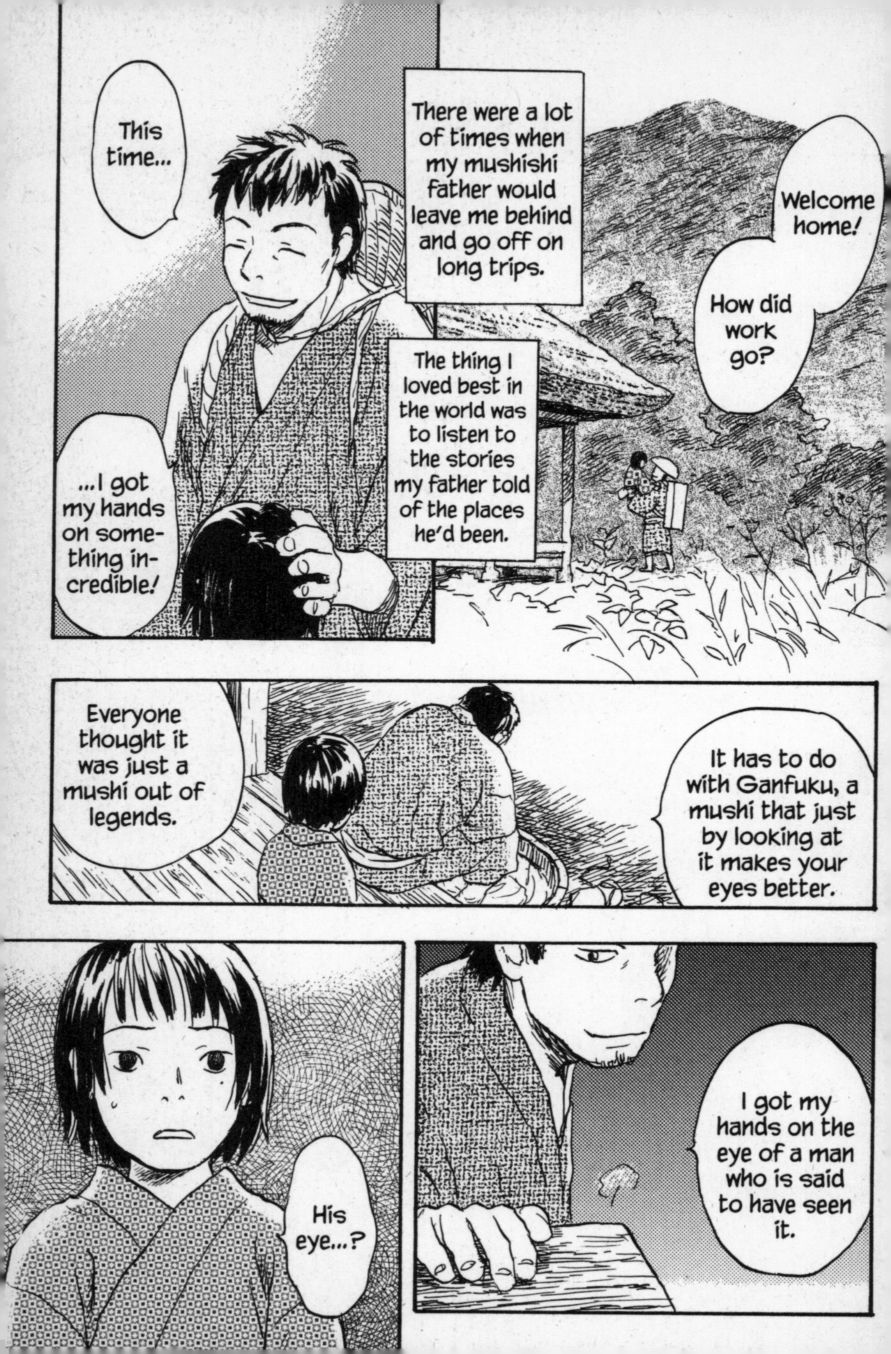
There were a lot of times when my mushishi father would leave me behind and go off on long trips.
Welcome home!
How did work go?
The thing I loved best in the world was to listen to the stories my father told of the places he'd been.
This time...
...I got my hands on some-thing in-credible!
It has to do with Ganfuku, a mushi that just by looking at it makes your eyes better.
Everyone thought it was just a mushi out of legends.
I got my hands on the eye of a man who is said to have seen it.
His eye...?

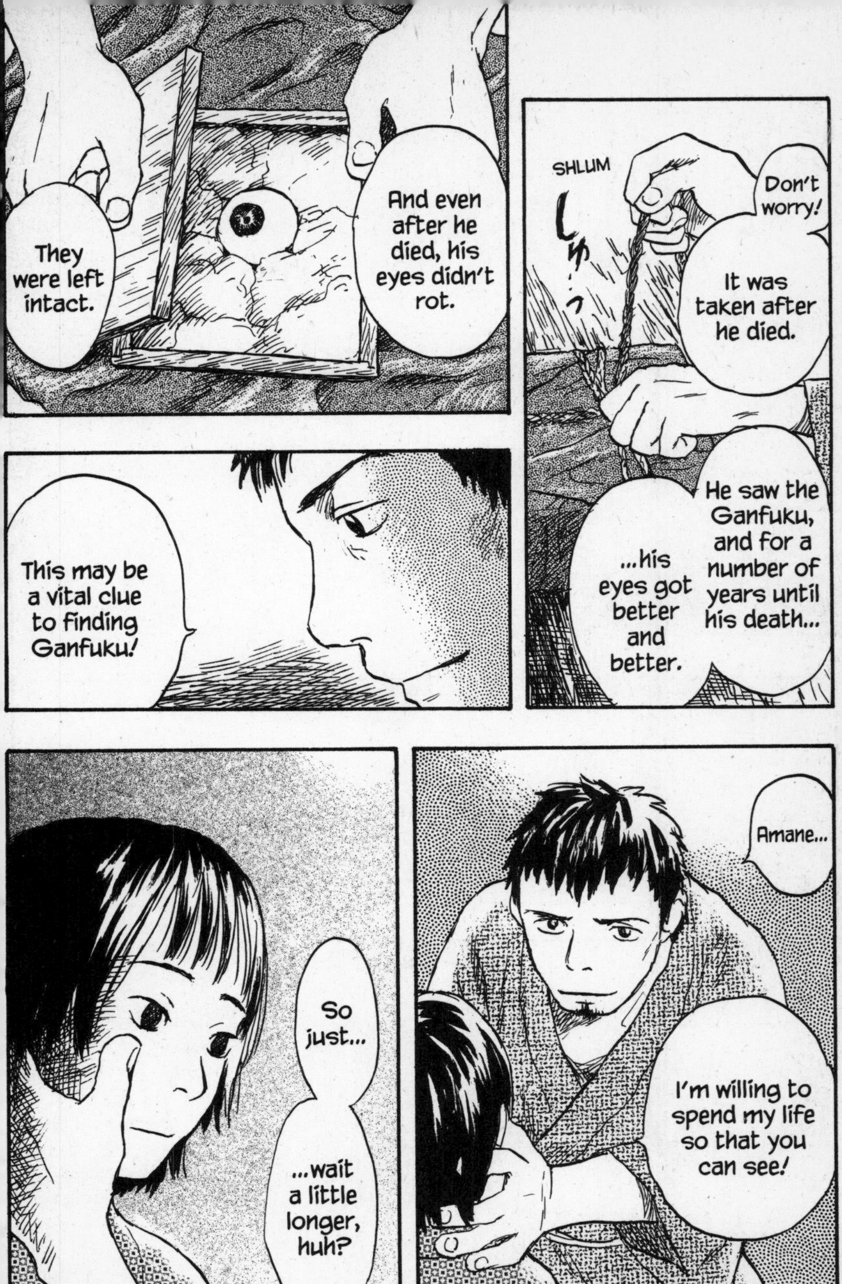
SHLUM
しゅっ
Don't worry!
It was taken after he died.
He saw the Ganfuku, and for a number of years until his death...
...his eyes got better and better.
And even after he died, his eyes didn't rot.
They were left intact.
This may be a vital clue to finding Ganfuku!
Amane...
I'm willing to spend my life so that you can see!
So just...
...wait a little longer, huh?

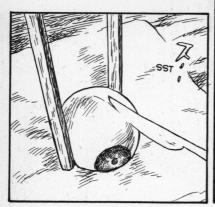

SST

?!

ZYUUM

Hm?

......

PIP
PIP

Father?

......

KRAK

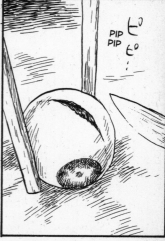

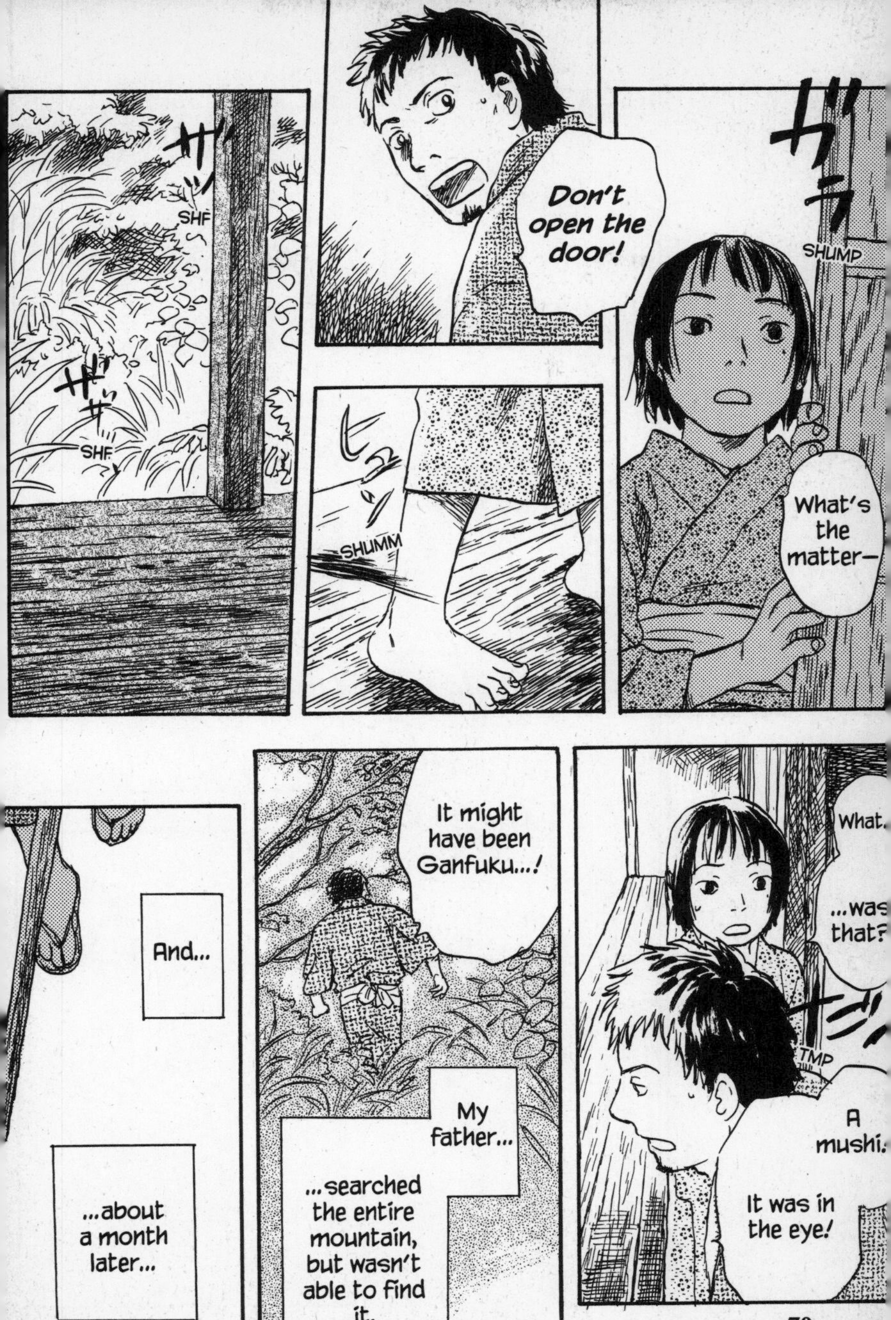
SHUMP
What's the matter—
Don't open the door!
SHUMM
SHF
SHF
What...
...was that?
TMP
A mushi.
It was in the eye!
It might have been Ganfuku...!
My father...
...searched the entire mountain, but wasn't able to find it.
And...
...about a month later...

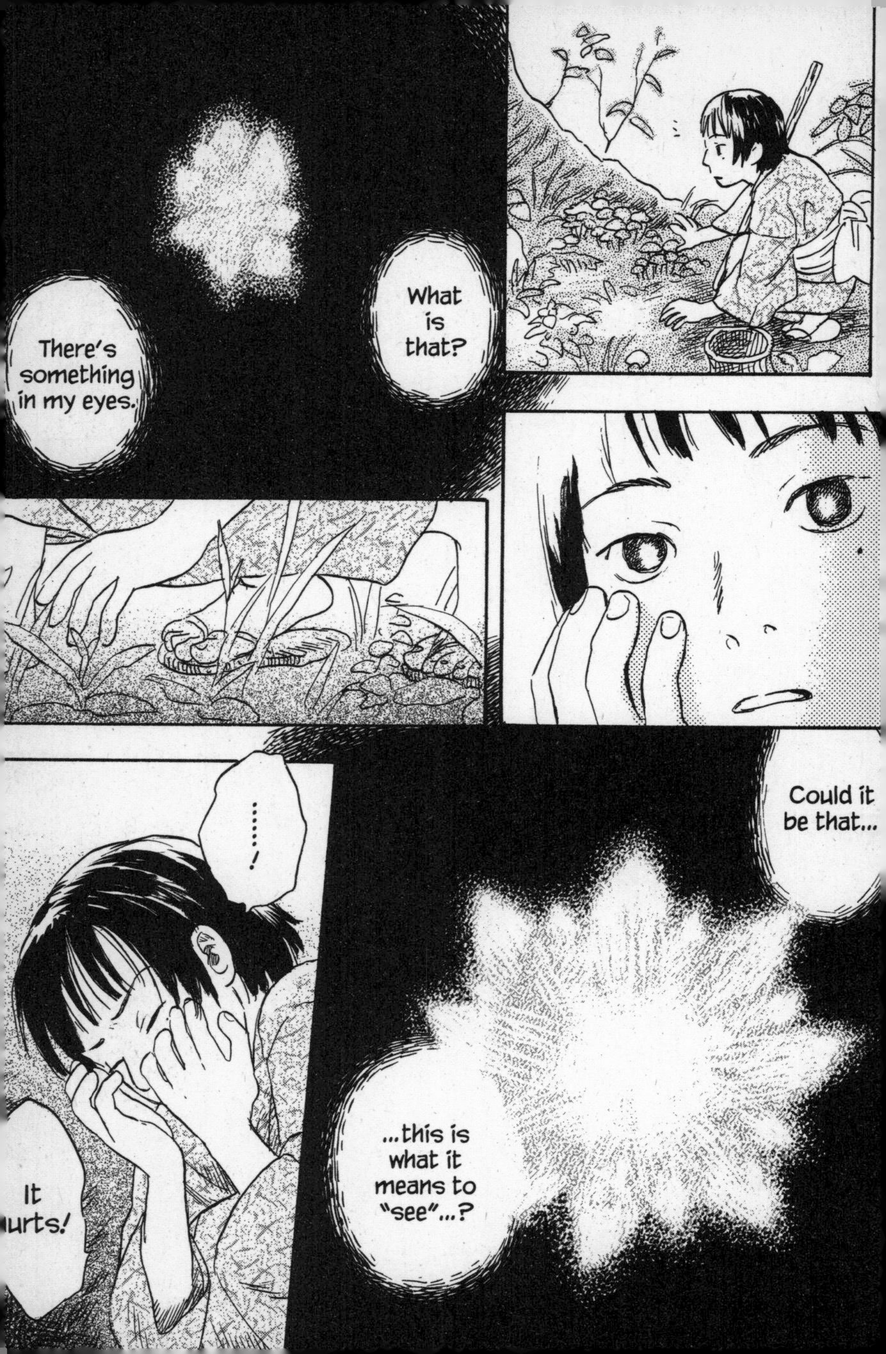
What is that?
There's something in my eyes.
Could it be that...
...this is what it means to "see"...?
......!
It urts!

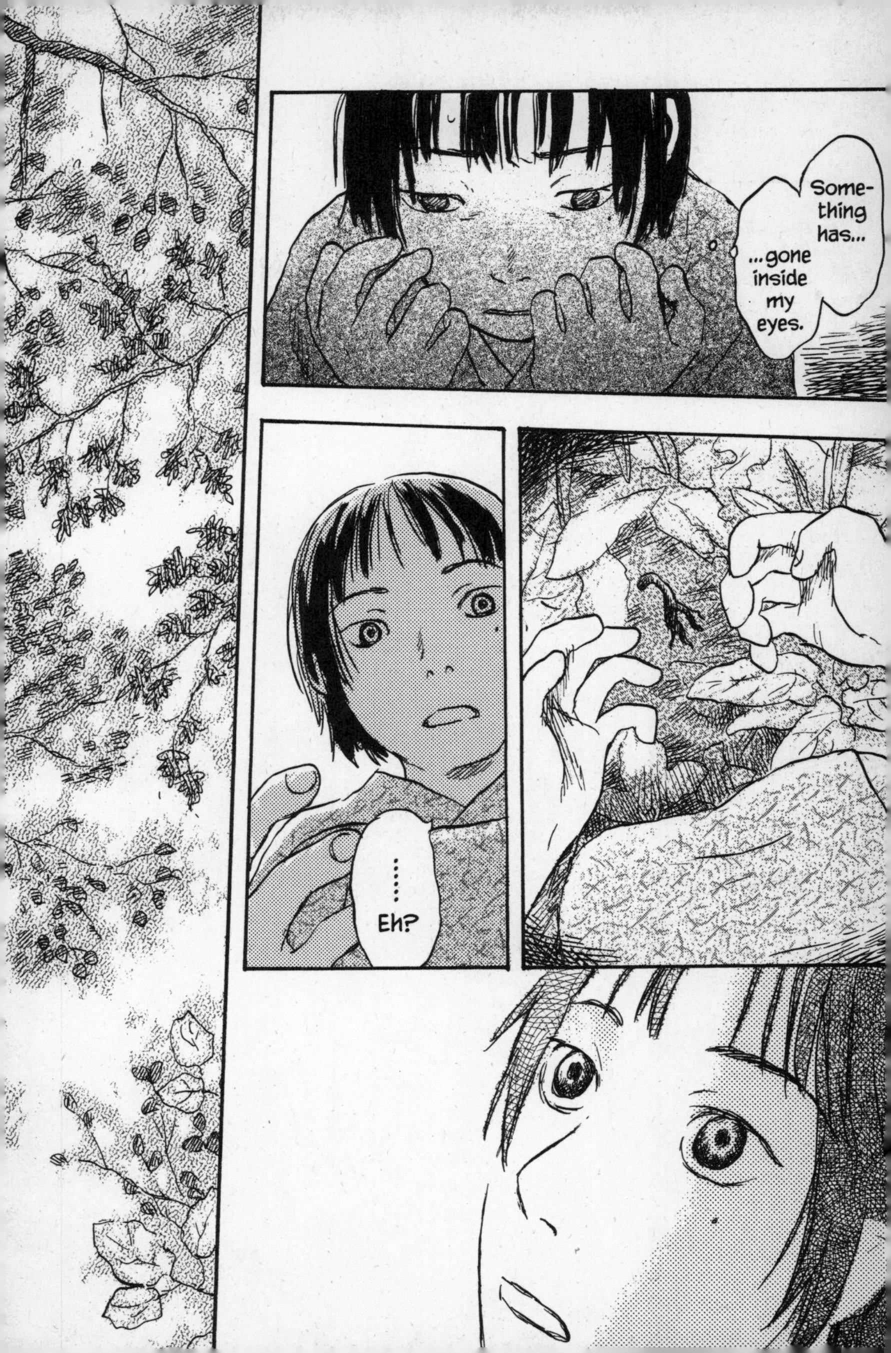
Something has...
...gone inside my eyes.
......
Eh?

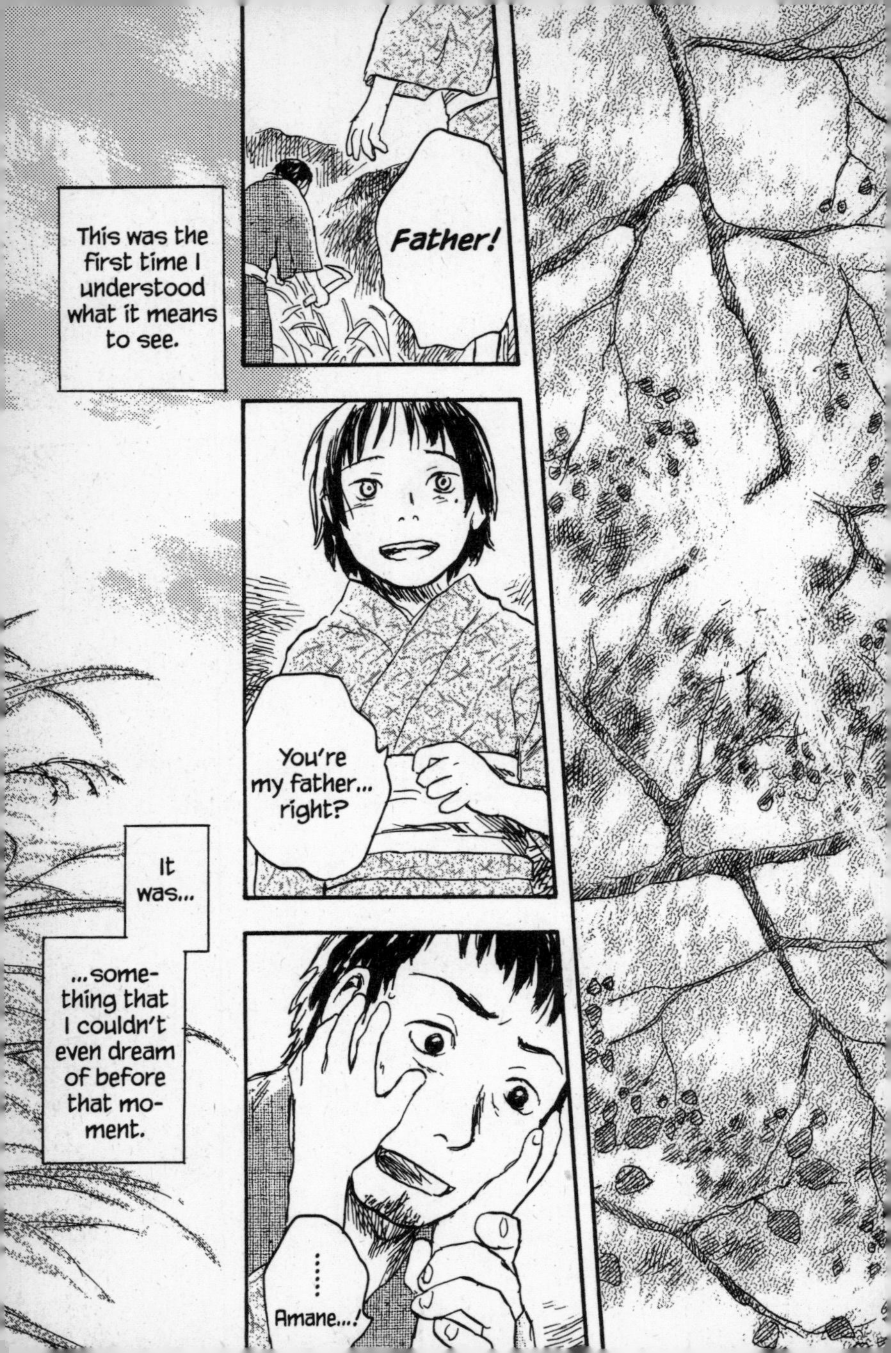
Father!
You're my father... right?
...... Amane...!
This was the first time I understood what it means to see.
It was...
...something that I couldn't even dream of before that moment.

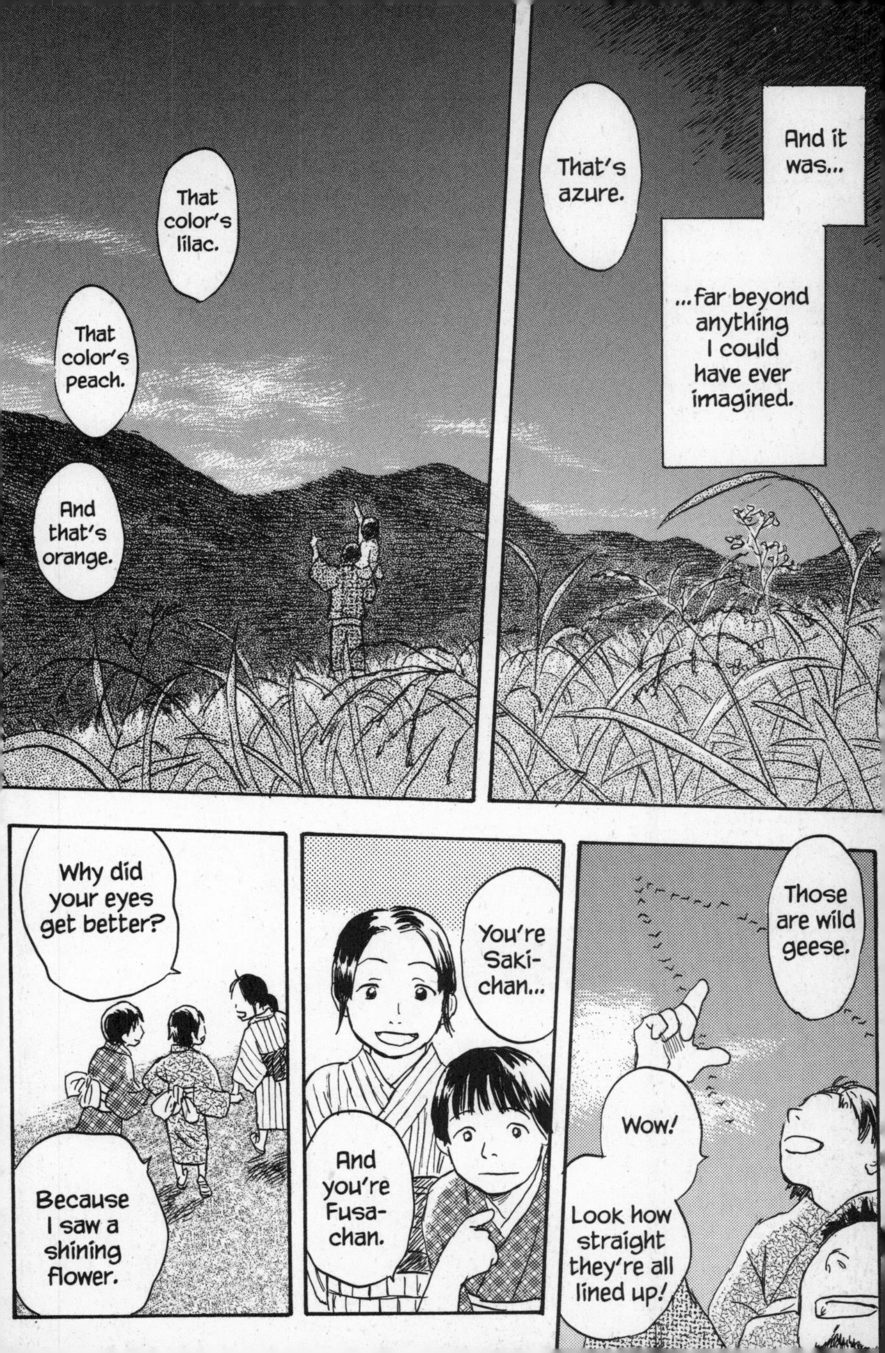
And it was...
That's azure.
...far beyond anything I could have ever imagined.
That color's lilac.
That color's peach.
And that's orange.
Those are wild geese.
Wow!
Look how straight they're all lined up!
You're Saki-chan...
And you're Fusa-chan.
Why did your eyes get better?
Because I saw a shining flower.

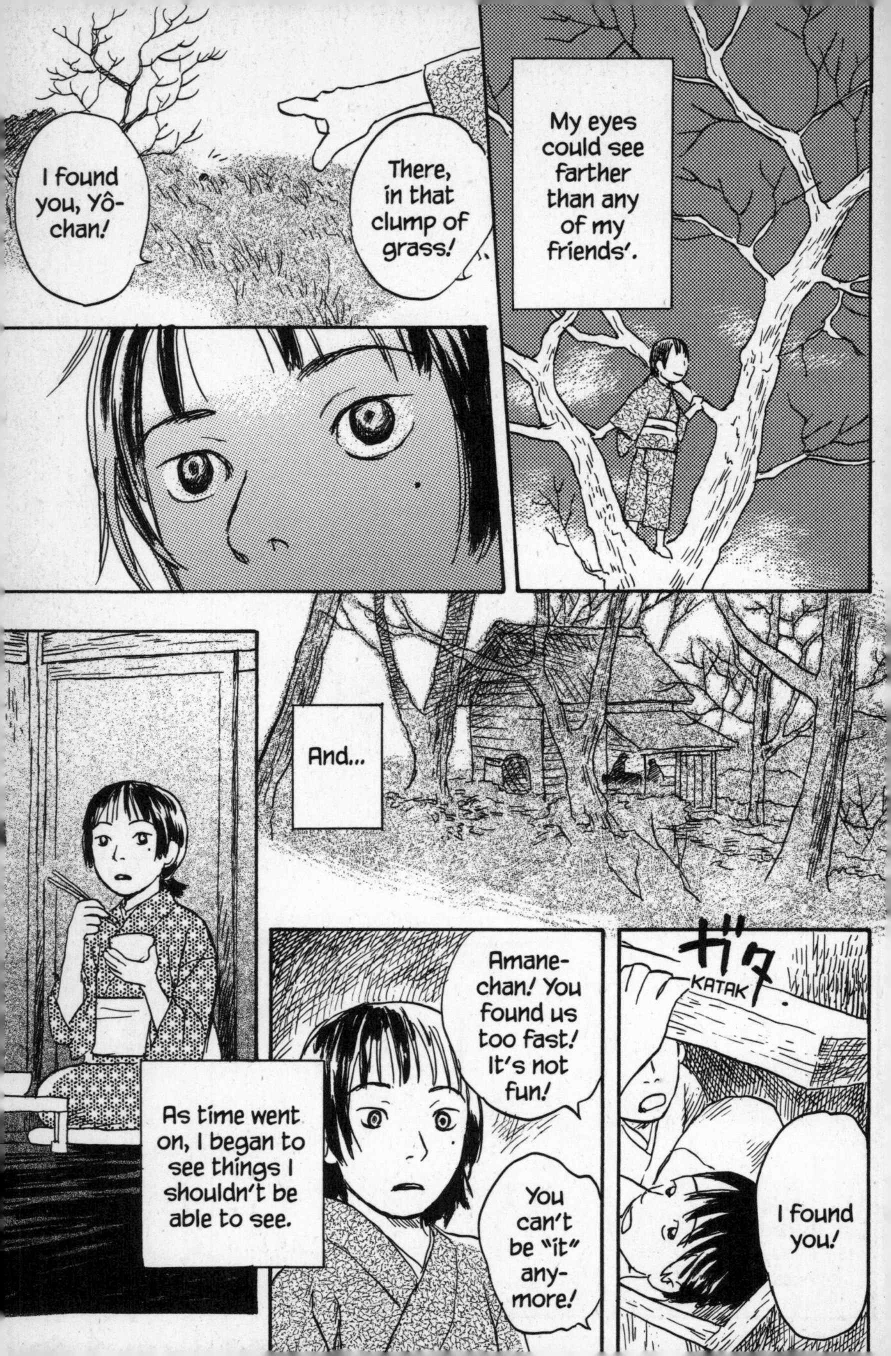
My eyes could see farther than any of my friends'.
There, in that clump of grass!
I found you, Yô-chan!
And...
ガタ
KATAK
I found you!
Amane-chan! You found us too fast! It's not fun!
You can't be "it" anymore!
As time went on, I began to see things I shouldn't be able to see.

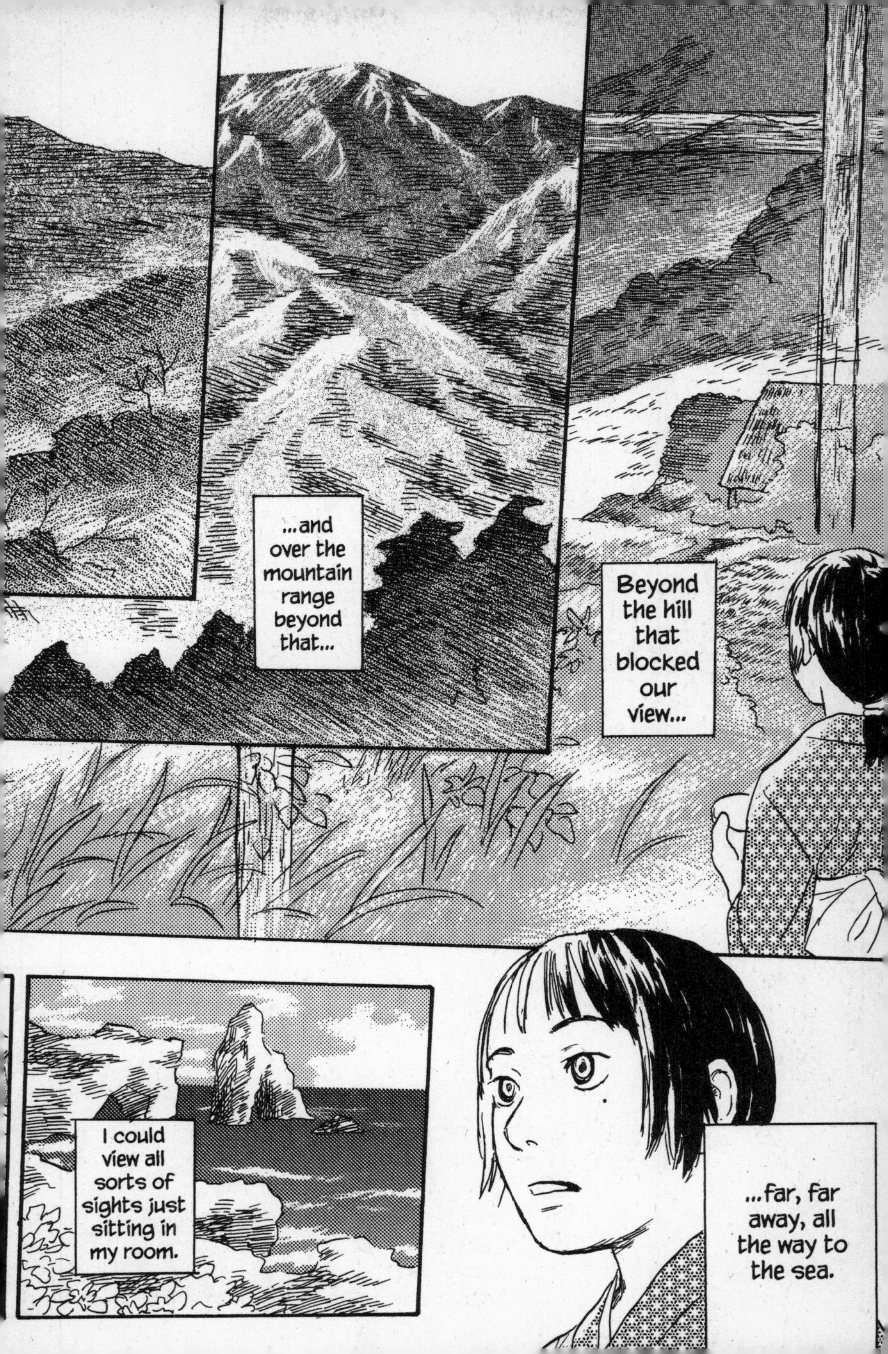
Beyond the hill that blocked our view...
...and over the mountain range beyond that...
...far, far away, all the way to the sea.
I could view all sorts of sights just sitting in my room.

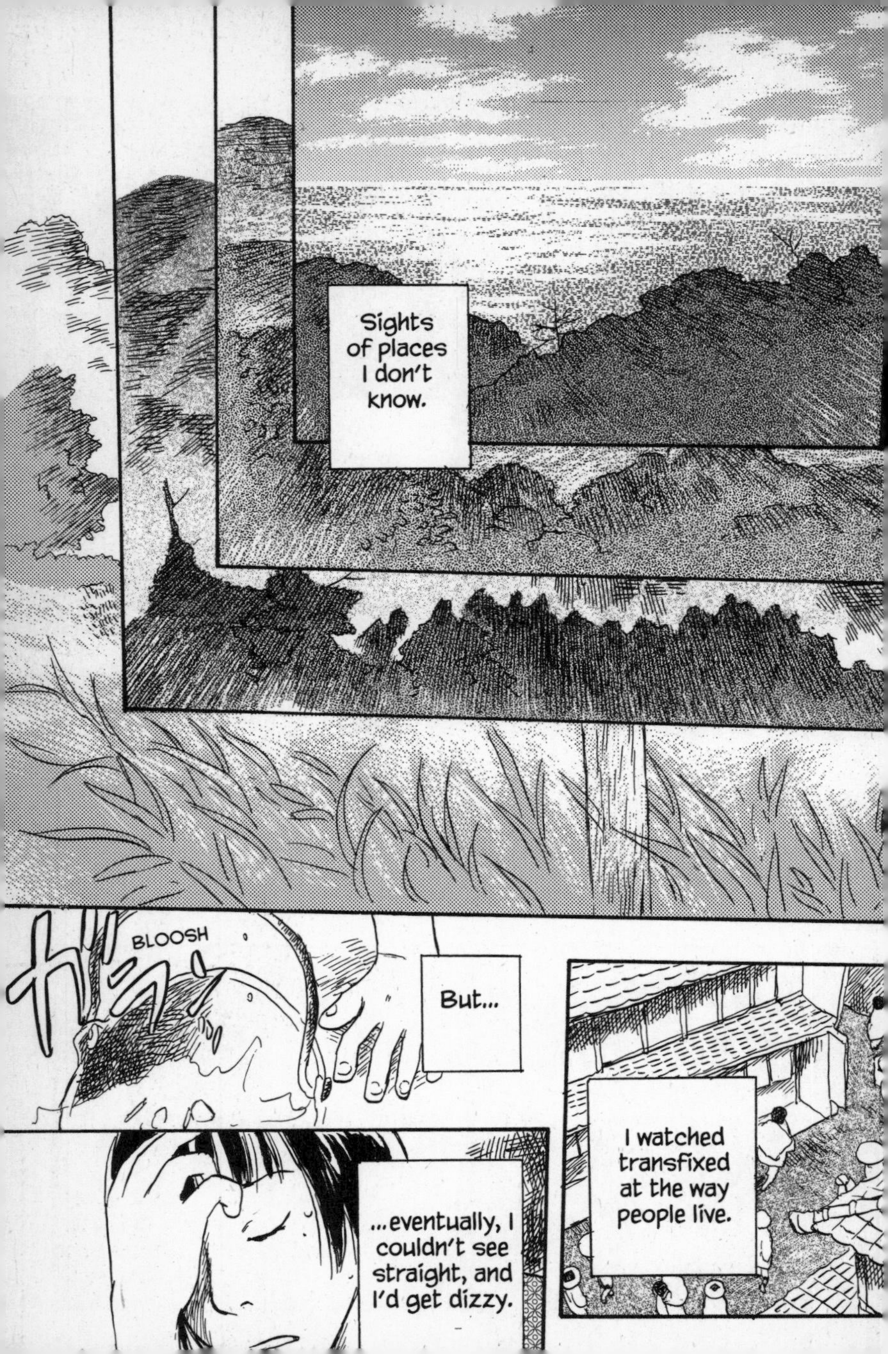
Sights of places I don't know.
I watched transfixed at the way people live.
BLOOSH
But...
...eventually, I couldn't see straight, and I'd get dizzy.

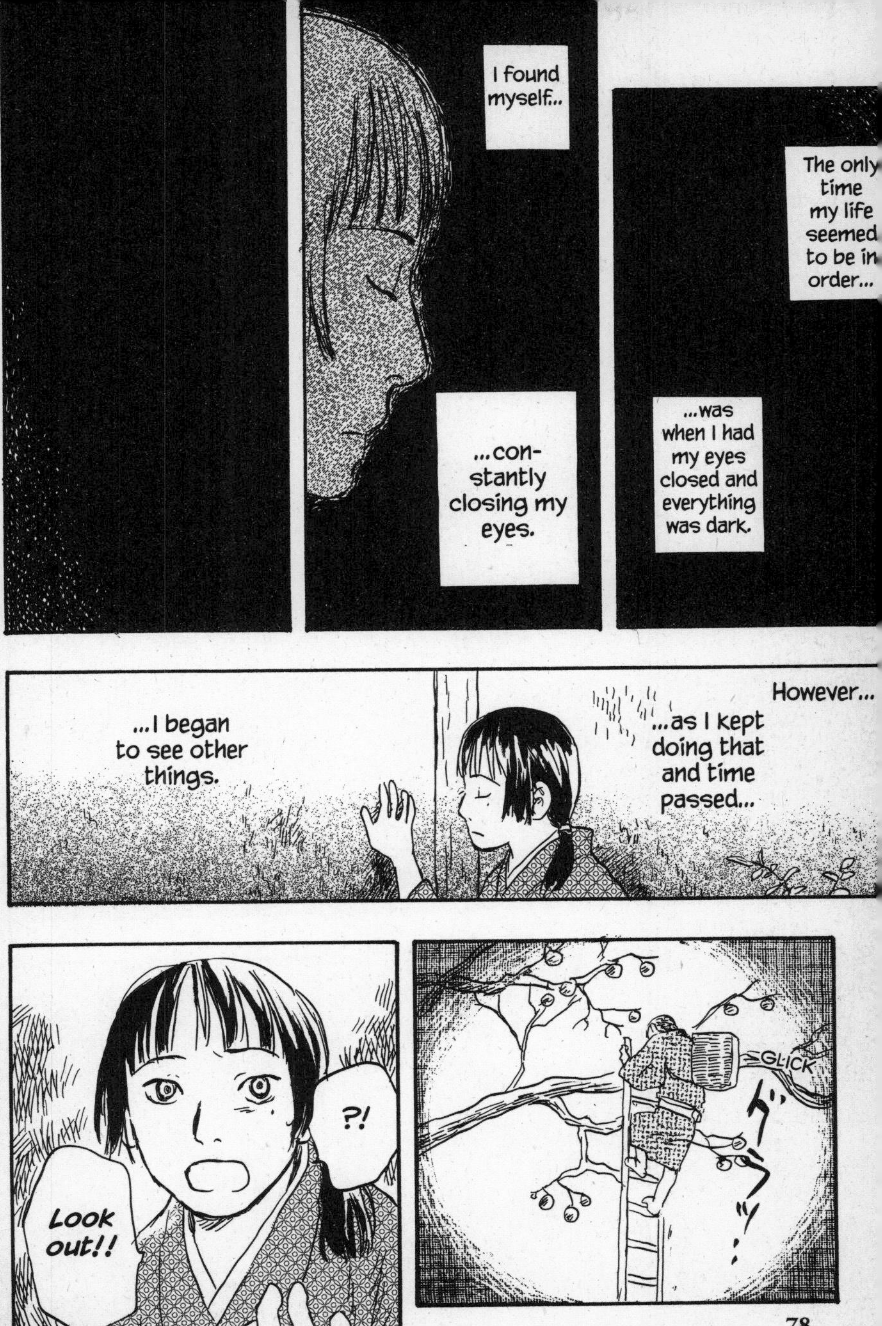
The only time my life seemed to be in order...
...was when I had my eyes closed and everything was dark.
I found myself...
...con-stantly closing my eyes.
However...
...as I kept doing that and time passed...
...I began to see other things.
GLICK
?!
Look out!!

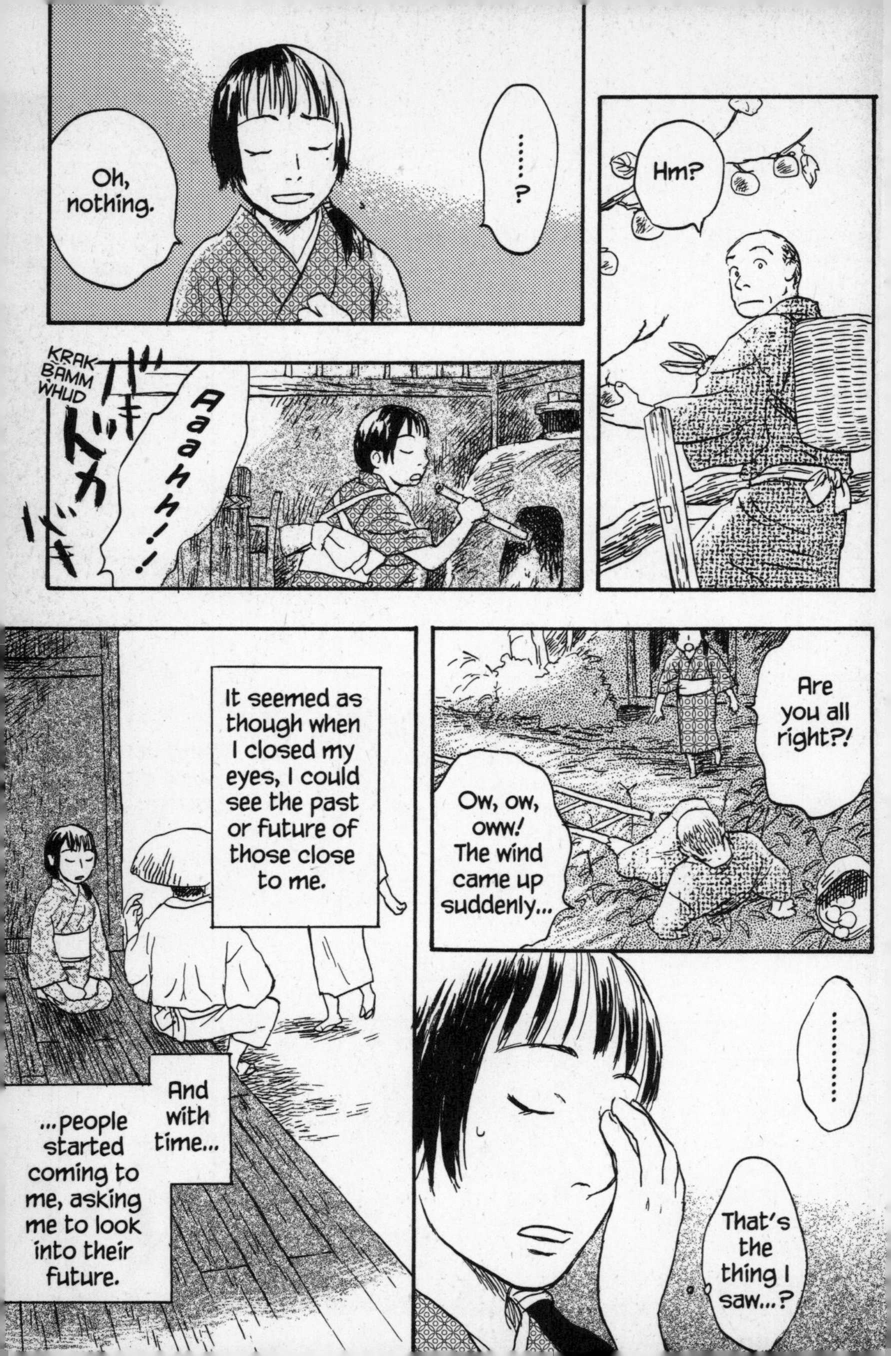
Hm?
......?
Oh, nothing.
Aaaahh!!
KRAK BAMM WHUD
Are you all right?!
Ow, ow, oww! The wind came up suddenly...
....
That's the thing I saw...?
It seemed as though when I closed my eyes, I could see the past or future of those close to me.
And with time...
...people started coming to me, asking me to look into their future.

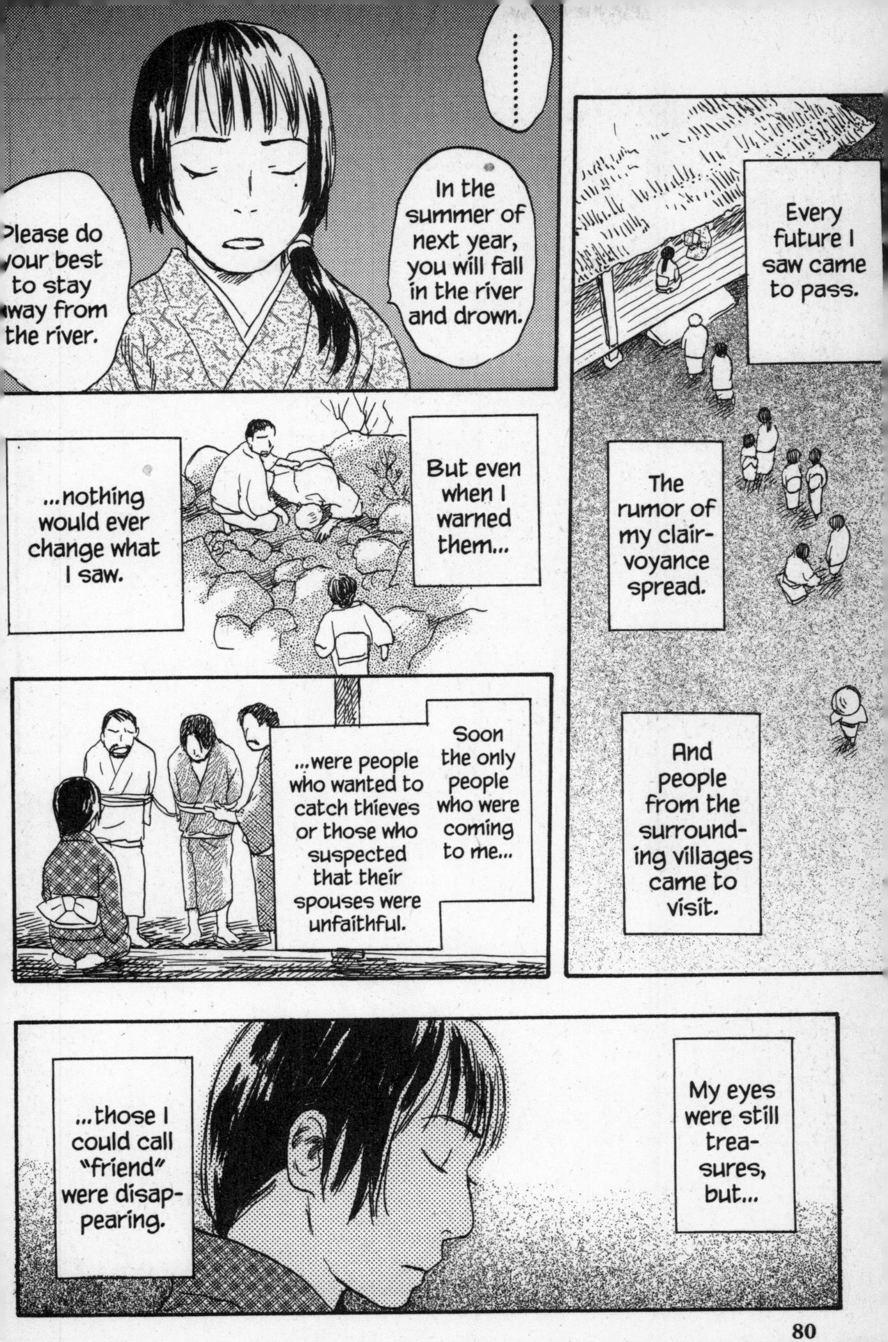
......
In the summer of next year, you will fall in the river and drown.
Please do your best to stay away from the river.
Every future I saw came to pass.
The rumor of my clair-voyance spread.
And people from the surround-ing villages came to visit.
But even when I warned them...
...nothing would ever change what I saw.
Soon the only people who were coming to me...
...were people who wanted to catch thieves or those who suspected that their spouses were unfaithful.
My eyes were still trea-sures, but...
...those I could call "friend" were disap-pearing.

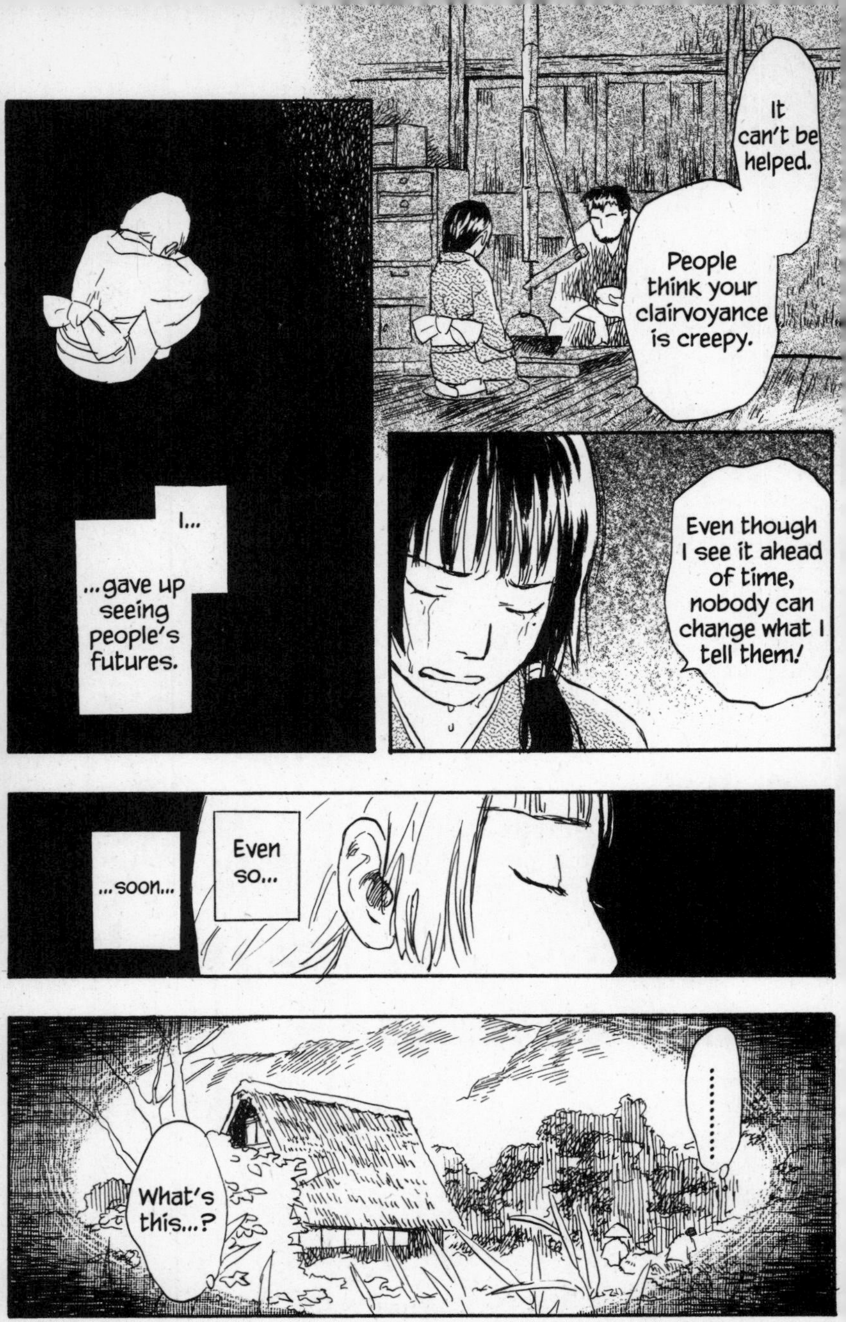
It can't be helped.
People think your clairvoyance is creepy.
Even though I see it ahead of time, nobody can change what I tell them!
I...
...gave up seeing people's futures.
Even so...
...soon...
......
What's this...?

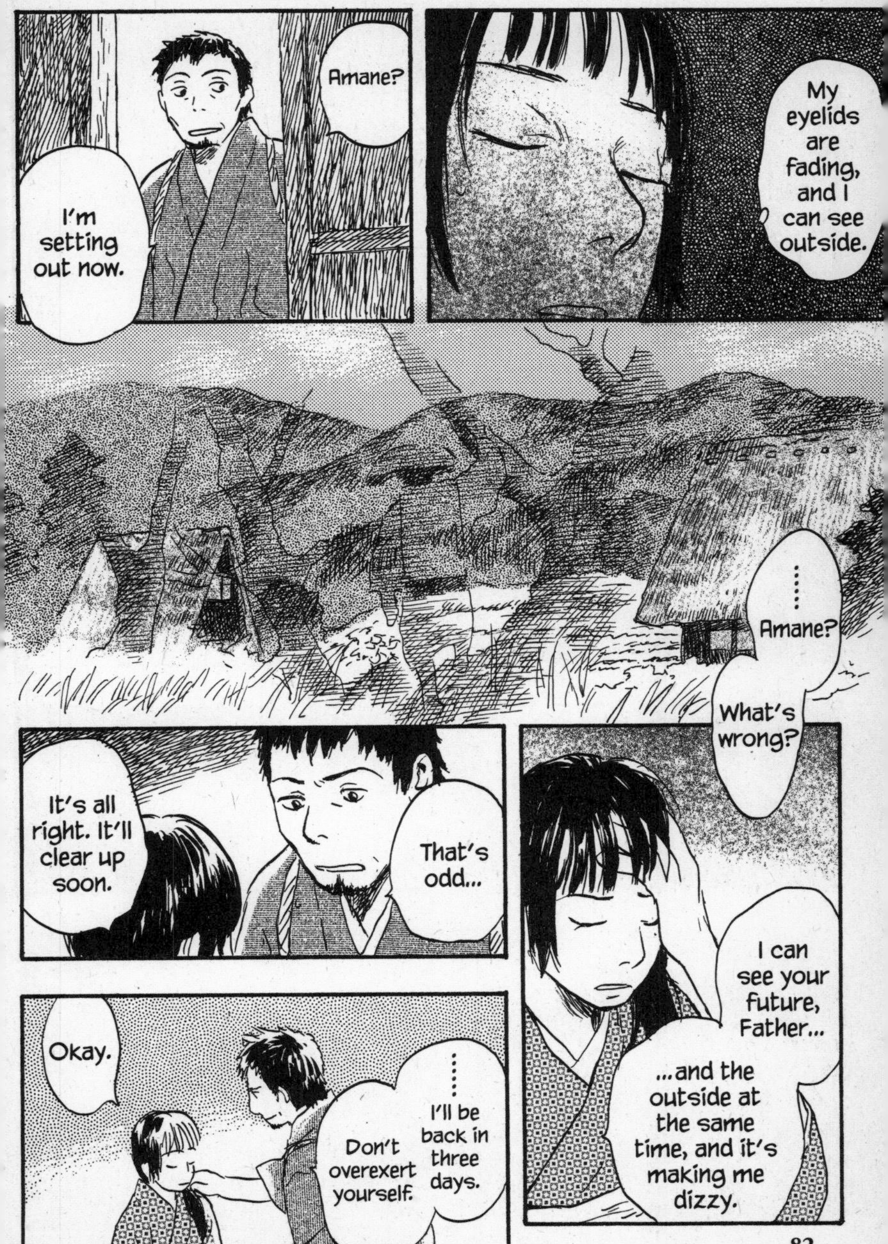
My eyelids are fading, and I can see outside.
Amane?
I'm setting out now.
...... Amane?
What's wrong?
I can see your future, Father...
...and the outside at the same time, and it's making me dizzy.
That's odd...
It's all right. It'll clear up soon.
......
I'll be back in three days.
Don't overexert yourself.
Okay.

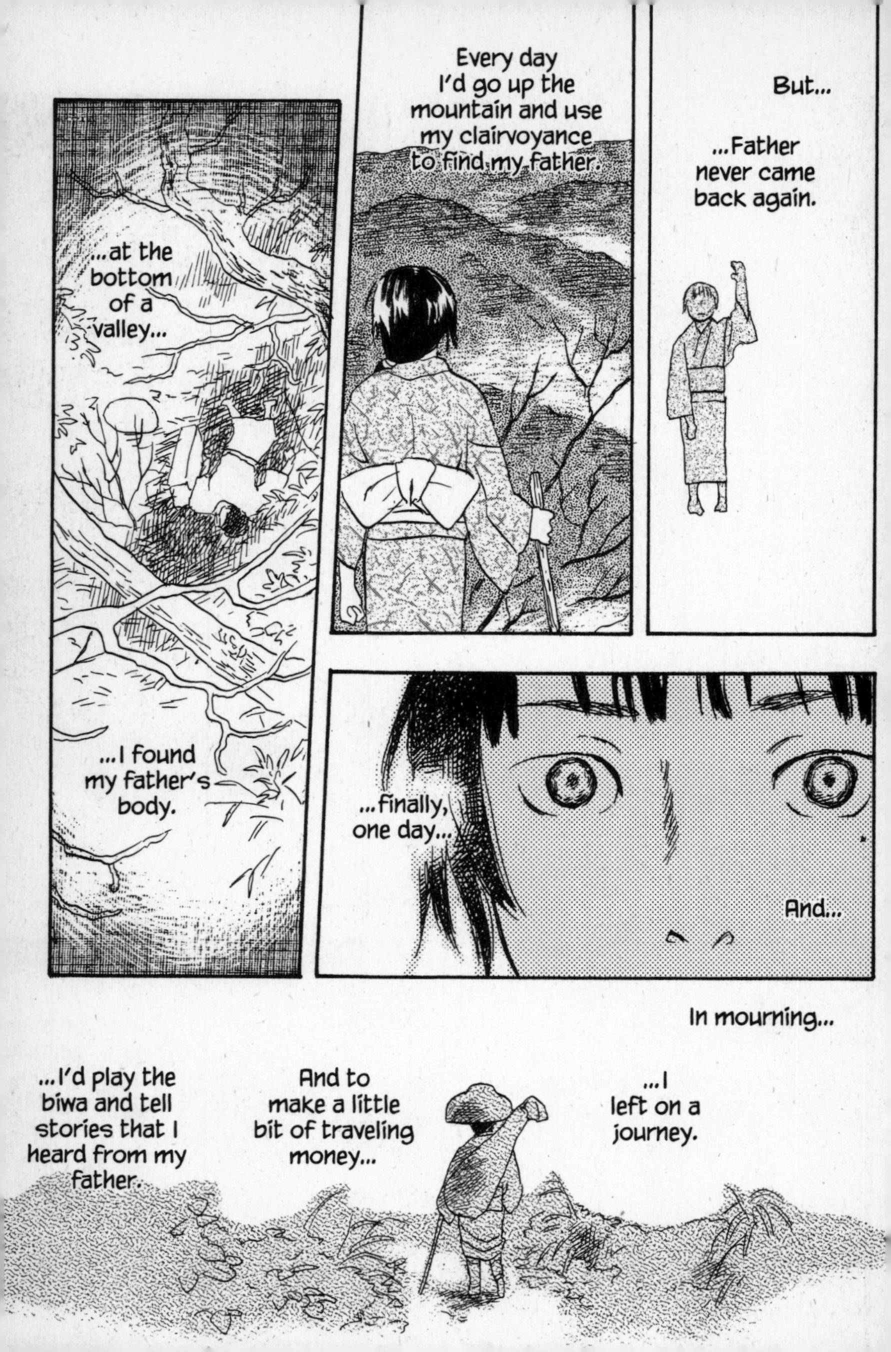
But...
...Father never came back again.
Every day I'd go up the mountain and use my clairvoyance to find my father.
And...
...finally, one day...
...at the bottom of a valley...
...I found my father's body.
In mourning...
...I left on a journey.
And to make a little bit of traveling money...
...I'd play the biwa and tell stories that I heard from my father.

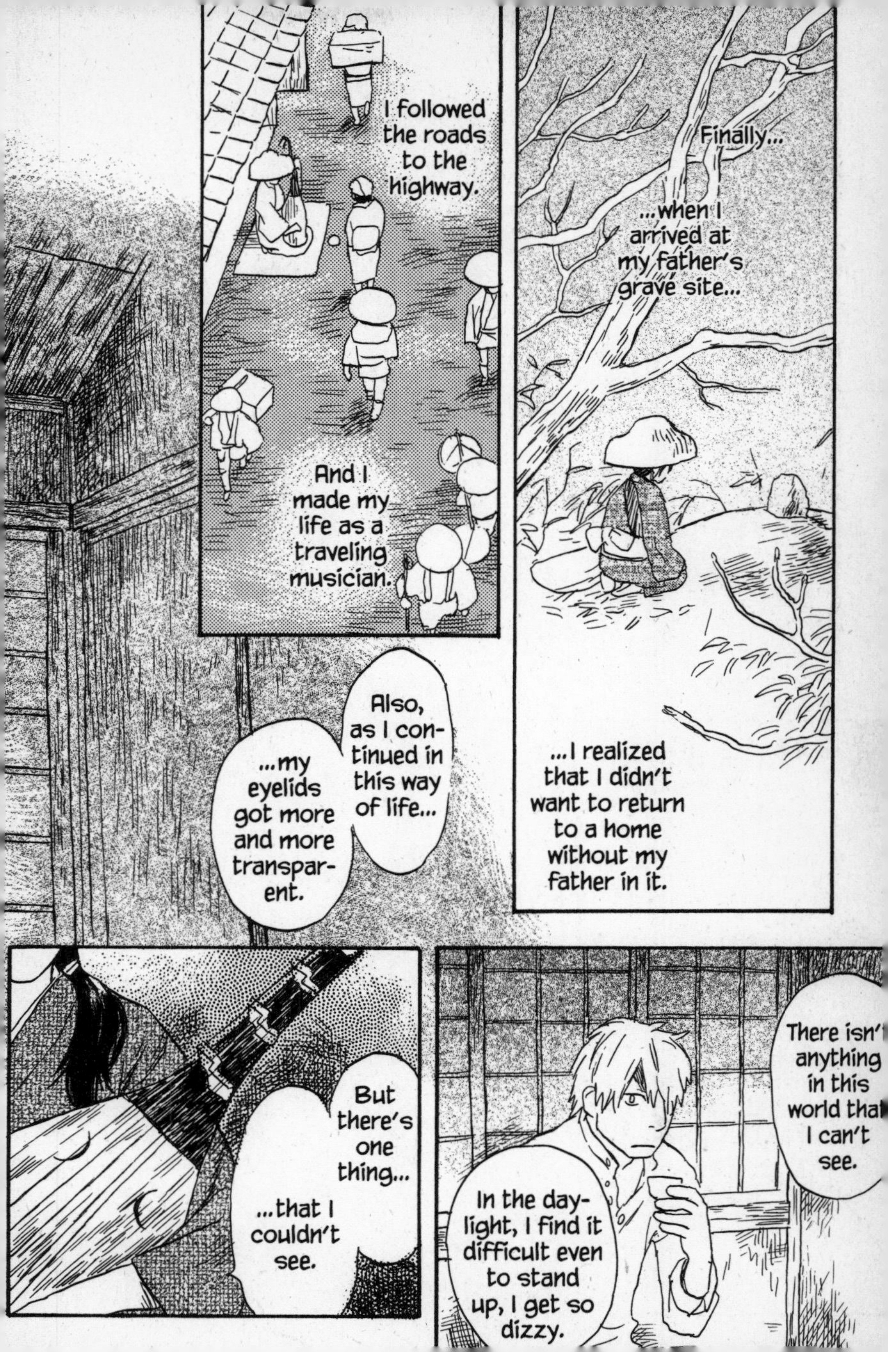

Finally...
...when I arrived at my father's grave site...
...I realized that I didn't want to return to a home without my father in it.
I followed the roads to the highway.
And I made my life as a traveling musician.
Also, as I continued in this way of life...
...my eyelids got more and more transparent.
There isn' anything in this world tha I can't see.
In the daylight, I find it difficult even to stand up, I get so dizzy.
But there's one thing...
...that I couldn't see.

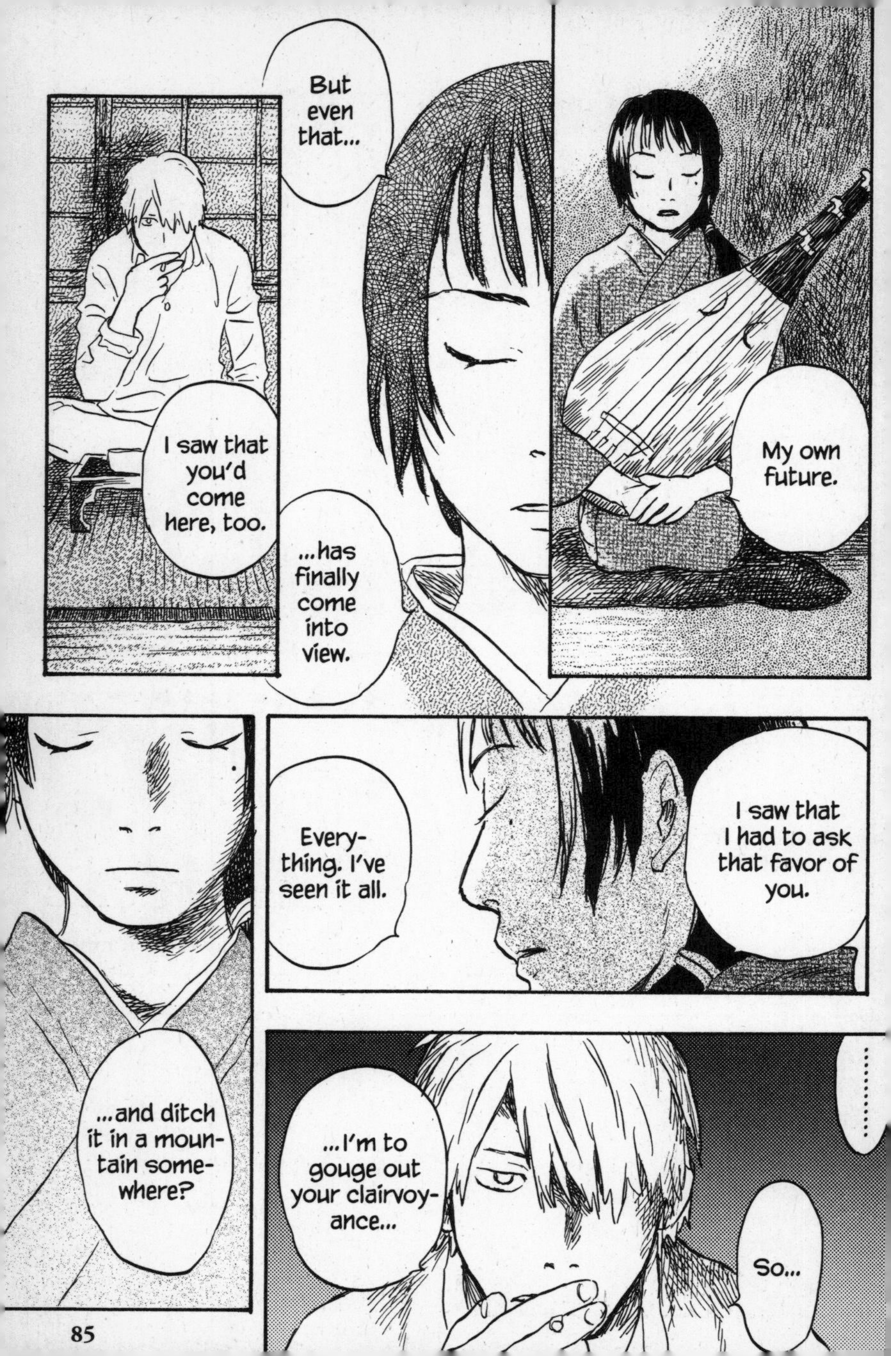
My own future.
But even that...
...has finally come into view.
I saw that you'd come here, too.
I saw that I had to ask that favor of you.
Every-thing. I've seen it all.
......
So...
...I'm to gouge out your clairvoy-ance...
...and ditch it in a moun-tain some-where?

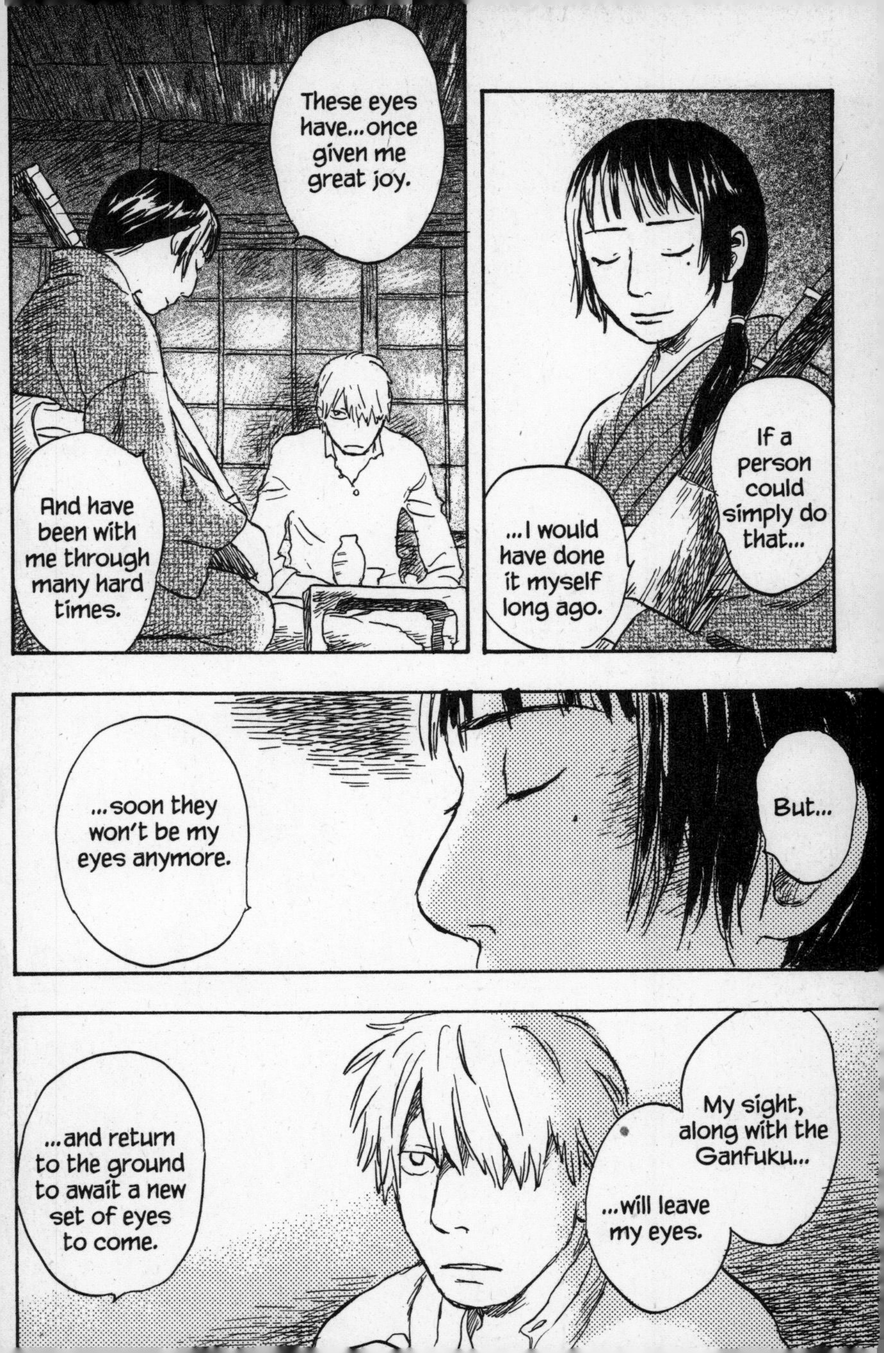
If a person could simply do that...
...I would have done it myself long ago.
These eyes have...once given me great joy.
And have been with me through many hard times.
But...
...soon they won't be my eyes anymore.
My sight, along with the Ganfuku...
...will leave my eyes.
...and return to the ground to await a new set of eyes to come.

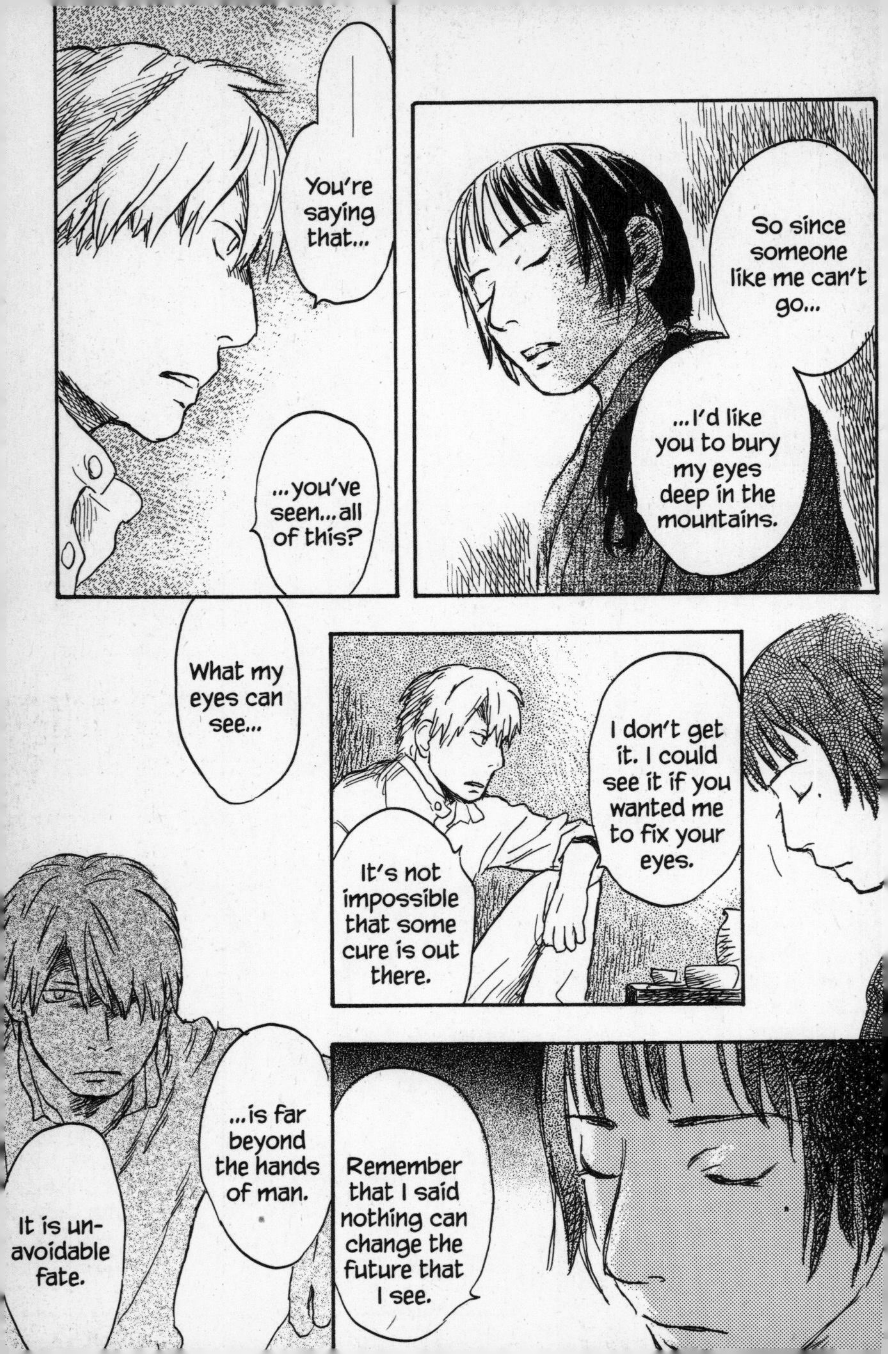
So since someone like me can't go...
...I'd like you to bury my eyes deep in the mountains.
You're saying that...
...you've seen...all of this?
I don't get it. I could see it if you wanted me to fix your eyes.
It's not impossible that some cure is out there.
What my eyes can see...
Remember that I said nothing can change the future that I see.
...is far beyond the hands of man.
It is unavoidable fate.

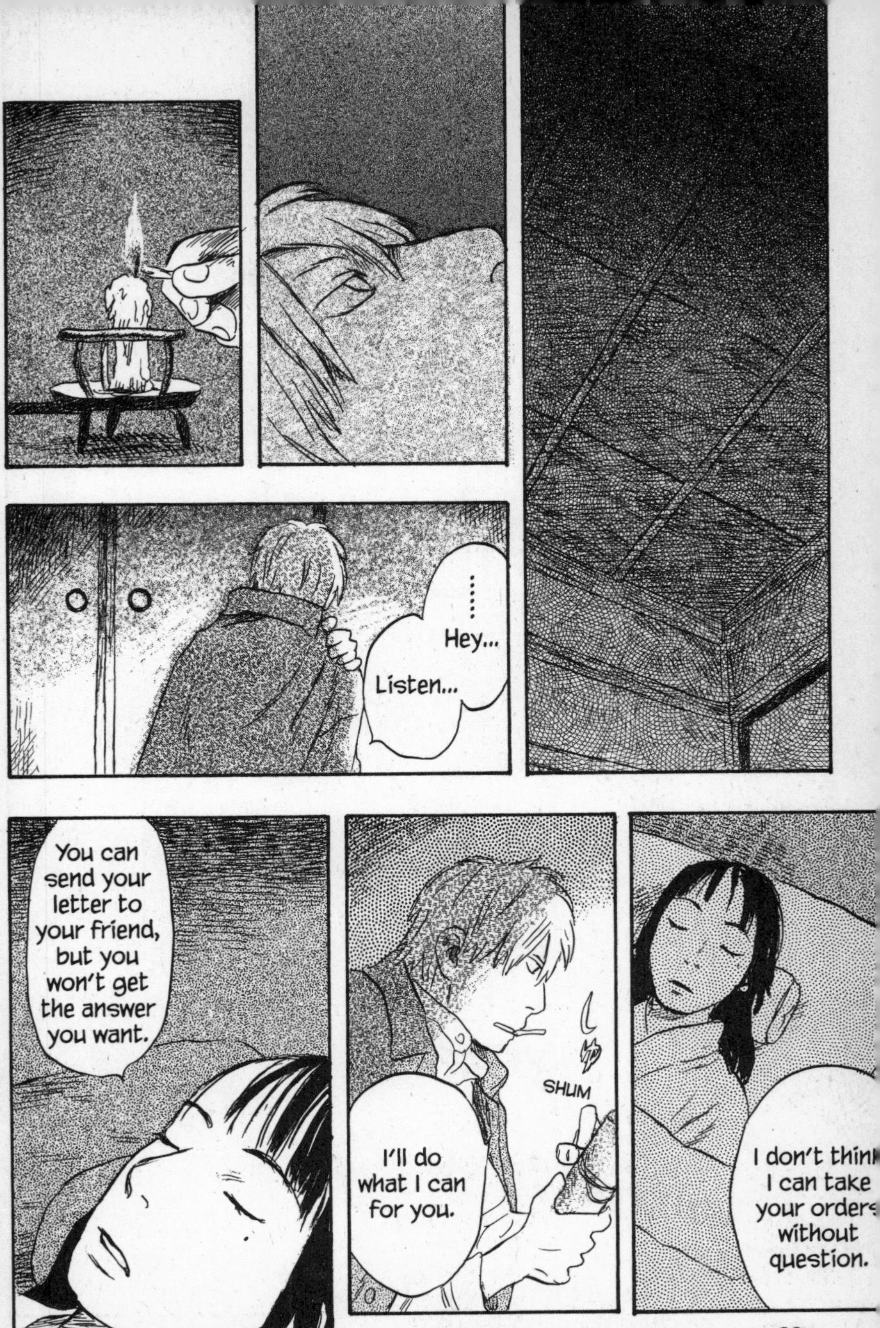
......
Hey...
Listen...
I don't think I can take your orders without question.
SHUM
I'll do what I can for you.
You can send your letter to your friend, but you won't get the answer you want.

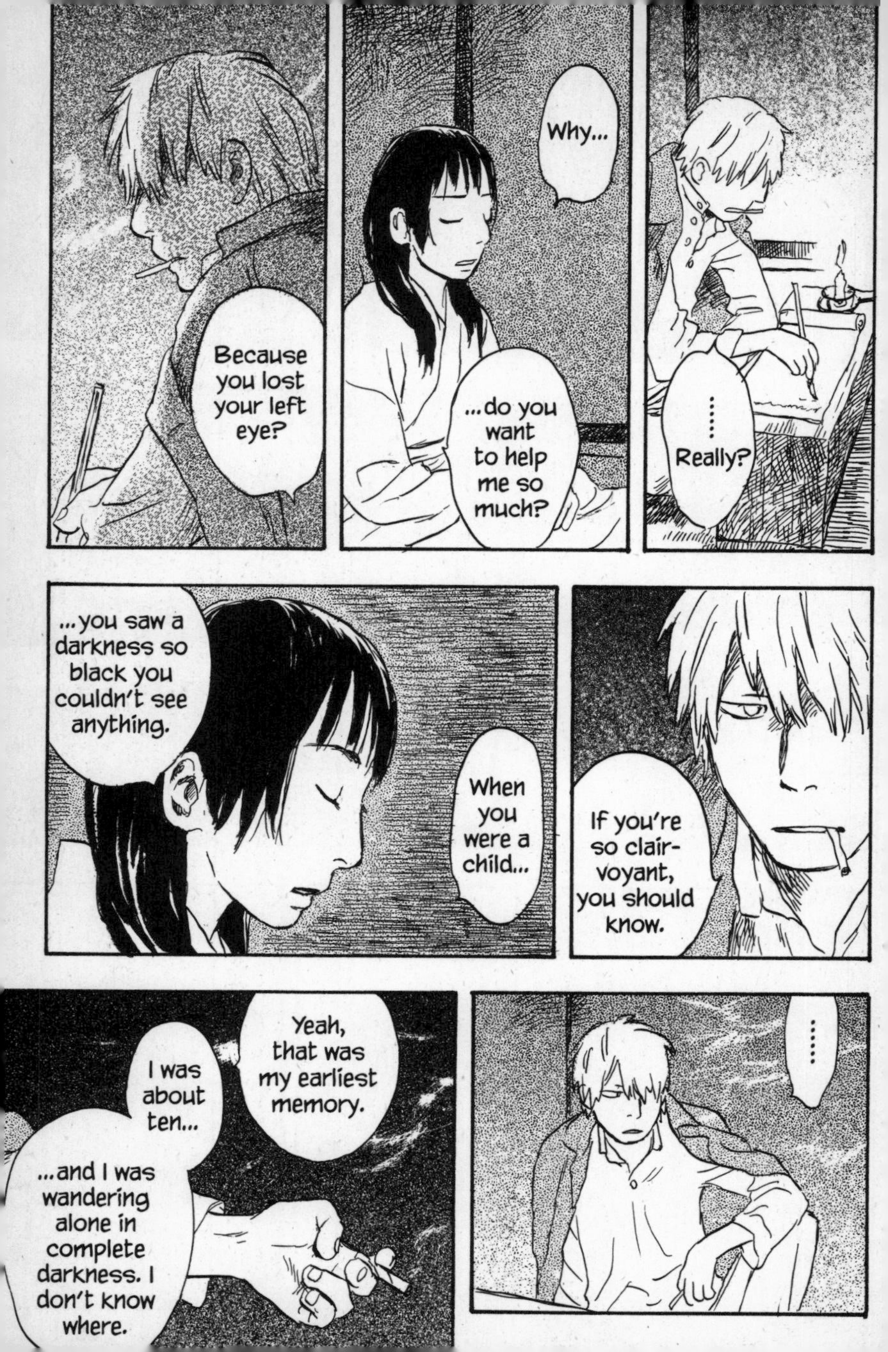
......
Really?
Why...
...do you want to help me so much?
Because you lost your left eye?
If you're so clair-voyant, you should know.
When you were a child...
...you saw a darkness so black you couldn't see anything.
......
Yeah, that was my earliest memory.
I was about ten...
...and I was wandering alone in complete darkness. I don't know where.

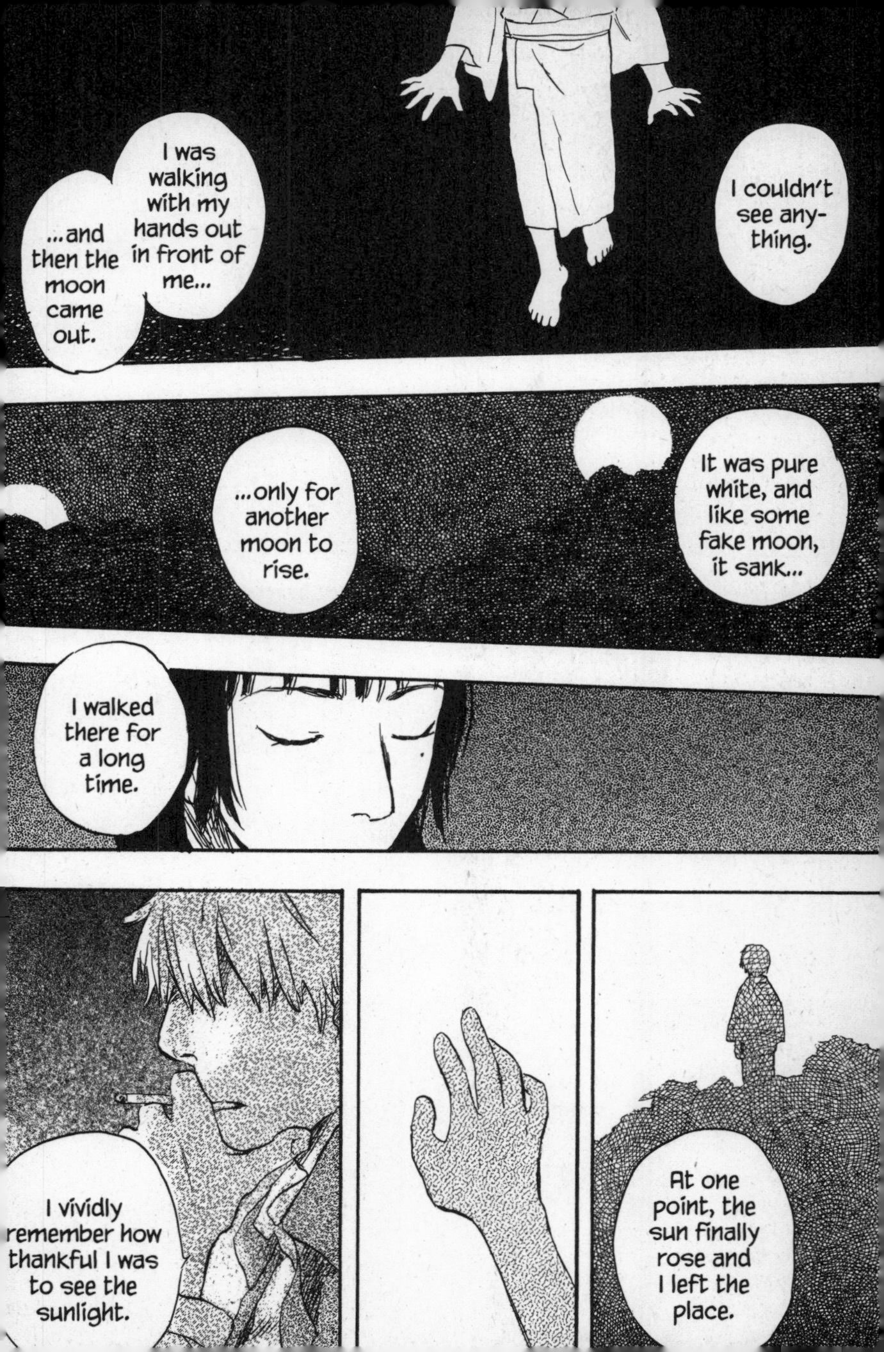
I couldn't see any-thing.
I was walking with my hands out in front of me...
...and then the moon came out.
It was pure white, and like some fake moon, it sank...
...only for another moon to rise.
I walked there for a long time.
At one point, the sun finally rose and I left the place.
I vividly remember how thankful I was to see the sunlight.

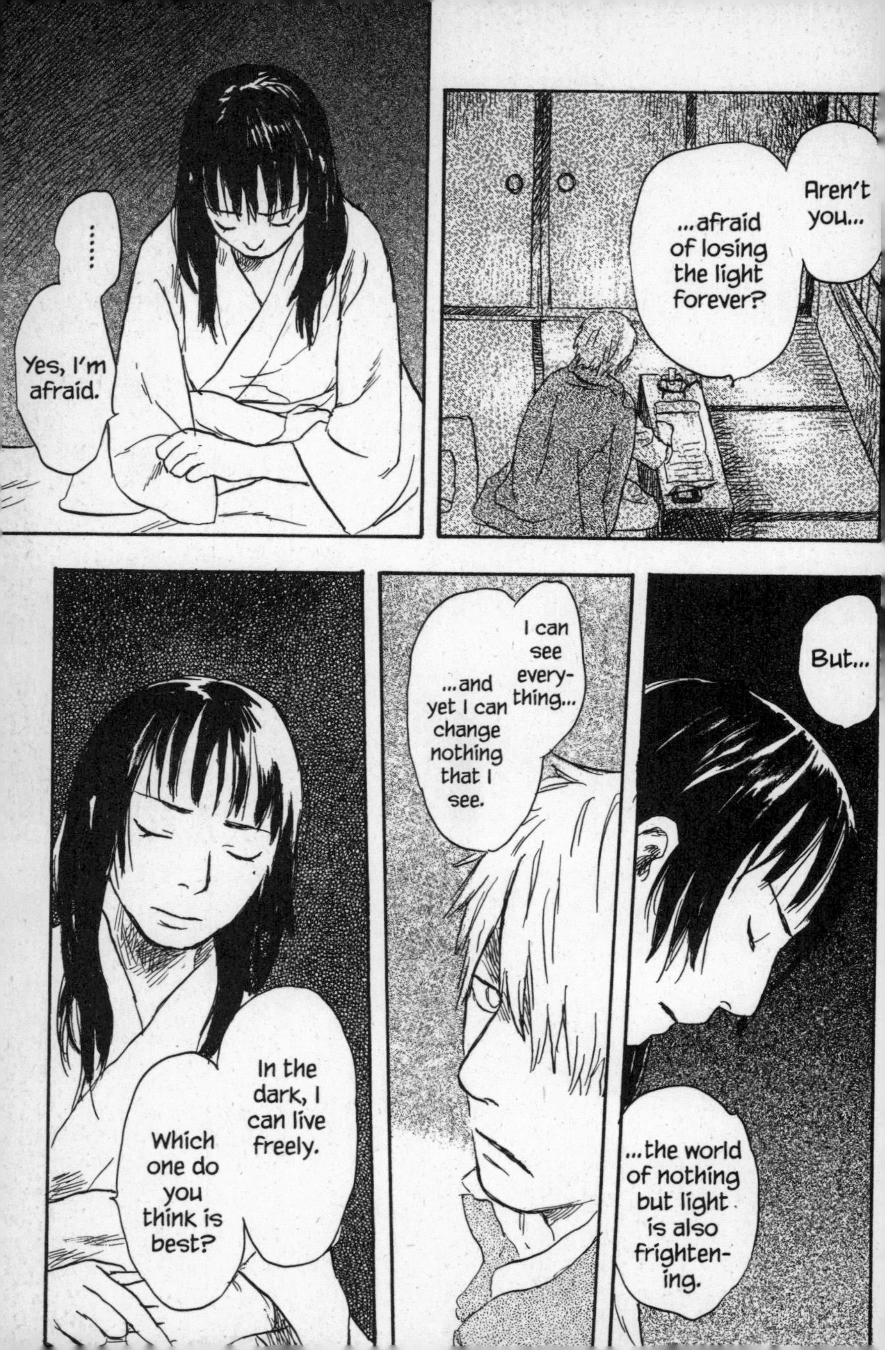

Aren't you...
...afraid of losing the light forever?
......
Yes, I'm afraid.
But...
...the world of nothing but light is also frighten-ing.
I can see every-thing...
...and yet I can change nothing that I see.
In the dark, I can live freely.
Which one do you think is best?

For me...

...I can remember the light even when I'm in the dark.

I think blind but still alive isn't a bad option.

.....
Uhn!

Ah!

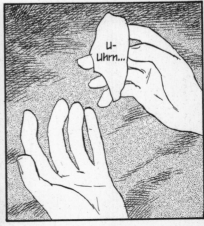

u-uhm...

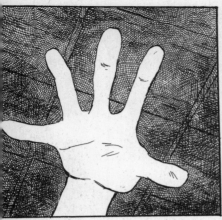
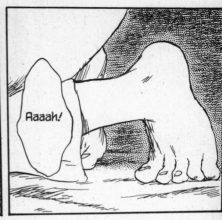

Aaaah!

Uhn...

Aaaa!!

SHUMP

What's wrong?!

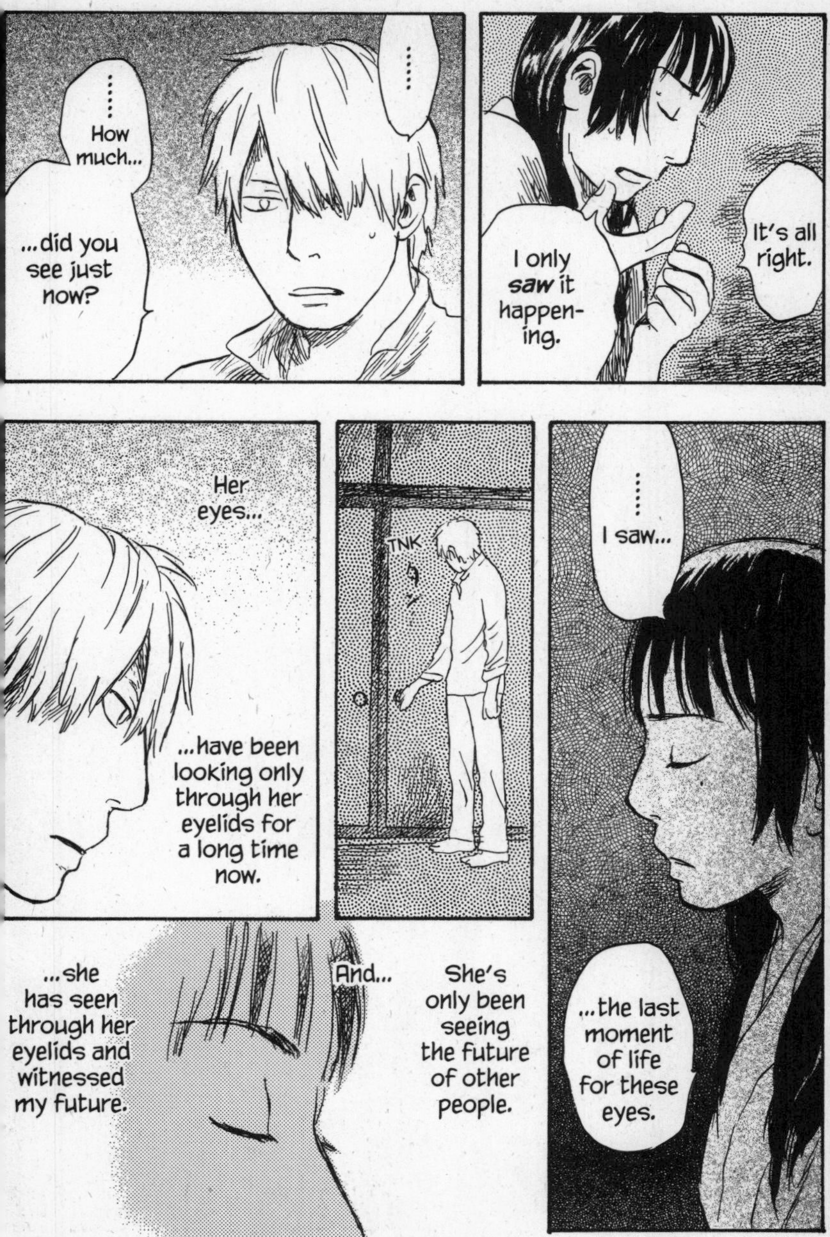

It's all right.
I only *saw* it happening.
......
...... How much...
...did you see just now?
...... I saw...
...the last moment of life for these eyes.
TNK
Her eyes...
...have been looking only through her eyelids for a long time now.
She's only been seeing the future of other people.
And...
...she has seen through her eyelids and witnessed my future.

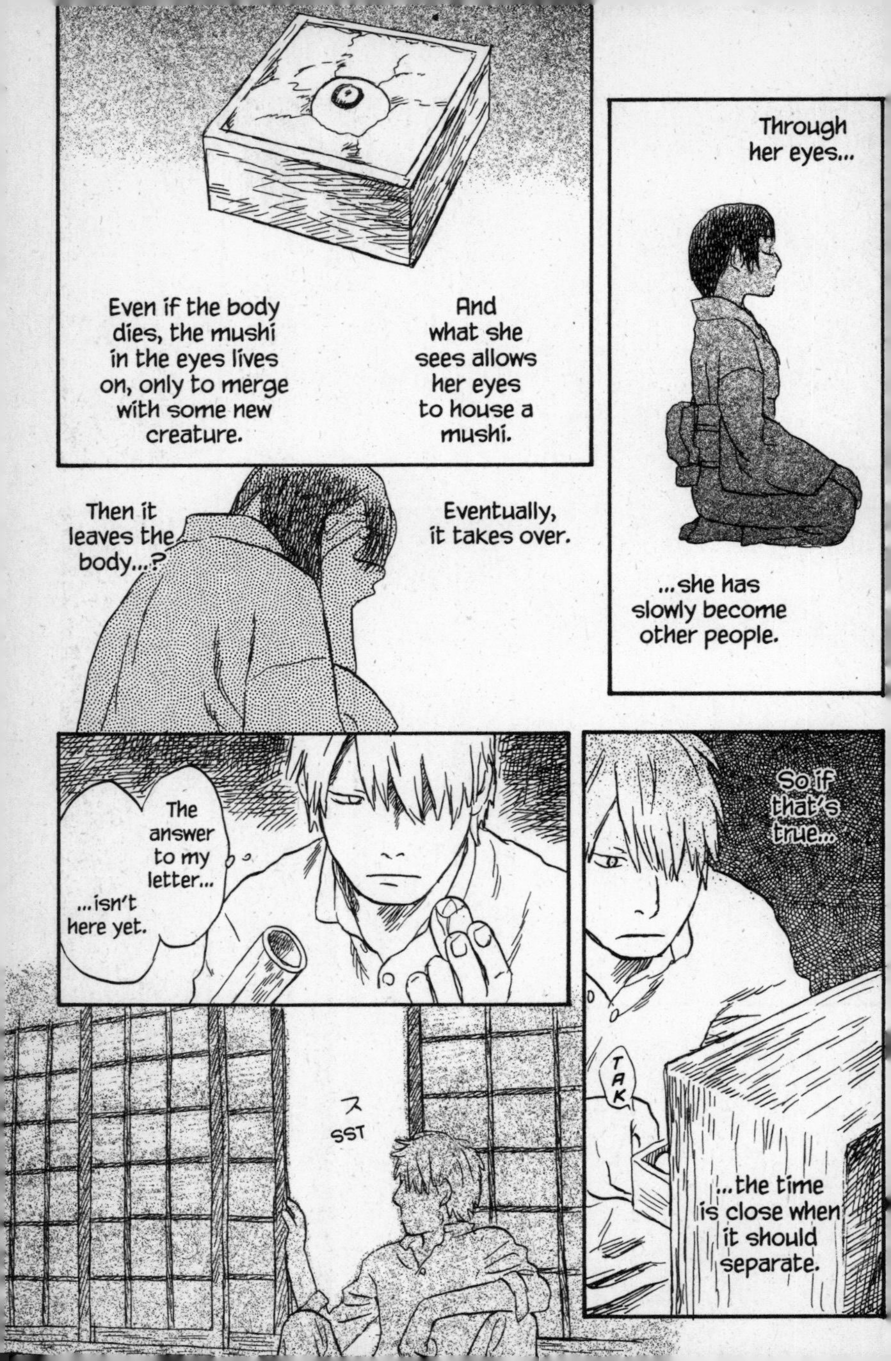

Through her eyes...
...she has slowly become other people.
And what she sees allows her eyes to house a mushi.
Even if the body dies, the mushi in the eyes lives on, only to merge with some new creature.
Eventually, it takes over.
Then it leaves the body...?
So if that's true...
TAK
...the time is close when it should separate.
The answer to my letter...
...isn't here yet.
ス
SST

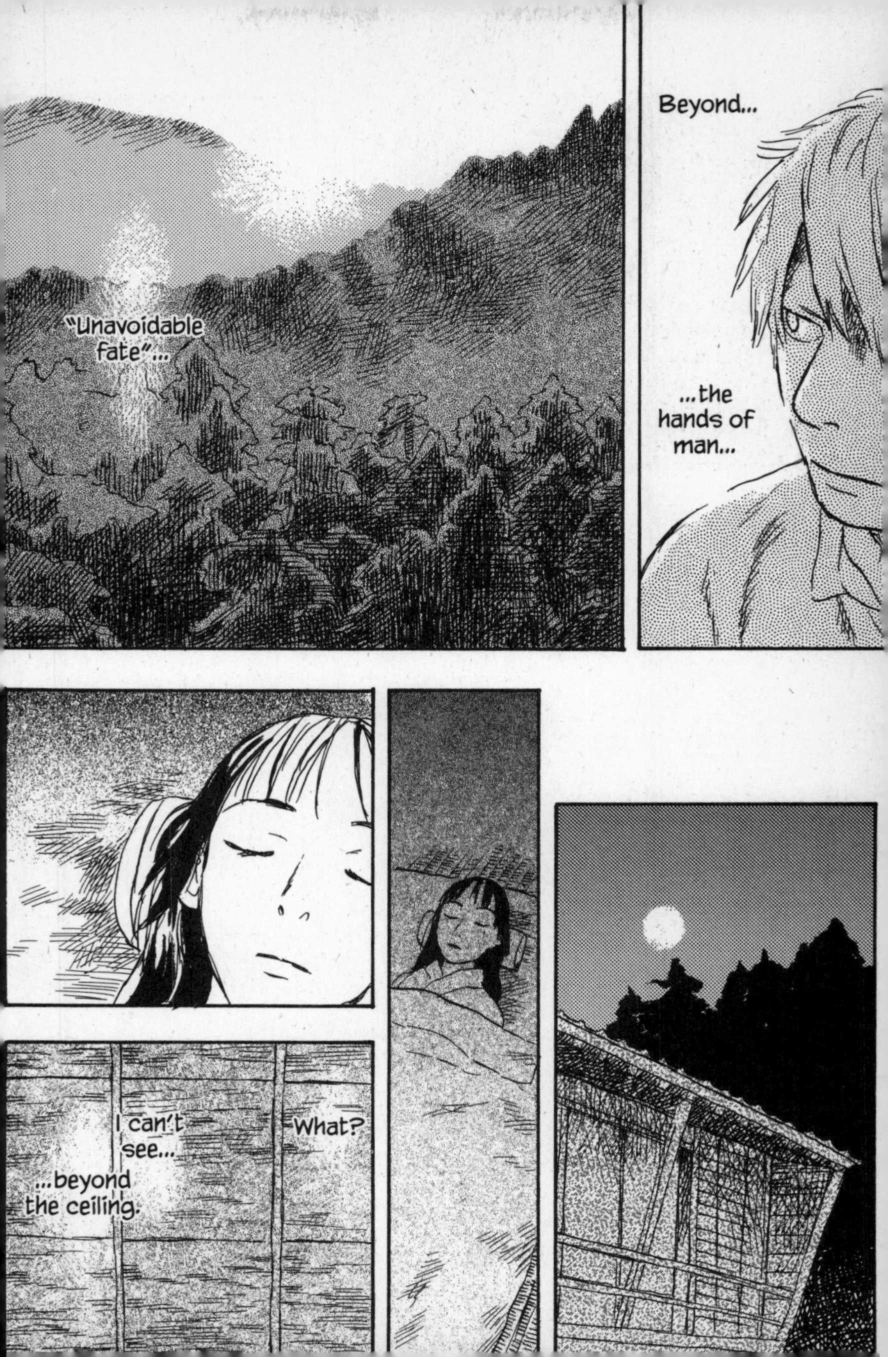
Beyond...
...the hands of man...
“Unavoidable fate”...
What?
I can't see...
...beyond the ceiling.

What's...

......?

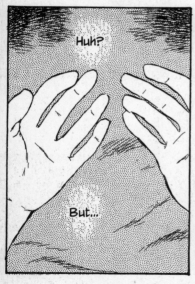

Huh?

But...

I can see normally!

...are moving on their own!

My eyes...

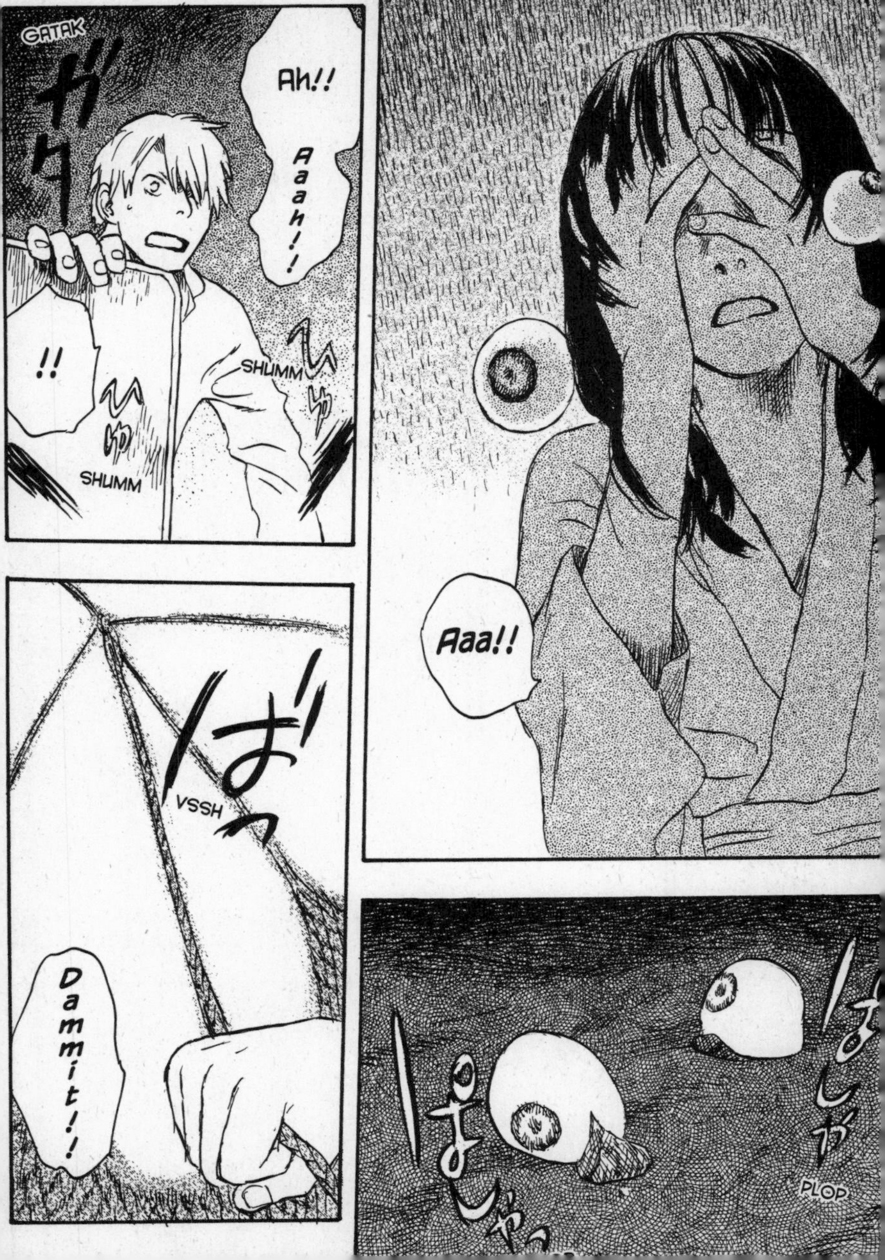
Aaa!!
PLOP
GATAK
Ah!!
Aaaah!!
SHUMM
!!
SHUMM
VSSH
Dammit!!

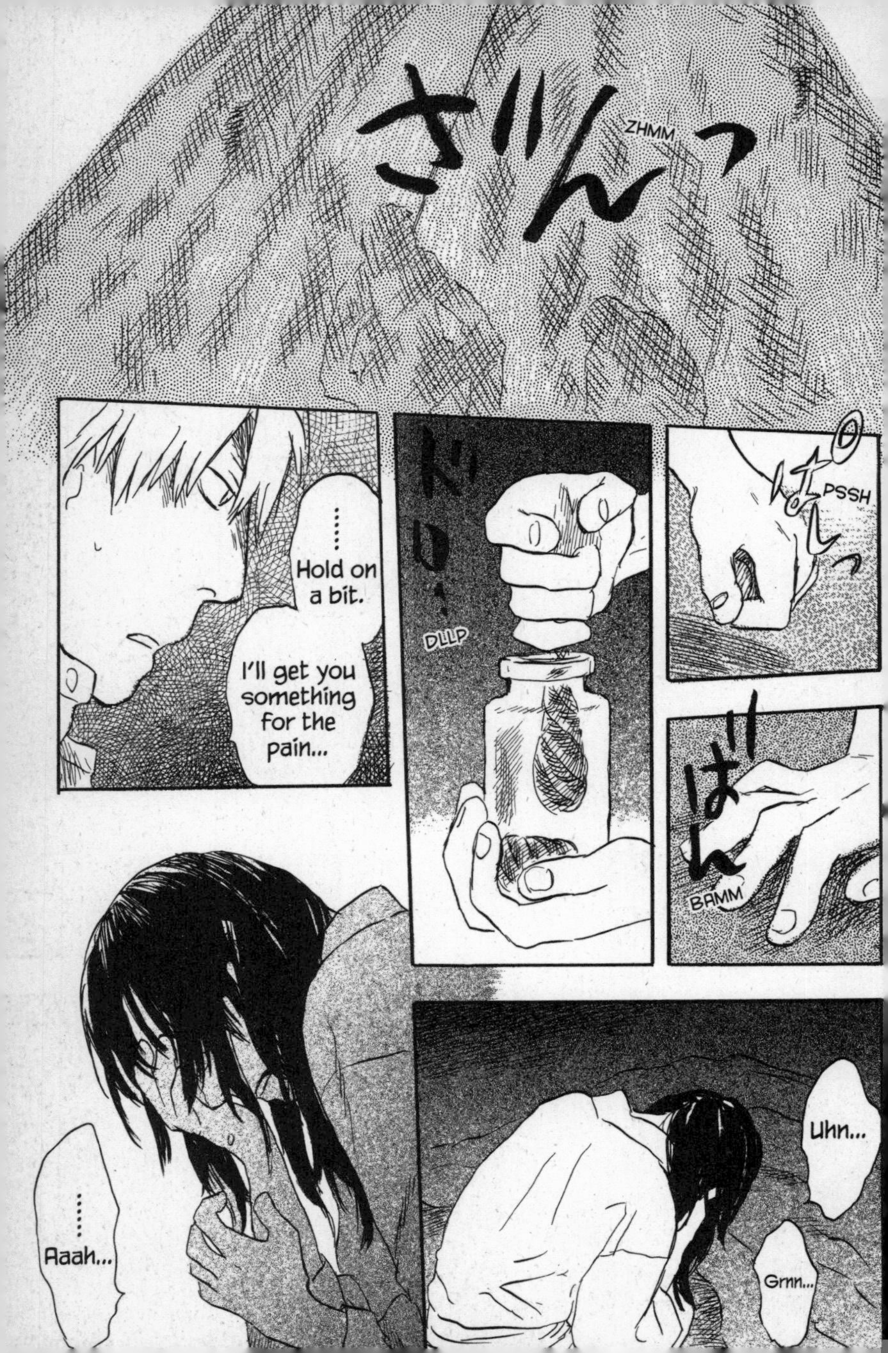

ZHMM
PSSH
BAMM
DLLP
......
Hold on a bit.
I'll get you something for the pain...
Uhn...
Grnn...
......
Aaah...

Even without eyes...

...we can still cry, can't we?

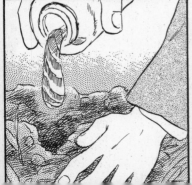

SHK

SHK

100

How much...
SHF SHF
...did you see just now?
......I saw...
...the last moment of life for these eyes.
After the eyes fell from me...
...they were buried beneath the earth.
Eventually a face came up from the ground.
Some animal looked its way.
And suddenly there was a beautiful flower reflected in the beast's eyes.

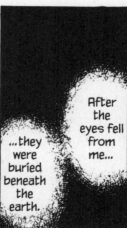

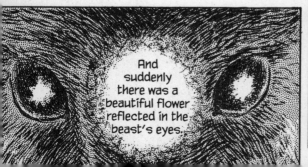

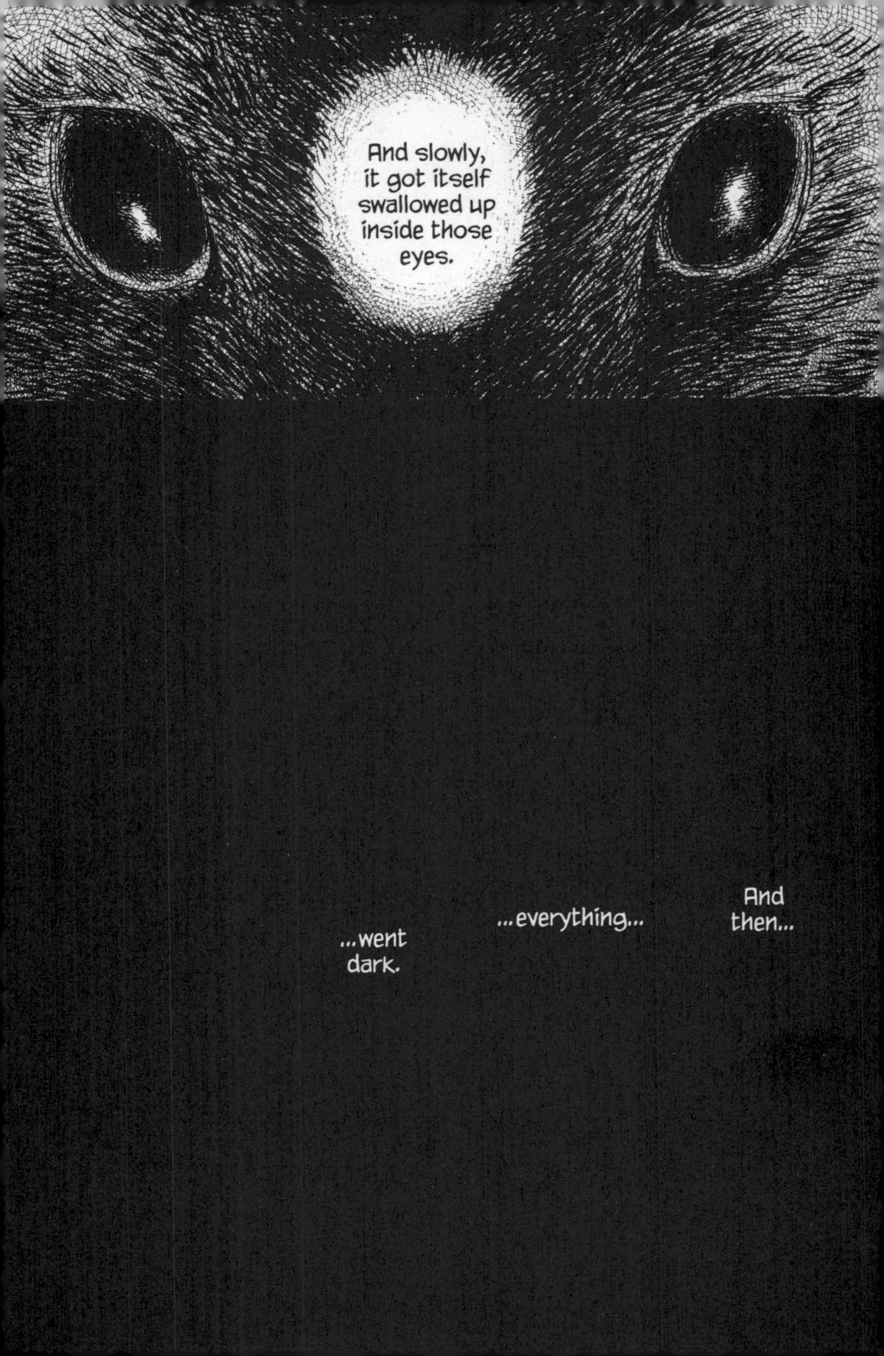
And slowly, it got itself swallowed up inside those eyes.
And then...
...everything...
...went dark.

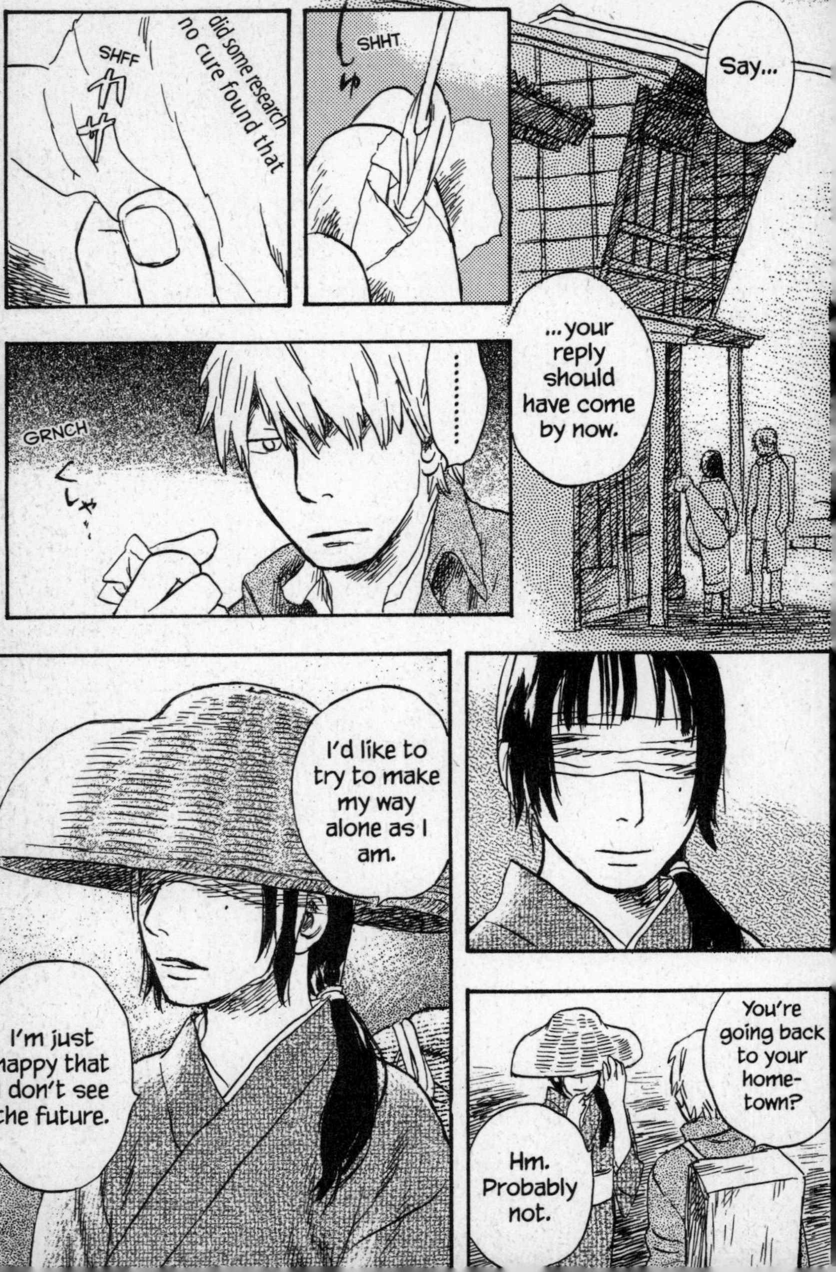
Say...
...your reply should have come by now.
SHHT
did some research
no cure found that
SHFF
カサ
......
GRNCH
くしゃ
You're going back to your home-town?
Hm. Probably not.
I'd like to try to make my way alone as I am.
I'm just happy that I don't see the future.

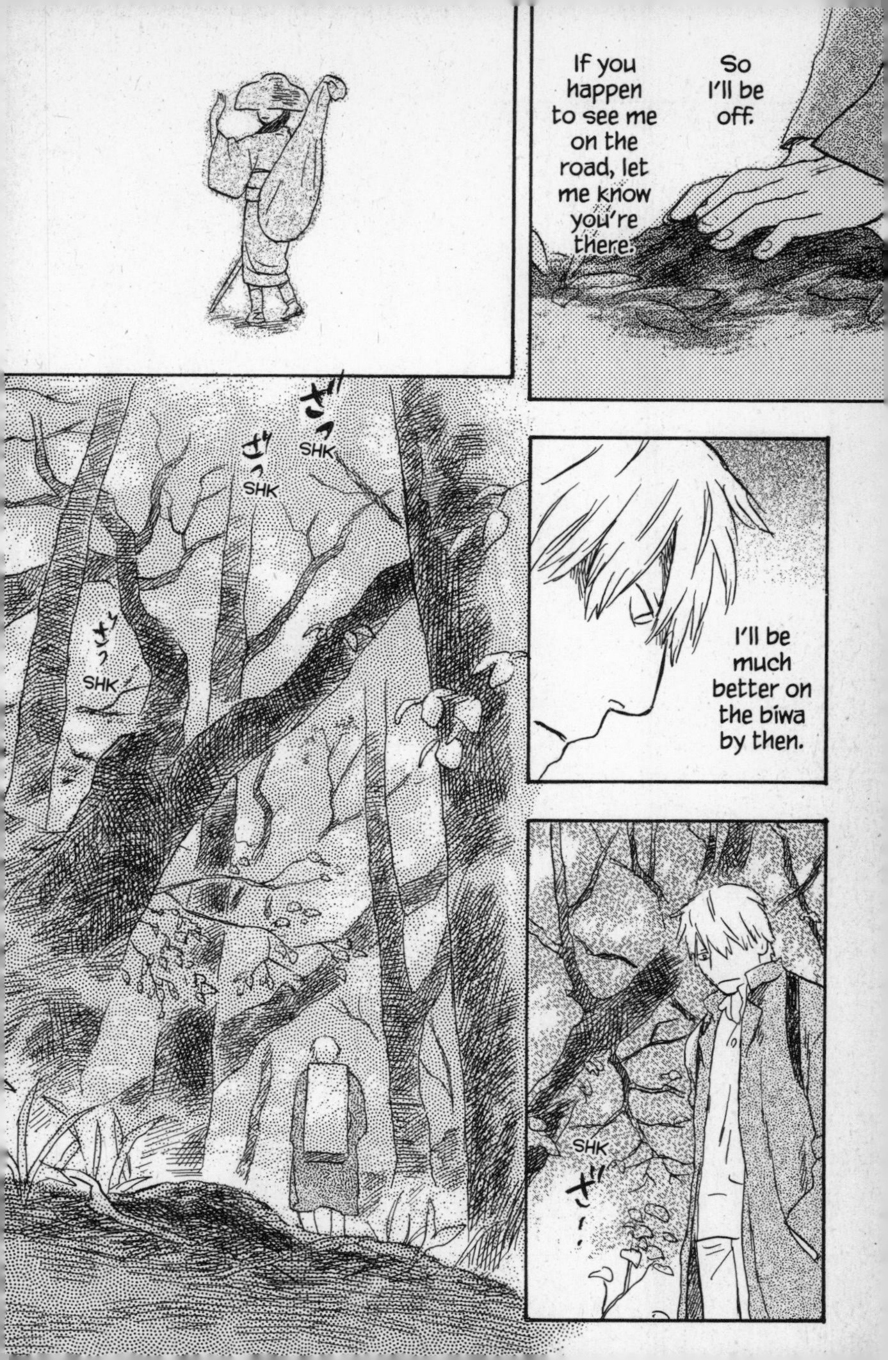
So I'll be off.
If you happen to see me on the road, let me know you're there.
I'll be much better on the biwa by then.
SHK
SHK
SHK
SHK

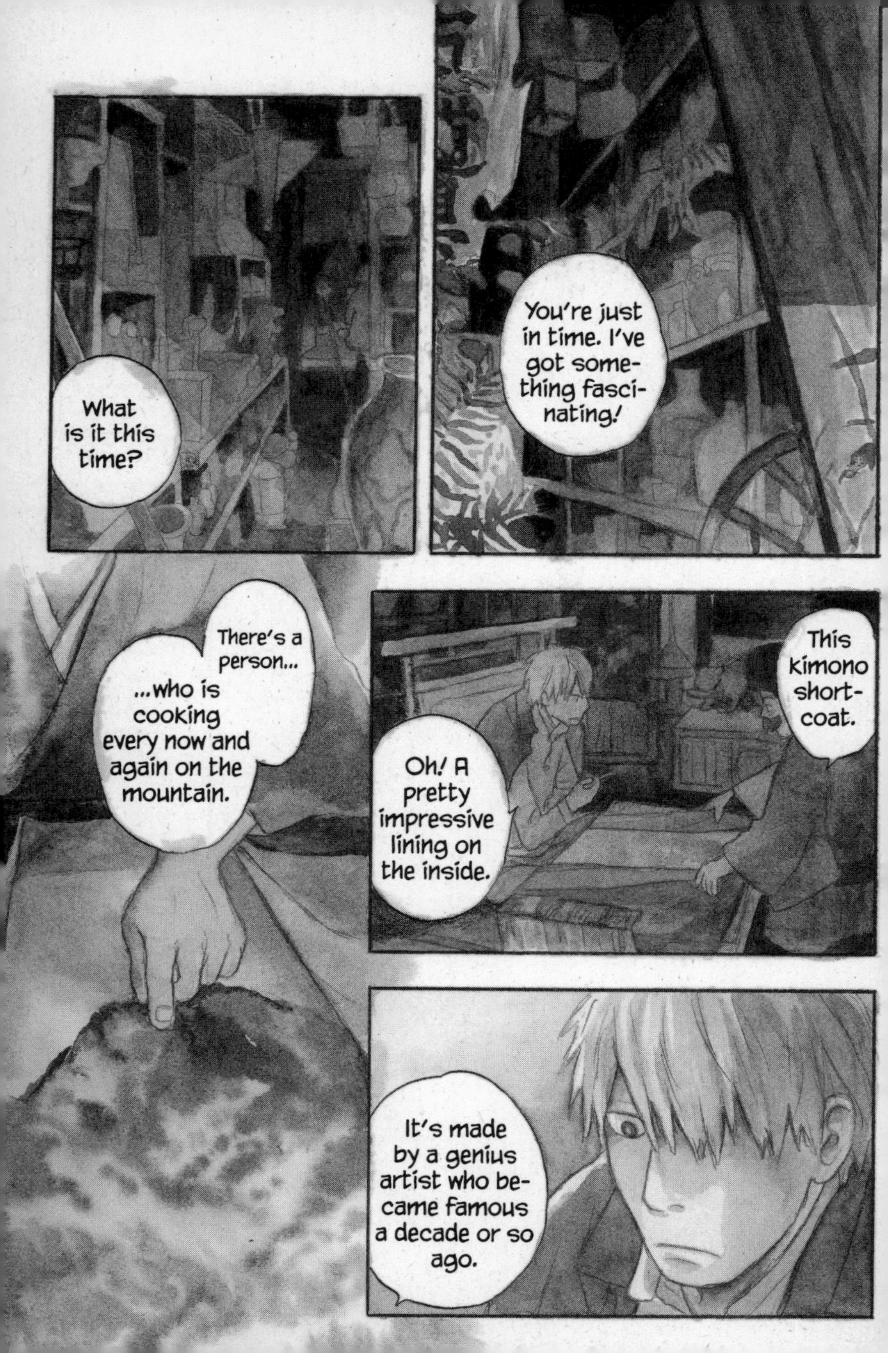
You're just in time. I've got some-thing fasci-nating!
What is it this time?
This kimono short-coat.
Oh! A pretty impressive lining on the inside.
It's made by a genius artist who be-came famous a decade or so ago.
There's a person...
...who is cooking every now and again on the mountain.

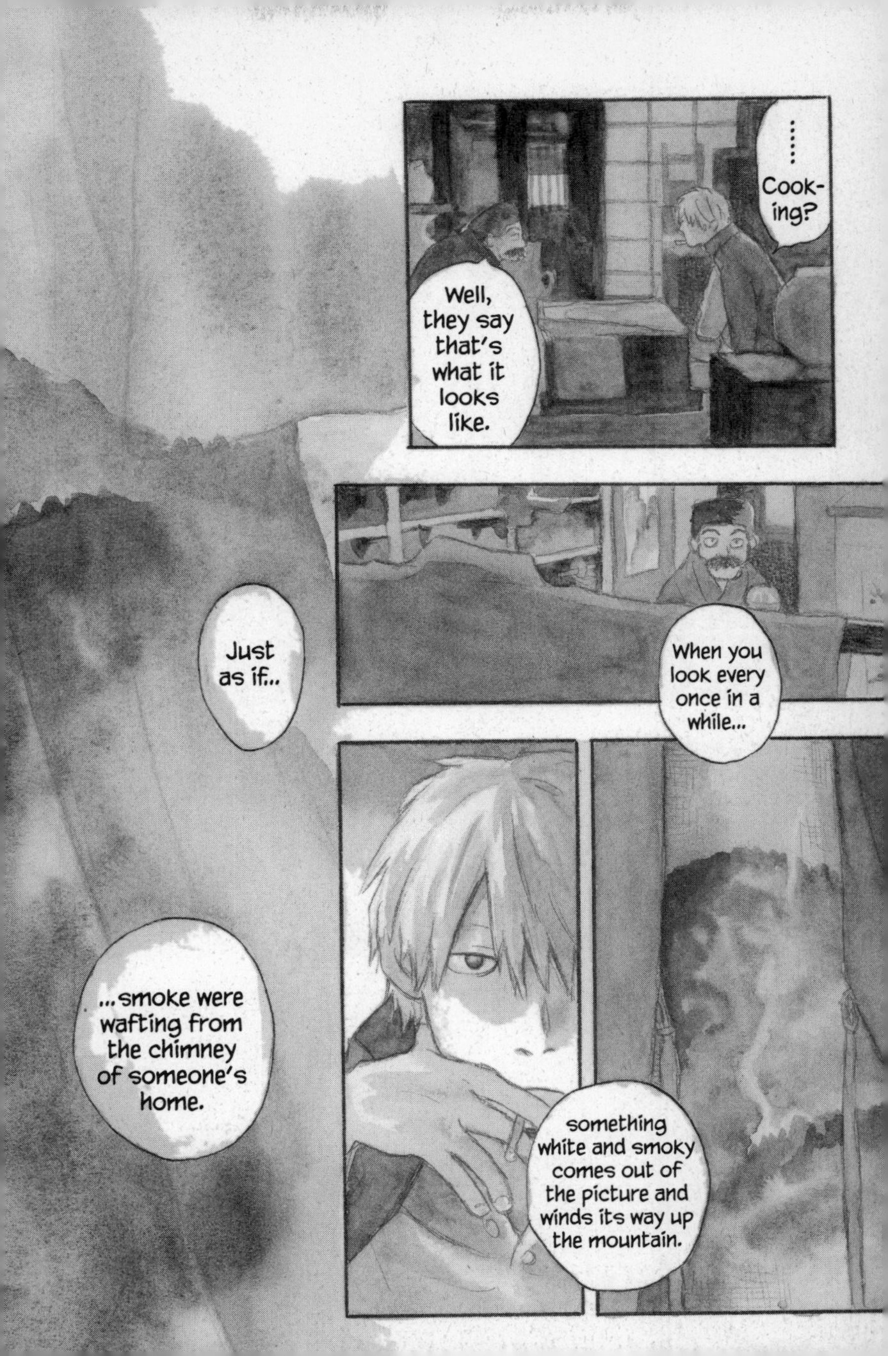
......
Cook-ing?
Well, they say that's what it looks like.
When you look every once in a while...
something white and smoky comes out of the picture and winds its way up the mountain.
Just as if...
...smoke were wafting from the chimney of someone's home.

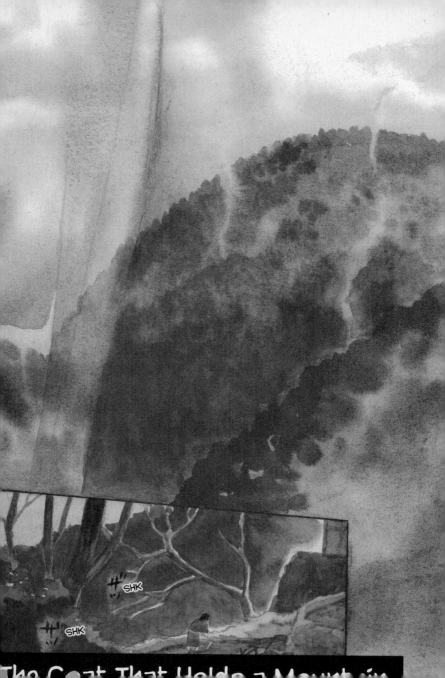

The Goat That Holds a Mountain

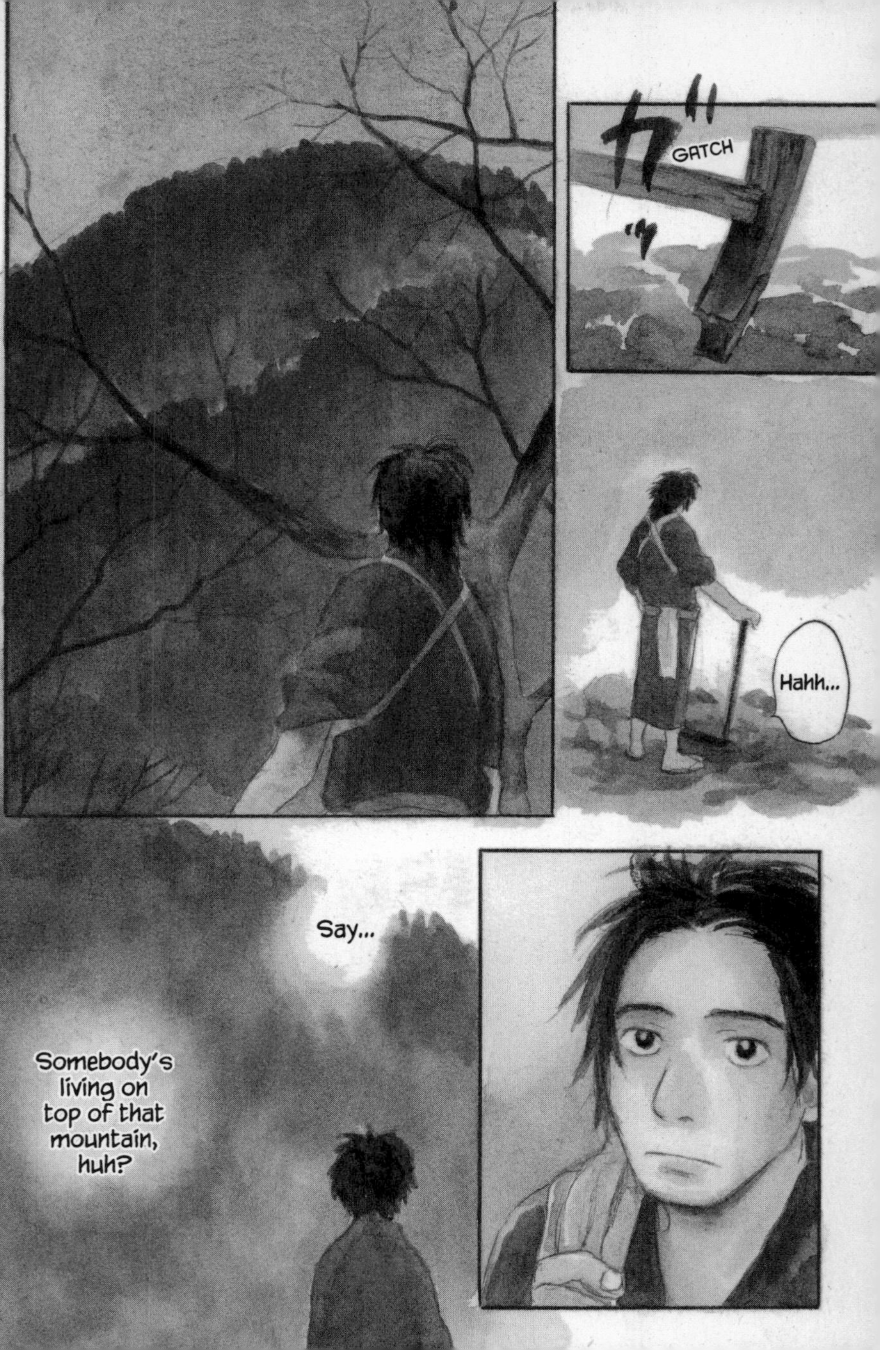
GATCH
Hahh...
Say...
Somebody's living on top of that mountain, huh?

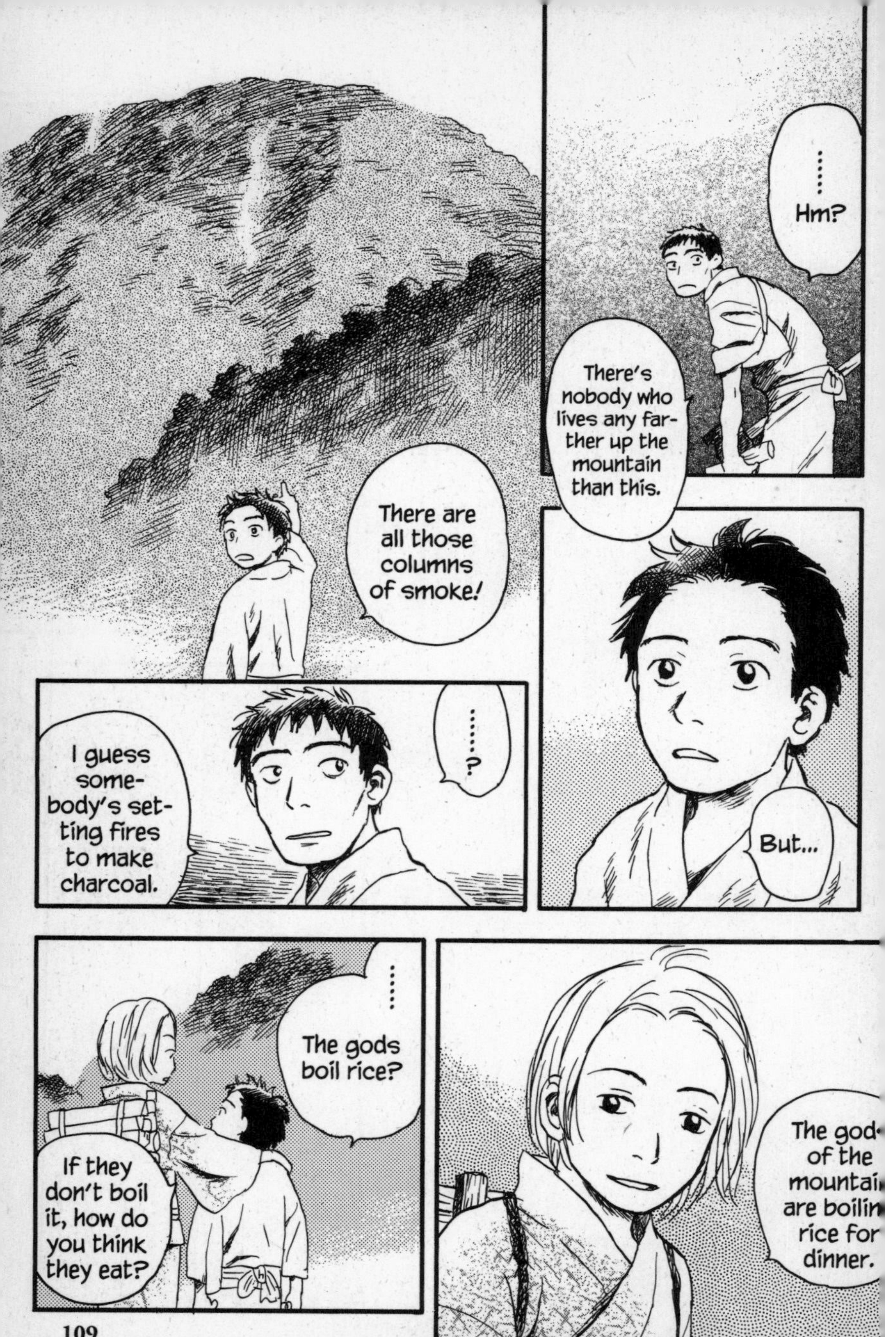

......
Hm?
There's nobody who lives any farther up the mountain than this.
There are all those columns of smoke!
But...
......?
I guess somebody's setting fires to make charcoal.
The god of the mountai are boilin rice for dinner.
......
The gods boil rice?
If they don't boil it, how do you think they eat?

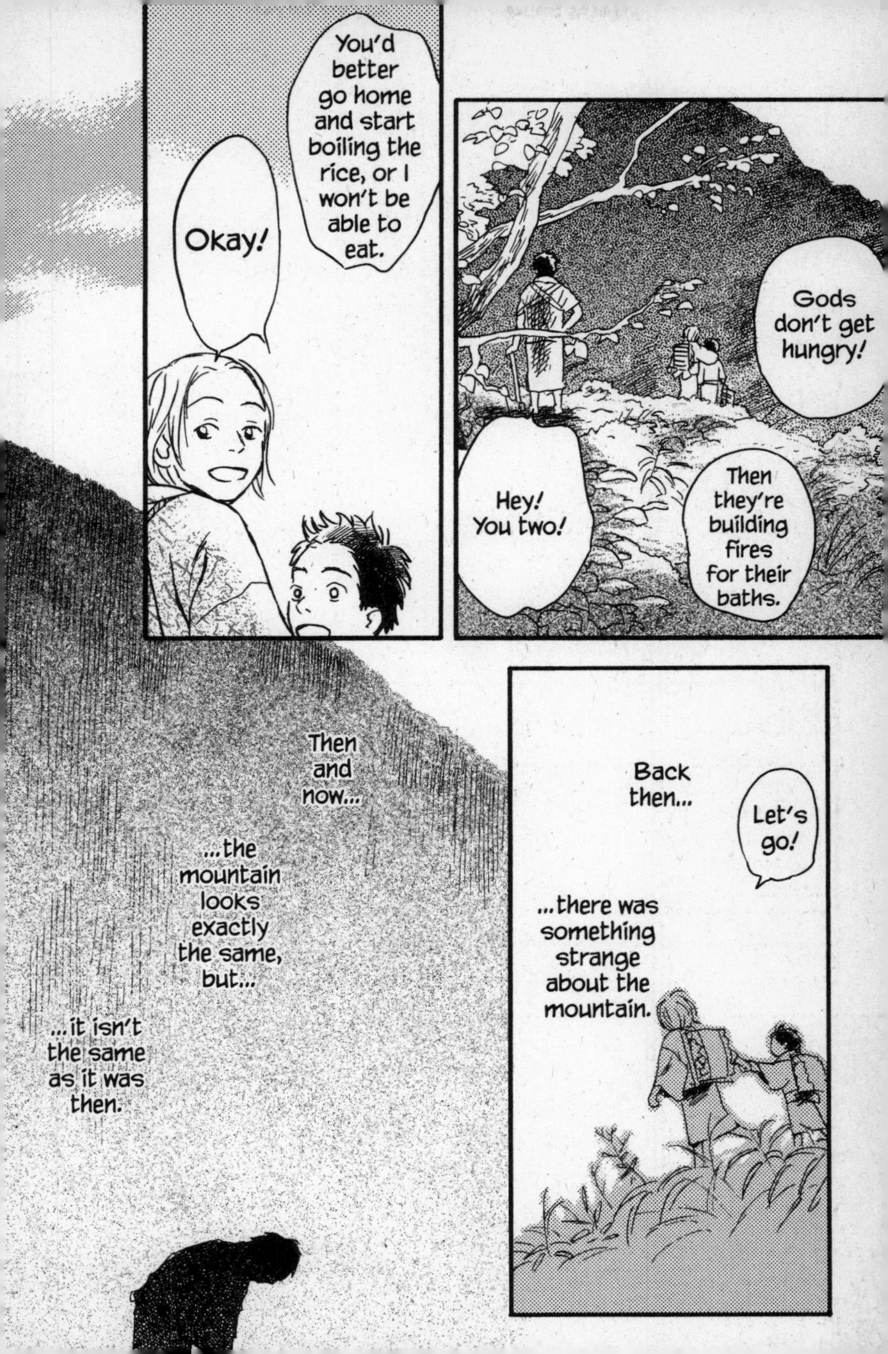
Gods don't get hungry!
Then they're building fires for their baths.
Hey! You two!
You'd better go home and start boiling the rice, or I won't be able to eat.
Okay!
Back then...
Let's go!
...there was something strange about the mountain.
Then and now...
...the mountain looks exactly the same, but...
...it isn't the same as it was then.

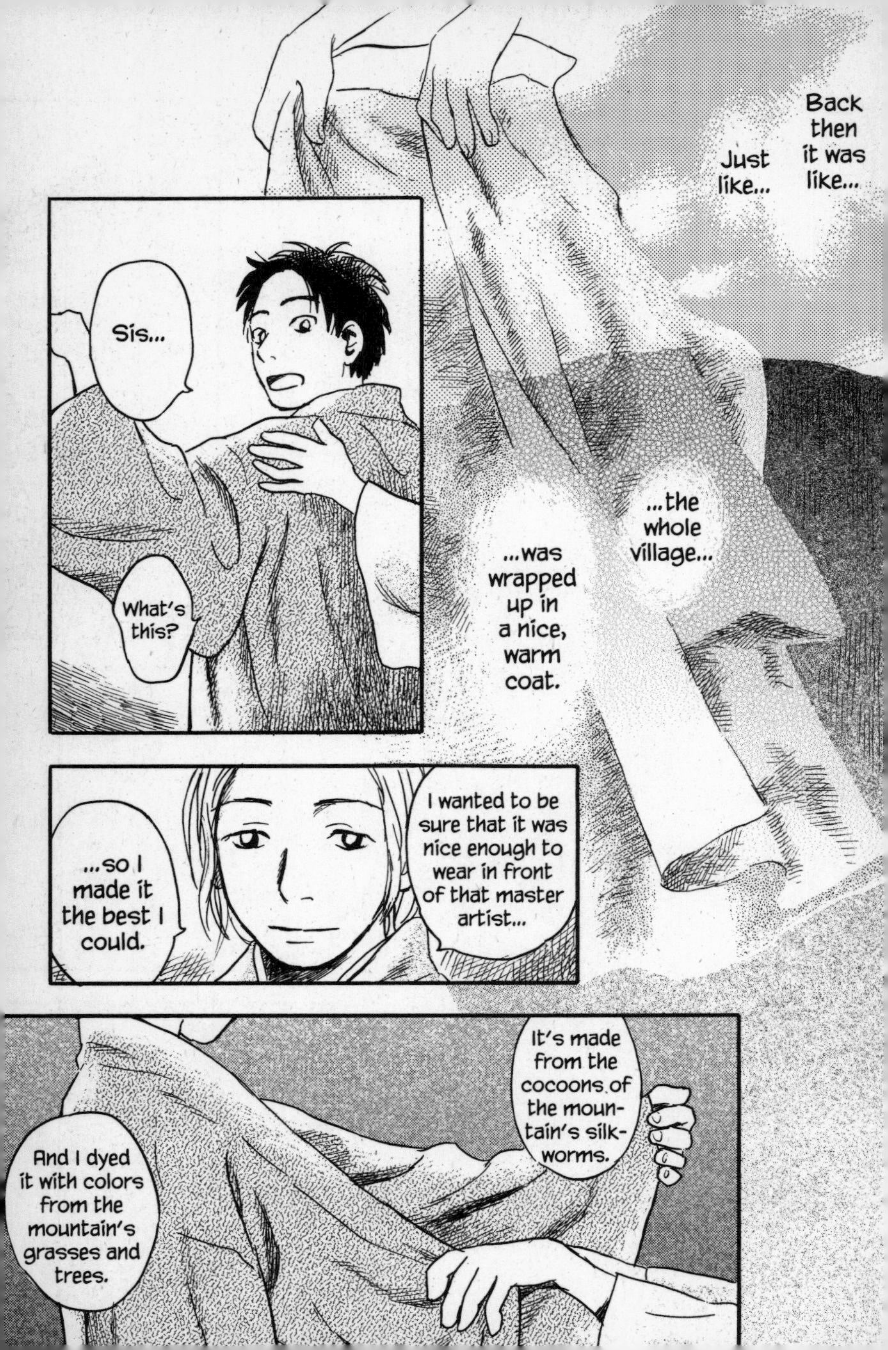
Back then it was like...
Just like...
...the whole village...
...was wrapped up in a nice, warm coat.
Sis...
What's this?
I wanted to be sure that it was nice enough to wear in front of that master artist...
...so I made it the best I could.
It's made from the cocoons of the mountain's silk-worms.
And I dyed it with colors from the mountain's grasses and trees.

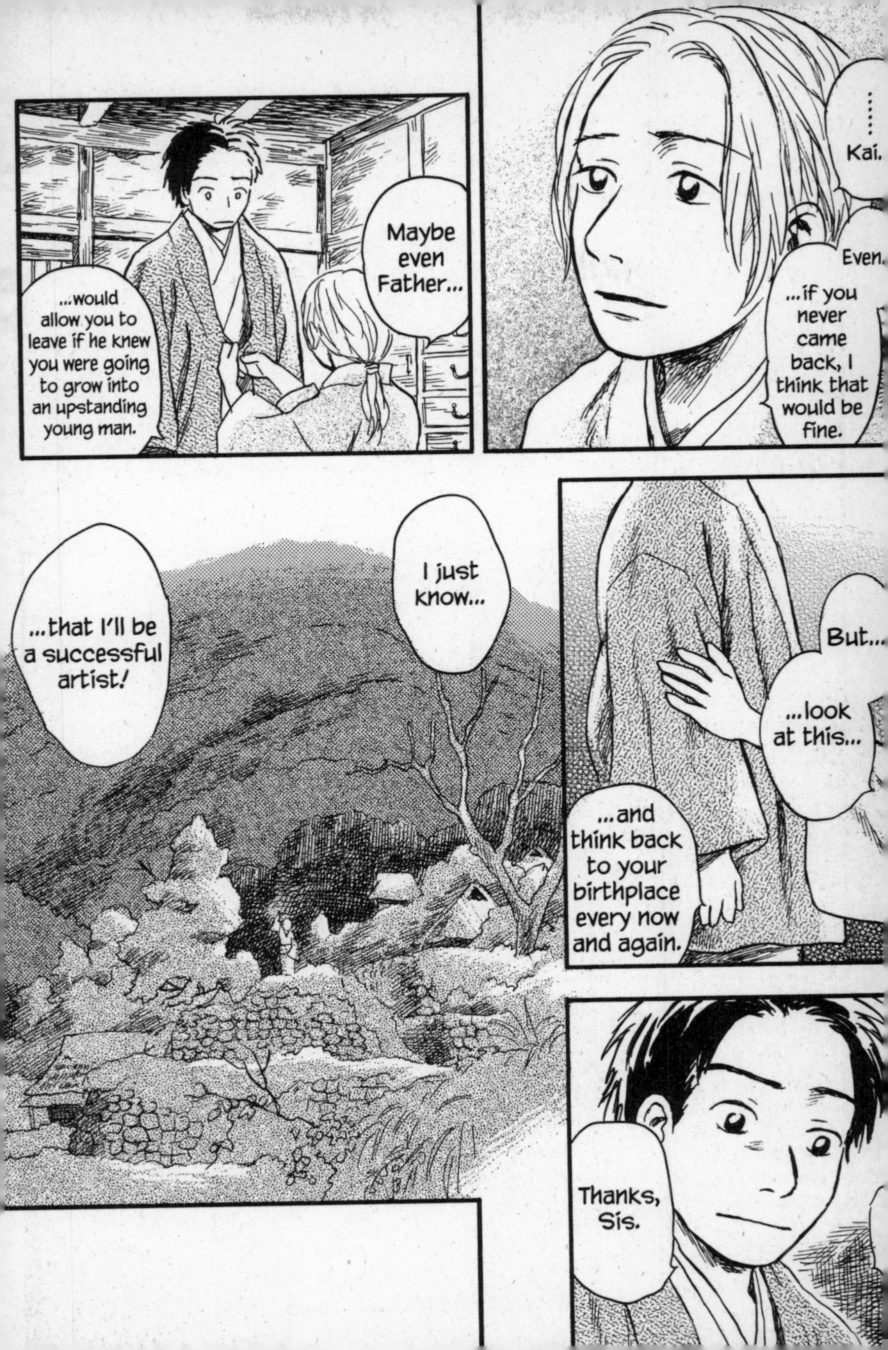
......
Kai.
Even.
...if you never came back, I think that would be fine.
Maybe even Father...
...would allow you to leave if he knew you were going to grow into an upstanding young man.
But...
...look at this...
...and think back to your birthplace every now and again.
Thanks, Sis.
I just know...
...that I'll be a successful artist!

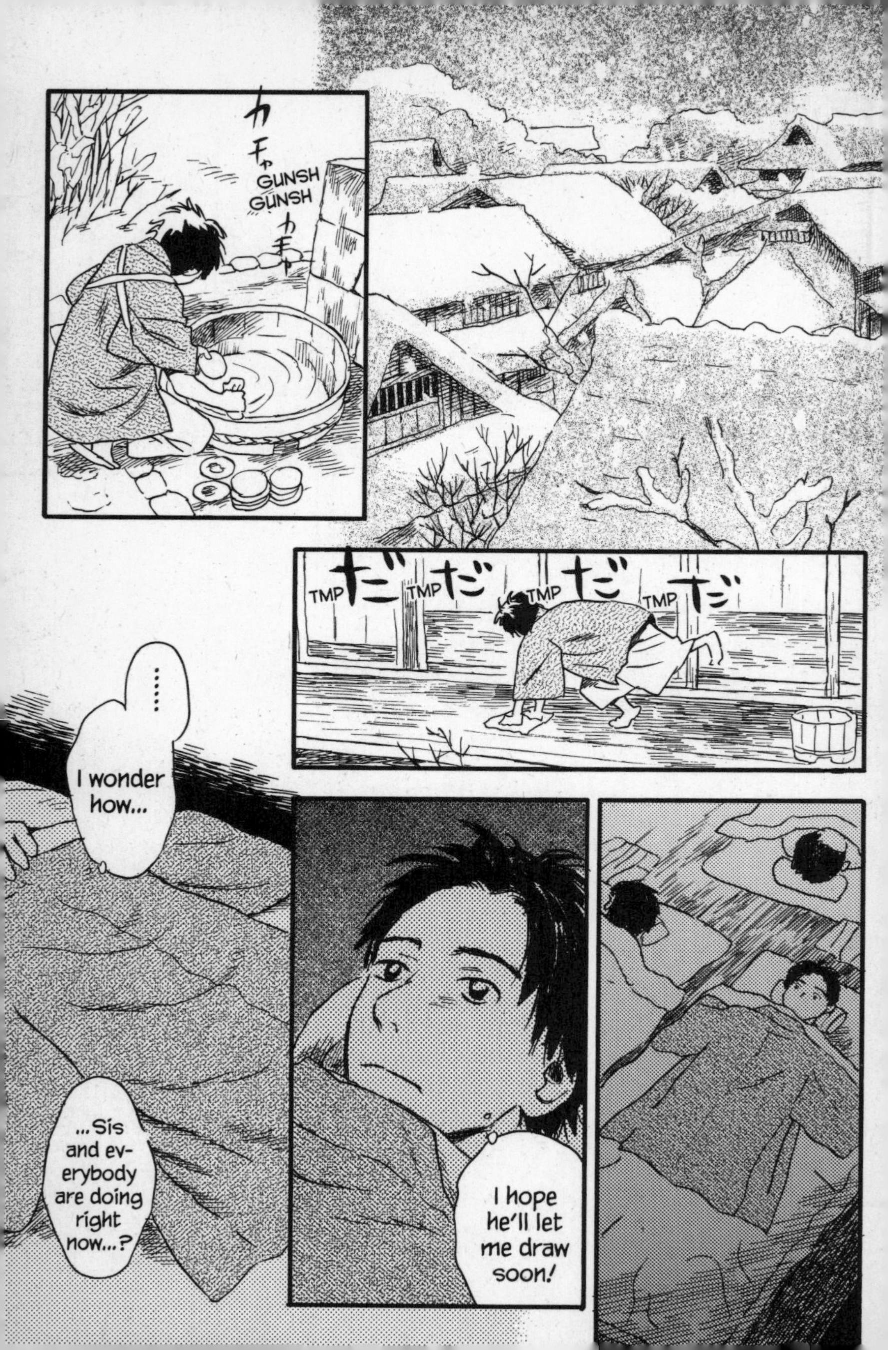
カチャ
GUNSH GUNSH
カチャ
TMP だ
TMP だ
TMP だ
TMP だ
I hope he'll let me draw soon!
......
I wonder how...
...Sis and everybody are doing right now...?

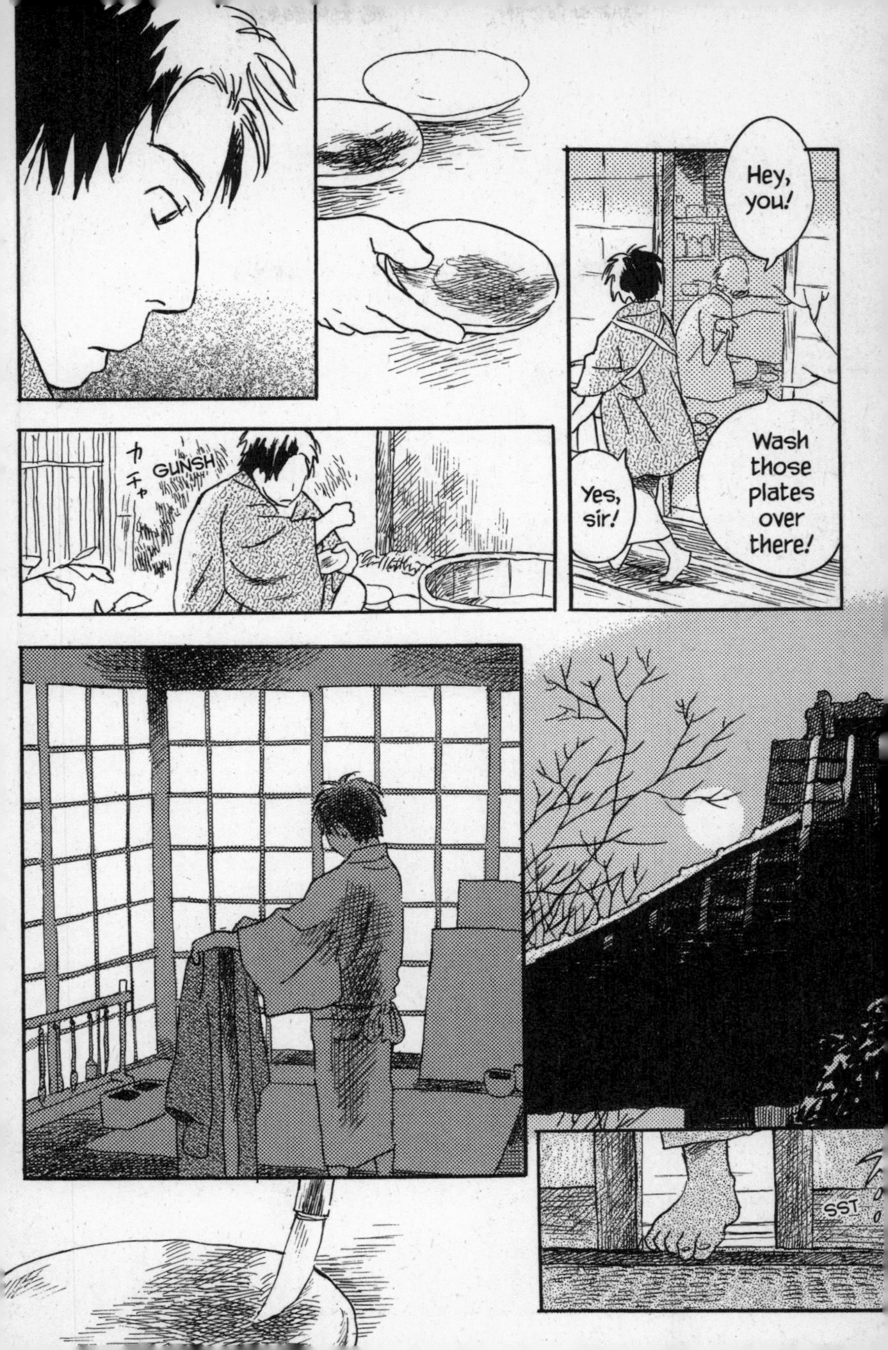
Hey, you!
Wash those plates over there!
Yes, sir!
カチャ
GUNSH
SST

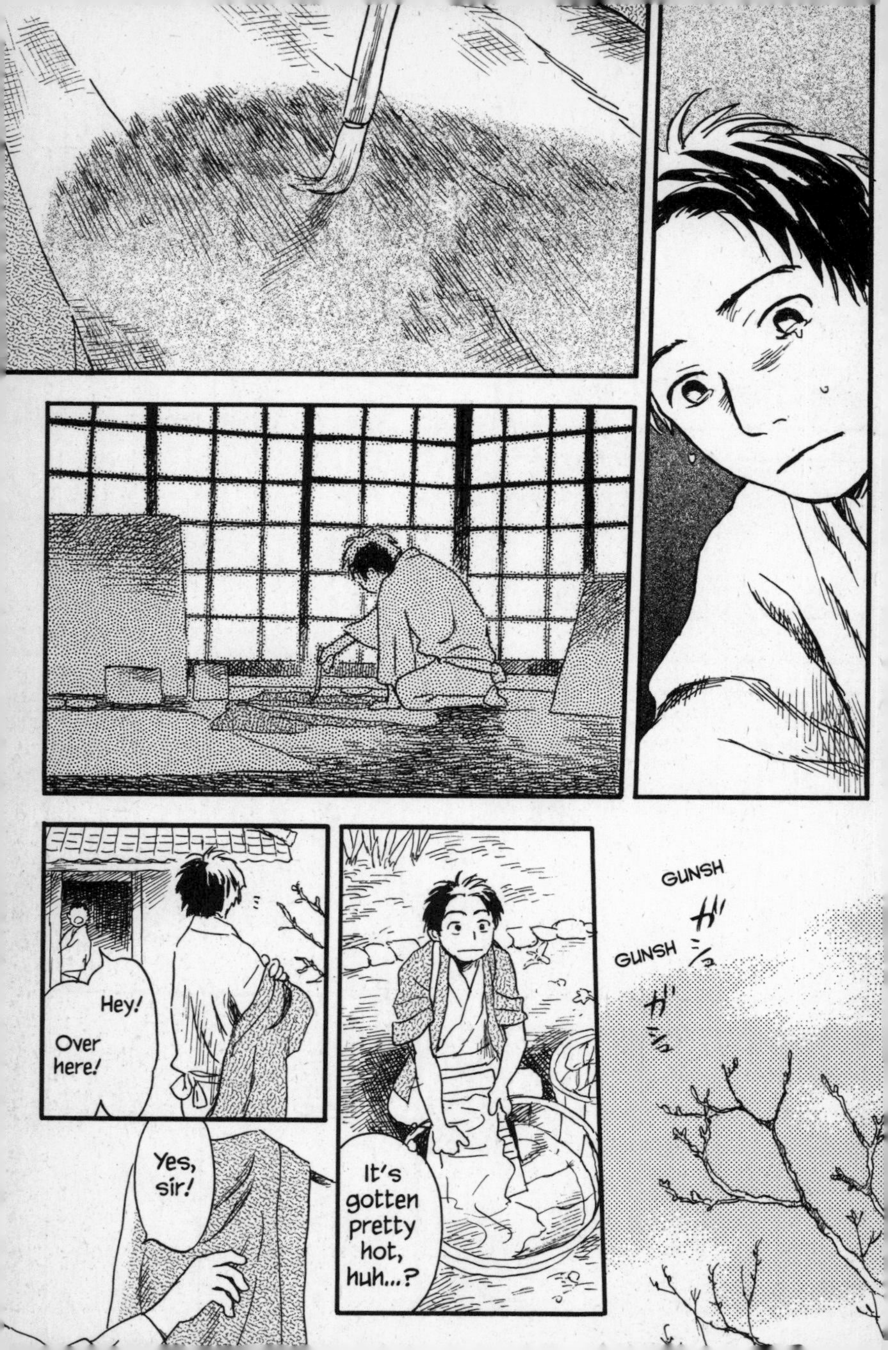
GUNSH
ガシュ
GUNSH
ガシュ
It's gotten pretty hot, huh...?
Hey! Over here!
Yes, sir!

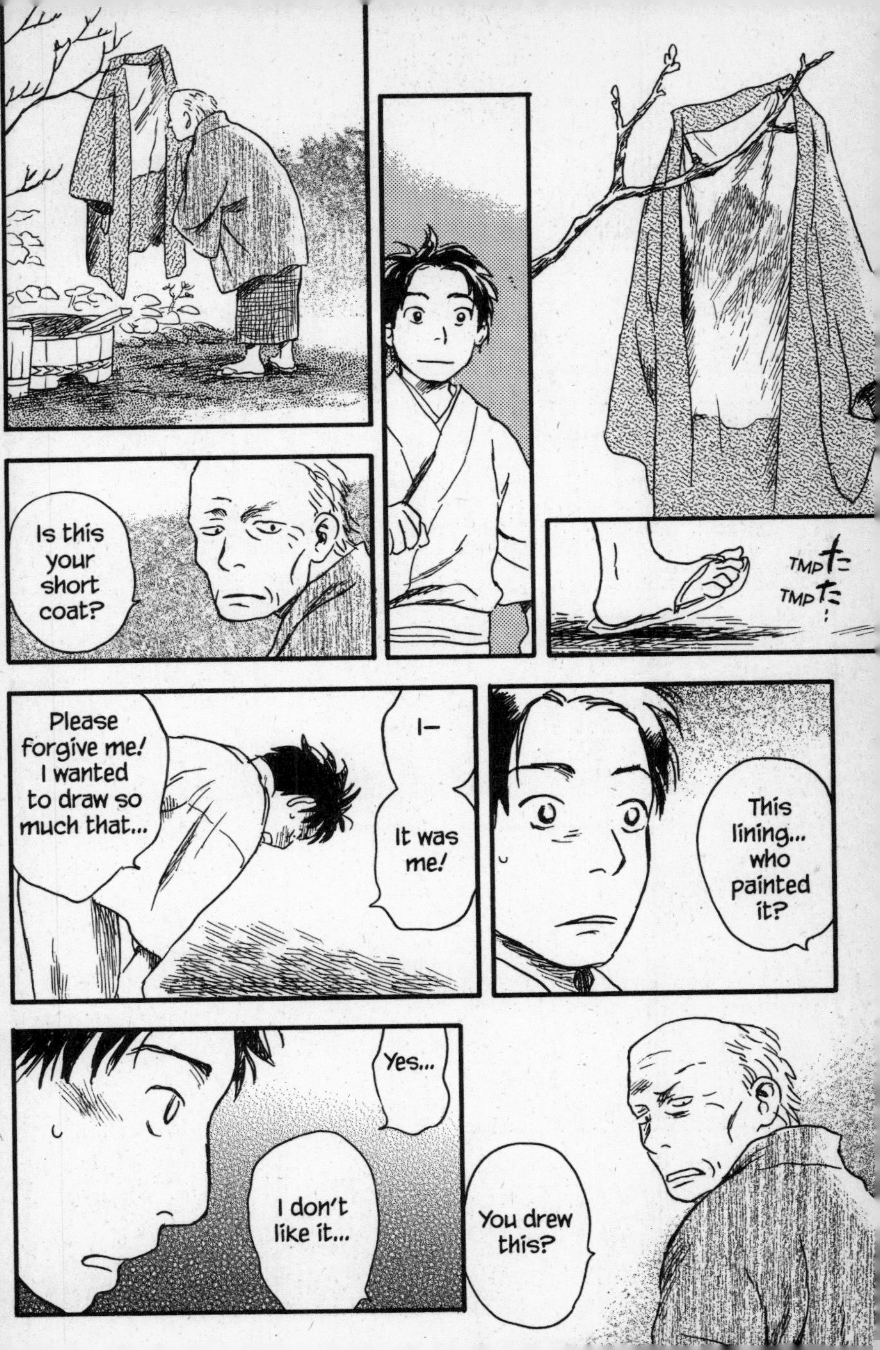
TMP た
TMP た
Is this your short coat?
This lining... who painted it?
I—
It was me!
Please forgive me! I wanted to draw so much that...
You drew this?
Yes...
I don't like it...

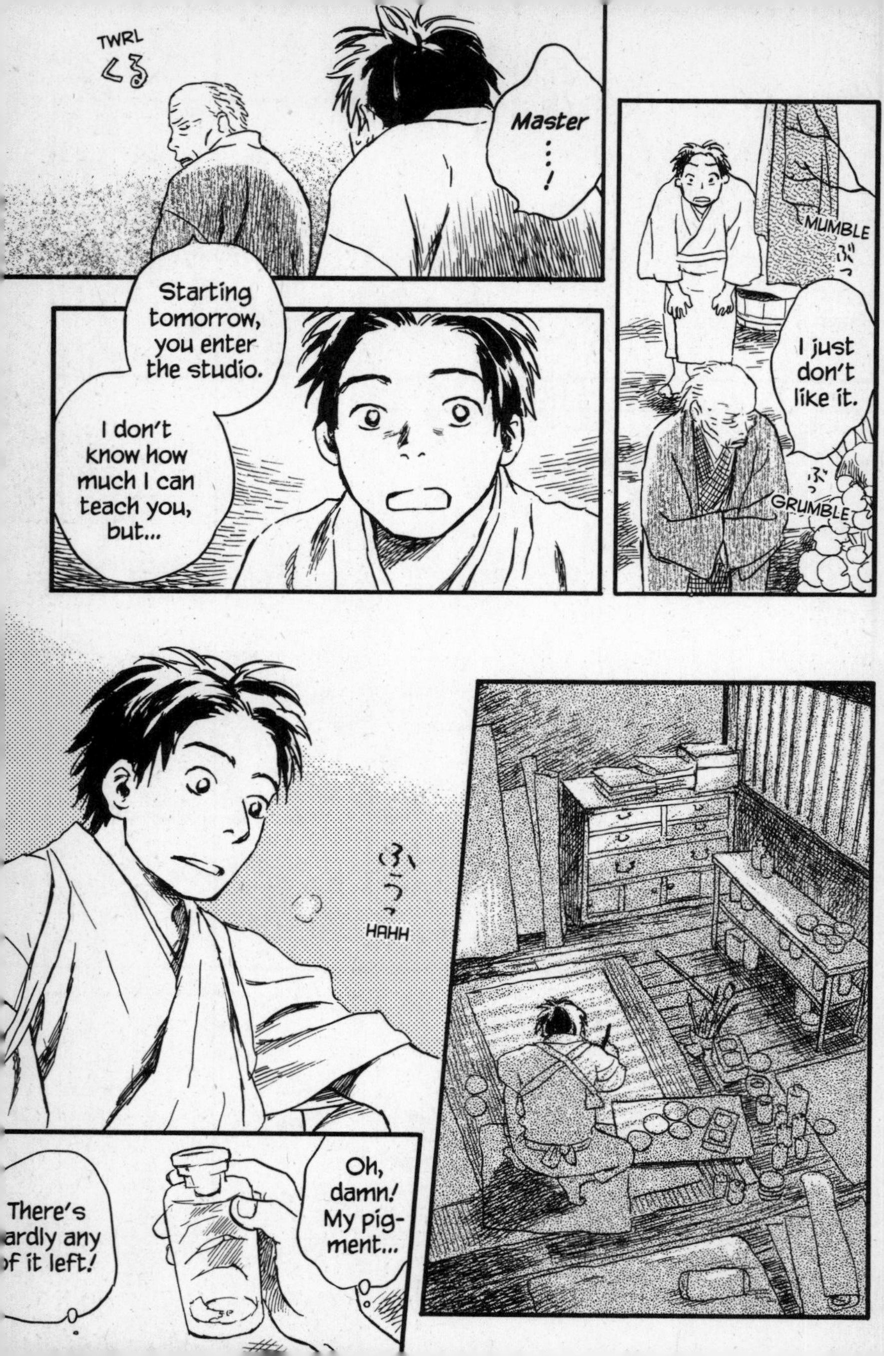

MUMBLE
ぶつ
I just don't like it.
ぶつ
GRUMBLE
TWRL
くる
Master...!
Starting tomorrow, you enter the studio.
I don't know how much I can teach you, but...
ふーっ
HAHH
Oh, damn! My pig-ment...
There's ardly any f it left!

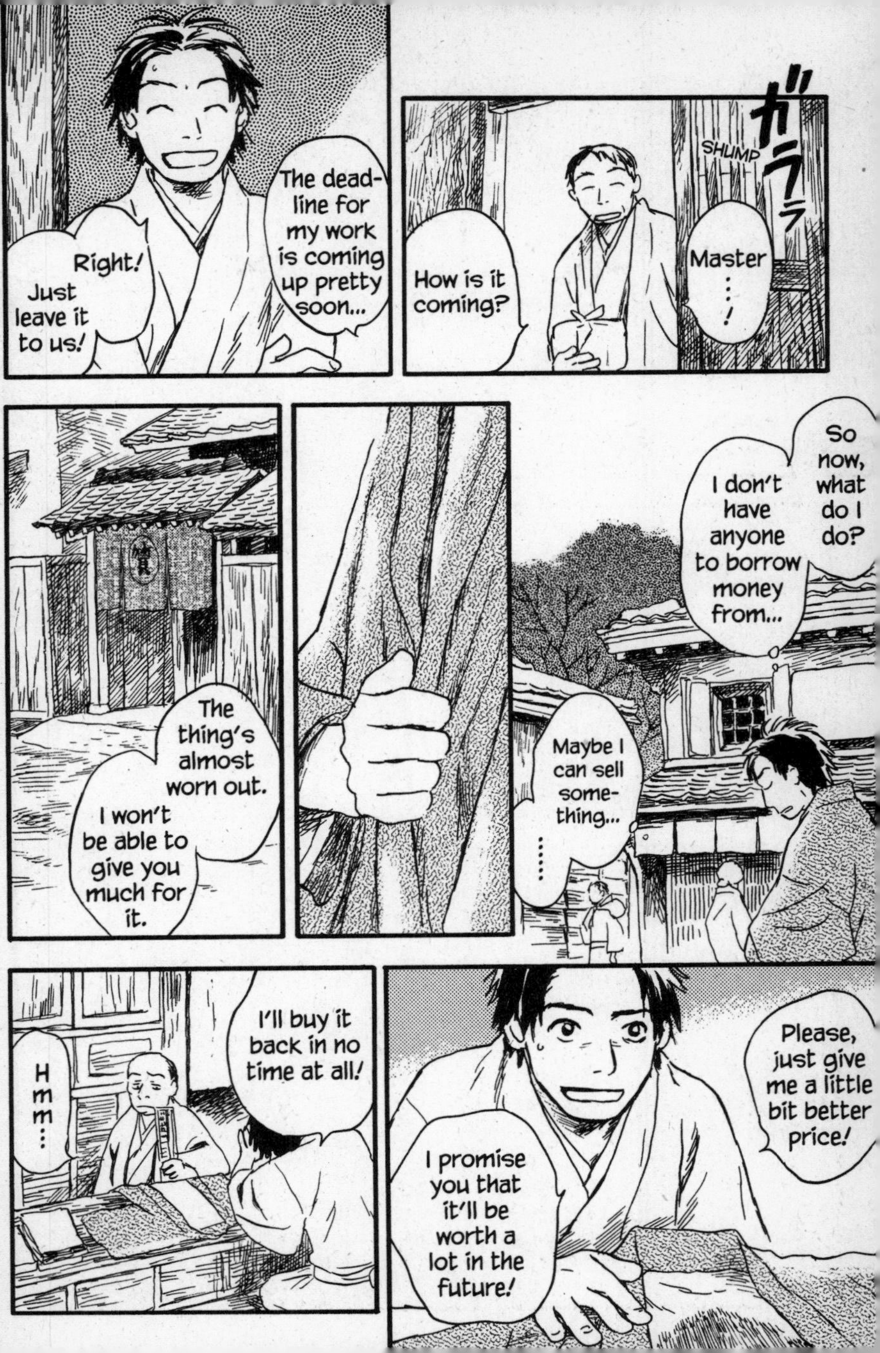
ガララ
SHUMP
Master ...!
How is it coming?
The deadline for my work is coming up pretty soon...
Right! Just leave it to us!
So now, what do I do?
I don't have anyone to borrow money from...
Maybe I can sell something...
......
The thing's almost worn out.
I won't be able to give you much for it.
Please, just give me a little bit better price!
I promise you that it'll be worth a lot in the future!
I'll buy it back in no time at all!
Hmm...

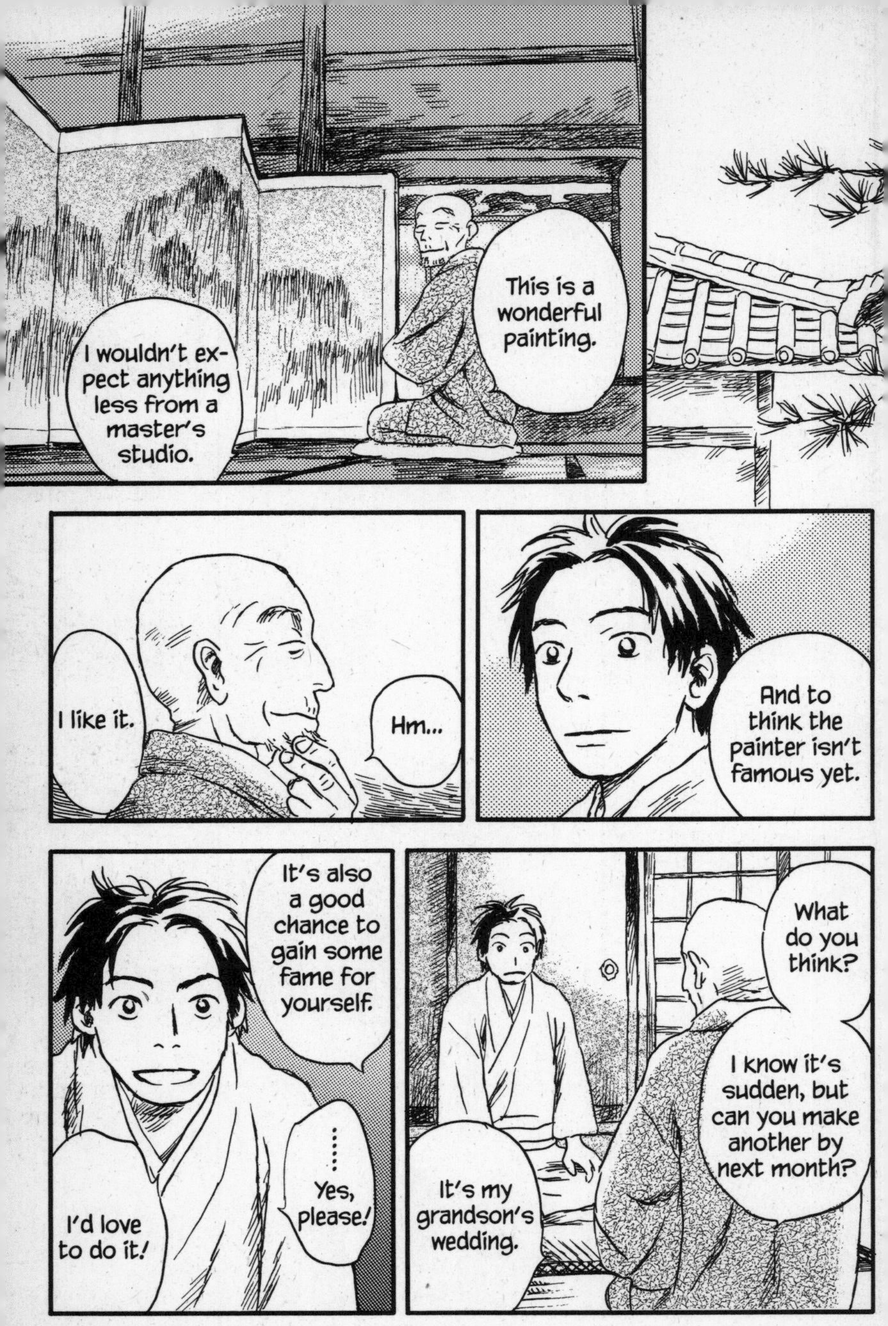
This is a wonderful painting.
I wouldn't expect anything less from a master's studio.
And to think the painter isn't famous yet.
Hm...
I like it.
What do you think?
I know it's sudden, but can you make another by next month?
It's my grandson's wedding.
It's also a good chance to gain some fame for yourself.
......
Yes, please!
I'd love to do it!

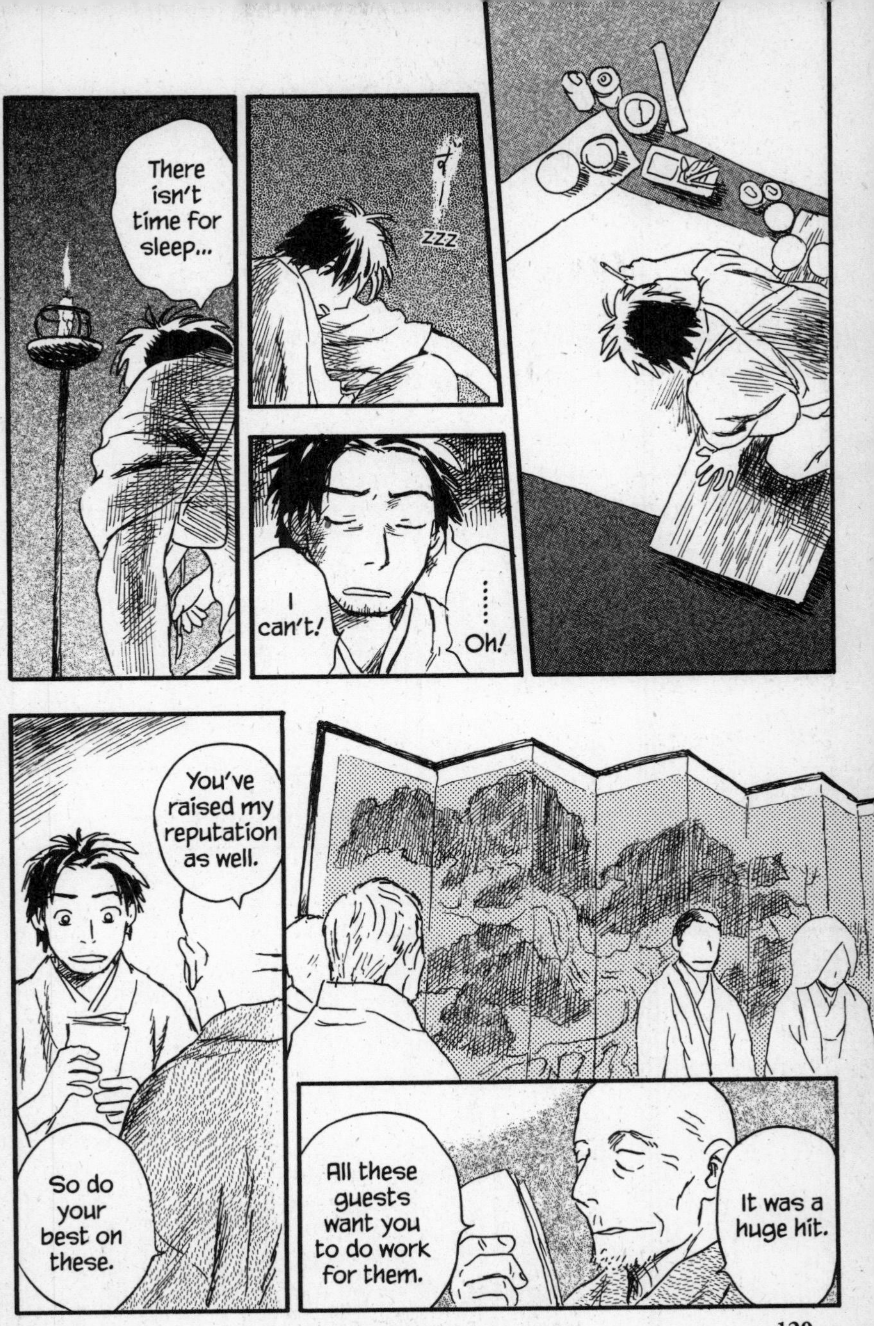
ZZZ
......Oh!
I can't!
There isn't time for sleep...
It was a huge hit.
All these guests want you to do work for them.
You've raised my reputation as well.
So do your best on these.

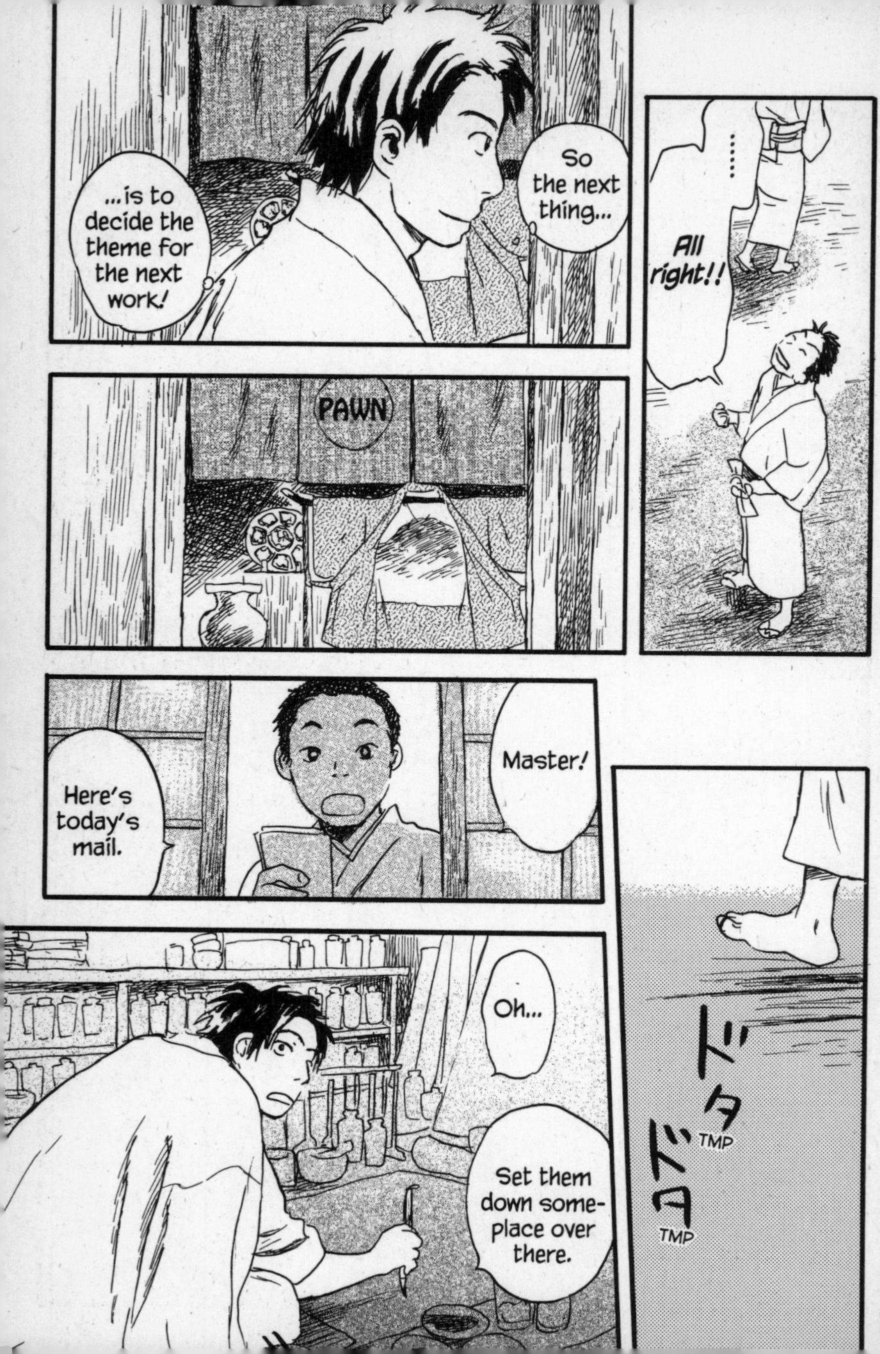
……
All right!!
So the next thing...
...is to decide the theme for the next work!
PAWN
ドタ TMP
ドタ TMP
Master!
Here's today's mail.
Oh...
Set them down some-place over there.

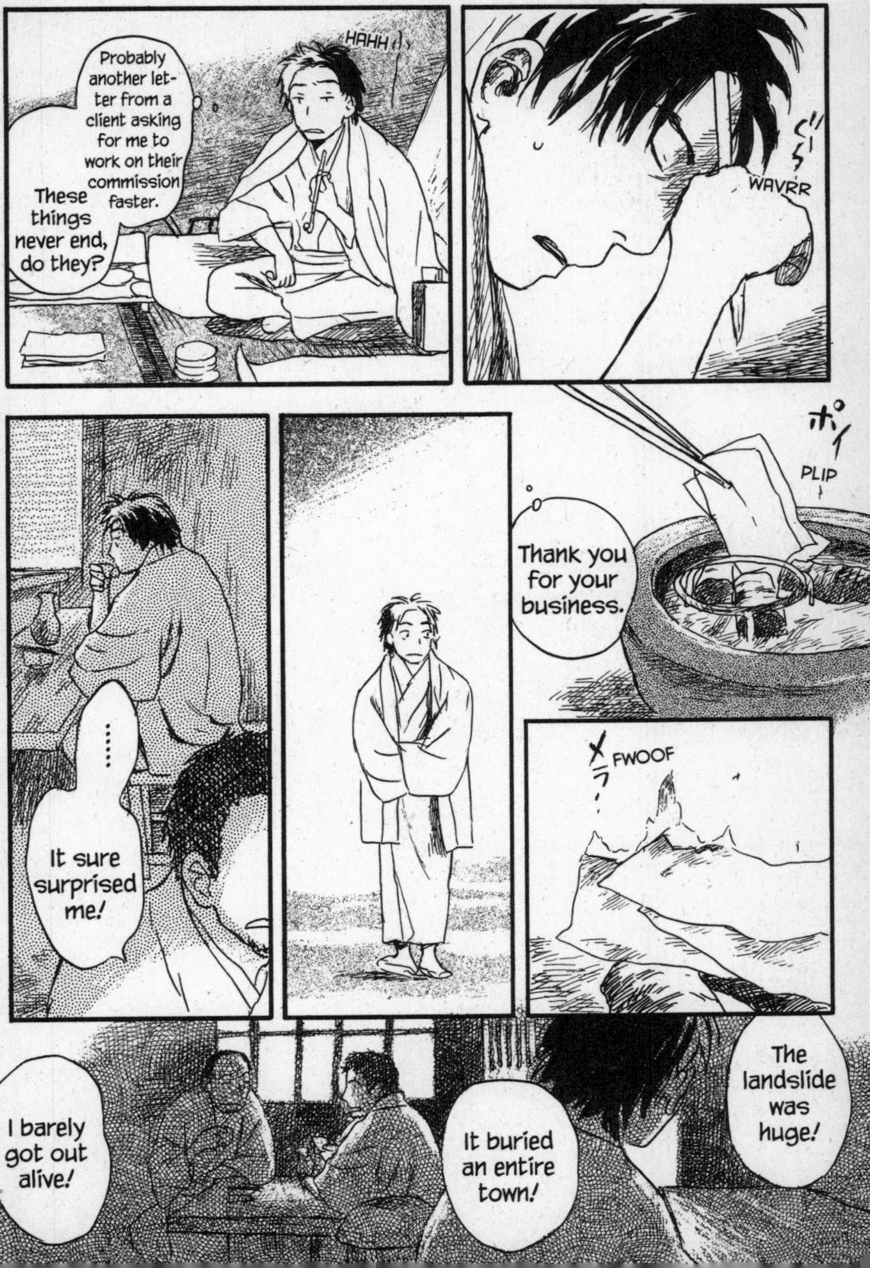

WAVRR
HAHH
Probably another letter from a client asking for me to work on their commission faster.
These things never end, do they?
ポイ
PLIP
Thank you for your business.
メラ
FWOOF
......
It sure surprised me!
The landslide was huge!
It buried an entire town!
I barely got out alive!

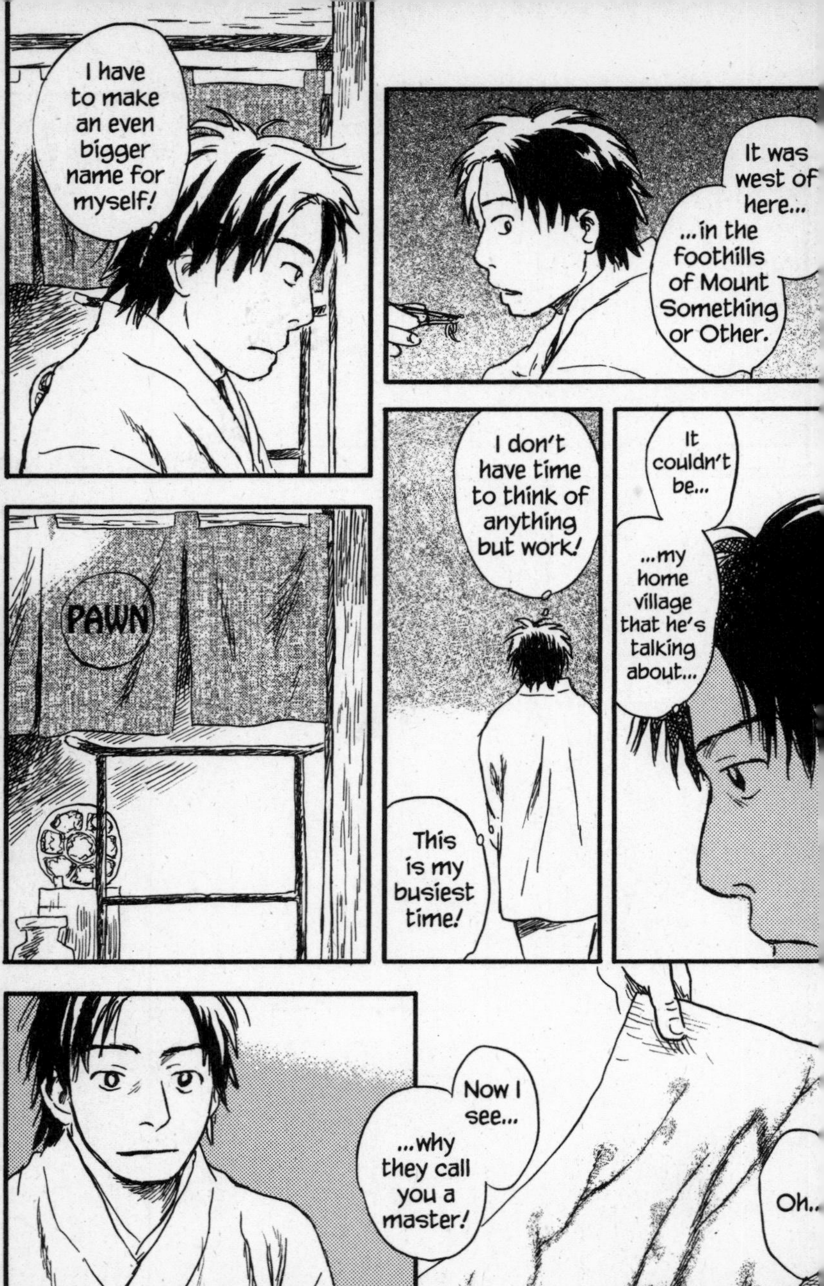
It was west of here...
...in the foothills of Mount Something or Other.
I have to make an even bigger name for myself!
It couldn't be...
...my home village that he's talking about...
I don't have time to think of anything but work!
This is my busiest time!
PAWN
Oh..
Now I see...
...why they call you a master!

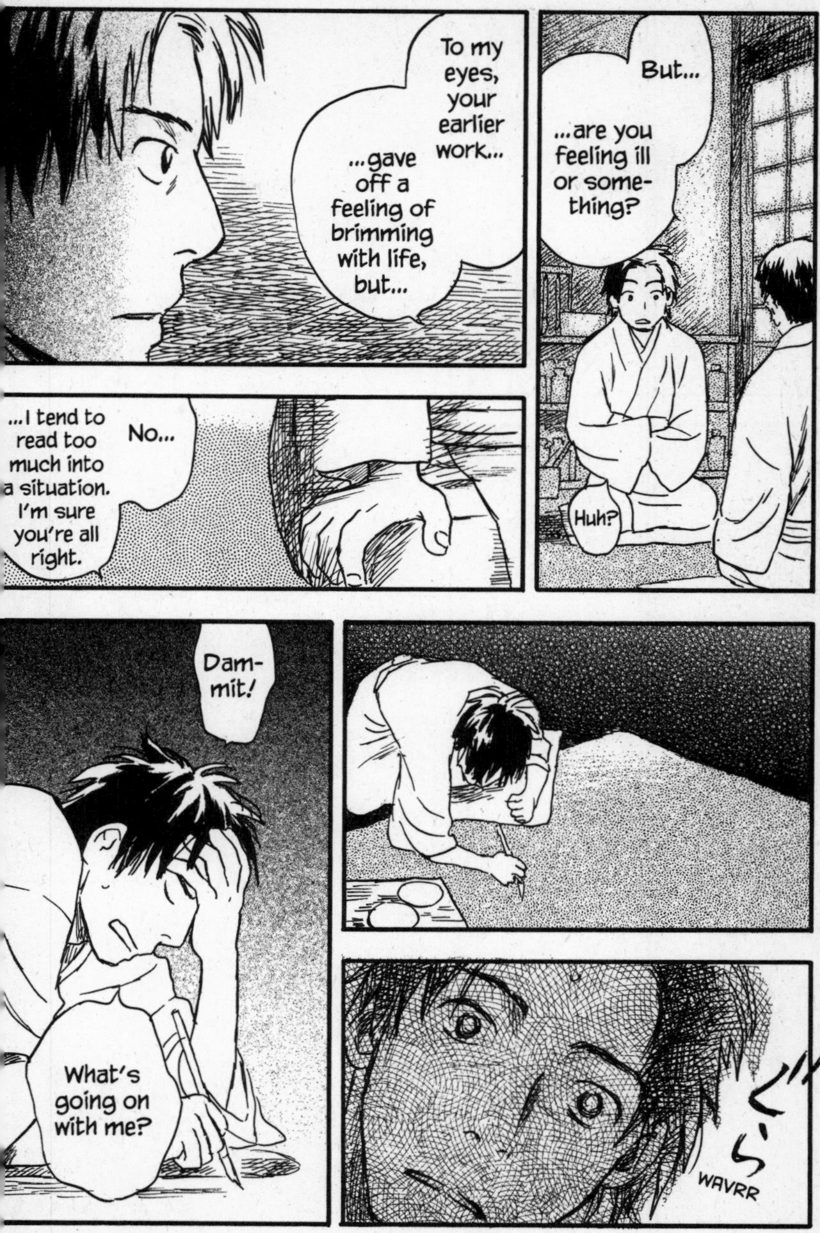

But...
...are you feeling ill or some-thing?
Huh?
To my eyes, your earlier work...
...gave off a feeling of brimming with life, but...
No...
...I tend to read too much into a situation. I'm sure you're all right.
ぐら
WAVRR
Dam-mit!
What's going on with me?

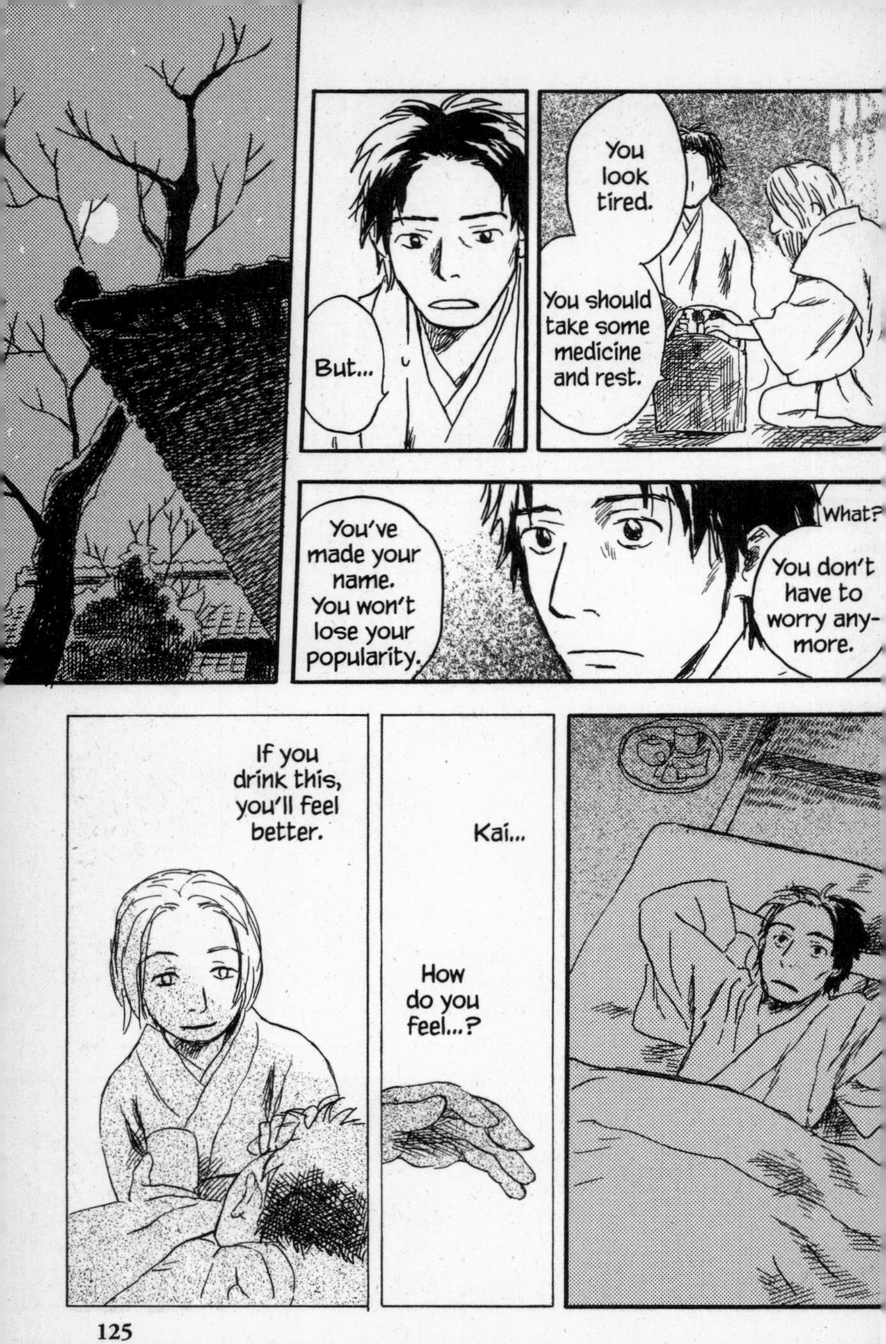
You look tired.
You should take some medicine and rest.
But...
What?
You don't have to worry anymore.
You've made your name. You won't lose your popularity.
Kai...
How do you feel...?
If you drink this, you'll feel better.

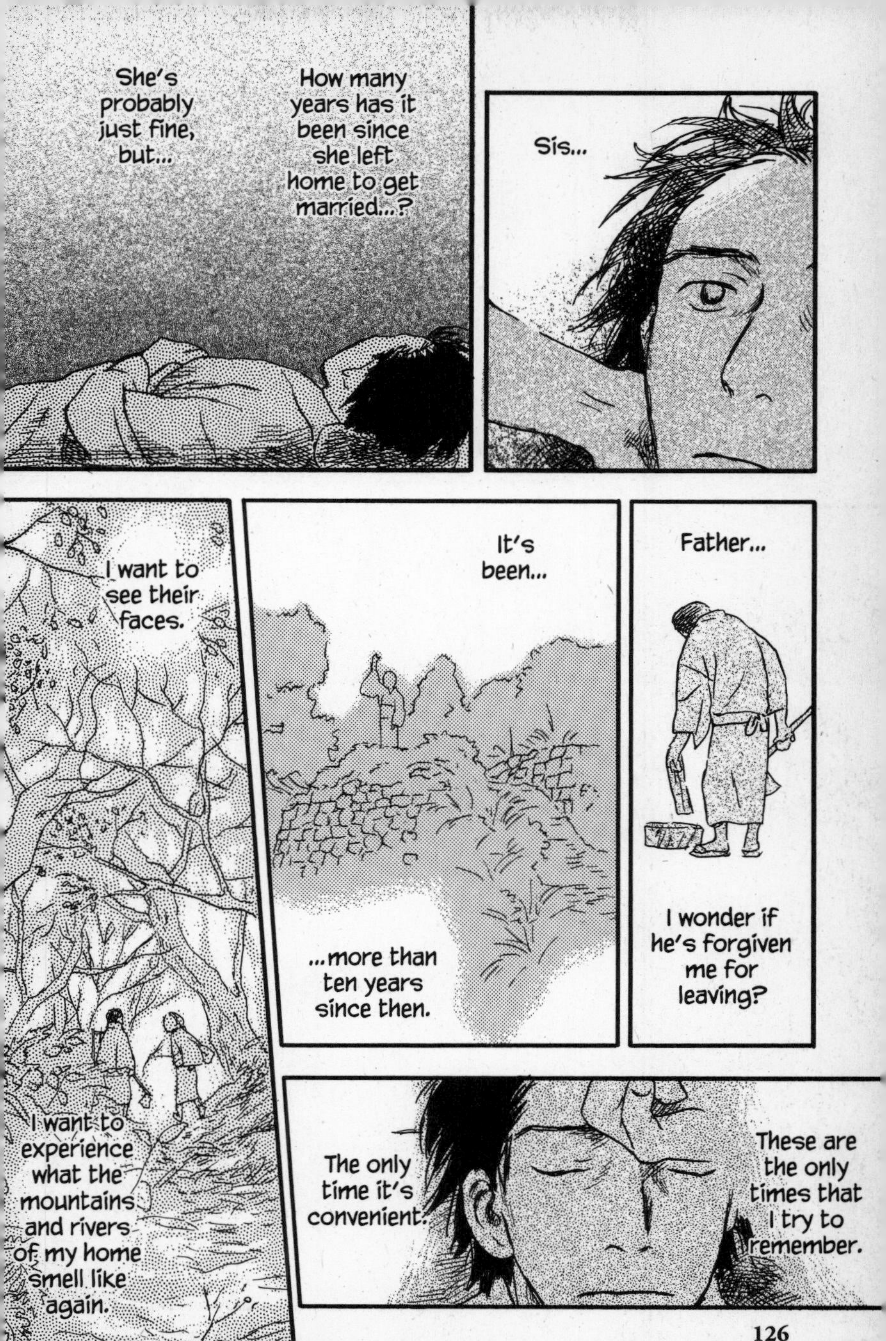

Sis...
How many years has it been since she left home to get married...?
She's probably just fine, but...
Father...
I wonder if he's forgiven me for leaving?
It's been...
...more than ten years since then.
These are the only times that I try to remember.
The only time it's convenient.
I want to see their faces.
I want to experience what the mountains and rivers of my home smell like again.

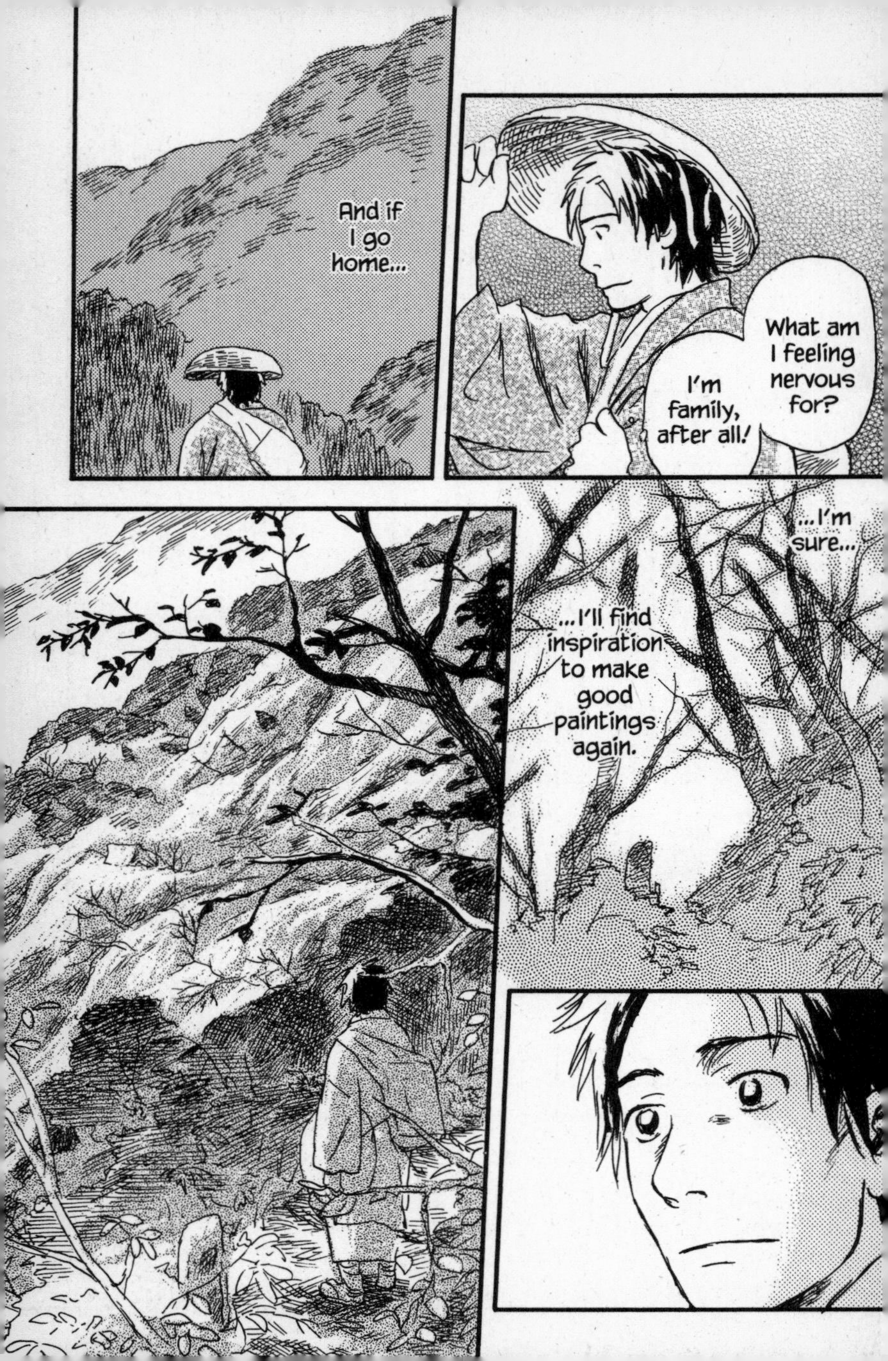
What am I feeling nervous for?
I'm family, after all!
And if I go home...
...I'm sure...
...I'll find inspiration to make good paintings again.

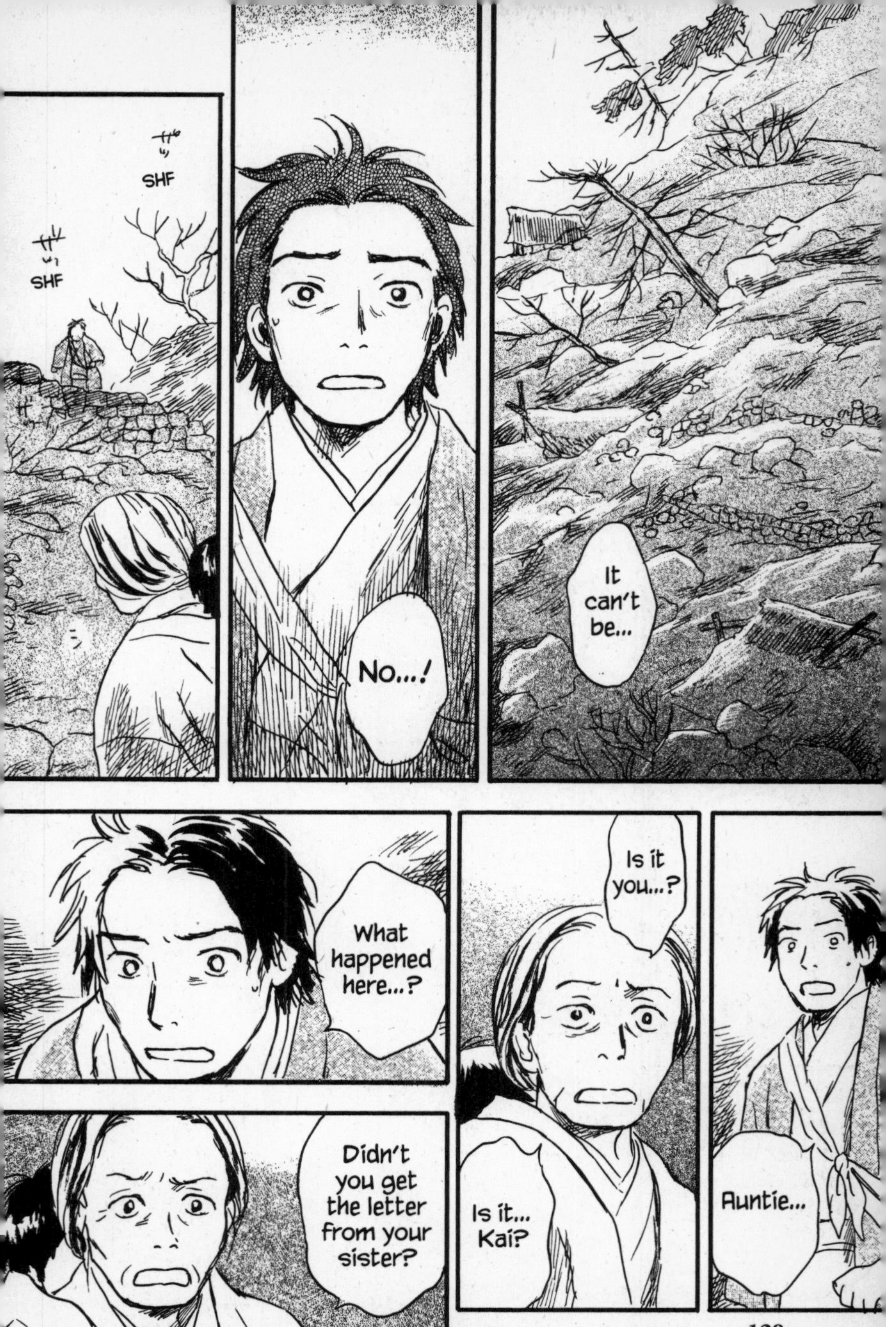
It can't be...
No...!
SHF
SHF
Auntie...
Is it you...?
Is it... Kai?
What happened here...?
Didn't you get the letter from your sister?

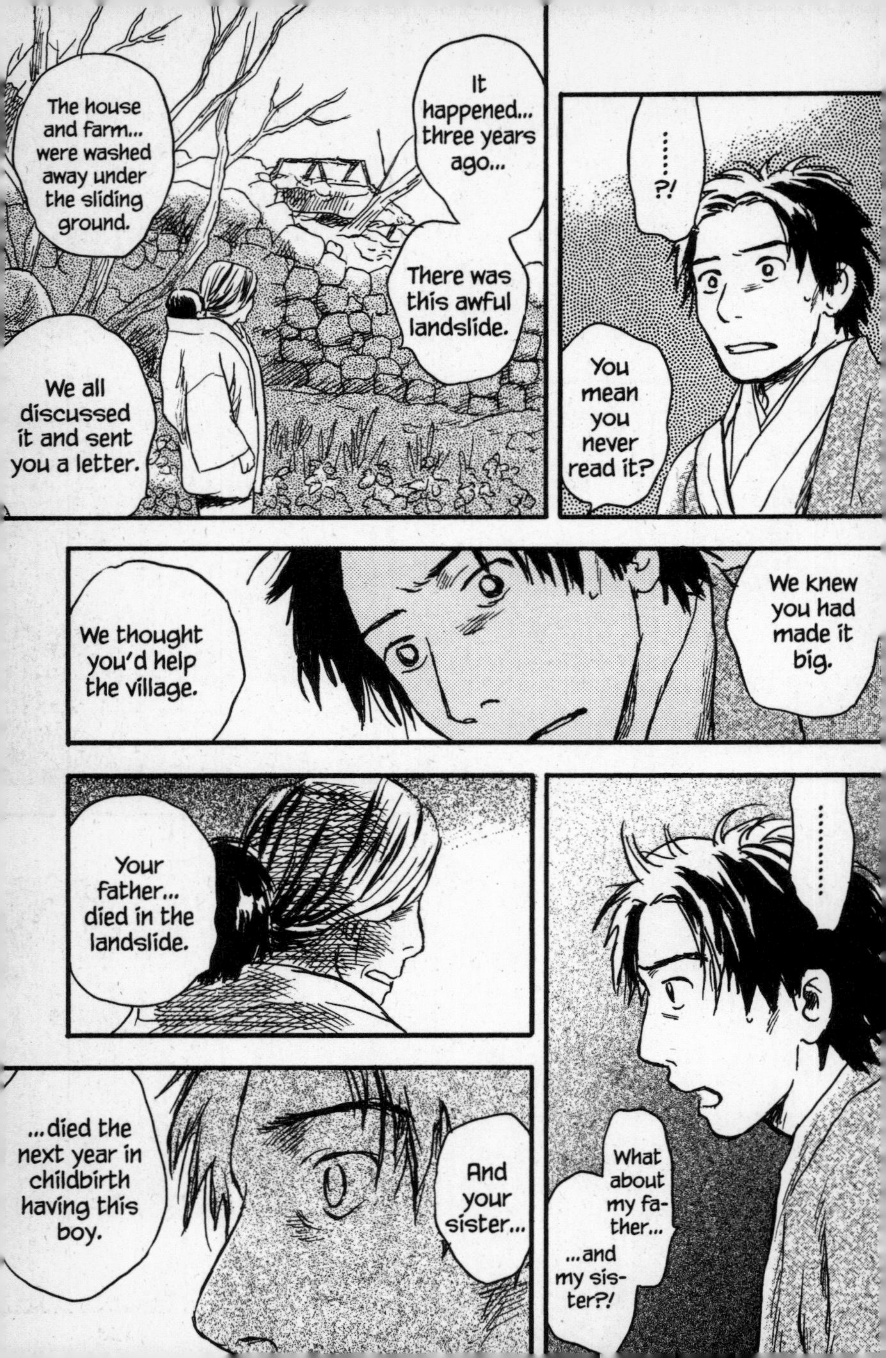
……?!
You mean you never read it?
It happened... three years ago...
There was this awful landslide.
The house and farm... were washed away under the sliding ground.
We all discussed it and sent you a letter.
We knew you had made it big.
We thought you'd help the village.
……
What about my father...
...and my sister?!
Your father... died in the landslide.
And your sister...
...died the next year in childbirth having this boy.

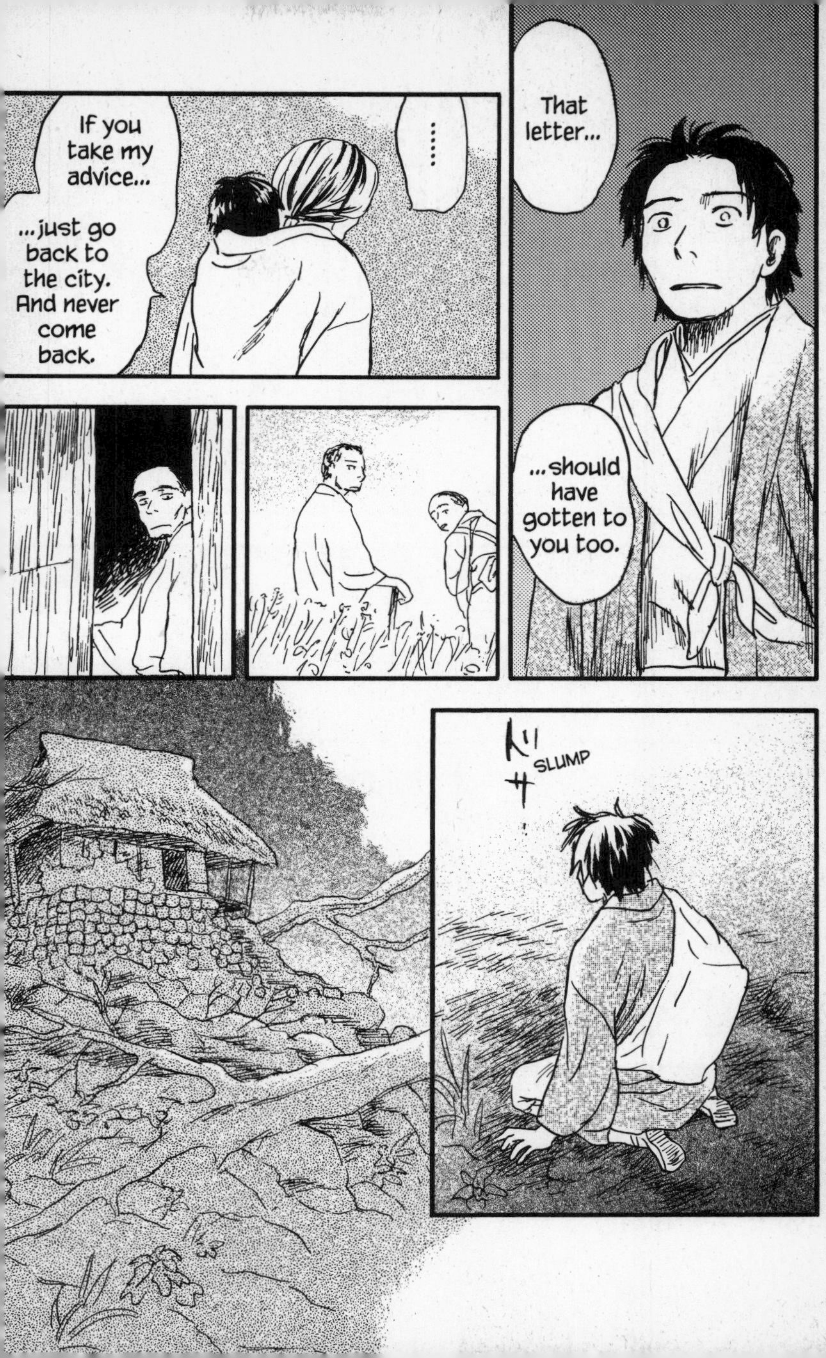
That letter...
...should have gotten to you too.
......
If you take my advice...
...just go back to the city. And never come back.
SLUMP

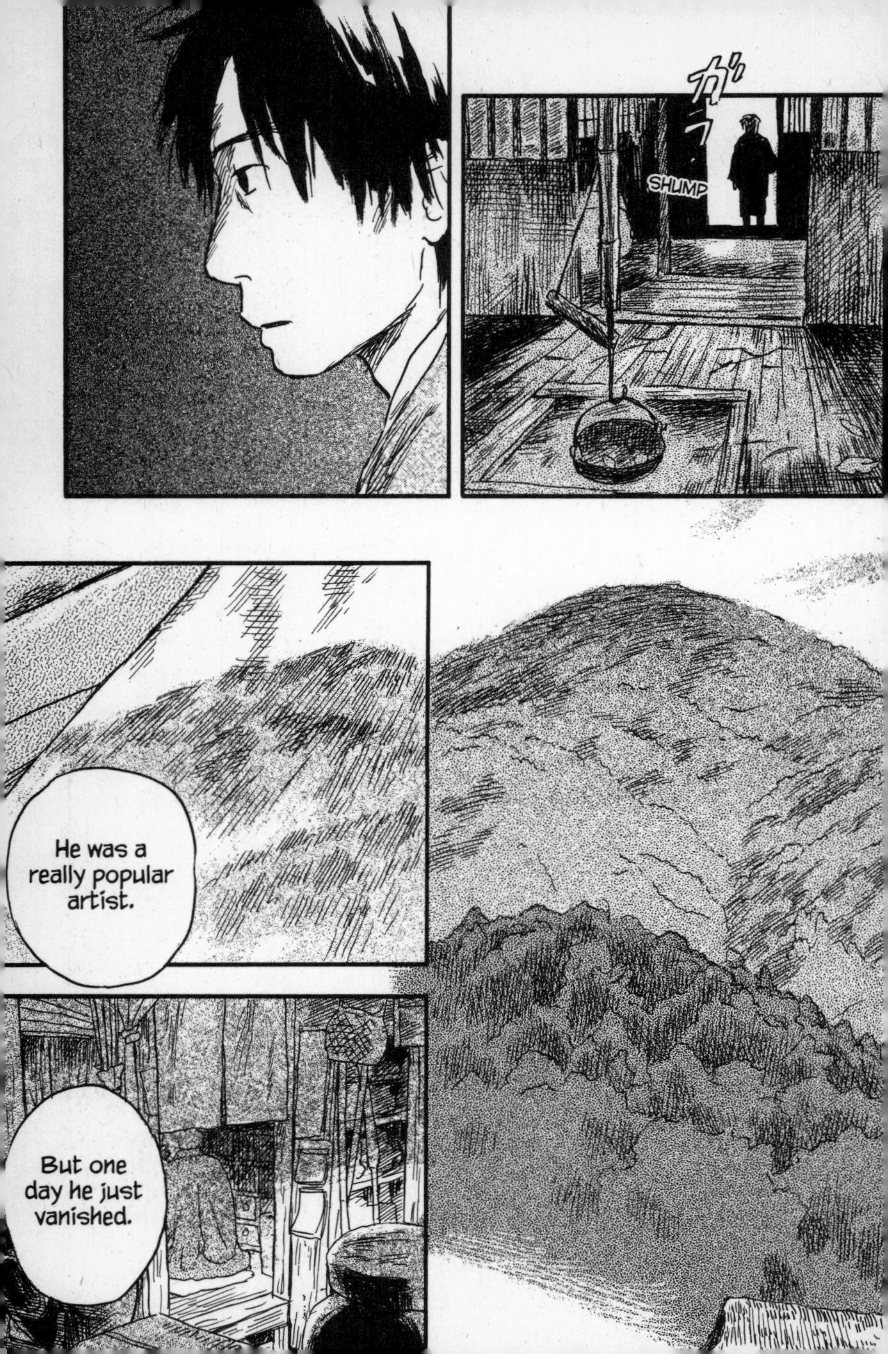
ガラ
SHUMP
He was a really popular artist.
But one day he just vanished.

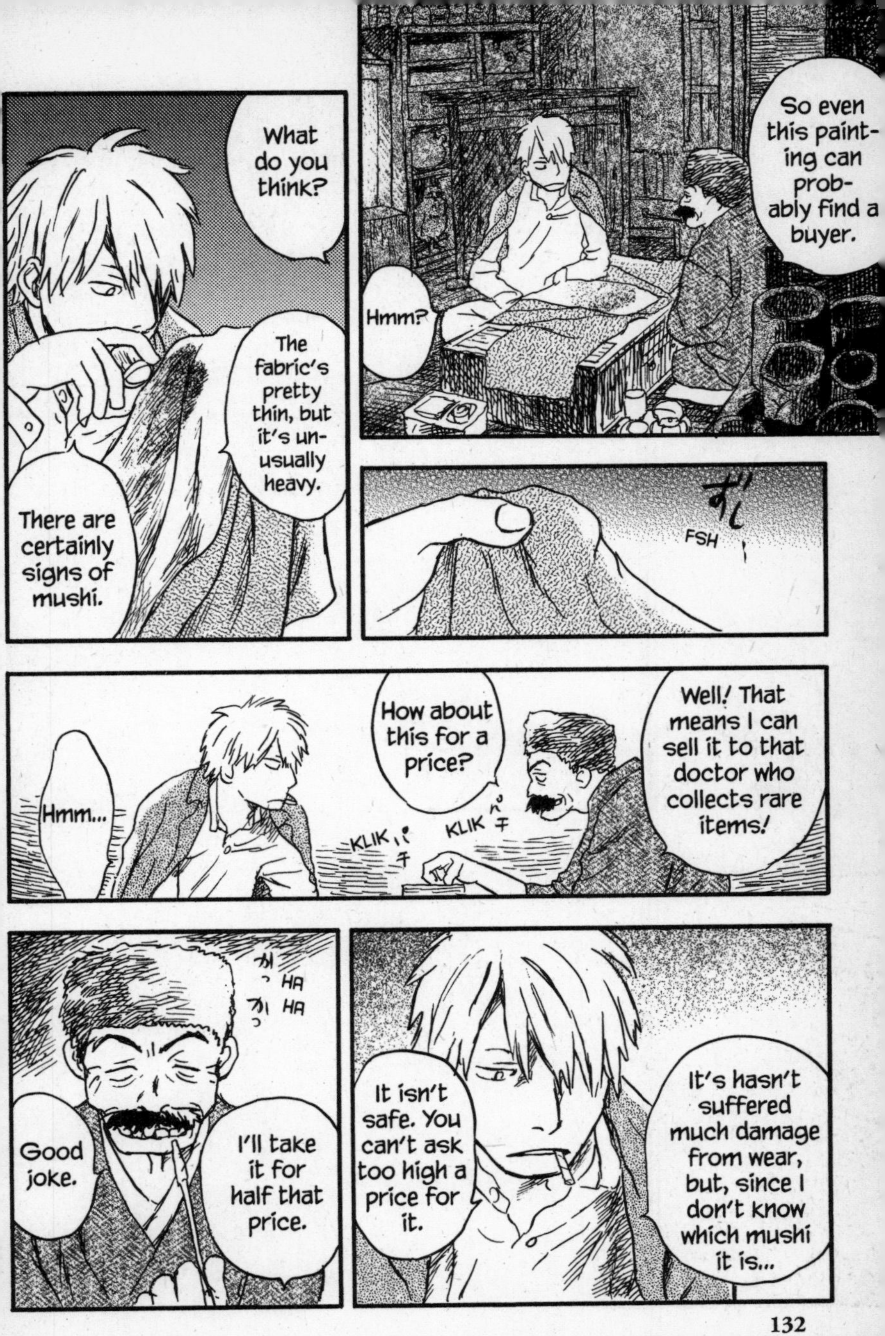

So even this painting can probably find a buyer.
Hmm?
FSH
What do you think?
The fabric's pretty thin, but it's unusually heavy.
There are certainly signs of mushi.
Well! That means I can sell it to that doctor who collects rare items!
How about this for a price?
KLIK
KLIK
Hmm...
It's hasn't suffered much damage from wear, but, since I don't know which mushi it is...
It isn't safe. You can't ask too high a price for it.
HA HA
I'll take it for half that price.
Good joke.

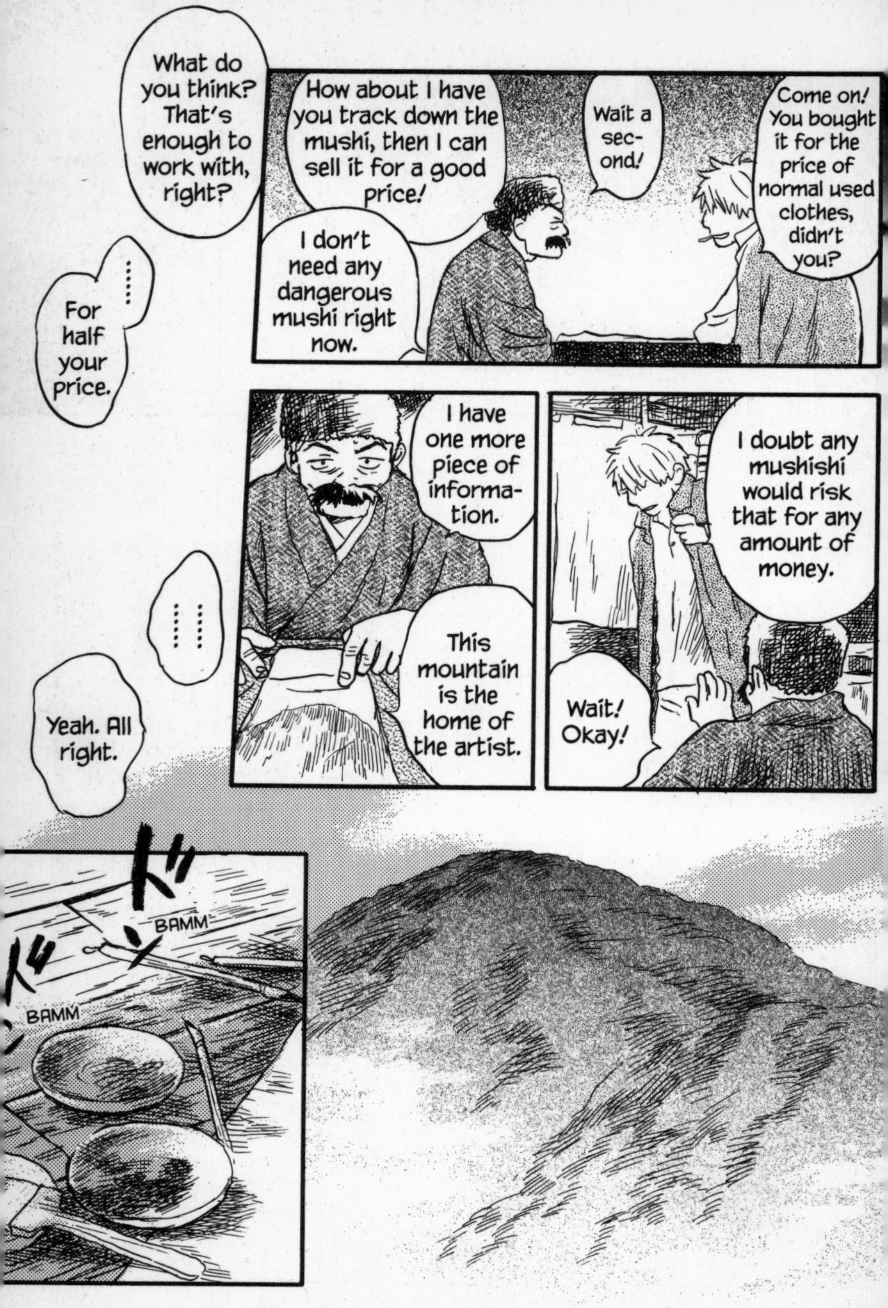
Come on! You bought it for the price of normal used clothes, didn't you?
Wait a second!
How about I have you track down the mushi, then I can sell it for a good price!
I don't need any dangerous mushi right now.
What do you think? That's enough to work with, right?
......
For half your price.
I doubt any mushishi would risk that for any amount of money.
Wait! Okay!
I have one more piece of information.
This mountain is the home of the artist.
....
Yeah. All right.
BAMM
BAMM

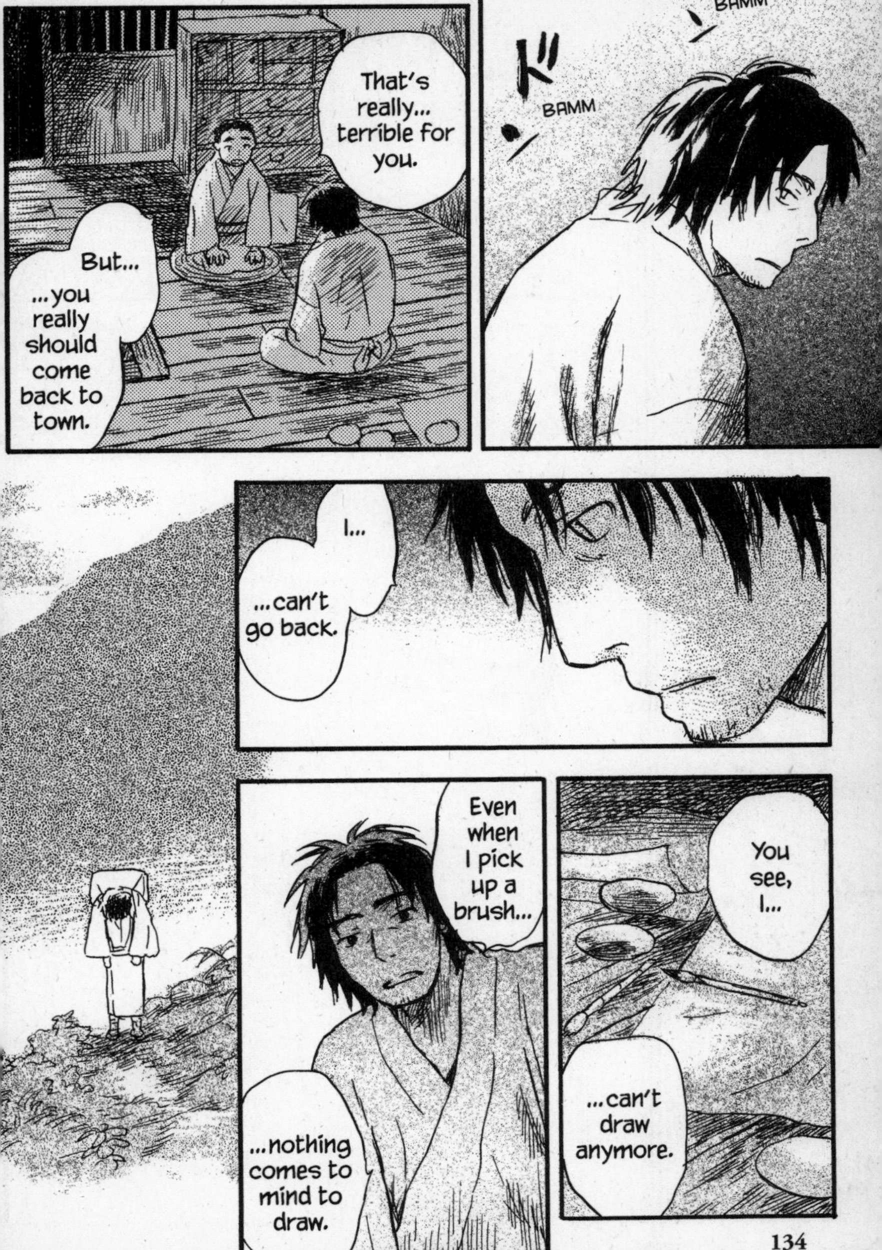

ド
BAMM
ド
BAMM
That's really... terrible for you.
But...
...you really should come back to town.
I...
...can't go back.
You see, I...
...can't draw anymore.
Even when I pick up a brush...
...nothing comes to mind to draw.

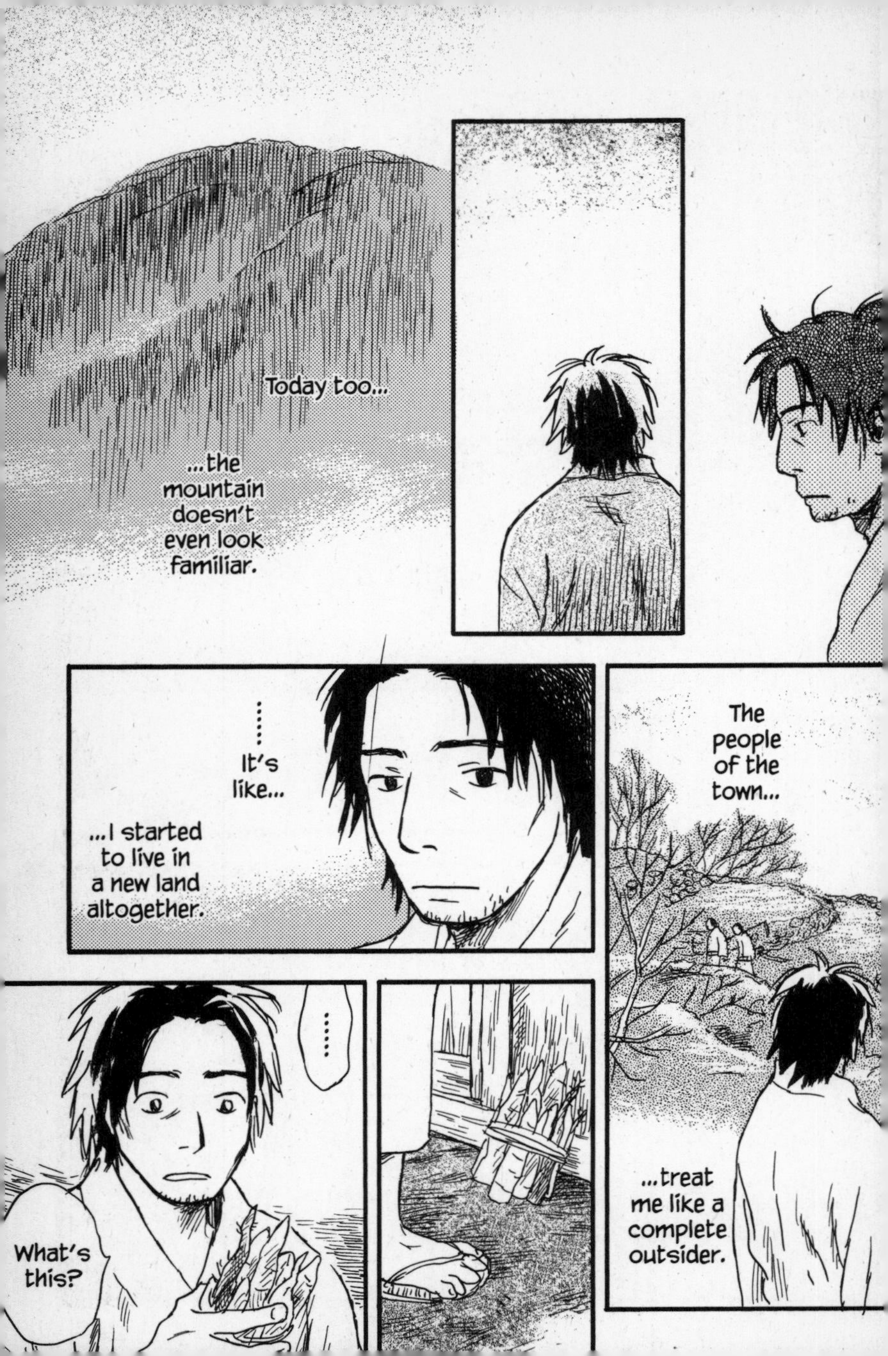
Today too...
...the mountain doesn't even look familiar.
The people of the town...
...treat me like a complete outsider.
......
It's like...
...I started to live in a new land altogether.
......
What's this?

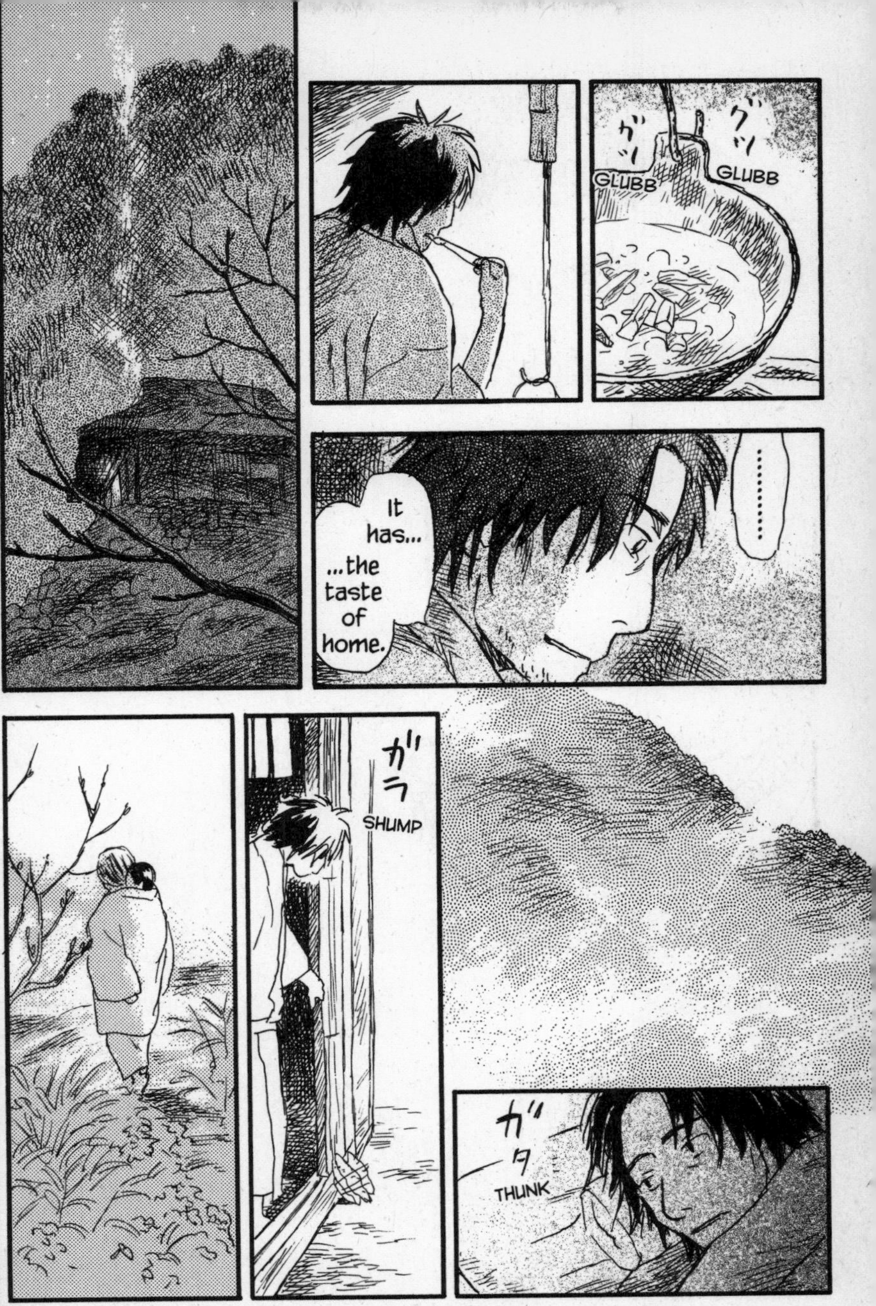
グツ
GLUBB
グツ
GLUBB
......
It has...
...the taste of home.
ガタ
THUNK
ガラ
SHUMP

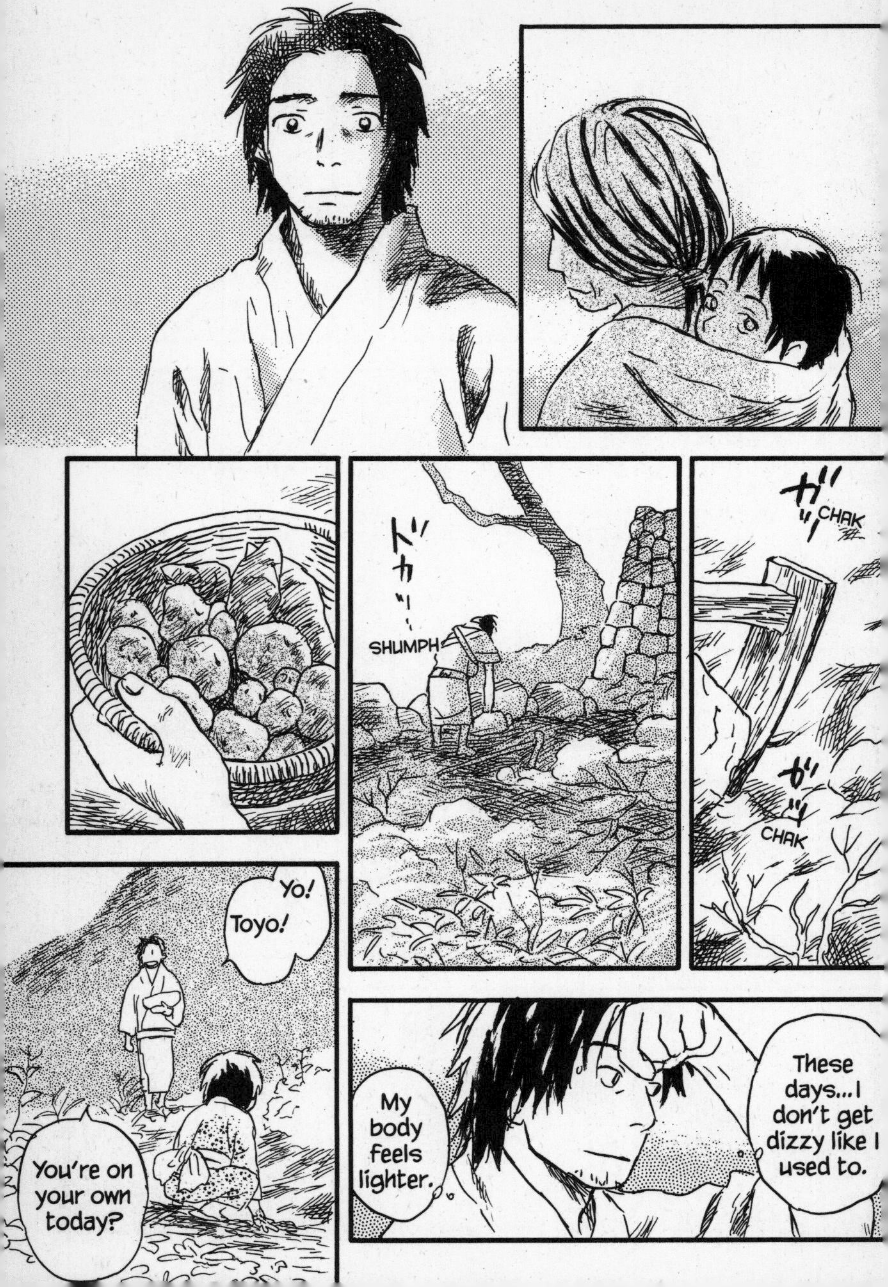
ガッ
CHAK
ガッ
CHAK
ドカッ
SHUMPH
These days...I don't get dizzy like I used to.
My body feels lighter.
Yo!
Toyo!
You're on your own today?

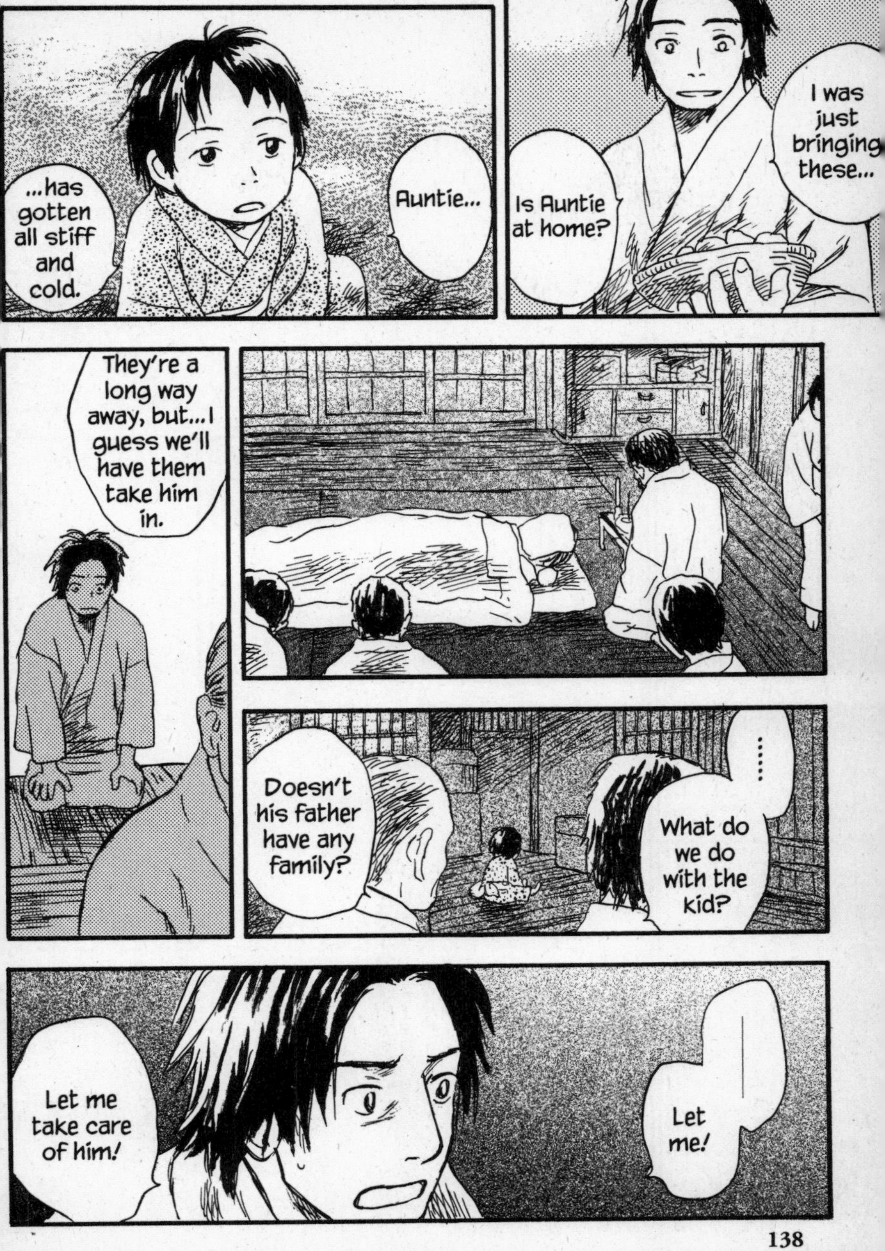
I was just bringing these...
Is Auntie at home?
Auntie...
...has gotten all stiff and cold.
......
What do we do with the kid?
Doesn't his father have any family?
They're a long way away, but...I guess we'll have them take him in.
Let me!
Let me take care of him!

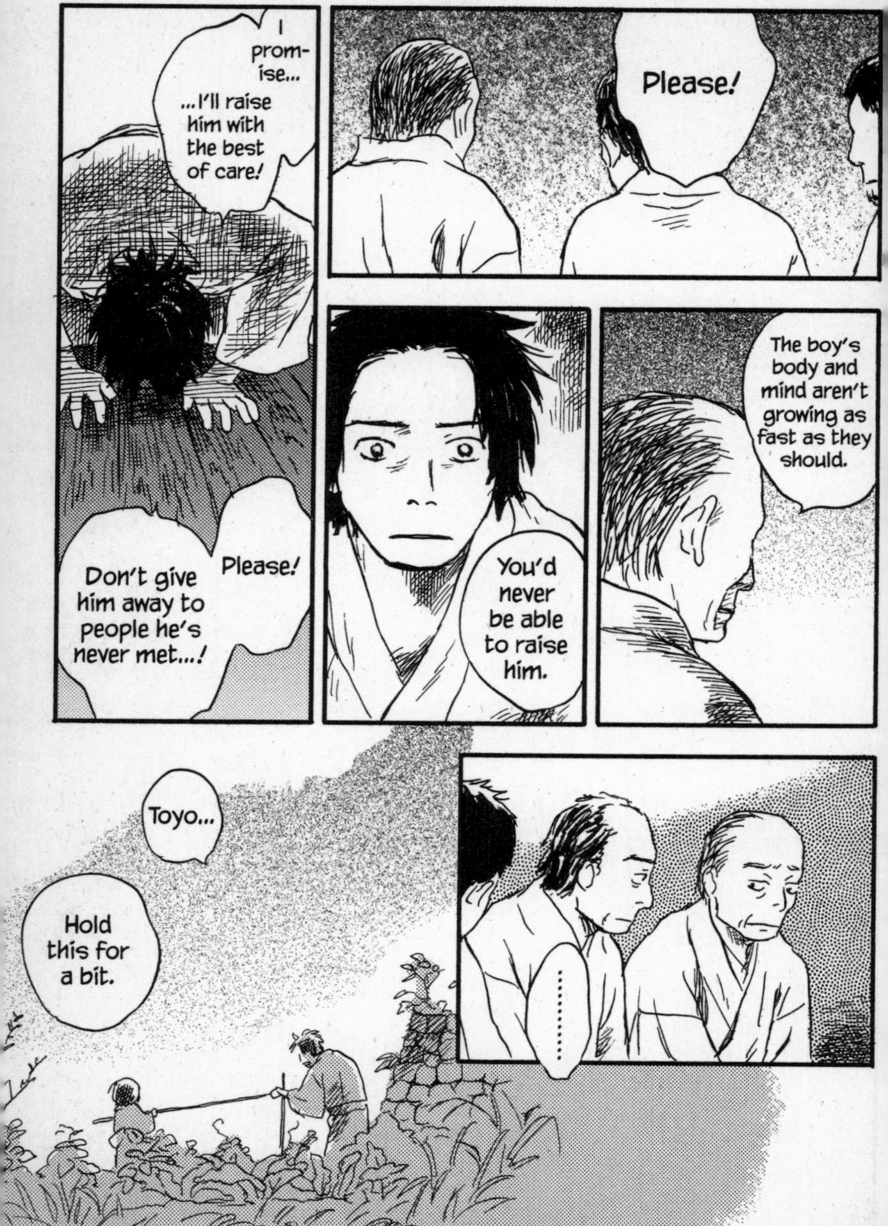

Please!
The boy's body and mind aren't growing as fast as they should.
You'd never be able to raise him.
I promise...
...I'll raise him with the best of care!
Please!
Don't give him away to people he's never met...!
....
Toyo...
Hold this for a bit.

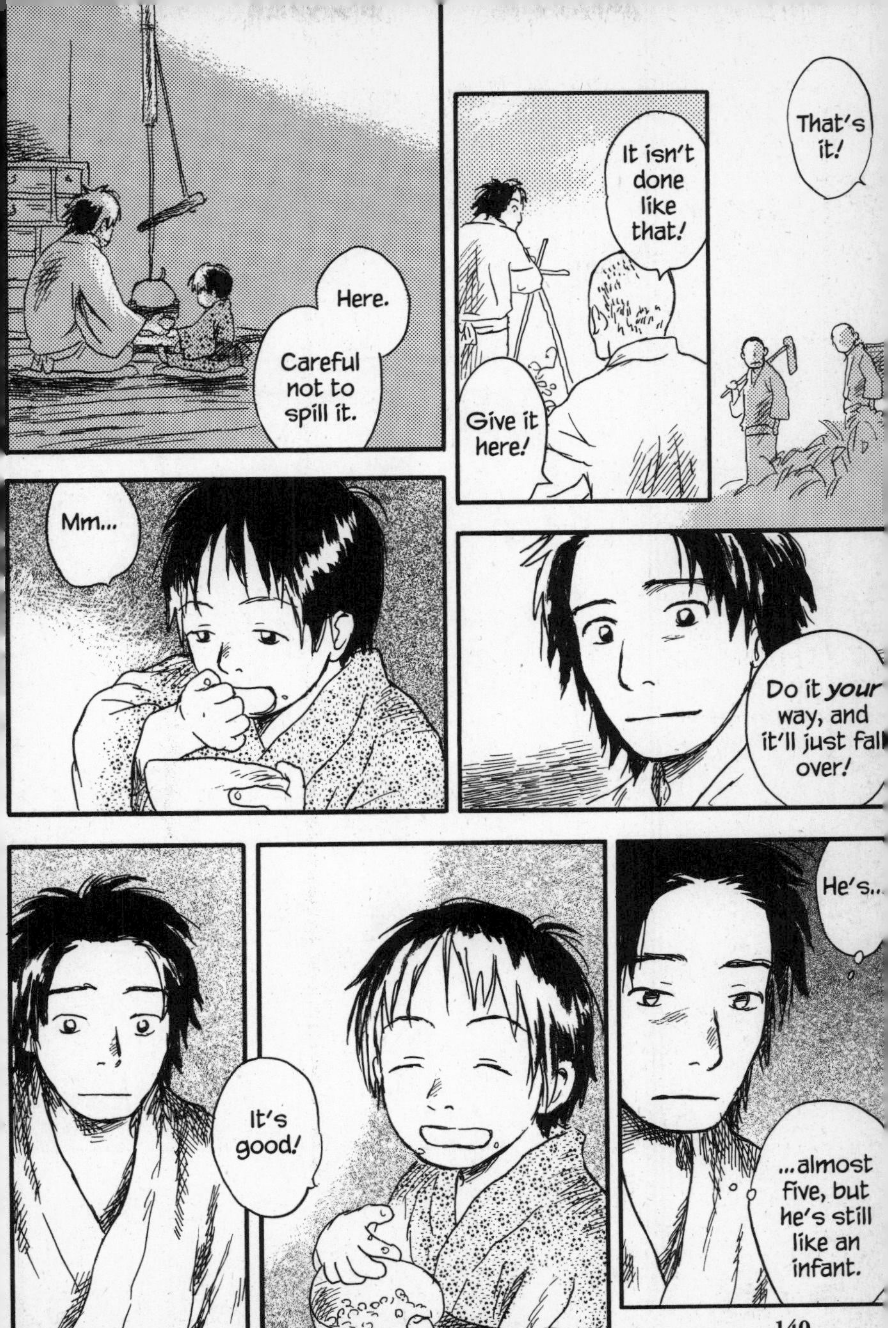
That's it!
It isn't done like that!
Give it here!
Here.
Careful not to spill it.
Do it *your* way, and it'll just fall over!
Mm...
He's...
...almost five, but he's still like an infant.
It's good!

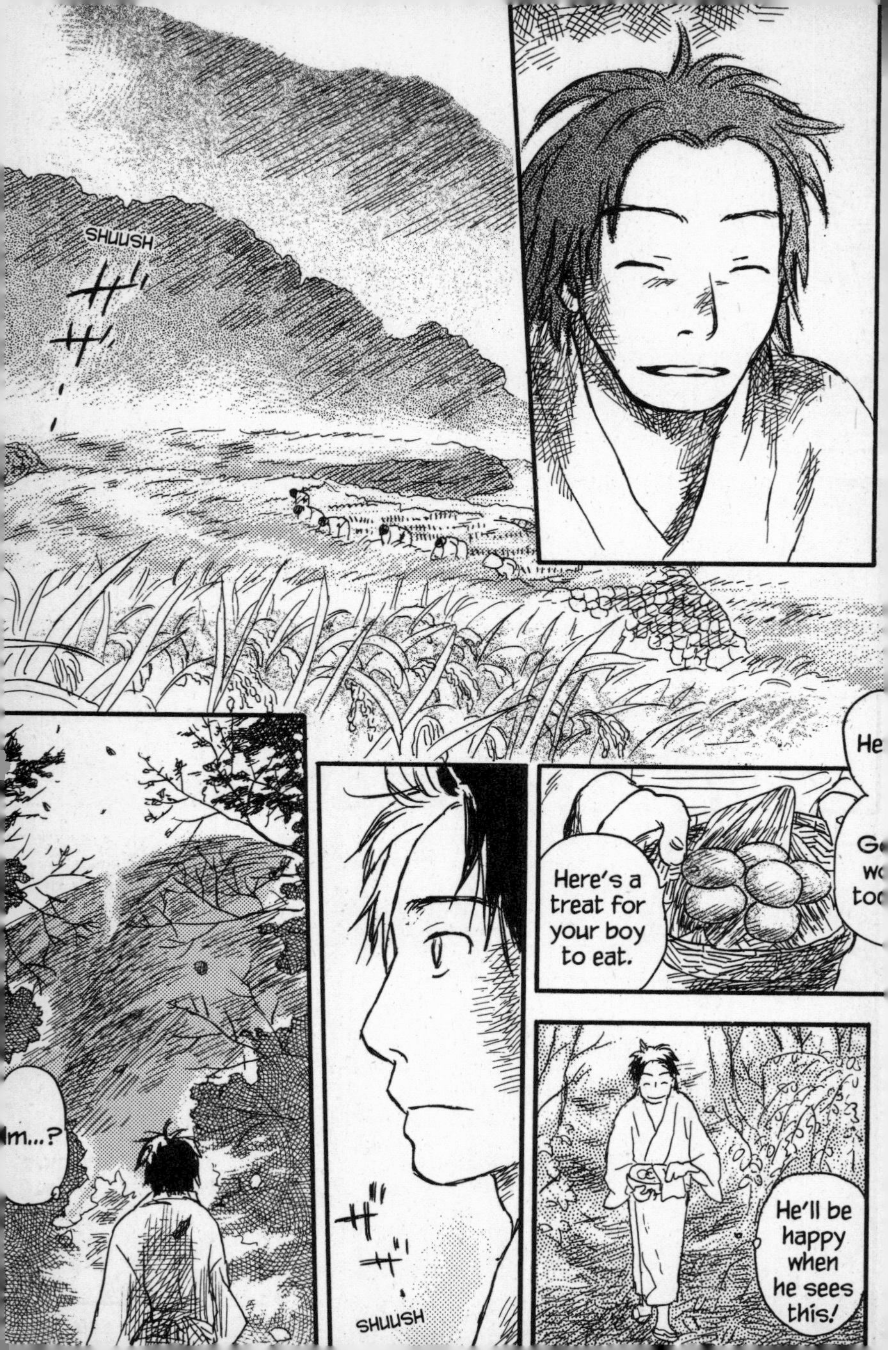
SHUUSH
He
Here's a treat for your boy to eat.
G
wo
too
He'll be happy when he sees this!
SHUUSH
m...?

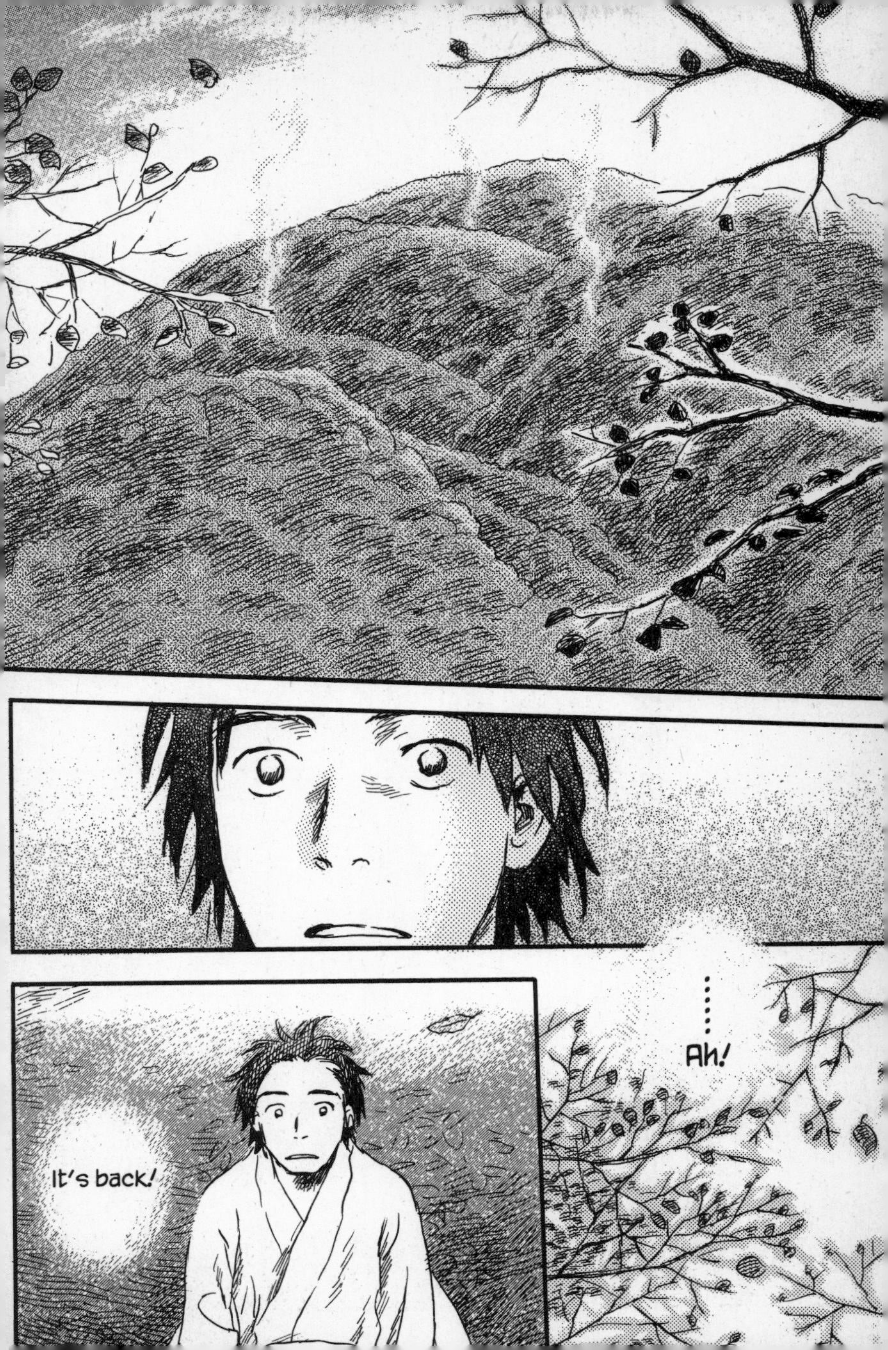

……
Ah!
It's back!

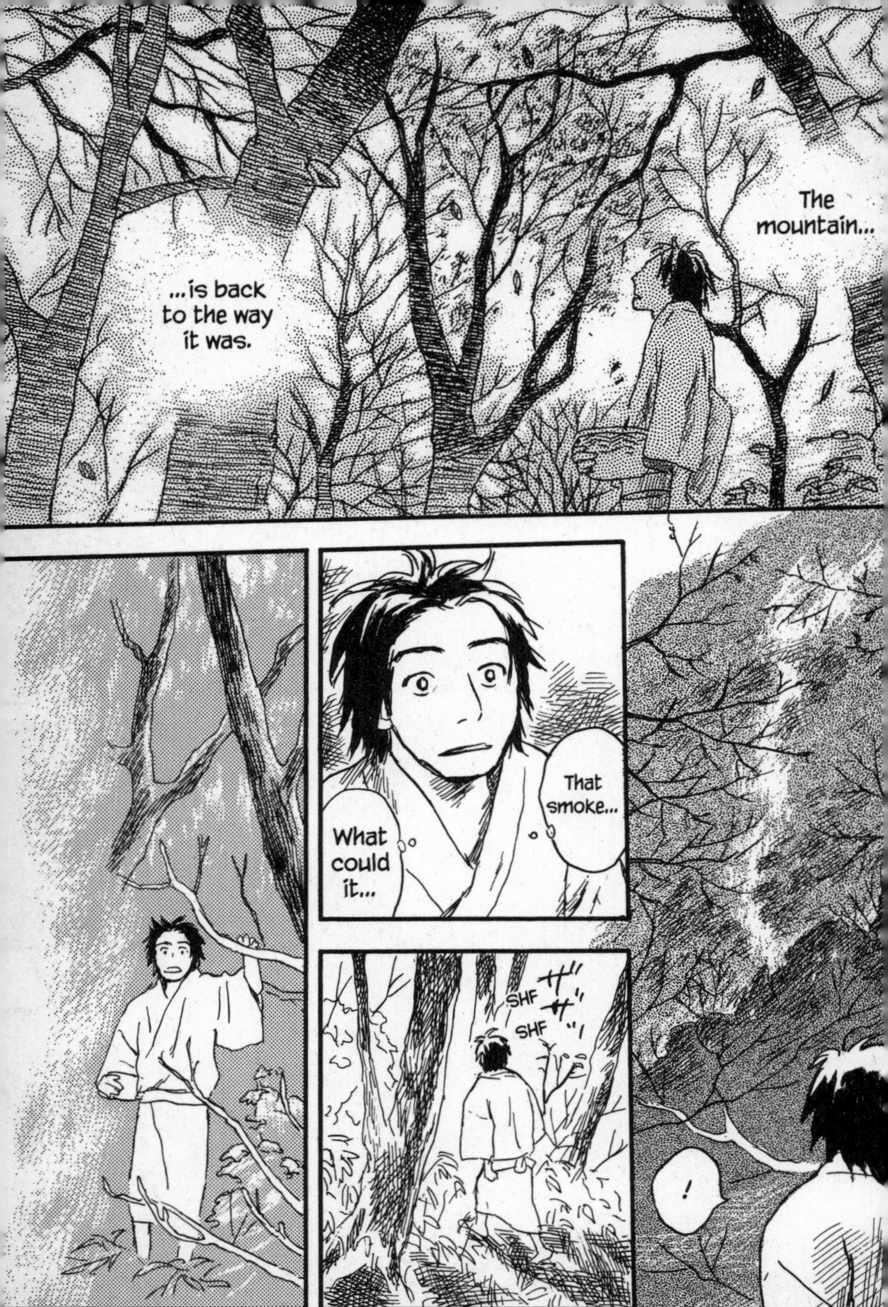
The mountain...
...is back to the way it was.
!
That smoke...
What could it...
SHF
SHF

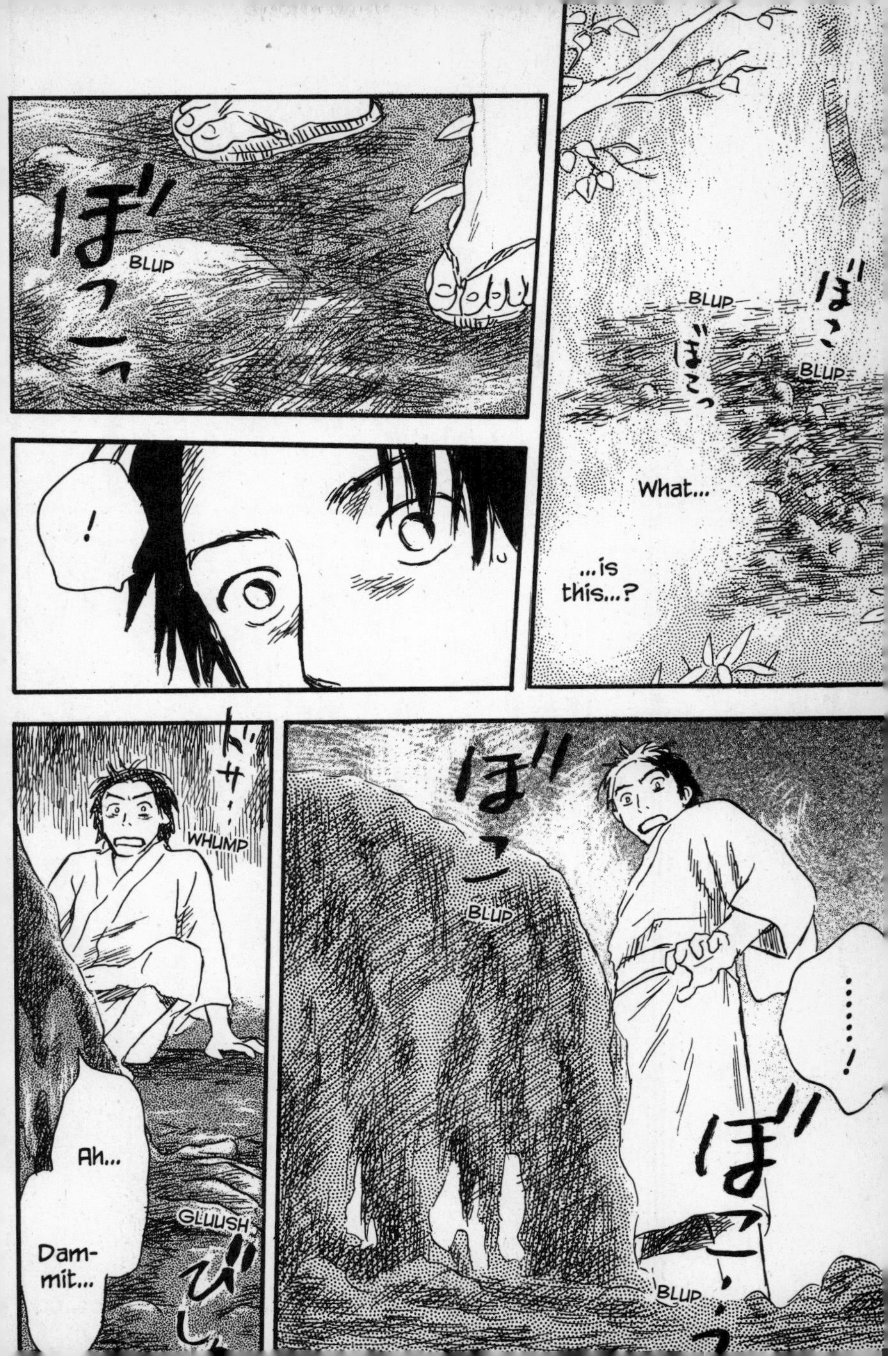
ぼこ
BLUP
ぼこっ
BLUP
What...
...is this...?
ぼっ
BLUP
!
ぼっ
BLUP
......!
ぼっ
BLUP
WHUMP
Ah...
Dam-
mit...
GLUUSH

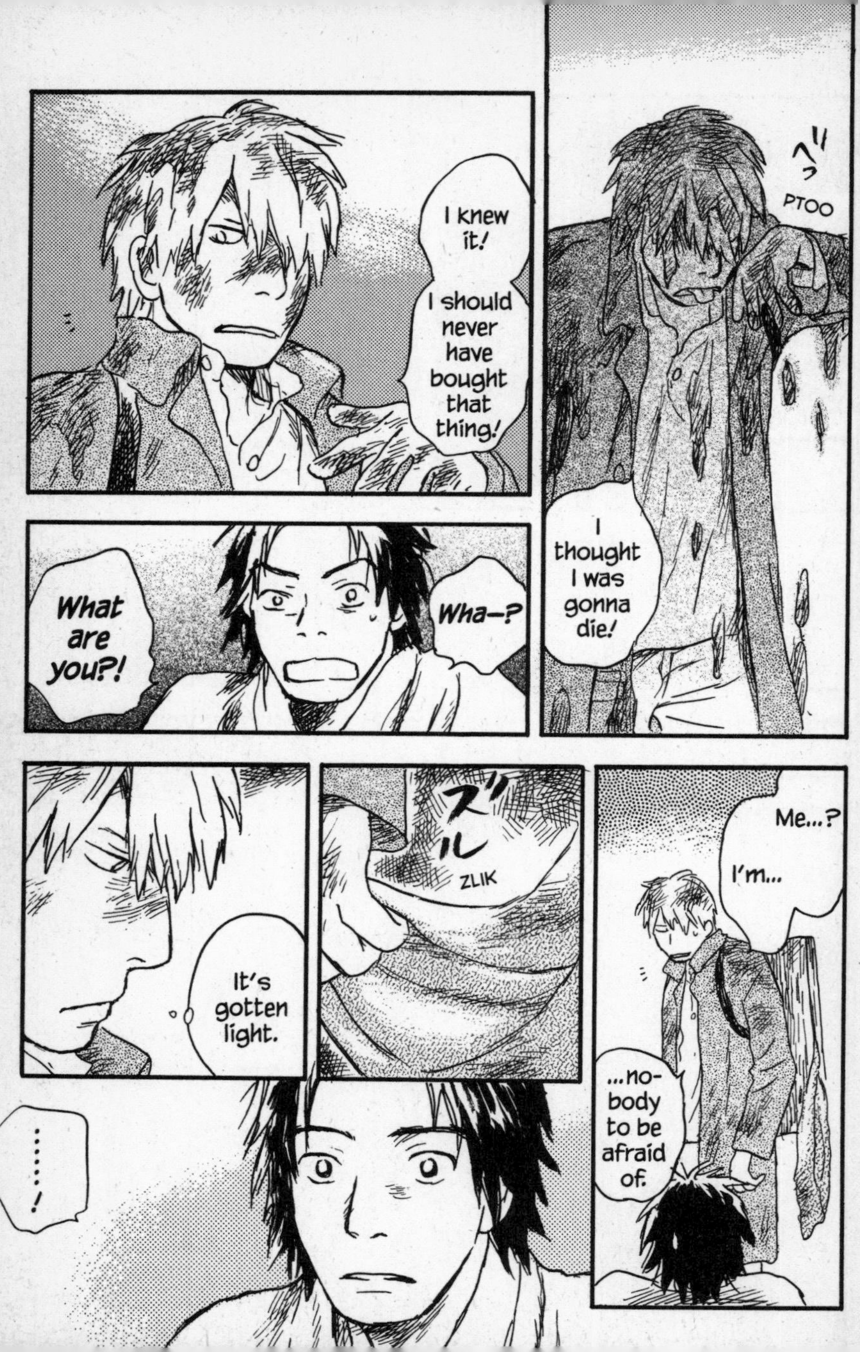
ベッ
PTOO
I thought I was gonna die!
I knew it!
I should never have bought that thing!
Wha–?
What are you?!
Me...?
I'm...
...nobody to be afraid of.
ズル
ZLIK
It's gotten light.
......!

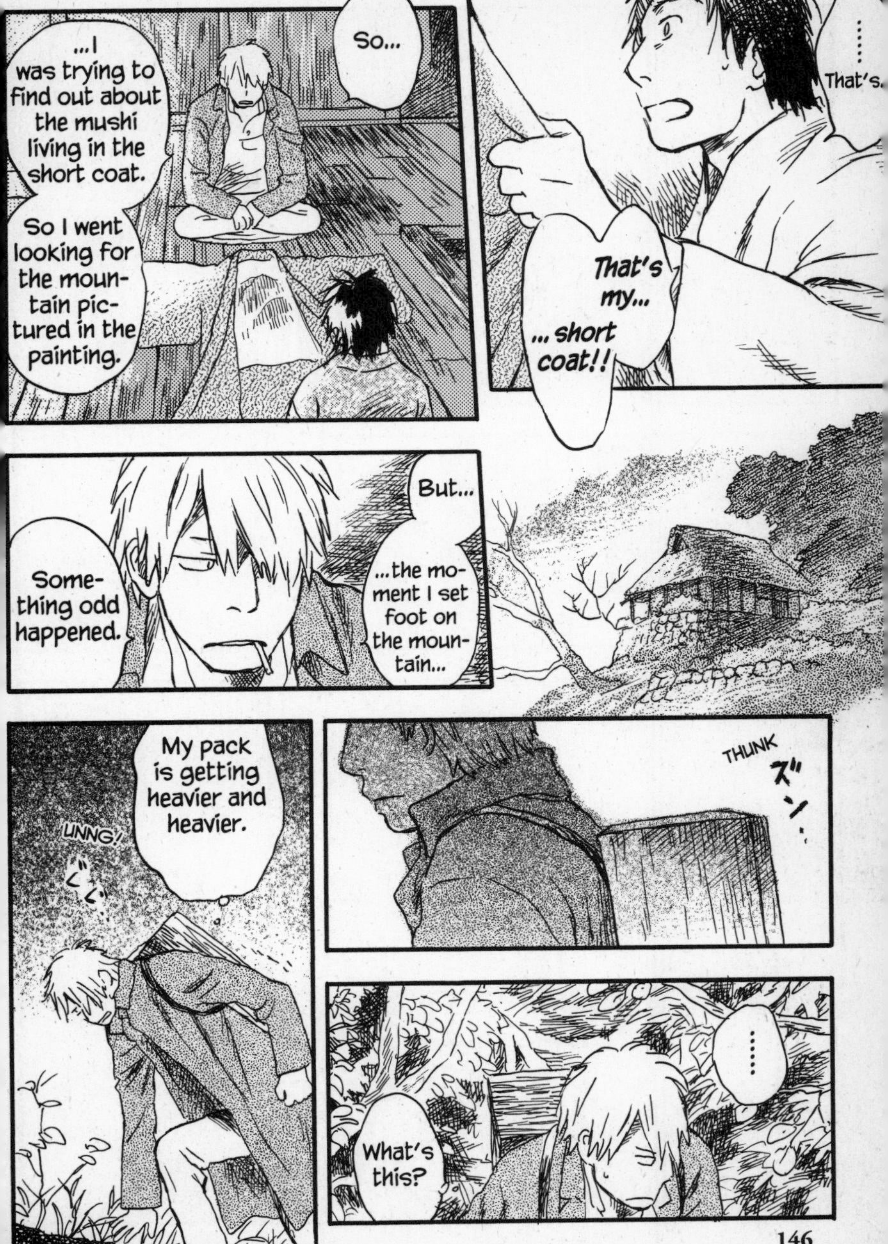
......
That's.
That's my... ...short coat!!
So...
...I was trying to find out about the mushi living in the short coat.
So I went looking for the mountain pictured in the painting.
But...
...the moment I set foot on the mountain...
Something odd happened.
THUNK
ズン
......
What's this?
My pack is getting heavier and heavier.
UNNG!
ぐぐ

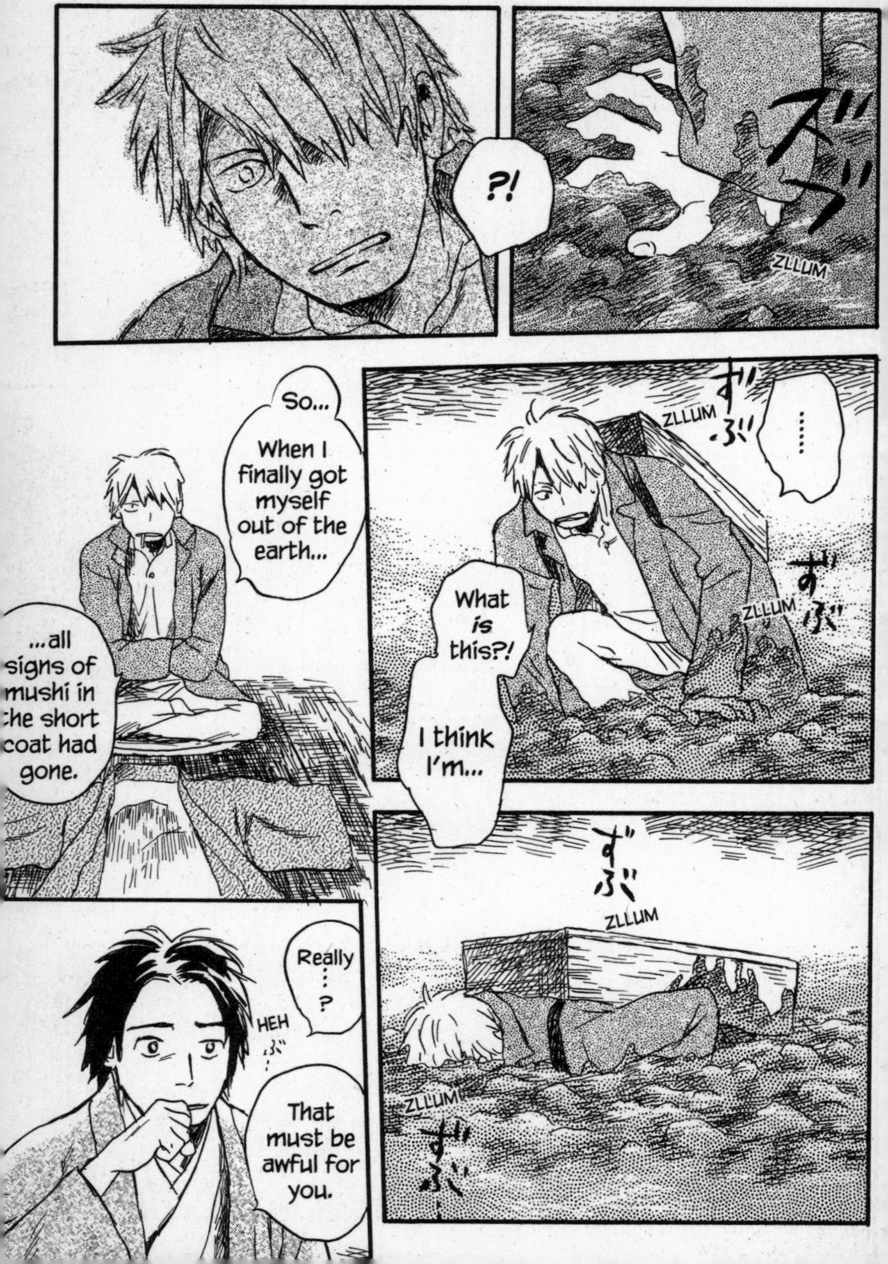
ZLLUM
?!
......
ずぶ
ZLLUM
ずぶ
ZLLUM
What is this?!
I think I'm...
So...
When I finally got myself out of the earth...
...all signs of mushi in the short coat had gone.
ずぶ
ZLLUM
ZLLUM
ずぶ
Really...?
HEH
That must be awful for you.

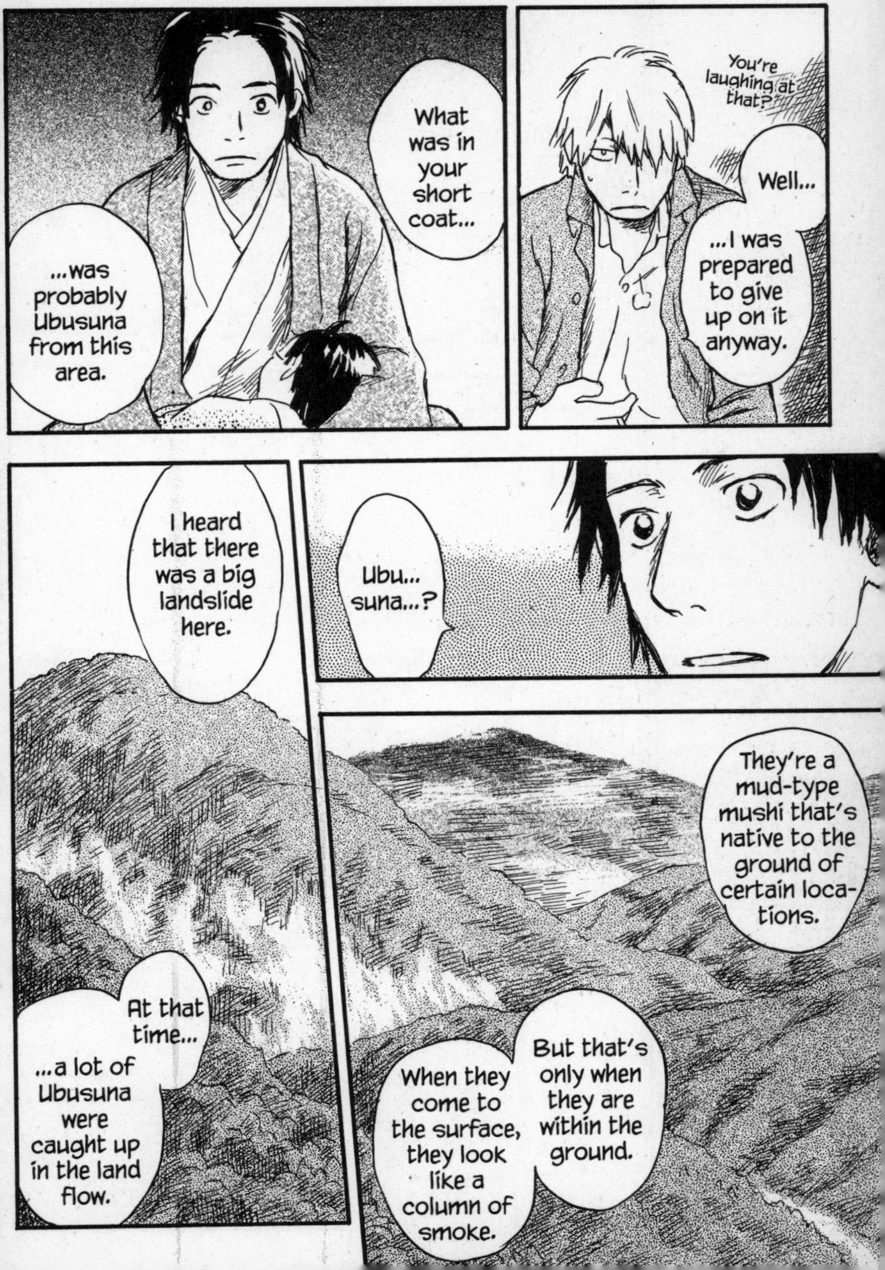
You're laughing at that?
Well...
...I was prepared to give up on it anyway.
What was in your short coat...
...was probably Ubusuna from this area.
Ubu... suna...?
They're a mud-type mushi that's native to the ground of certain loca-tions.
But that's only when they are within the ground.
When they come to the surface, they look like a column of smoke.
I heard that there was a big landslide here.
At that time...
...a lot of Ubusuna were caught up in the land flow.

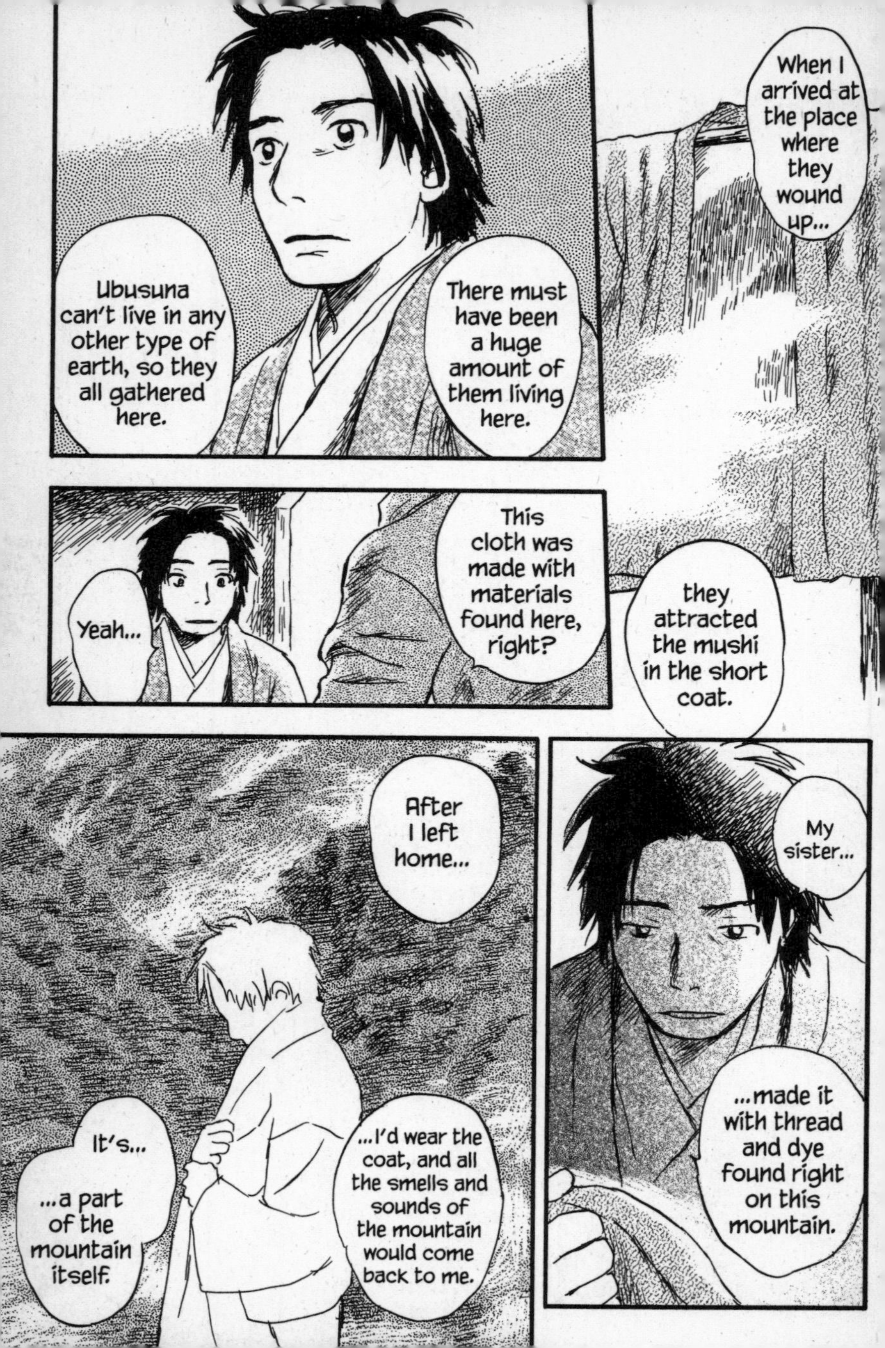
When I arrived at the place where they wound up...
they attracted the mushi in the short coat.
There must have been a huge amount of them living here.
Ubusuna can't live in any other type of earth, so they all gathered here.
This cloth was made with materials found here, right?
Yeah...
My sister...
...made it with thread and dye found right on this mountain.
After I left home...
...I'd wear the coat, and all the smells and sounds of the mountain would come back to me.
It's...
...a part of the mountain itself.

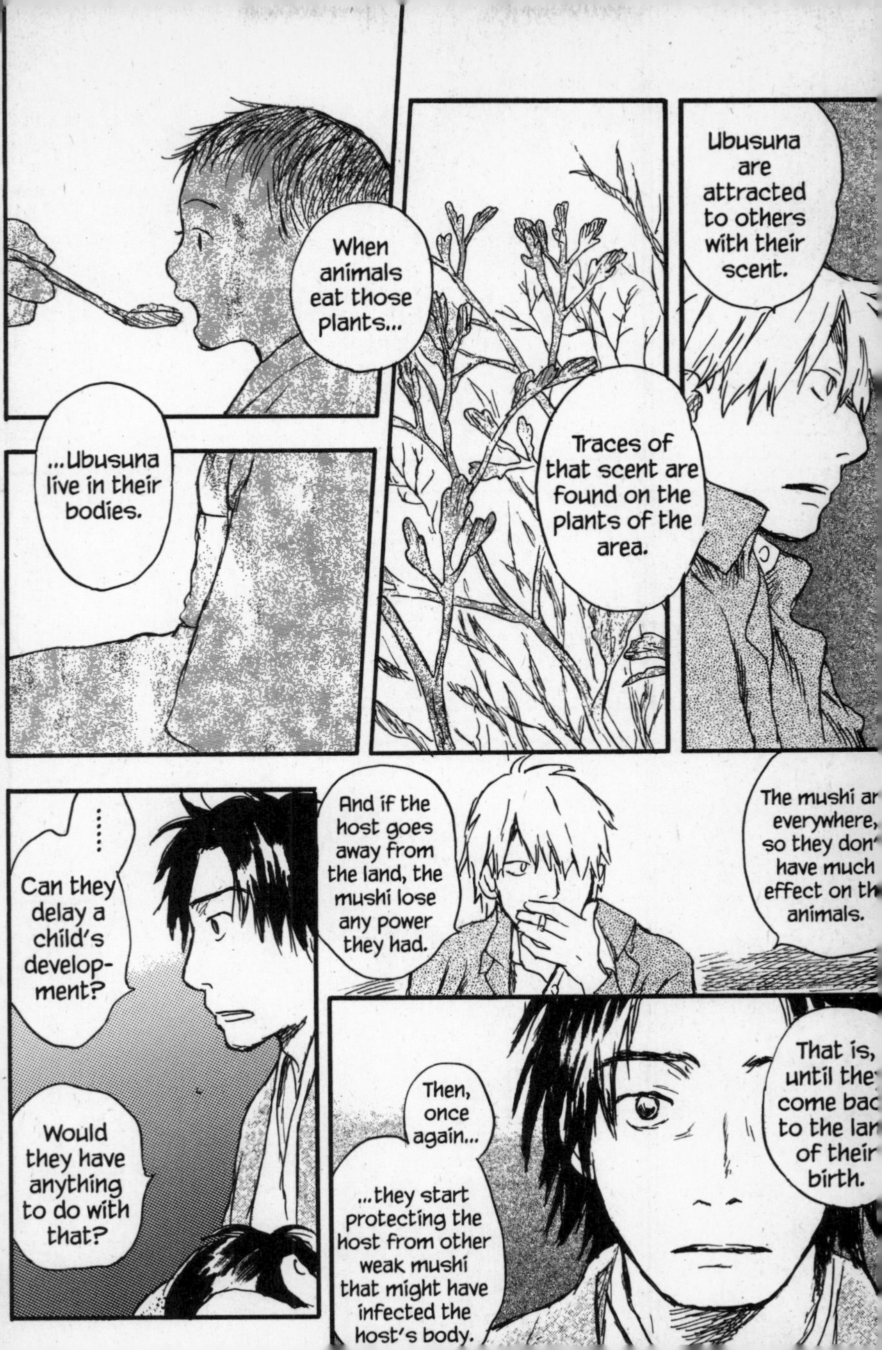

Ubusuna are attracted to others with their scent.
Traces of that scent are found on the plants of the area.
When animals eat those plants...
...Ubusuna live in their bodies.
The mushi ar everywhere, so they don' have much effect on th animals.
And if the host goes away from the land, the mushi lose any power they had.
That is, until the come bac to the lar of their birth.
Then, once again...
...they start protecting the host from other weak mushi that might have infected the host's body.
......
Can they delay a child's develop-ment?
Would they have anything to do with that?

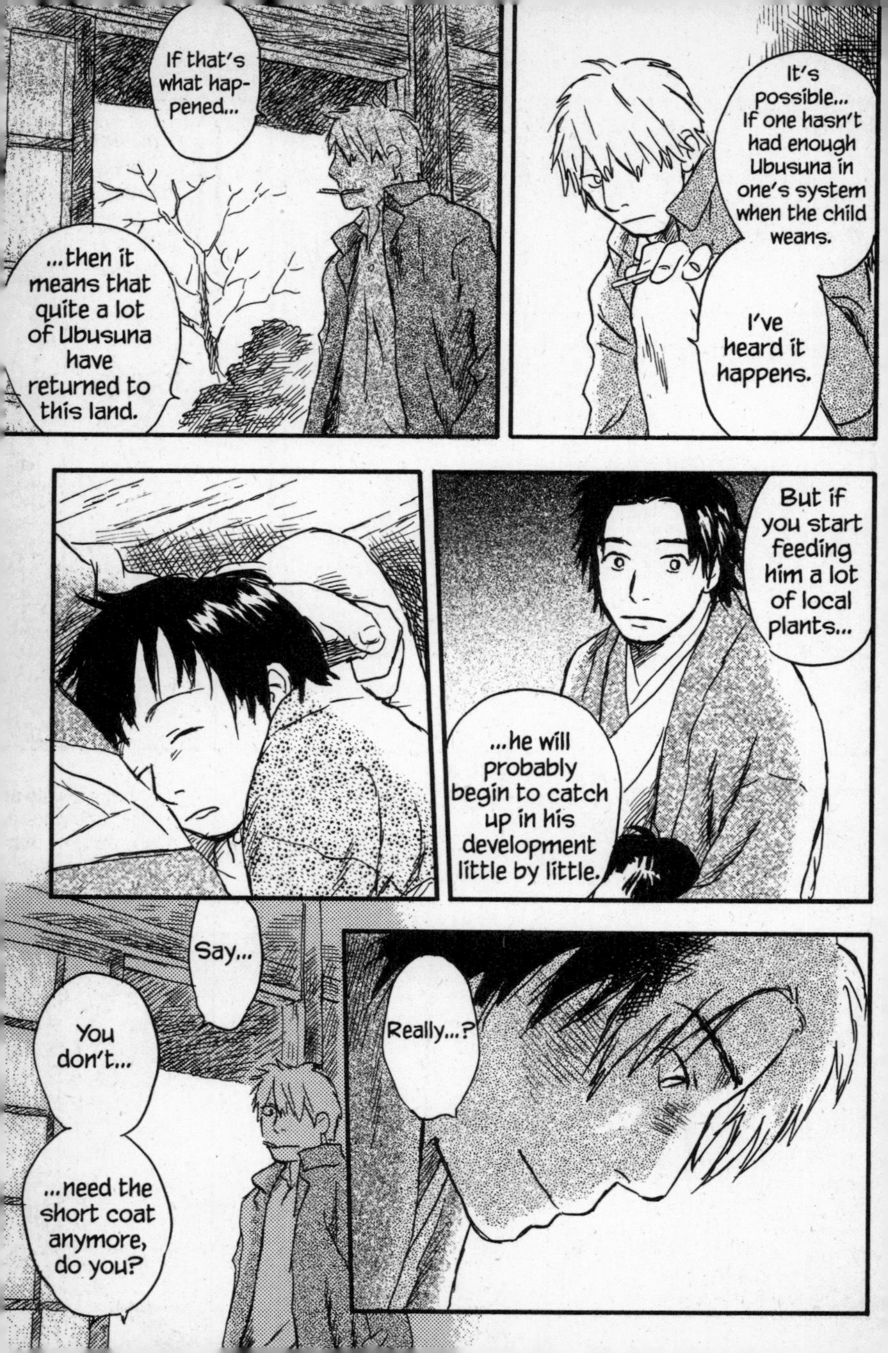
It's possible... If one hasn't had enough Ubusuna in one's system when the child weans.
I've heard it happens.
If that's what hap-pened...
...then it means that quite a lot of Ubusuna have returned to this land.
But if you start feeding him a lot of local plants...
...he will probably begin to catch up in his development little by little.
Really...?
Say...
You don't...
...need the short coat anymore, do you?

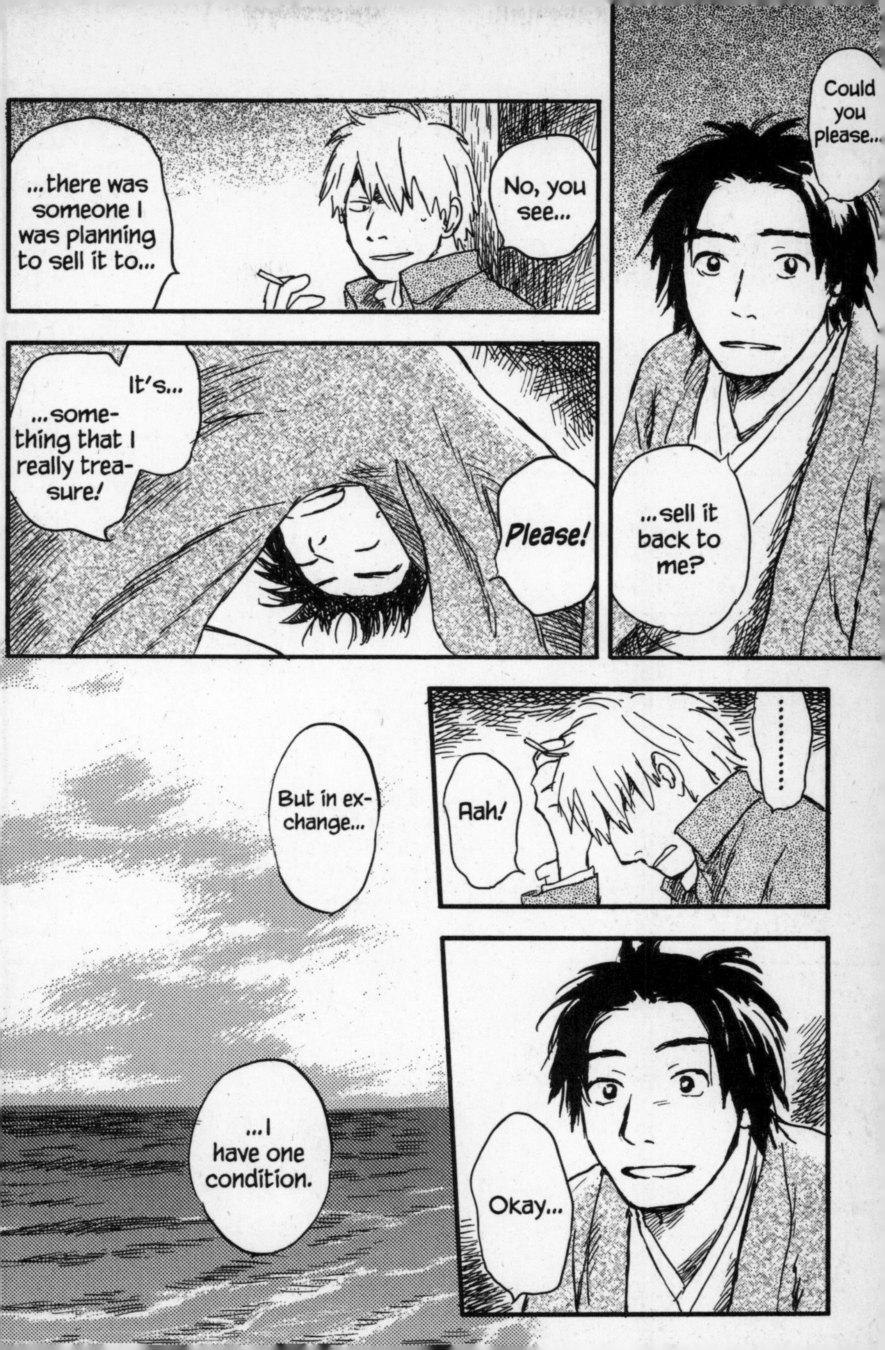
Could you please...
...sell it back to me?
No, you see...
...there was someone I was planning to sell it to...
Please!
It's...
...some-thing that I really trea-sure!
......
Aah!
Okay...
But in ex-change...
...I have one condition.

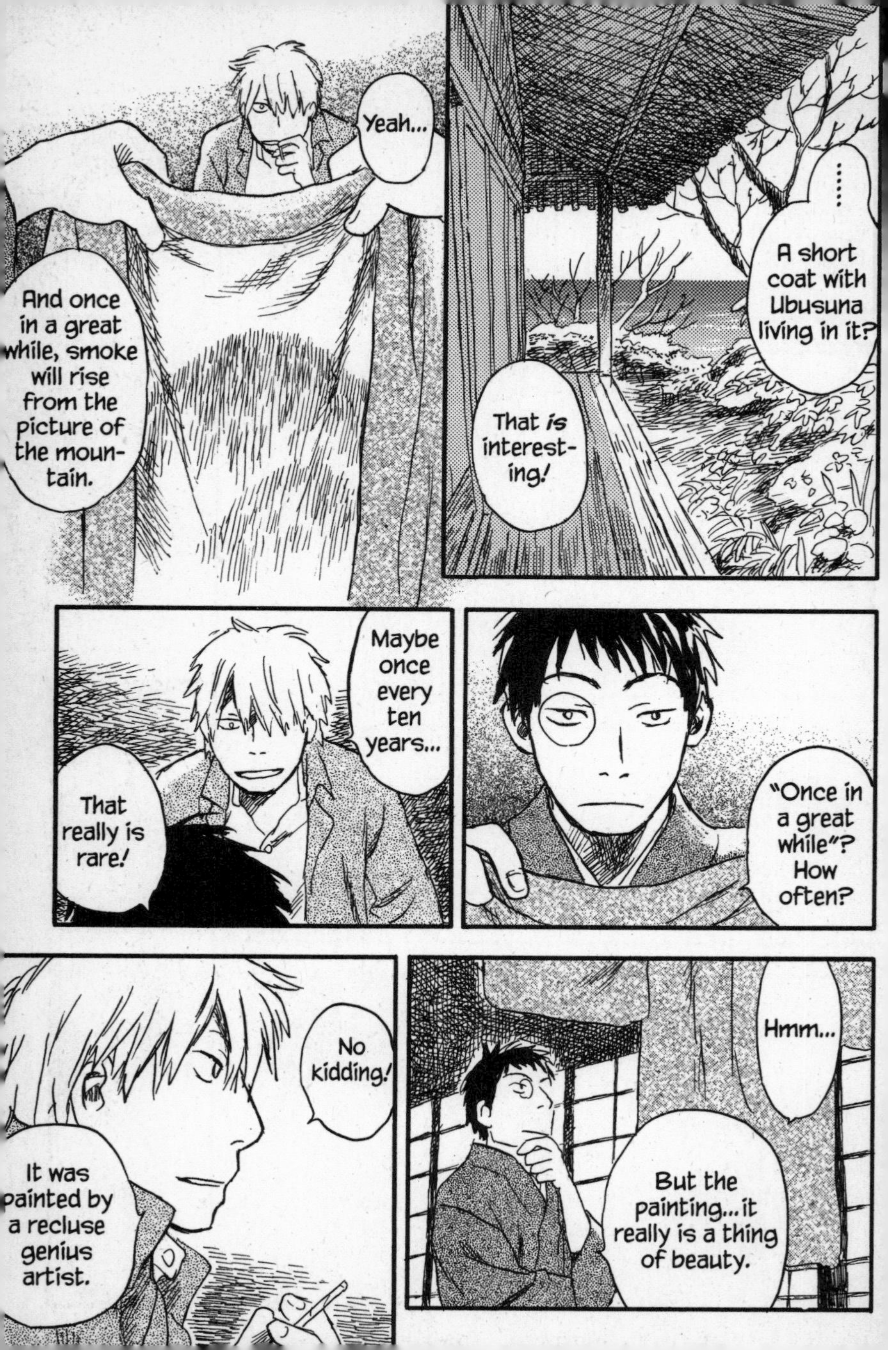
......
A short coat with Ubusuna living in it?
That *is* interesting!
Yeah...
And once in a great while, smoke will rise from the picture of the moun-tain.
"Once in a great while"? How often?
Maybe once every ten years...
That really is rare!
Hmm...
But the painting...it really is a thing of beauty.
No kidding!
It was painted by a recluse genius artist.

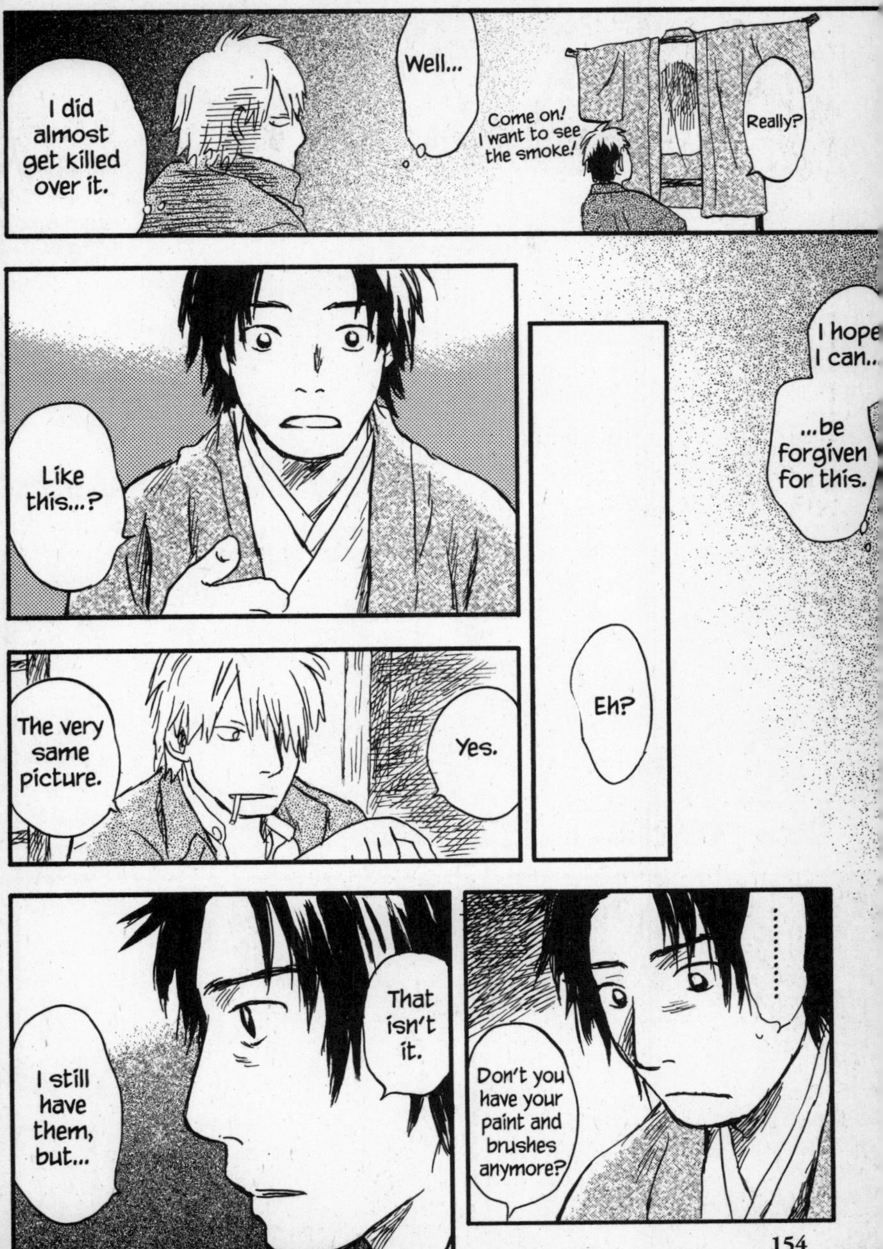

Really?
Come on! I want to see the smoke!
Well...
I did almost get killed over it.
I hope I can...
...be forgiven for this.
Eh?
Like this...?
Yes.
The very same picture.
......
Don't you have your paint and brushes anymore?
That isn't it.
I still have them, but...

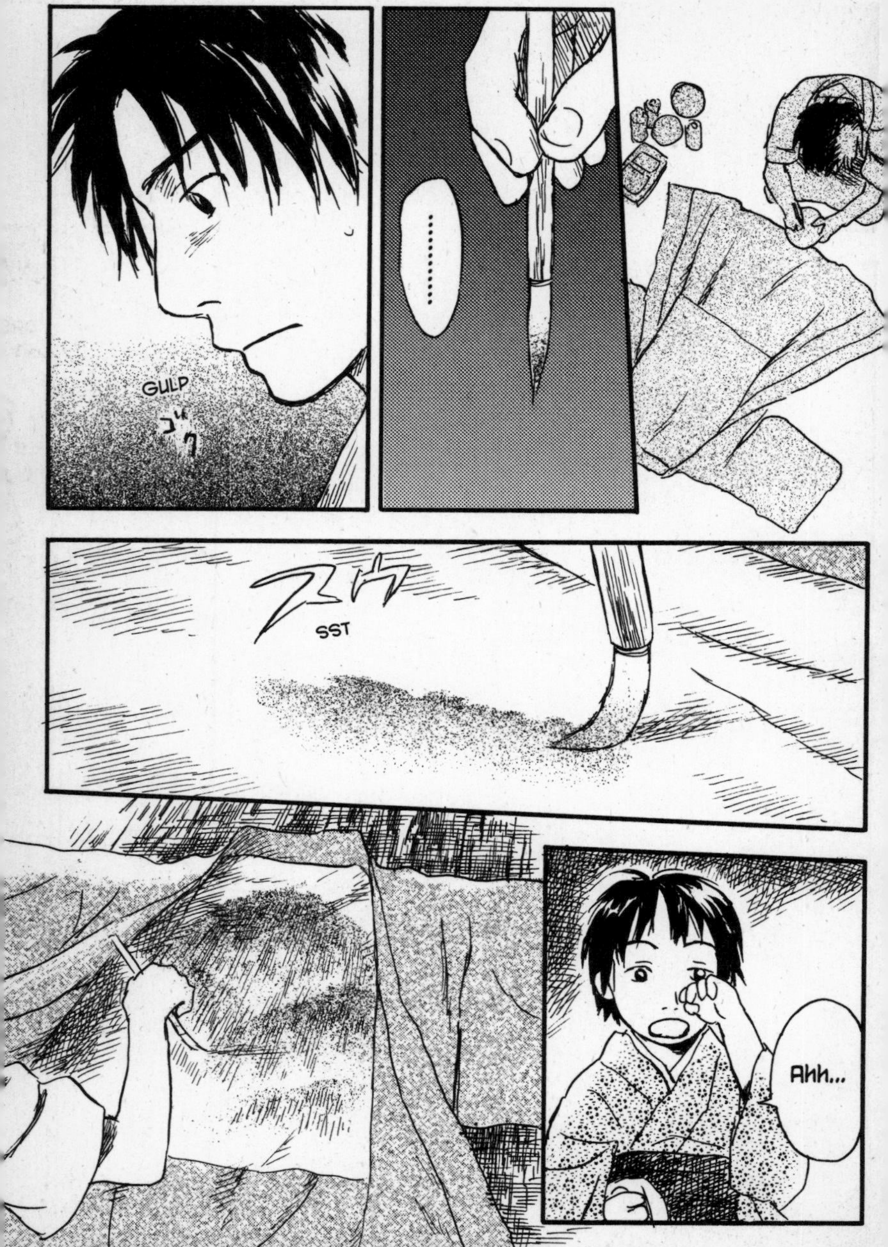
......
GULP
SST
Ahh...

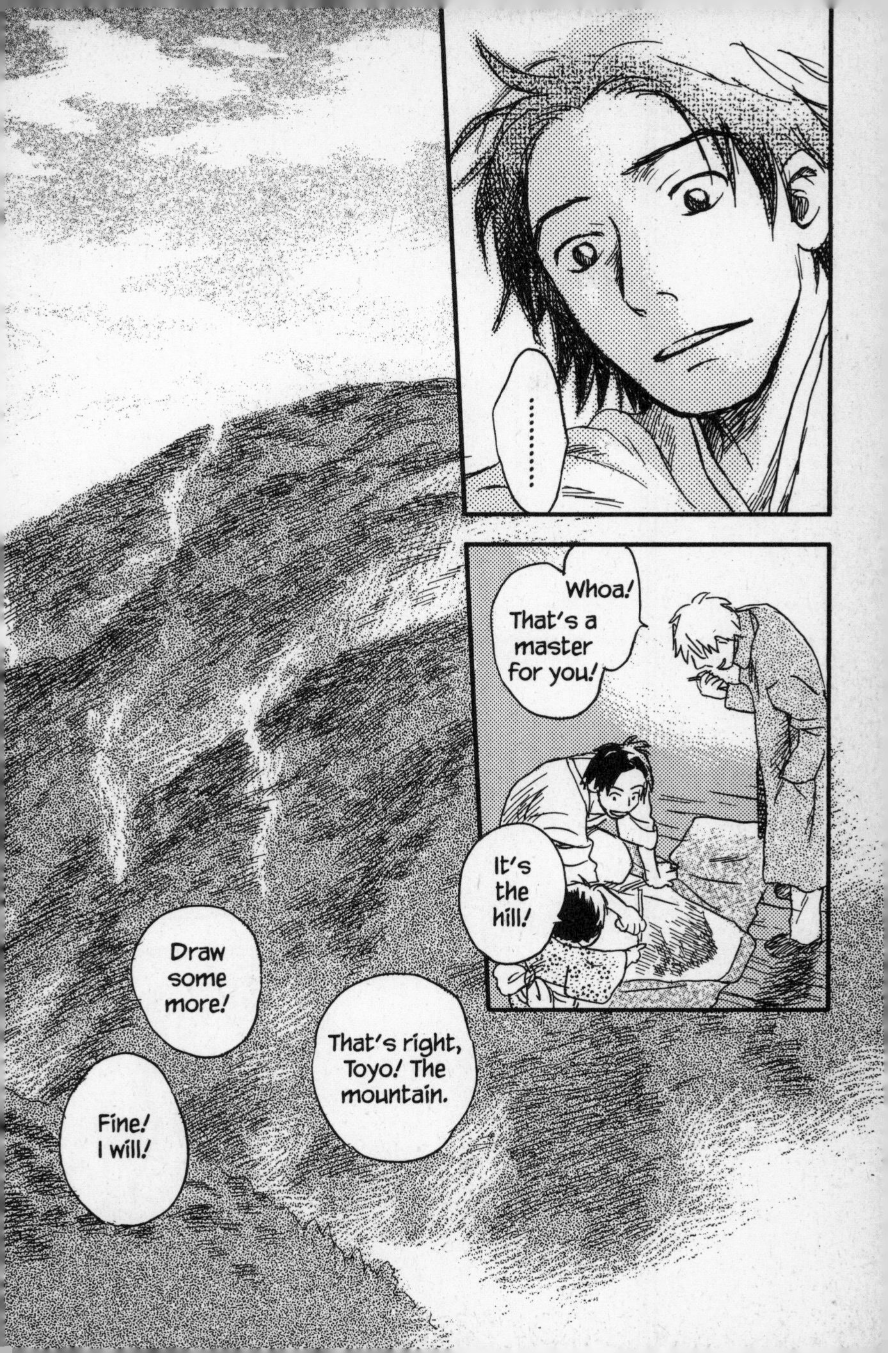
......
Whoa! That's a master for you!
It's the hill!
That's right, Toyo! The mountain.
Draw some more!
Fine! I will!

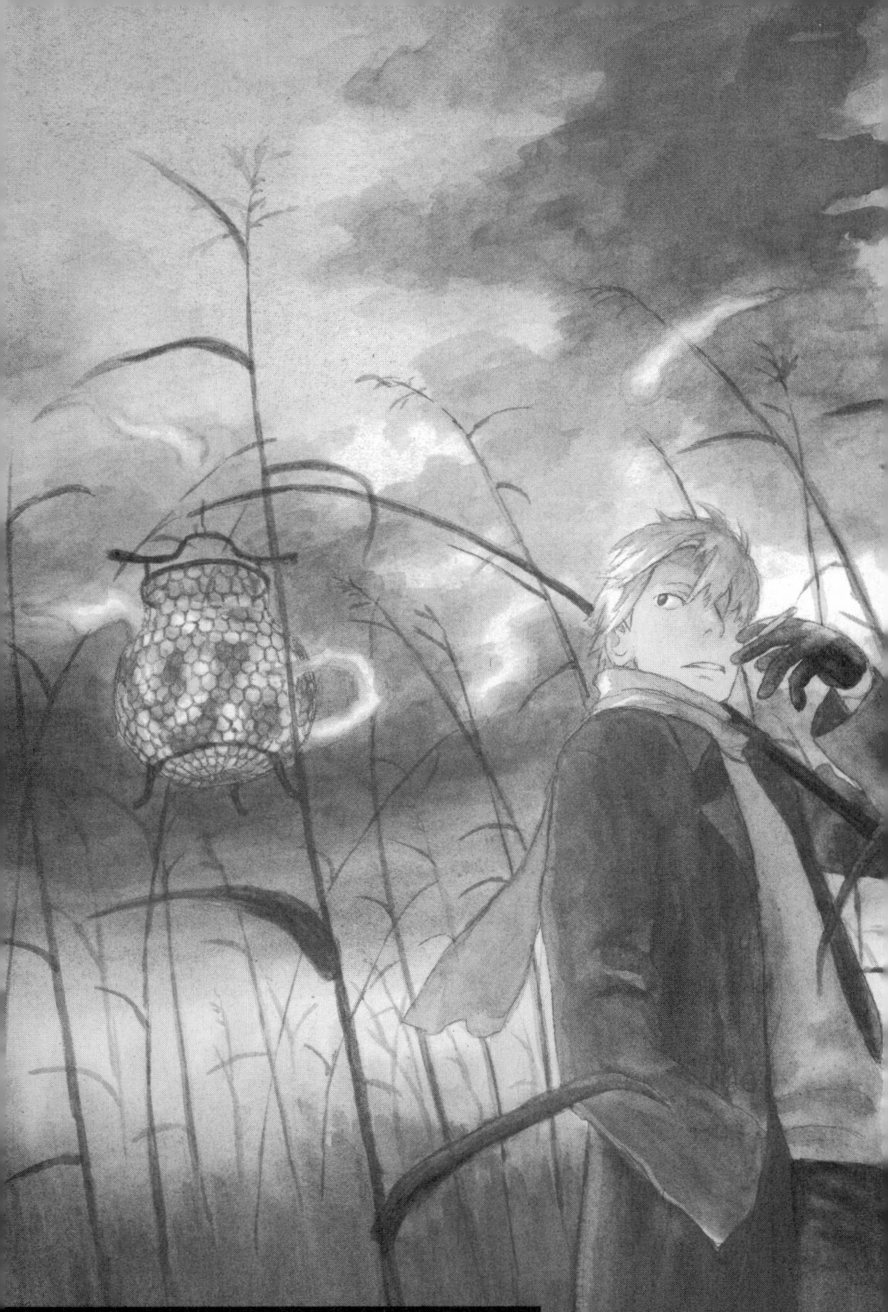

Flames of the Fields

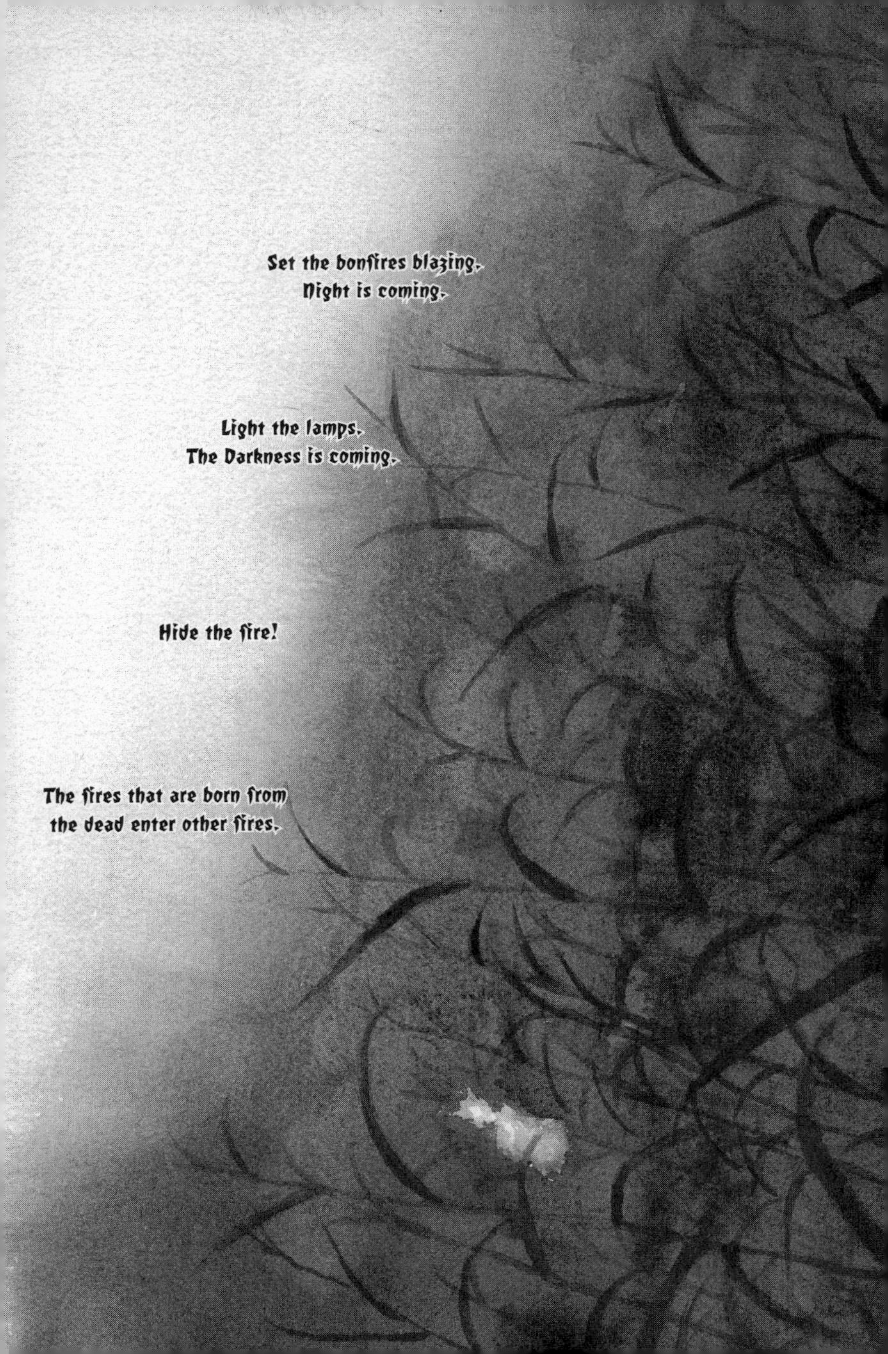
Set the bonfires blazing.
Night is coming.
Light the lamps.
The Darkness is coming.
Hide the fire!
The fires that are born from
the dead enter other fires.

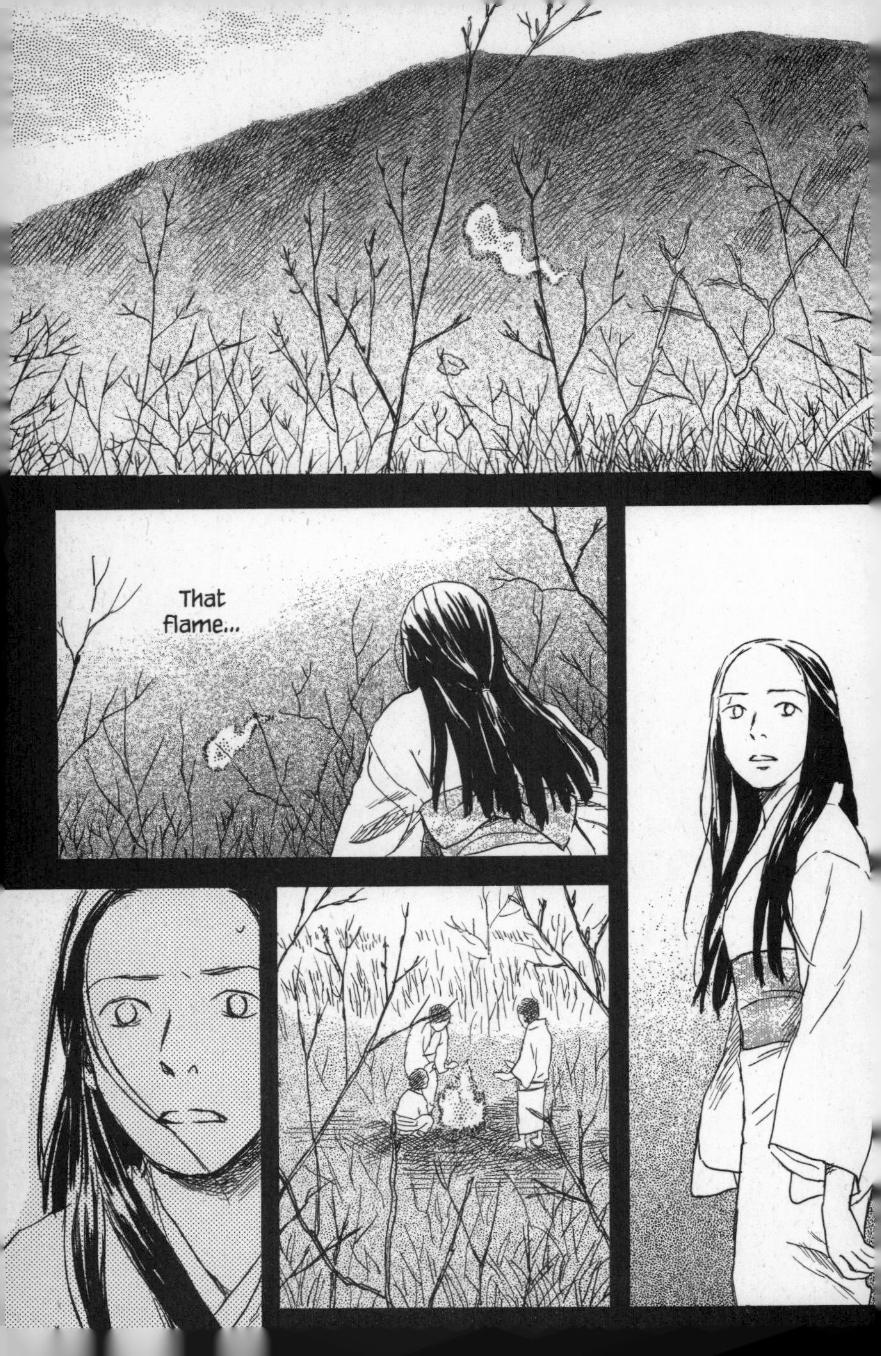
That flame...

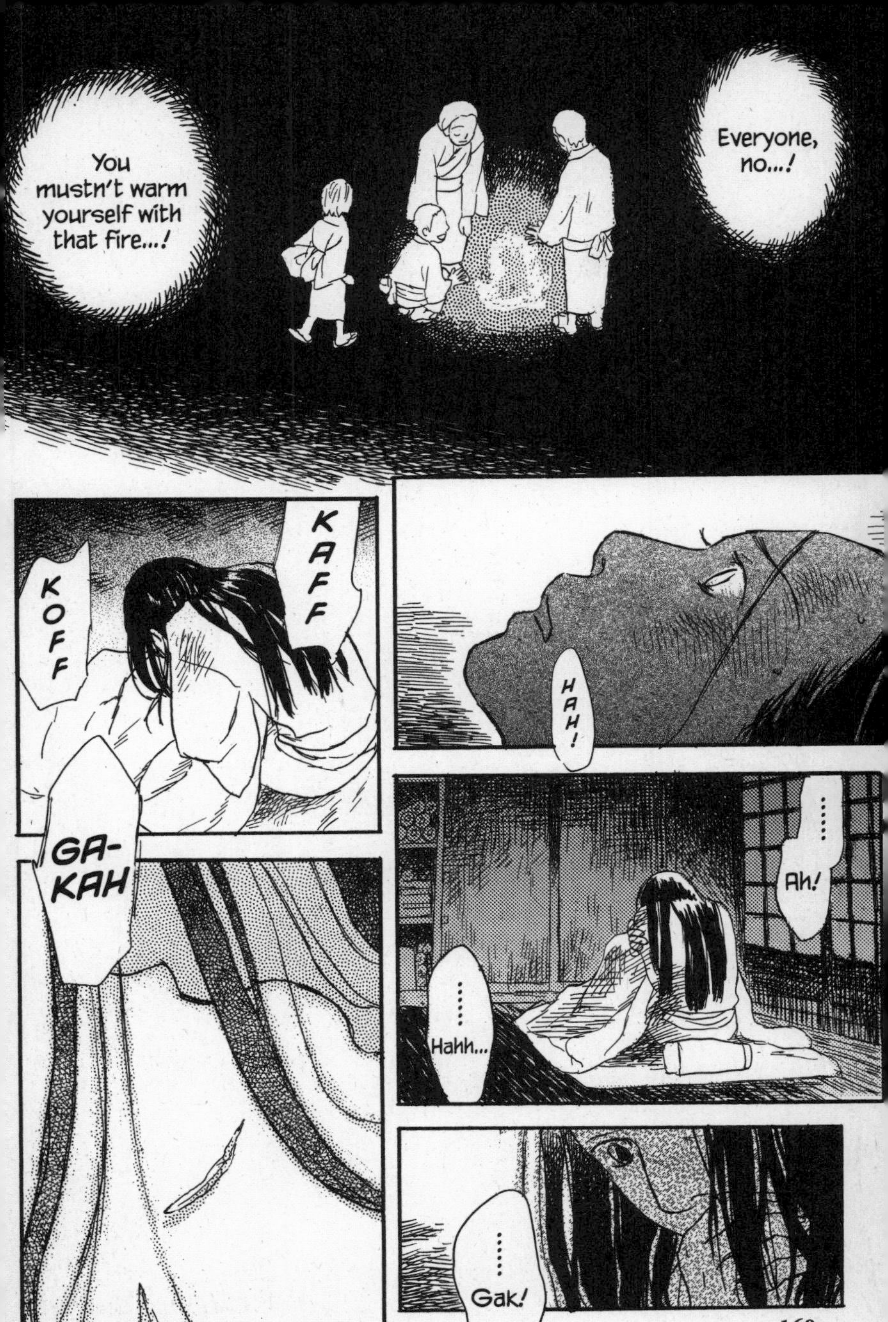
Everyone, no...!
You mustn't warm yourself with that fire...!
HAH!
...... Ah!
...... Hahh...
...... Gak!
KAFF
KOFF
GA-KAH

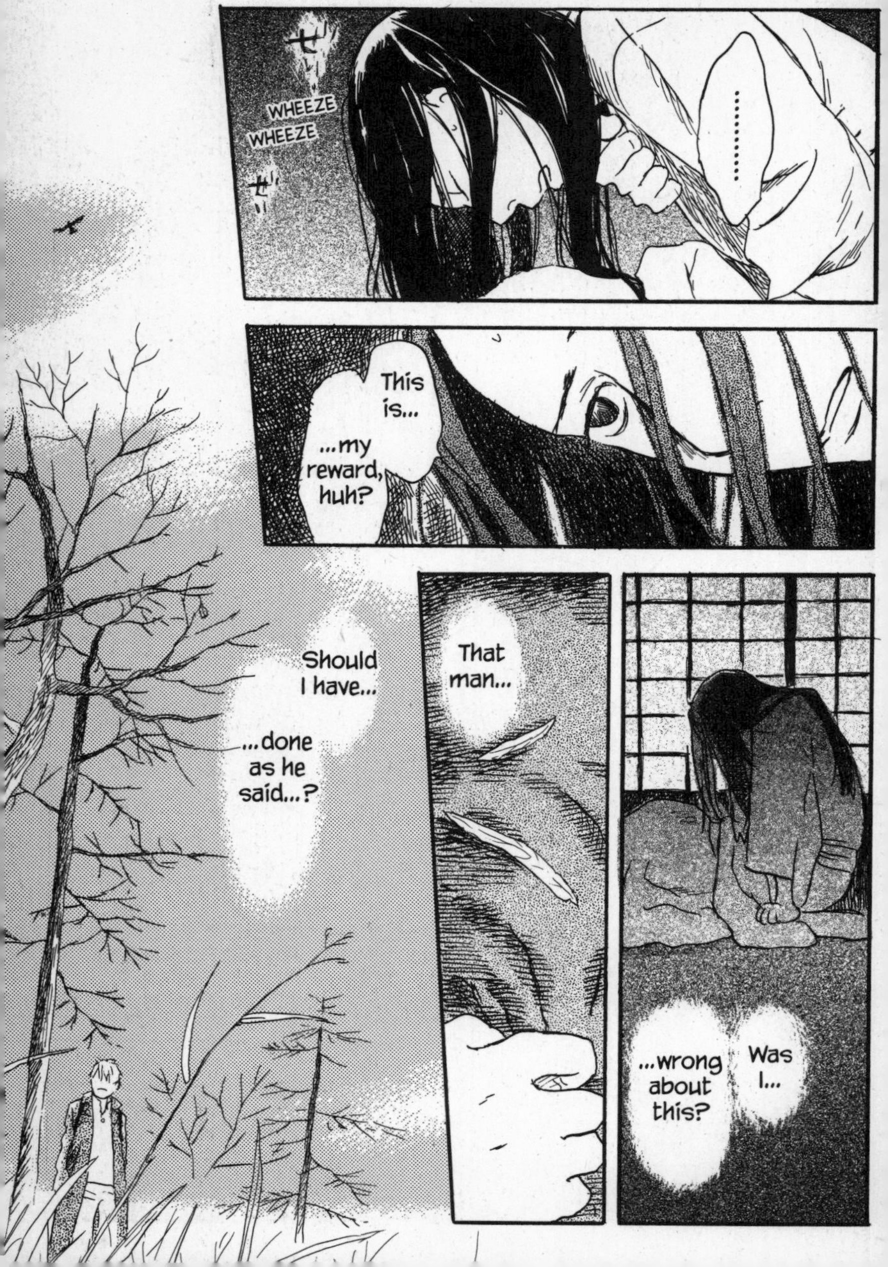
......
WHEEZE WHEEZE
This is...
...my reward, huh?
Was I...
...wrong about this?
That man...
Should I have...
...done as he said...?

It looks like this is the place.

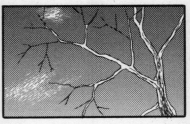

KRKKL

Is there a mushishi living in this village?

Yo!

Maybe he's talking about Nohagi?

Mushi-shi?

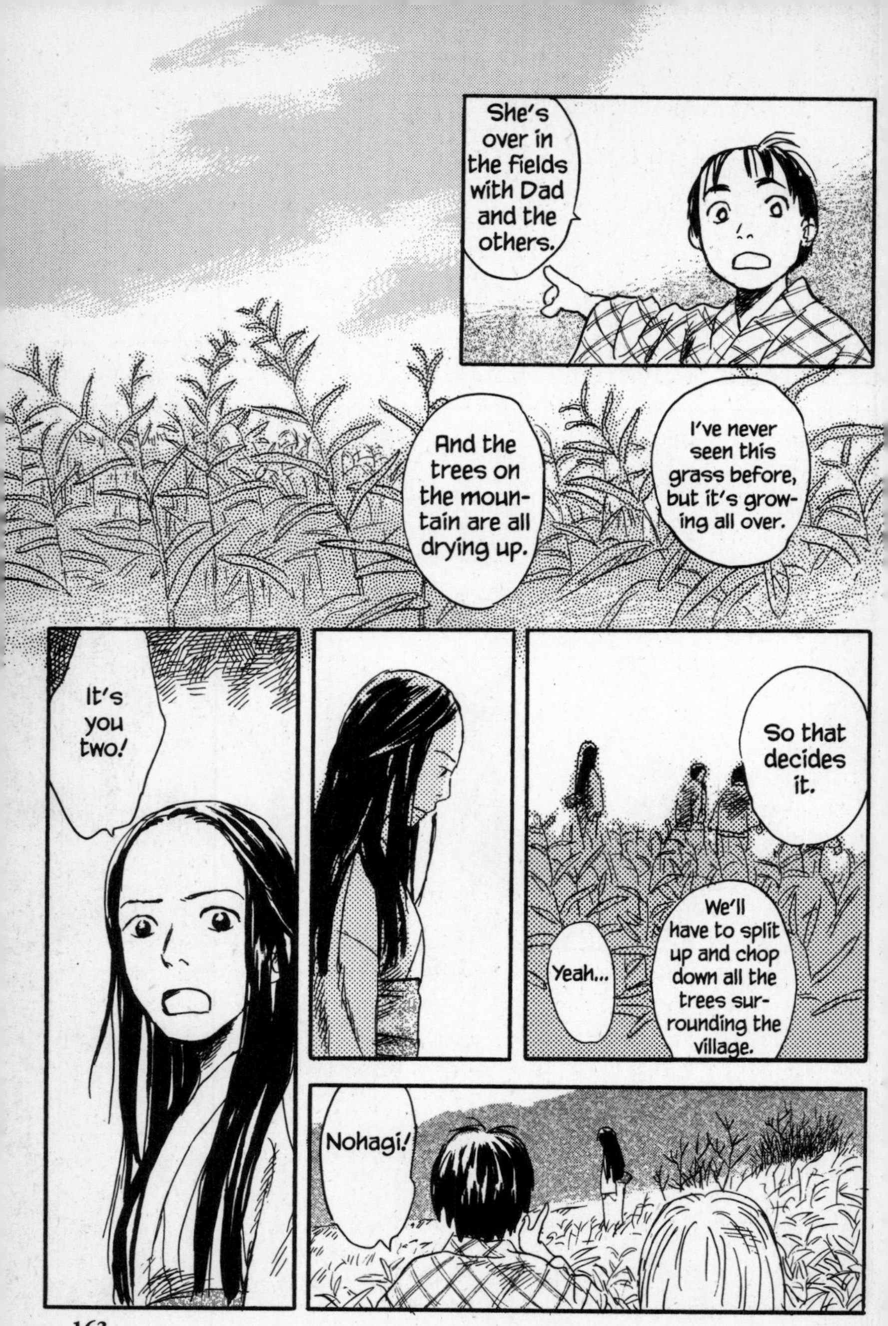

She's over in the fields with Dad and the others.
I've never seen this grass before, but it's growing all over.
And the trees on the mountain are all drying up.
So that decides it.
We'll have to split up and chop down all the trees surrounding the village.
Yeah...
Nohagi!
It's you two!

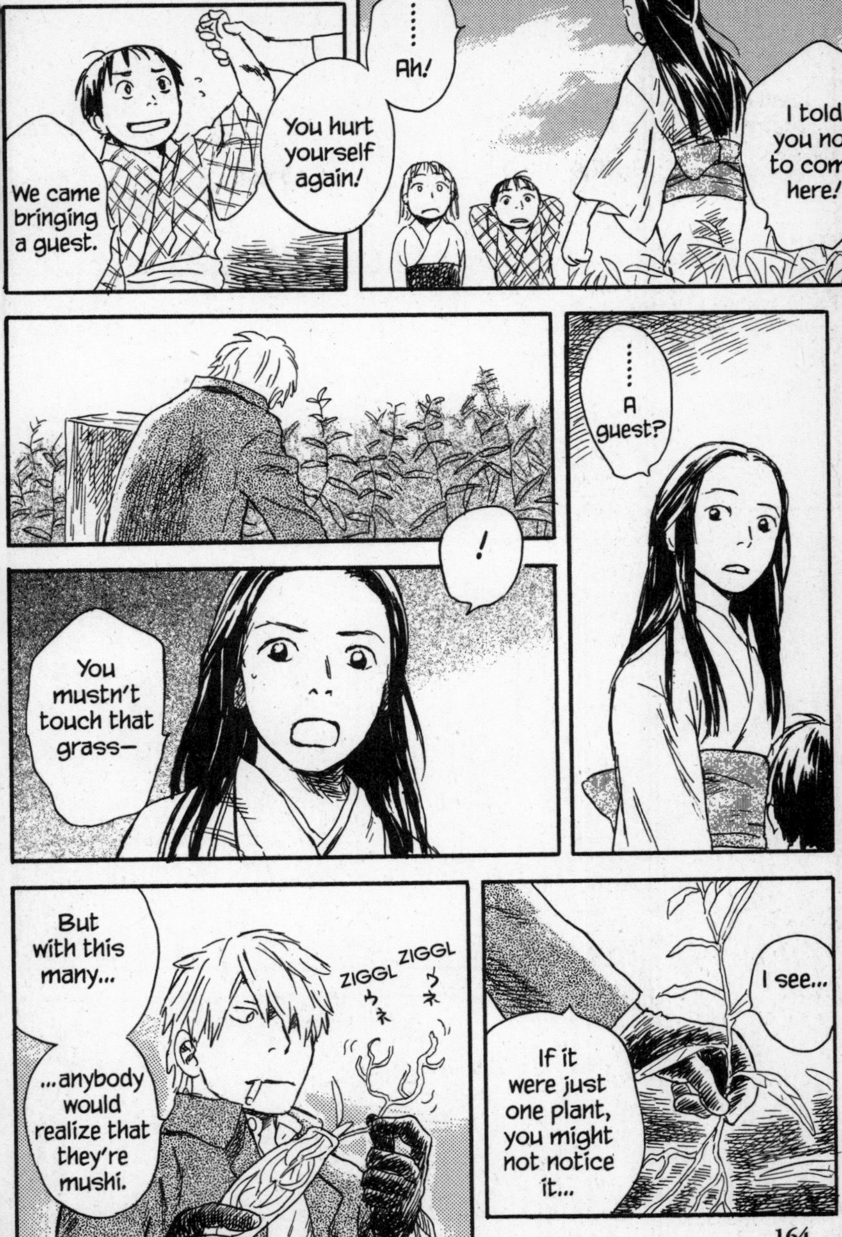
I told you not to come here!
……
Ah!
You hurt yourself again!
We came bringing a guest.
……
A guest?
!
You mustn't touch that grass—
I see...
If it were just one plant, you might not notice it...
But with this many...
ZIGGL ウネ
ZIGGL ウネ
...anybody would realize that they're mushi.

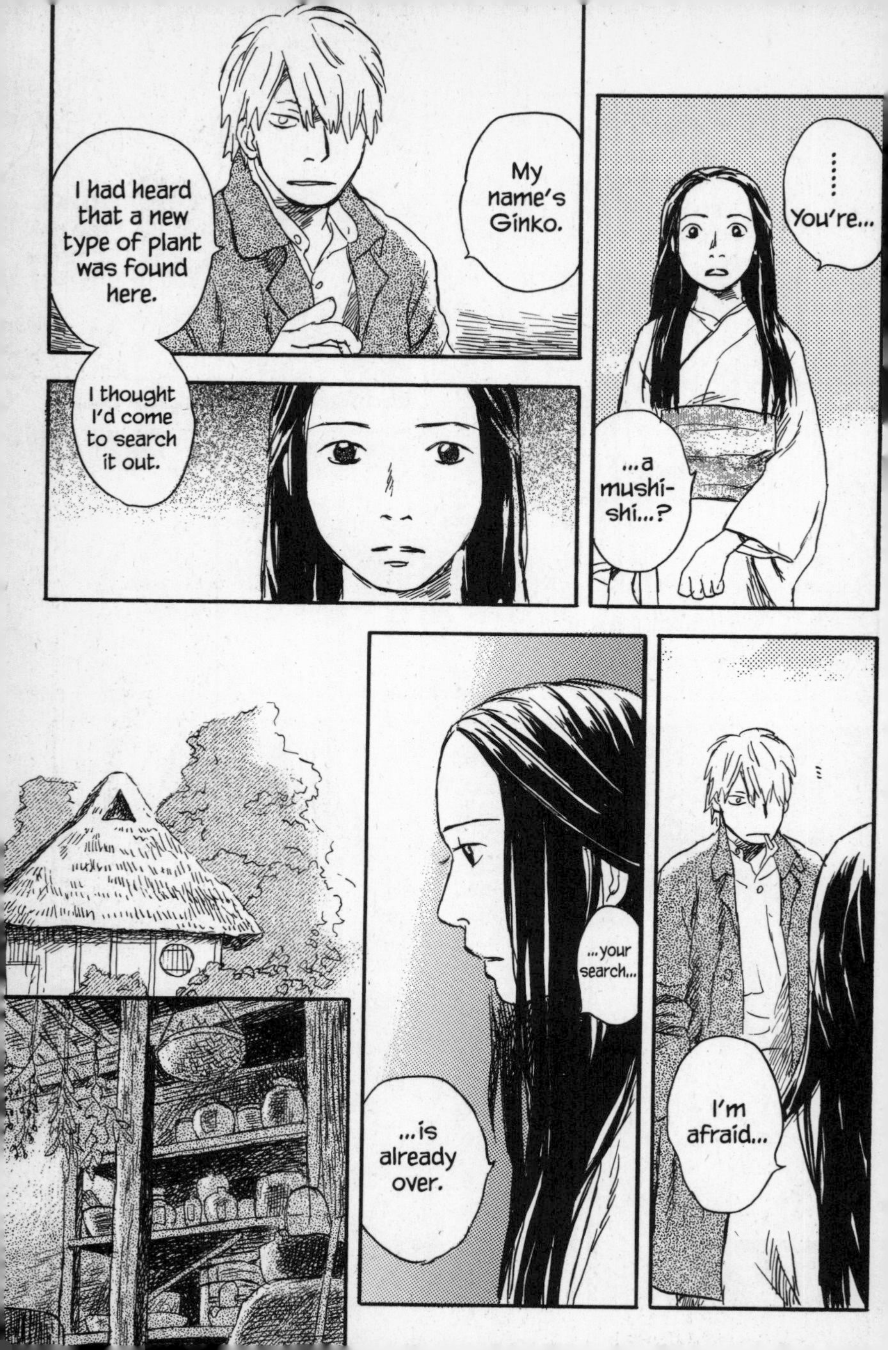
……
You're...
...a mushi-shi...?
My name's Ginko.
I had heard that a new type of plant was found here.
I thought I'd come to search it out.
…
I'm afraid...
...your search...
...is already over.

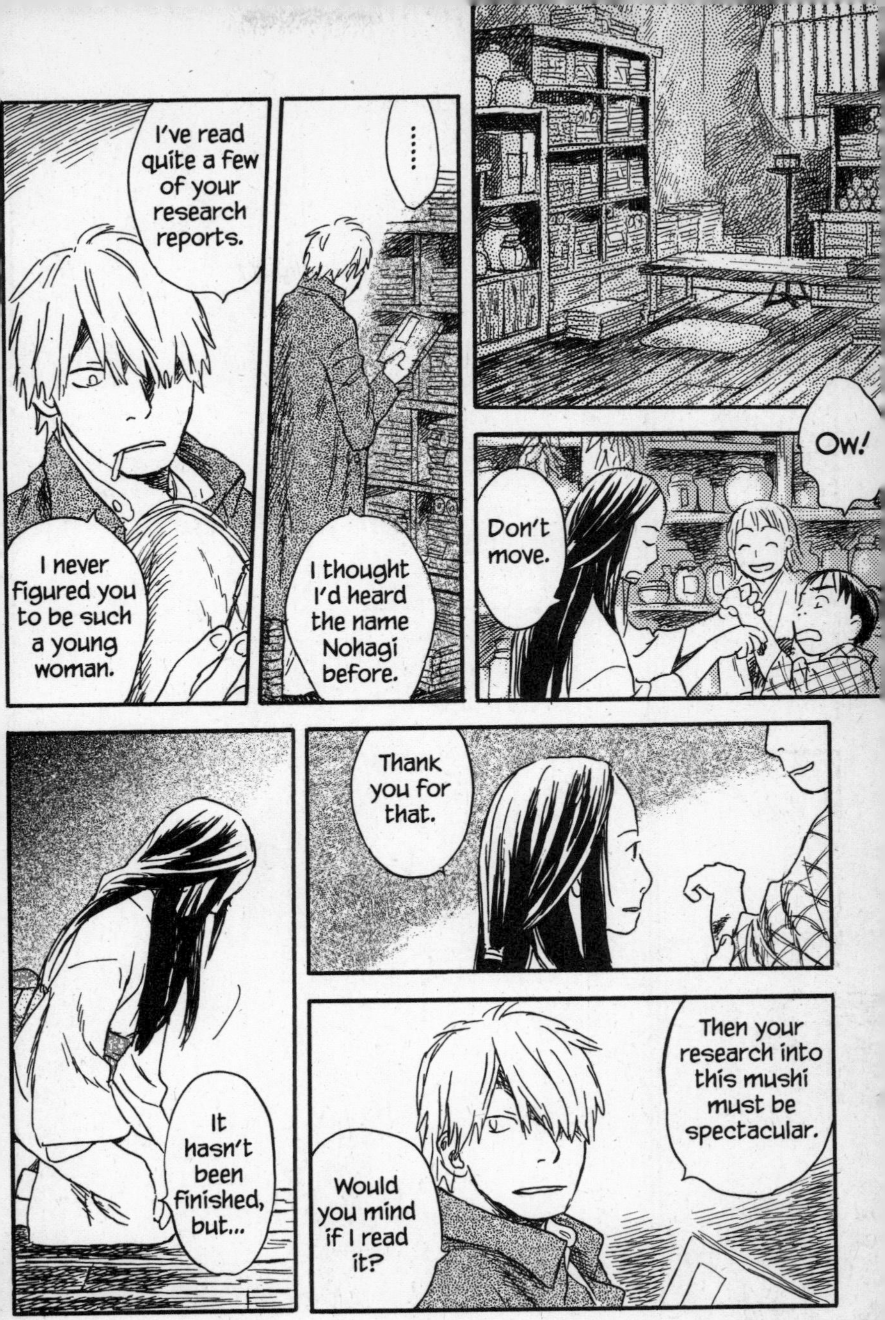
Ow!
Don't move.
......
I thought I'd heard the name Nohagi before.
I've read quite a few of your research reports.
I never figured you to be such a young woman.
Thank you for that.
Then your research into this mushi must be spectacular.
Would you mind if I read it?
It hasn't been finished, but...

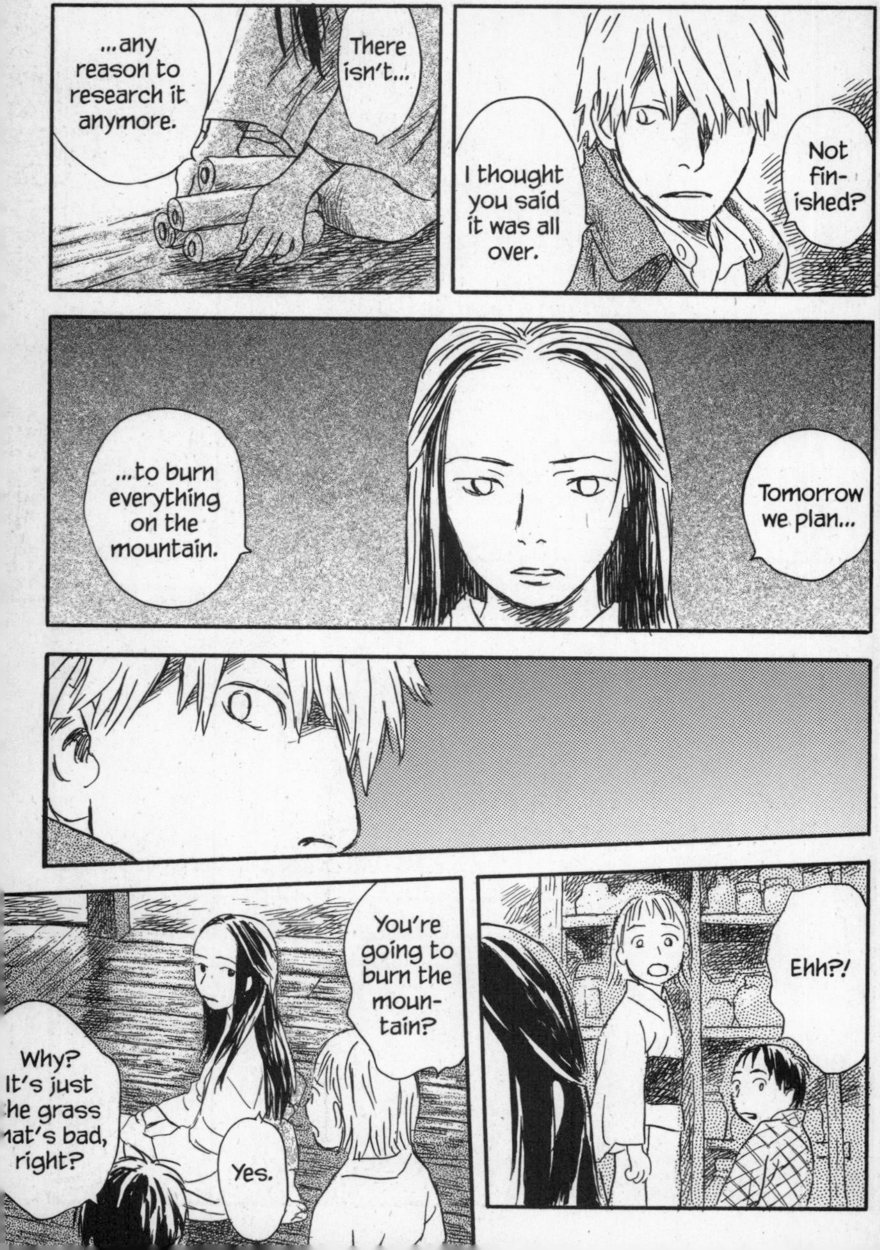
Not fin-ished?
I thought you said it was all over.
There isn't...
...any reason to research it anymore.
Tomorrow we plan...
...to burn everything on the mountain.
Ehh?!
You're going to burn the mountain?
Why? It's just he grass hat's bad, right?
Yes.

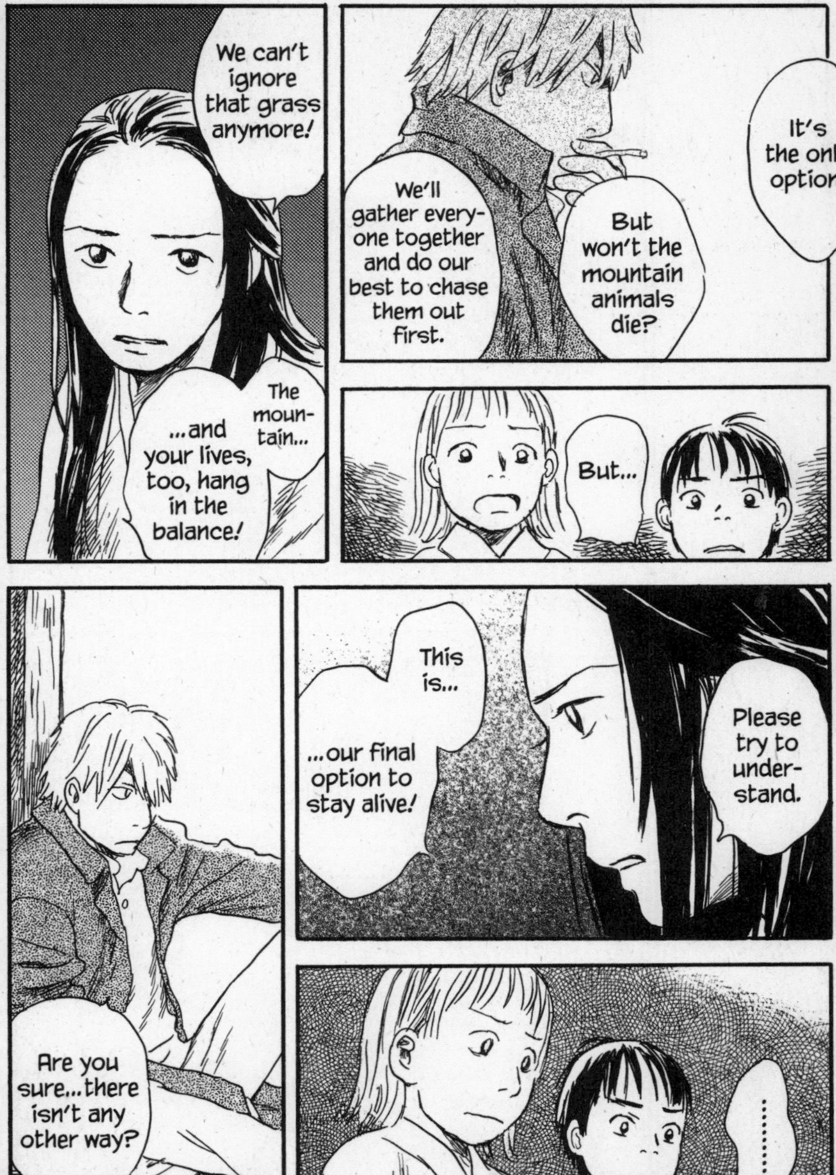
It's the only option.
But won't the mountain animals die?
We'll gather every-one together and do our best to chase them out first.
But...
We can't ignore that grass anymore!
The moun-tain...
...and your lives, too, hang in the balance!
Please try to under-stand.
This is...
...our final option to stay alive!
......
Are you sure...there isn't any other way?

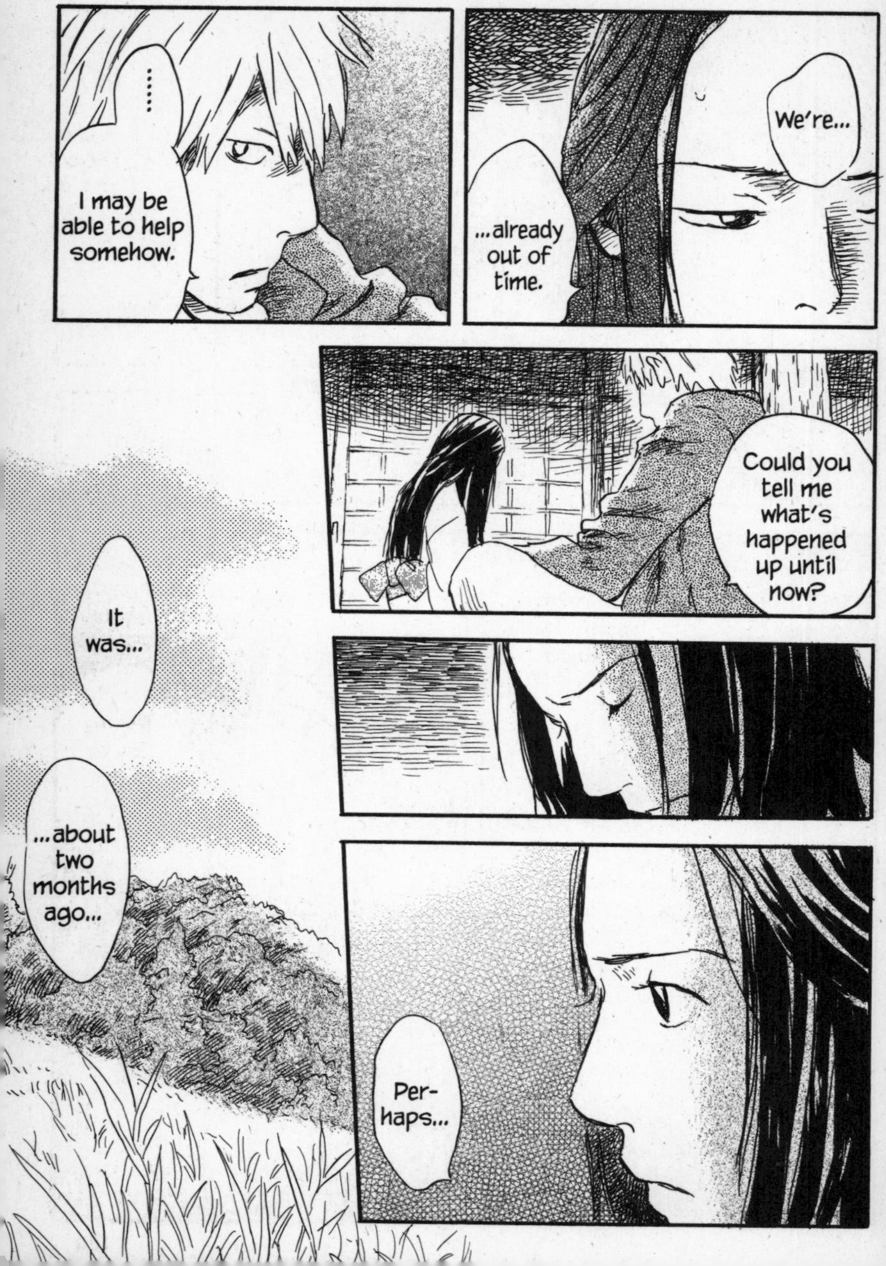
We're...
...already out of time.
......
I may be able to help somehow.
Could you tell me what's happened up until now?
Per-haps...
It was...
...about two months ago...

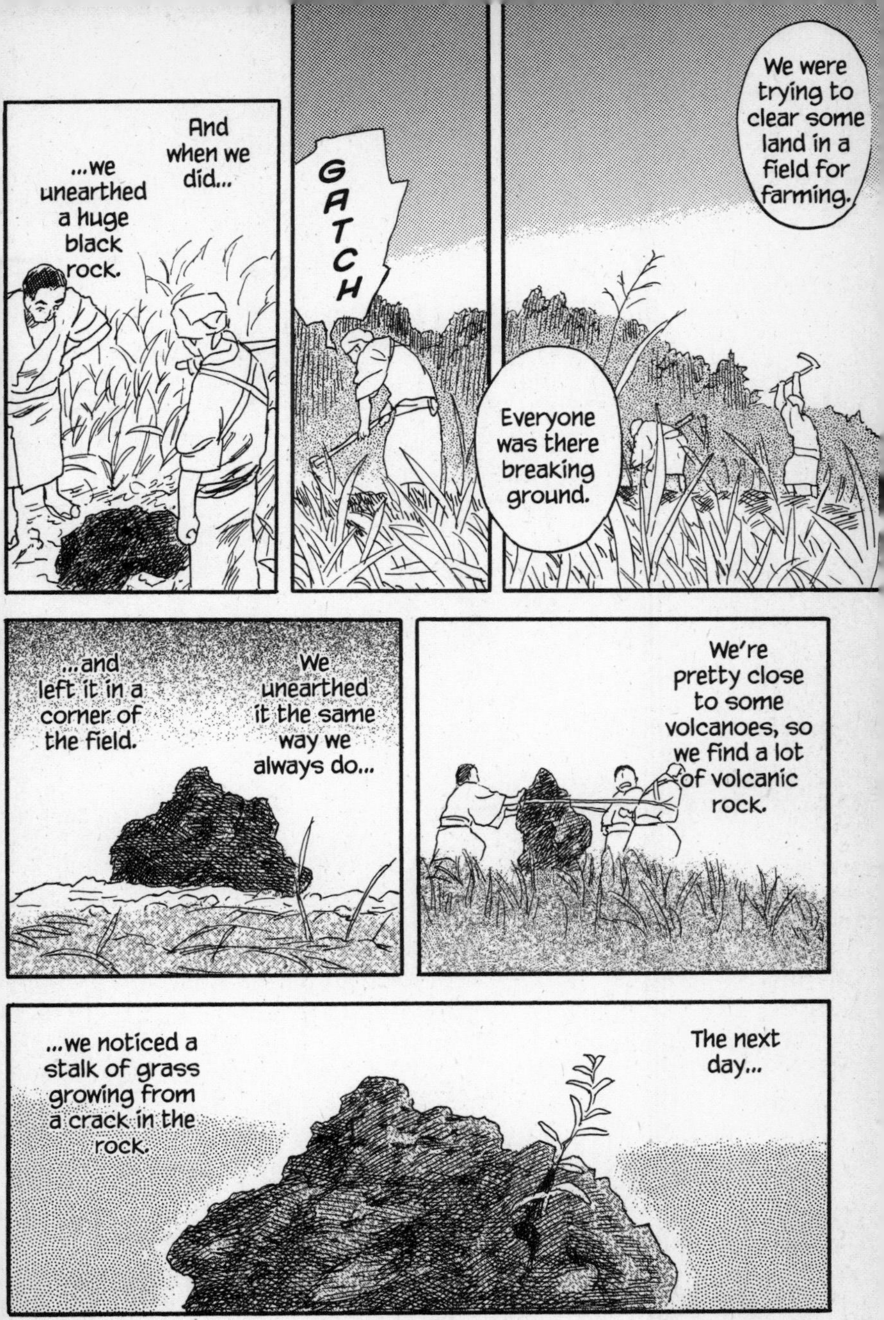
We were trying to clear some land in a field for farming.
Everyone was there breaking ground.
GATCH
And when we did...
...we unearthed a huge black rock.
We're pretty close to some volcanoes, so we find a lot of volcanic rock.
We unearthed it the same way we always do...
...and left it in a corner of the field.
The next day...
...we noticed a stalk of grass growing from a crack in the rock.

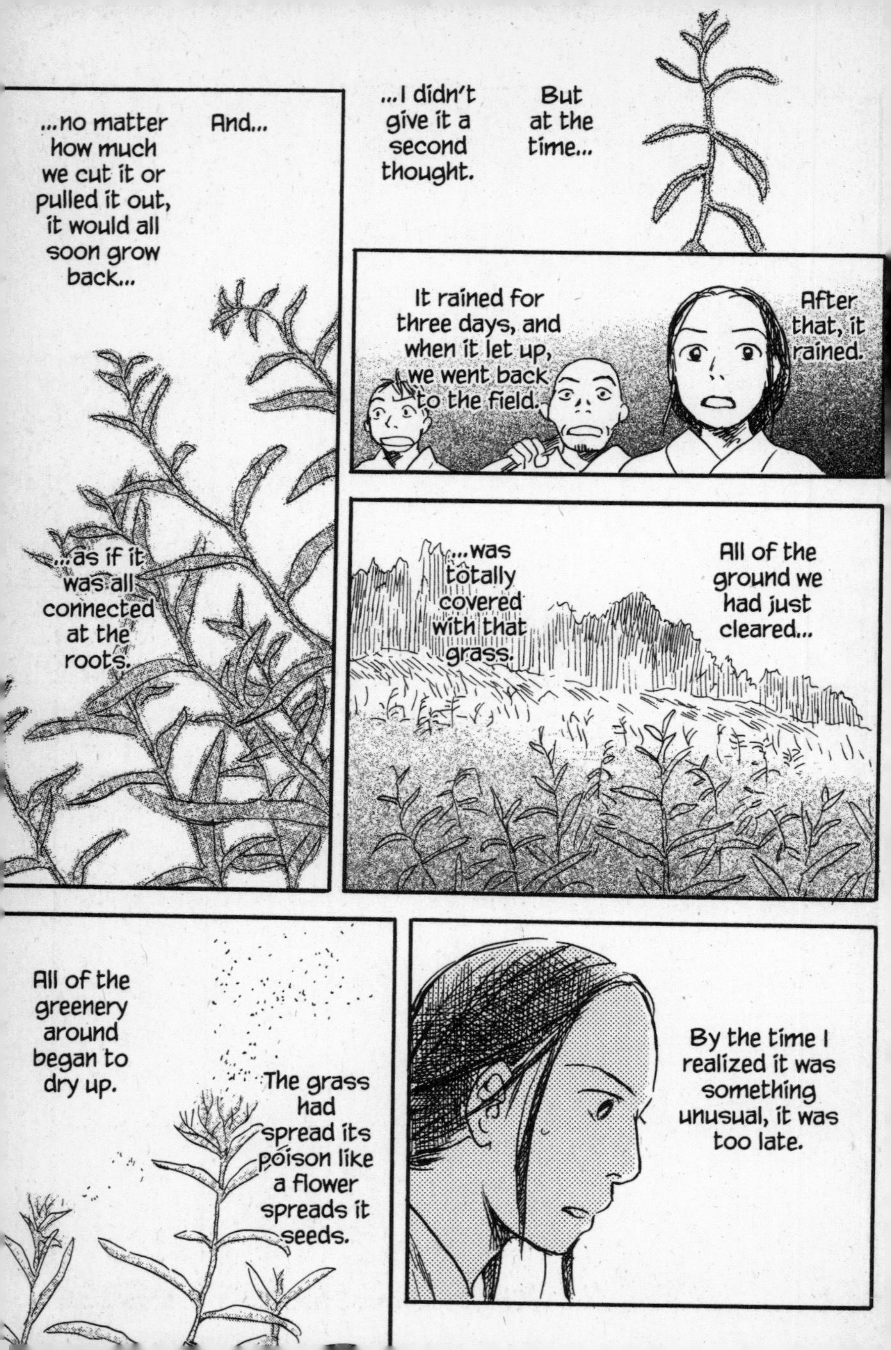
But at the time...
...I didn't give it a second thought.
After that, it rained.
It rained for three days, and when it let up, we went back to the field.
All of the ground we had just cleared...
...was totally covered with that grass.
And...
...no matter how much we cut it or pulled it out, it would all soon grow back...
...as if it was all connected at the roots.
By the time I realized it was something unusual, it was too late.
The grass had spread its poison like a flower spreads it seeds.
All of the greenery around began to dry up.

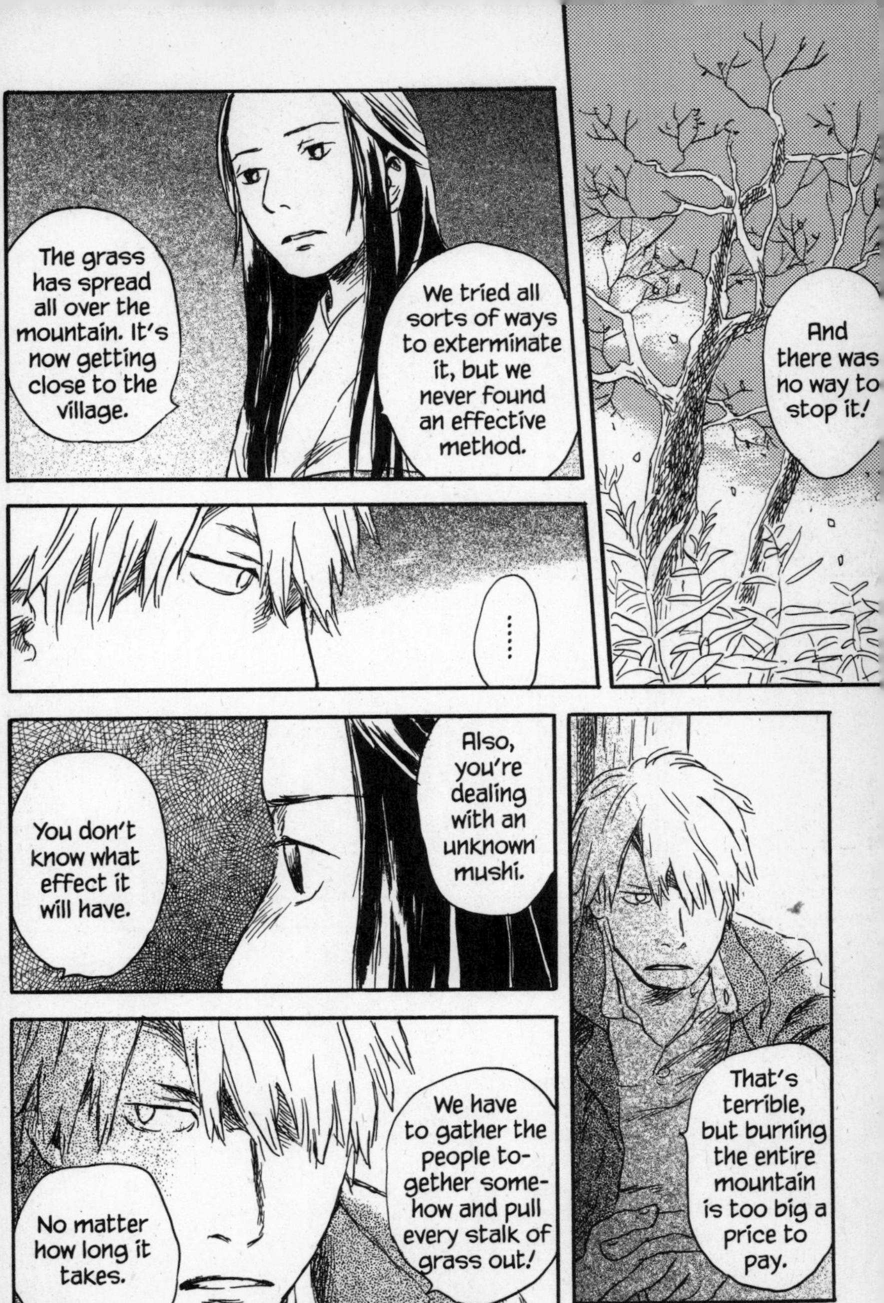
And there was no way to stop it!
We tried all sorts of ways to exterminate it, but we never found an effective method.
The grass has spread all over the mountain. It's now getting close to the village.
......
That's terrible, but burning the entire mountain is too big a price to pay.
Also, you're dealing with an unknown mushi.
You don't know what effect it will have.
We have to gather the people to-gether some-how and pull every stalk of grass out!
No matter how long it takes.

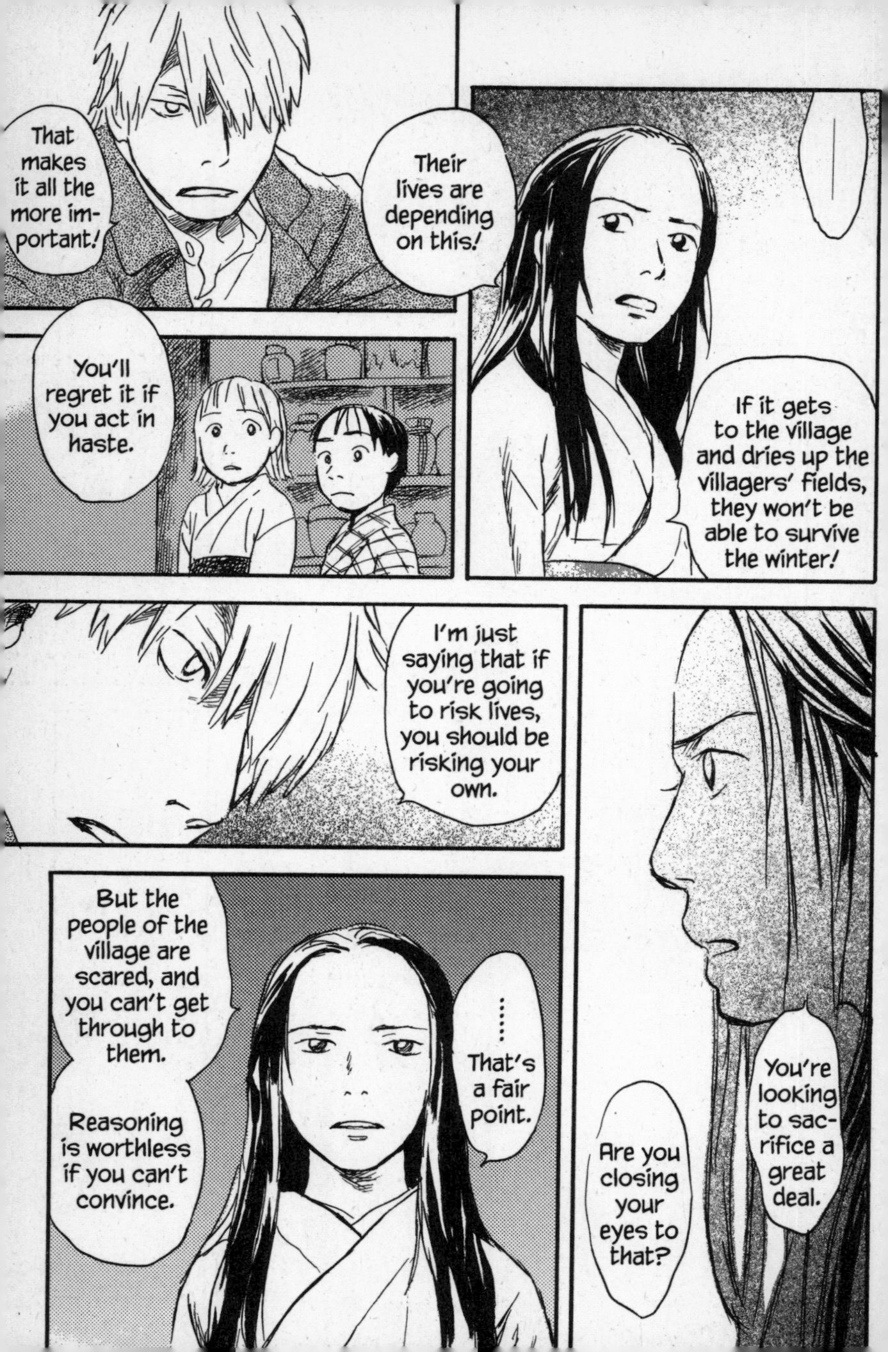

Their lives are depending on this!
If it gets to the village and dries up the villagers' fields, they won't be able to survive the winter!
That makes it all the more important!
You'll regret it if you act in haste.
You're looking to sacrifice a great deal.
Are you closing your eyes to that?
I'm just saying that if you're going to risk lives, you should be risking your own.
......
That's a fair point.
But the people of the village are scared, and you can't get through to them.
Reasoning is worthless if you can't convince.

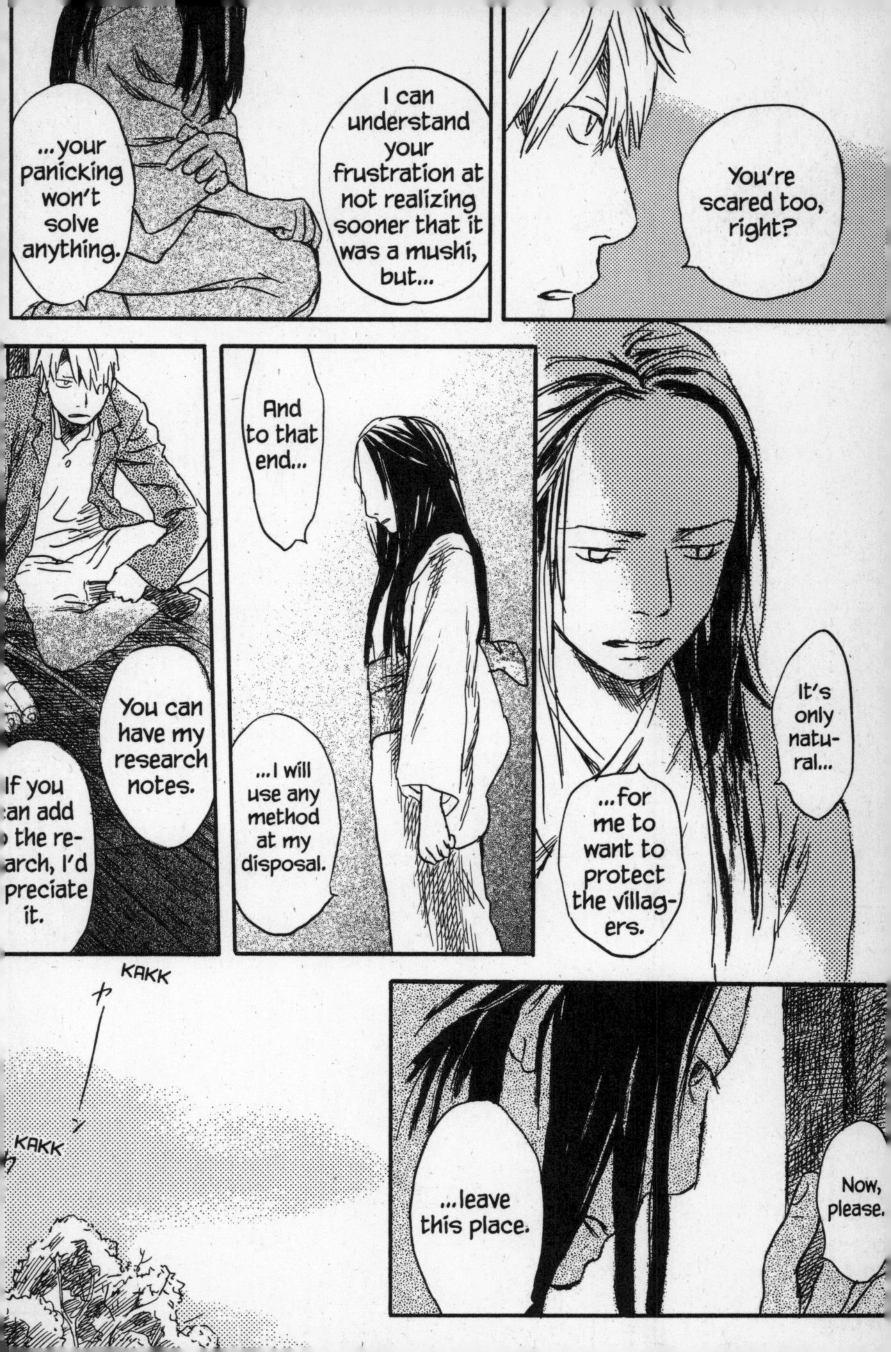
You're scared too, right?
I can understand your frustration at not realizing sooner that it was a mushi, but...
...your panicking won't solve anything.
It's only natural...
...for me to want to protect the villagers.
And to that end...
...I will use any method at my disposal.
You can have my research notes.
If you an add the re- arch, I'd preciate it.
Now, please.
...leave this place.
KAKK
KAKK

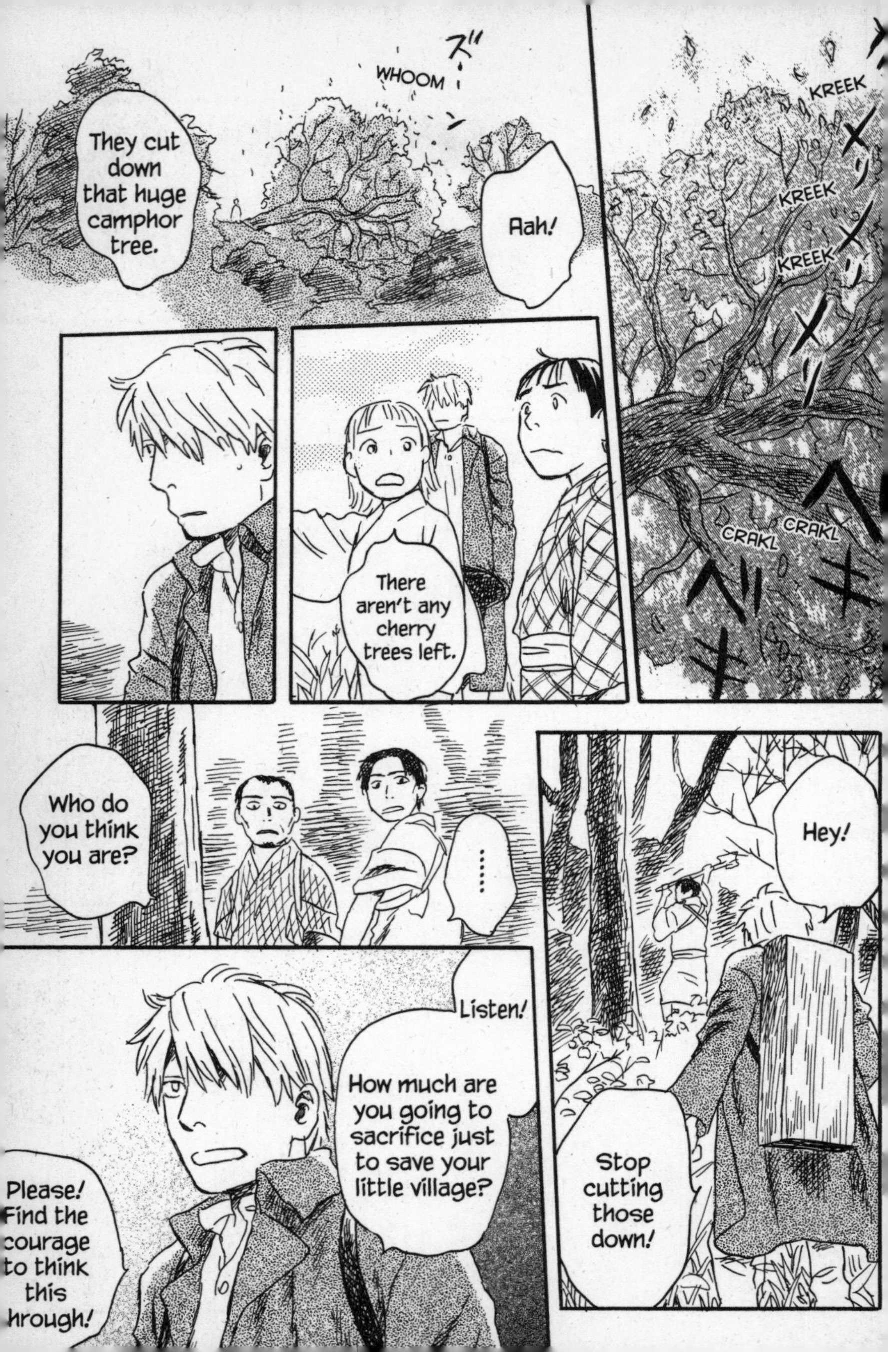
KREEK
KREEK
KREEK
CRAKL
CRAKL
WHOOM
Aah!
They cut down that huge camphor tree.
There aren't any cherry trees left.
Hey!
Stop cutting those down!
......
Who do you think you are?
Listen!
How much are you going to sacrifice just to save your little village?
Please! Find the courage to think this hrough!

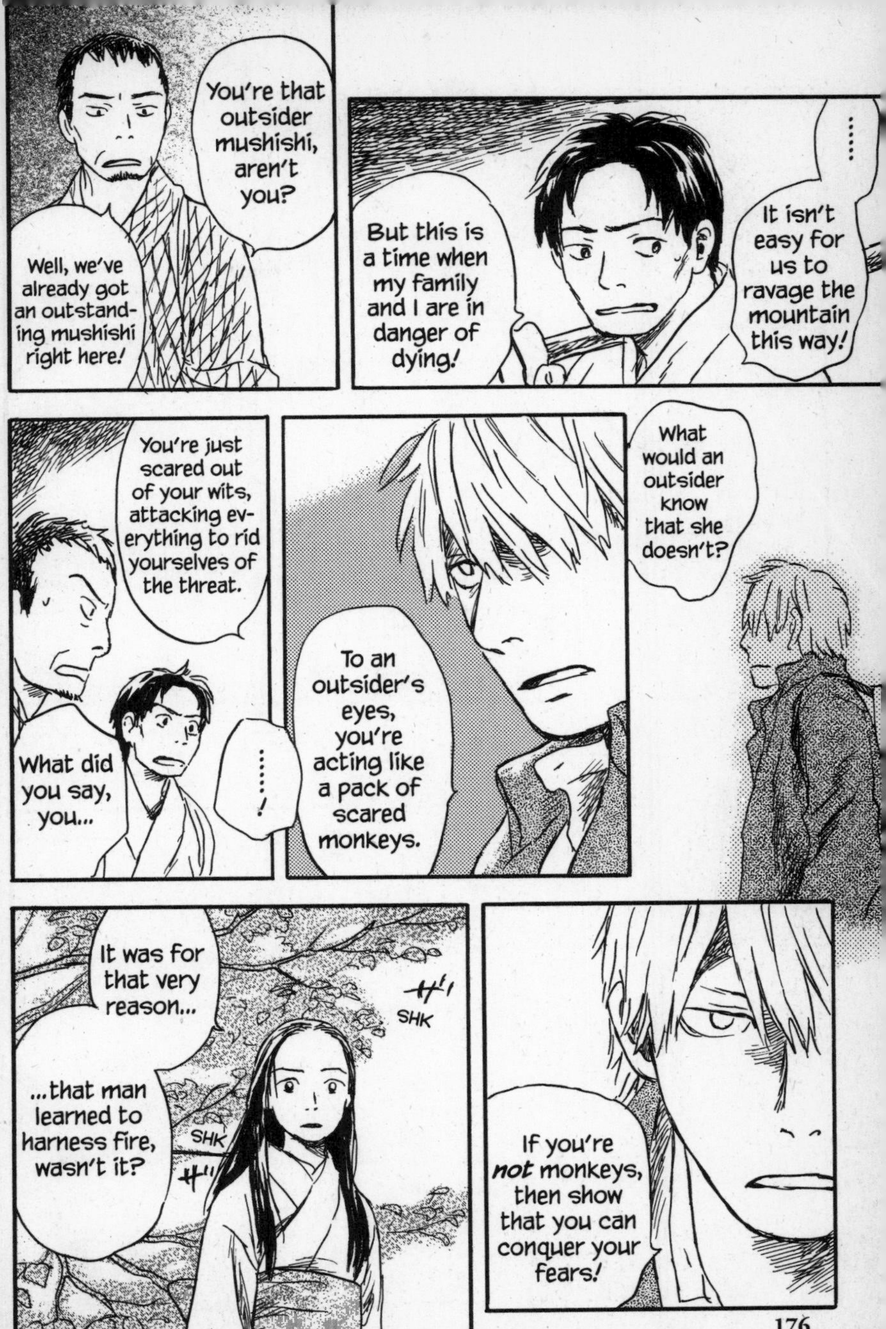
……
It isn't easy for us to ravage the mountain this way!
But this is a time when my family and I are in danger of dying!
You're that outsider mushishi, aren't you?
Well, we've already got an outstand-ing mushishi right here!
What would an outsider know that she doesn't?
To an outsider's eyes, you're acting like a pack of scared monkeys.
You're just scared out of your wits, attacking ev-erything to rid yourselves of the threat.
……!
What did you say, you...
If you're *not* monkeys, then show that you can conquer your fears!
It was for that very reason...
SHK
...that man learned to harness fire, wasn't it?
SHK

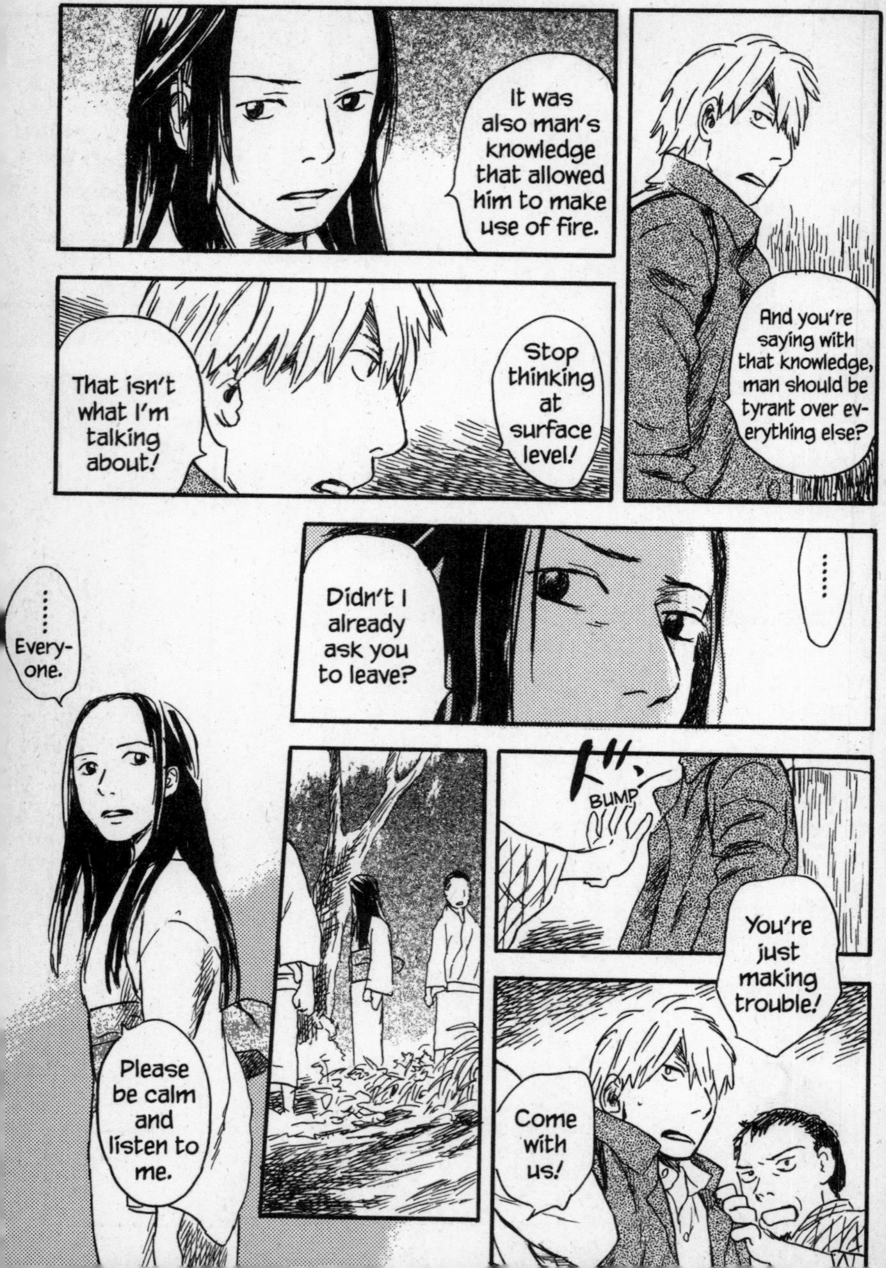

And you're saying with that knowledge, man should be tyrant over ev-erything else?
It was also man's knowledge that allowed him to make use of fire.
Stop thinking at surface level!
That isn't what I'm talking about!
……
Didn't I already ask you to leave?
ドッ
BUMP
You're just making trouble!
Come with us!
…… Every-one.
Please be calm and listen to me.

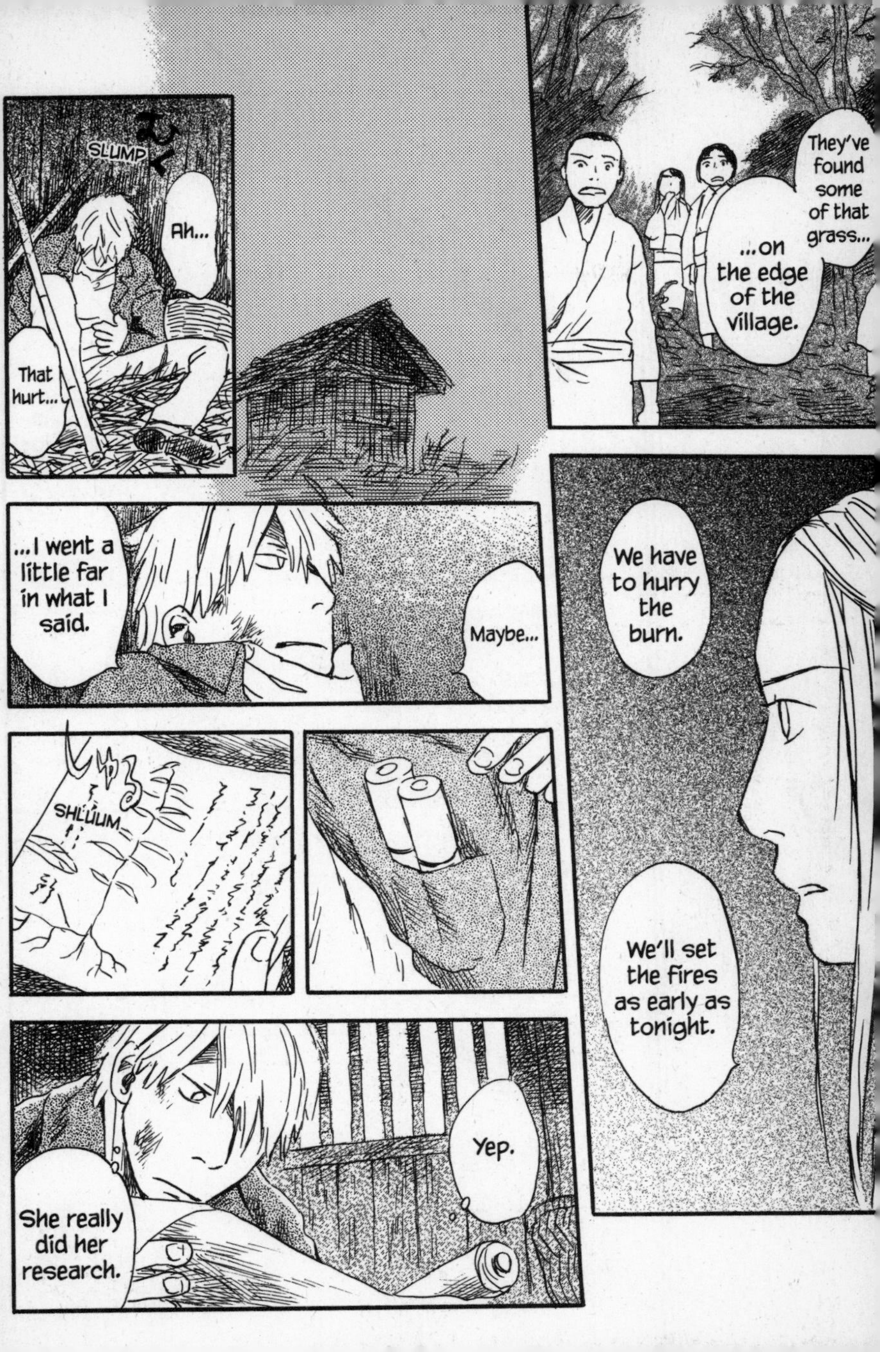
They've found some of that grass...
...on the edge of the village.
SLUMP
Ah...
That hurt...
We have to hurry the burn.
We'll set the fires as early as tonight.
Maybe...
...I went a little far in what I said.
SHLUUM
Yep.
She really did her research.

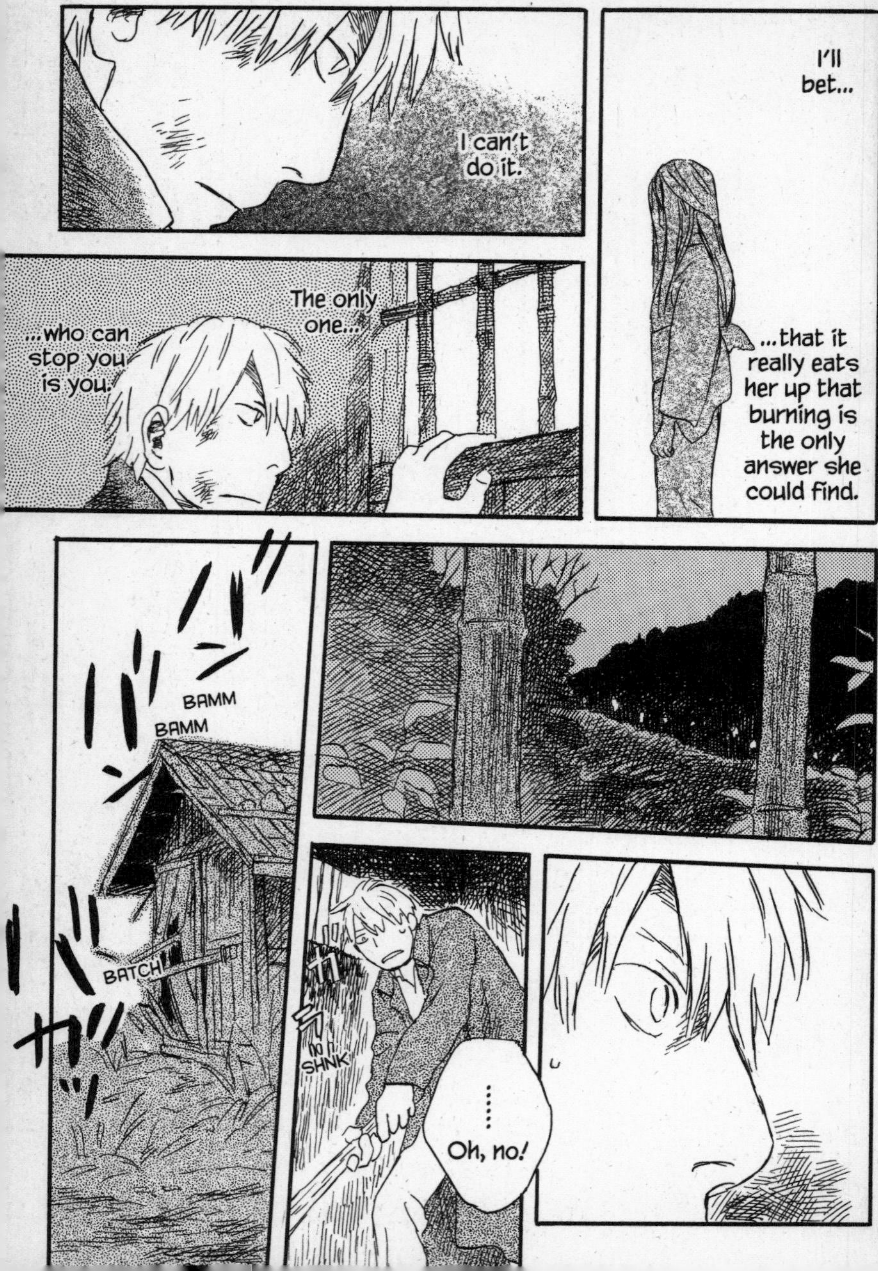
I'll bet...
...that it really eats her up that burning is the only answer she could find.
I can't do it.
The only one...
...who can stop you is you.
......
Oh, no!
SHNK
BAMM
BAMM
BATCH

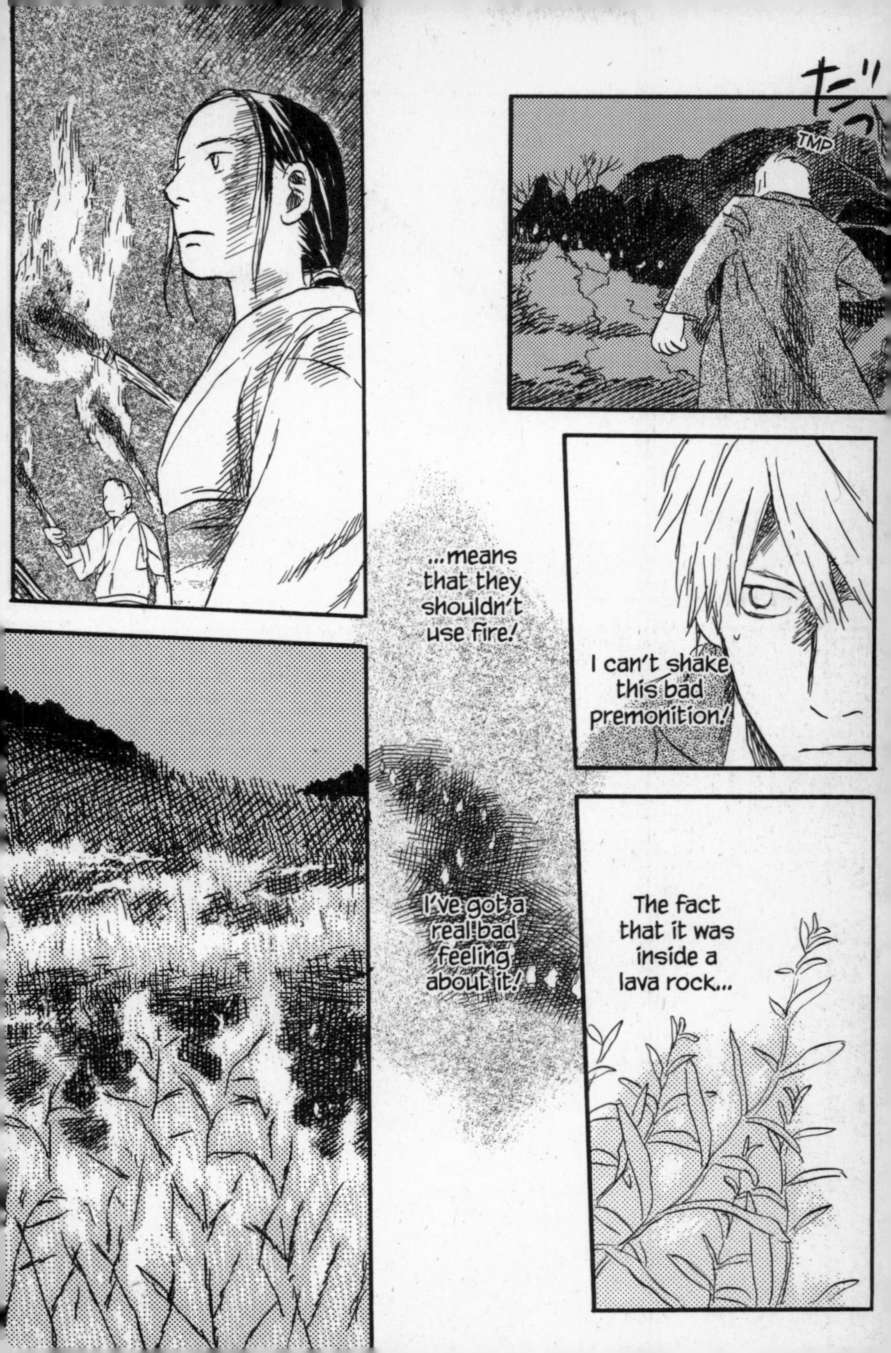
TMP
I can't shake this bad premonition!
...means that they shouldn't use fire!
The fact that it was inside a lava rock...
I've got a real bad feeling about it!

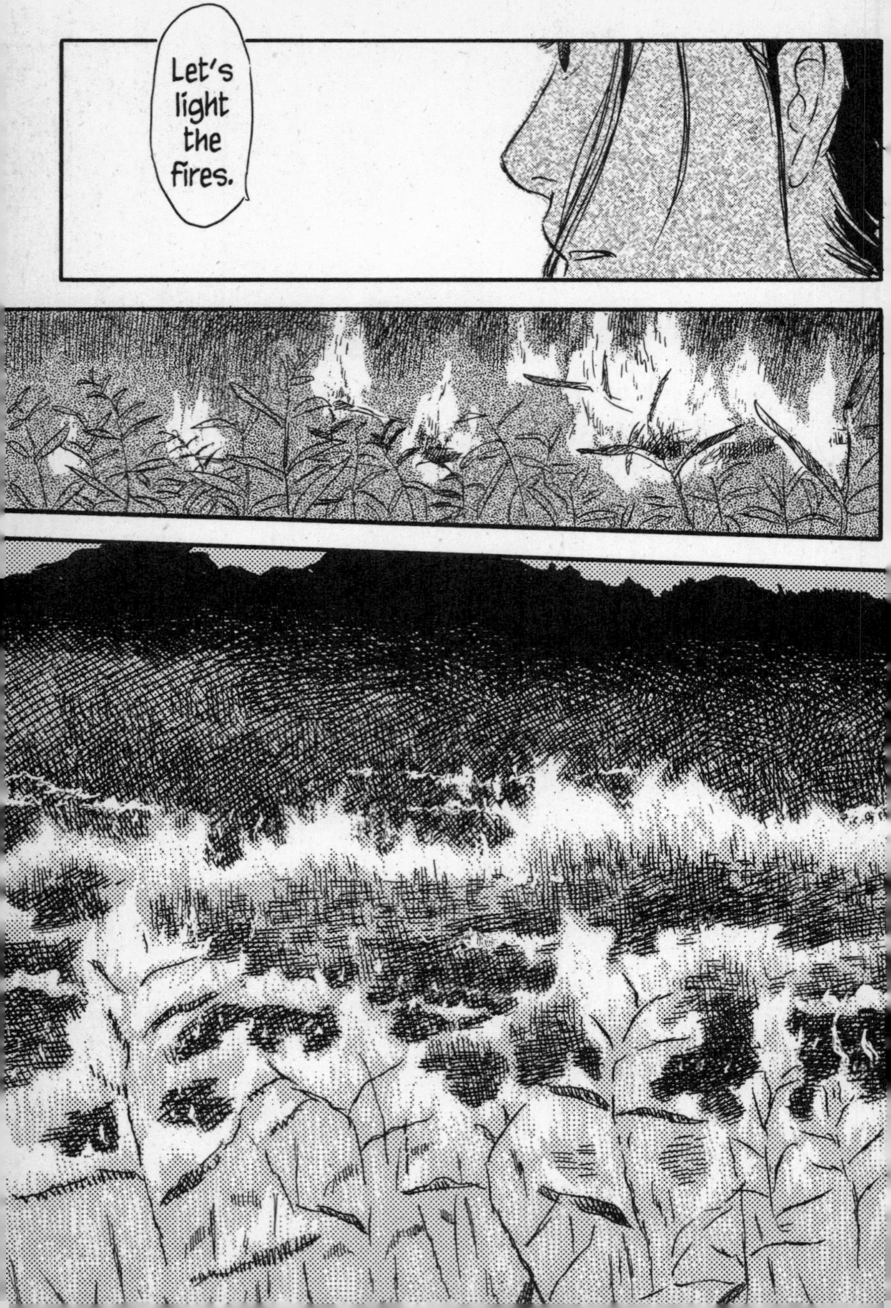
Let's light the fires.

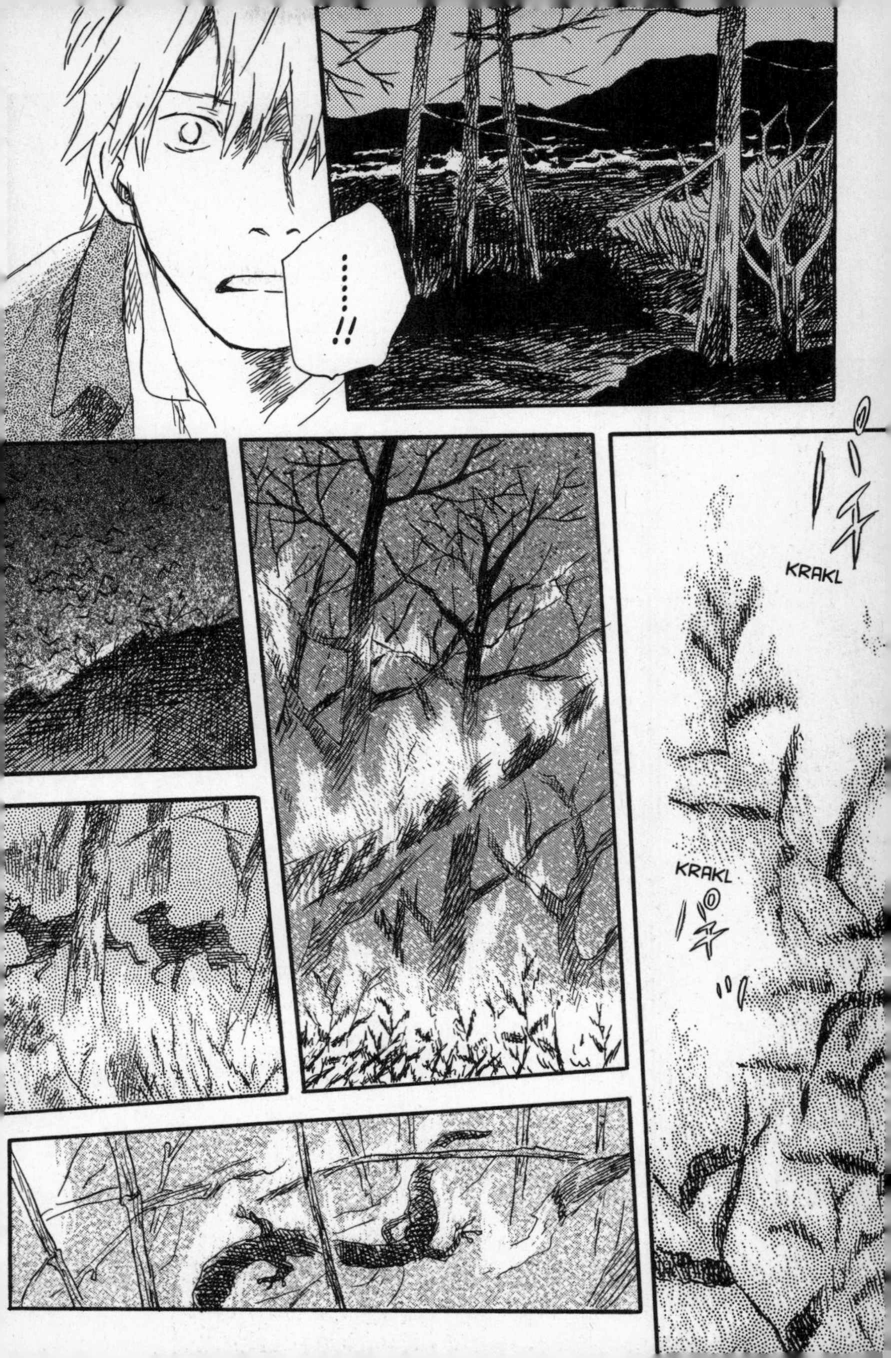
......!!
KRAKL
KRAKL

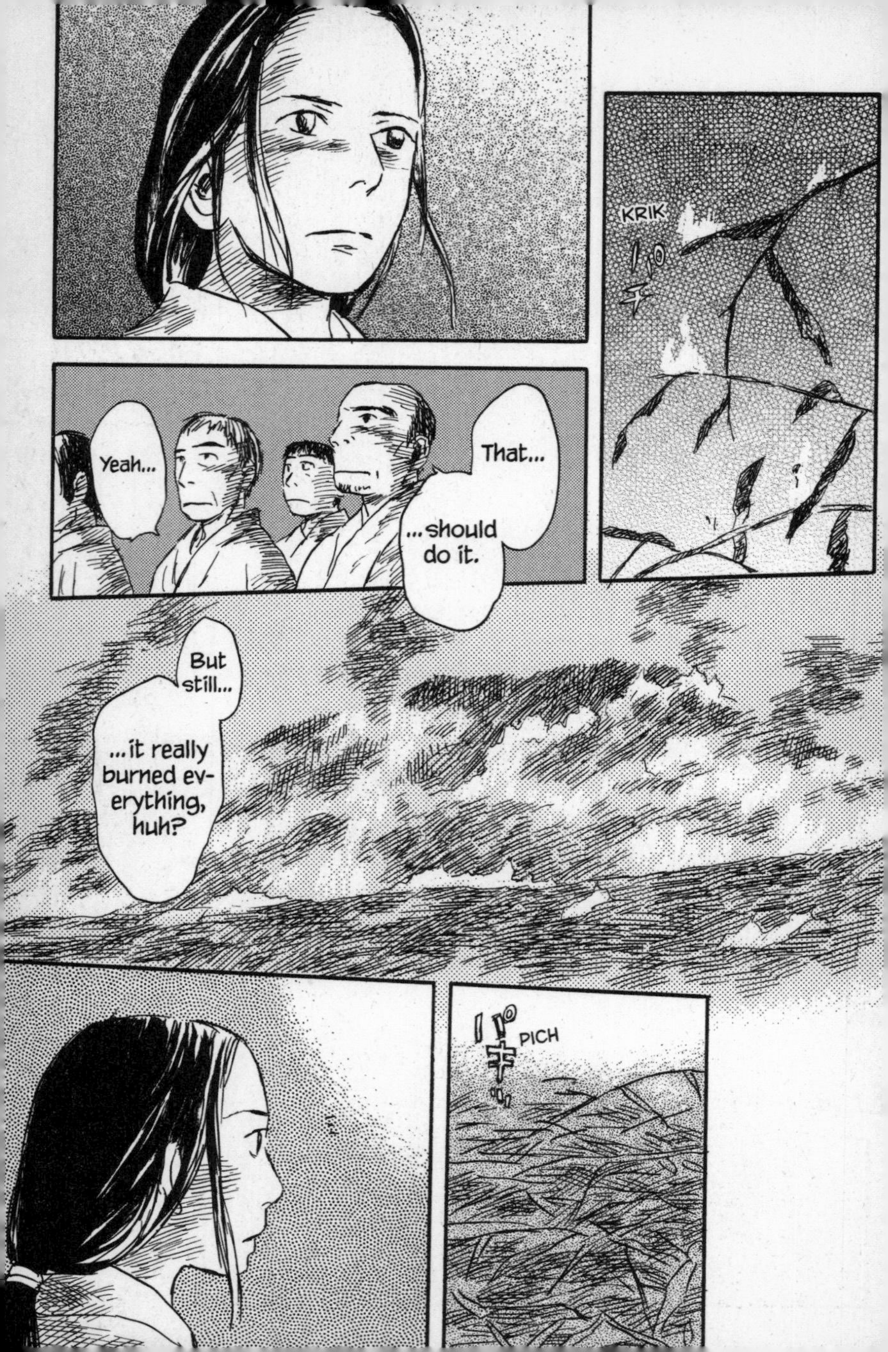
KRIK
That...
...should do it.
Yeah...
But still...
...it really burned everything, huh?
PICH

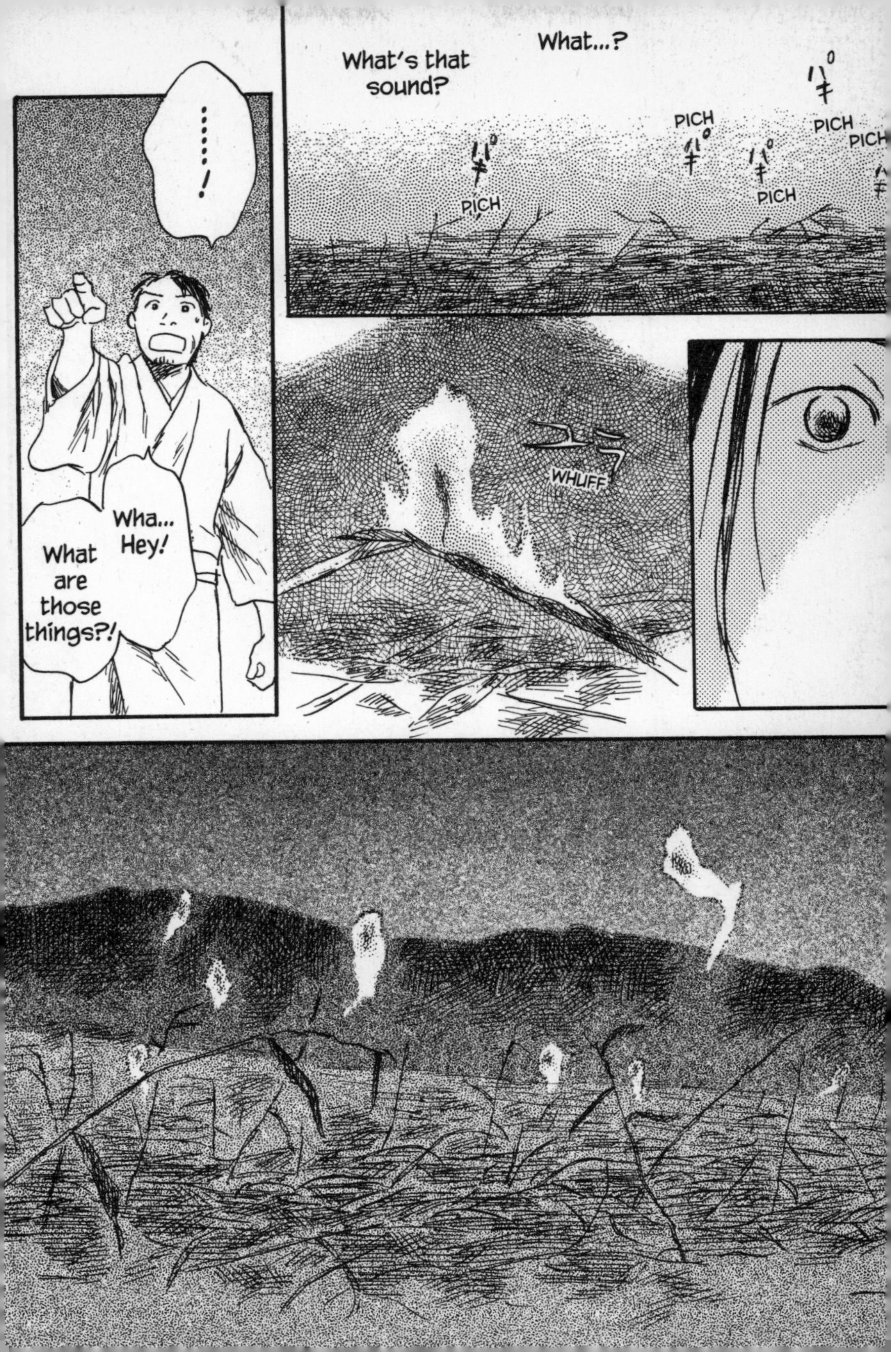
What...?
What's that sound?
パキ
PICH
PICH
PICH
PICH
PICH
WHUFF
......!
Wha... Hey!
What are those things?!

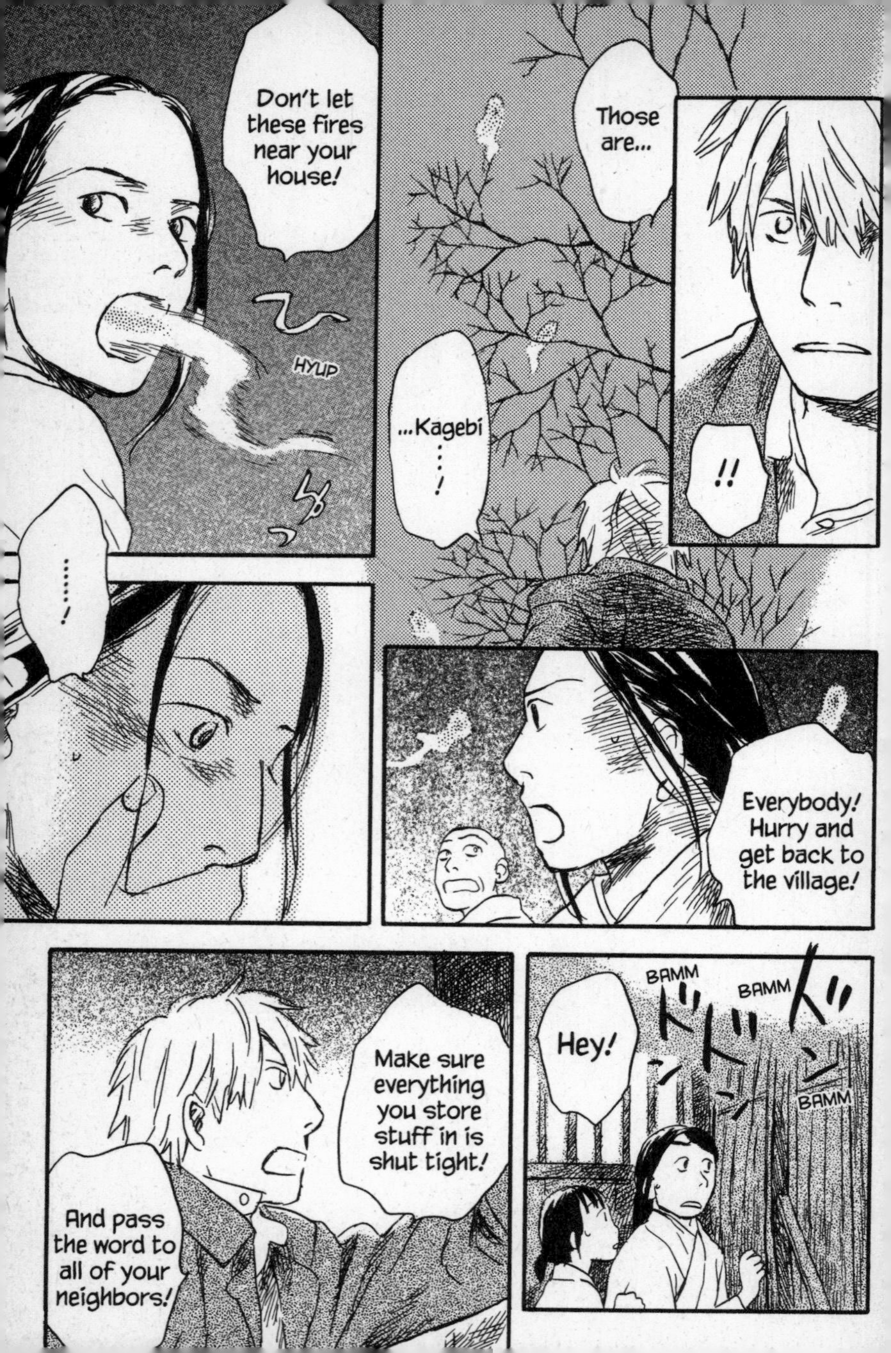

Those are...
!!
...Kagebi...!
Don't let these fires near your house!
HYUP
Everybody! Hurry and get back to the village!
......!
Hey!
BAMM
BAMM
BAMM
Make sure everything you store stuff in is shut tight!
And pass the word to all of your neighbors!

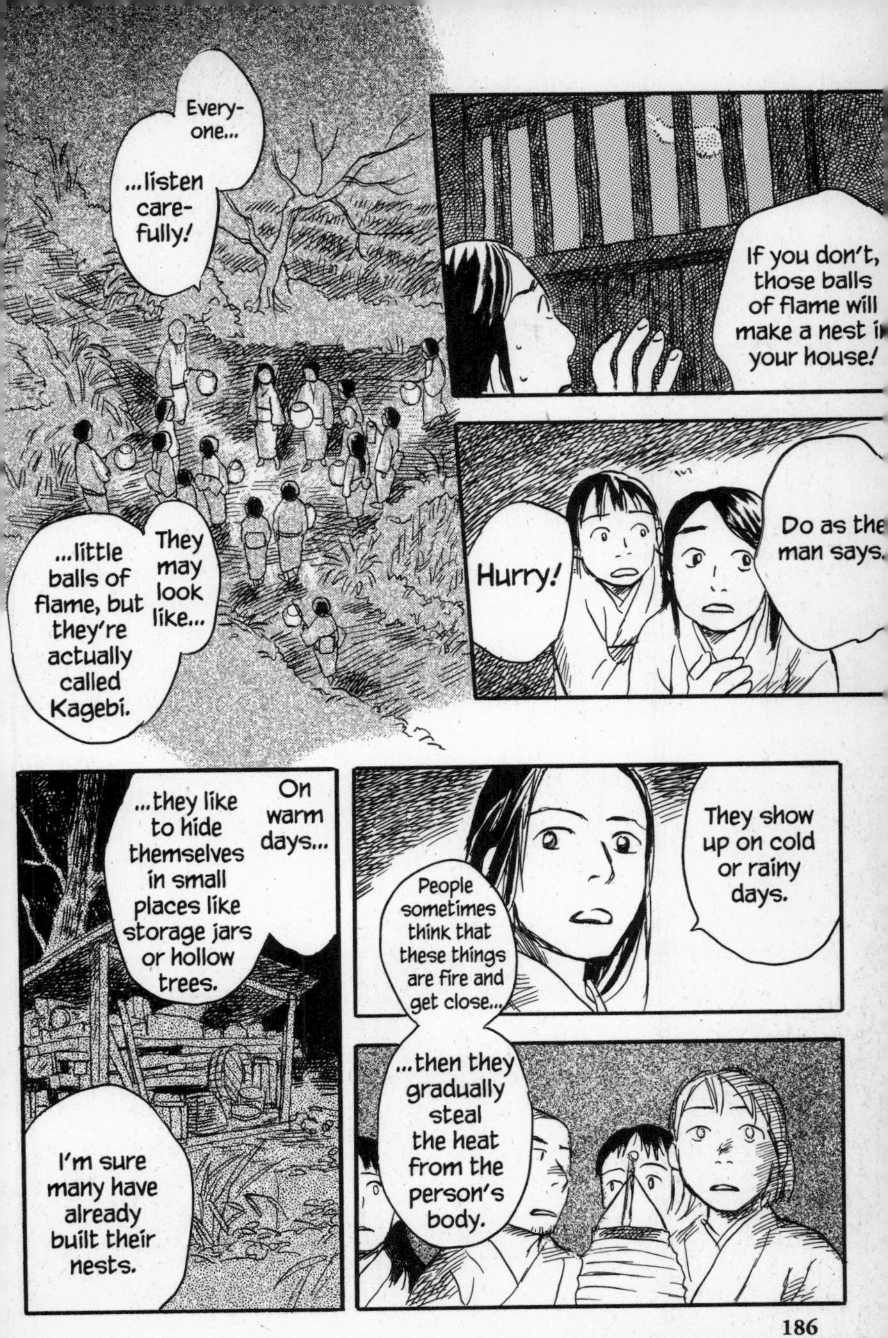
If you don't, those balls of flame will make a nest i[n] your house!
Do as the man says.
Hurry!
Every-one...
...listen care-fully!
They may look like...
...little balls of flame, but they're actually called Kagebi.
They show up on cold or rainy days.
People sometimes think that these things are fire and get close...
...then they gradually steal the heat from the person's body.
On warm days...
...they like to hide themselves in small places like storage jars or hollow trees.
I'm sure many have already built their nests.

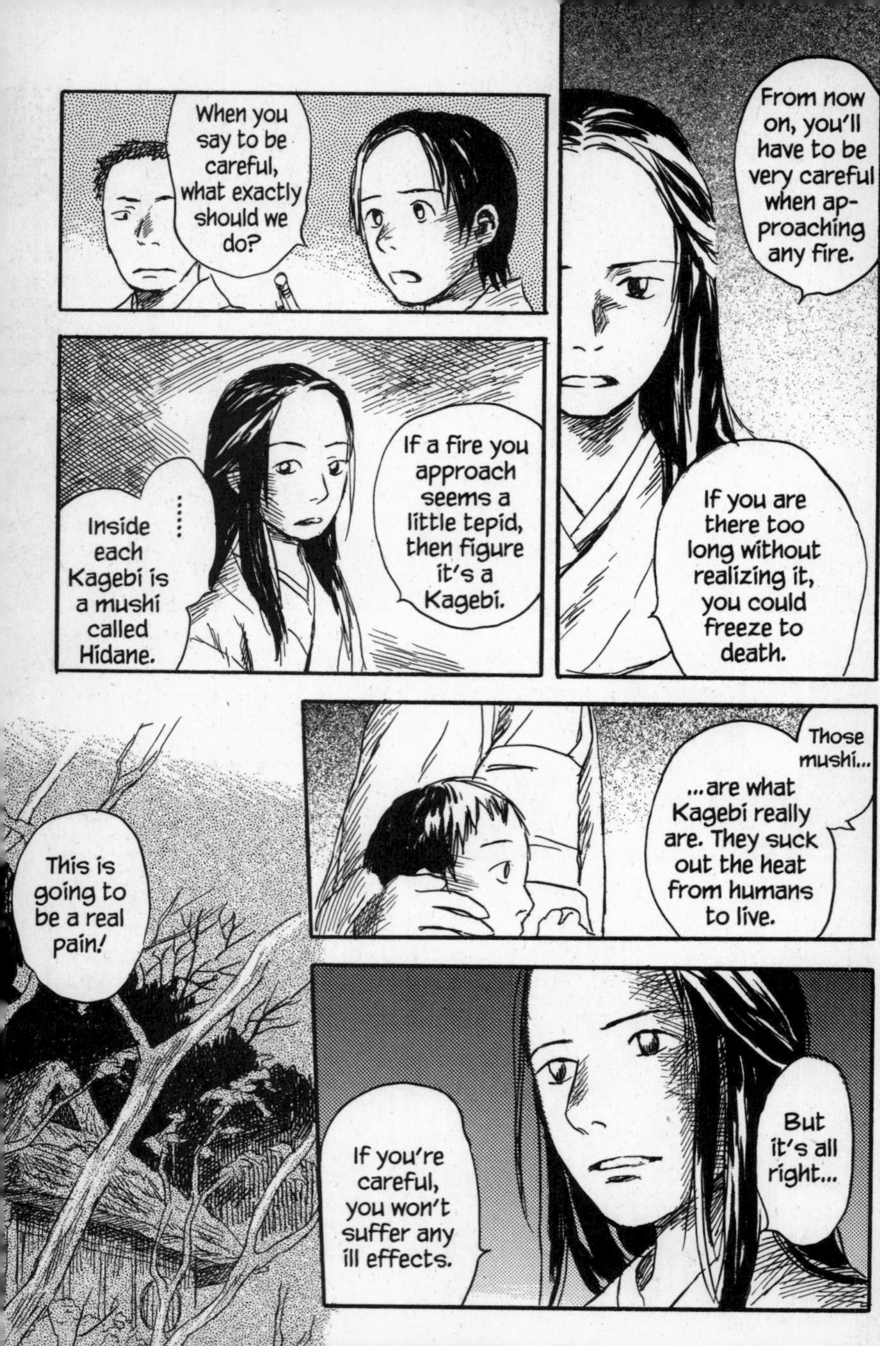
From now on, you'll have to be very careful when approaching any fire.
If you are there too long without realizing it, you could freeze to death.
When you say to be careful, what exactly should we do?
If a fire you approach seems a little tepid, then figure it's a Kagebi.
......
Inside each Kagebi is a mushi called Hidane.
Those mushi...
...are what Kagebi really are. They suck out the heat from humans to live.
But it's all right...
If you're careful, you won't suffer any ill effects.
This is going to be a real pain!

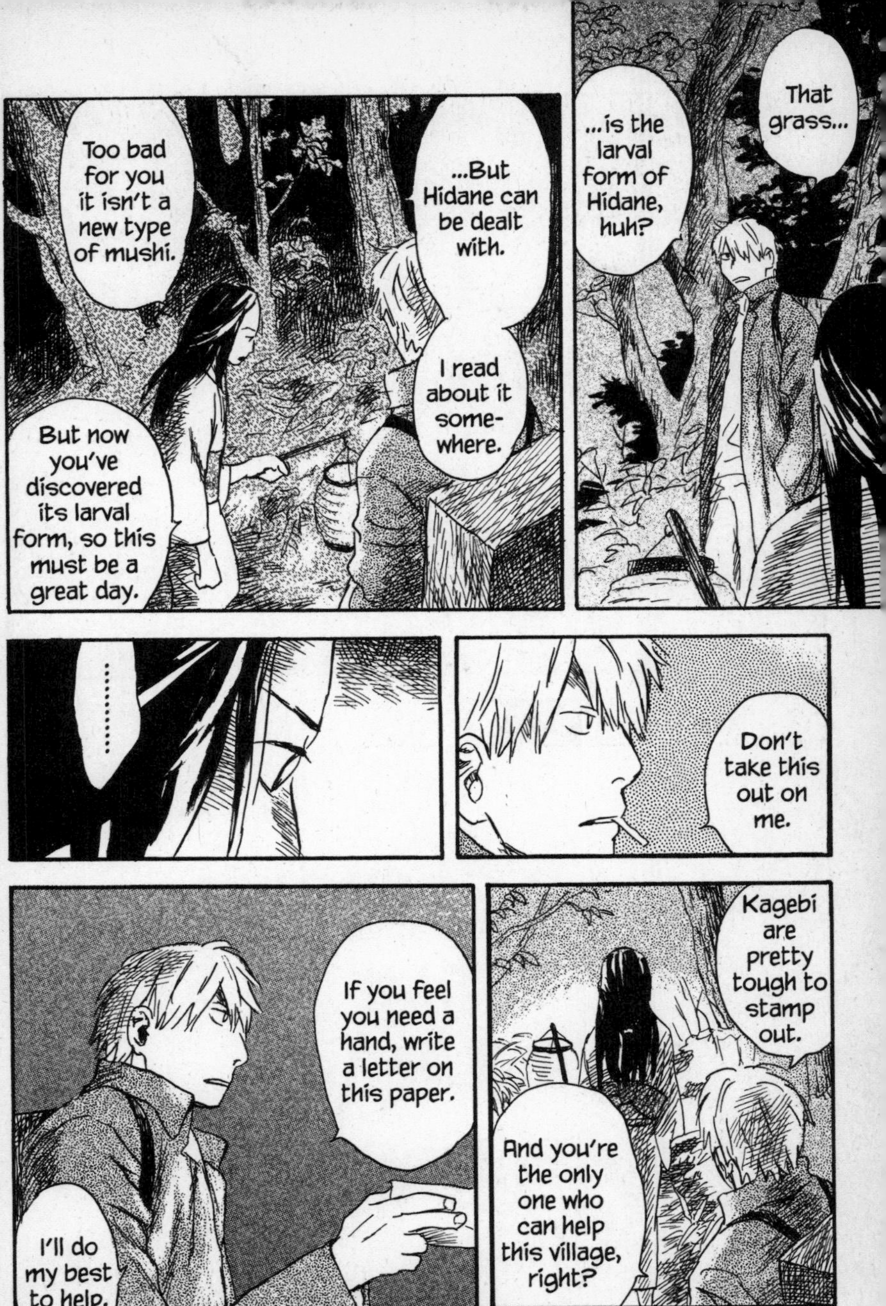
That grass...
...is the larval form of Hidane, huh?
...But Hidane can be dealt with.
I read about it some-where.
Too bad for you it isn't a new type of mushi.
But now you've discovered its larval form, so this must be a great day.
Don't take this out on me.
......
Kagebi are pretty tough to stamp out.
And you're the only one who can help this village, right?
If you feel you need a hand, write a letter on this paper.
I'll do my best to help.

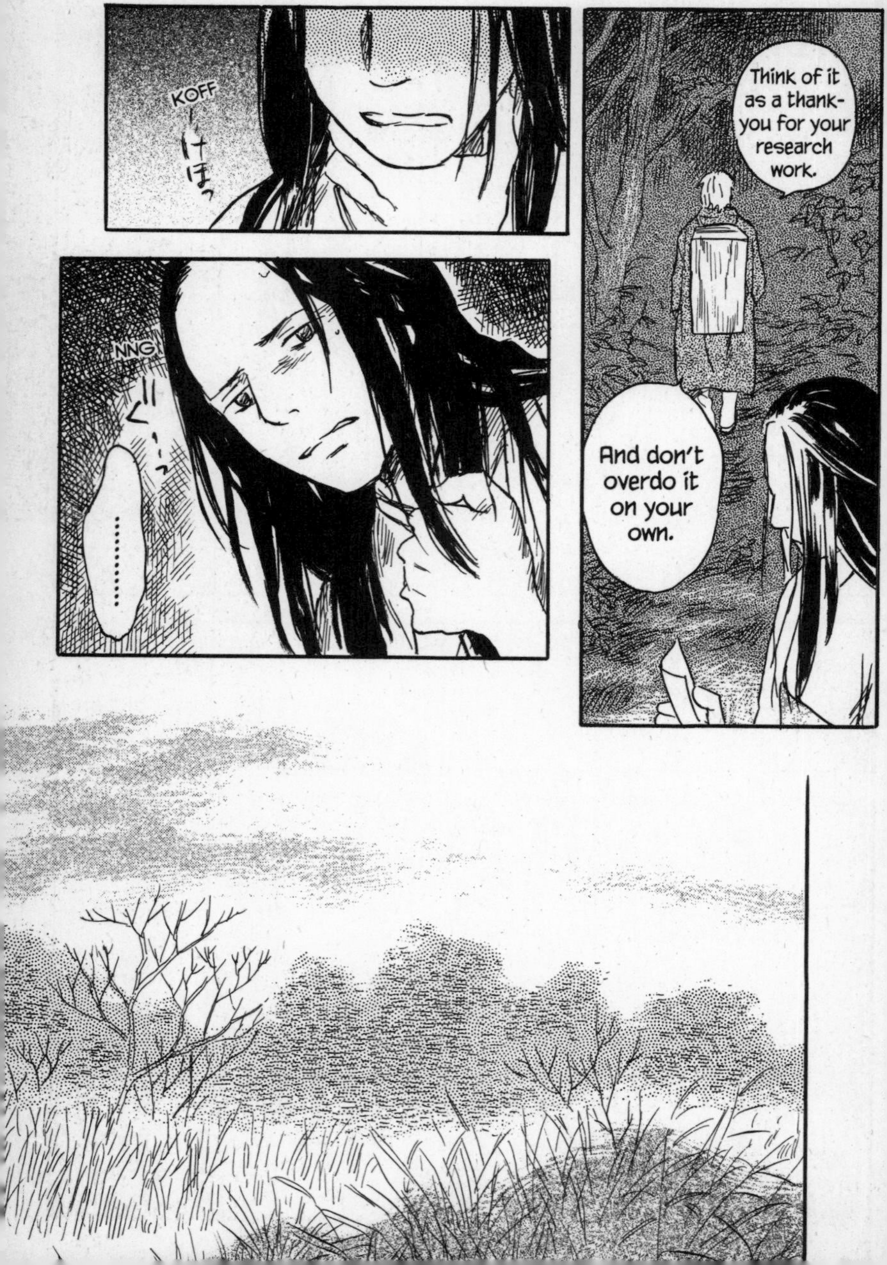
Think of it as a thank-you for your research work.
And don't overdo it on your own.
KOFF
けほっ
NNG
くっ
......

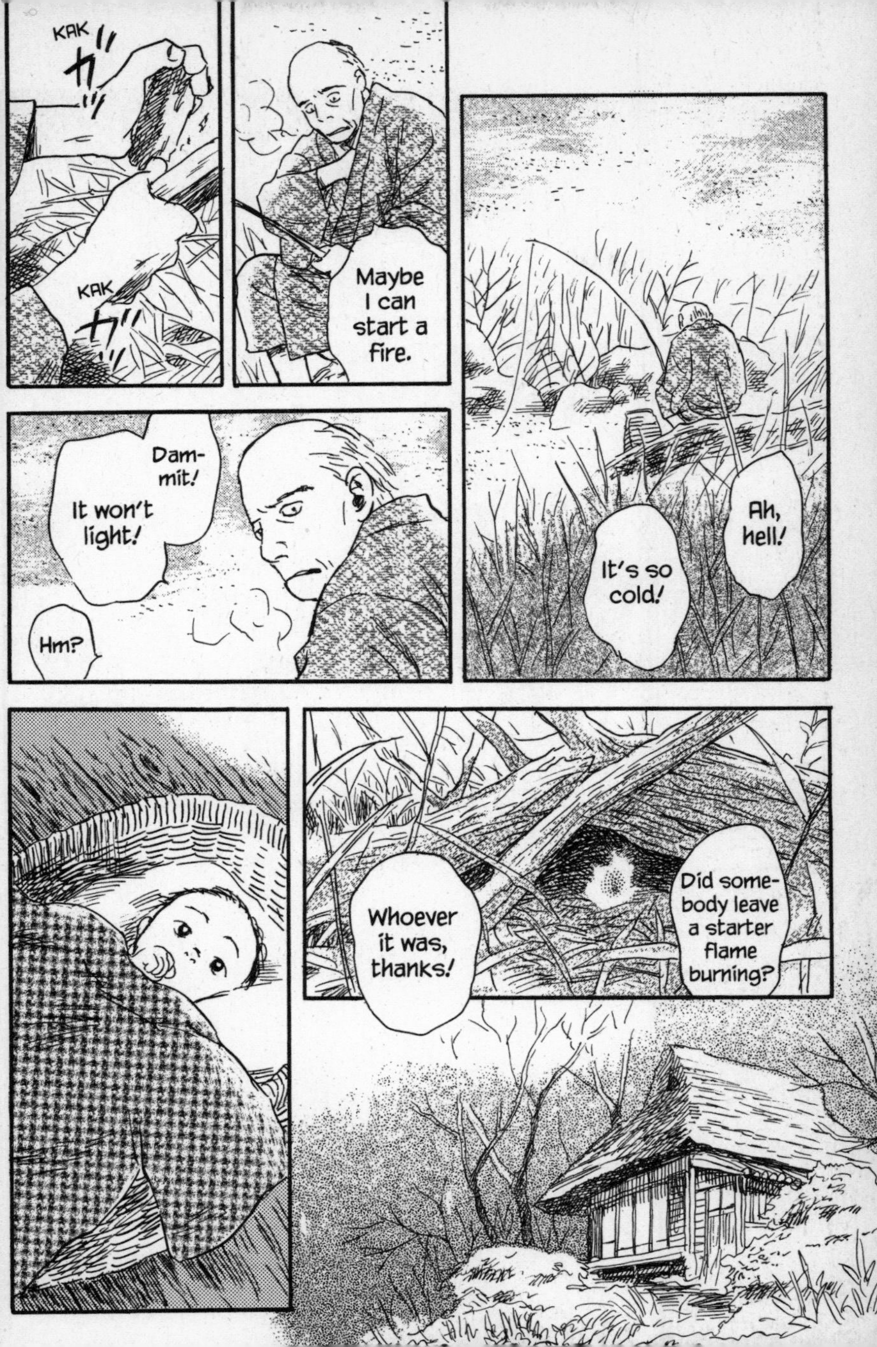

Ah, hell!
It's so cold!
Maybe I can start a fire.
KAK
ガ
KAK
ガ
Dam-mit!
It won't light!
Hm?
Did some-body leave a starter flame burning?
Whoever it was, thanks!

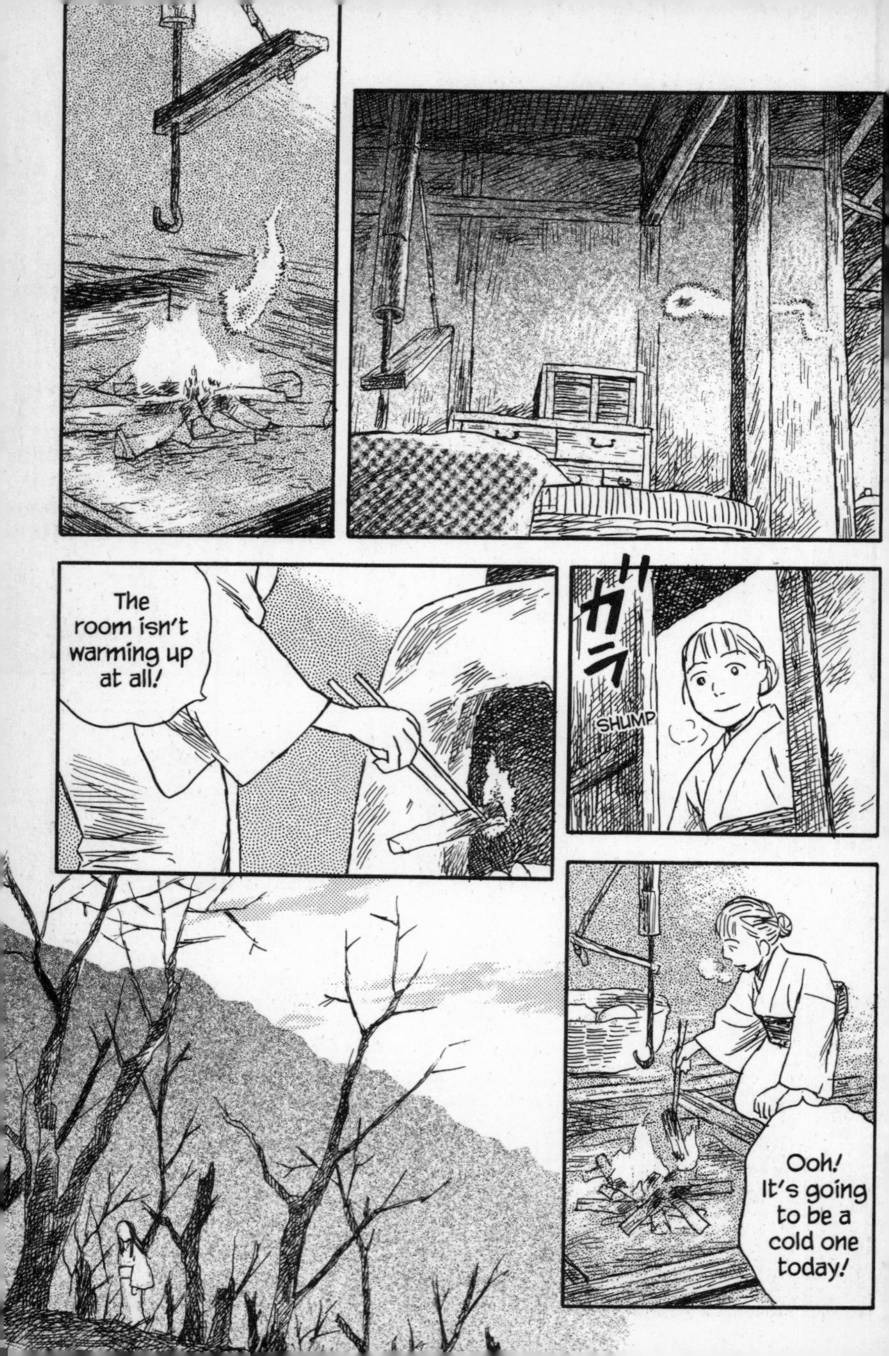
ガラ
SHUMP
The room isn't warming up at all!
Ooh! It's going to be a cold one today!

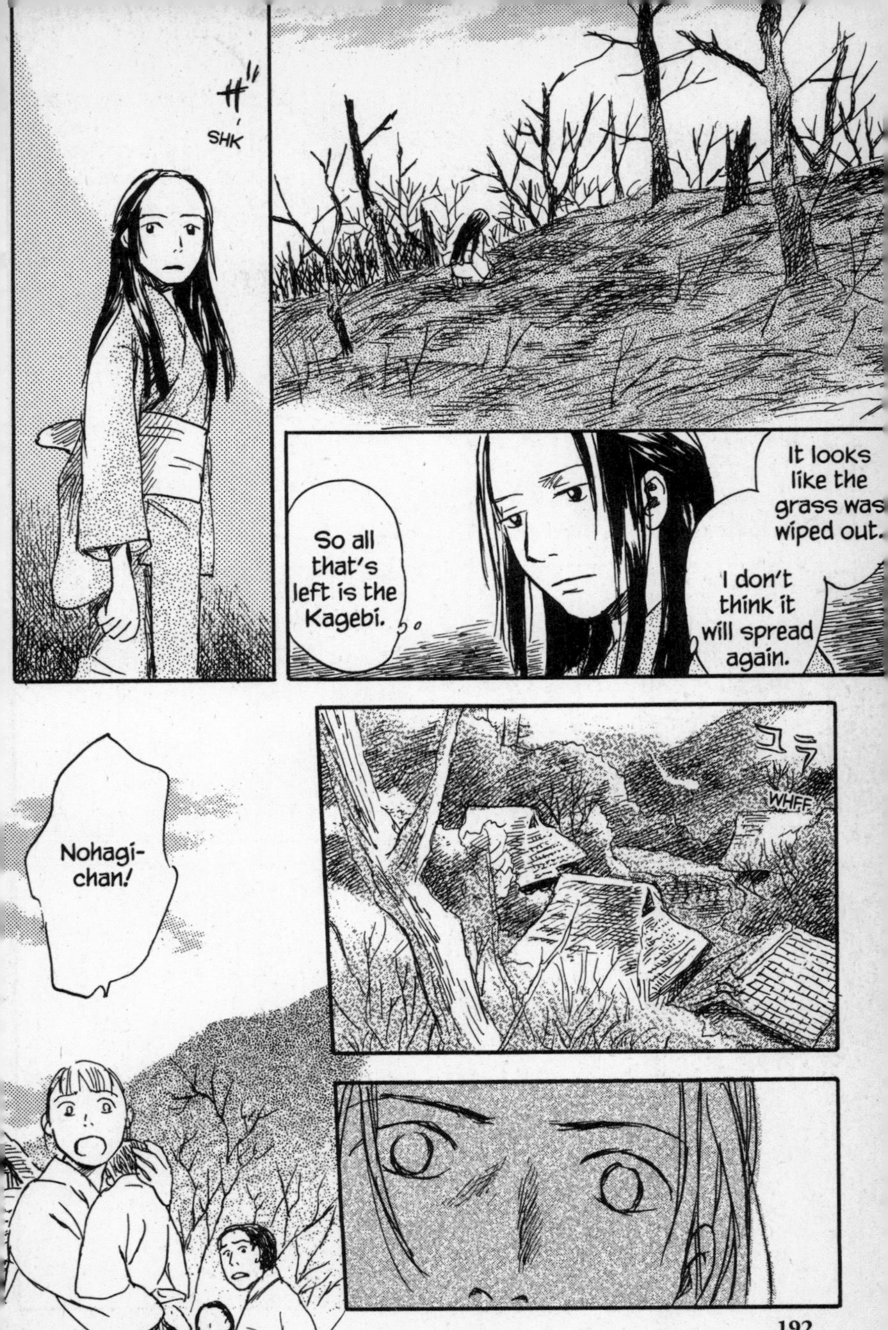
It looks like the grass was wiped out.
I don't think it will spread again.
So all that's left is the Kagebi.
SHK
WHFF
Nohagi-chan!

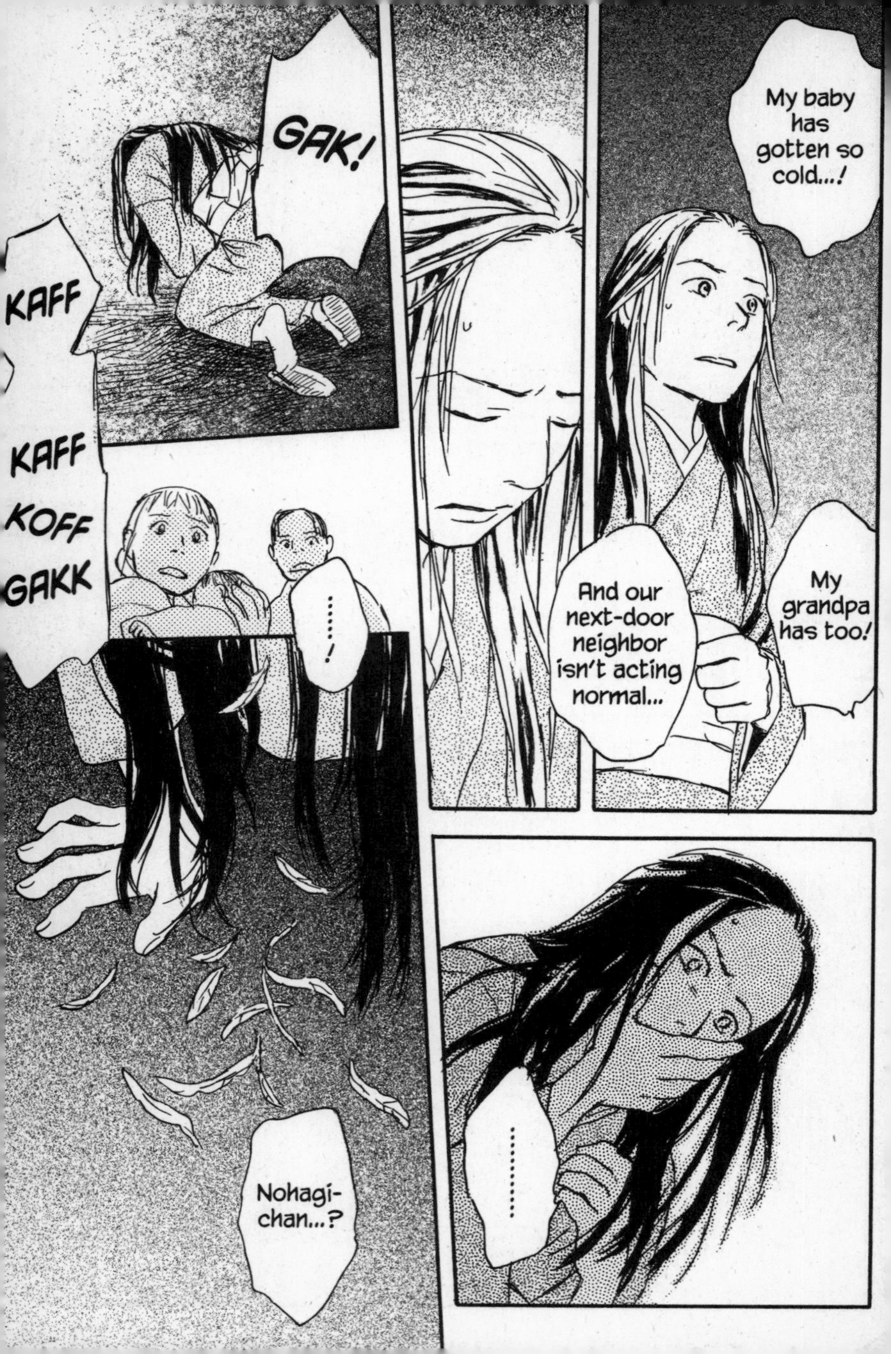
My baby has gotten so cold...!
My grandpa has too!
And our next-door neighbor isn't acting normal...
GAK!
KAFF
KAFF
KOFF
GAKK
......!
....
Nohagi-chan...?

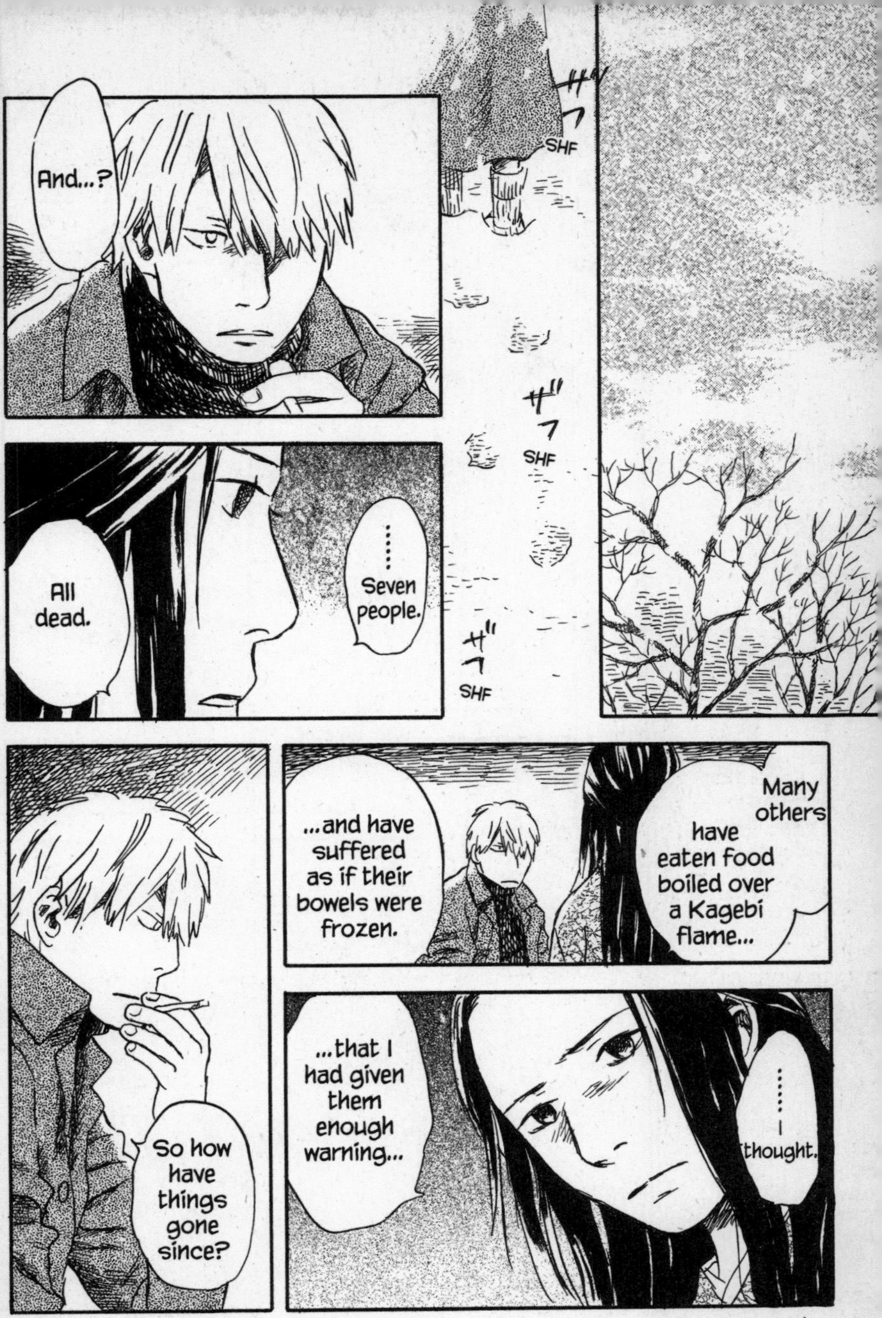
SHF
SHF
SHF
And...?
...... Seven people.
All dead.
Many others have eaten food boiled over a Kagebi flame...
...and have suffered as if their bowels were frozen.
...... I thought.
...that I had given them enough warning...
So how have things gone since?

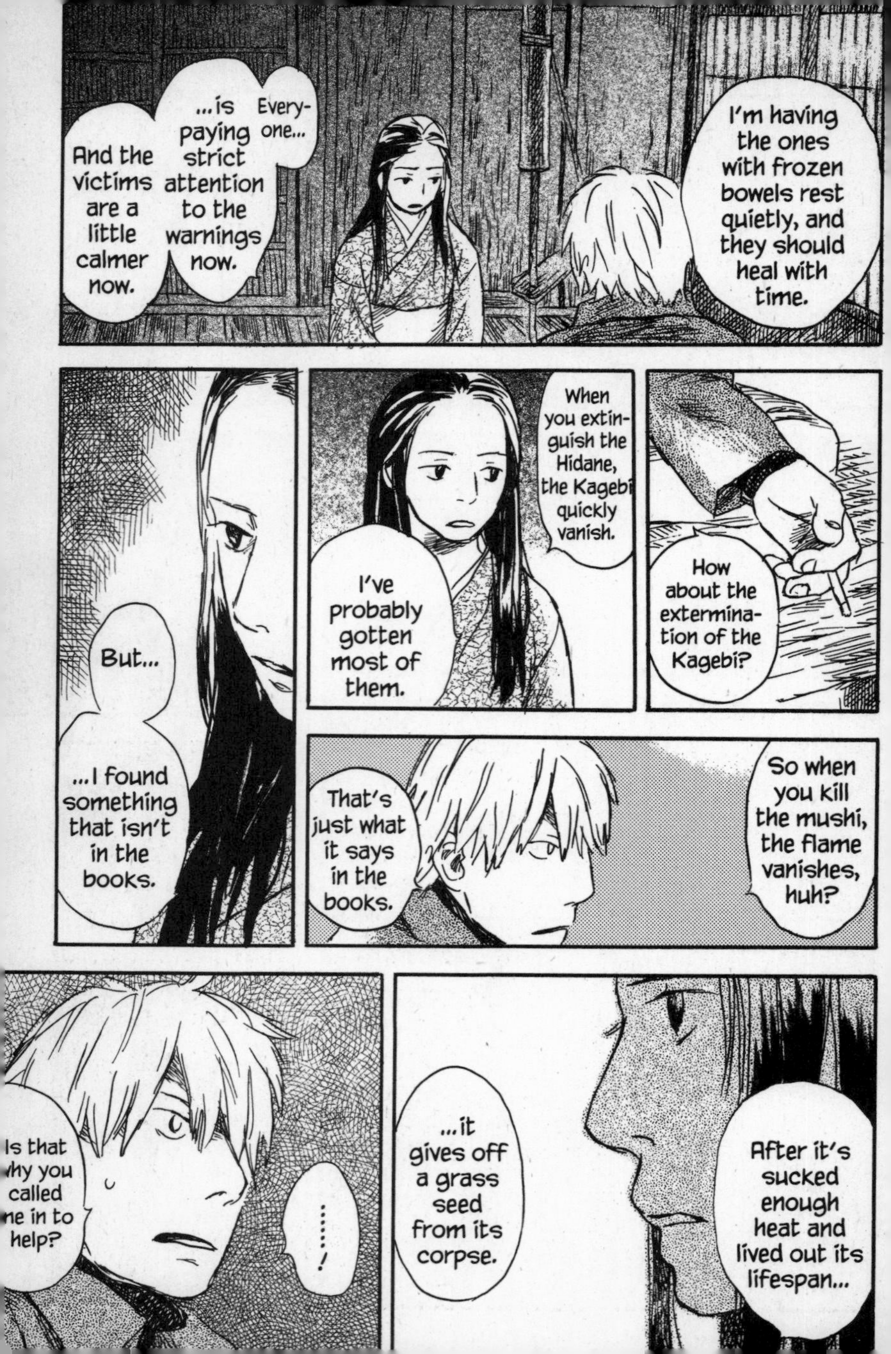
I'm having the ones with frozen bowels rest quietly, and they should heal with time.
Every-one...
...is paying strict attention to the warnings now.
And the victims are a little calmer now.
How about the extermina-tion of the Kagebi?
When you extin-guish the Hidane, the Kagebi quickly vanish.
I've probably gotten most of them.
So when you kill the mushi, the flame vanishes, huh?
That's just what it says in the books.
But...
...I found something that isn't in the books.
After it's sucked enough heat and lived out its lifespan...
...it gives off a grass seed from its corpse.
......!
Is that hy you called ne in to help?

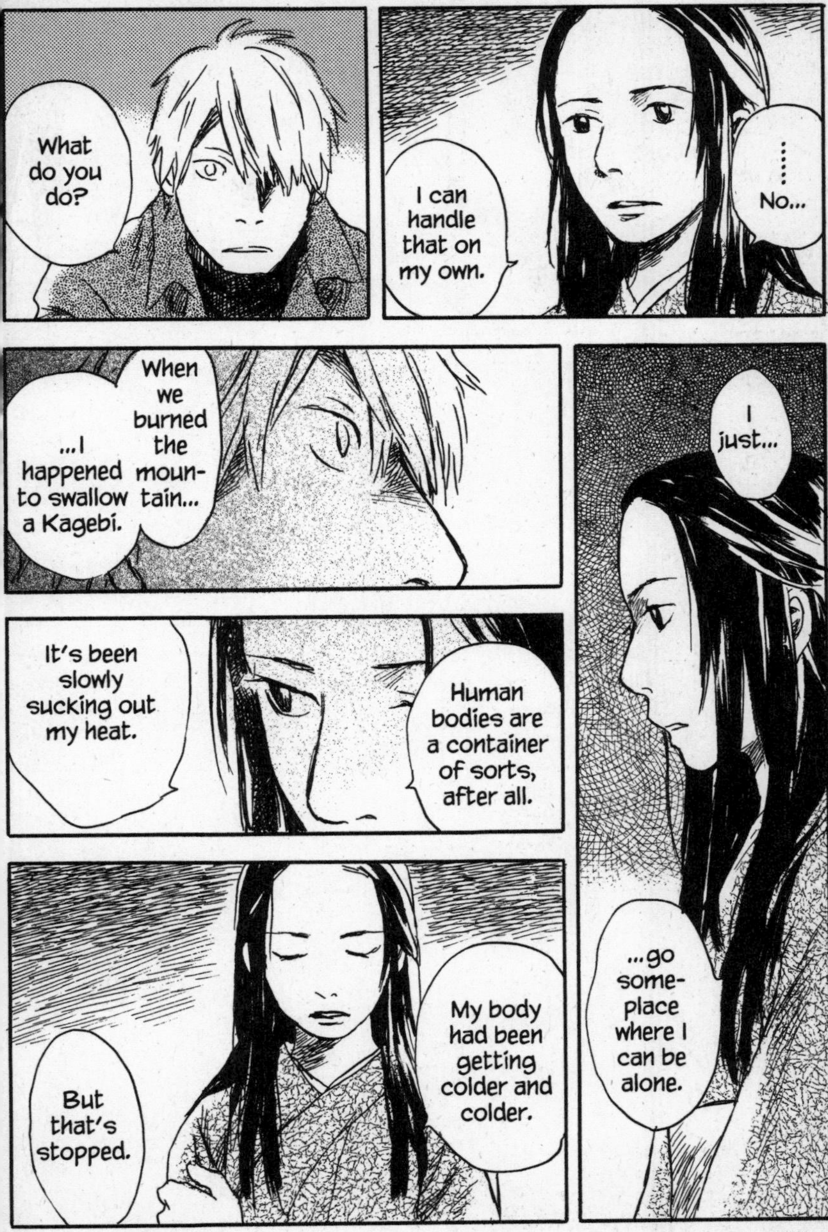
......
No...
I can handle that on my own.
What do you do?
I just...
...go someplace where I can be alone.
When we burned the mountain...
...I happened to swallow a Kagebi.
Human bodies are a container of sorts, after all.
It's been slowly sucking out my heat.
My body had been getting colder and colder.
But that's stopped.

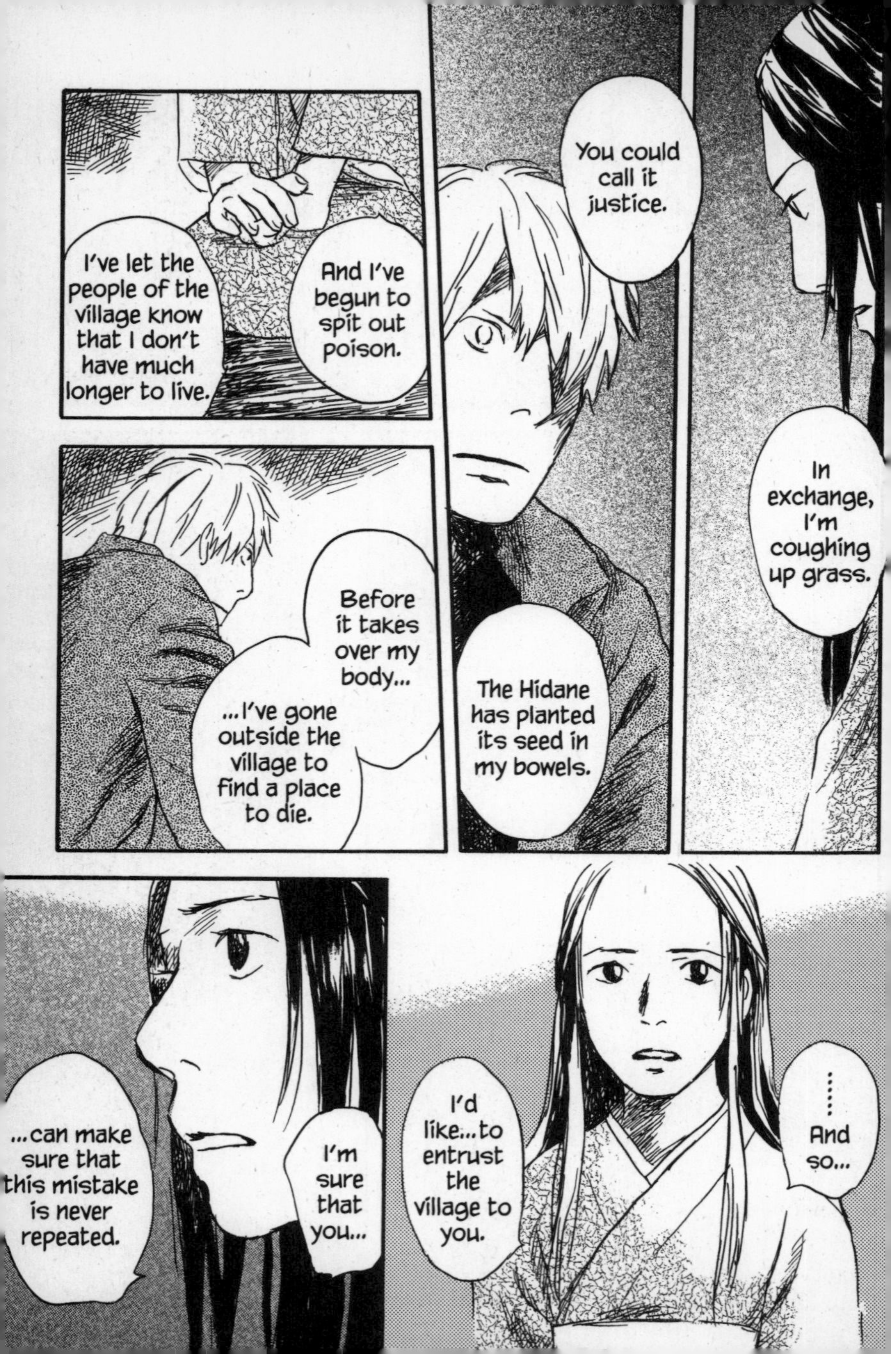
In exchange, I'm coughing up grass.
You could call it justice.
The Hidane has planted its seed in my bowels.
And I've begun to spit out poison.
I've let the people of the village know that I don't have much longer to live.
Before it takes over my body...
...I've gone outside the village to find a place to die.
......
And so...
I'd like...to entrust the village to you.
I'm sure that you...
...can make sure that this mistake is never repeated.

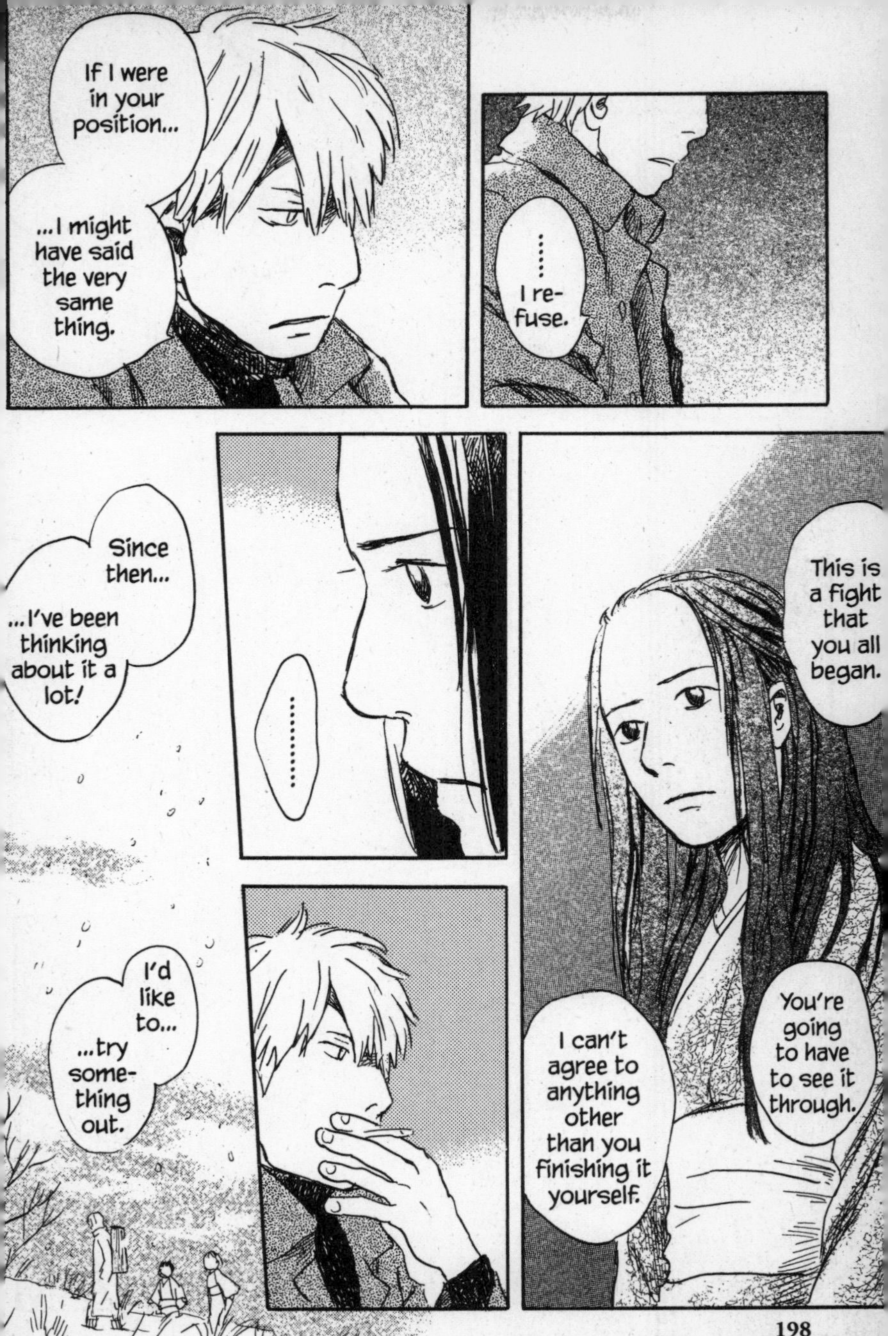
......
I re-fuse.
If I were in your position...
...I might have said the very same thing.
This is a fight that you all began.
You're going to have to see it through.
I can't agree to anything other than you finishing it yourself.
......
Since then...
...I've been thinking about it a lot!
I'd like to...
...try some-thing out.

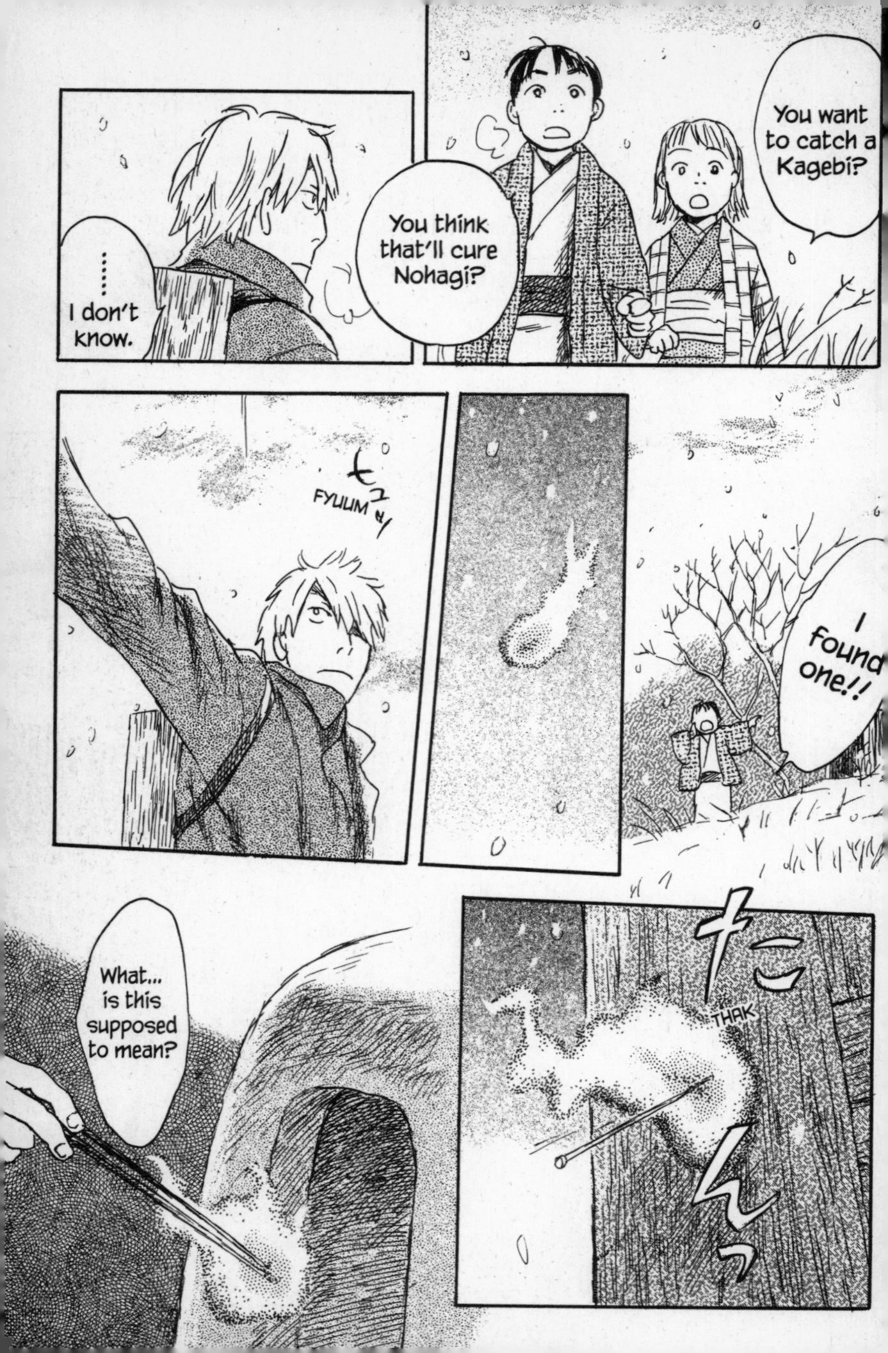
You want to catch a Kagebi?
You think that'll cure Nohagi?
......
I don't know.
I found one!!
FYUUM
THAK
What... is this supposed to mean?

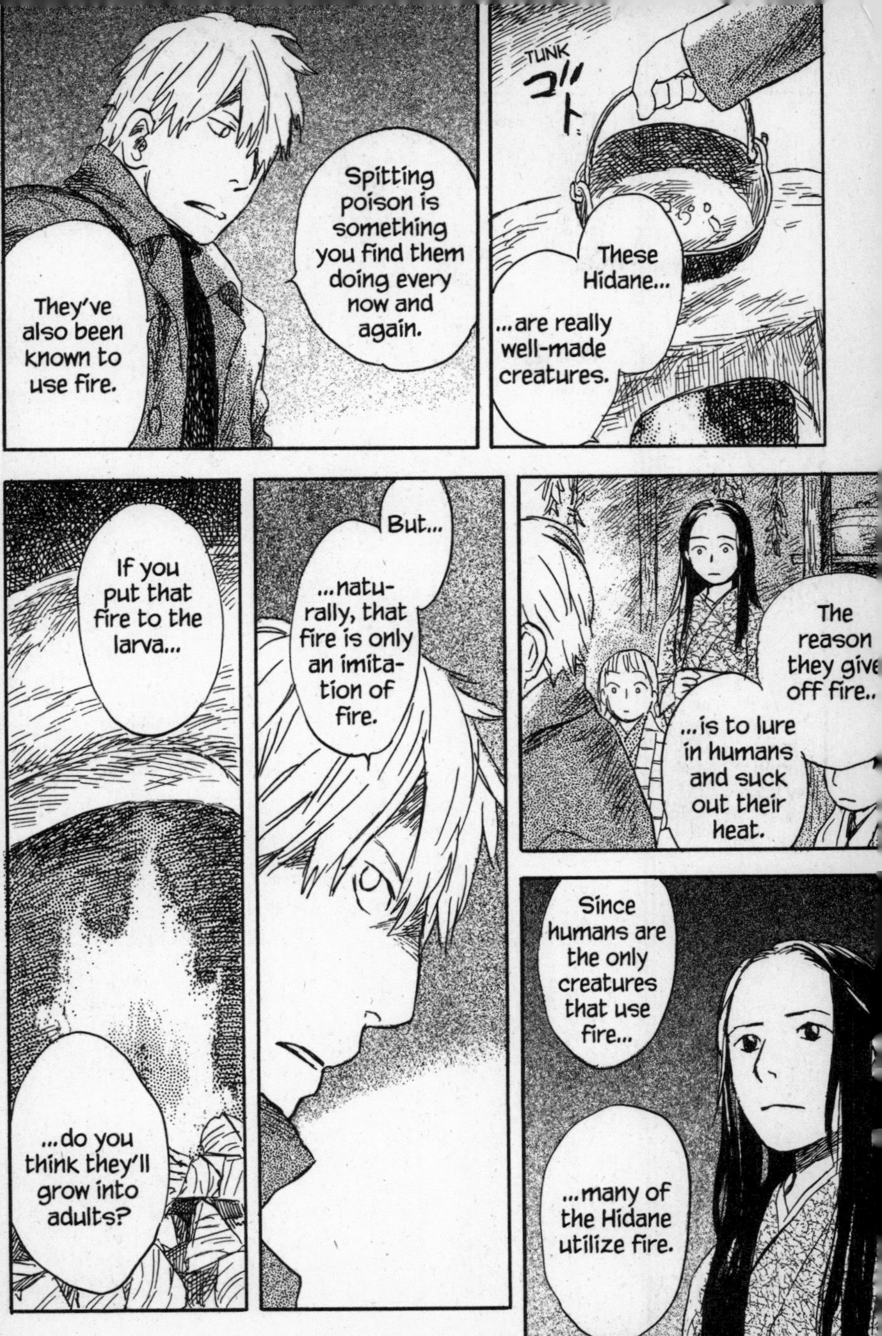
TUNK
ゴト
These Hidane...
...are really well-made creatures.
Spitting poison is something you find them doing every now and again.
They've also been known to use fire.
The reason they give off fire..
...is to lure in humans and suck out their heat.
Since humans are the only creatures that use fire...
...many of the Hidane utilize fire.
But...
...naturally, that fire is only an imitation of fire.
If you put that fire to the larva...
...do you think they'll grow into adults?

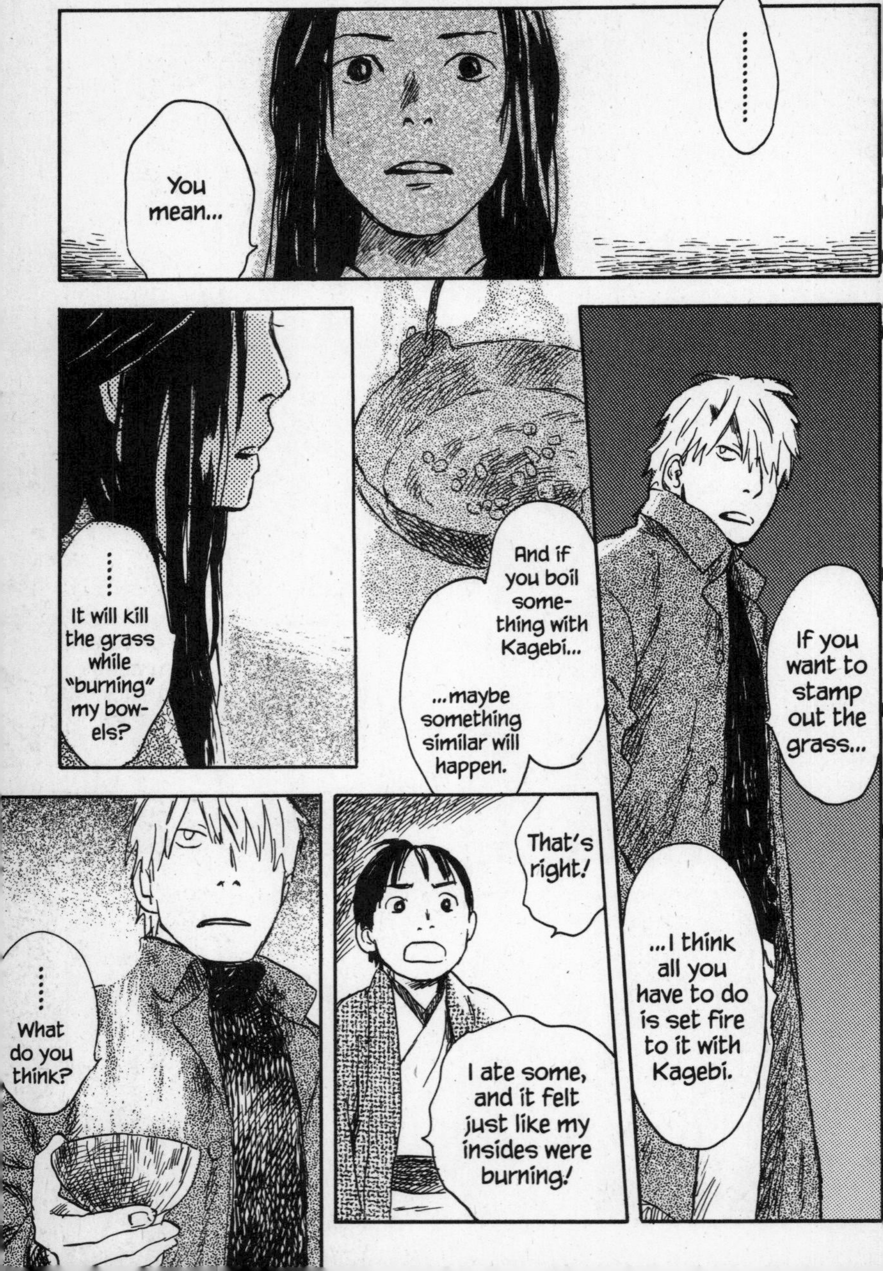
……
You mean...
If you want to stamp out the grass...
...I think all you have to do is set fire to it with Kagebi.
And if you boil something with Kagebi...
...maybe something similar will happen.
……
It will kill the grass while "burning" my bowels?
That's right!
I ate some, and it felt just like my insides were burning!
……
What do you think?

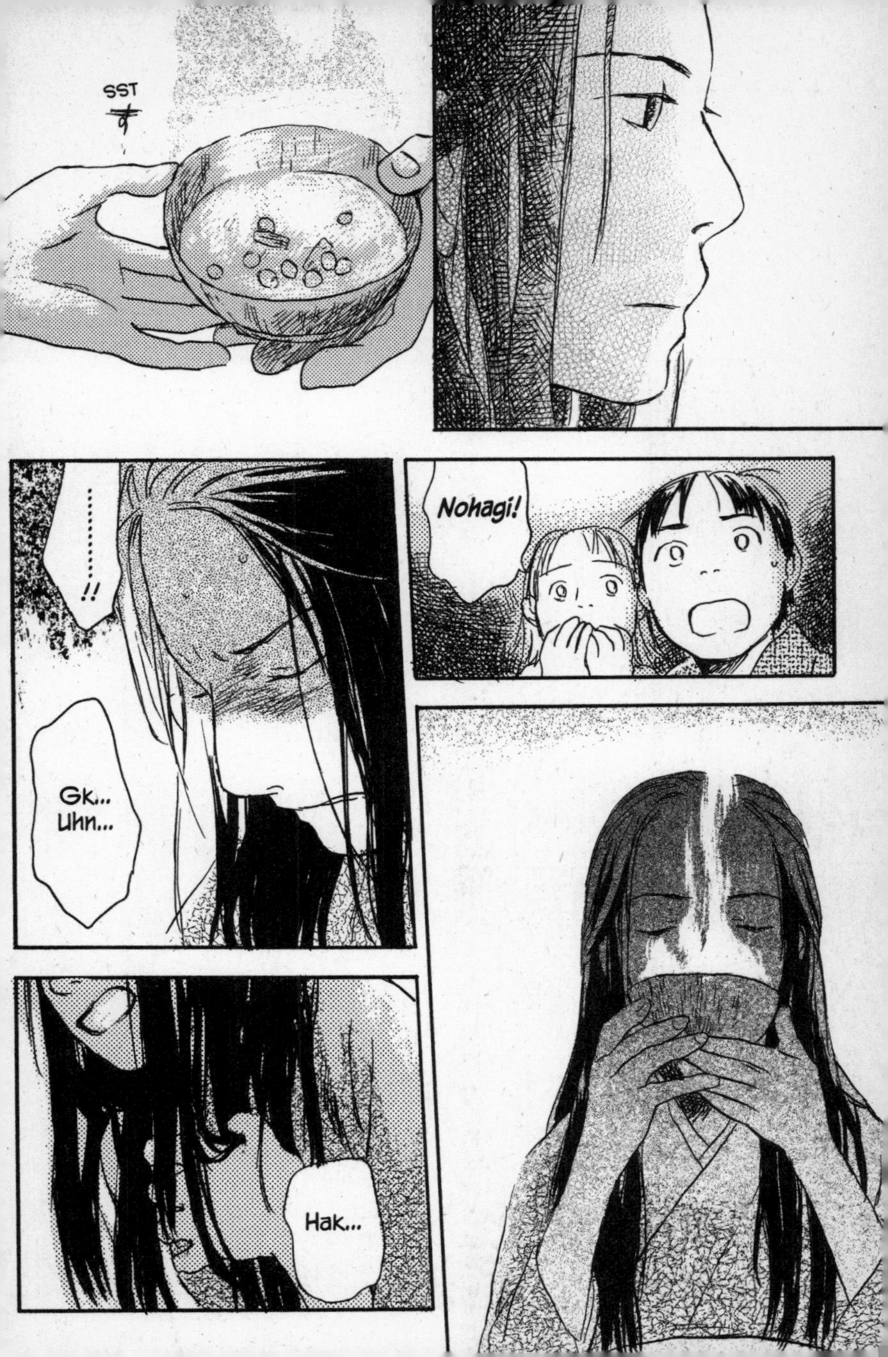

SST
す
Nohagi!
......!!
Gk... Uhn...
Hak...

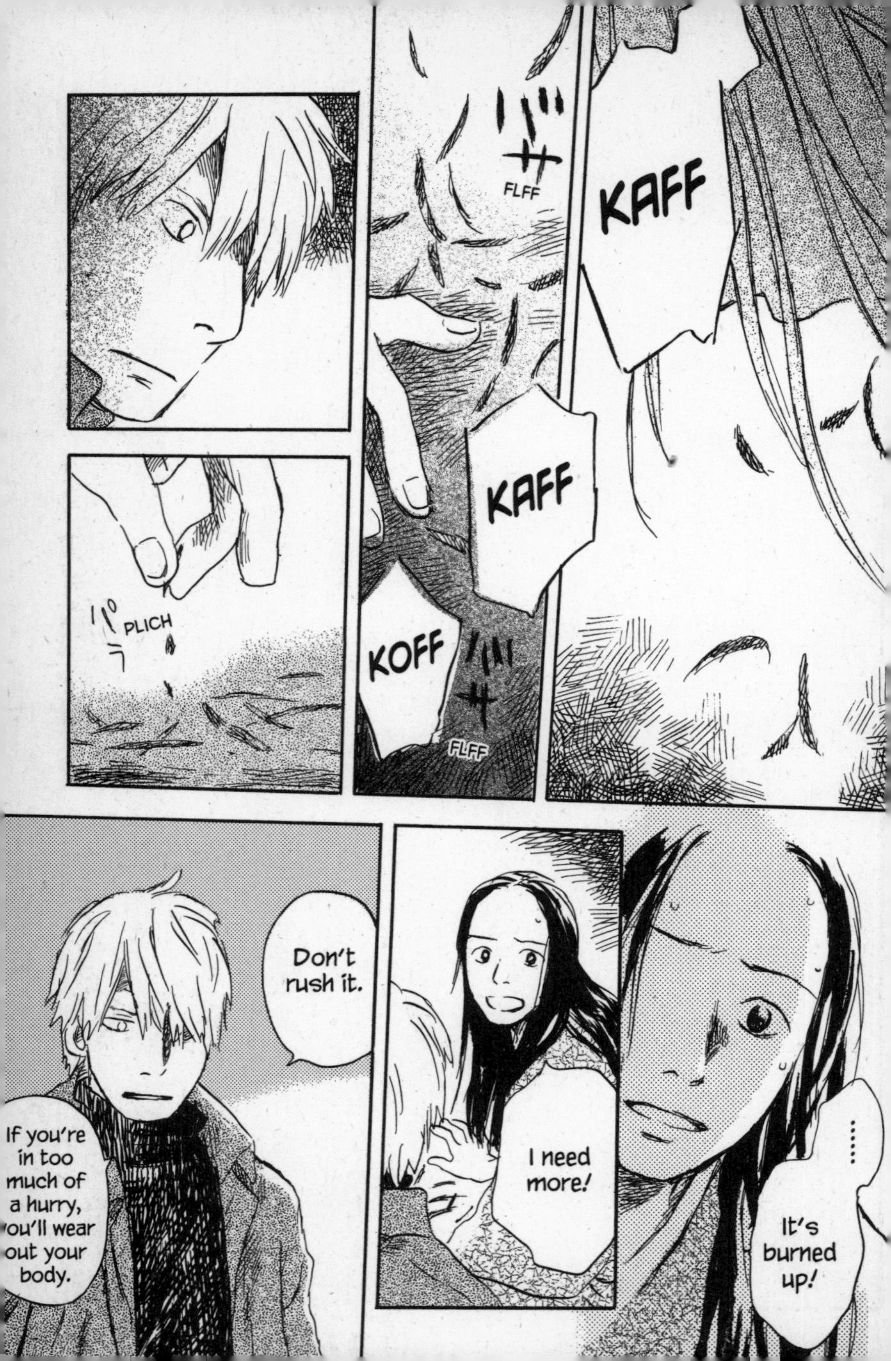
KAFF
FLFF
KAFF
KOFF
FLFF
PLICH
......
It's burned up!
I need more!
Don't rush it.
If you're in too much of a hurry, ou'll wear out your body.

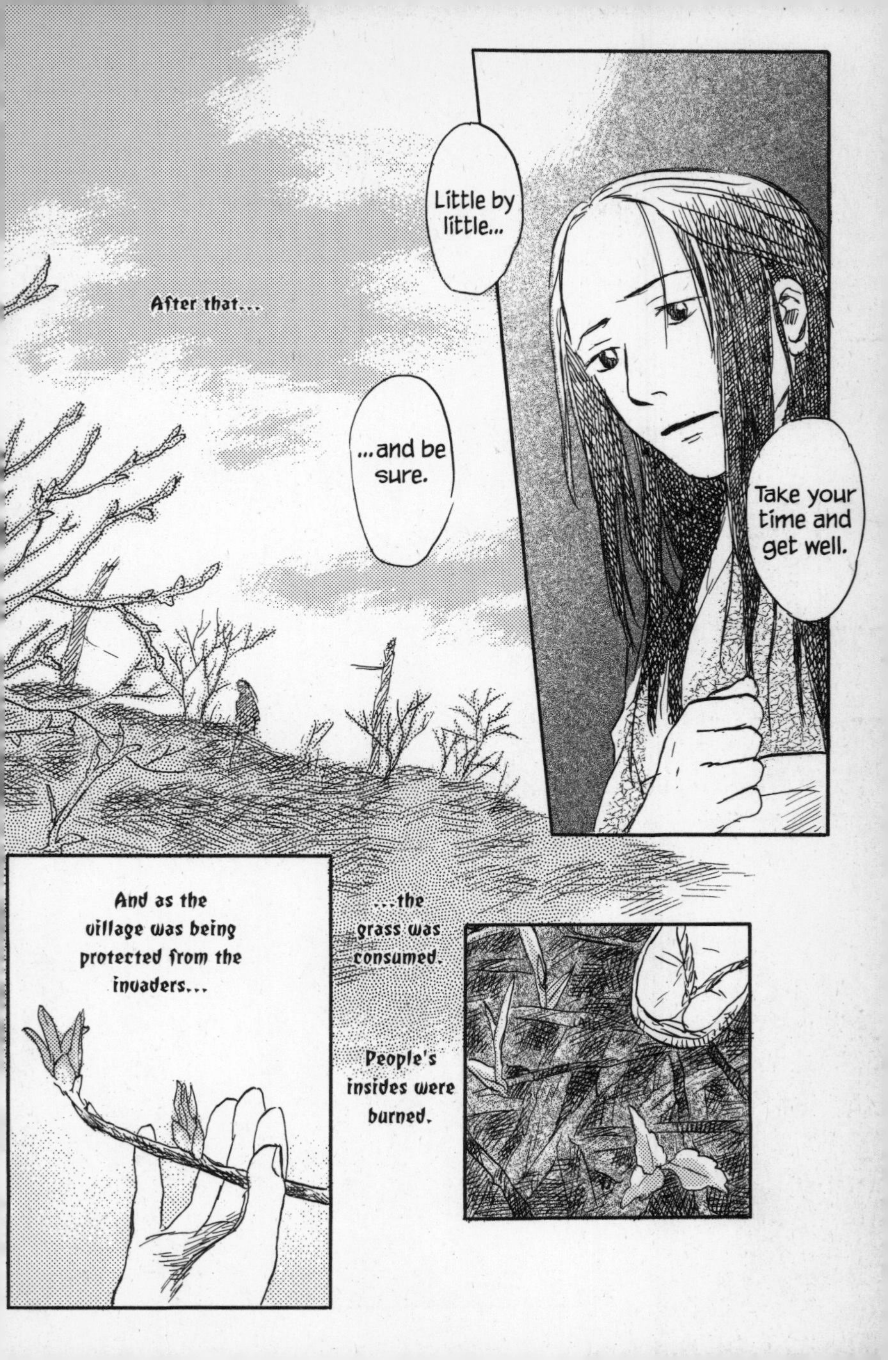
Take your time and get well.
Little by little...
...and be sure.
After that...
And as the village was being protected from the invaders...
...the grass was consumed.
People's insides were burned.

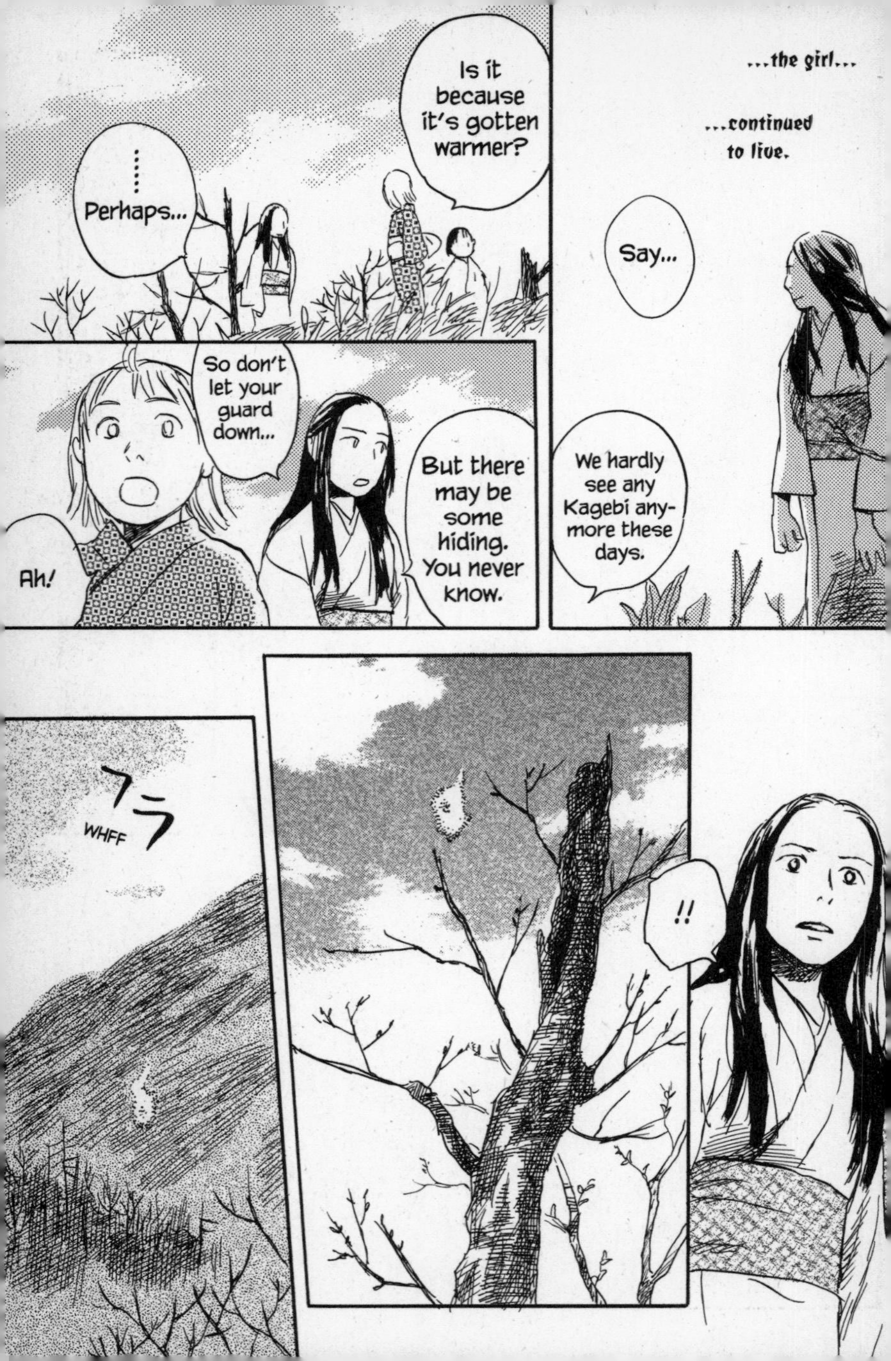
...the girl...
...continued to live.
Say...
We hardly see any Kagebi anymore these days.
Is it because it's gotten warmer?
......
Perhaps...
But there may be some hiding. You never know.
So don't let your guard down...
Ah!
!!
フラ
WHFF

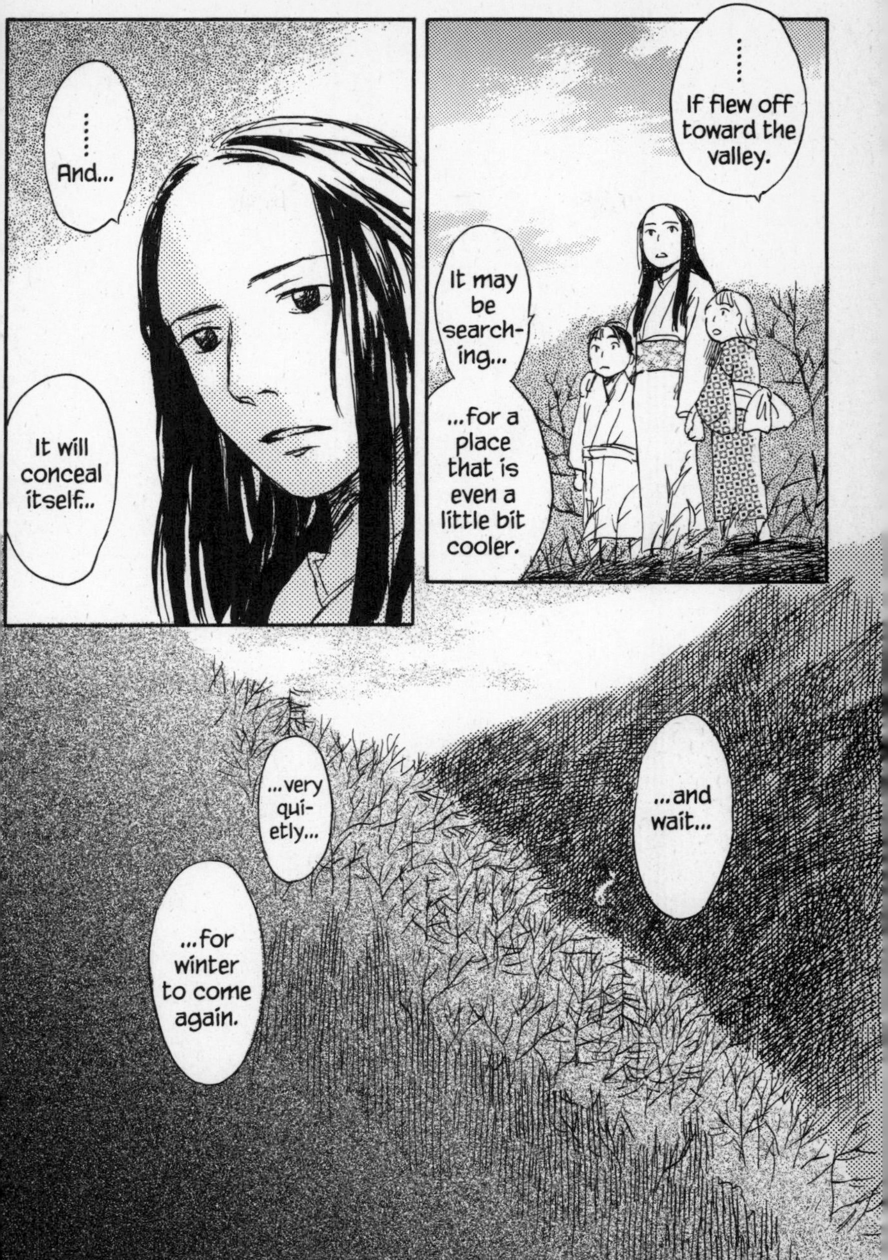
......
If flew off toward the valley.
It may be searching...
...for a place that is even a little bit cooler.
......
And...
It will conceal itself...
...and wait...
...very quietly...
...for winter to come again.

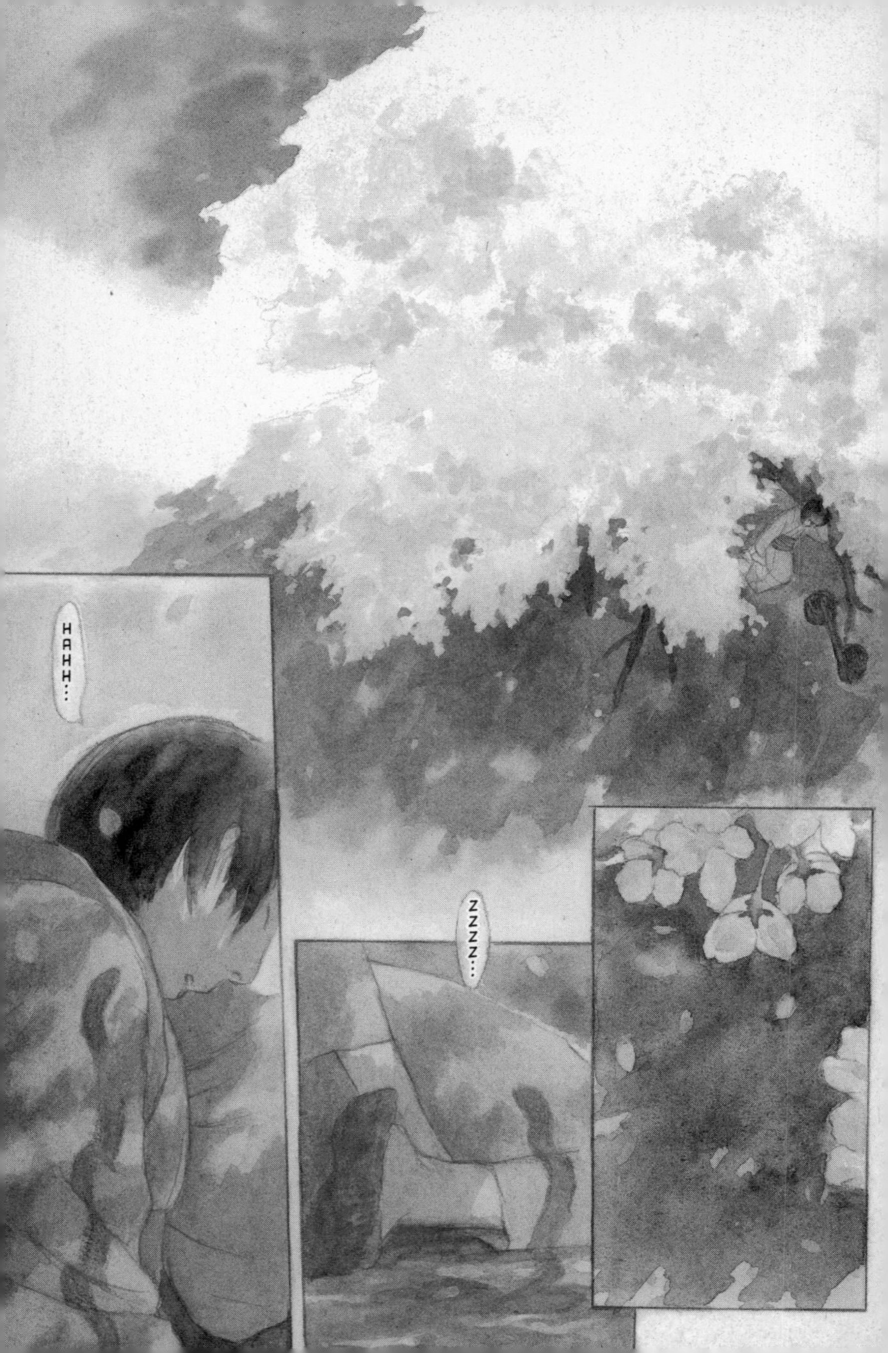
ZZZZ...
HAHH...

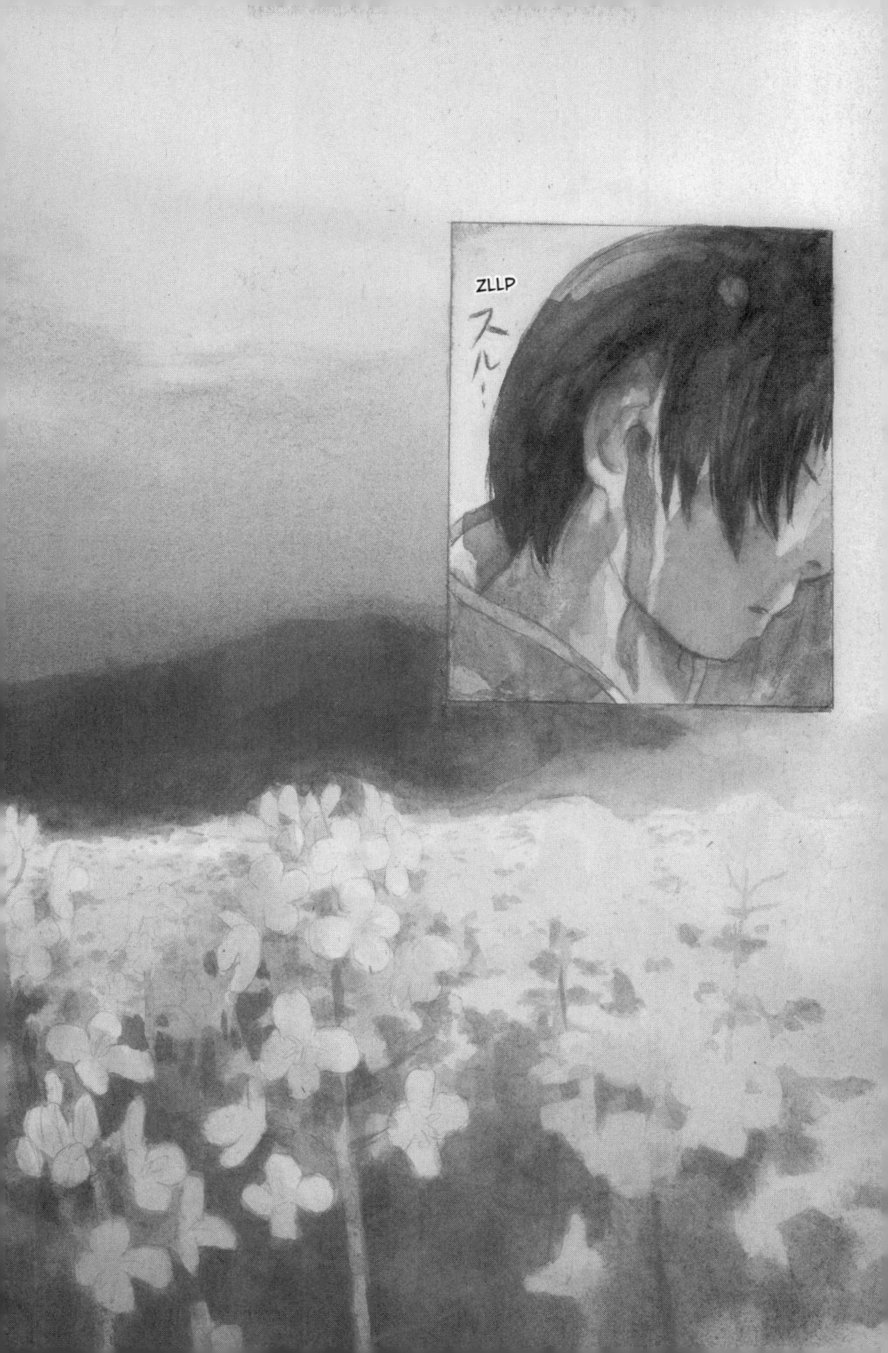
ZLLP
スル

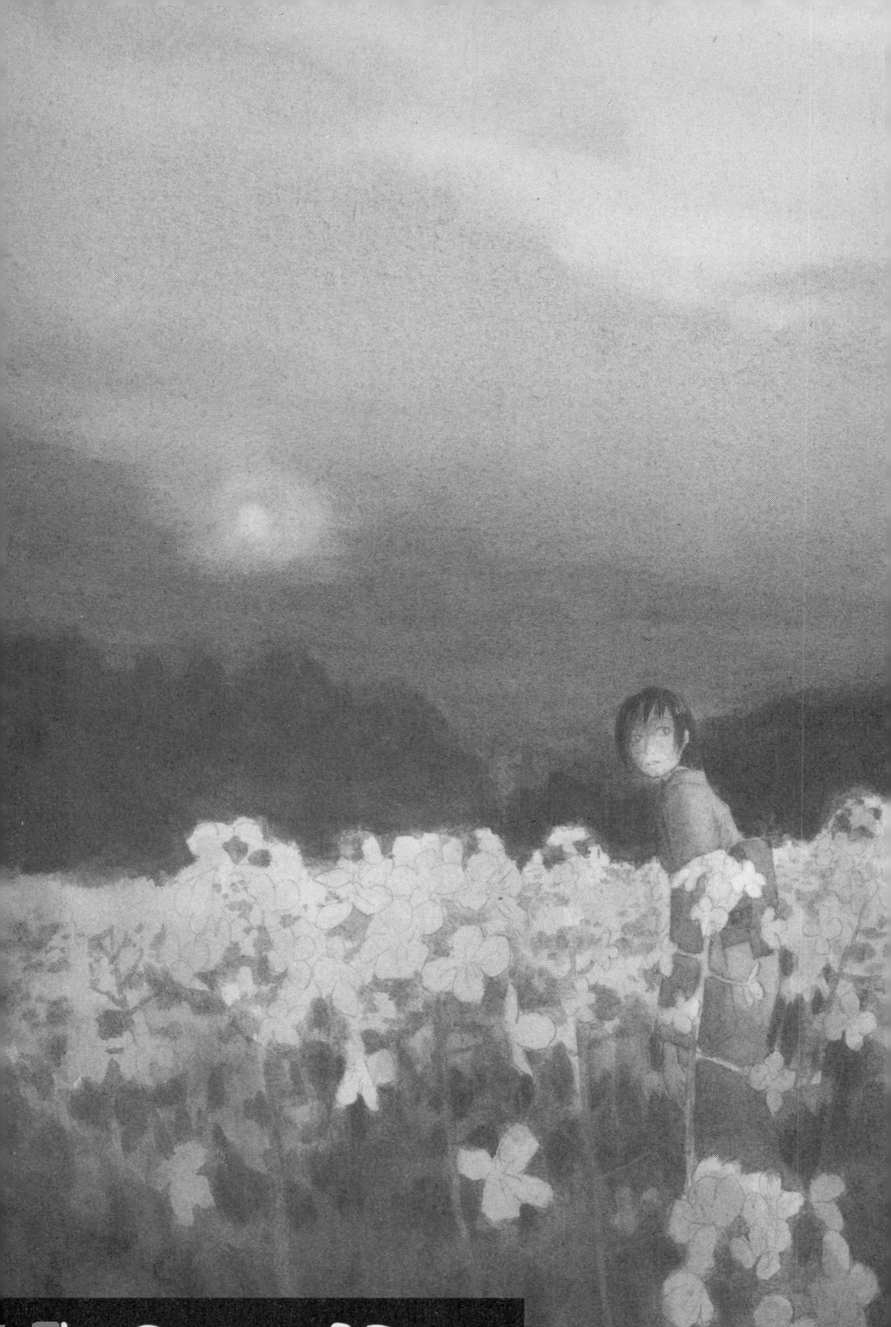

The Snake of Dawn

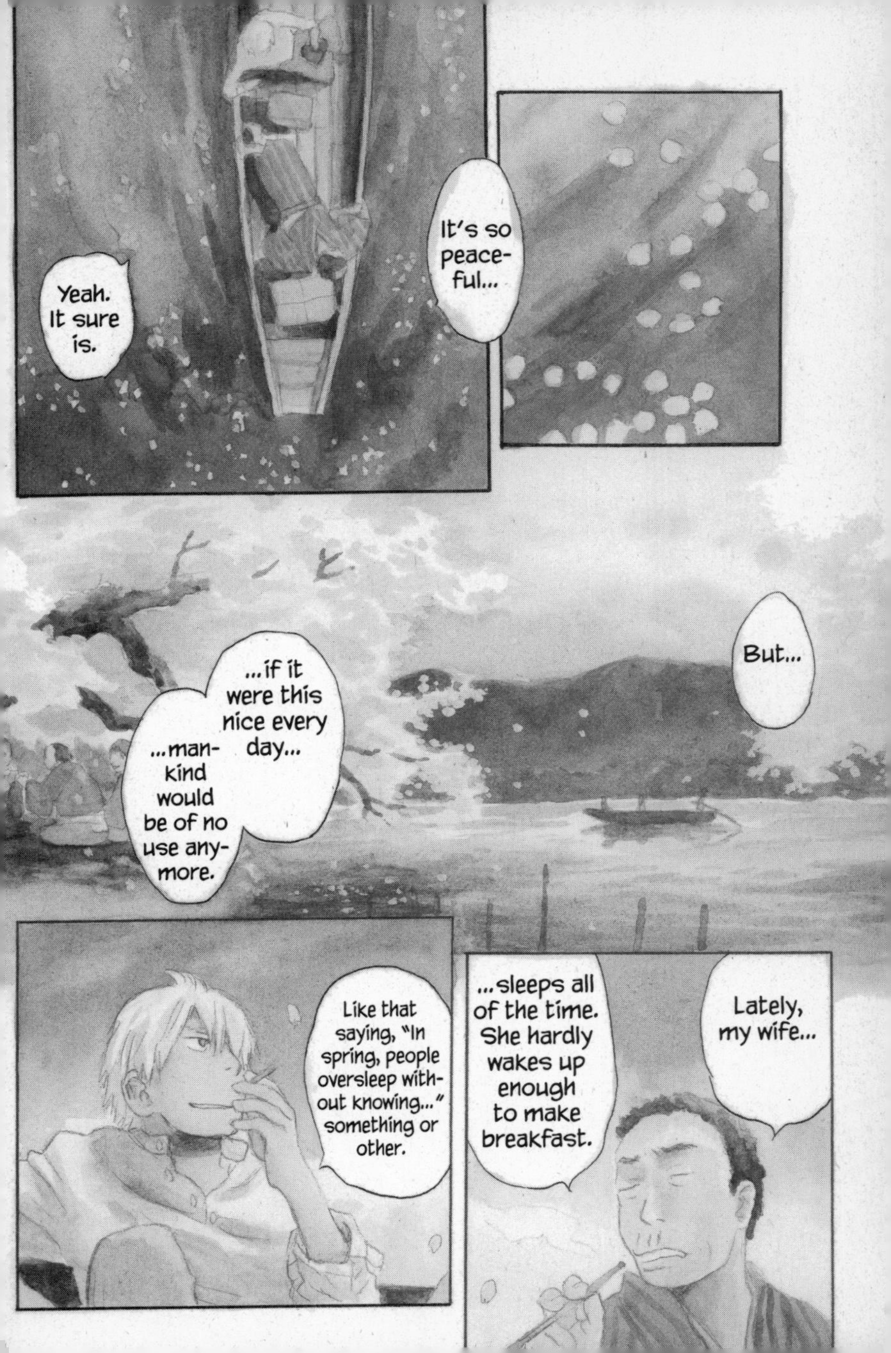
It's so peaceful...
Yeah. It sure is.
But...
...if it were this nice every day...
...mankind would be of no use anymore.
Lately, my wife...
...sleeps all of the time. She hardly wakes up enough to make breakfast.
Like that saying, "In spring, people oversleep without knowing..." something or other.

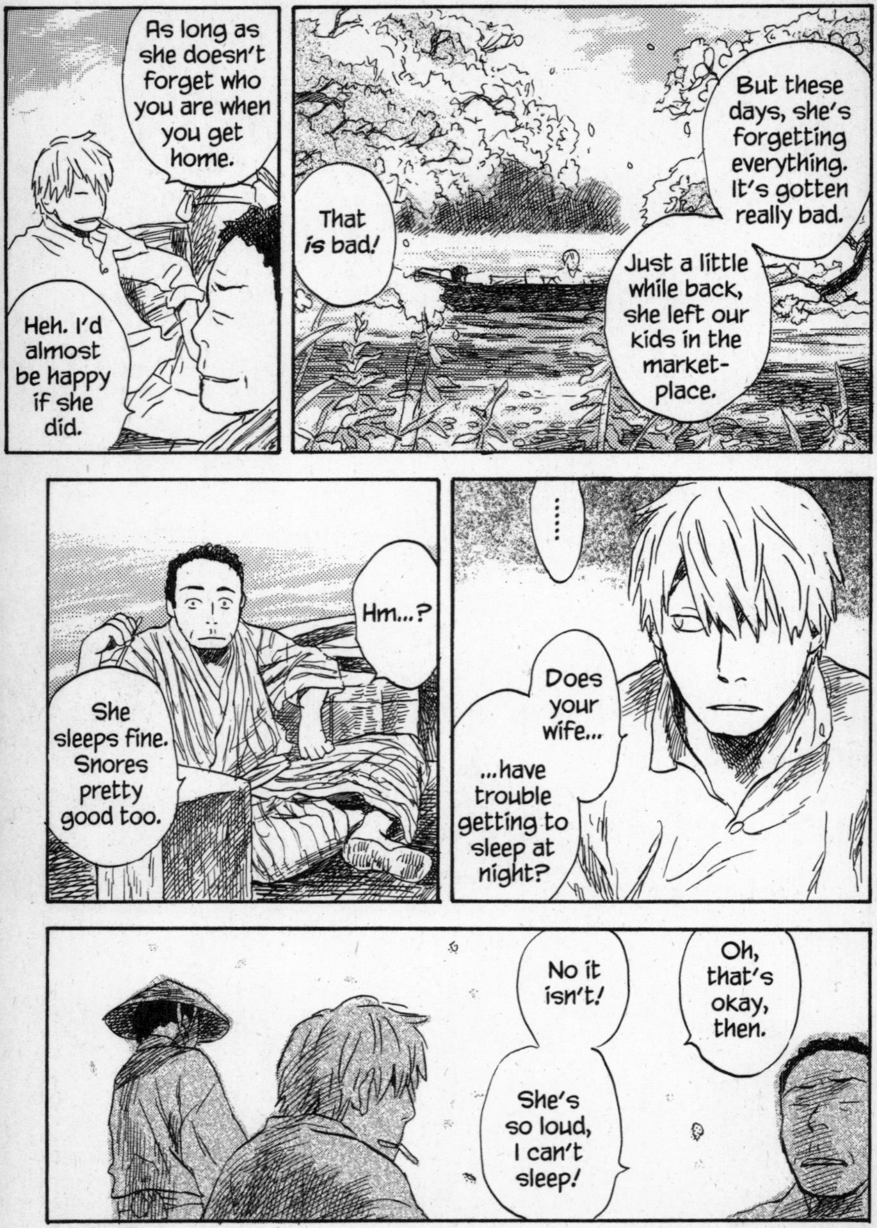
But these days, she's forgetting everything. It's gotten really bad.
Just a little while back, she left our kids in the market-place.
That *is* bad!
As long as she doesn't forget who you are when you get home.
Heh. I'd almost be happy if she did.
......
Does your wife...
...have trouble getting to sleep at night?
Hm...?
She sleeps fine. Snores pretty good too.
Oh, that's okay, then.
No it isn't!
She's so loud, I can't sleep!

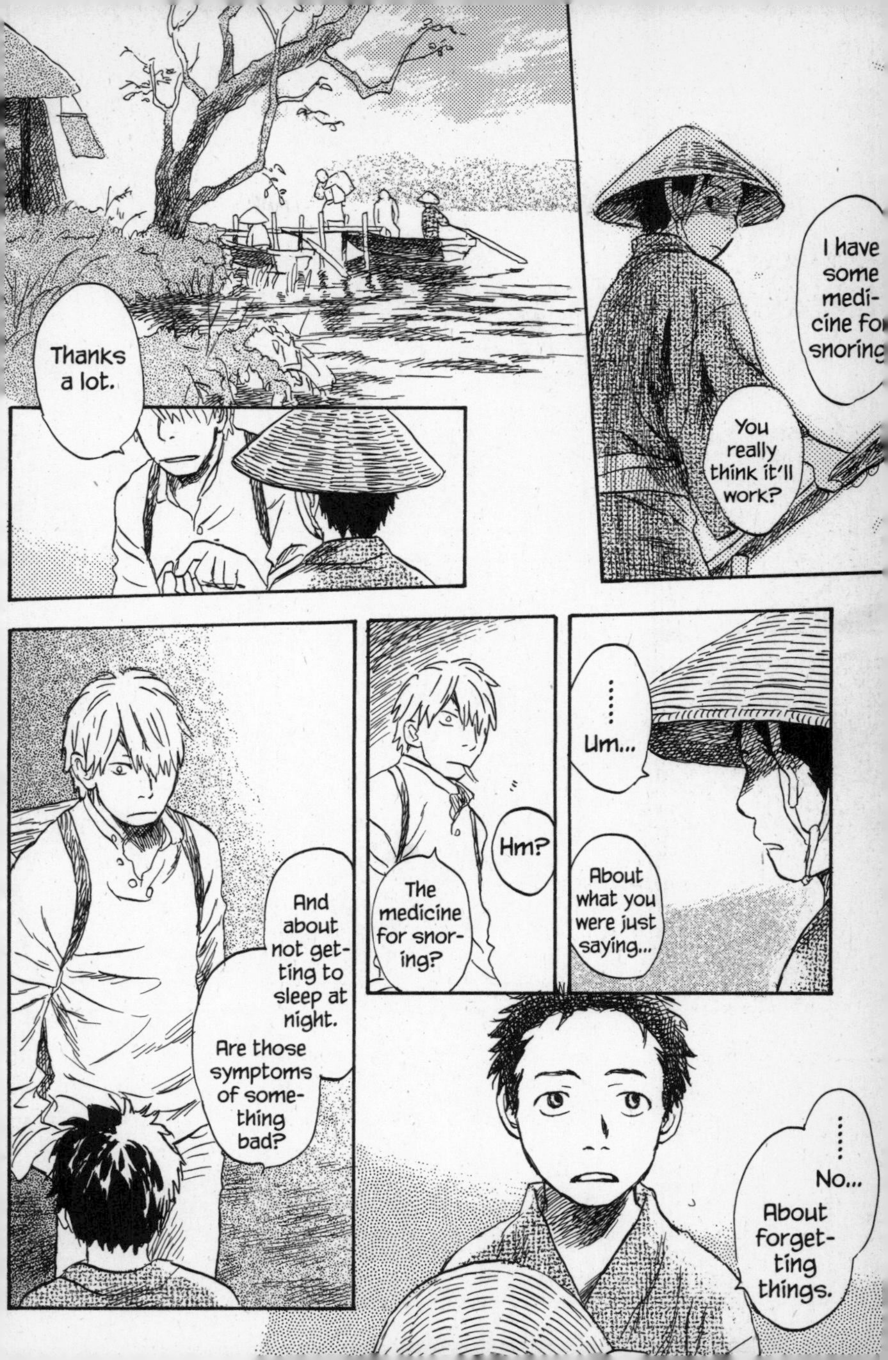

I have some medi-cine fo snoring
You really think it'll work?
Thanks a lot.
...... Um...
About what you were just saying...
Hm?
The medicine for snor-ing?
And about not get-ting to sleep at night.
Are those symptoms of some-thing bad?
...... No...
About forget-ting things.

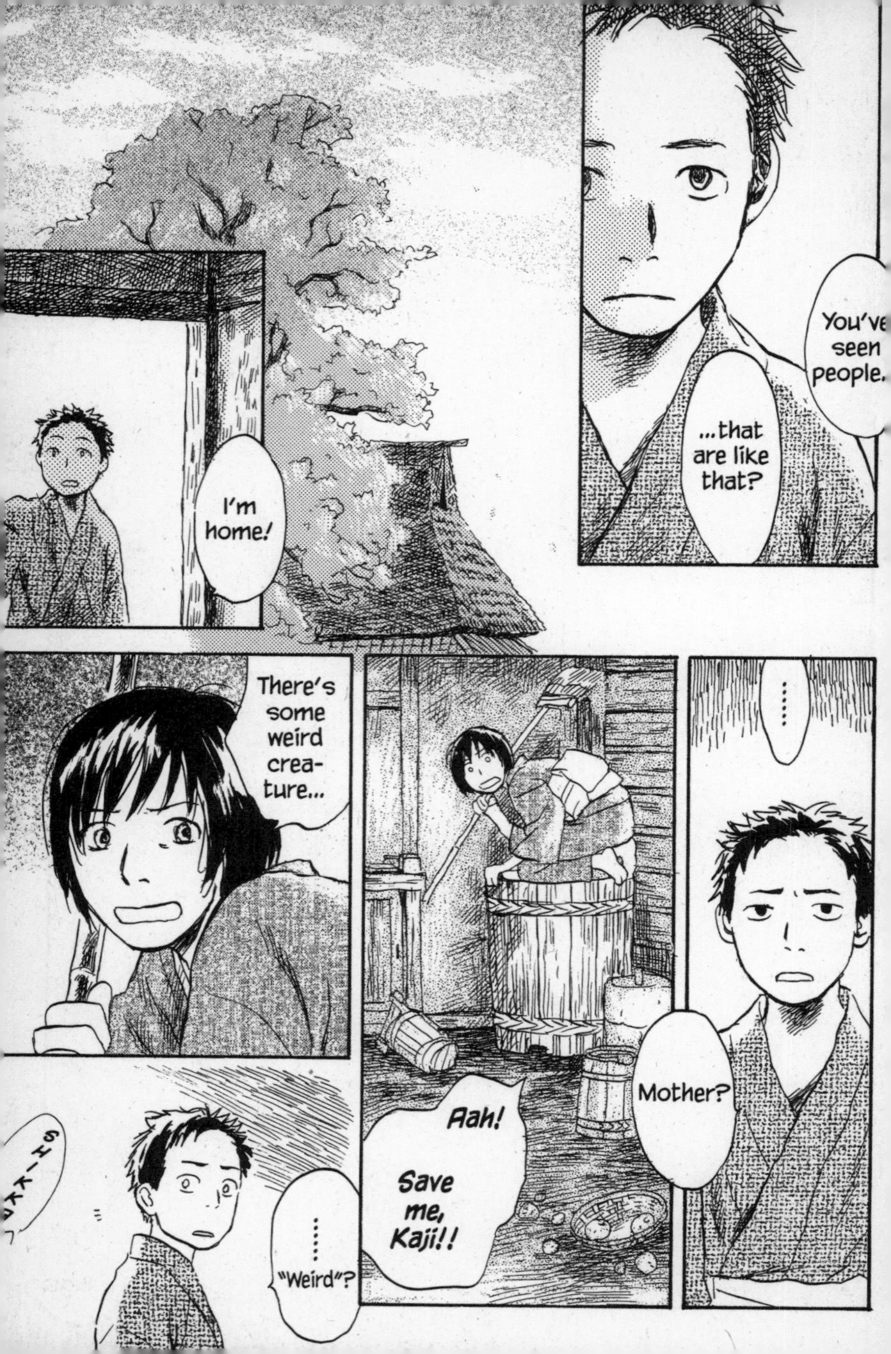
You've seen people.
...that are like that?
I'm home!
......
Mother?
Aah!
Save me, Kaji!!
There's some weird crea-ture...
SHIKK
......
"Weird"?

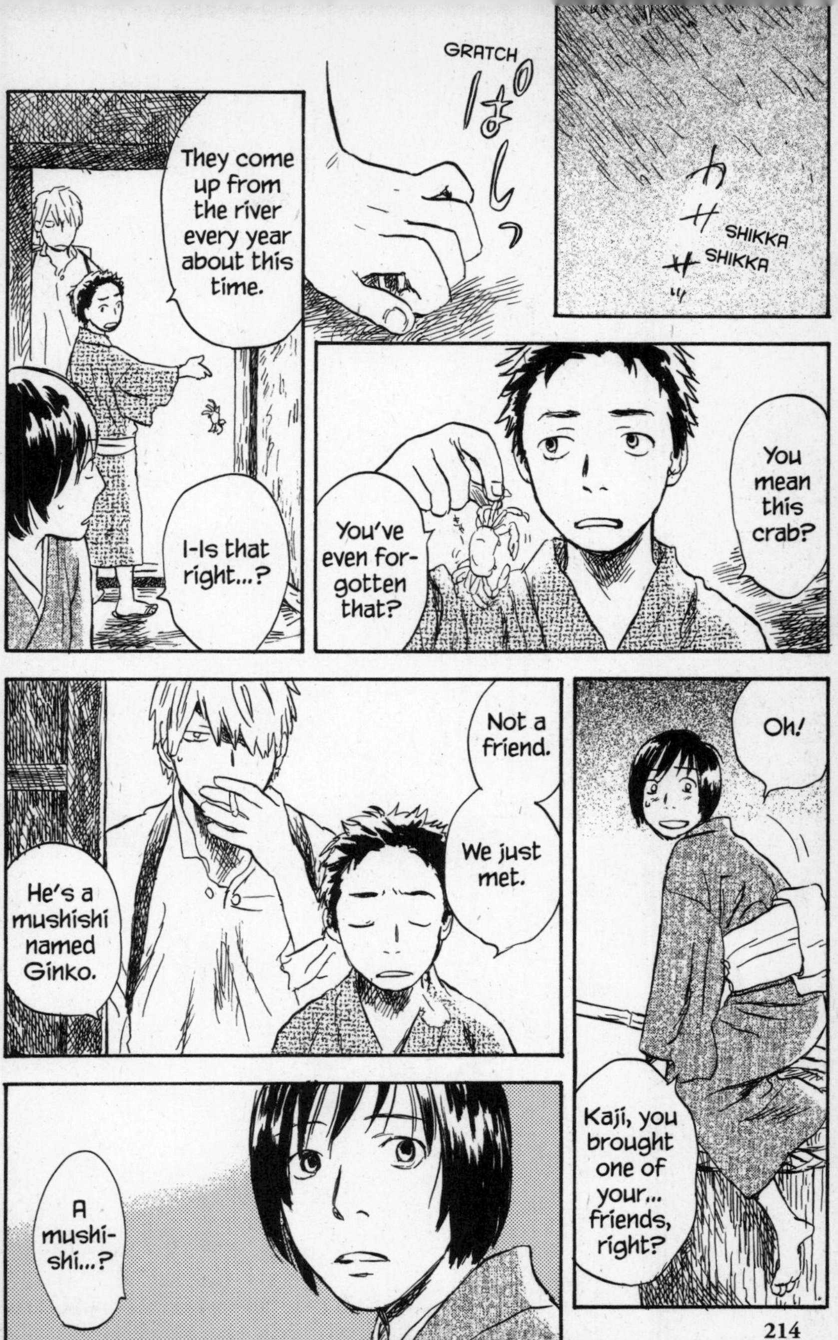
カサ
カサ
SHIKKA
SHIKKA
ぱしっ
GRATCH
You mean this crab?
You've even forgotten that?
They come up from the river every year about this time.
I-Is that right...?
Oh!
Kaji, you brought one of your... friends, right?
Not a friend.
We just met.
He's a mushishi named Ginko.
A mushi-shi...?

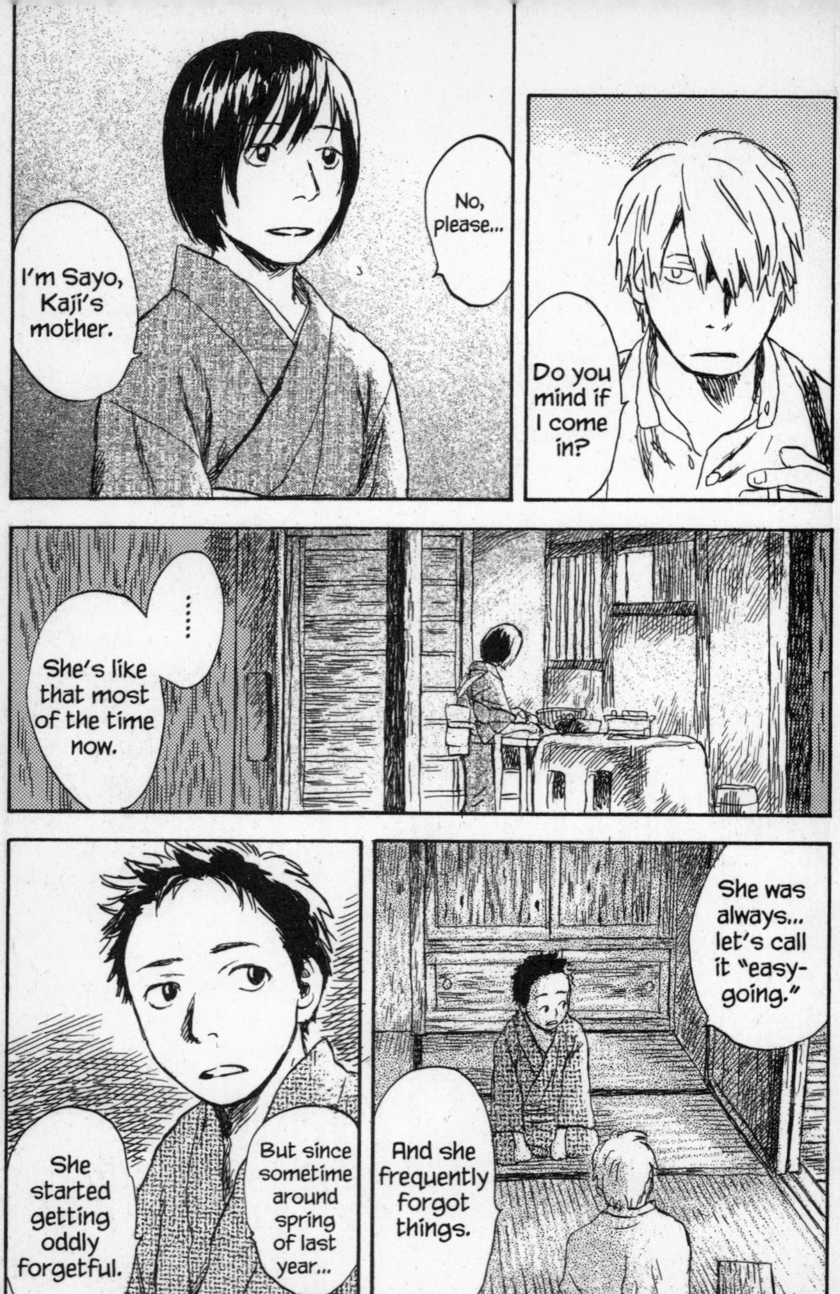
Do you mind if I come in?
No, please...
I'm Sayo, Kaji's mother.
......
She's like that most of the time now.
She was always... let's call it "easy-going."
And she frequently forgot things.
But since sometime around spring of last year...
She started getting oddly forgetful.

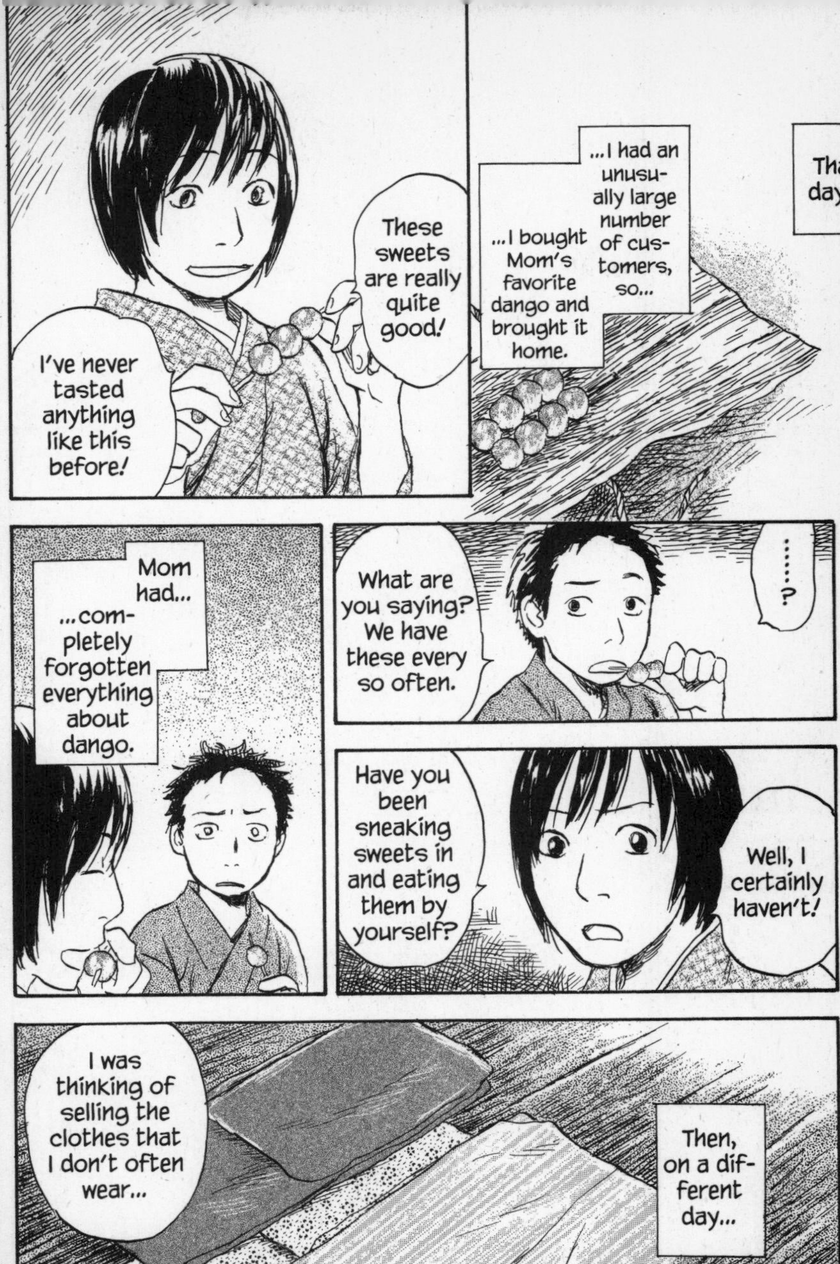
That day...
...I had an unusually large number of customers, so...
...I bought Mom's favorite dango and brought it home.
These sweets are really quite good!
I've never tasted anything like this before!
......?
What are you saying? We have these every so often.
Well, I certainly haven't!
Have you been sneaking sweets in and eating them by yourself?
Mom had... ...completely forgotten everything about dango.
Then, on a different day...
I was thinking of selling the clothes that I don't often wear...

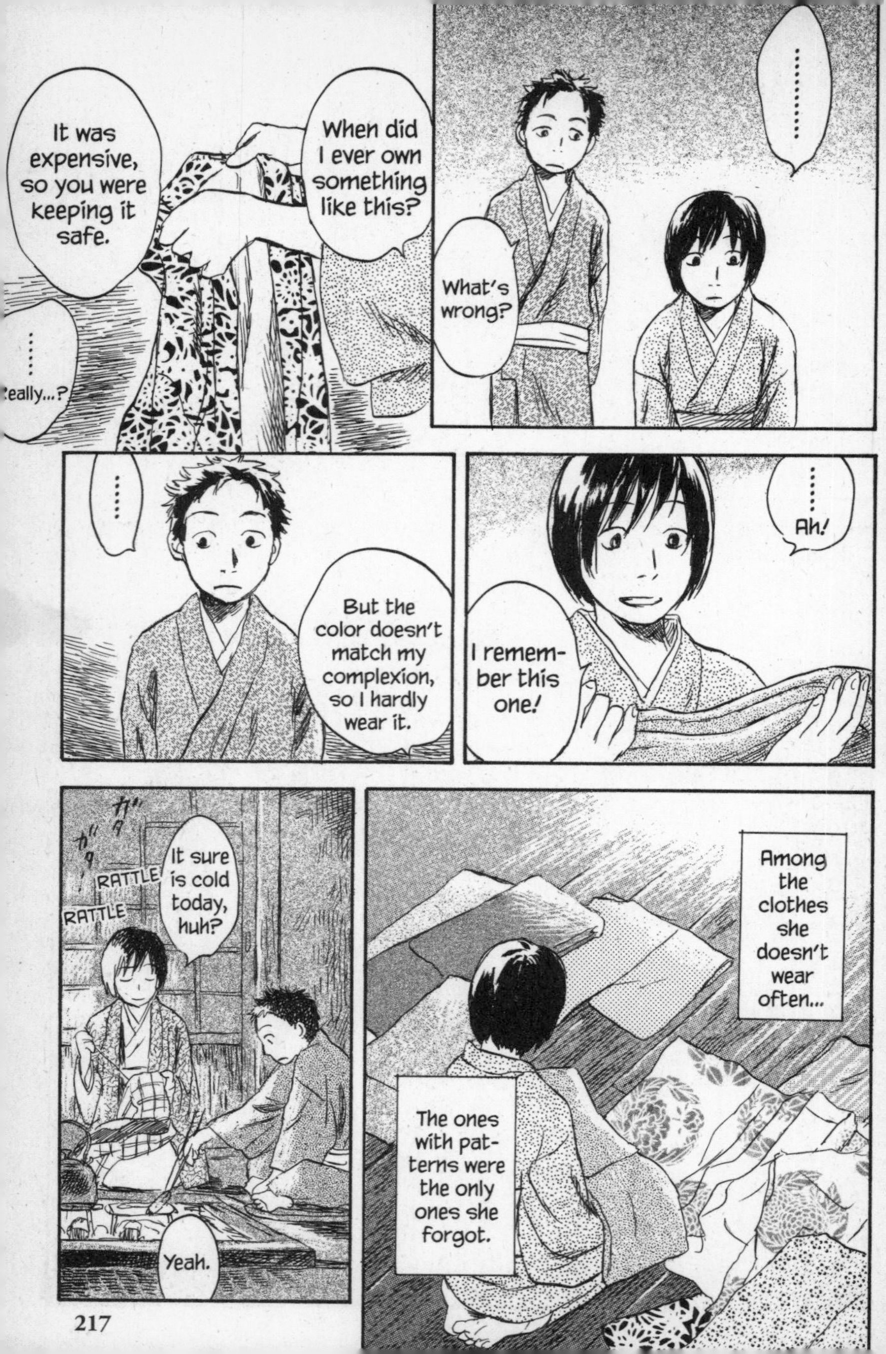
……
What's wrong?
When did I ever own something like this?
It was expensive, so you were keeping it safe.
……
eally...?
……
Ah!
I remember this one!
……
But the color doesn't match my complexion, so I hardly wear it.
Among the clothes she doesn't wear often...
The ones with patterns were the only ones she forgot.
RATTLE
RATTLE
It sure is cold today, huh?
Yeah.

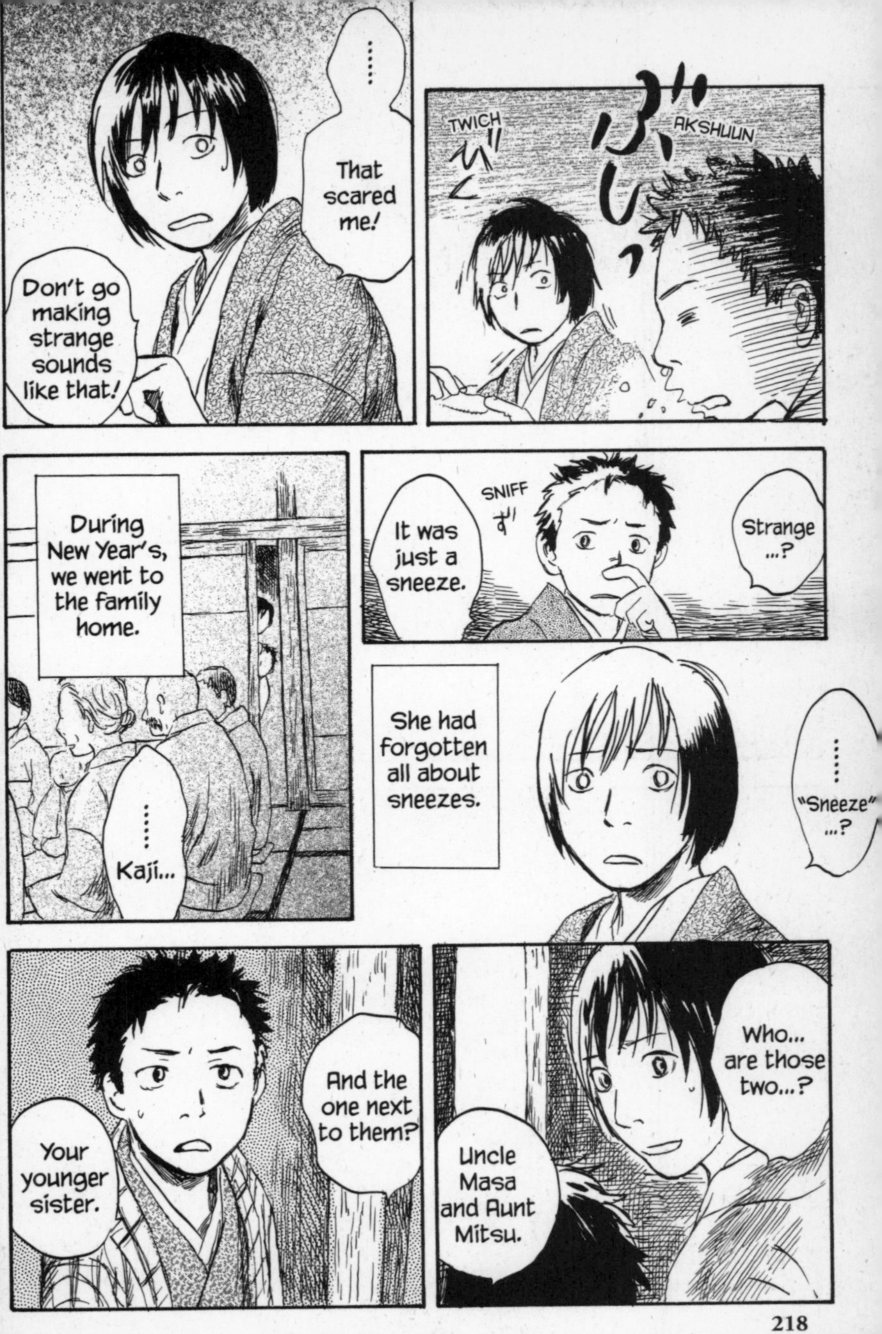

ぶしっ
AKSHUUN
びく
TWICH
......
That scared me!
Don't go making strange sounds like that!
Strange ...?
ず
SNIFF
It was just a sneeze.
......
"Sneeze" ...?
She had forgotten all about sneezes.
During New Year's, we went to the family home.
......
Kaji...
Who... are those two...?
Uncle Masa and Aunt Mitsu.
And the one next to them?
Your younger sister.

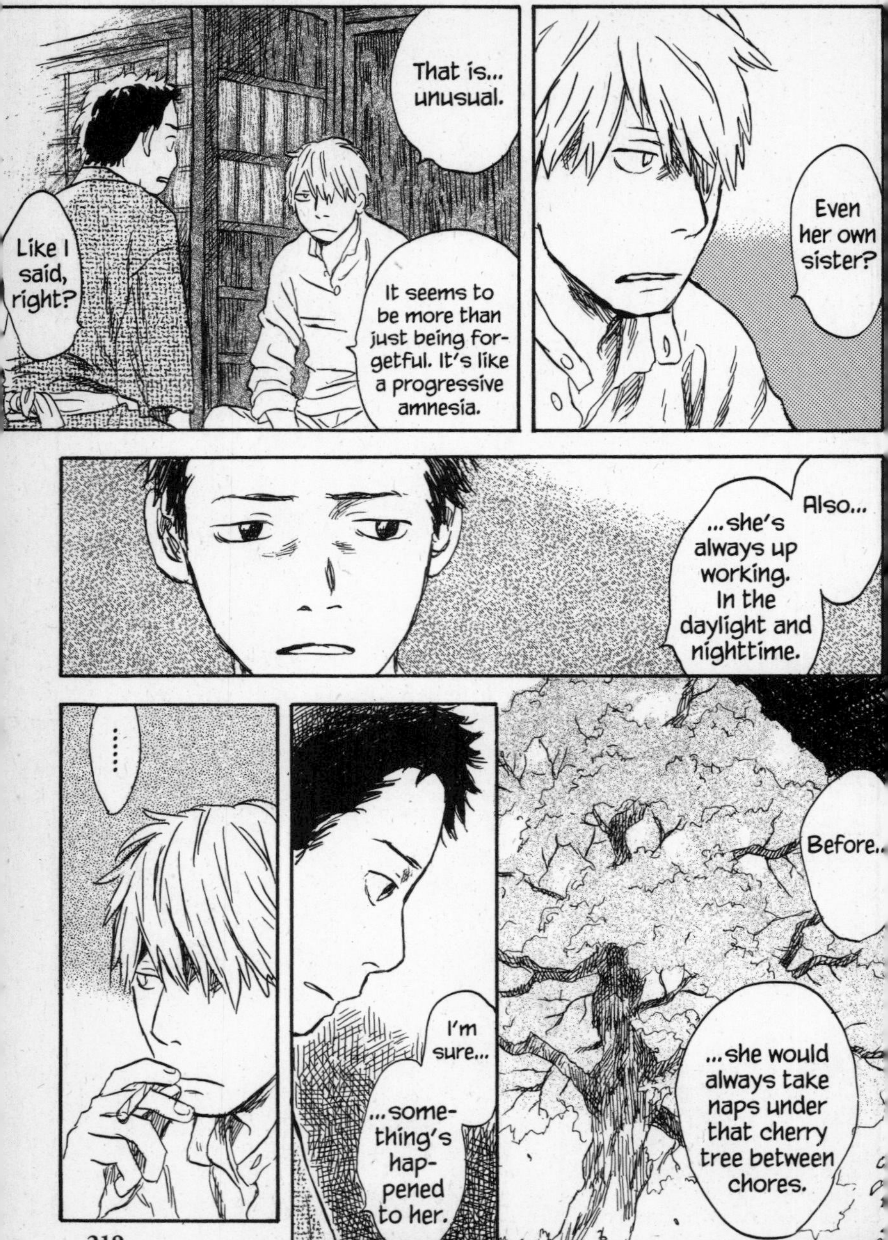
Even her own sister?
That is... unusual.
It seems to be more than just being forgetful. It's like a progressive amnesia.
Like I said, right?
Also...
...she's always up working. In the daylight and nighttime.
Before...
...she would always take naps under that cherry tree between chores.
I'm sure...
...something's happened to her.
......

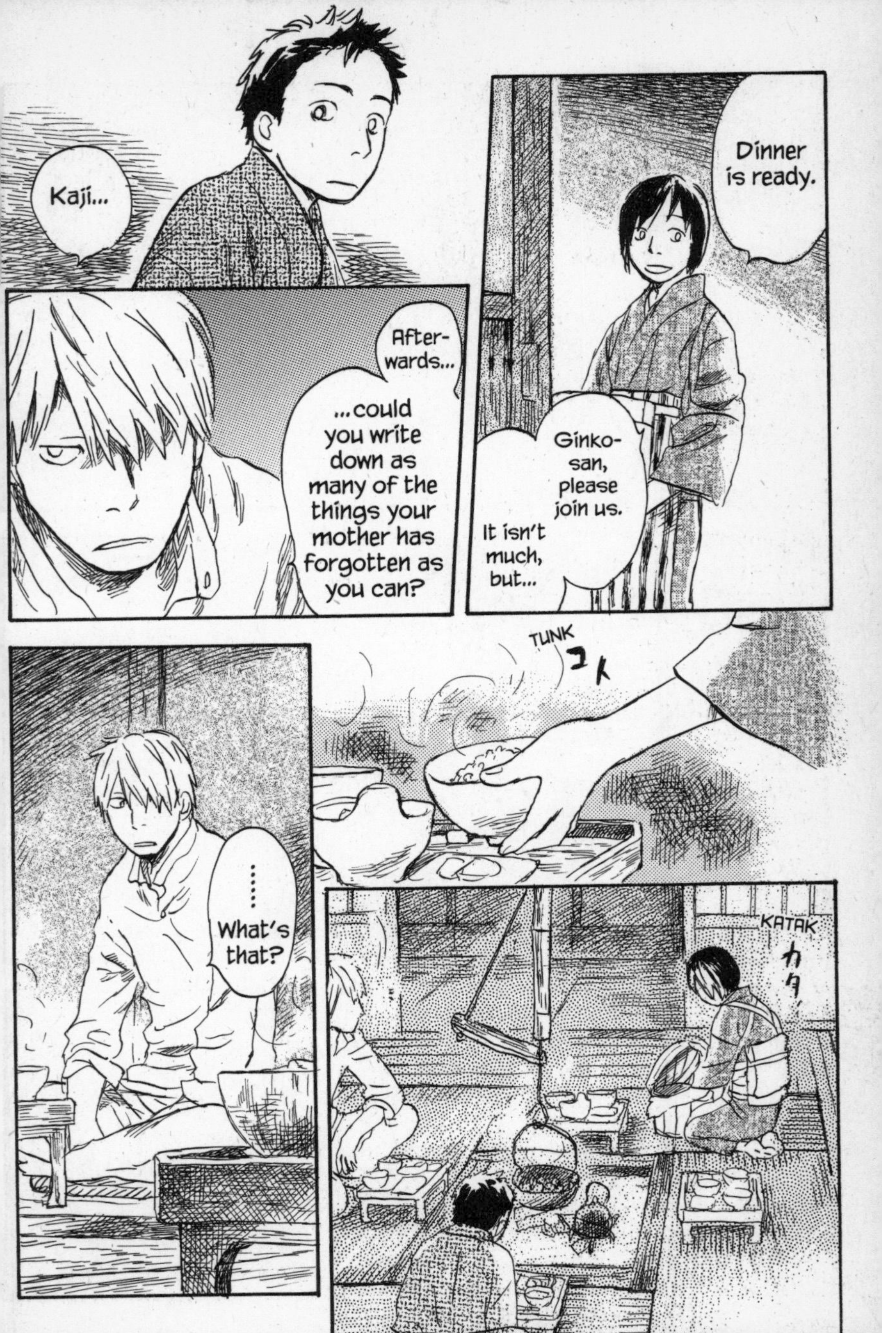
Dinner is ready.
Ginko-san, please join us.
It isn't much, but...
Kaji...
Afterwards...
...could you write down as many of the things your mother has forgotten as you can?
TUNK
コト
KATAK
カタ
......
What's that?

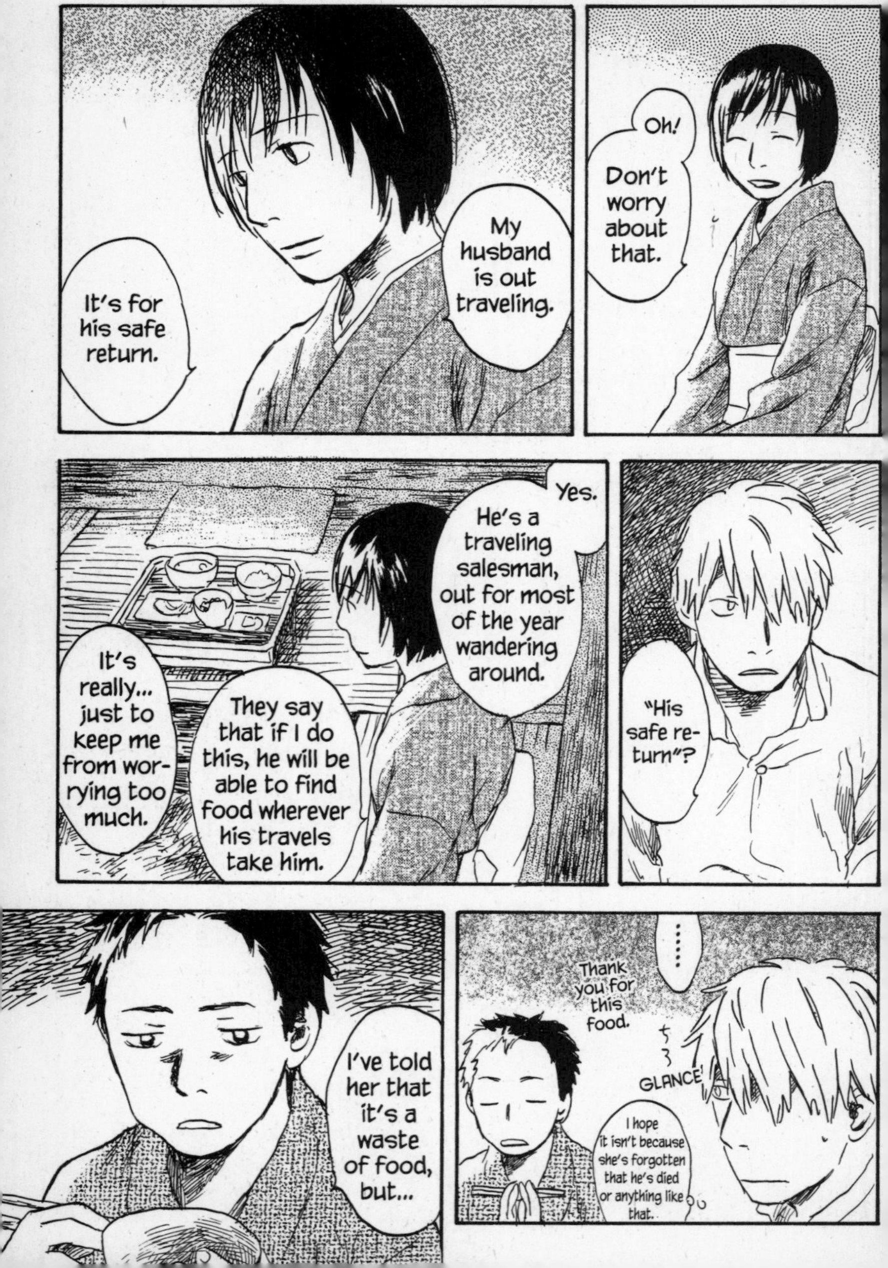
Oh!
Don't worry about that.
My husband is out traveling.
It's for his safe return.
"His safe re-turn"?
Yes.
He's a traveling salesman, out for most of the year wandering around.
They say that if I do this, he will be able to find food wherever his travels take him.
It's really... just to keep me from wor-rying too much.
......
Thank you for this food.
ちろ
GLANCE
I hope it isn't because she's forgotten that he's died or anything like that.
I've told her that it's a waste of food, but...

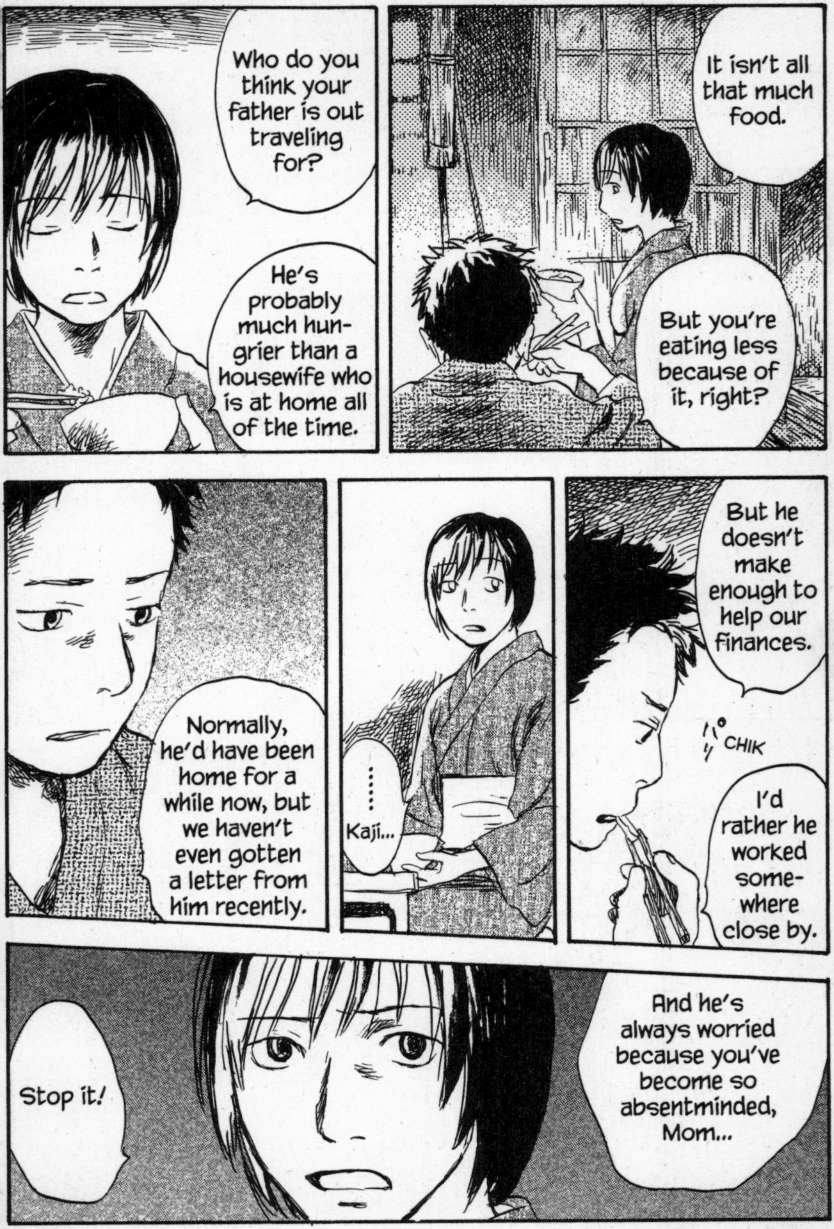
It isn't all that much food.
But you're eating less because of it, right?
Who do you think your father is out traveling for?
He's probably much hungrier than a housewife who is at home all of the time.
But he doesn't make enough to help our finances.
CHIK
I'd rather he worked somewhere close by.
......
Kaji...
Normally, he'd have been home for a while now, but we haven't even gotten a letter from him recently.
And he's always worried because you've become so absentminded, Mom...
Stop it!

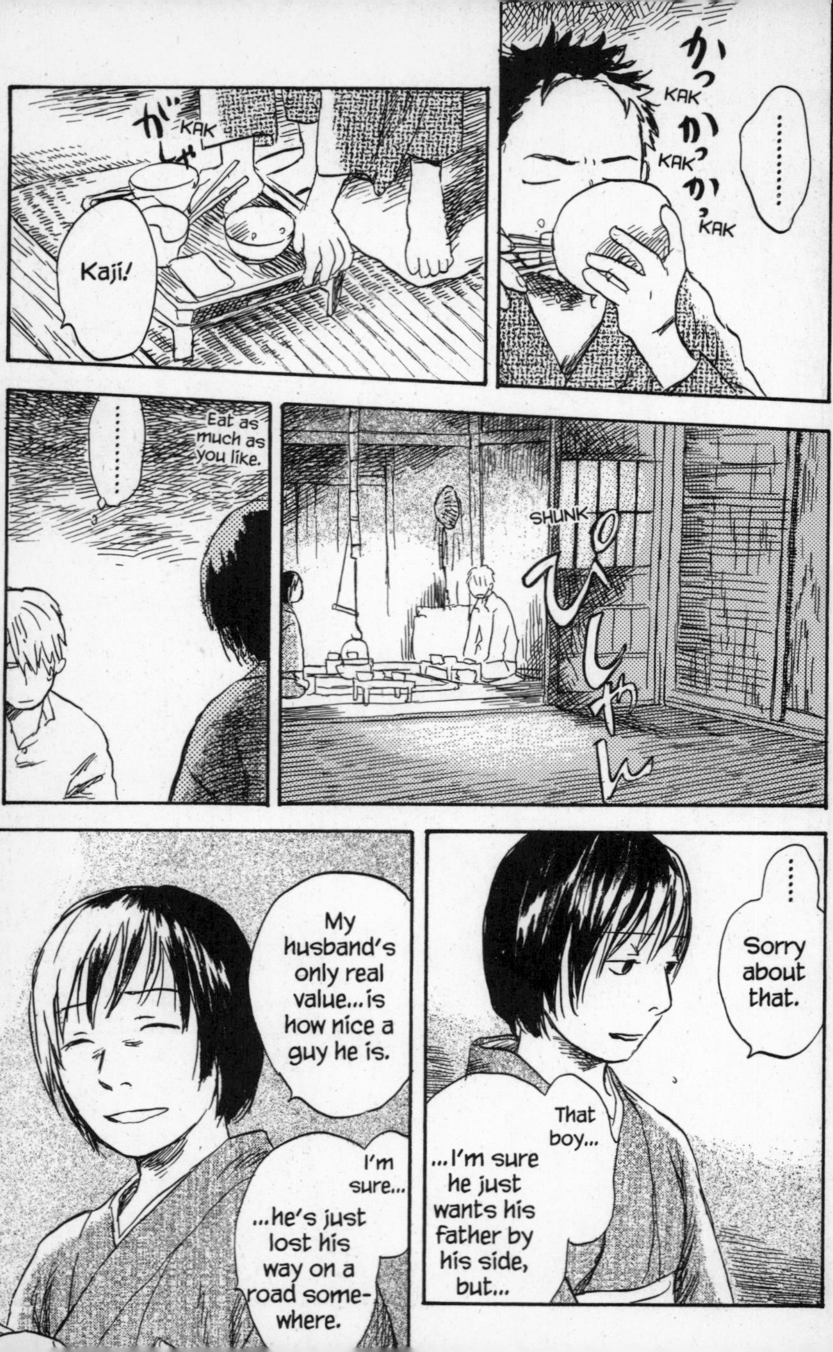
……
かっかっかっ
KAK KAK KAK
がしゃ
KAK
Kaji!
ぴしゃん
SHUNK
Eat as much as you like.
……
……
Sorry about that.
That boy...
...I'm sure he just wants his father by his side, but...
My husband's only real value...is how nice a guy he is.
I'm sure...
...he's just lost his way on a road somewhere.

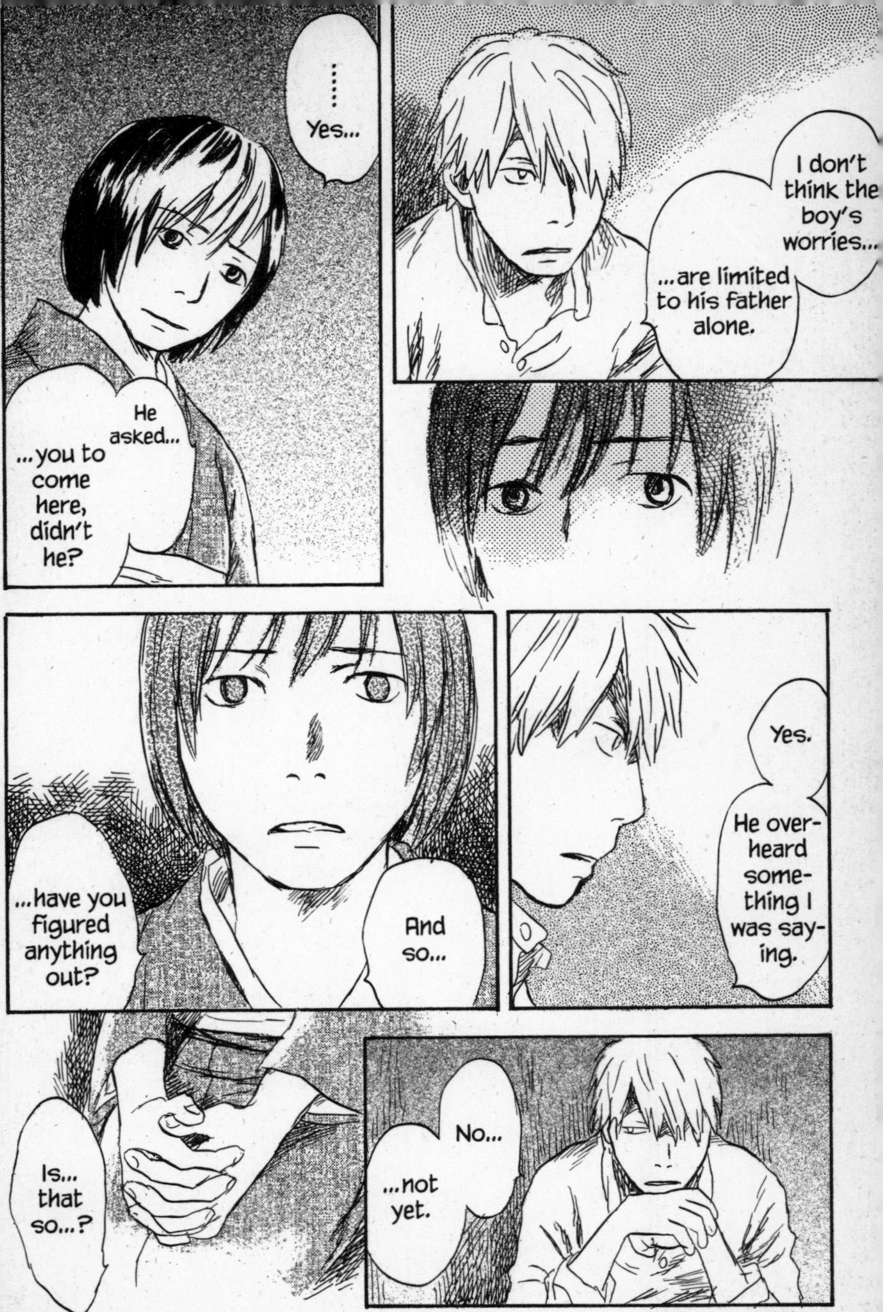
I don't think the boy's worries...
...are limited to his father alone.
......
Yes...
He asked...
...you to come here, didn't he?
Yes.
He over-heard some-thing I was say-ing.
And so...
...have you figured anything out?
No...
...not yet.
Is... that so...?

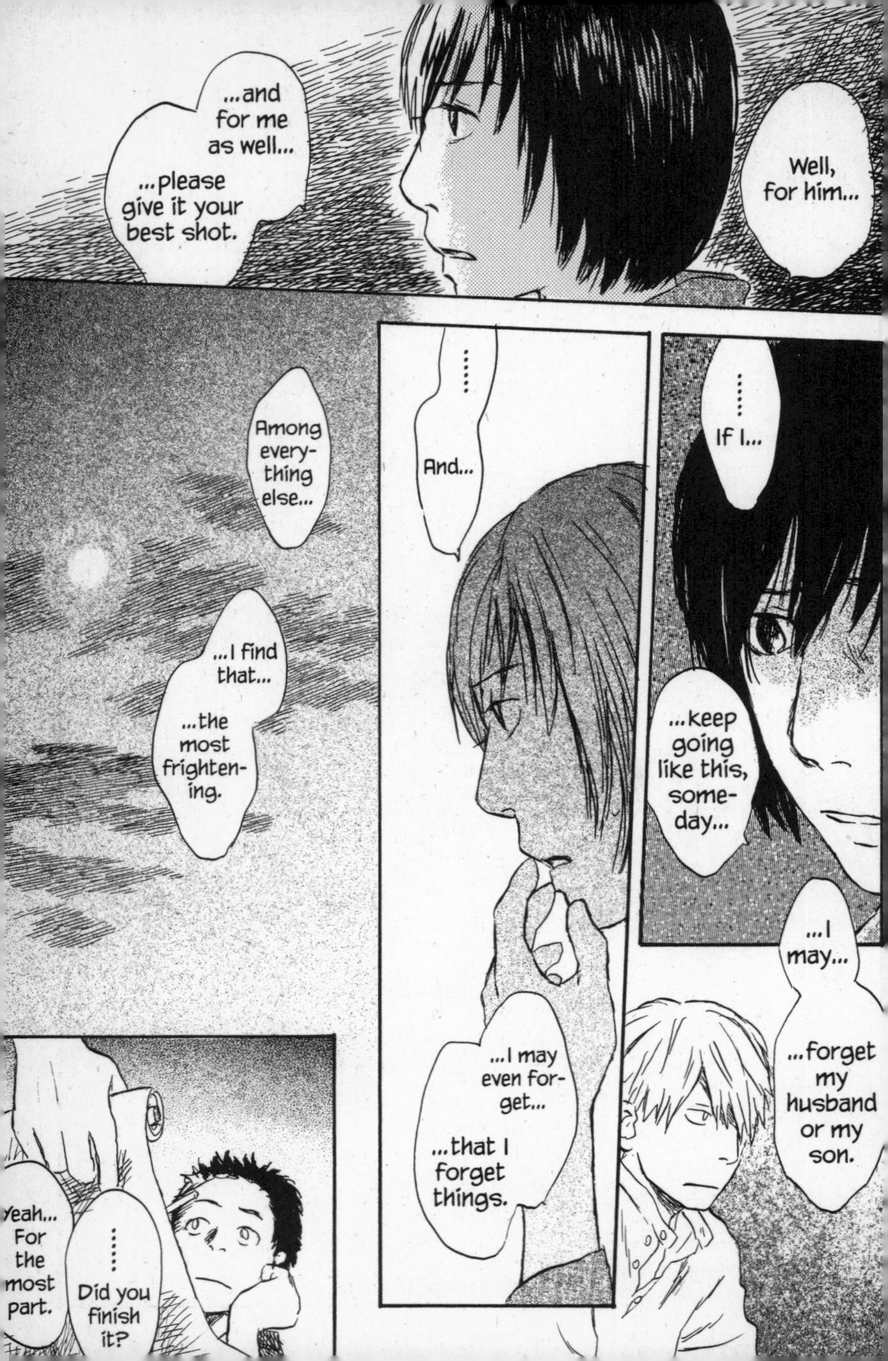
Well, for him...
...and for me as well...
...please give it your best shot.
......
If I...
...keep going like this, someday...
...I may...
...forget my husband or my son.
......
And...
...I may even forget...
...that I forget things.
Among everything else...
...I find that...
...the most frightening.
......
Did you finish it?
Yeah... For the most part.

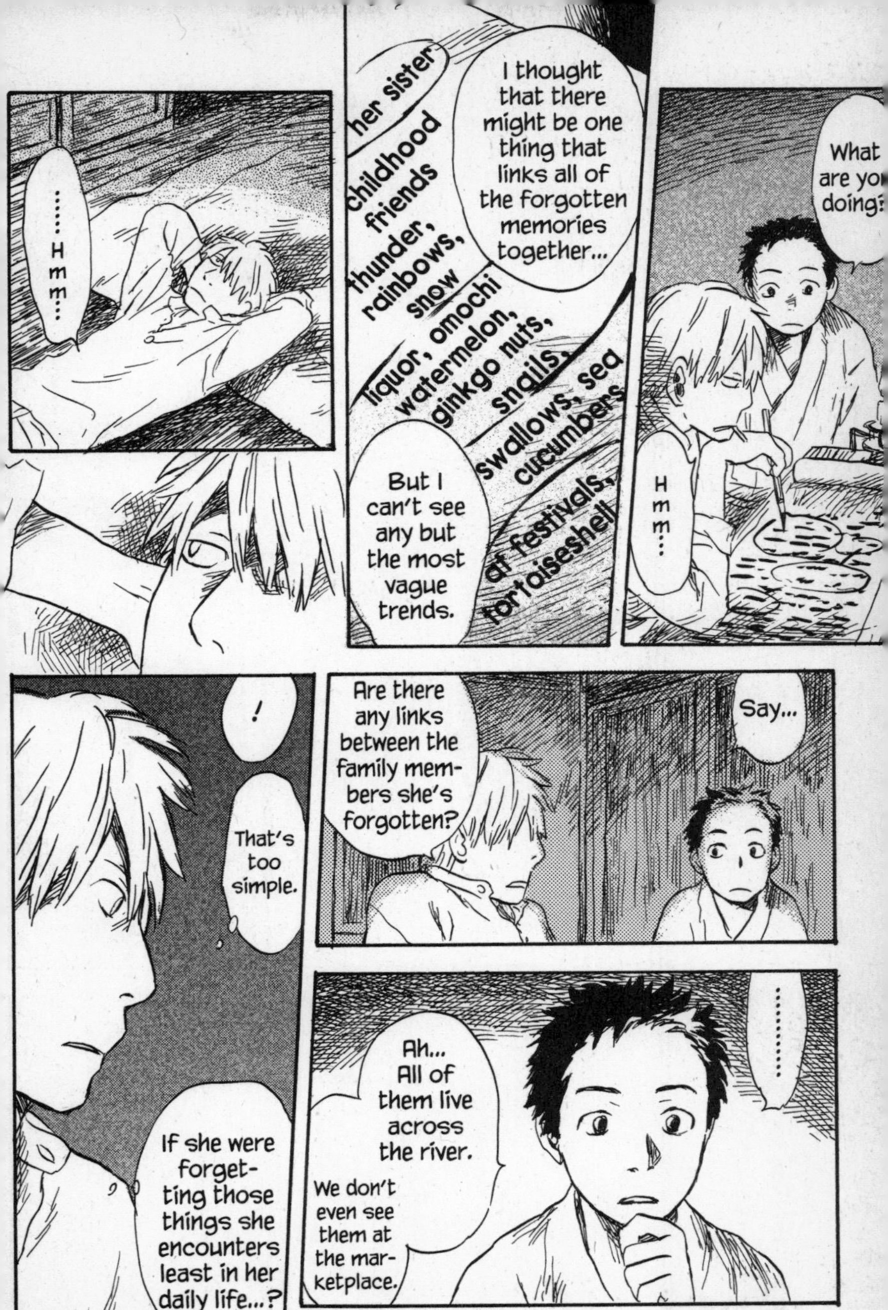

What are yo doing?
Hmm...
I thought that there might be one thing that links all of the forgotten memories together...
her sister
childhood friends
thunder, rainbows, snow
liquor, omochi
watermelon, ginkgo nuts, snails,
swallows, sea cucumbers
at festivals, tortoiseshell
But I can't see any but the most vague trends.
......Hmm...
Say...
Are there any links between the family members she's forgotten?
....
Ah... All of them live across the river.
We don't even see them at the marketplace.
!
That's too simple.
If she were forgetting those things she encounters least in her daily life...?

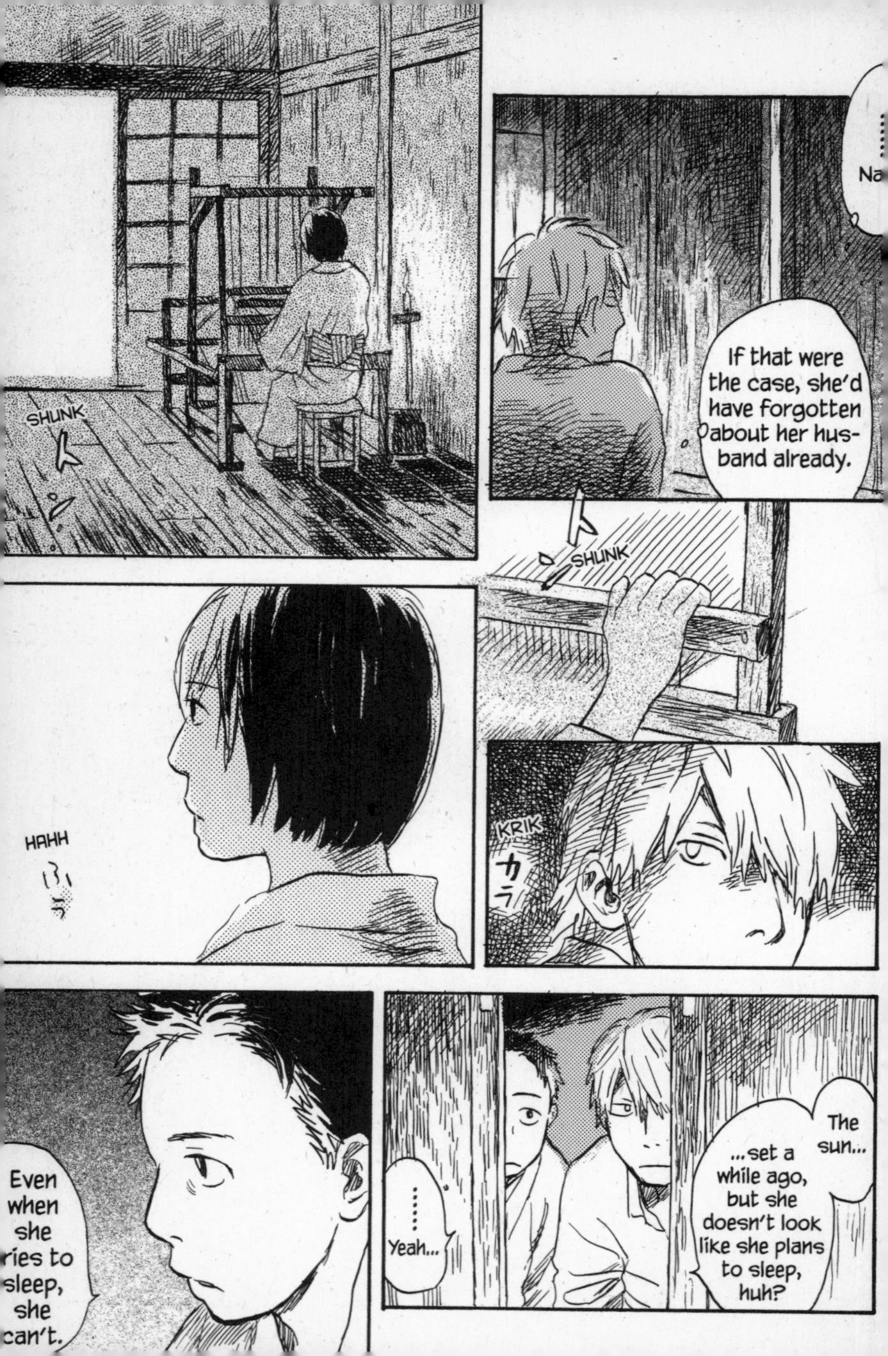

Na
If that were the case, she'd have forgotten about her husband already.
SHUNK
SHUNK
KRIK
HAHH
The sun...
...set a while ago, but she doesn't look like she plans to sleep, huh?
......
Yeah...
Even when she ries to sleep, she can't.

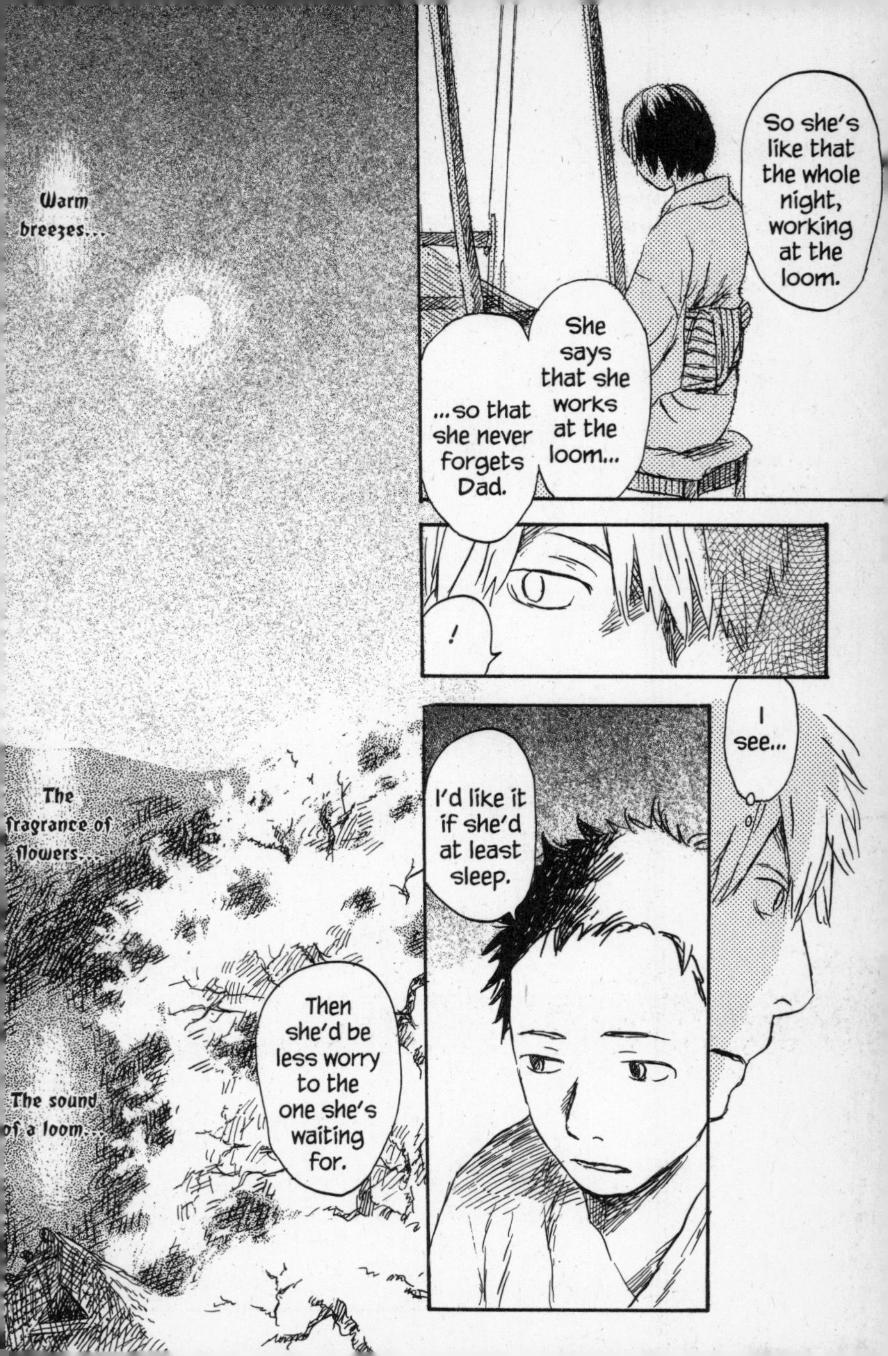
So she's like that the whole night, working at the loom.
She says that she works at the loom...
...so that she never forgets Dad.
!
I see...
I'd like it if she'd at least sleep.
Then she'd be less worry to the one she's waiting for.
Warm breezes...
The fragrance of flowers...
The sound of a loom...

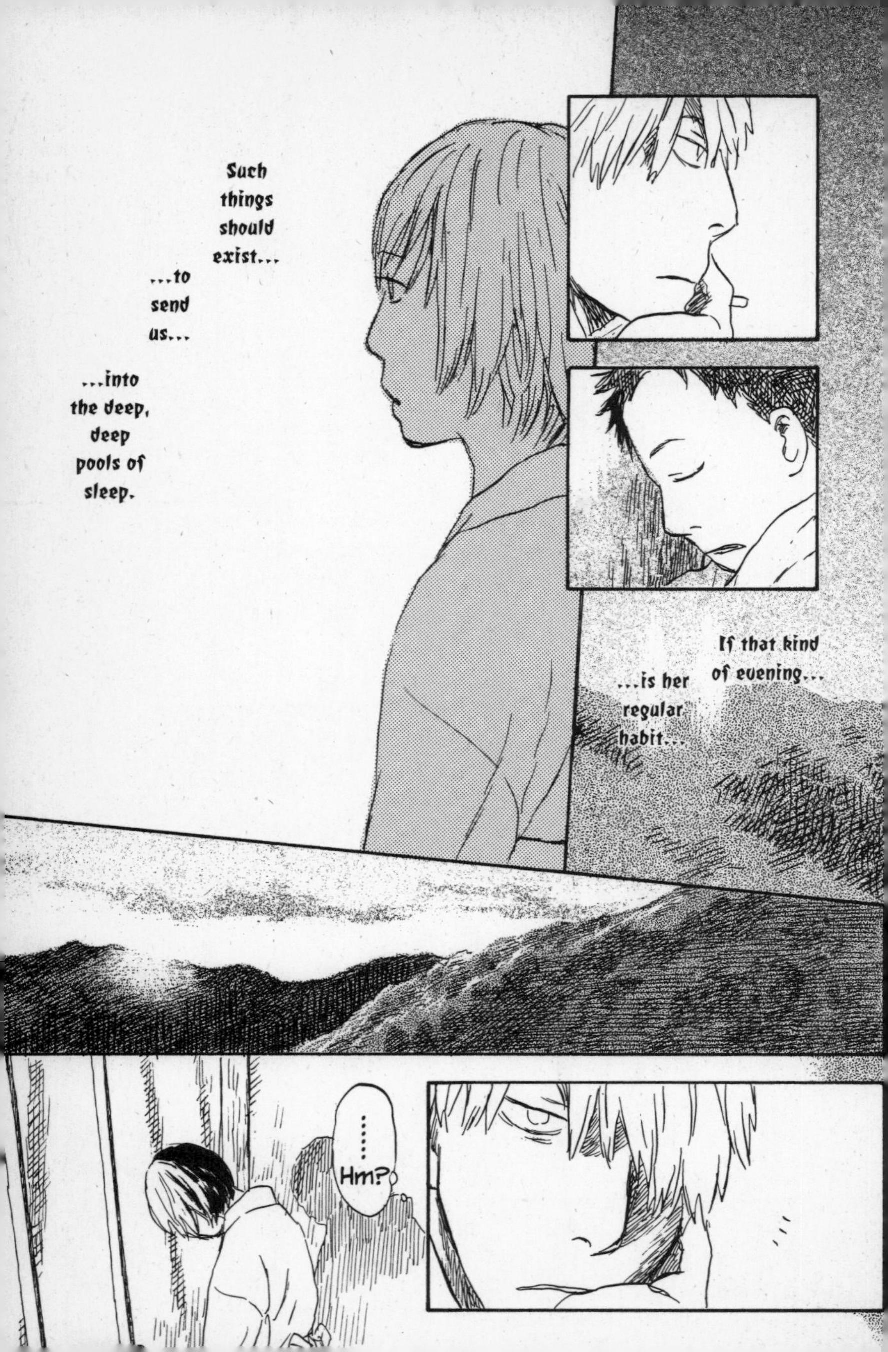
If that kind of evening...
...is her regular habit...
Such things should exist...
...to send us...
...into the deep, deep pools of sleep.
......
Hm?

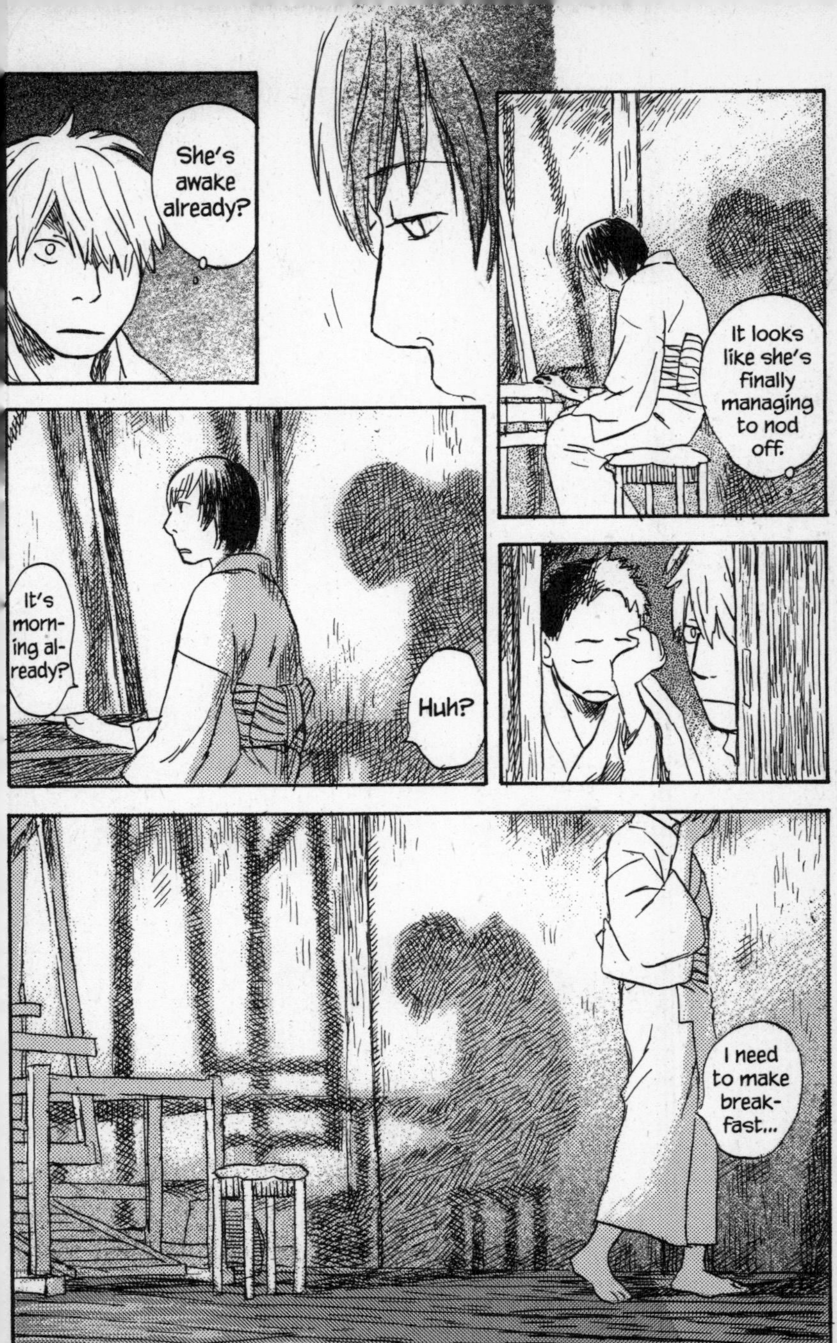
It looks like she's finally managing to nod off.
She's awake already?
Huh?
It's morn-ing al-ready?
I need to make break-fast...

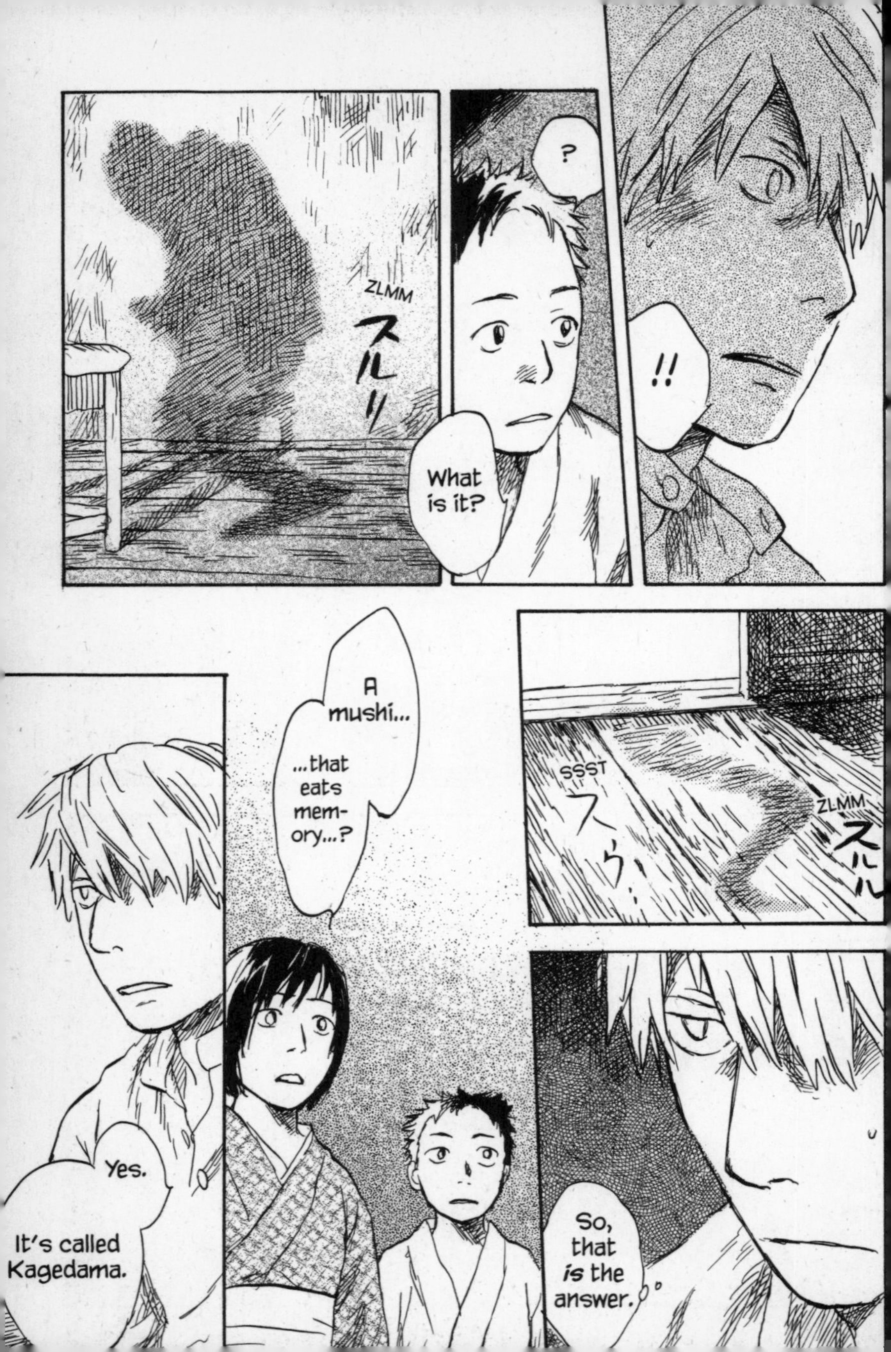
!!
?
What is it?
ZLMM
スルリ
ZLMM
スルル
SSST
スぅ
So, that *is* the answer.
A mushi...
...that eats mem-ory...?
Yes.
It's called Kagedama.

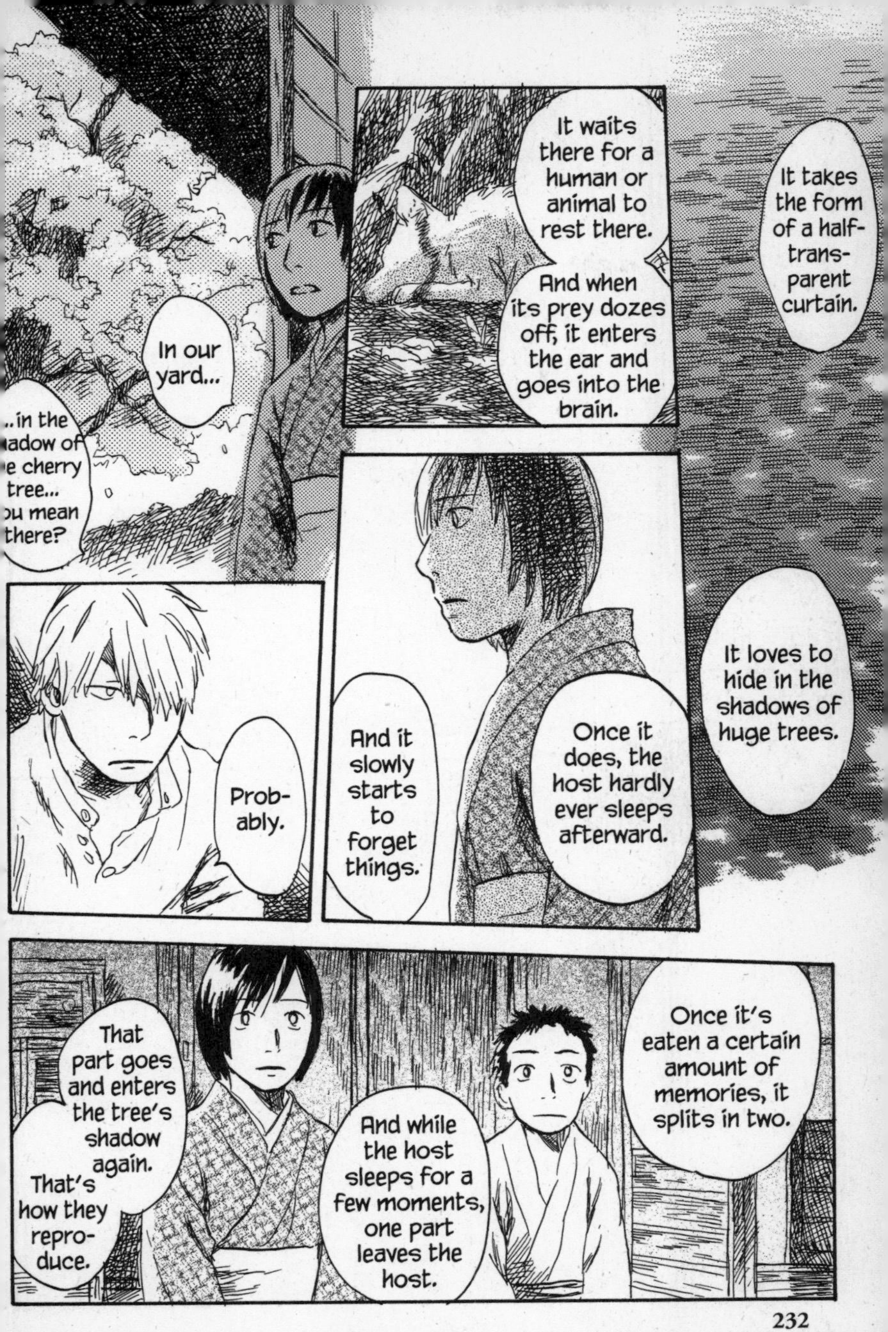
It takes the form of a half-transparent curtain.
It waits there for a human or animal to rest there.
And when its prey dozes off, it enters the ear and goes into the brain.
Once it does, the host hardly ever sleeps afterward.
And it slowly starts to forget things.
It loves to hide in the shadows of huge trees.
In our yard...
..in the adow of e cherry tree... ou mean there?
Prob-ably.
Once it's eaten a certain amount of memories, it splits in two.
And while the host sleeps for a few moments, one part leaves the host.
That part goes and enters the tree's shadow again.
That's how they repro-duce.

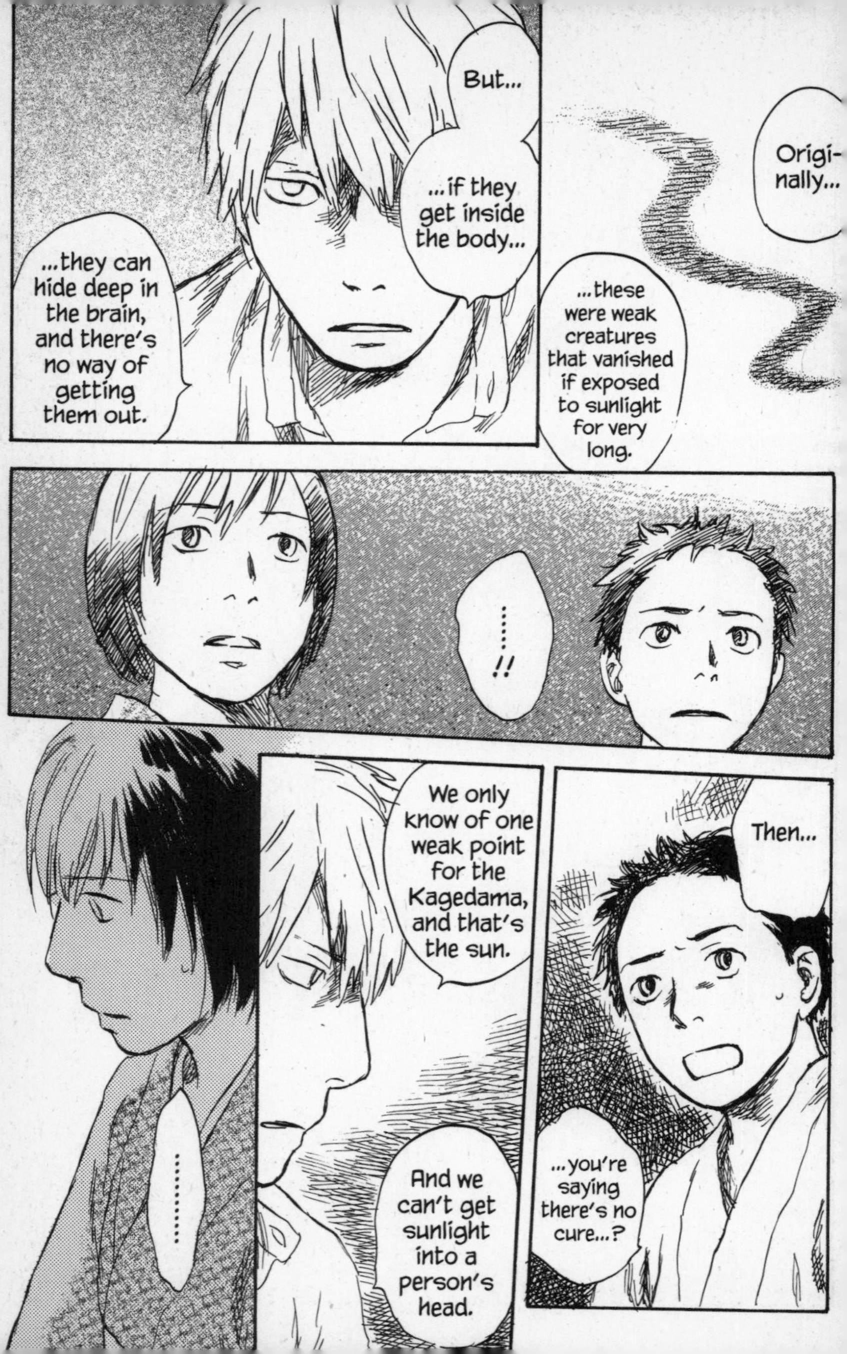
Originally...
...these were weak creatures that vanished if exposed to sunlight for very long.
But...
...if they get inside the body...
...they can hide deep in the brain, and there's no way of getting them out.
......!!
Then...
...you're saying there's no cure...?
We only know of one weak point for the Kagedama, and that's the sun.
And we can't get sunlight into a person's head.
....

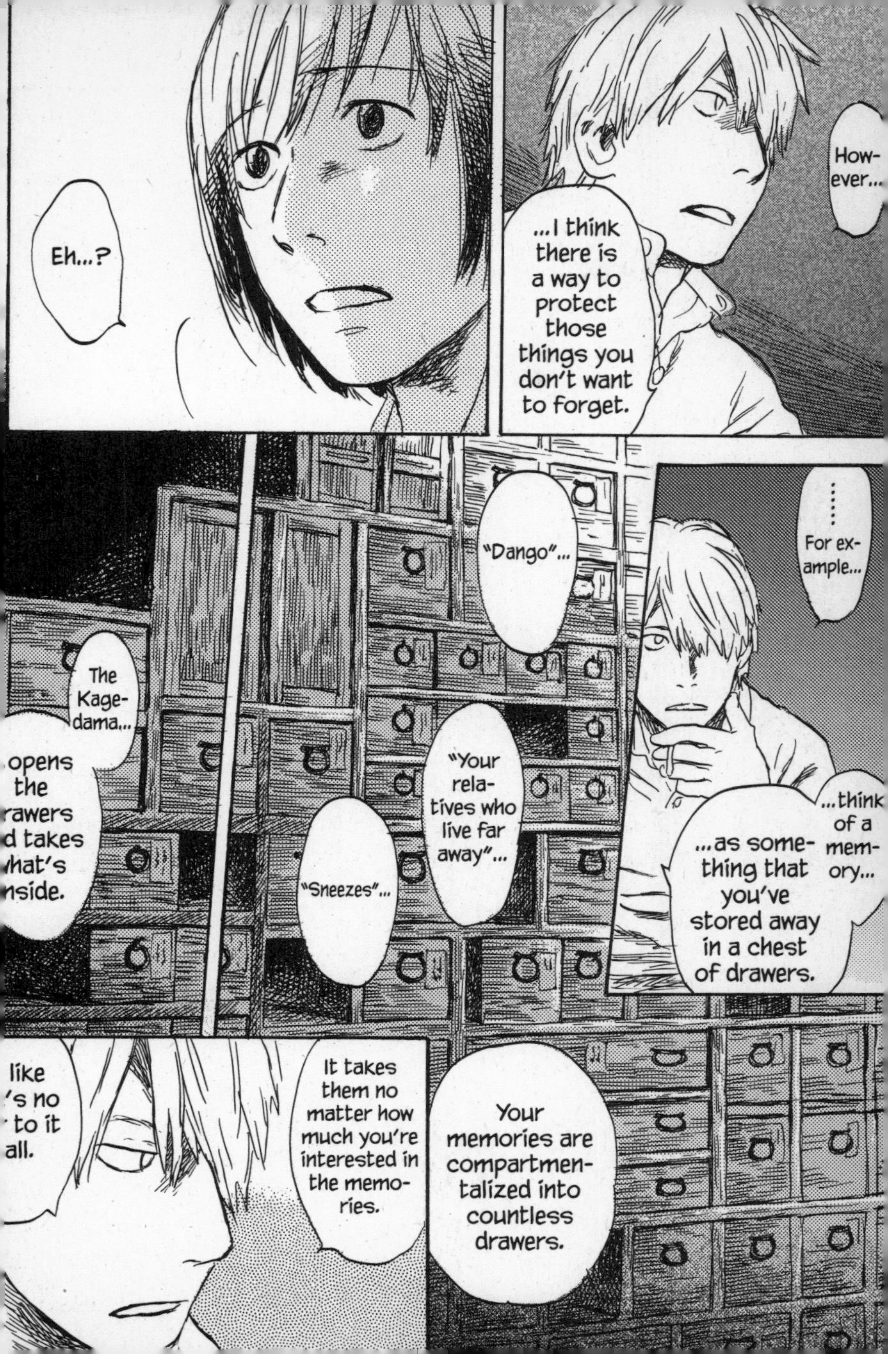

How-ever...
...I think there is a way to protect those things you don't want to forget.
Eh...?
......
For ex-ample...
...think of a mem-ory...
...as some-thing that you've stored away in a chest of drawers.
"Dango"...
"Your rela-tives who live far away"...
"Sneezes"...
The Kage-dama...
opens the rawers d takes hat's nside.
Your memories are compartmen-talized into countless drawers.
It takes them no matter how much you're interested in the memo-ries.
like 's no to it all.

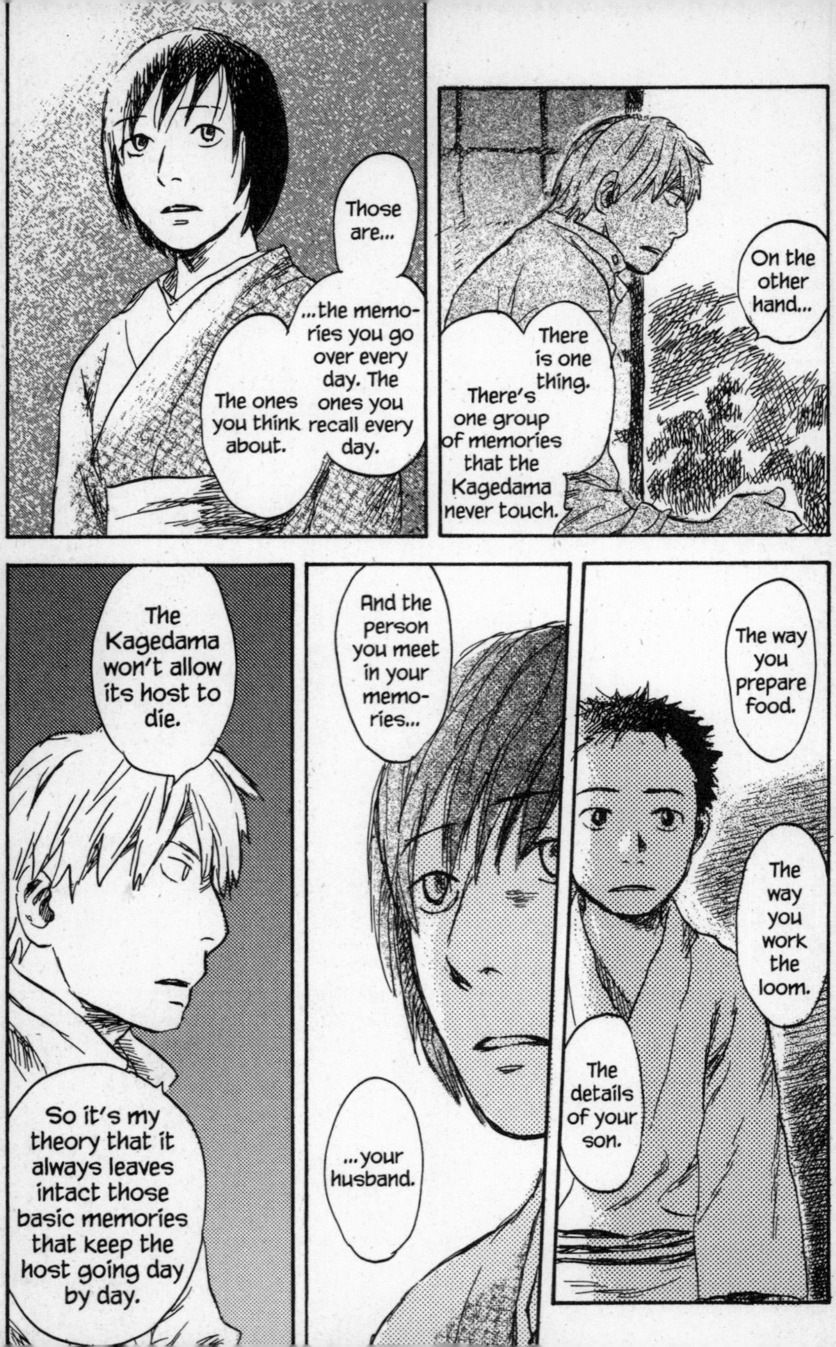
On the other hand...
There is one thing.
There's one group of memories that the Kagedama never touch.
Those are...
...the memories you go over every day. The ones you recall every day.
The ones you think about.
The way you prepare food.
The way you work the loom.
The details of your son.
And the person you meet in your memories...
...your husband.
The Kagedama won't allow its host to die.
So it's my theory that it always leaves intact those basic memories that keep the host going day by day.

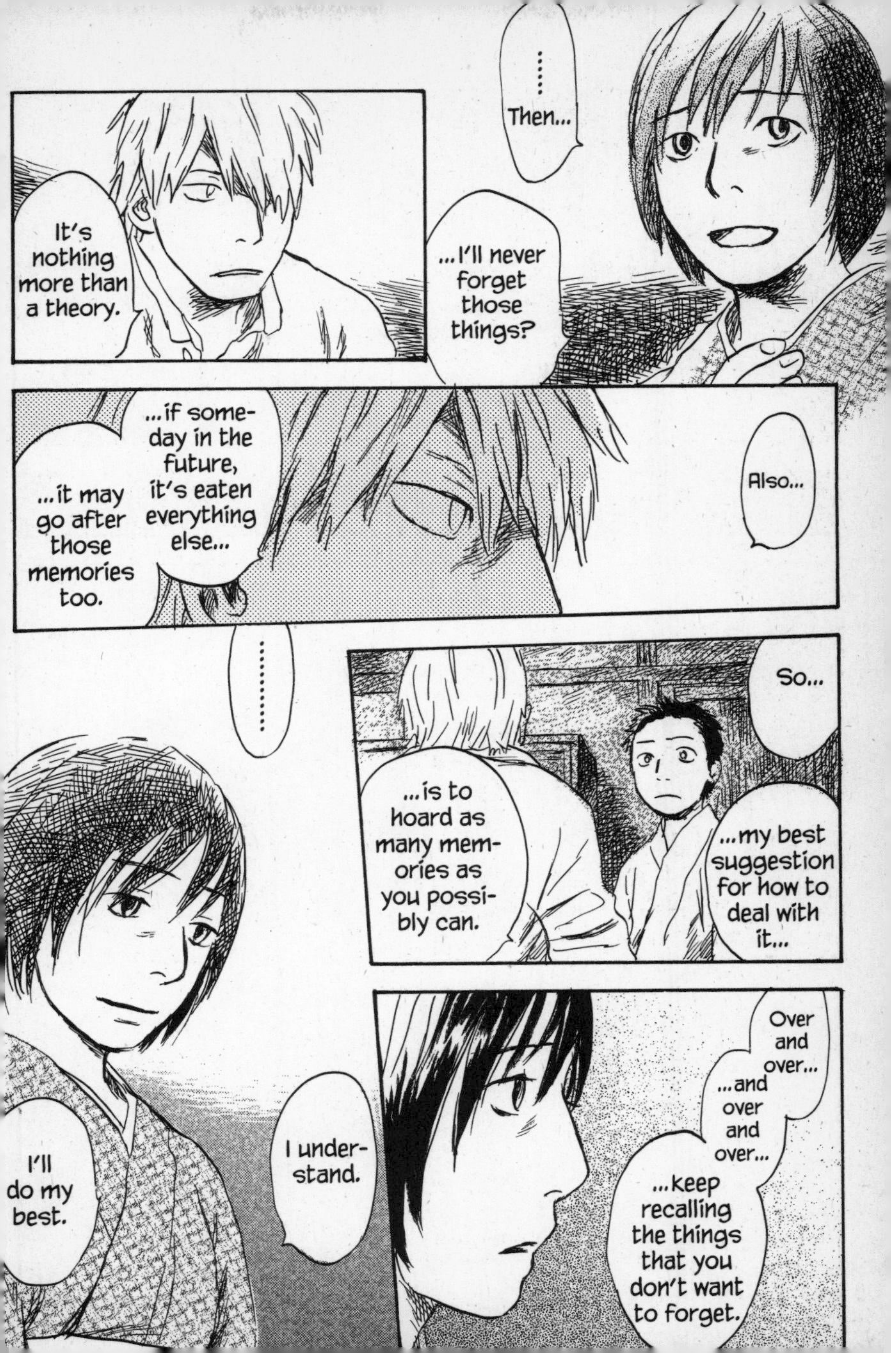
......
Then...
...I'll never forget those things?
It's nothing more than a theory.
Also...
...if someday in the future, it's eaten everything else...
...it may go after those memories too.
So...
...my best suggestion for how to deal with it...
...is to hoard as many memories as you possibly can.
Over and over...
...and over and over...
...keep recalling the things that you don't want to forget.
I understand.
......
I'll do my best.

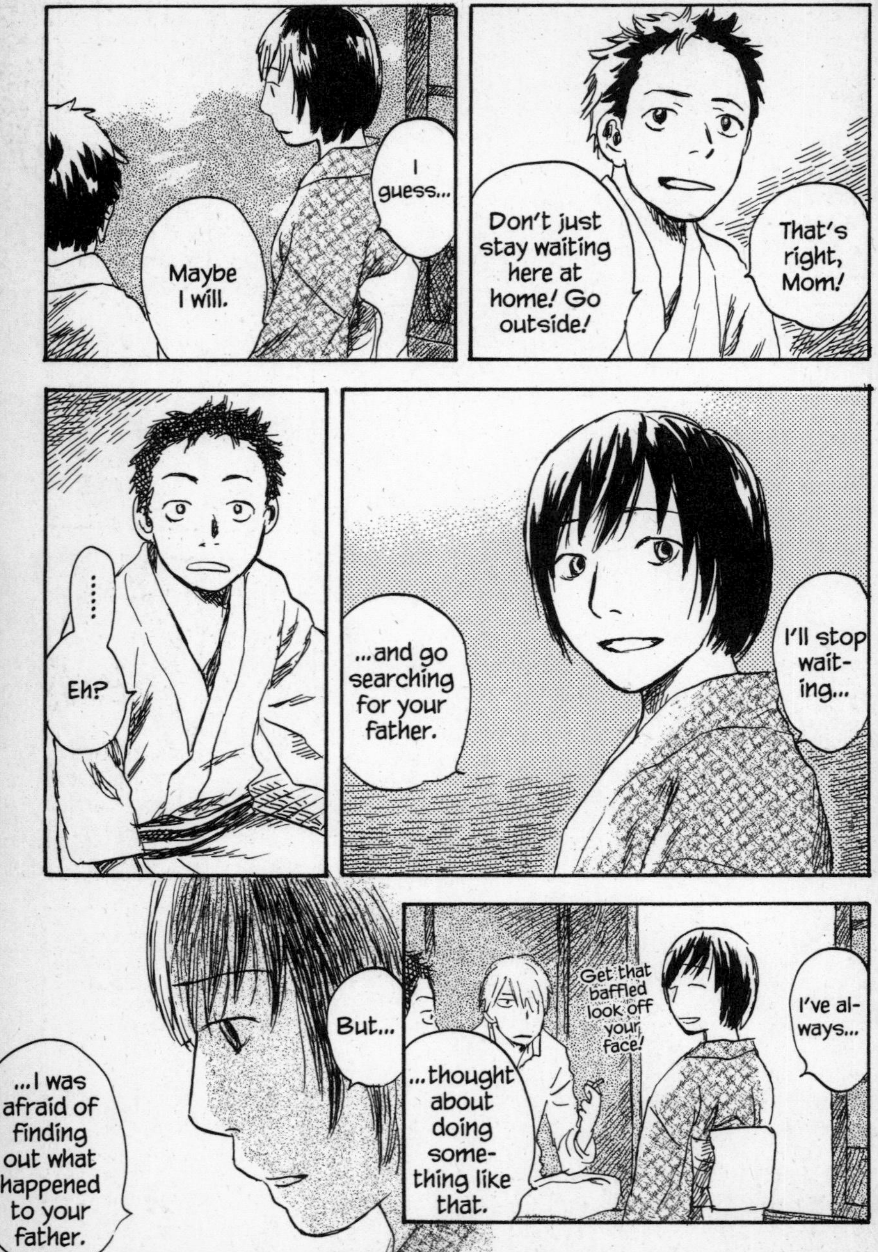
That's right, Mom!
Don't just stay waiting here at home! Go outside!
I guess...
Maybe I will.
I'll stop waiting...
...and go searching for your father.
......
Eh?
I've always...
Get that baffled look off your face!
...thought about doing something like that.
But...
...I was afraid of finding out what happened to your father.

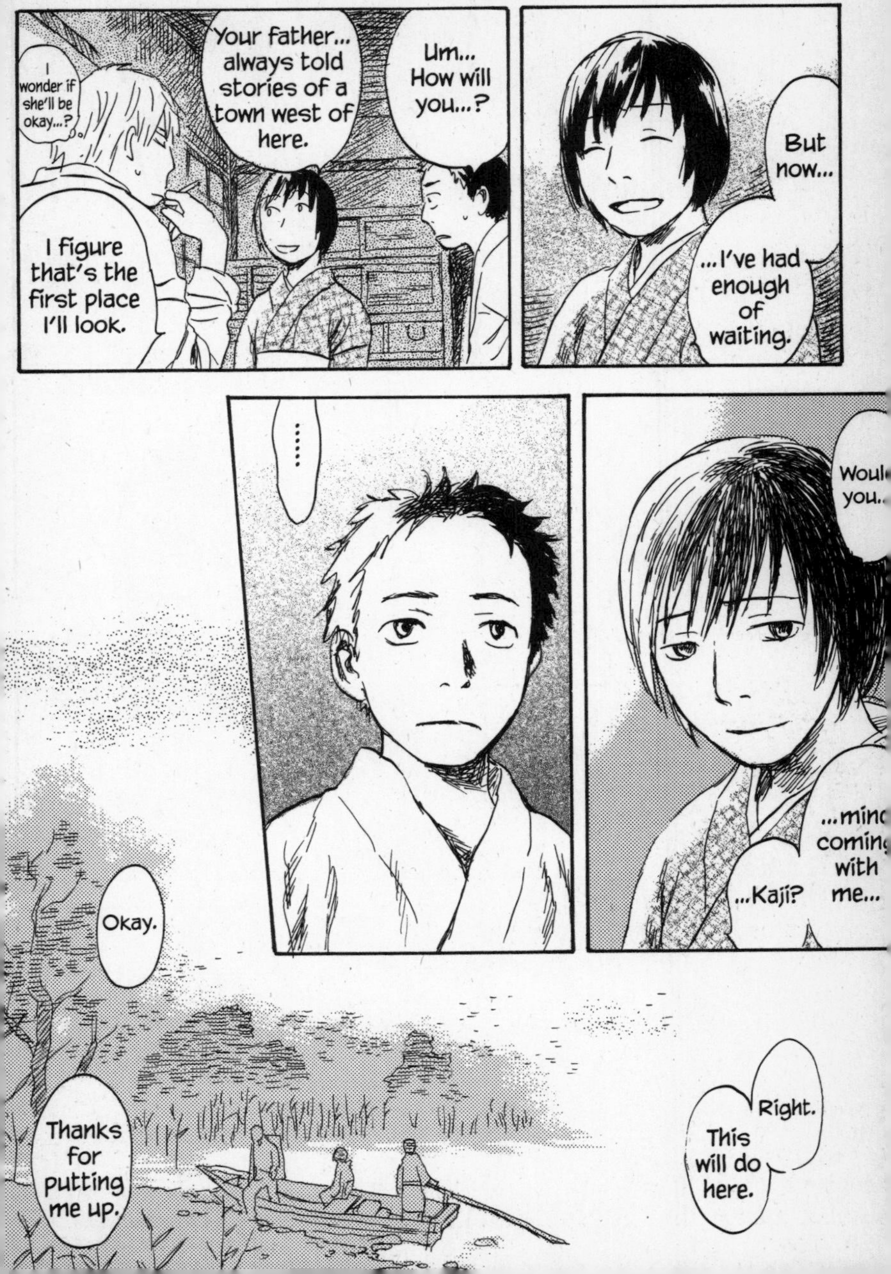
But now...
...I've had enough of waiting.
Um... How will you...?
Your father... always told stories of a town west of here.
I wonder if she'll be okay...?
I figure that's the first place I'll look.
Woul you..
...min comin with me...
...Kaji?
......
Okay.
Right. This will do here.
Thanks for putting me up.

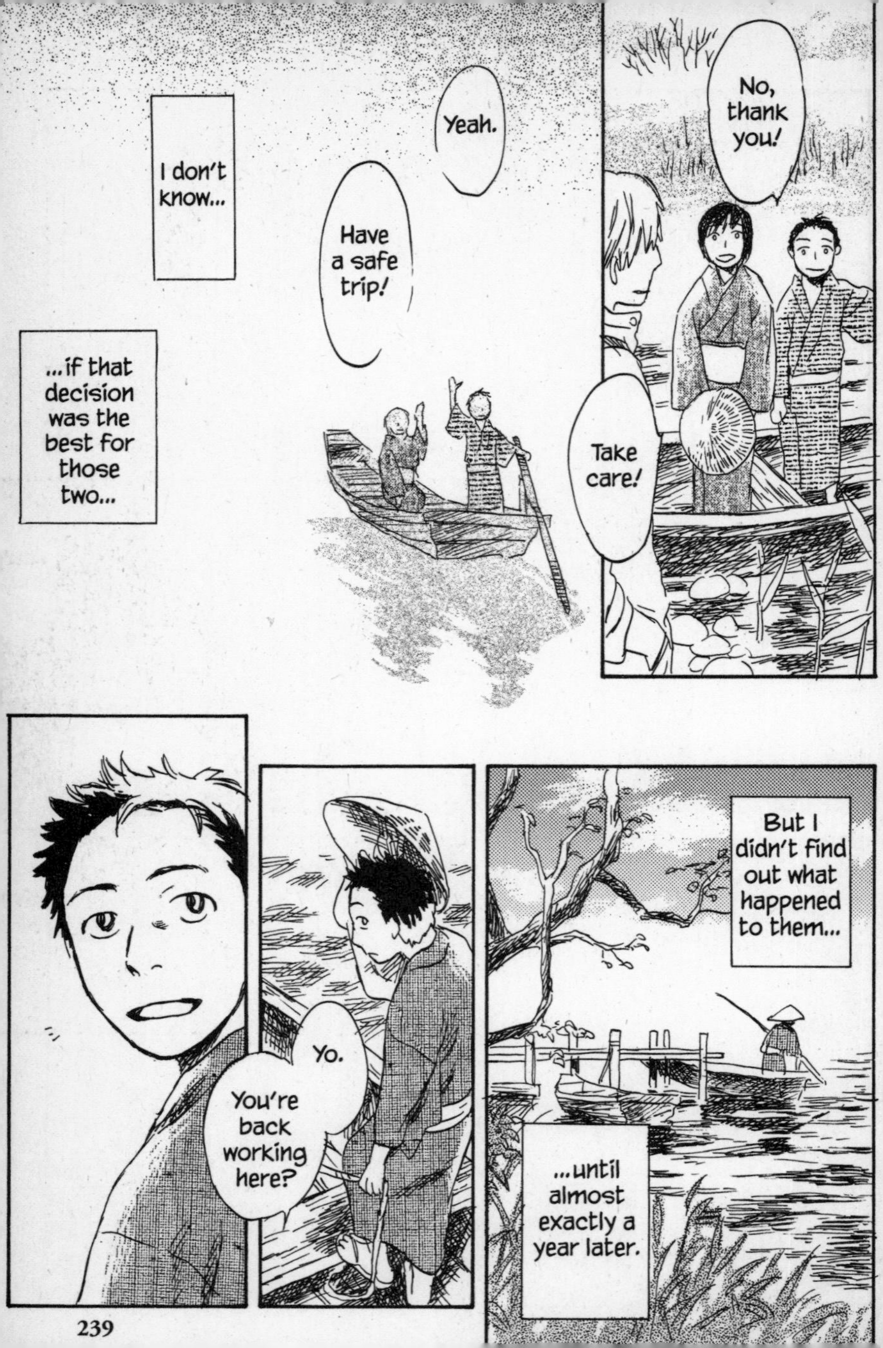
No, thank you!
Take care!
Yeah.
Have a safe trip!
I don't know...
...if that decision was the best for those two...
But I didn't find out what happened to them...
...until almost exactly a year later.
Yo.
You're back working here?

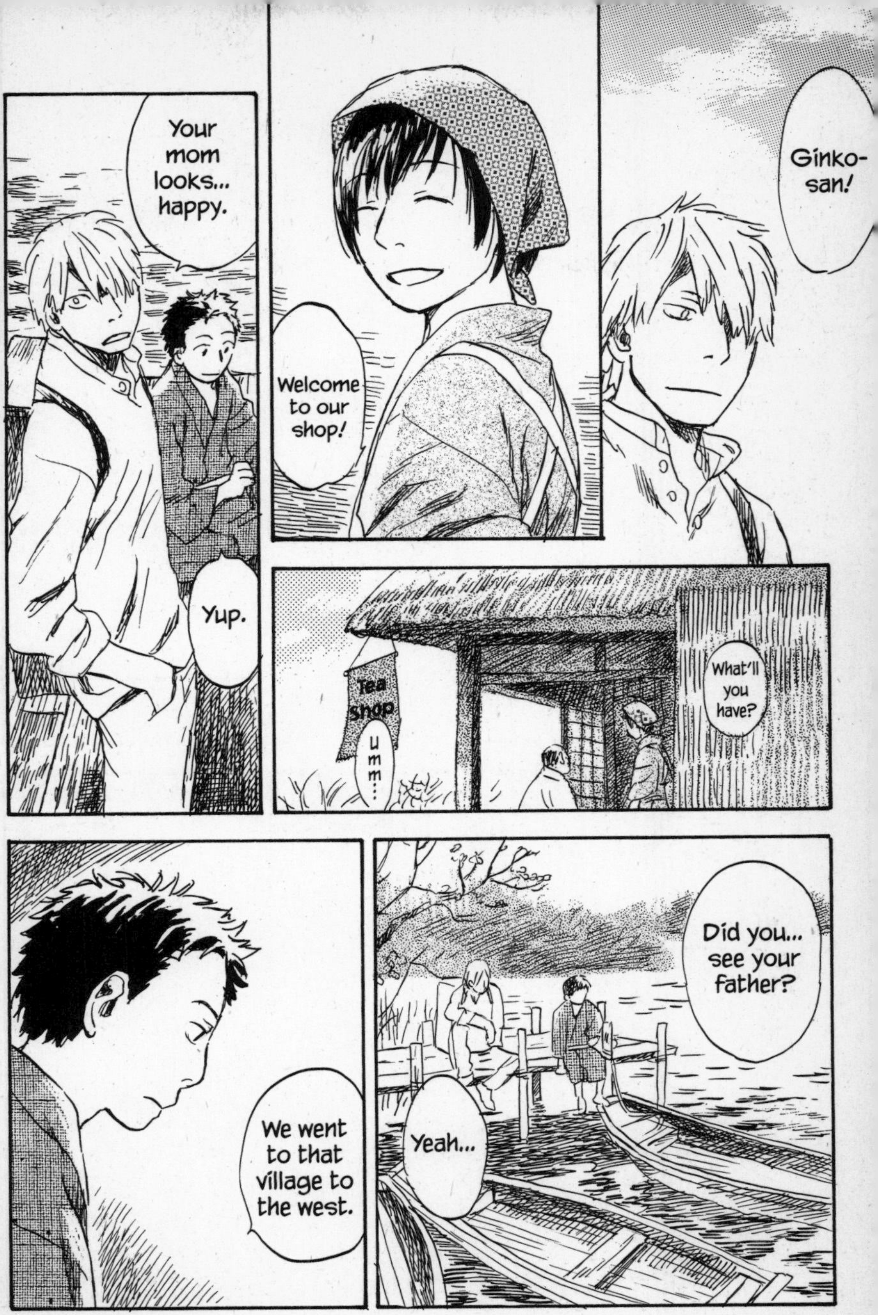
Ginko-san!
Welcome to our shop!
Tea shop
What'll you have?
Umm...
Your mom looks... happy.
Yup.
Did you... see your father?
Yeah...
We went to that village to the west.

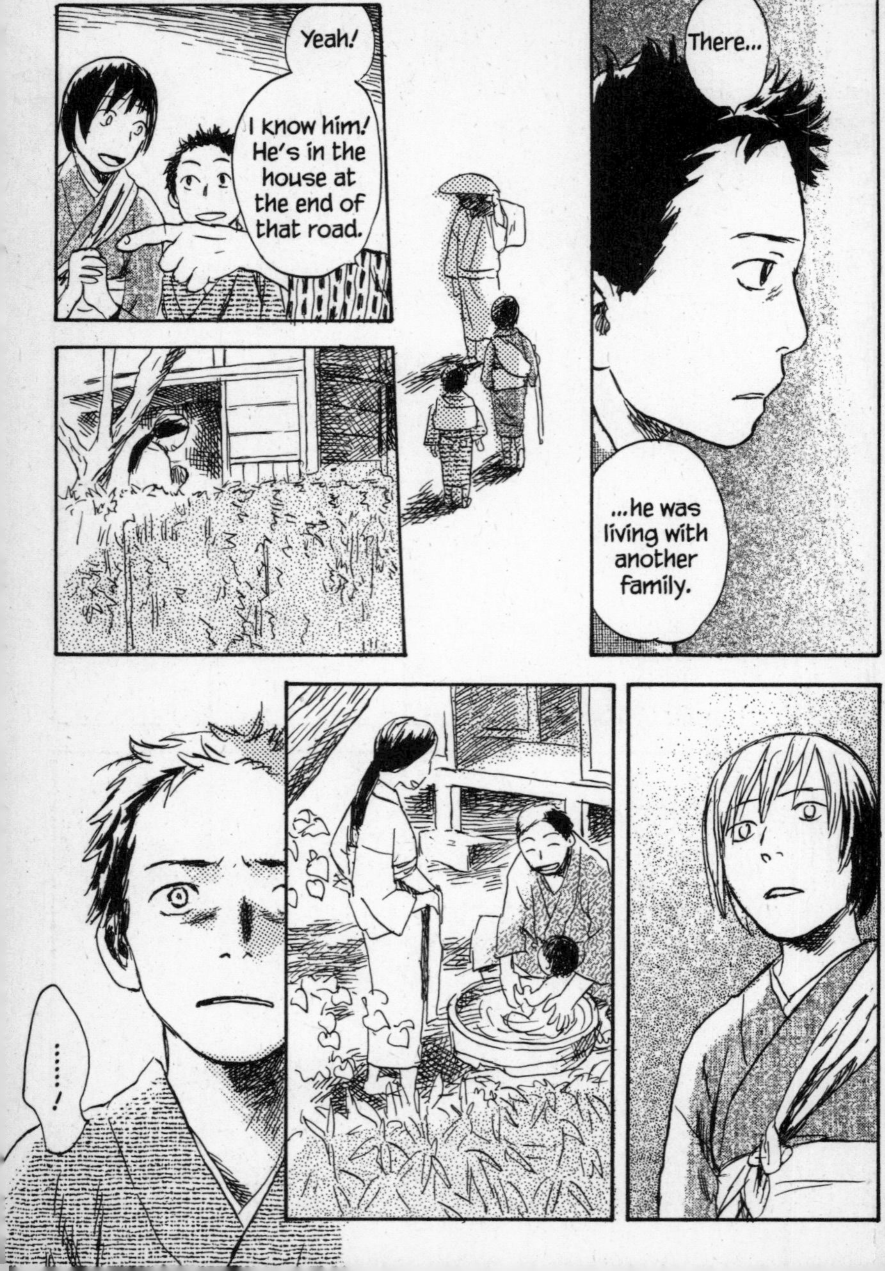
There...
...he was living with another family.
Yeah!
I know him! He's in the house at the end of that road.
......!

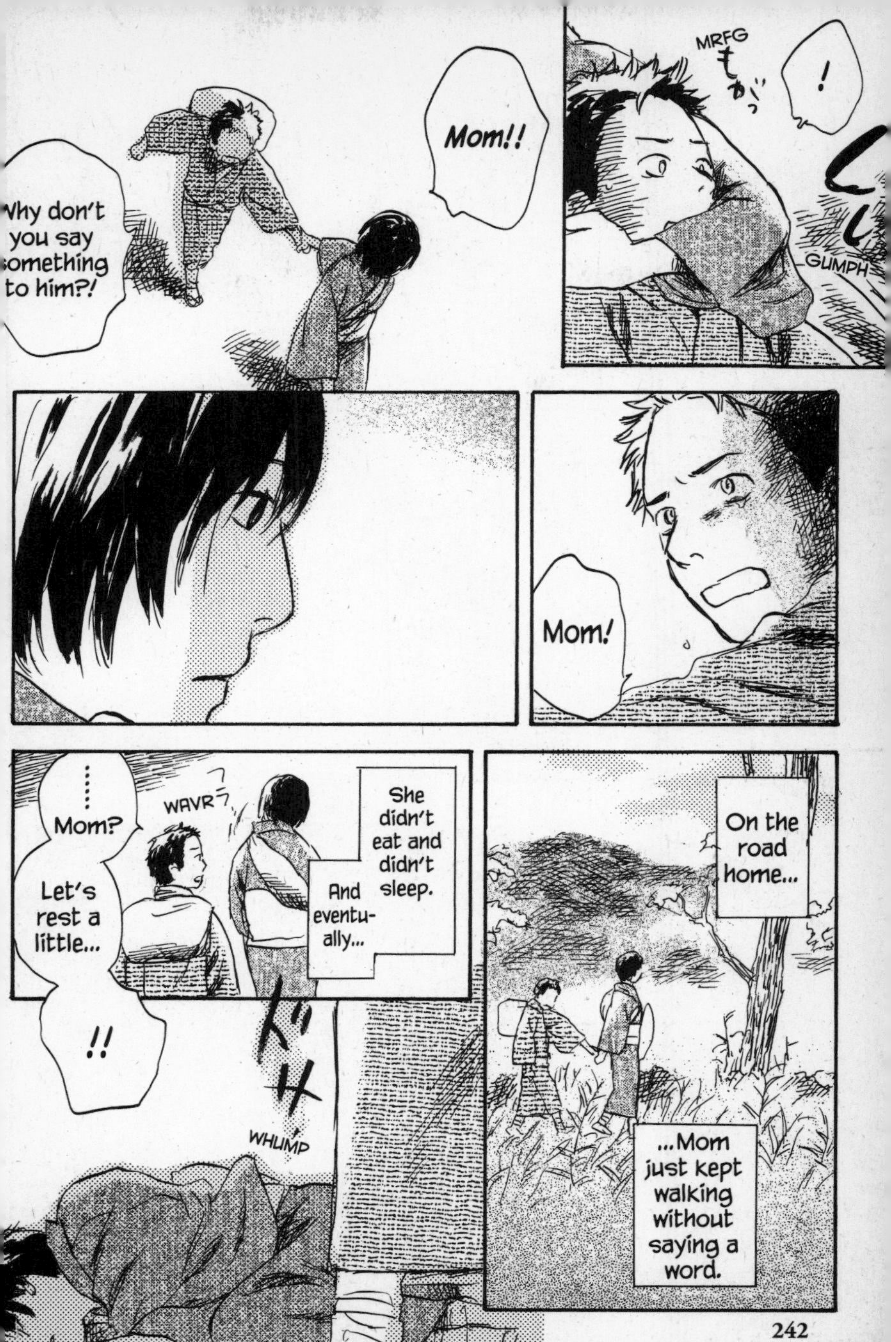
MRFG
!
GUMPH
Mom!!
Why don't you say something to him?!
Mom!
On the road home...
...Mom just kept walking without saying a word.
She didn't eat and didn't sleep.
And eventually...
WAVR
......Mom?
Let's rest a little...
!!
WHUMP

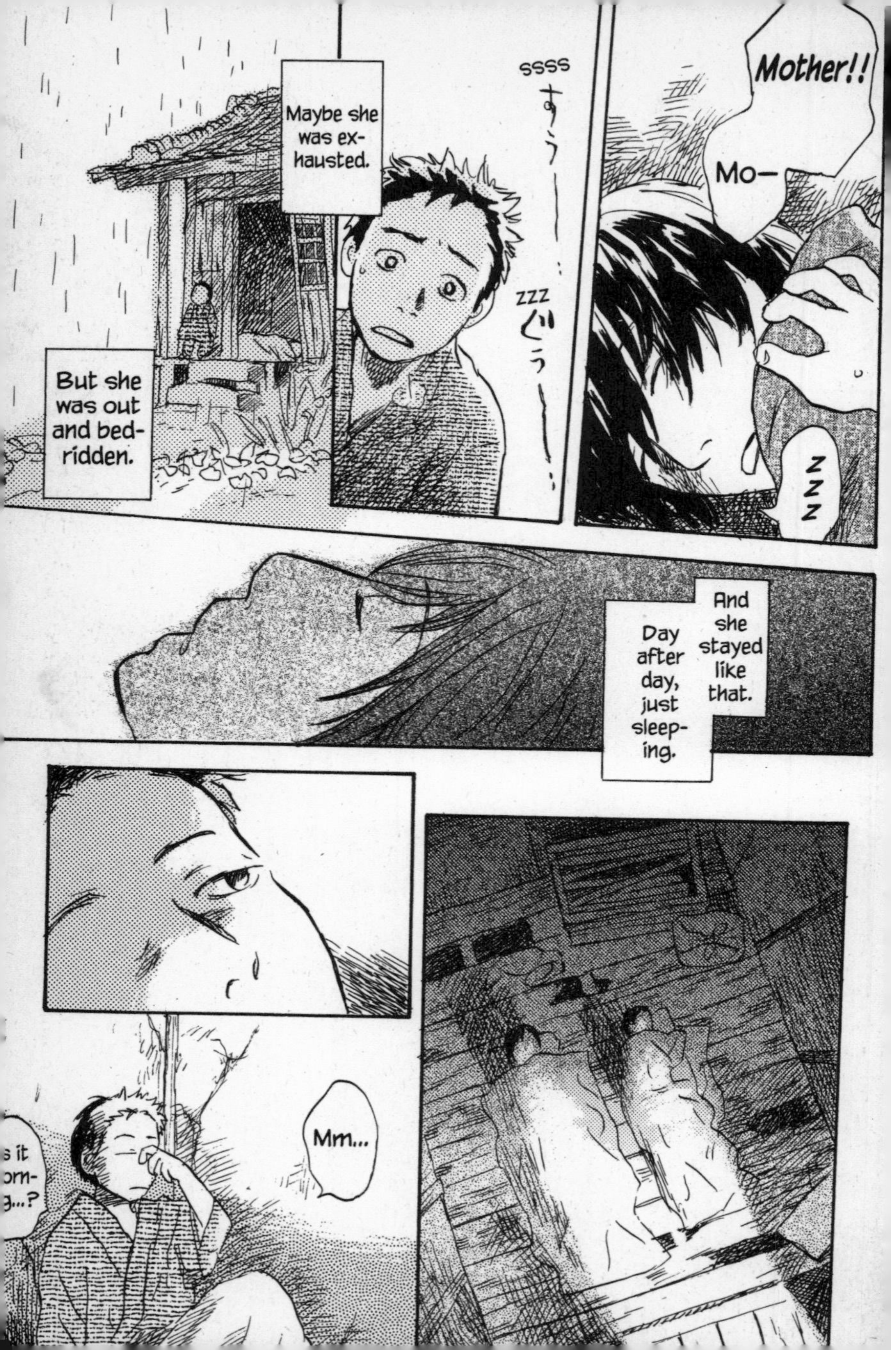

Mother!!
Mo—
ZZZ
ssss すぅー…
zzz ぐぅー…
Maybe she was ex-hausted.
But she was out and bed-ridden.
And she stayed like that.
Day after day, just sleep-ing.
Mm...
s it orn- g...?

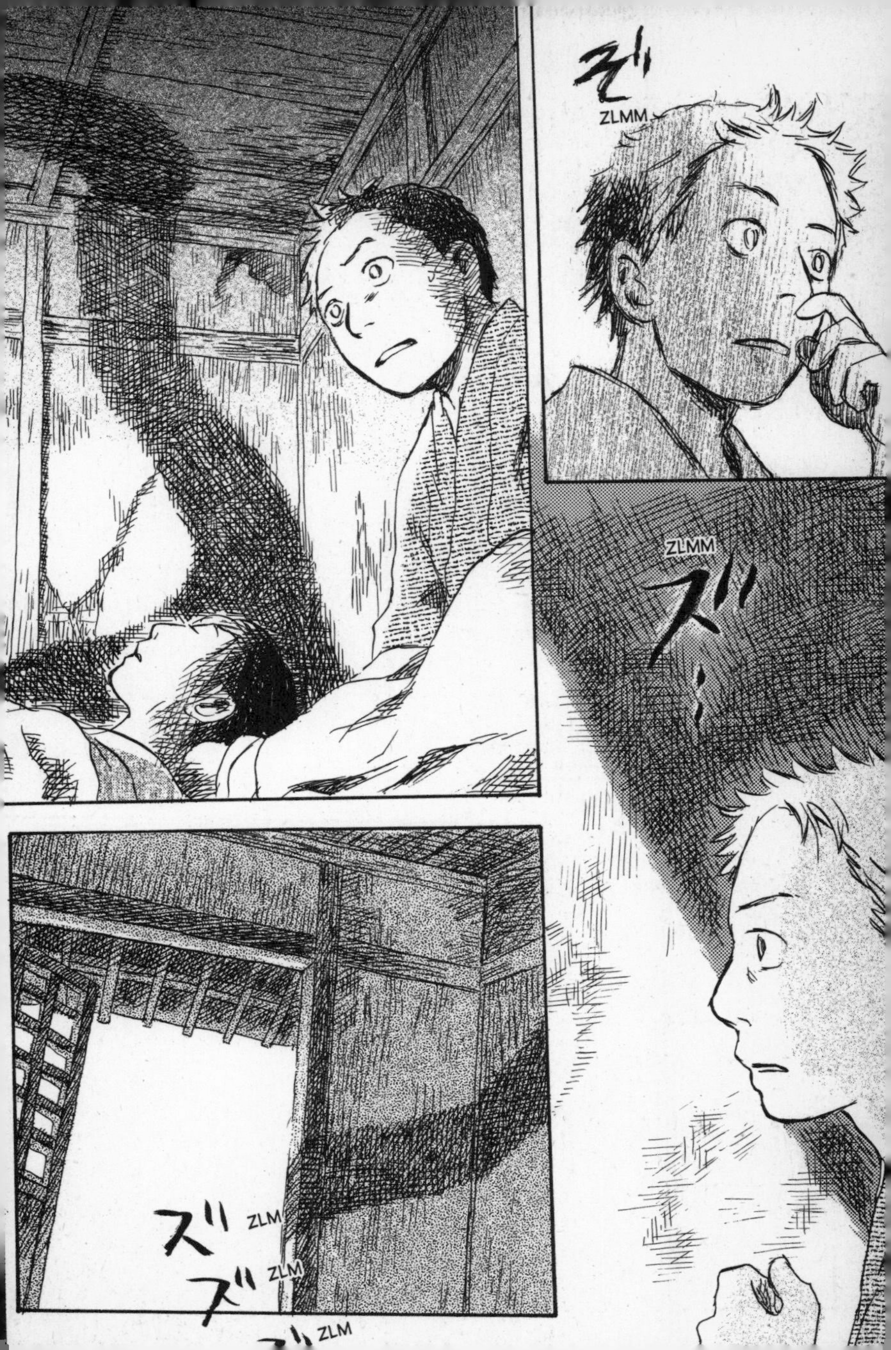
ズ
ZLMM
ZLMM
ズ
ズ
ZLM
ズ
ZLM
ZLM

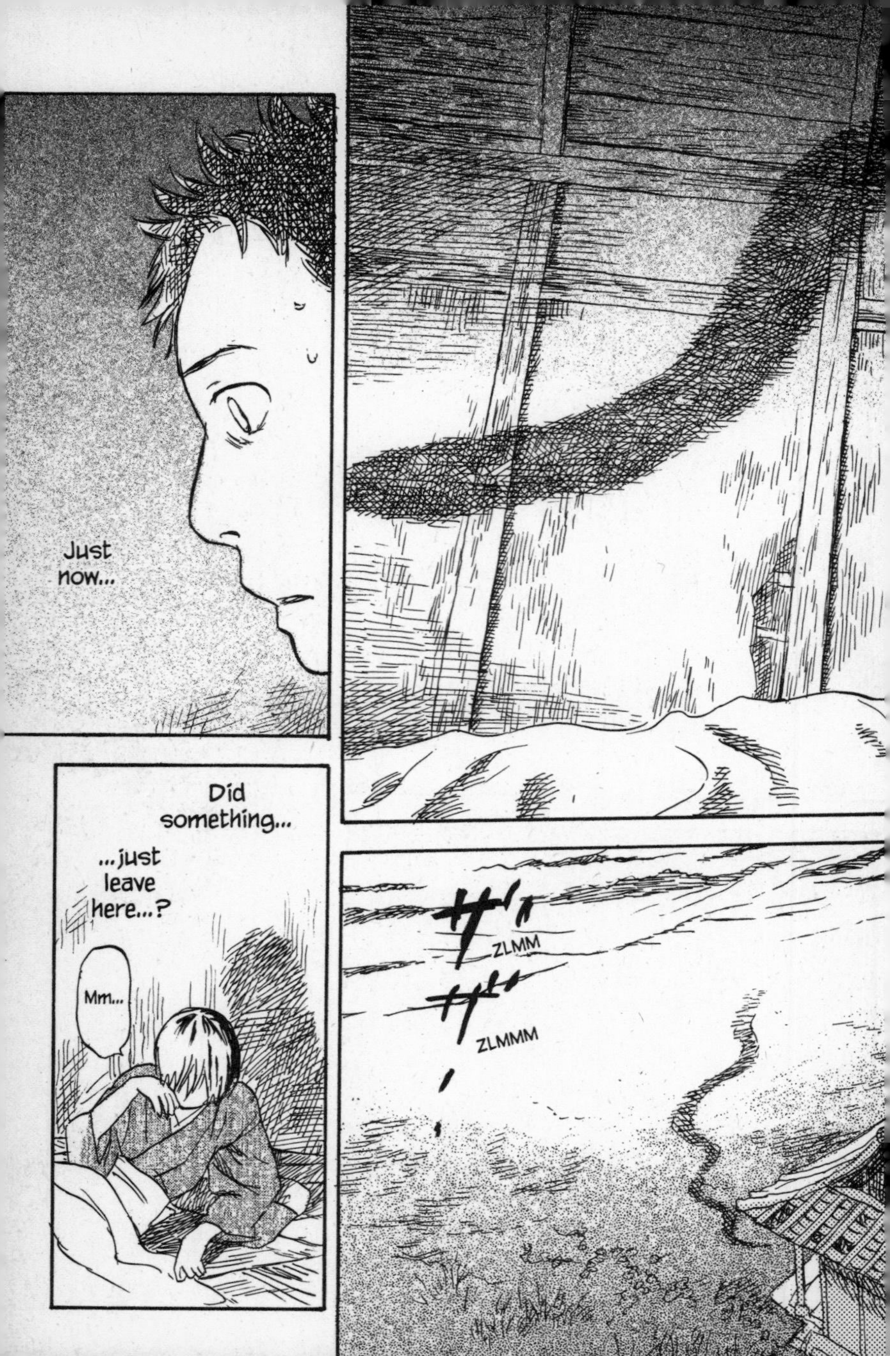
Just now...
ZLMM
ZLMMM
Did something...
...just leave here...?
Mm...

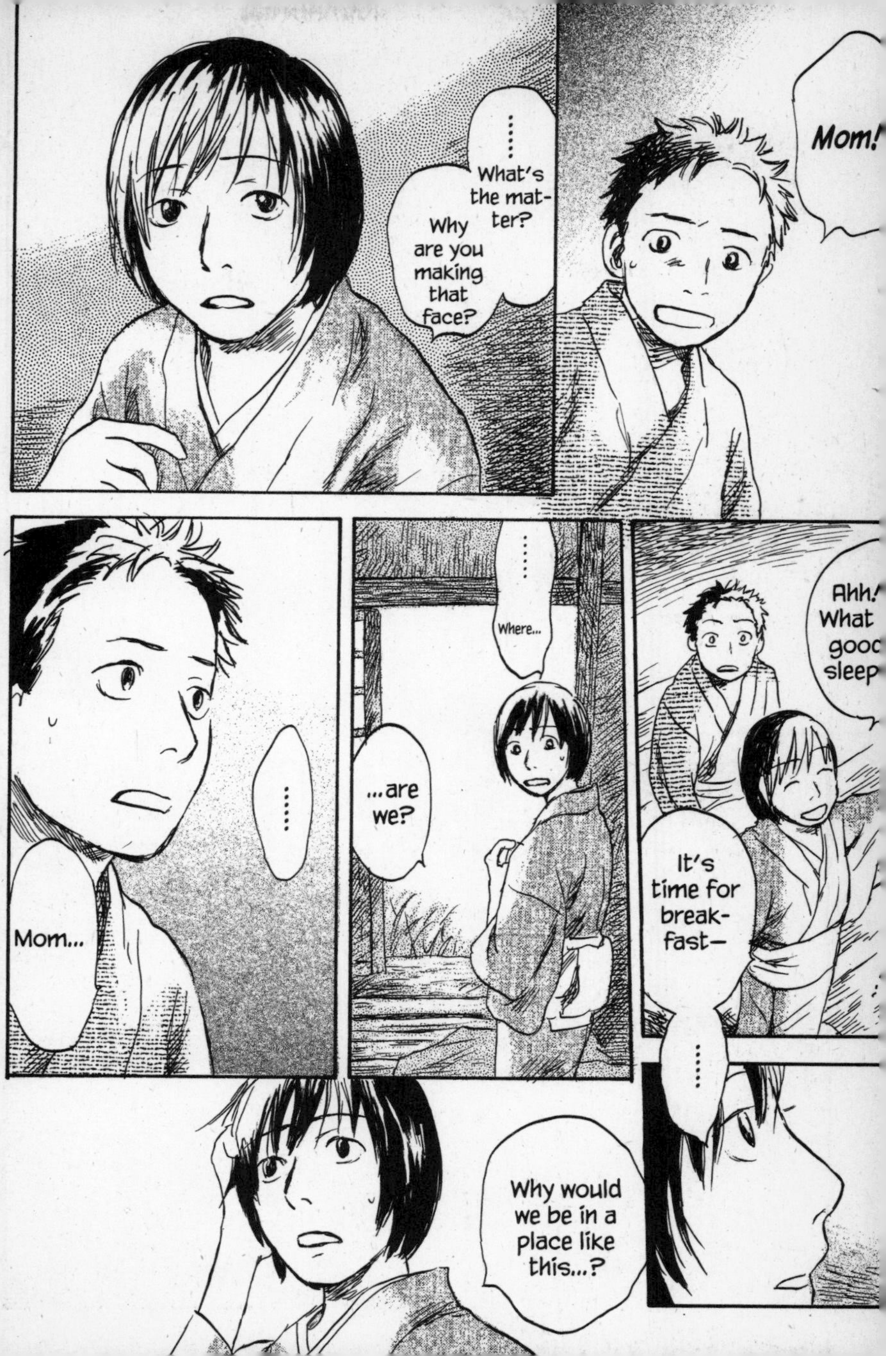
Mom!
......
What's the matter?
Why are you making that face?
Ahh! What goo sleep
It's time for break-fast–
......
Where...
...are we?
......
Mom...
......
Why would we be in a place like this...?

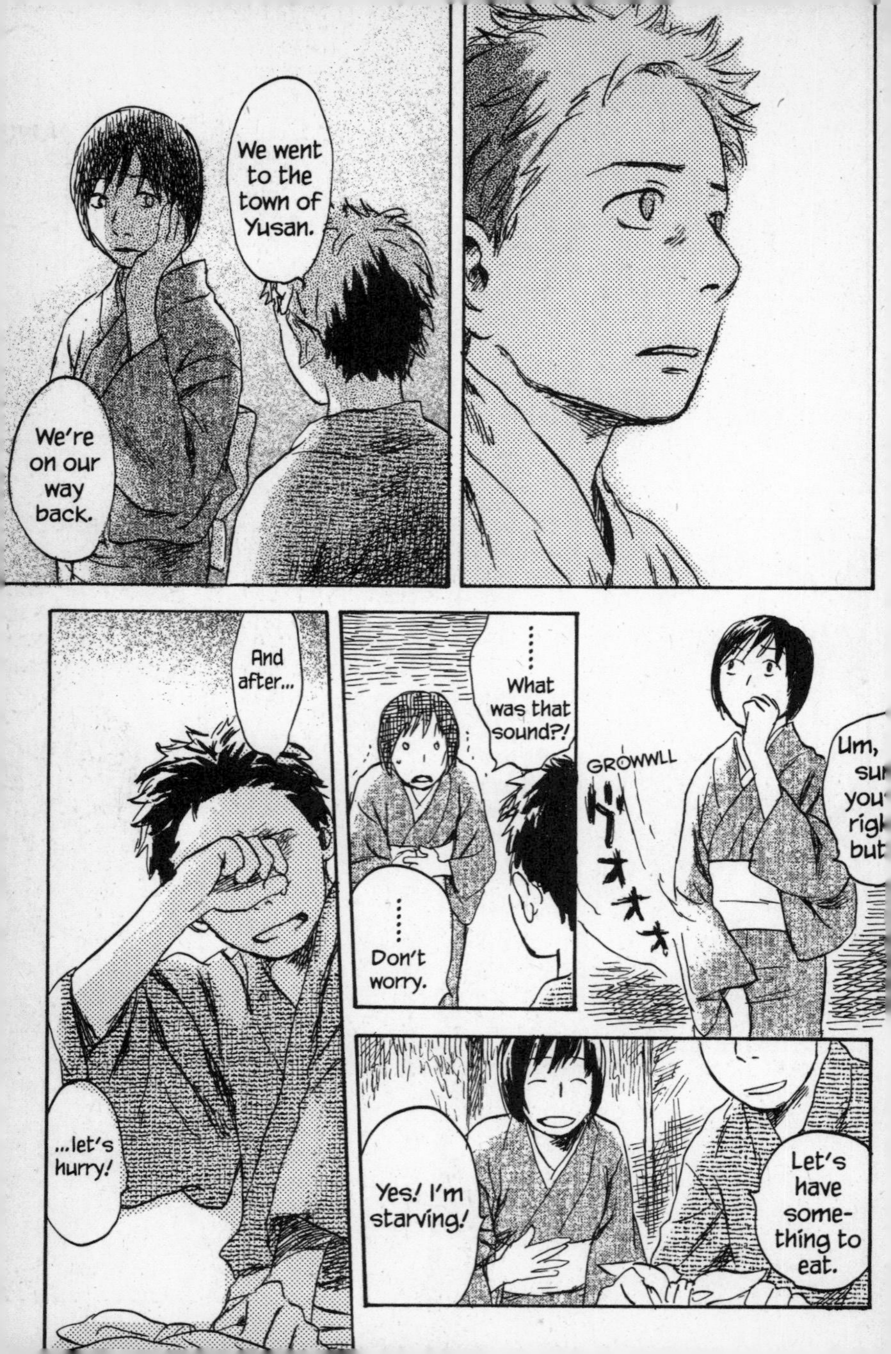
We went to the town of Yusan.
We're on our way back.
Um,
GROWWLL
What was that sound?!
...Don't worry.
Let's have something to eat.
Yes! I'm starving!
And after...
...let's hurry!

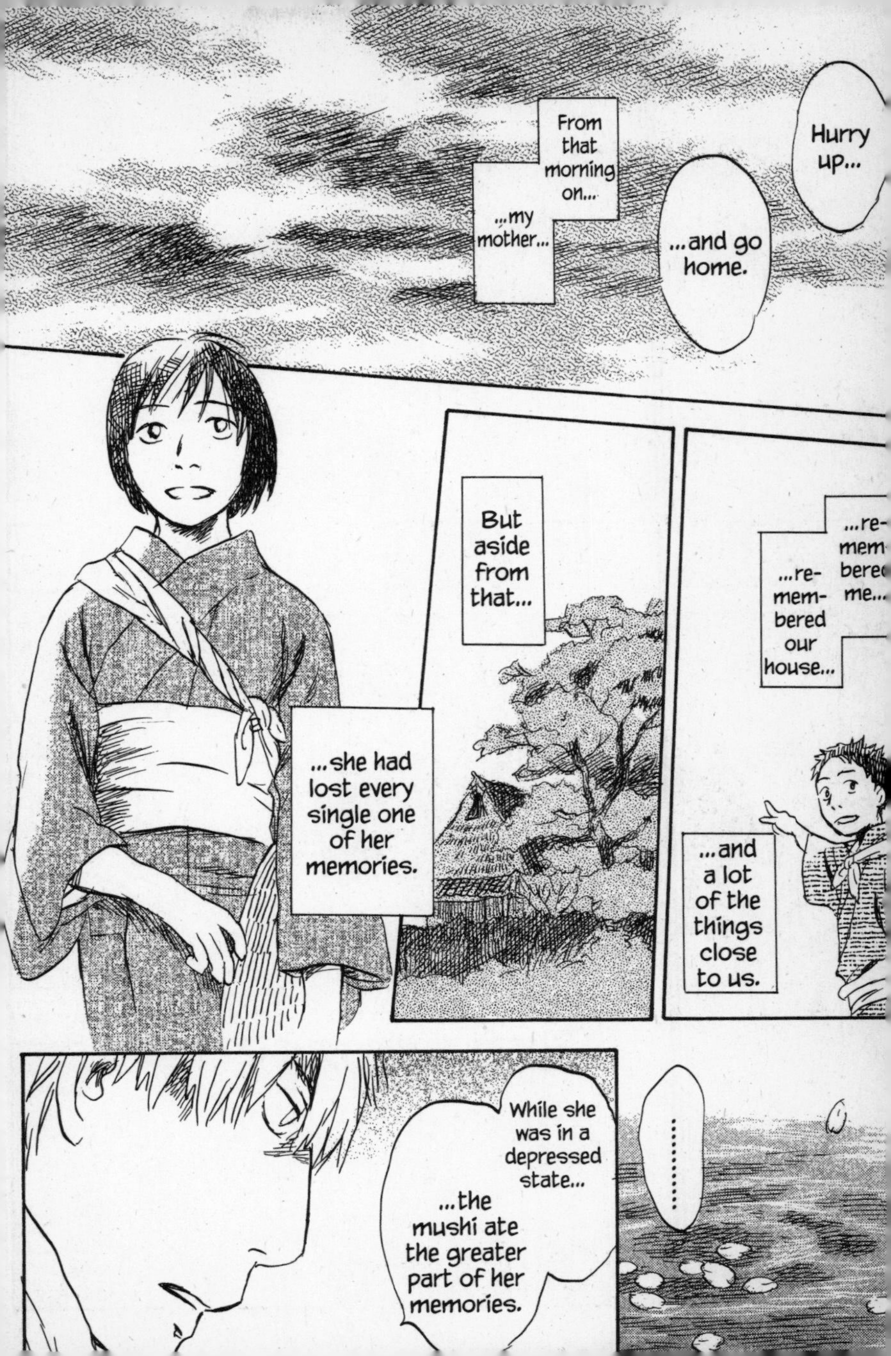
Hurry up...
...and go home.
From that morning on...
...my mother...
...re-mem-bered me...
...re-mem-bered our house...
...and a lot of the things close to us.
But aside from that...
...she had lost every single one of her memories.
......
While she was in a depressed state...
...the mushi ate the greater part of her memories.

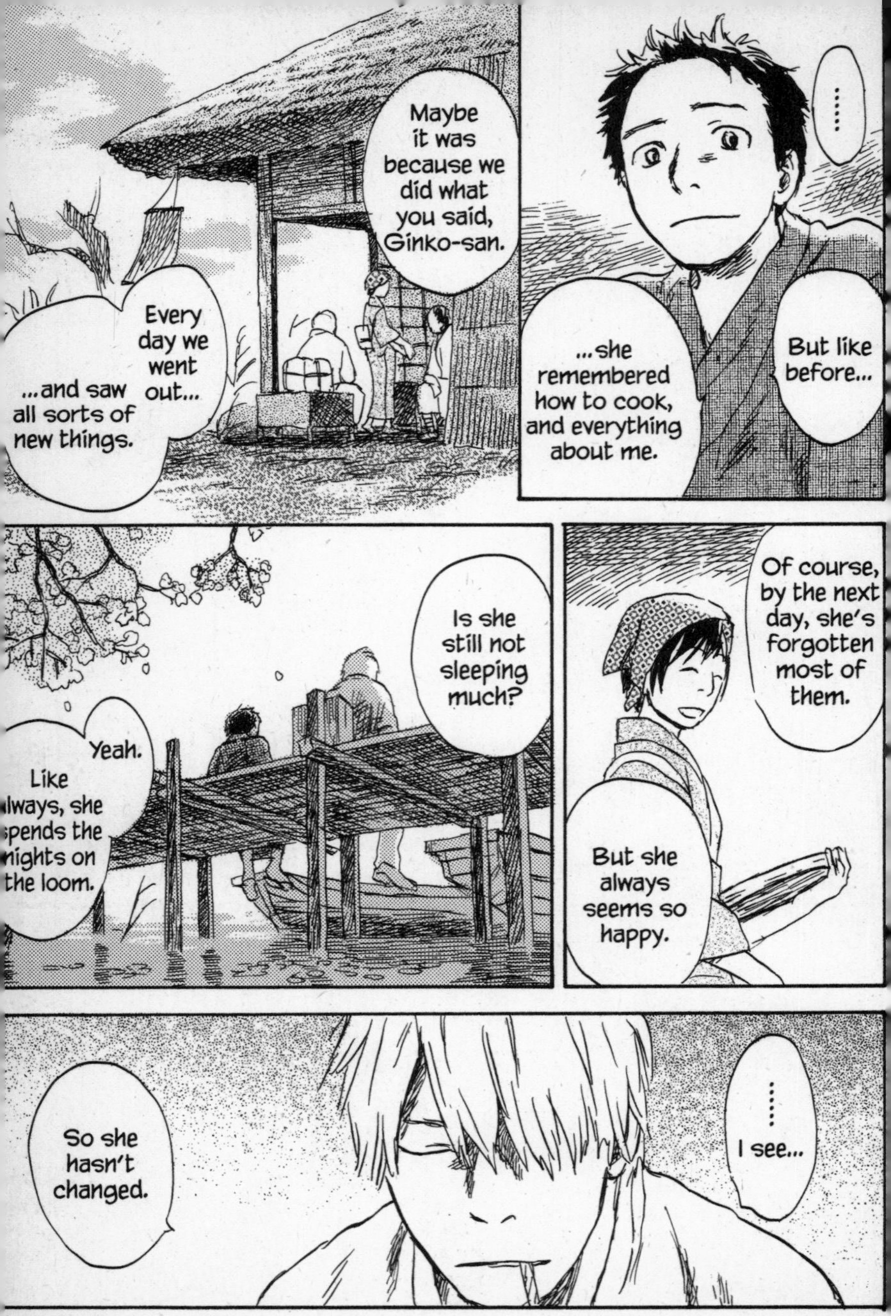
......
But like before...
...she remembered how to cook, and everything about me.
Maybe it was because we did what you said, Ginko-san.
Every day we went out...
...and saw all sorts of new things.
Of course, by the next day, she's forgotten most of them.
But she always seems so happy.
Is she still not sleeping much?
Yeah.
Like lways, she pends the ights on the loom.
......
I see...
So she hasn't changed.

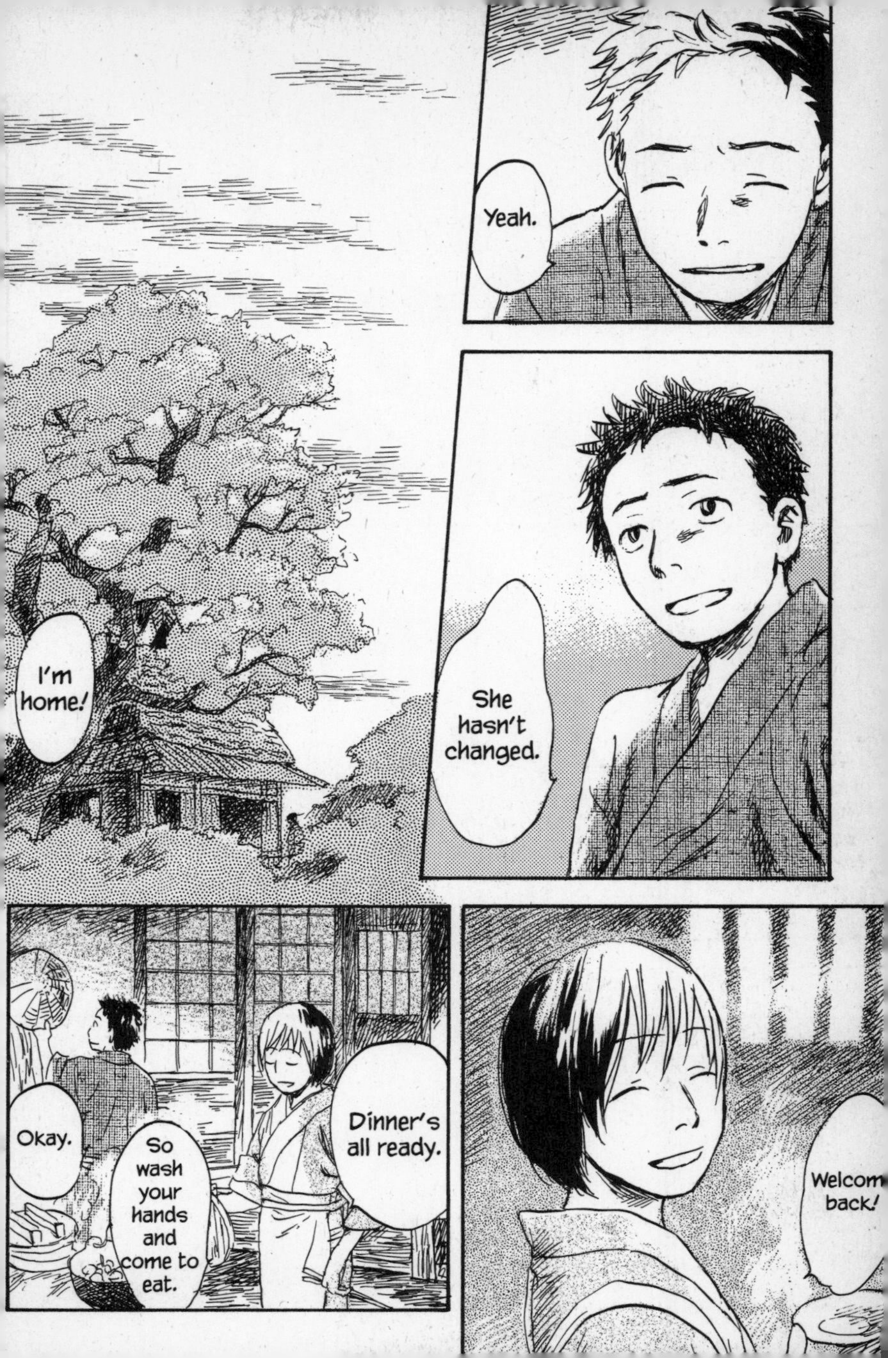
Yeah.
She hasn't changed.
I'm home!
Welcom back!
Dinner's all ready.
So wash your hands and come to eat.
Okay.

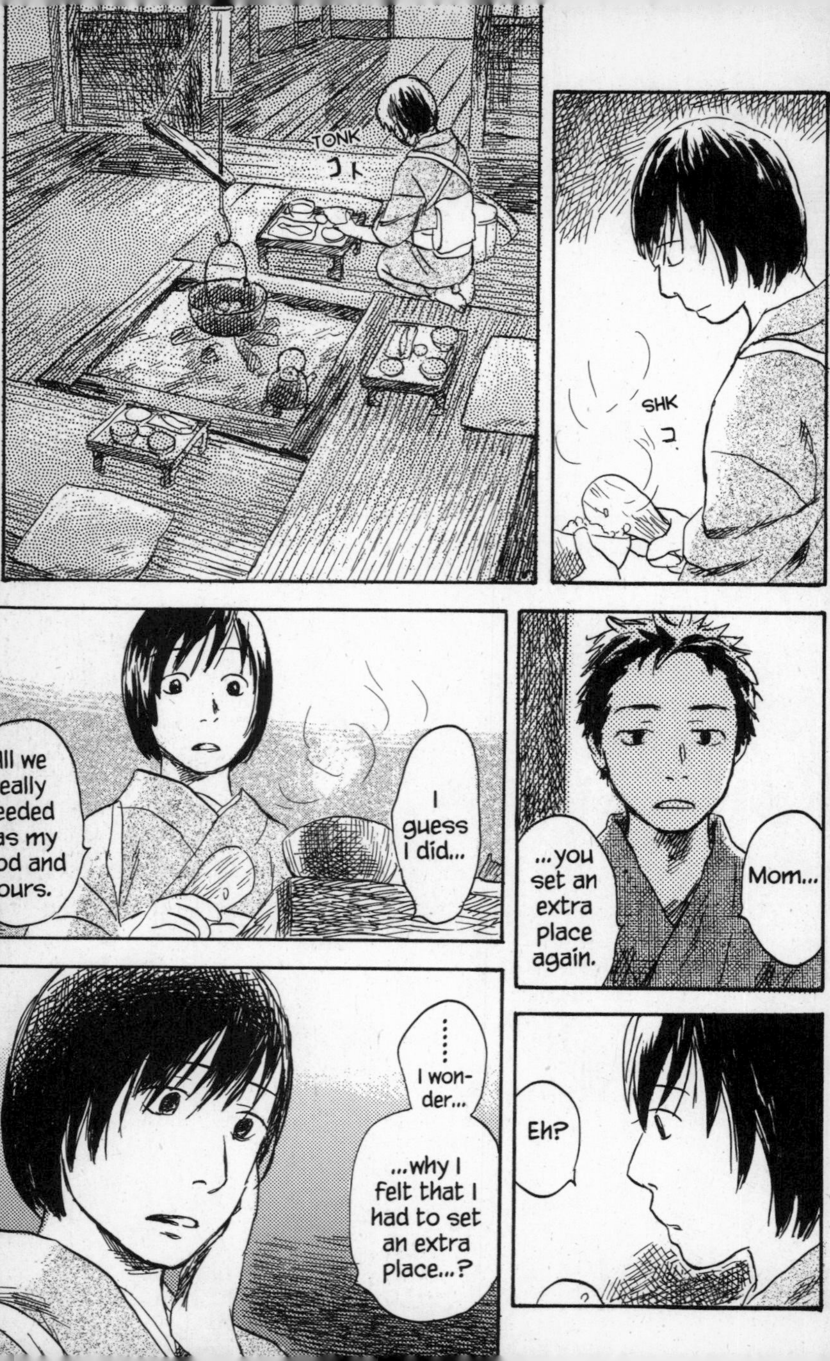
SHK
コ
TONK
コト
Mom...
...you set an extra place again.
I guess I did...
All we really needed was my food and yours.
Eh?
......
I won-der...
...why I felt that I had to set an extra place...?

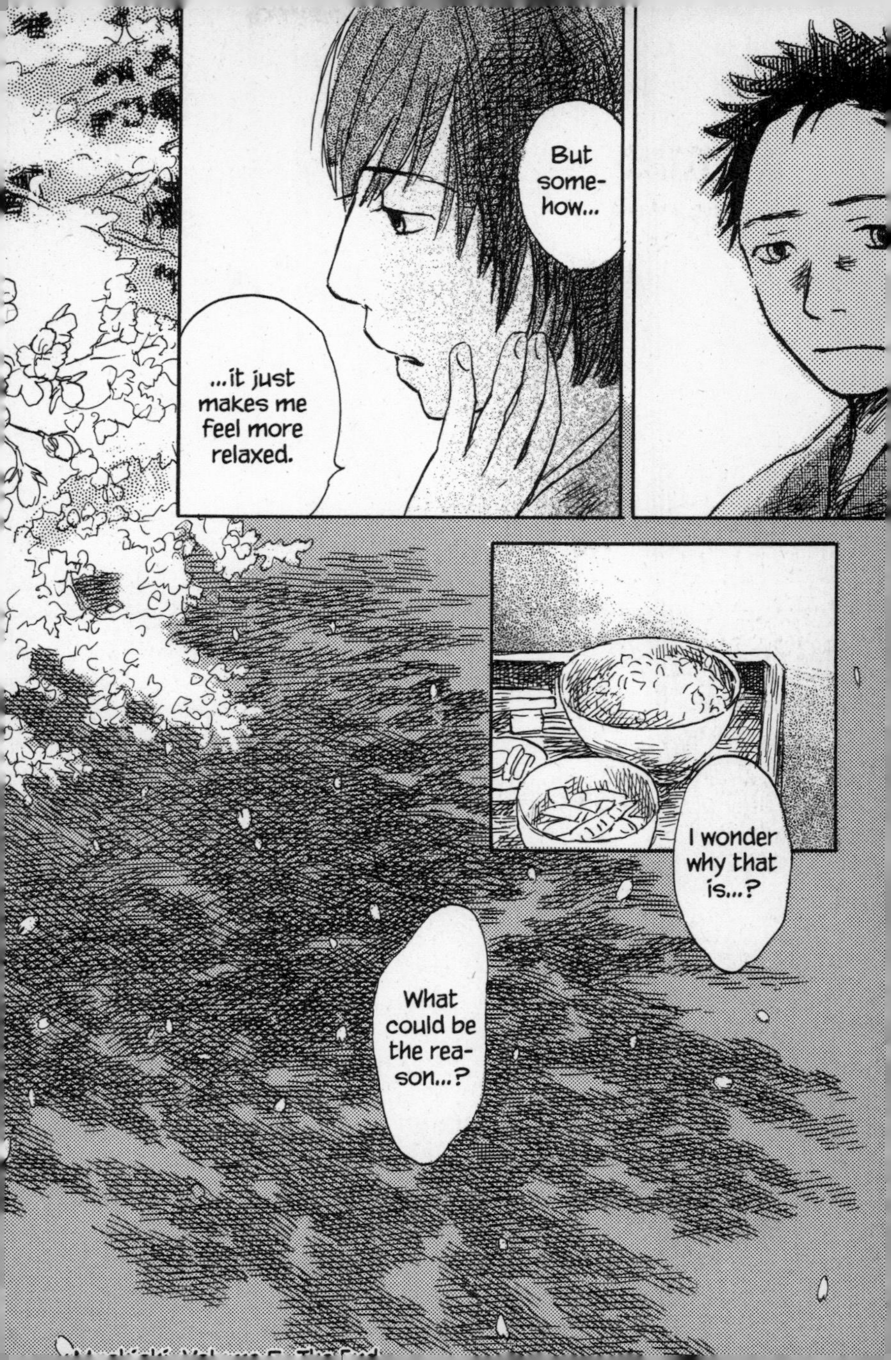
But some-how...
...it just makes me feel more relaxed.
I wonder why that is...?
What could be the rea-son...?

Bonus Manga

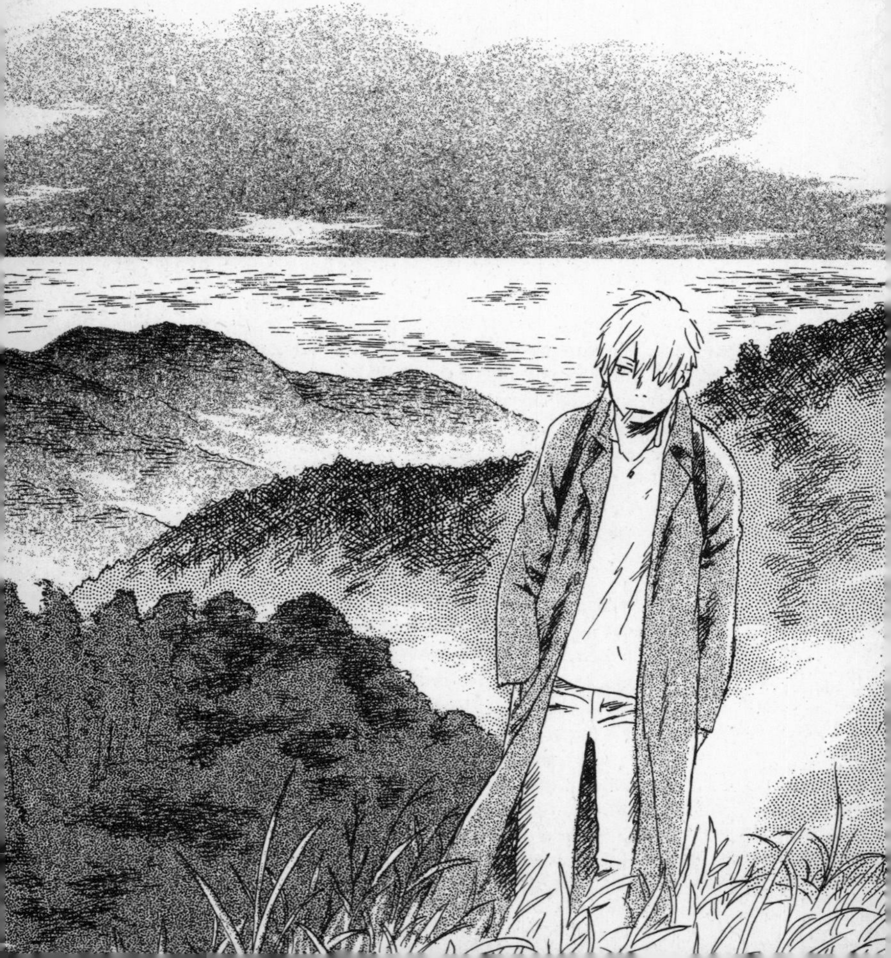

Just a little bit.

I tried walking the ancient road of Kumano.

In April of this year (2004), for some reason I got the itch to try walking the ancient road of Kumano, so I went there. I say that, but I actually stayed in the area for only one night. There were other places I wanted to visit, so this time I went to see the Nachi Grand Shrine.

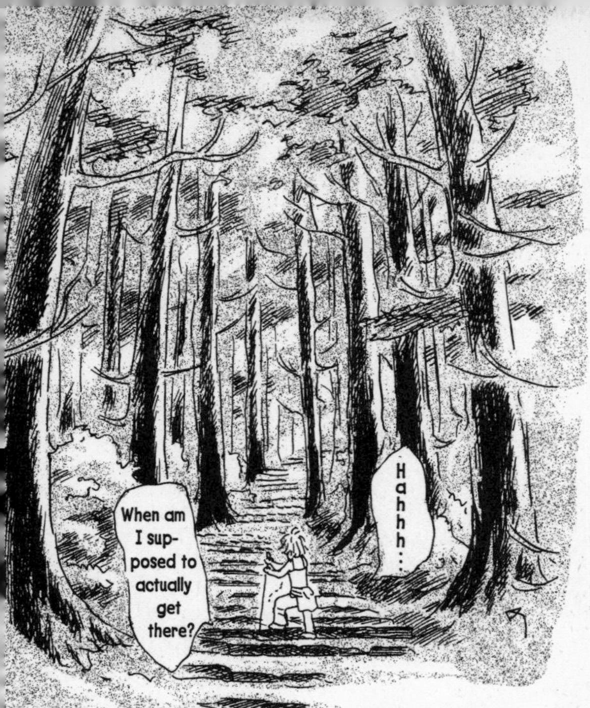

Hahhh...
When am I supposed to actually get there?

This is the Grand Gate Hill (Ōmon-saka) and the huge trees lining the route. The sign says it takes about twenty minutes to climb, but it took me more than half an hour. There's a married couple hiking along easily on the JR poster, but in reality, you'll be covered in sweat. The towering cedars look like gods, and the view is wonderful. And as your body reaches its physical limits (ha ha), it's a place where you really might see things that aren't there.

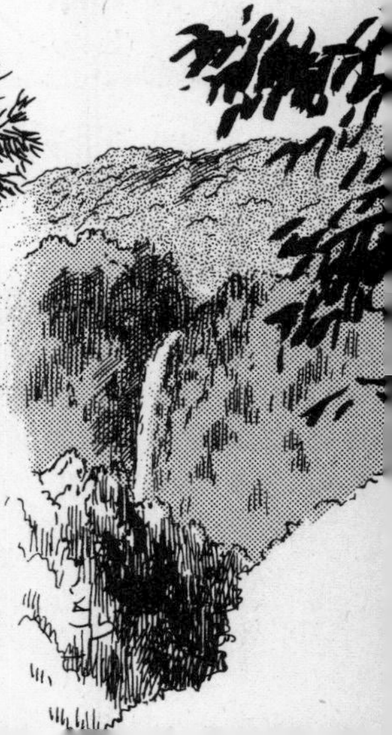

Eventually through the trees you can see gorgeous Nachi Falls, which is said to house gods. Its beauty makes you want to clap your hands together in prayer even if you don't have a reason to pray. It wasn't any kind of religious fervor that brought me there, of course. I always thought that those three mountains would be a very hard climb, but after going, I find that I want to go back. It's a place where I have a great desire to see what's farther in. Eventually I'd like to be sure of my abilities and challenge the road again.

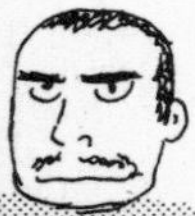

By the way, ne of the other ices I wanted to was the Minakata magusu Museum. ere are numerous ns he left behind various specimens of microscopic ganisms. But the seum was smaller an I imagined it to be.

Afterword

This is the fifth volume, which means it's already been five years since I started drawing *Mushishi*. Which also means that Ginko, who I always pictured as being in his late twenties, has become younger than me. An occurrence that pains me. Ginko, as well, has seemed to age a little over the years of telling this story, but the flow of time for him is quite a bit slower, so I am very jealous. To tell the truth, at first, I never thought for a second that the series would go on as long as it has. But, somehow, it seems like it can continue on. If you can come with me from here on out, too, it will make me very happy.

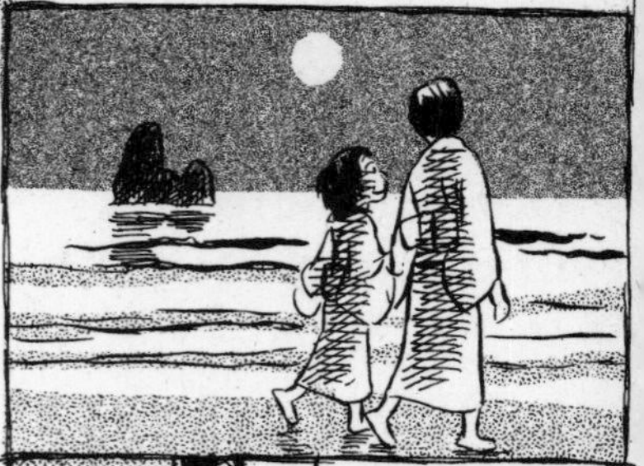

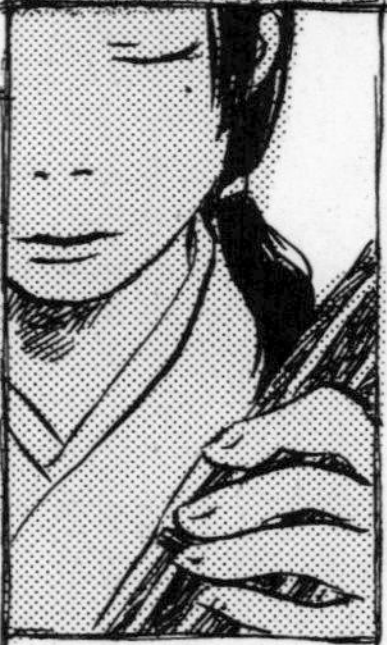

<The Sea Palace> The scene where the eggs rise from the coral is the motif for this story. It's one of the things I'd love to see in person.

<Eye's Fortune, Eye's Misfortune> I'm terribly afraid of losing my eyes, and that's probably why I draw it so much.

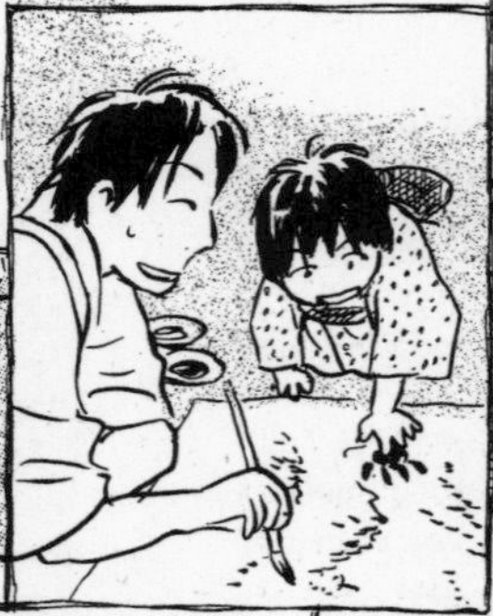

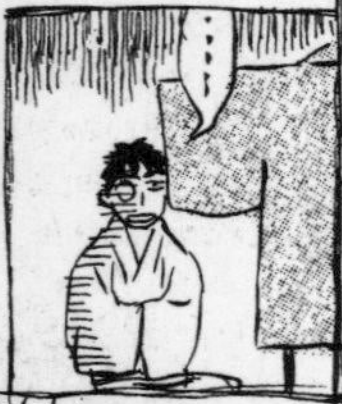

<The Coat That Holds a Mountain> Back in the Edo Period, during the reigns of emperors Bunka and Bunsei (1804–1830), they started making the inside of coats even showier than the outside. Pretty stylish, huh...

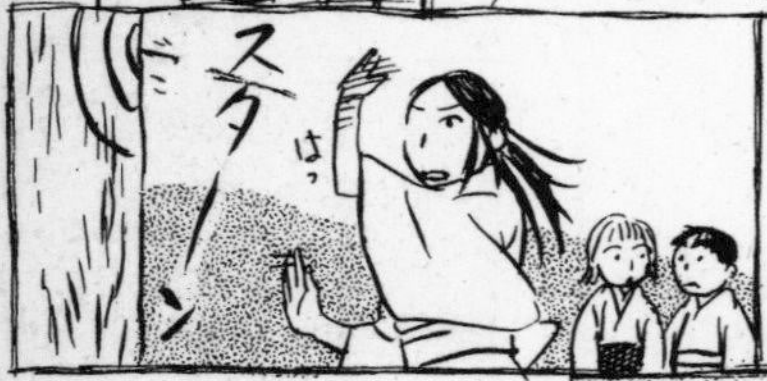
はっ

<Flames of the Fields> The thing we call fire is beautiful, frightening, transient, powerful. I love it so much, I never get sick of watching it. But it's so hard to draw...

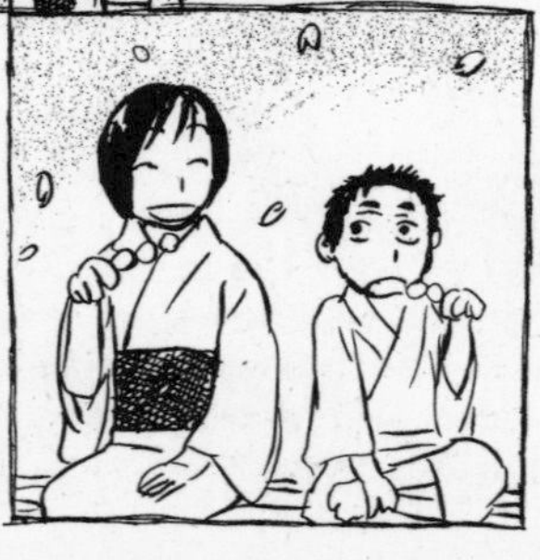

<The Snake of Dawn> It was fun drawing the naturally absentminded mother. I feel sorry for her son, but...

The people who helped me out this time: Mmasu Tnaka, Mami-chin, Hiro, Yayoi-chan, Yōko-chan, Yone, and my grandmother,

Thank you!!

Translation Notes

Japanese is a tricky language for most Westerners, and translation is often more an art than a science. For your edification and reading pleasure, here are notes on some of the places where we could have gone in a different direction, or where a Japanese cultural difference is used.

General notes on *mushi* and *mushishi*

The kanji for *mushi* is made of three kanji meaning bug (also called *mushi*) put together. The kanji can be used interchangeably for insect, but they can easily take on other meanings. In CLAMP's *xxxHolic*, the kanji was introduced as the name for a type of magical vermin.

Mushishi can be translated as "*mushi* master." Ginko is a man who made a study of *mushi* and seems to have learned to control some through his own senses and others through medicines, remedies, or just a knowledge of their nature. Ginko probably learned his craft from other older *mushishi* who wander Japan.

The highway, page 60

There are several major historical thoroughfares in Japan. The Tôkai road was probably the most famous, stretching from Osaka through Kyoto, past Mt. Fuji and on to Tokyo. Travel was pretty common along the road, since most Japanese wanted to take at least one pilgrimage in their life.

Biwa, page 60

A type of lute that originated reportedly in ancient Persia and worked its way along the Silk Road to end up in Japan. There are illustrations of the *biwa* in *The Tale of Genji* (eleventh century), but the most prevalent image of the *biwa* in Japan today is its use during the Edo period by Buddhist monks as they traveled the country telling stories. This was probably the model for Urushibara's creation of the character Amane, with his monklike round straw hat and storytelling on the street.

Master *(danna)*, page 62

One of the Japanese words for master, *danna* can be used for the male owner or manager of a store, restaurant, or inn (a common word for a female owner or manager is *kami-san*). The English word "master" is also used for the owners of bars in Japan today.

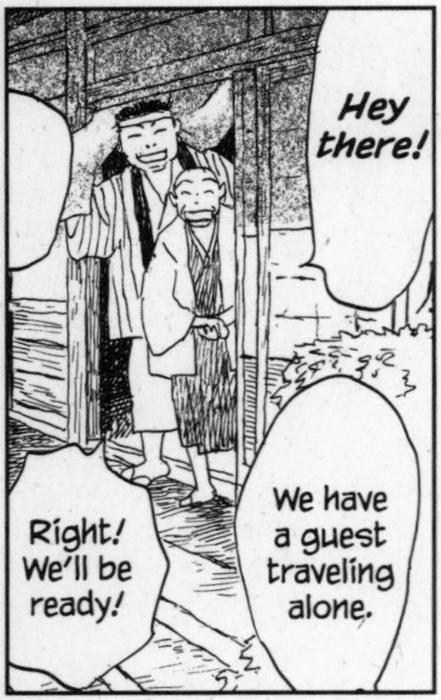
Hey there!
We have a guest traveling alone.
Right! We'll be ready!

Picking up customers *(Kyaku-hiki)*, page 63

According to some Japanese historians, female employees of restaurants, bars, and inns along the great highways of Japan were pretty forceful when it came to drawing customers into their establishments. Some were even known to tackle potential customers and drag them bodily into the place of business. The practice of drawing in customers is still in force today (but not quite so forcefully) in the downtown entertainment districts of Japanese cities.

Kimono short coat (*Haori*), page 105

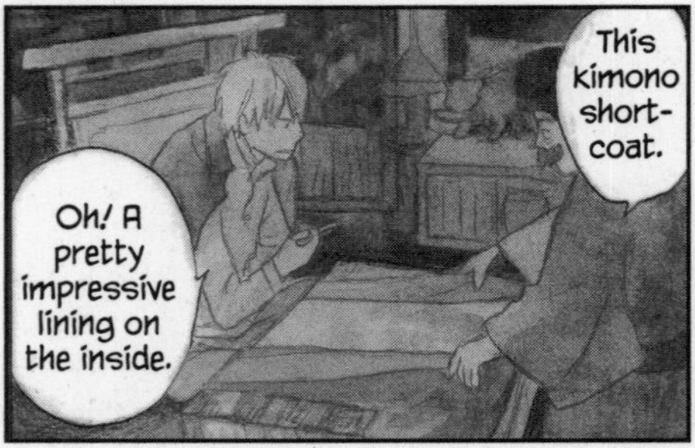
This kimono short-coat.
Oh! A pretty impressive lining on the inside.

Haori, which we call the short coat in the text, is traditionally a man's garment meant to be worn over a kimono to keep the kimono clean and the wearer warm. After the end of the Edo period, women's *haori* became very popular as well.

Ubusuna, page 148

The first kanji in the *mushi* name *Ubusuna* means to cultivate or to give birth. The second kanji means earth.

Kagebi, page 185

The first kanji for *Kagebi* is *kage,* which means shadow. The second means fire. So the name for this phenomenon is something like a "shadowy fire."

Hidane, page 187

If a fire you approach seems a little tepid, then figure it's a Kagebi.
......
Inside each Kagebi is a mushi called Hidane.

There is a real-world item called *hidane* in Japanese that refers to coal. The kanji are made up of the Japanese words for "fire" and "seed." (So it's easy to see why the *mushi* are also called "fire seeds.")

The cherry tree *(Sakura),* page 207

The cherry tree is perhaps Japan's most prominent symbol. As well as symbolizing Japan as a country, it is a potent symbol of spring. Every year in late March or early April the cherry trees blossom, creating cloudlike canopies of pinkish white. So merely by drawing a blooming cherry tree, the author lets his readers know the time of year.

In spring, people oversleep without knowing..., page 210

Like that saying, "In spring, people oversleep without knowing..." something or other.

The actual saying is, *Shûmin akatsuki wo oboezu,* which translated literally means "Spring people forget dawn." The actual meaning is that people tend to sleep late in spring, not realizing that dawn has arrived. But since *akatsuki* (dawn) is in the title of the chapter and a failure of memory is the theme, Urushibara-sensei had Ginko forget what it is that people in spring don't "know."

Dango, page 216

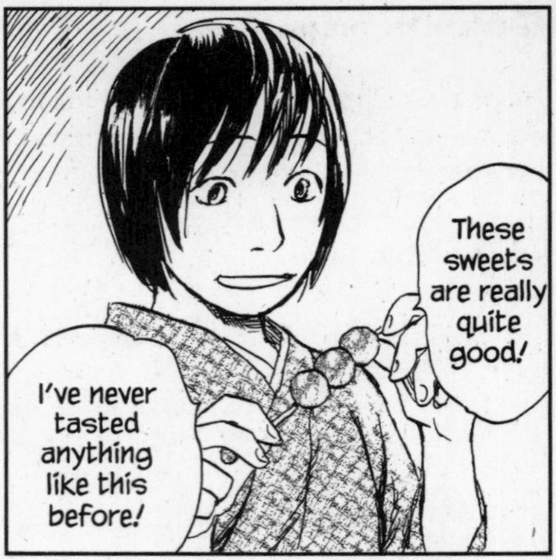
These sweets are really quite good!
I've never tasted anything like this before!

Dango, or skewered dumpling, is perhaps the most popular festival snack in Japan. It is usually made of rice flour dumplings (although there are plenty of other recipes) that have been treated with different types of sauce to give them various flavors. *An*, the sweet-bean sauce, is probably the most prevalent since it is so popular with the kids, but tastes and flavors abound. There are usually three on a skewer, which prompted the late 1990s smash-hit children's song "Dango San Kyodai" (The Three Dango Brothers).

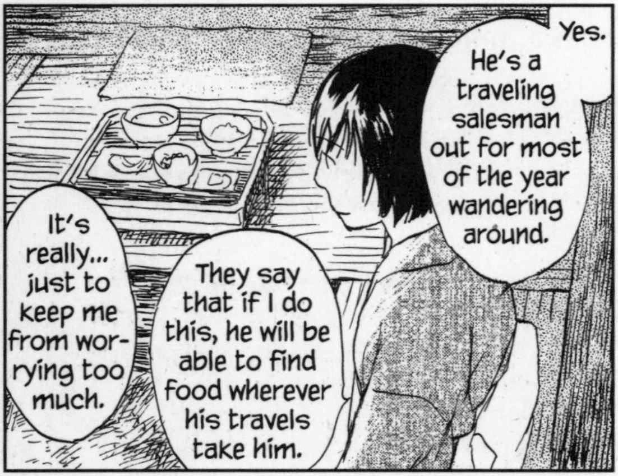
Yes. He's a traveling salesman out for most of the year wandering around.
They say that if I do this, he will be able to find food wherever his travels take him.
It's really... just to keep me from worrying too much.

Kagezen, page 221

This is a full meal prepared for someone who is not present as a prayer for their safe return.

Thank you for this food, page 221

One of the standard phrases of Japanese life is a word said before eating, "*Itadakimasu!*" Like the Christian tradition of grace, the word is usually said to give thanks for the meal. (Thanks to whom depends on the traditions in which the Japanese person is raised. In some cases it is to God or gods, and in other cases it is to the food itself which was sacrificed so the one eating can be nourished.)

Omochi, page 226

A rice paste that can be found in many forms. There are *omochi* snacks with sweet-bean paste inside for a sweet snack, but it can also be found unsweetened in soups or as a side dish.

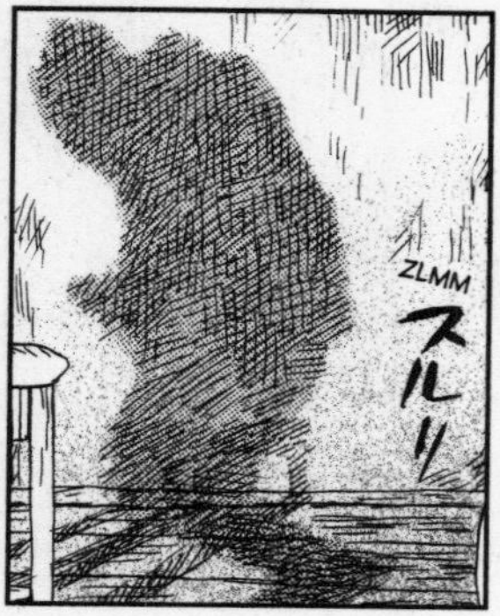
ZLMM
ズルリ

Kagedama, page 231

Like *Kagebi* above, the first kanji is one that means "shadow." The second kanji is the character meaning "soul."

Kumano old road, page 254

One of the old highways of Japan (see above note), but in a somewhat remote location at the southern point of Wakayama prefecture south of Osaka and Nara. The remoteness meant that the main people traveling the old road were pilgrims on the way to see the Nachi Grand Shrine that Yuki-sensei mentions.

Minakata Kumagusu Museum, page 254

Also in Wakayama prefecture, but toward its westernmost point, is the Minakata Kumagusu Museum, listed as one of UNESCO's World Heritage Sites. Kumagusu Minakata (1867–1941) was one of Japan's leading naturalists after the end of Japan's isolation. He published articles in the British journal *Nature* and was known as a walking encyclopedia, especially in his favorite area of study, slime molds.

We're please to present you with a preview of volume 6. Please check our website (www.delreymanga.com) to see when this volume will be available in English. For now you'll have to make do with Japanese!

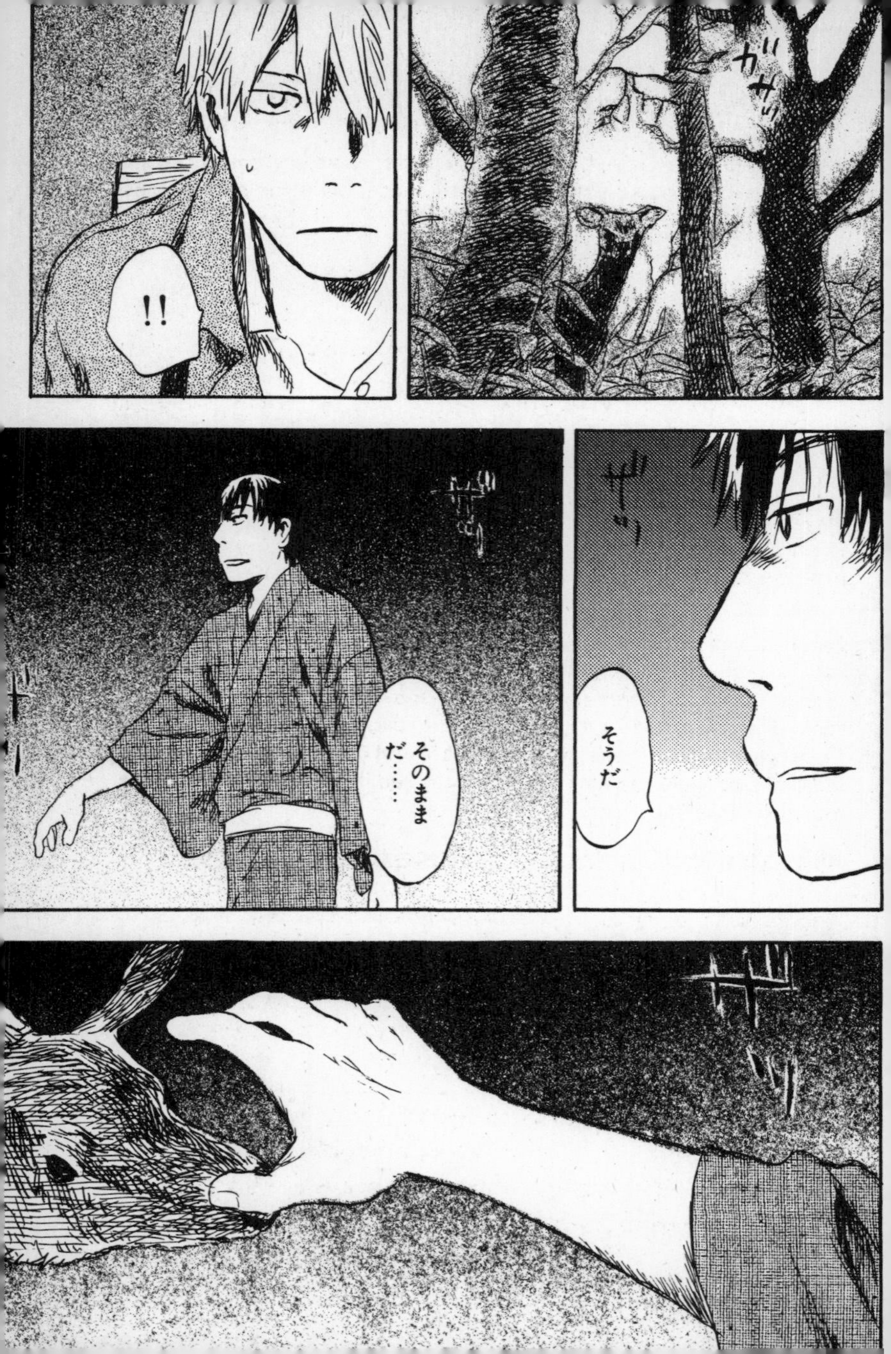
!!
そうだ
そのままだ……

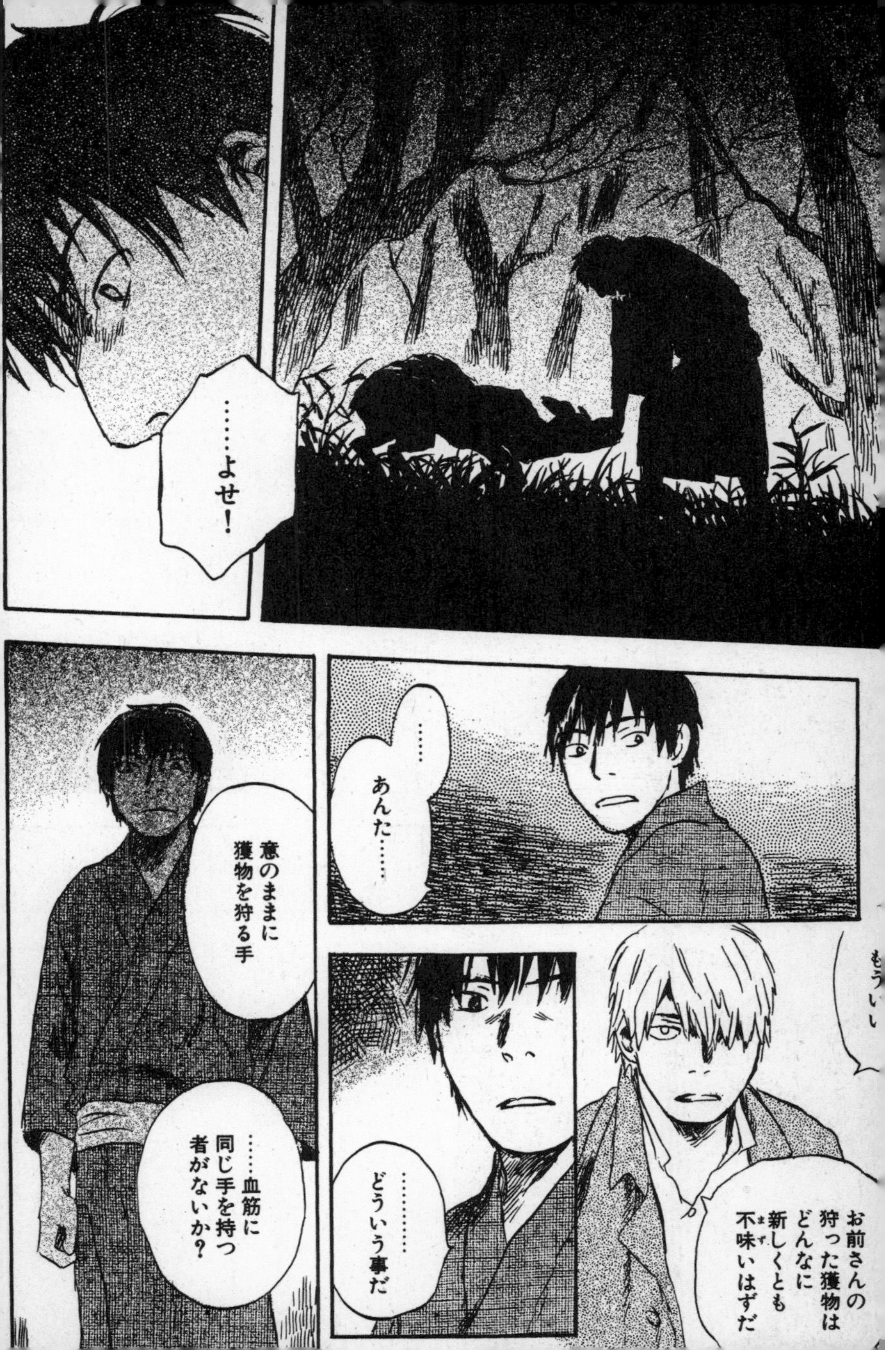
……よせ!
……あんた……
もういい
お前さんの狩った獲物はどんなに新しくとも不味いはずだ
………どういう事だ
意のままに獲物を狩る手
……血筋に同じ手を持つ者がないか?

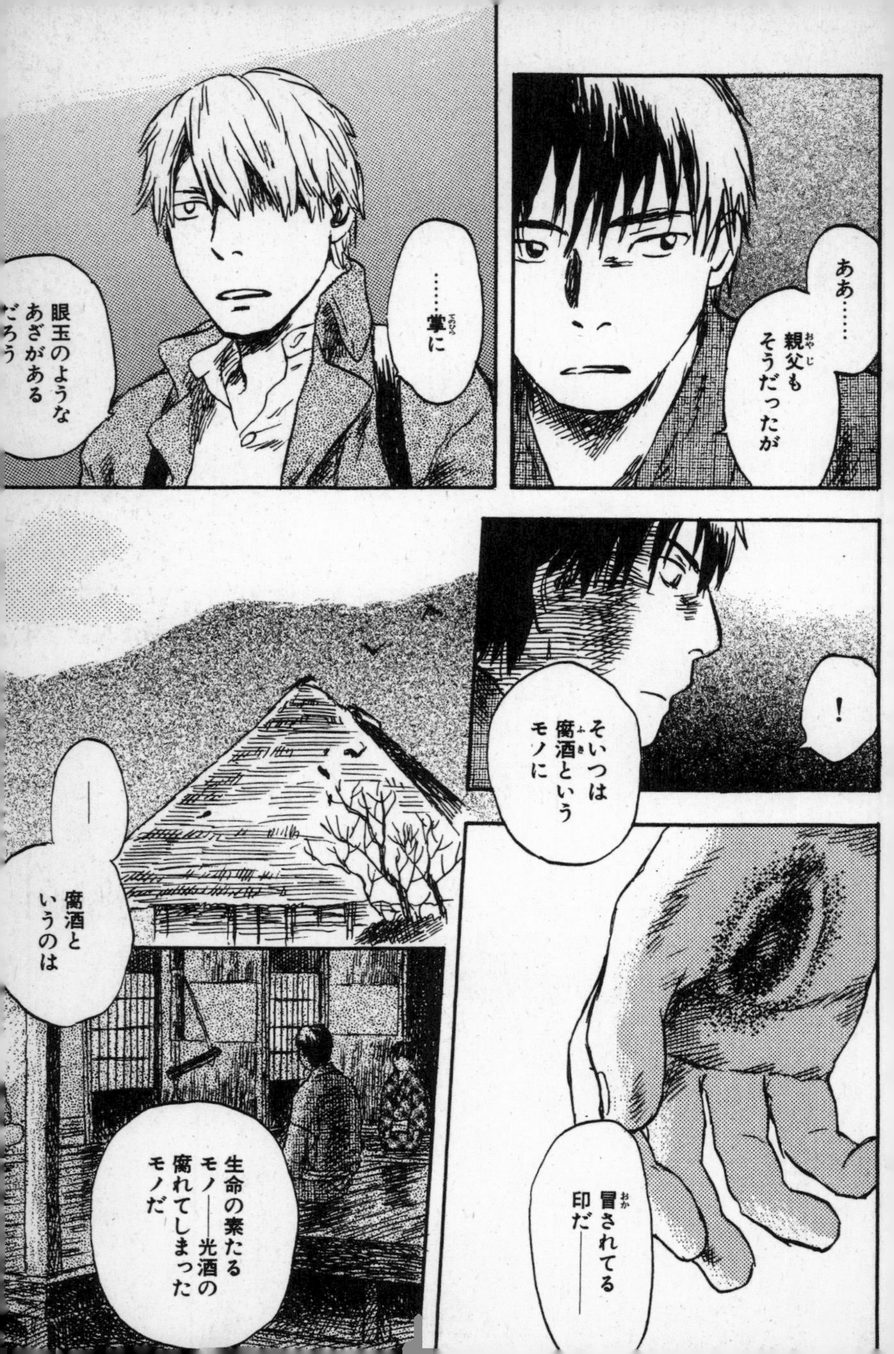
ああ……
親父もそうだったが
……掌に
眼玉のようなあざがあるだろう
!
そいつは腐酒というモノに
冒されてる印だ――
――
腐酒というのは
生命の素たるモノ――光酒の腐れてしまったモノだ

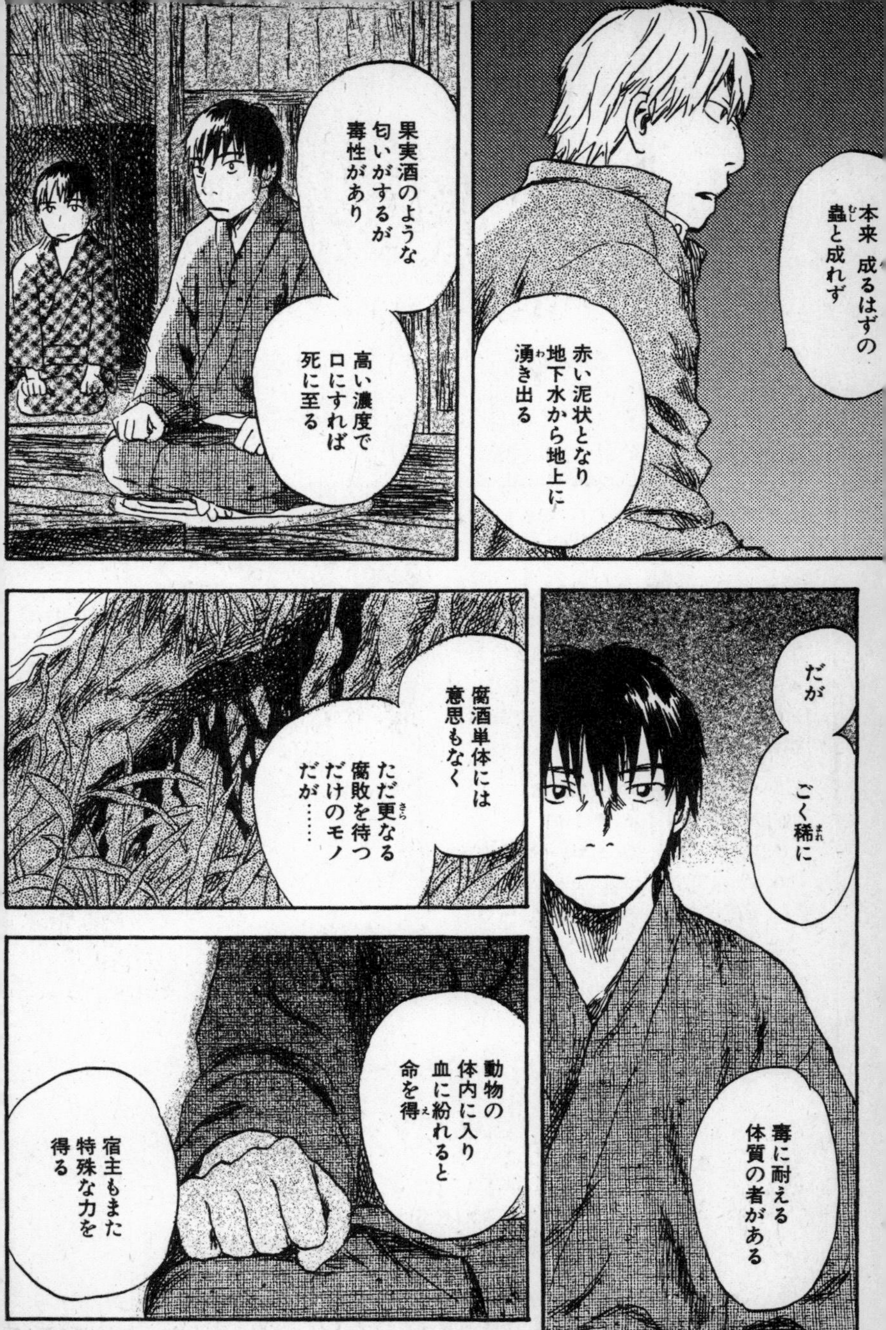
本来 成るはずの蟲と成れず
赤い泥状となり地下水から地上に湧き出る
果実酒のような匂いがするが毒性があり
高い濃度で口にすれば死に至る
だが
ごく稀に
毒に耐える体質の者がある
腐酒単体には意思もなくただ更なる腐敗を待つだけのモノだが……
動物の体内に入り血に紛れると命を得
宿主もまた特殊な力を得る

School Rumble

BY JIN KOBAYASHI

SUBTLETY IS FOR WIMPS!

She . . . is a second-year high school student with a single all-consuming question: Will the boy she likes ever really notice her?

He . . . is the school's most notorious juvenile delinquent, and he's suddenly come to a shocking realization: He's got a huge crush, and now he must tell her how he feels.

Life-changing obsessions, colossal foul-ups, grand schemes, deep-seated anxieties, and raging hormones—School Rumble portrays high school as it really is: over-the-top comedy!

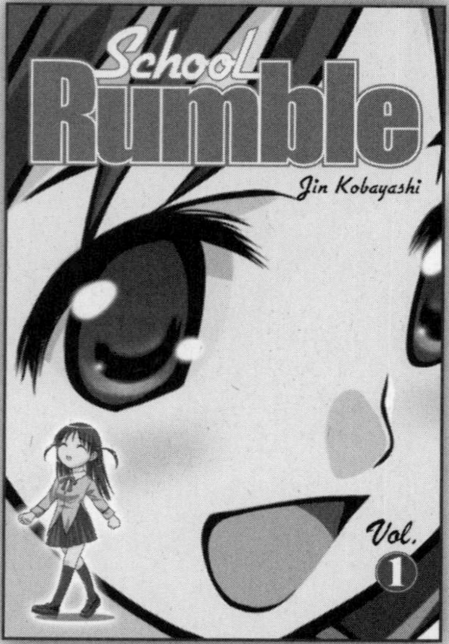
School Rumble
Jin Kobayashi
Vol. 1

Ages: 13+

Special extras in each volume! Read them all!

DEL REY

VISIT WWW.DELREYMANGA.COM TO:
- Read sample pages
- View release date calendars for upcoming volumes
- Sign up for Del Rey's free manga e-newsletter
- Find out the latest about new Del Rey Manga series

[STOP!]

You are going the wrong way!

Manga is a completely different
type of reading experience.

To start at the *beginning*, go to the *end*!

That's right! Authentic manga is read the traditional Japanese
way—from right to left. Exactly the *opposite* of how American
books are read. It's easy to follow: Just go to the other end of
the book, and read each page—and each panel—from right side
to left side, starting at the top right. Now you're experiencing
manga as it was meant to be.